EARLY TOWNS

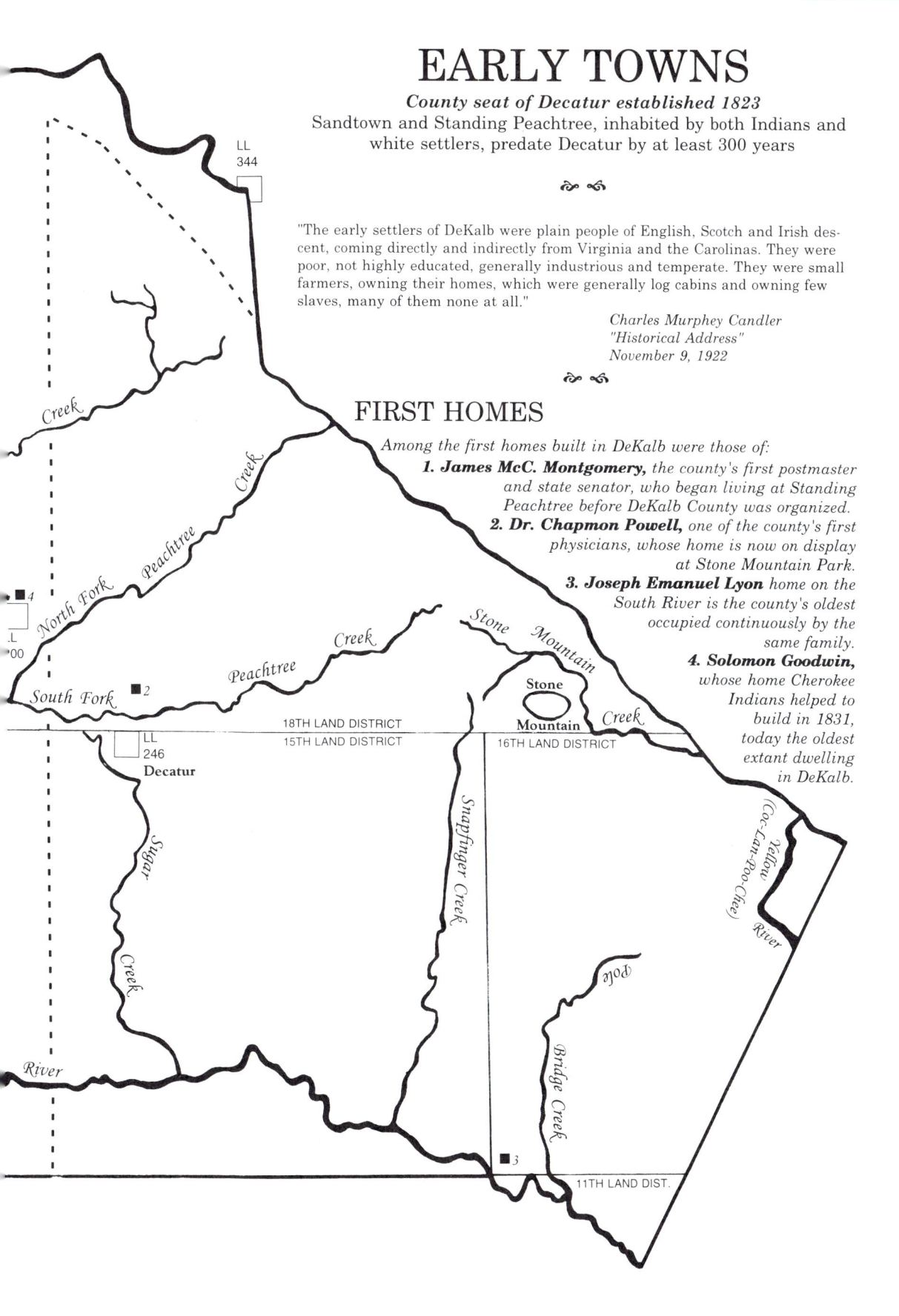

County seat of Decatur established 1823
Sandtown and Standing Peachtree, inhabited by both Indians and white settlers, predate Decatur by at least 300 years

&

"The early settlers of DeKalb were plain people of English, Scotch and Irish descent, coming directly and indirectly from Virginia and the Carolinas. They were poor, not highly educated, generally industrious and temperate. They were small farmers, owning their homes, which were generally log cabins and owning few slaves, many of them none at all."

Charles Murphey Candler
"Historical Address"
November 9, 1922

&

FIRST HOMES

Among the first homes built in DeKalb were those of:
1. **James McC. Montgomery,** *the county's first postmaster and state senator, who began living at Standing Peachtree before DeKalb County was organized.*
2. **Dr. Chapmon Powell,** *one of the county's first physicians, whose home is now on display at Stone Mountain Park.*
3. **Joseph Emanuel Lyon** *home on the South River is the county's oldest occupied continuously by the same family.*
4. **Solomon Goodwin,** *whose home Cherokee Indians helped to build in 1831, today the oldest extant dwelling in DeKalb.*

The History Of DeKalb County, Georgia

THE
HISTORY
OF
DeKalb County, Georgia
1822-1900

By Vivian Price

*published on the occasion
of the 175th anniversary of DeKalb County
and the 50th anniversary of the DeKalb Historical Society*

Copyright 1997 DeKalb Historical Society
All rights reserved

Library of Congress Catalog Card Number
97-62098
ISBN Number
1-883793-27-0

Wolfe Publishing Company
P. O. Box 8036
Fernandina Beach, FL 32035
Printed in the United States of America

For additional copies, phone or write:
DeKalb Historical Society
101 E. Court Square
Decatur, GA 30030
404/373-1088
$45

Cover artwork based on a DeKalb County Courthouse Replica design copyrighted by, and used with permission of, Hometowne Collectibles, Inc., P. O. Box 468 Bowmansville, Pa. 17507.
Replicas on sale at DeKalb Historical Society

FOREWORD

The History of DeKalb County, a very important addition to the roster of published histories of Georgia counties, is now in print. The author, Vivian Price, has every right to be proud of her accomplishment.

Indeed, this excellent account of an important Georgia county will be a prime source of information for both scholars and the numerous persons interested in local history.

In common with most worthwhile endeavors, the preparation of this history required intensive research and many long hours of reading of primary and secondary sources.

Most of what is now Fulton County was for a number of years part of DeKalb until Fulton County was created in 1853. DeKalb County is named for Baron Johan DeKalb, a native German, who made the supreme sacrifice on behalf of American freedom at the Battle of Camden, South Carolina in 1780.

Vivian Price and the DeKalb Historical Society have made a fine contribution to the lengthening list of Georgia county histories in substantial book form.

Franklin M. Garrett

PROLOGUE

From the Ice Age to yesterday's newspaper headline, DeKalb County has a rich history, as dramatic and compelling as any novel.

The story extends to a time that most of us cannot really comprehend. Imagine: human beings lived here 10,000 years ago. Although that history may seem so remote as to be inconsequential, it was quite important, relative to its time and place. James McConnell Montgomery lived with Creek and Cherokee Indians along the banks of the Chattahoochee River in territory that would become DeKalb County. While he struggled to carve a home out of the wilderness, the new nation struggled with important moral and constitutional issues. DeKalb County was the birthplace of that upstart little village called Atlanta, which was still a collection of shacks years after Decatur was a cultured county seat. Union and Confederate troops did not clash in Atlanta in 1864, as the name of the battle suggests. It is DeKalb County soil that bears the scars of cannon wheels and retains the vestiges of blood spilled by thousands of young men. When the fires died out and the gunsmoke cleared, Atlanta began its rise to becoming a booming, bustling city. "Old DeKalb" set its sights on becoming the place Atlanta's workers wanted to come home to after a hard day at the office. It remains that kind of place, thriving, but content to let Atlanta be the "big city."

No history of DeKalb County can be completed without consulting Charles Murphey Candler's "Historical Address," The Story of Decatur by Caroline McKinney Clarke, Mary Gay's Life In Dixie During The War, the works of Levi Willard, Carl T. Hudgins and J. B. Bond, as well as the unpublished research of former DeKalb Historical Society director Dorothy Nix. But, the primary resource has been, and continues to be, Franklin M. Garrett's work, Atlanta and Environs.

Mr. Garrett spent 25 years researching the area's history and four years writing his 2000-page, two-volume history. This work has been completed in less than one quarter of that time.

That is, unless you count what might be called pre-planning. A written history of DeKalb County was first mentioned in 1930, when Murphey Candler Sr. (at the time the "official county historian") announced he would write a book, authorized by the Georgia General Assembly. All totaled, it has taken 67 years for a DeKalb County history book to become a reality, six years longer than it took to complete the Stone Mountain carving.

The goal in writing has been to create a factual work that can be enjoyed by both scholars and casual readers alike. The hope is that it has been worth the wait.

Vivian Price
Chamblee, Ga.
December, 1997

🌸 THANKS 🌸

my husband
Michael C. Saffold

my family
Frances McGraw Price • Grover Cleveland Price

Col. James G. Bogle, Ruth Fruit, Franklin M. Garrett, Barbara Loar, Robert Pendergrast, Kenneth H. Thomas Jr.

Johnnie Woodward, research assistant

Mrs. L. D. Askew; Sgt. Roy Baker, DeKalb Sheriff's Department; Laura and Ken Barre'; Margaret Calhoun, Georgia Power Company; Alvin Del Chamblee; Anne Barrett and Tilmon P. Chamlee; Linda and J. David Chesnut; Donald Stephen Clarke; James T. Cochran; Confident Software, Inc.; Dian Cross; Alfred C. Ellis; Fran Broadnax Franz; Matt Fulgham, National Archives; Jeff Gaston; Delia Gilliland; Mary Grant; Samuel J. Hardman; Richard Harris, Norfolk Southern Corporation; Michael Hitt; Adrian Hopkins; Dr. Fredrick C. (Cris) House; Susan Illis; Fannie Mae Jett; John Carrol Jones; Mark Kirkpatrick, Tucker Federal Savings and Loan Association; Michael C. Kitchens; Dot Lassiter, Old Campbell County Historical Society; Rob Levin, Riverbend Books; Betty and George Lyon; Albert Martin Jr.; Alice McCabe, Gwinnett Historical Society; Walter McCurdy Jr.; Lawrence W. Meier; Dorothy Nix; Otis Norcross; Elsie Olson; Sue Ellen Owens; Jim Perkins; Dolly Purvis, Agnes Scott College; Kathleen Robinson, Smithsonian Institution Archives; Melody Selvage, U. S. Postal Service; Katherine Southard Stiltner; D'Ann Stoddard; Larry Taulbee; Tim Thompson, Muskogee Creek Nation, Okmulgee, Okla.; H. Parks Tilly; Gordon Wallace; Commander Bennie Wilkins; and John E. Worth, Ph.D., Fernbank Museum of Natural History.

the staffs of
the Atlanta History Center
the DeKalb Historical Society
the Emory University Woodruff Library
the Georgia Department of Archives and History
the Georgia Department of Natural Resources, Historic Preservation Division
the Georgia Room of the Cobb County Public Library

and Boo, the dedicated lap cat

TABLE OF CONTENTS

Chapter 1: Prehistoric DeKalb 1
Chapter 2: The Legends of Stone Mountain 15
Chapter 3: Spanish Explorers Were First Europeans 25
Chapter 4: Creek and Cherokee Indian Hunting Grounds 31
Chapter 5: Transition from Indian to White Man 41
Chapter 6: Indian Trails in DeKalb 51
Chapter 7: Baron Johann de Kalb 59
Chapter 8: DeKalb County Firsts 63
Chapter 9: DeKalb's Revolutionary Veterans 75
Chapter 10: Early Settlers in South DeKalb 85
Chapter 11: Standing Peachtree and the Montgomerys 101
Chapter 12: Pioneers of North DeKalb 109
Chapter 13: Decatur's First Settlers 123
Chapter 14: Early Days in Decatur 135
Chapter 15: Two Influential Families 151
Chapter 16: Rebecca Latimer Felton 165
Chapter 17: Stone Mountain, the Town and the Mountain 177
Chapter 18: 1825-1829 -- Pushing Back the Wilderness 185
Chapter 19: 1830-1835 -- Building Communities 193
Chapter 20: 1835-1839: The End of the Indian Era 207
Chapter 21: 1840-1845 -- Railroad Terminus Becomes a New Town 229
Chapter 22: 1845-1847 -- First Southeastern Fair Comes to Stone Mountain 251
Chapter 23: 1848-1849 -- Railroad Brings Crime and Commerce 273
Chapter 24: 1850-1859 -- Bustling, Boisterous Atlanta and Peaceful, Prosperous Decatur 291
Chapter 25: 1860-1863 -- Men Go Off to War 323
Chapter 26: 1864 -- Fighting Close to Home 345
Chapter 27: 1865-1869 -- Rebuilding and Reconstruction 373
Chapter 28: 1870-1879 -- Post-War Struggle Comes to an End 401
Chapter 29: 1880-1889 -- Prosperity Returns 433
Chapter 30: 1889-1900 -- Preparing for the Twentieth Century 473
Epilogue 493
Appendices i
Index 495

ILLUSTRATIONS

1818 map showing "Rock Mountain"	45
1821 map showing Indian cession	46
1824 map Indian territory	70
1829 map of showing DeKalb County	186
1829 map showing "Hightowa" Trail	188
1845 engraving of Stone Mountain	178
1849 engraving of Stone Mountain	179
1867 map of DeKalb County	387
1879 map of Decatur	426
1898 grand jury	484
1898 DeKalb County Courthouse	485
Agnes Irvine Scott	461
Agnes Scott College	462-463
Alf and Delilah Rachel Chewning	475
Amanda (Katie) Powell Houston	363
Asa Griggs Candler Sr. House	481
Avary-Fulton House	Appendix
B. F. White and Thurza G. White	421
Baron Johan de DeKalb	60
Brown's Mill	465
Calhoun-Jones House	143
Chamblee Depot	437
Chamblee shoe shop	438
Chapman Powell Cabin	154
Charles H. Cobb House with cotton	451
Charles Murphey	327
Charles Murphey Candler	86
Clarkston City Hall and mayor	417
Commodore Stephen Decatur	66
Hampton Holleyman House	Appendix
Daniel E. Jackson House	65
Decatur Baptist Church	406
Decatur Female Academy	434
Decatur lamplighter Joe Osborne	477
Decatur third graders	448
DeKalb Courthouse with public well	482
DeKalb County Jail	277
DeKalb County jail (Civil War era)	357
DeKalb public officials	447
DeKalb's third courthouse	234
Donald Fraser School	404
Dr. Chapman Powell	155
Elijah Henry Clarke	333
Elijah Henry Clarke itinerant sawmill	377
Elizabeth (Betsy) Hardman Powell	155
First Methodist Church of Decatur	131
George A. Ramspeck House	435
George A. Ramspeck Store	435
George Washington Scott	461
Harwell Parks Tilly and family	113
High House	137
Home of Samuel House	346
J. B. Bond	479
James Francis Akin	118
James Oliver Powell House	351
Joberry Cheek's cotton gin and mill	442
John Brown Gordon House	487
John Llewlyn Brown	465
John Montgomery House	476
John William Fletcher Tilly	114
Joseph Emanuel Lyon House	88
Jud and Dora Braswell Tapp	408
Macedonia Baptist Church	93
Macedonia Baptist Church sign	92
Map of the Battle of Atlanta	360
Map of the Battle of Decatur	355
Map of B. F. Swanton industries	254
Map of Indian trails in DeKalb	54-55
Map of original county boundary	68
Map of prehistoric sites in DeKalb	4-5
Margaret Malinda Tilly McElroy	112
Martha Lumpkin Compton House	235
Mary Ann Harris Gay	329
Methodist Children's home	395-396
Nancy Evins and Georgia Ann Evins	110
Nettie Southern and Glen G. Austin	488
Ollie and Hannah Weaver farm	459
Orphan's Message newspaper	397
Panola Light and Power Company	474
Piromis Hulsey Bell	325
Prospect Methodist Church	115
Prosperity Presbyterian Church	213
Rebecca Latimer Felton	167
Rehoboth Baptist Church singers	312
Rev. John S. Wilson	129
Rev. William Henry Clarke	242
Robert A. Alston	423
Robert A. Alston House	424
Robert Asbury Chamblee	438
Roswell Railroad	441
Seminary, The	Appendix
Sketch of Oliver Powell House	156
Solomon Goodwin House	202
Stephen Tilly McElroy	114
Sacred harp singing students	420
Sacred Harp songbook	422
Smith-Benning House	Appendix
Stonecutters	468
Stone Mountain Presbyterian Church	457
Stone Mountain granite quarry	467

Stone Mountain with farmer 180	Tullie Smith House 199
Soapstone bowl pre-form 2	Turn-of-the-century downtown Decatur . . 480
Soapstone bowl fragment 7	Washington J. Houston Jr. House 477
Stone Mountain 17	Washington J. Houston Sr. House 418
Swanton House 53	Weekes Brothers Grocery Store 478
Thankful Baptist Church 444	William R. Wallace family 390
Thankful Baptist Church leaders 444	William Turner Southard and family . . . 440
Thomas Holly Chivers 261	
Thomas Holly Chivers House 261	

Chapter 1

Of DeKalb County's ancient landscape few elements remain constant. Today as then the land is flanked by two great rivers -- the Chattahoochee and the South -- and is crisscrossed by many creeks. It was to these lifegiving waterways that man first came.

Almost twelve thousand years ago when man first walked into the Georgia Piedmont [1] from the Mississippi River in the west and from the Tennessee River to the north [2] he found vast woodlands dominated by towering white oak, mockernut hickory and southern pine trees. [3] He found plentiful drinking water, as well as fish and shellfish to supplement a diet of leaves, stems, roots, nuts and fruits. Game animals on foot and wing were abundant.

Because there have been no cataclysmic changes in weather since man's arrival, he lived among many of the same plants and trees we know today. He marveled at the vivid springtime orange of "flame" azaleas. He inhaled the spicy fragrance of sweet shrub blooms. He learned the hard way about the perils of poison ivy. [4]

During what is called the PaleoIndian Period (10,000 B.C. to 8,000 B.C.), people were nomadic, traveling in family groups of 25 to 50 members, [5] moving on as seasons changed and food supplies became exhausted. They would return to a promising site at the right time for harvesting ripe muscadines and blackberries [6] or acorns and hickory nuts. [7] They anticipated when the tide would be low to make harvesting fresh-water clams easier. [8] They followed the migration patterns of game animals.

A keen understanding of the earth and all its resources was vital to their survival.

Hunting was arduous and dangerous work, performed almost exclusively by men of the band. [9] Modern man will never know the feeling of facing teeth, tusks and claws, armed with only your wits and a stick topped with a sharply hewn stone, depending on killing the beast in order to feed his family.

Small groups of men herded large now-extinct animals, including the mammoth, mastodon, giant beaver, ground sloth and musk ox [10] into bogs where, impeded by the mud, they made easier targets.

Another tactic was to hunt younger, less dangerous animals contributing, it has been claimed, to the extinction of such game as the mammoth. [11] The diminutive rhinoceros relative, the tapir, the armadillo and the small nocturnal wild boar called peccary also were killed for food and many other uses. Skins were made into shoes, clothing and shelter. Antlers, teeth, bones and sinew became parts for tools for pounding, puncturing, drilling, cutting and scraping. [12]

Man's primary weapon was the spear. Some time during the Archaic Period (8,000 B.C. to 1,000 B.C.), he developed the atlatl, which served to increase his power and leverage when hurling a spear. Equipped with a stone to balance the weight of the spear, the atlatl created, in effect, a sling shot, designed to hurtle the spear farther, faster and deadlier. [13] Made out of wood or antler, the spear thrower looked like a foot-long crochet hook and increased the spear's range and speed in much the same way the curved basket speeds the ball in the game of jai-alai. [14] Whereas man might be able to hurl a spear 70 yards, with an effective killing range of 15 yards, the spear thrower increased that range to 150 yards and allowed him to kill effectively at 30 yards. [15]

These nomadic people built no permanent houses. [16] Their tools were generally primitively made. [17] Many of them have been found in modern times presumably where they were dropped by their users thousands of years ago. [18]

By 3000 B.C., man's more efficient hunting-gathering techniques allowed the bands a more sedentary life. They began to remain in one place for longer periods of time and to roam ever-smaller territories. [19] Instead of wandering an entire watershed, they could find all the food, clothing and shelter necessary to sustain life in a single section of a river valley. [20] One of the places they chose to live and work was the Soapstone Ridge area of what is now southwest DeKalb County.

Between the South River and Conley Creek they found a congenial year-round climate and generous food sources. More significantly, they found a unique natural phenomenon that aided in development of a new way of life. On and close to the surface of the rolling ridges and valleys were huge boulders, malleable rocks made up in large part of talc, the softest mineral known. Technically called ultramafic, the rock would become known as soapstone.

Soapstone carvers first located a "bump" in a rock that was likely to form a suitable bowl. The bump was further shaped before being separated from the main rock. (Photo by Vivian Price)

In addition to thirty-one kinds of trees, twenty-five varieties of ferns and forty-two different wildflowers, they found a type of western bluegrass that grows only on soils derived from mafic rocks.[21]

The soft stone, gray-green in color, has a soapy feel, vastly different from the flinty granitic rock which underlies most of the region.[22] Thus, nature provided these early settlers with both the carving tool and the medium in close proximity. But the fact that it is easily carved was not the only valuable quality of soapstone. The rock can withstand temperature changes, can be heated red hot, and will not crack. The talc gives it a non-stick surface.[23] Weather does not erode or deteriorate soapstone. Scars made in soapstone boulders 3,000 years ago can easily be seen today.[24]

Soapstone would have a vast impact on the way people lived, the way they prepared their food and even their politics.

Five thousand years ago on the banks of the South River, man discovered that soapstone could facilitate the heating of water to cook the leaves and shoots of giant cane or bracken fern or to make sassafras tea.[25]

"Stone cooking" was accomplished when a piece of soapstone called a spall was heated and then placed in a container of water with food.[26] The cooking apparatus could be as simple as a pit dug into the ground and lined with bark, clay or skins.[27]

Because of its "thermal shock resistance,"[28] soapstone was the preferred material for cooking stones. The sixteen-square-mile area of Soapstone Ridge in south DeKalb County contained the only soapstone deposit for many miles around. It remains one of the largest soapstone deposits in North America.[29]

Beginning about 3000 B.C. perforated soapstone slabs were manufactured on Soapstone Ridge and traded as far away as Louisiana and the Great Lakes.[30] The rarity of the material made the slabs quite a valuable trading commodity.

Access to soapstone is thought to be one basis for political power among Archaic people.[31] The individual who controlled the production and exchange of soapstone slabs could command a high price in terms of allegiance, as well as currency.

Thus, the development of pottery about 2500 B.C. near the mouth of the Savannah River[32] must have caused quite a furor when news reached Soapstone Ridge. Clay pots could be placed directly over open flame, rendering soapstone slabs obsolete.

By 2200 B.C. coastal societies had stopped using soapstone slabs, although the practice continued in inland communities until 1400 B.C.[33] Not to be outdone, however, Soapstone Ridge residents began to fashion stone bowls to compete with pottery.[34]

While men hunted, the majority of the quarry chores were performed by women.[35]

After locating a likely bulge in a soapstone boulder, they began by outlining a bowl of the size they wanted. They slowly chipped away the surrounding rock with picks and axes made of harder stone

PREHISTORIC SITES
• IN •
DeKALB COUNTY
GEORGIA

Almost twelve thousand years ago man first walked into the oak-hickory woodlands crisscrossed by the many creeks and rivers in prehistoric DeKalb County. In addition to plentiful drinking water, he found fish and shellfish to supplement his diet of game animals and birds, as well as the leaves, stems, roots, nuts and fruits he harvested from wild plants.

Between 10,000 B.C. and the end of the prehistoric period -- around 1450 A.D. -- DeKalb residents evolved from being nomadic hunter-gatherers to living in stable villages and surviving primarily through agriculture. Primary crops among aboriginal DeKalb residents were maize, pumpkins and squash.

ARCHAEOLOGICIAL TIME PERIODS

Historic — Present to European Contact (mid-1500s)
Mississippian — European Contact to A.D. 900
Woodland — A.D. 900 to 1,000 B.C.
Archaic — 1,000 B.C. to 8,000 B.C.
Paleo-Indian — 8,000 B.C. to 10,000 B.C.

Prehistoric settlements ....

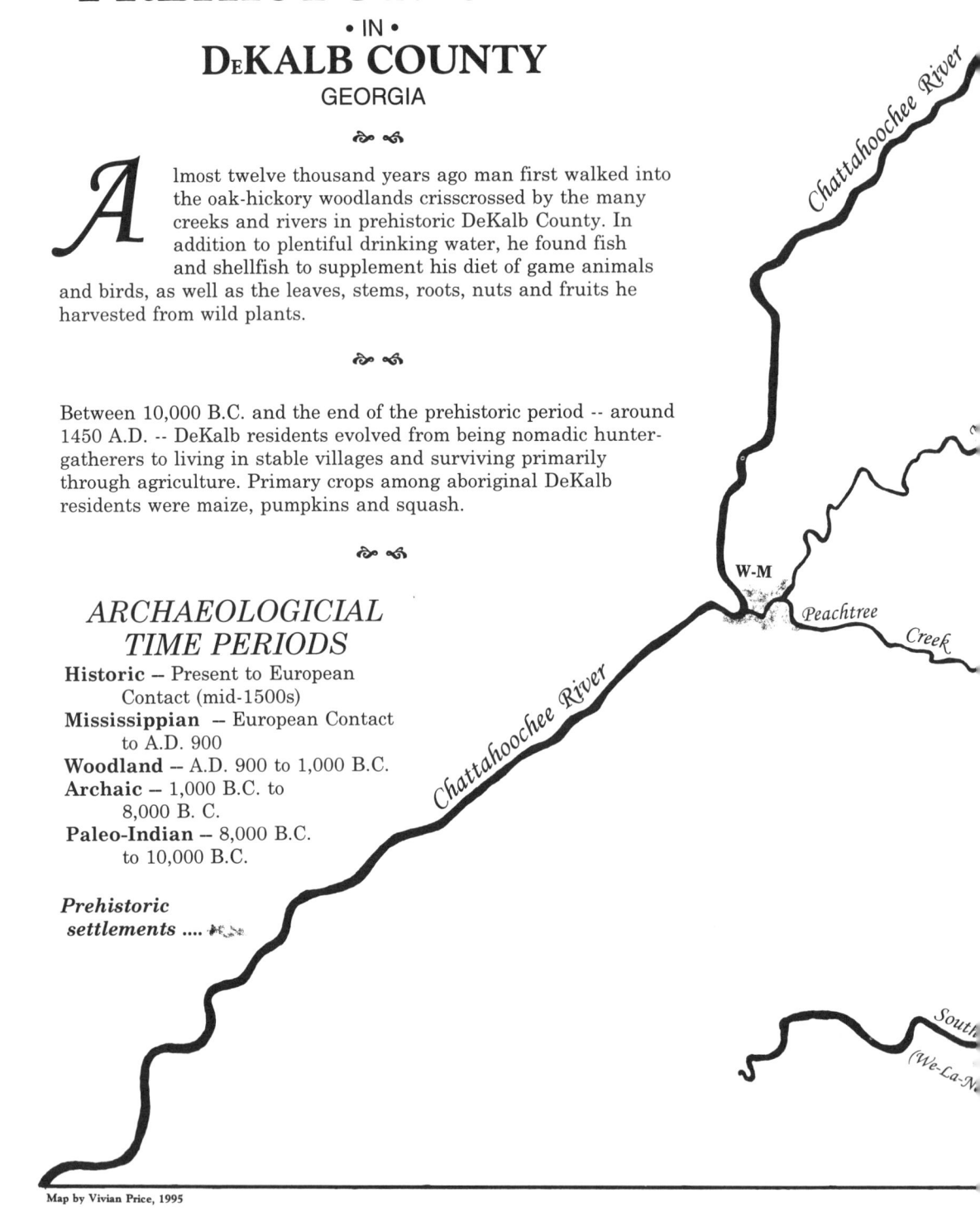

Map by Vivian Price, 1995

Map shows some of the sites of prehistoric camps and workshops.

SOAPSTONE RIDGE
THE FIRST INDUSTRIAL PARK
• IN •
DeKALB COUNTY
GEORGIA

Between 3000 B.C. and 1500 B.C., Soapstone Ridge in the area of the South River was one of the most important places in what would become North America. The soft, gray-green stone known as soapstone has unique qualities that made it a valuable commodity among prehistoric people.

Soapstone is easily carved, can be heated red hot without breaking and resists deterioration. Ridge inhabitants operated a soapstone quarry and factory where they made cooking slabs, bowls and tools with a non-stick surface caused by the talc content of the rock.

Bowls manufactured in DeKalb County were traded as far away as the Great Lakes. Twenty-two separate quarries have been documented in the South River area.

THE HISTORY OF DeKALB COUNTY, GA. 1822-1900 • CHAPTER 1

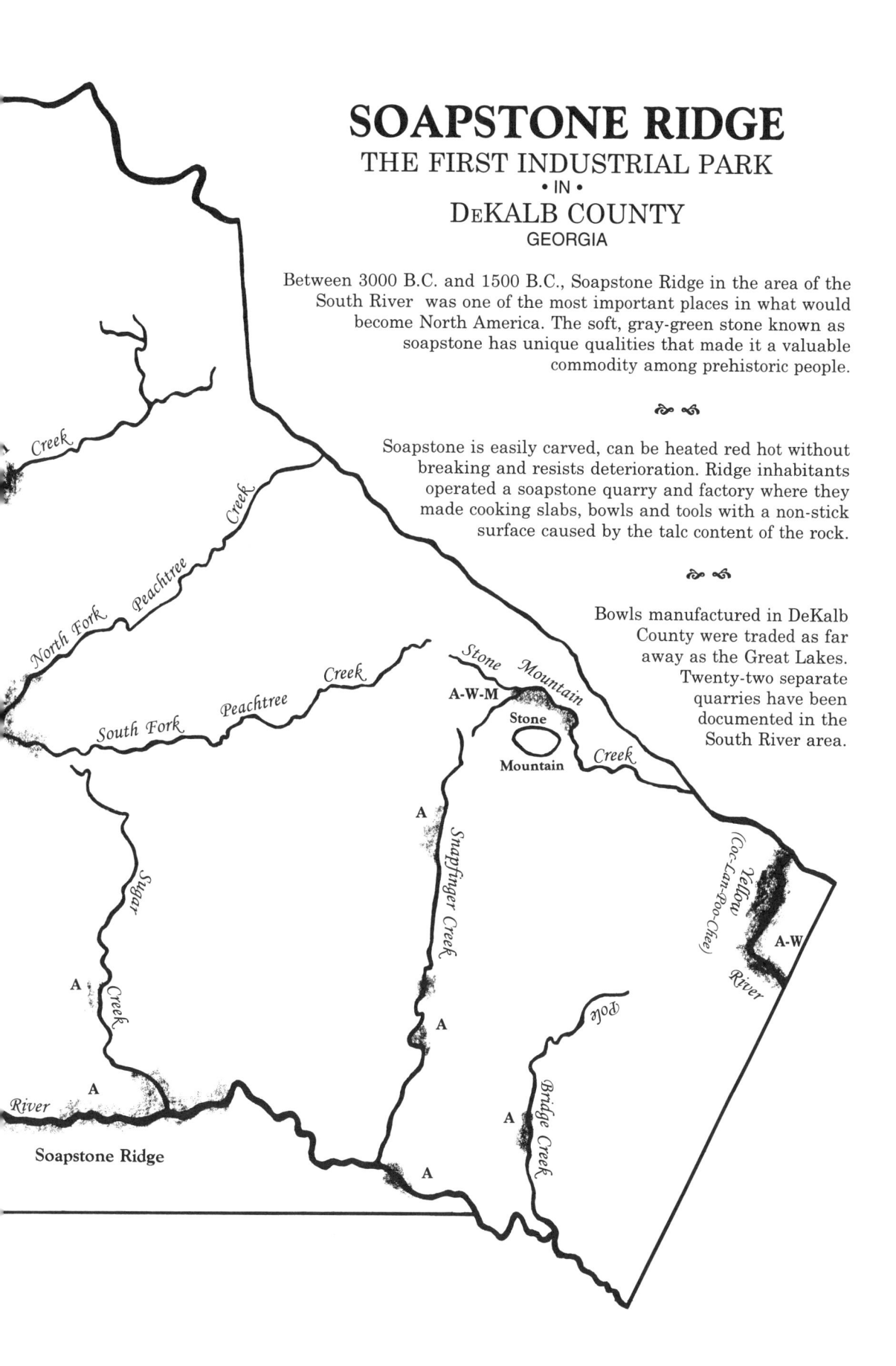

like quartz or gneiss, until a half-sphere was attached to the main stone by small stem. [36] The women then wedged saplings in behind the bowl form and snapped it off. They hollowed it out until they had a two-inch-thick preform. The preform was taken to a nearby campsite, where the women removed still more of the stone until the bowl was one-half to one-eighth inches thick. [37] Using chisels, gouges and scrapers made of animal antlers, wood and quartz, [38] finishing a bowl from an already-separated preform could take as long as twenty hours. [39]

The women made deep bowls with flat bottoms, as well as shallow oval and circular platters, some with opposing handles. [40] That the bowls were considered valuable is apparent from evidence found that cracks were mended with lacings and worn-through bottoms were patched with adhesive. [41]

Trading the heavy stone bowls must have been a laborious process. Man had not yet begun to domesticate animals for use in hauling goods. [42] Bowls were carried overland to the South River, the Chattahoochee or the Flint and shipped by dugout canoe to their destination. [43]

In addition to bowls, soapstone was carved into fishing net sinkers, atlatl weights, smoking pipes, gaming stones and ornaments. [44]

Thus, two thousand years before the Mexican pyramids were built and one thousand years before Stonehenge, DeKalb County was the site of an extensive quarrying and manufacturing operation and commercial enterprise. [45]

Twenty-two separate documented quarries were located in the area known as Live Oak Quarry (now the county's Live Oak Landfill), with twenty-two corresponding workshops. [46] There were 12 family camp sites along the South River, with 11 more on Conley Creek. [47]

As pottery became more widely used, the use of soapstone bowls and spalls gradually faded. The soapstone bowl industry lasted only 300 years in the Late Archaic period -- 1400-1000 B.C.[48] Although Cherokee Indians still carved soapstone smoking pipes into the 1700s, [49] soapstone had lost its trade value. The people moved on, abandoning their campsites on Soapstone Ridge.

The vast majority of DeKalb County's Archaic period campsites were located south of today's Interstate 20 highway. While Soapstone Ridge sites were occupied almost exclusively during the Archaic period, other locations in DeKalb served as homes almost continuously from the Archaic period until the arrival of the white man.

As man began to understand that he was not strictly at the mercy of nature, he became more selective when looking for a place to live. Instead of camping immediately adjacent to waterways where his home was prone to flooding, he moved his campsite to well-drained, slightly elevated sites overlooking the floodplains where he planted his garden. [50] He built small villages where he lived almost year-round in sturdy houses.

He still gathered pokeweed, wild onions and other vegetables, as well as fruits and nuts in season. He hunted deer, turkey, rabbit, doves [51] and "tygers" (the panthers of today's Panthersville)[52] with the newly developed efficiency of the bow and arrow. He created dams to trap trout, bluegill and bass.[53] Remnants of just such an aboriginal dam remained in the Chattahoochee River well into the twentieth century.[54] As interaction among bands increased in appeal, a man might round up his family and travel to a summer social gathering on the coast. [55]

The era called the Woodland period (1500 B.C. to 900 A.D.) also is characterized by more ornate pottery, a more organized social structure, clearly defined religious beliefs and burial customs, ritualism and the beginnings of mound building, a phenomenon which continued until around 500 A.D.[56]

DeKalb County had many Woodland period communities. The largest concentration of small camps and larger villages could be found along the North and South forks of Peachtree Creek in the area of today's Clairmont Road between the Interstate 85 highway and the Veterans Administration Hospital.[57]

Fragments of soapstone bowls, like this one, have been found in several locations along the South River. Photo by Vivian Price

Small settlements were scattered in the today's Redan area along Barbashela and Snapfinger creeks,[58] in Chamblee along Nancy Creek where today children play on ballfields at Murphey Candler Park,[59] along the Yellow River near now Lithonia [60] and near a tributary of Nancy Creek in the Oglethorpe University area. [61] Prehistoric man also returned to the north banks of the South River between 300 B.C. and 500 A.D. [62] Prehistoric man inhabited at least five separate campsites spread across 8,000 acres along Stone Mountain Creek in now DeKalb and Gwinnett counties. [63] Sites also have been documented along Susan Creek, Entrenchment Creek and Shoal Creek. [64]

Indeed, it would not be unreasonable to assume that prehistoric man lived and farmed along virtually every creekbank and hunted in every woodland in DeKalb County.

Habitation of many of these sites began during the Archaic period and continued through the Mississippian, some may have been occupied as late as 1000 A.D. [65]

At least two Archaic, Woodland and Mississippian settlements were located on the banks of the Chattahoochee River in what would become DeKalb County -- one at Morgan Falls [66] and one at the Shallow Ford of the Chattahoochee River [67] near the contemporary Roswell Road bridge.

During the Mississippian period (900 A.D.-1500 A.D.), people settled in villages, often surrounded by palisades and ditches. They were organized into chiefdoms with a well-developed social order. Dependent upon agriculture and confined to smaller territories, they were often at war over land[68] on which to grow maize, squash, beans and pumpkins. [69] Mississippian artifacts were elaborate, as were ceremonies. Mississippian inhabitants constructed the vast flat-topped earth pyramids that can be seen today in many parts of the country, including north and central Georgia. [70]

Religion played an important role in the lives of these Indians, who were most like the Creeks and Cherokees of later years. During elaborate ceremonies, the first corn of the annual harvest was always offered to their deity, "the Master of Breath." The dead were buried wearing ornate costumes; interred along with them were items of religious or cultural significance. [71]

With two notable exceptions, the territory that would become DeKalb County ceased to be occupied by prehistoric Indians after around 1100 A.D. [71] The exceptions -- Sandtown and Standing Peachtree -- were the only settlements in the area to be occupied by prehistoric and historic period Indians, as well as later by the white man.

The area's most prominent area Mississippian settlement was located at what would become the southwestern tip of DeKalb County. Sandtown also is the only community that was called by the white man by the same name given to it by the Indians. The translation of the Creek Indian Oktahasasi is "place where sand is abundant." [72] Ironically, there is no sand at Sandtown, only the familiar clay of the Piedmont. The name probably comes from a tribe of Hillibee Indians who moved there from an Alabama town of the same name. [73] The community near the intersection of Campbellton Road and Camp Creek Parkway in south Fulton County is still called Sandtown today.

Once described as a "provincial center of some importance," Sandtown was the site of extensive archaeological work in 1938. At that time, archaeologists found remains of a house and two human skeletons, one seated upright and cross-legged leaning against stone slab backrest, arms crossed at wrists. [74]

Standing Peachtree, located at the confluence of Peachtree Creek and the Chattahoochee River, was first occupied between 1034 and 1154 A.D., almost 400 years before the first European set foot on the American continent. [75] The Indian village from which many Atlanta place names are derive would provide the setting for momentous happenings in the DeKalb County that was to come.

Chapter 1 Notes

1. Anderson, David G., Ledbetter, R. Jerald and O'Steen, Lisa 1990, "PaleoIndian Period Archaeology of Georgia," Laboratory of Archaeology Series Report No. 28, Georgia Archaeology Research Design Paper No. 6, page 1. Garrow, Patrick H., n.d., "The Archaeology of DeKalb County: A Summary," page 1.

2. Anderson, David G., Ledbetter, R. Jerald and O'Steen, Lisa 1990, "PaleoIndian Period Archaeology of Georgia," Laboratory of Archaeology Series Report No. 28, Georgia Archaeology Research Design Paper No. 6, page 3.

3. Anderson, David G., Ledbetter, R. Jerald and O'Steen, Lisa 1990, "PaleoIndian Period Archaeology of Georgia," Laboratory of Archaeology Series Report No. 28, Georgia Archaeology Research Design Paper No. 6, page 5. Garrow, Patrick H., n.d., "The Archaeology of DeKalb County: A Summary," page 1. Bunch, Robyn L. 1982, "Fork Creek Mountain on Soapstone Ridge: Defining the Quarry Site in its Environmental Setting," page 29.

4. Bunch, Robyn L., 1982, "Fork Creek Mountain on Soapstone Ridge: Defining the Quarry Site in its Environmental Setting," page 29.

5. Justus, Lucy, July 28, 1974, "Atlanta's Lost Green Island," The Atlanta Journal and Constitution Magazine, page 27.

6. Bunch, Robyn L., 1982, "Fork Creek Mountain on Soapstone Ridge: Defining the Quarry Site in its Environmental Setting," page 37. Dickens, Roy S., Jr. and Barber, Gary D. January 1, 1976, "An Archaeological Survey in Clayton, DeKalb, and Gwinnett Counties, Georgia," Laboratory of Archaeology, Georgia State University, Georgia Department of Natural Resources.

7. Wagner, John A., Spring, summer, 1981, "Fork Creek Mountain Vegetative Study, Soapstone Ridge, DeKalb County, Ga.," independent study, page 11.

8. Justus, Lucy, July 28, 1974, "Atlanta's Lost Green Island," The Atlanta Journal and Constitution Magazine, page 29.

9. Winn, Bill, April 14, 1968, "The First Georgians (No. 1) -- Their Destiny: Extinction," The Atlanta Journal, page 24A.

10. Author unknown, November 7, 1979, "A Summary of the Archaeological Sequence of Georgia."

11. Winn, Bill, April 14, 1968, "The First Georgians (No. 1) -- Their Destiny: Extinction," The Atlanta Journal, page 24A.

12. Author unknown, November 7, 1979, "A Summary of the Archaeological Sequence of Georgia."

13. Winn, Bill, April 14, 1968, "The First Georgians (No. 1) -- Their Destiny: Extinction," The Atlanta Journal, page 24A.

14. Prideaux, Tom and the Editors of Time-Life Books, 1973, "The Emergency of Man: Cro-Magnon Man."

15. Lambert, David and the Diagram Group, 1987, "The Field Guide to Early Man," page 160.

16. Winn, Bill, April, 14, 1968, "The First Georgians (No. 1) -- Their Destiny: Extinction, "The Atlanta Journal," page 24A.

17. Anderson, David G., Ledbetter, R. Jerald and O'Steen, Lisa, 1990, "PaleoIndian Period Archaeology of Georgia," Laboratory of Archaeology Series Report No. 28, Georgia Archaeology Research Design Paper No. 6, page 5.

18. Elliott, Daniel T., 1986, "The Live Oak Quarry, DeKalb County, Ga.," Garrow and Associates, Inc., Patrick H. Garrow, principal investigator, page 3.

19. Law Environmental, 1992, "Cultural Resources Assessment of a Proposed Solid Waste Landfill Site and Evaluative Testing at Archaeological Site 9DA67, DeKalb County, Ga.," page 21.

20. Worth, Dr. John, Fall, 1994, "The First Georgians -- The Late Archaic Period, 3,000-1,000 B.C.," Fernbank Quarterly, page 27.

21. Wagner, John A., Spring, summer, 1981, "Fork Creek Mountain Vegetative Study, Soapstone Ridge, DeKalb County, Ga.," independent study, page 4.

22. Justus, Lucy, July 28, 1974, "Atlanta's Lost Green Island," The Atlanta Journal and Constitution Magazine, page 9.

23. Elliott, Daniel T., 1986, "The Live Oak Quarry, DeKalb County, Ga.," Garrow and Associates, Inc., Patrick H. Garrow, principal investigator, page 1. Justus, Lucy, July 28, 1974, "Atlanta's Lost Green Island," The Atlanta Journal and Constitution Magazine, page 31.

24. Bunch, Robyn L., 1982, "Fork Creek Mountain on Soapstone Ridge: Defining the Quarry Site in its Environmental Setting," page 3. Elliott, Daniel T. 1986, "The Live Oak Quarry, DeKalb County, Ga.," Garrow and Associates, Inc., Patrick H. Garrow, principal investigator, page 1. Justus, Lucy, July 28, 1974, "Atlanta's Lost Green Island," The Atlanta Journal and Constitution Magazine, page 29.

25. Wagner, John A., Spring, summer, 1981, "Fork Creek Mountain Vegetative Study, Soapstone Ridge, DeKalb County, Ga.," independent study, pages 25-26.

26. Worth, Dr. John, Fall, 1994, "The First Georgians -- The Late Archaic Period, 3,000-1,000 B.C.," Fernbank Quarterly, page 23.

27. Winn, Bill, April, 14, 1968, "The First Georgians (No. 1) -- Their Destiny: Extinction, "The Atlanta Journal," page 6A. Worth, Dr. John, Fall, 1994, "The First Georgians -- The Late Archaic Period, 3,000-1,000 B.C.," Fernbank Quarterly, page 24.

28. Worth, Dr. John, Fall, 1994, "The First Georgians -- The Late Archaic Period, 3,000-1,000 B.C.," Fernbank Quarterly, page 24.

29. Worth, Dr. John, Fall, 1994, "The First Georgians -- The Late Archaic Period, 3,000-1,000 B.C.," Fernbank Quarterly, page 24.

30. Worth, Dr. John, Fall, 1994, "The First Georgians -- The Late Archaic Period, 3,000-1,000 B.C.," Fernbank Quarterly, page 28.

31. Worth, Dr. John, Fall, 1994, "The First Georgians -- The Late Archaic Period, 3,000-1,000 B.C.," Fernbank Quarterly, page 28.

32. Worth, Dr. John, Fall, 1994, "The First Georgians -- The Late Archaic Period, 3,000-1,000 B.C.," Fernbank Quarterly, page 25.

33. Worth, Dr. John, Fall, 1994, "The First Georgians -- The Late Archaic Period, 3,000-1,000 B.C.," Fernbank Quarterly, page 29.

34. Worth, Dr. John, Fall, 1994, "The First Georgians -- The Late Archaic Period, 3,000-1,000 B.C.," Fernbank Quarterly, page 30.

35. Justus, Lucy, July 28, 1974, "Atlanta's Lost Green Island," The Atlanta Journal and Constitution Magazine, page 29.

36. Carnes, Linda F. 1983, "Archaeological Investigations at the Fork Creek Mountain Quarry Site (9Da18), DeKalb County, Georgia," prepared for DeKalb County Division of Recreation, Parks and Cultural Affairs, page 21. Justus, Lucy, July 28, 1974, "Atlanta's Lost Green Island," The Atlanta Journal and Constitution Magazine, page 29.

37. Justus, Lucy, July 28, 1974, "Atlanta's Lost Green Island," The Atlanta Journal and Constitution Magazine, page 29. Carnes, Linda F., 1983, "Archaeological Investigations at the Fork Creek Mountain Quarry Site (9Da18), DeKalb County, Georgia," prepared for DeKalb County Division of Recreation, Parks and Cultural Affairs, page 26.

38. Carnes, Linda F., 1983, "Archaeological Investigations at the Fork Creek Mountain Quarry Site (9Da18), DeKalb County, Georgia," prepared for DeKalb County Division of Recreation, Parks and Cultural Affairs, page 26.

39. Bunch, Robyn L., 1982, "Fork Creek Mountain on Soapstone Ridge: Defining the Quarry Site in its Environmental Setting, page 30.

40. Elliott, Daniel T., 1986, "The Live Oak Quarry, DeKalb County, Ga.," Garrow and Associates, Inc., Patrick H. Garrow, principal investigator, page 15.

41. Justus, Lucy, July 28, 1974, "Atlanta's Lost Green Island," The Atlanta Journal and Constitution Magazine, page 29.

42. Elliott, Daniel T., 1986, "The Live Oak Quarry, DeKalb County, Ga.," Garrow and Associates, Inc., Patrick H. Garrow, principal investigator, page 106.

43. Elliott, Daniel T., 1986, "The Live Oak Quarry, DeKalb County, Ga.," Garrow and Associates, Inc., Patrick H. Garrow, principal investigator, page 106.

44. Law Environmental, 1992, "Cultural Resources Assessment of a Proposed Solid Waste Landfill Site and Evaluative Testing at Archaeological Site 9Da67 DeKalb County, Ga.," page 22.

45. Justus, Lucy, July 28, 1974, "Atlanta's Lost Green Island," The Atlanta Journal and Constitution Magazine, page 27.

46. Dickens/Carnes, 1983. Elliott, Daniel T., 1986, "The Live Oak Quarry, DeKalb County, Ga.," Garrow and Associates, IInc., Patrick H. Garrow, principal investigator, page 28.

47. Elliott, Daniel T., 1986, "The Live Oak Quarry, DeKalb County, Ga.," Garrow and Associates, Inc., Patrick H. Garrow, principal investigator, page 28.

48. Worth, Dr. John, Fall, 1994, "The First Georgians -- The Late Archaic Period, 3,000-1,000 B.C.," Fernbank Quarterly, page 24.

49. Elliott, Daniel T., 1986, "The Live Oak Quarry, DeKalb County, Ga.," Garrow and Associates, Inc., Patrick H. Garrow, principal investigator, page 13.

50. Dickens, Roy S., Jr. and Barber, Gary D., January 1, 1976, "An Archaeological Survey in Clayton, DeKalb, and Gwinnett Counties, Georgia," conducted by the Laboratory of Archaeology, Georgia State University for the Georgia Department of Natural Resources, page 10.

51. Bunch, Robyn L., 1982, "Fork Creek Mountain on Soapstone Ridge: Defining the Quarry Site in its Environmental Setting," page 30. Dickens, Roy S., Jr. and Barber, Gary D., January 1, 1976, "An Archaeological Survey in Clayton, DeKalb, and Gwinnett Counties, Georgia," conducted by the Laboratory of Archaeology, Georgia State University, for the Georgia Department of Natural Resources, page 9.

52. Bartram, William, 1792, 1973, "Travels Through North and South Carolina, Georgia, East and West Florida," page 46.

53. Dickens, Roy S., Jr. and Barber, Gary D., January 1, 1976, "An Archaeological Survey in Clayton, DeKalb, and Gwinnett Counties, Georgia," conducted by the Laboratory of Archaeology, Georgia State University, for the Georgia Department of Natural Resources, page 9.

54. Dickens, Roy S., Jr. and Barber, Gary D., January 1, 1976, "An Archaeological Survey in Clayton, DeKalb, and Gwinnett Counties, Georgia," conducted by the Laboratory of Archaeology, Georgia State University for the Georgia Department of Natural Resources, page 17.

55. Worth, Dr. John, Fall, 1994, "The First Georgians -- The Late Archaic Period, 3,000-1,000 B.C.," Fernbank Quarterly, page 26-27.

56. Garrow, Patrick H., n.d., "The Archaeology of DeKalb County: A Summary," pages 8-9. Author unknown, November 7, 1979, "A Summary of the Archaeological Sequence of Georgia." Elliott, Daniel T., 1986, "The Live Oak Quarry, DeKalb County, Ga.," Garrow and Associates, Inc., Patrick H. Garrow, principal investigator, page 13.

57. Dickens, Roy S., Jr. and Barber, Gary D., January 1, 1976, "An Archaeological Survey in Clayton, DeKalb, and Gwinnett Counties, Georgia," conducted by the Laboratory of Archaeology, Georgia State University for the Georgia Department of Natural Resources, page 28-31.

58. Dickens, Roy S., Jr. and Barber, Gary D., January 1, 1976, "An Archaeological Survey in Clayton, DeKalb, and Gwinnett Counties, Georgia," conducted by the Laboratory of Archaeology, Georgia State University for the Georgia Department of Natural Resources, page 28-31.

59. Dickens, Roy S., Jr. and Barber, Gary D., January 1, 1976, "An Archaeological Survey in Clayton, DeKalb, and Gwinnett Counties, Georgia," conducted by the Laboratory of Archaeology, Georgia State University for the Georgia Department of Natural Resources, pages 28-31. Wilkie, Hugh, 1969, "Amerinds of North Georgia (A Study of Stone-Age Man): About A Prehistoric Indian site in Greater Atlanta (North DeKalb County)," page 12.

60. Wauchope, Robert, July, 1966, "Archaeological Survey of Northern Georgia with a Test of Some Cultural Hypotheses," Memoirs of the Society for American Archaeology (issued as American Antiquity, Vol. 31, No. 5, Part 2), page 391.

61. Cooper, Walter G., 1924, "Official History of Fulton County," page 8.

62. Chase, David, December, 1988, "Archaeological Excavations of the Miner's Creek Site," The Profile, Number 63, page 92.

63. Dickens, Roy S., Jr., December, 1965, "The Stone Mountain Salvage Project, DeKalb and Gwinnett Counties, Georgia, Part II, The Stone Mountain Creek Site (9Da2)," Journal of Alabama Archaeology, Vol. XI, No. 2, pages 123-125. Dickens, Roy S., Jr. and Barber, Gary D., January 1, 1976, "An Archaeological Survey in Clayton, DeKalb, and Gwinnett Counties, Georgia," conducted by the Laboratory of Archaeology, Georgia State University for the Georgia Department of Natural Resources, page 19.

64. Dickens, Roy S., Jr., and Barber, Gary D., January 1, 1976, "An Archaeological Survey in Clayton, DeKalb, and Gwinnett Counties, Georgia," conducted by the Laboratory of Archaeology, Georgia State University for the Georgia Department of Natural Resources, page 19.

65. Dickens, Roy S., Jr. and Barber, Gary D., January 1, 1976, "An Archaeological Survey in Clayton, DeKalb, and Gwinnett Counties, Georgia," conducted by the Laboratory of Archaeology, Georgia State University for the Georgia Department of Natural Resources, page 28-31.

66. De Baillou, Clemens, 1959, "Morgan Falls Reservoir Study and Excavation," Historic Preservation Section, Georgia Department of Natural Resources. Hally, David J. and Rudolph, James L., n.d, "Mississippi Period Archaeology of the Georgia Piedmont," Department of Anthropology, University of Georgia, Georgia Archaeological Research Design Paper No. 2, University of Georgia Laboratory of Archaeology Series Report No. 24, page ??

67. Wauchope, Robert, July, 1966, "Archaeological Survey of Northern Georgia with a Test of Some Cultural Hypotheses," Memoirs of the Society for American Archaeology (issued as American Antiquity, Vol. 31, No. 5, Part 2), pages 406-407.

68. Law Environmental, 1992, "Cultural Resources Assessment of a Proposed Solid Waste Landfill Site and Evaluative Testing at Archaeological Site 9DA67, DeKalb County, Ga.," page 26.

69. Elliott, Daniel T., 1986, "The Live Oak Quarry, DeKalb County, Ga.," Garrow and Associates, Inc., Patrick H. Garrow, principal investigator, page 13. Wilkie, Hugh, 1969, "Amerinds of North Georgia (A Study of Stone-Age Man): About A Prehistoric Indian site in Greater Atlanta (North DeKalb County)," page 10.

70. Elliott, Daniel T., 1986, "The Live Oak Quarry, DeKalb County, Ga.," Garrow and Associates, Inc., Patrick H. Garrow, principal investigator, page 13.

71. Winn, Bill, April 17, 1968, The First Georgians No. 4 -- Temple Mounds and Religion, The Atlanta Journal, page 18A.

71. Worth, Dr. John, anthropologist, Fernbank Museum of Natural History, August 25, 1994, personal interview.

72. Goff, John H., December, 1966, "The Sandtown Trail," Atlanta Historical Bulletin Vol. XI, No. 4, page 34.

73. Goff, John H., December, 1966, "The Sandtown Trail," Atlanta Historical Bulletin Vol. XI, No. 4, page 35.

74. Wauchope, Robert, July, 1966, "Archaeological Survey of Northern Georgia with a Test of Some Cultural Hypotheses," Memoirs of the Society for American Archaeology (issued as American Antiquity, Vol. 31, No. 5, Part 2), pages 467-468.

75. Meier, Lawrence W., May, 1973, "A Preliminary Report of Research at 9Co1, Standing Peachtree Site, Cobb County, Georgia," SPEGH Newsletter No. 6, The Profile Papers, The Society for Georgia Archaeology Special Publication No. 1, page 2.

Chapter 2

*T*owering over the prolonged process of evolution of mankind in DeKalb County was Stone Mountain. Indeed, the great gray rock predates not only man but all living creatures on earth by thousands of years.

Formed at least 200 million years ago [1] and possibly as much as 510 million years ago, [2] the giant monadnock is one of the oldest rock formations on the planet earth. [3]

Geologist Poole Maynard: "Stone Mountain had passed through millions of years of its life history before the Island Empire of England was formed; before the Alps, the Rockies, the Pyrenees and the Himalayas were conceived; millions of years before the atmosphere carried enough oxygen for land animals to exist. Stone Mountain has been a witness to the growth and development of every great division of the animal kingdom; the advent of the vertebrates; the age of the greatest luxuriance of plant growth the world has ever seen, when the land was full of strange creatures, amphibians, great hosts of lizards, crocodiles, dinosaurs, ichthyosaurs and flying saurians. It witnessed the most remarkable change in the world's atmosphere when the great plant growth absorbed the carbonic acid gas to form the coal deposits of the Carboniferous, resulting in an atmosphere enriched by oxygen, paving the way for an atmosphere in which man could live. [4]

Geologically, Maynard calls Stone Mountain a "great book of rocks" which tells the story of its making. "No section of the world's rocks is more intricate in its folding; no rock structures are more difficult to untangle; no section of the world has been subjected to greater metamorphism than have the rocks of the Stone Mountain District... In this great complex of rocks, the most striking geologic and physical feature is Stone Mountain which has shot up from a deep seated magma." [5]

Stone Mountain was originally a mass of molten minerals, rich in silica, alumna, potash and soda, which seeped upward through weak spots in the earth's crust. Erosion of the soil that once covered Stone Mountain exposed a single huge igneous rock containing mica, feldspar and quartz. [6] As erosion continues, Stone Mountain grows in relation to the surrounding landscape. [7]

Soil that remained on the mountain formed the habitat for 17 species of plant life that grow nowhere else in the world. Stone Mountain gets its gray-green color from a covering of lichens which can make climbing treacherous. The mossy fungus turns to powder underfoot in dry weather and becomes slippery when wet. [8]

Craters that pock the mountain top -- caused by lightning -- are home to tiny crabs and "fairy shrimp" during spring and fall rains. [9]

The high quality of Stone Mountain granite, with its unique swirling pattern of sparkling highlights, [10] has made it a much-sought-after paving and building material all over the world. Structures from locks in the Panama Canal to post offices in small towns all over America were built with Stone Mountain granite. [11]

There is literally nothing like Stone Mountain anywhere on the planet Earth. [12] School children learn to place Stone Mountain eighth on the list of natural wonders of the world.

Elliptical in shape, the dome's two-mile axis runs east to west. The mountain is seven miles in circumference at the base. [13] It is a relatively easy climb up the south side, but the north face is a sheer 1000-foot vertical face. At its highest point, the giant rock is 1686 feet above sea level. It rises 686 feet above the surrounding terrain, which in itself is a ridge that forms a natural watershed. [14]

Geologists have estimated that the exposed portion of mountain contains more than seven and one-half billion cubic feet of granite, weighing more than one and one-quarter billion pounds.[15]

Writes Maynard: "If the granite alone in sight was loaded in freight cars carrying fifty tons each, it would require ten million, five hundred and seventy-two thousand, nine hundred and eighteen cars to carry it and the train would extend two and a half times around the earth." [16]

And, the exposed rock is only a small portion of the granite formation which spreads beneath the earth's crust, surfacing periodically, through several area counties. Stone Mountain is actually part of the Appalachian Mountain chain, which sinks below ground for many miles before reemerging in DeKalb County. [17]

Anthropologists and historians speculate that prehistoric Indians took refuge atop the mountain from fierce animals who themselves were fleeing advancing sheets of ice. [18]

They also speculate that prehistoric Indians viewed the mountain "with superstitious awe." [19] When Creek Indians roamed the land, it is said they lit signal fires that could be seen for miles around. [20] We will never know for certain how they perceived the mountain or if, like the white men who supplanted them, thought of the mountain as a somewhat useless curiosity.

Two stone formations once atop the mountain were said to have been the handiwork of prehistoric Indians, a relatively easy deduction since the oddities were in place when white men first saw Stone Mountain and created beyond the memory of Creek and Cherokee Indians.

One of the constructions was a wall made of loose granite boulders that circled the mountain near the summit. The four-foot-high wall had only one opening, the size and height of which would allow only

Stone Mountain must have appeared to the first human who saw it much the way it looks in this old postcard. (Lee Collection, DeKalb Historical Society)

one person at a time to crawl into the enclosure. [21]

Most writers on the subject of Stone Mountain discount the theory that the enclosure was a fortification. As historian Willard Neal wrote: "The most ignorant savage certainly would have realized that the top of Stone Mountain would be untenable in a siege, since there was no water and no access to food. It is the last place anyone would want to be caught when the shooting started." [22]

Although one historian [23] claimed that the military strategy of the seige had yet to be invented, this seems unlikely for a people who demonstrated their understanding of the importance of a readily available source of water.

More likely, as Neal and others agree, the wall had some "religious or ceremonial significance." Some even speculate on the possibility of its use as a setting for sacrifices to the gods. [24]

Elizabeth Austin Ford describes the circle on Stone Mountain as "somewhat reminiscent of Druid places of worship in Britain." Ford also contends that there was a similar wall around the base of the mountain. [25] Without drawing any conclusion as to the wall's possible purpose, Leila Venable Mason Eldridge points out its similarity to a formation on Fort Mountain in Chatsworth, Georgia. [26]

Today's sophisticated anthropological tests cannot determine any new information about the wall; the last of its boulders were rolled off the mountainside in 1923. [27] A security fence was later constructed in much the same place as the old rock wall. [28]

Even more curious was a stone formation atop the mountain called "Devil's Cross Roads." A huge rock 200 feet in diameter and five to ten feet thick was rent by two fissures which began as cracks, then widened and deepened and crossed at right angles. They reached a width and depth of five feet at their intersection. The cracks were of different lengths, with the longer extending about 400 feet. One crevice ran exactly north and south, the other east and west. The granite compass was covered at its junction by a flat rock about 20 feet in diameter. [29]

Theories on how the formation came to be are wildly varied. One historian wrote that the rent was made "when this old world shook at the crucifixion of Christ." [30] Another writer claims that the Devil's Cross Roads was related in some way to the Rock Eagle Mound in Eatonton and the shell mound at Sea Pines Plantation in Hilton Head, South Carolina. All three were said to have been made in 2450 B. C. by the Eagle Division of the Four Corners Engineer and Construction Utd. [31]

The Devil's Cross Roads may have been nothing more mysterious than a giant hearth. Trenches were cut into the granite by the Indians to channel rainwater away from their fires, and raised platforms constructed of stone for use much as today's kitchen counters. [32]

Regardless of its original purpose, capitalism was to be the ultimate undoing of the Devil's Cross Roads. The stones were found to be of superior building quality, and quarrymen hauled the stones down the mountain in 1896. [33]

Stone Mountain has long inspired its viewers to wax poetic.

Geologist M. F. Stephenson called it "the most profound geologic phenomenon in the United States east of the Rockies and surpasses anything of its kind yet known in grandeur."

This "unparalled curiosity of nature" has inspired countless poems and odes to the "majestic and sublime cone" [34]... "the Great Blue Ball." [35]

Perhaps the best description was by historian Percy Plant:

"Stone Mountain has a grandeur and ever-changing beauty which cannot be expressed by an artist or captured by a photographer.

"On a clear morning it sparkles with the promise of a new day... In the rain it broods with a dismal and foreboding look... In the glare of the midday sun the huge rock seems to move as it shimmers with the heat... During a storm the sides of the mountain become a mighty waterfall... After the storm its sides are streaked with rivulets of silver and it glows with a radiant freshness... Late in the afternoon its majesty is emphasized by a purple haze... When partly shrouded by mist or fog, the ancient stone appears to cling to the secrets of its mysterious past... On rare occasions a crystal mountain glistens in the splendor of a mantle of white... About twice a century it is glorified by a rainbow which starts at the base, climbs the side and seems to leave a pot of gold on the summit... Its many charms are mirrored in its nearby lakes... Each sunrise and each sunset at the mountain is a silent sermon.

"Stone Mountain never looks the same. From a long distance it appears a gray, mysterious mound with little or no hint as to its size or actual appearance. From a short distance it will appear vividly close on one day; on another day from the same spot it will seem far distant. The mountain has a particular beauty in each season: winter with bare gnarled trees; spring with the budding of rare plants found in no other place on earth; summer with acres of yellow flower which grow only in granite soil; and autumn with a breath-taking display of fall foliage.

"The big rock has a changing personality and many moods. It can appear proud and independent with the wisdom of countless centuries. It can seem lonesome, a solitary sentinel far from others of its kind. It can appear weary from the buffeting of the ages. It can be peaceful, friendly and inviting, or it can be wild and violent in the lightning flashes of a midnight storm. When its laws are ignored, the big rock can be stern and merciless.

"Pictures and words cannot describe Stone Mountain by moonlight! Thousands of lovers who have climbed the old Indian trail attest the magical lure and mystical beauty of two hundred million years.

"The Stone Mountain panorama, through the ages, unfolds with an ever-changing spiritual beauty of infinite variety." [36]

Born in violence, Stone Mountain has survived violence both natural and manmade --- from the earthquake that created the Cartersville Fault [37] to the Civil War and cross burnings by the Ku Klux Klan. No doubt Stone Mountain will bear witness to profound changes during the coming millennia.

Geologist Maynard had no qualms about the mountain's ability to endure. Calling it "one of the pillars of the earth itself," he wrote that the mountain "has passed through the ages with only superficial decomposition." [38] Wrote Maynard: "... there can be no appreciable weathering of the mountain or the carved cavalcade for thousands of years." [39]

And, despite 150 years of quarrying and carving, man has managed to remove only "insignificant peelings," according to historian Neal. [40]

"Here stands a monument which, conceived in the belly of the earth, born midst the travail of the fires of hell has risen from its sepulcher, an inanimate body, transformed to a perfect crystal complex. It has risen and continues to rise higher and higher. One of the wonders of the world, it is more than forty-eight times larger around its base and a hundred and twenty times larger than the Pyramid of Gizeh.

"We shall never cease to marvel at its majesty, sometimes at the dawn of a day, sometimes in the hours of twilight. Even more fascinating than its outward splendor is the visualizing of its birth." [41]

Stone Mountain has long captured the imagination of man, inspiring deeds from writing passionate poetry to concocting tall tales by the campfire to encouraging hatred and bigotry with mountaintop fires at midnight.

Even the first ownership of the mountain is the stuff of legend.

John W. Beauchamp's descendants tell the story that their ancestor gave Indians $40, a horse and some whiskey for the mountain. Beauchamp apparently thought it was worth more than a man who is said to have walked 60 miles only to find that his newly-acquired land "wouldn't grow beans." He traded the mountain for a mule to ride back home. E. V. Sanford is said to have traded the mountain for a rifle with which he could hunt his dinner. [42]

William Garrard captures "The Romance of Old Stone Mountain" with this legend of caves and bats and eyeless fish in a clear underground stream:

It seems there was a dancing pavillion on the mountain, with a bar and a gambling room. Visitors came from as far as Charleston and Savannah to drink and play cards and try to steal a kiss while dancing with a beautiful girl.

"Young `Beau' Stephens, as they called him, heir to the finest rice plantation on the Carolina rivers, sat one night in a poker game. Above, on the pavillion, the little feet of Emily, fairest flower of old Charleston, danced to minuet music. Stephens loved Emily. So did other men. And, because he thought Emily's favors were not for him, the young planter sought solace in whisky and poker.

"The game was going against him. His losses mounted into the hundreds; the thousand mark was passed, and still young Stephens could not win. Drinking heavily, he became posessed of a recklessness that would win or lose all. Play at the other tables stopped; men gathered around where Stephens sat. Finally, he lost ten thousand dollars when a straight flush beat him. He was a good loser. Writing out a check for the money, laughing while he did it, Stephens walked out into the blackness of the mountain side.

He went up the steps to the pavillion. Reeling slightly, he strode to where Emily was sitting out a dance. He told her good-by, saying he was going away that night. But his eyes gleamed queerly; this manner frightened the girl. Some instinct warned her.

"She followed secretly when he went from the pavillion. He did not go towards the lights of the cottages in the village, but started through the blackness around the giant rock. Down the steep slopes he leaped, the girl calling to him. Apparently he did not hear.

"They reached the deep mouth of the cave. The man plunged into it, the girl following, crying for him to stop. Snakes hissed at them; bats flapped dirty wings in their faces. The man turned, seized the girl around the waist, and ran forward over the slippery rocks, straight into the bowels of the earth. They came to the black stream in which eyeless fishes swam; a splash; ripples of black water, and the man and girl sank to the unseen bottom. Then the dancers on the pavillion felt a tremor like an earthquake; and the cave was never again discovered...

"Whether or not this legend is true, it is a strange fact that Stephens and Emily were never seen alive since that night, nor were their bodies found at the foot of any of the mountain cliffs... Incidentally, Stephens' $10,000 check proved to be worthless...

"This is a little cave half-way down the steep side of the mountain. It is about as tall as a man, and only seven feet deep. An adventurous stone-cutter, working in the quarries leased by the Venables, the owners of the mountain, lowered himself by a rope to this cave. Inside he found a folded piece of paper wedged behind a splinter of rock. Opening it, he read: `You are not the first darn fool who has been here.'" [43]

Chapter 2 Notes

1. Neal, Willard, 1963, "The Story of Stone Mountain."

2. Bunch, Robyn L., 1982, "Fork Creek Mountain on Soapstone Ridge: Defining the Quarry Site in its Environmental Setting," page 18-19.

3. Maynard, Poole, Ph.D., 1929, "How Stone Mountain Was Created," page 11.

4. Maynard, Poole, Ph.D., 1929, "How Stone Mountain Was Created," pages 8-9.

5. Maynard, Poole, Ph.D., 1929, "How Stone Mountain Was Created," page 7.

6. Maynard, Poole, Ph.D., 1929, "How Stone Mountain Was Created," pages 9-11.

7. Price, Vivian, November, 1987, "Stone Mountain Around Long Before Animals Roamed Earth," Georgia's Stone Mountain Park Guide-Gazette, page 14.

8. Neal, Willard, 1963, "The Story of Stone Mountain," pages 21-22.

9. Price, Vivian, November, 1987, "Stone Mountain Around Long Before Animals Roamed Earth," Georgia's Stone Mountain Park Guide-Gazette, page 14.

10. Price, Vivian, September 30, 1992, "Lithonia built on foundation of solid granite," Fall Granite Heritage Festival special section, DeKalb News/Sun, page 2.

11. Price, Vivian, November, 1987, "Stone Mountain Around Long Before Animals Roamed Earth," Georgia's Stone Mountain Park Guide-Gazette, page 14.

12. Maynard, Poole, Ph.D., 1929, "How Stone Mountain Was Created," page 5.

13. Maynard, Poole, Ph.D., 1929, "How Stone Mountain Was Created," page 7.

14. Neal, Willard, 1963, "The Story of Stone Mountain," page 3.

15. Maynard, Poole, Ph.D., 1929, "How Stone Mountain Was Created," page 18.

16. Maynard, Poole, Ph.D., 1929, "How Stone Mountain Was Created," page 18.

17. Price, Vivian, November, 1987, "Stone Mountain Around Long Before Animals Roamed Earth," Georgia's Stone Mountain Park Guide-Gazette, page 14.

18. Maynard, Poole, 1929, "How Stone Mountain Was Created," page 9.

19. Eldridge, Leila Venable Mason, 1951, "Stone Mountain," page 7, quoting Lucian Lamar Knight in <u>Georgia Landmarks, Memorials and Legends</u>.

20. Miller, Dorothy Burke, 1952, <u>The Collections of the DeKalb Historical Society,</u> Vol. 1, page 7.

21. Price, Vivian, November, 1987, "Mysterious Granite Formations Older Than The Indians," Georgia's Stone Mountain Park Guide-Gazette, page 3.

22. Neal, Willard, 1963, "The Story of Stone Mountain," page 14.

23. Jones, Charles C., Jr., 1873, "Antiquities of the Southern Indians, Particularly of the Georgia Tribes," page 208.

24. Neal, Willard, 1963, "The Story of Stone Mountain," page 14.

25. Ford, Elizabeth Austin, 1959, "Stone Mountain," page 15.

26. Eldridge, Leila Venable Mason, 1951, "Stone Mountain," page 8.

27. Neal, Willard, 1963, "The Story of Stone Mountain," page 15.

28. Neal, Willard, 1963, "The Story of Stone Mountain," page 22.

29. Neal, Willard, 1963, "The Story of Stone Mountain," page 15.

30. Hill, Mrs. J. F., n. d., "The History of Stone Mountain," DeKalb Historical Society, page 2.

31. McCall, Howard McCall, n. d. "The eagles have landed, long ago," Eatonton Messenger.

32. Jones, Charles C., Jr., 1873, "Antiquities of the Southern Indians, Particularly of the Georgia Tribes," page 208.

33. Neal, Willard, 1963, "The Story of Stone Mountain," page 15.

34. Eldridge, Leila Venable Mason, 1951, "Stone Mountain," page 21, quoting F. M. Stephenson in Geology and Minerology of Georgia.

35. Hill, Mrs. J. F., n. d., The History of Stone Mountain, page 2.

36. Plant, Percy, August-September, 1961, "Work Progresses on Stone Mountain Memorial Park," Georgia magazine, pages 44-45.

37. Maynard, Poole, Ph.D., 1929, "How Stone Mountain Was Created," page 19.

38. Maynard, Poole, Ph.D., 1929, "How Stone Mountain Was Created," page 19.

39. Maynard, Poole, Ph.D., 1929, "How Stone Mountain Was Created," page 20.

40. Neal, Willard, 1963, "The Story of Stone Mountain," page 4.

41. Maynard, Poole, Ph.D., 1929, "How Stone Mountain Was Created," page 20.

42. Patton, Kathryn, n. d., A Sketchbook of Stone Mountain, page 6.

43. Knight, Lucian Lamar, n.d., L. L. Knight's Georgia Scrapbook, Vol. 13, pages 30-31.

Chapter 3

*W*e may never know the identity of the first white man to set foot on Stone Mountain, nor his impressions of a great mountain made of a single rock rising abruptly out of the surrounding level sea of treetops.

No Spanish explorer ventured as far into the interior of what would become Georgia than the Indian town of Ocute, on the Ocmulgee River just south of today's Milledgeville. [1]

Hernando de Soto bypassed DeKalb on his explorations from 1539-1543; although he was advised to travel the Hightower Trail, he did not. [2] The Tristan de Luna march from Pensacola, Florida into north Georgia (1559-1561) stayed well to the east. Subsequent Spanish explorers traveled primarily to the same towns de Soto had visited during their explorations of 1566. [3]

No route taken by these early Spanish explorers came close enough to Stone Mountain to account for such descriptions of the monolith as "Crystal Mountain" attributed by modern-day historians to Capt. Juan Pardo. Certainly, no diamonds and rubies were ever lying on the ground waiting to be picked up by the ambitious Spaniards.

The first written mention of Stone Mountain appears to be from the journals of the Pedro de Chozas expedition to Ocute in 1596. Indians told de Chozas of a mountain "very high, shining when the sun set set like a fire" which could be found several days' travel from Ocute. On the other side of this mountain lived a "short-haired" people. Signs of pine trees cut with axes could be found in this area. Perhaps the Indians at Ocute could have been referring to Stone Mountain and people who lived along the Chattahoochee River basin. [4]

It was about this time peaches brought across the Atlantic Ocean by the Spaniards reached the interior of Georgia. Little did the Spanish know they would be contributing a name and an icon to a vast city of millions. [5]

The Spanish occupation of Georgia (1566-1702) triggered changes among the prehistoric Indians of the late Mississippian period that would change Indian civilization forever. The prehistoric Indian chiefdoms encountered by the Spanish in the mid-1500s began collapsing around 1570.[6]

Disease, war and slavery, all introduced by the Europeans, resulted in the rapid political disintegration of Indian societies[7] and the depreciation of the Indian population which had been estimated to be at least at 170,000 in 1540.[8]

More than half, and conceivably as much as 90 percent, of the population of Southeastern American Indians died from smallpox, bubonic plague, measles and yellow fever, diseases against which the Indians had no defense.[9] As late as 1783, epidemics ravaged the Indian populations, cutting tribal numbers in half with each wave of sickness.[10]

European cultural practices also resulted in the decimation of the aboriginal populations. Trading strategies, slavery and political struggles contributed to their ultimate transformation.

Southeastern Indians began trading with Europeans as early as 1513.[11] By 1670, and the establishment of Charles Town in South Carolina, north Georgia Indians traded regularly with Europeans. DeKalb County and all of Georgia became crisscrossed with paths over which white and Indian traders carried on their business. Trade, carried on in the early years primarily between Charles Town and villages on the Chattahoochee River, was a major cause of the Indians' metamorphosis.[12] Fur skins were much in demand, as were Indian slaves who were often shipped to the West Indies to work on plantations.[13] "Trade in Indian slaves and deer skins became the primary occupation of many Indian males."[14] In return, the Indians received clothing, blankets, jewelry, horses, liquor and weapons.[15]

Firearms, heretofore unknown to the Indians, upset the balance of power among the remaining tribes, and caused their final cataclysmic decline.[16]

"From that time on, the Indians of the Southern region of North America rarely knew peace among themselves or with the white man... Competition for the fur trade developed into a bitter struggle that brought out the worst in both the whites and the Indians."[17]

Before the arrival of the white man, land was plentiful and boundary lines mapping the territories of Indian tribes was at best an informal arrangement. Competition for hunting grounds to supply white traders with furs caused Indians "to murder each other in a frenzy -- egged on by the Europeans, who wanted the tribes weak and docile."[18]

As more European countries began to compete for the newly discovered soil, the Indians became caught up in the colonial politics of the English, Spanish and French governments. Later, the Indians's dilemma was further complicated by the American colonists, principally the Carolinians, as well as the Georgia settlers and the state government.

The Indians were "drawn into a deadly game in which the Indians were often the diplomatic and military pawns to further the interest of the white man."[19]

The history of Georgia's Indians between 1550 and 1650 may never be adequately documented. It was a century during which the indigenous societies fell apart and reformed. Georgia's share of that reformation evolved into the tribes of the Creek Confederation and the Cherokee Indian nation. [20]

Changes the Indians never could have anticipated put them on the move again, in search, not of food like their prehistoric predecessors, but of other refugees with whom they could unite. The result, in the case of the Creeks, was a diverse alliance of culturally and geographically diverse peoples whose main bond was language.

Interior Georgia became "a vast abandoned zone" between territory claimed by the Spanish to the south and English conquests to the north. [21]

By 1700, Georgia's Indian population was confined to the Cherokee nation in northwest Georgia and settlements below the fall line that separates the Piedmont from the Coastal Plain, along the Chattahoochee, Flint, Ocmulgee, Altamaha and Savannah rivers. [22]

With the Spanish and French explorers driven out and the nearest English colony hundreds of miles away at Charles Town, the Georgia Indians enjoyed a quarter century of relative peace. They could not have known that the real onslaught was just beginning.

Chapter 3 Notes

1. Worth, Dr. John E., anthropoligist/educational coordinator, Fernbank Museum of Natural History, interview, August 25, 1994.

2. Worth, Dr. John E., anthropoligist/educational coordinator, Fernbank Museum of Natural History, interview, August 25, 1994.

3. Patterson, Isabel Garrard, May 13, 1934, "Despite Ancient Maps and Documents of Early Explorers But Little Is Known About Lives and Habits of Original Natives of Georgia," Atlanta Constitution, page 7C.

4. Worth, Dr. John E., 1993, "Prelude to Abandonment: the Interior Provinces of Early 17th Century Georgia," Early Georgia, Vol. 21, No. 1, The Society for Georgia Archaeology, page 49.

5. Worth, Dr. John E., anthropologist/educational coordinator, Fernbank Museum of Natural History, interview, August 25, 1994.

6. Worth, Dr. John E., n. d., "Before Creek and Cherokee: Georgia Indians during the Early Colonial Era," Fernbank Quarterly, Fernbank Museum of Natural History, page 23.

7. Smith, Martin T., June, 1990, "Historic Period Indian Archaeology of Northern Georgia," Department of Anthropology, Georgia State University, page 28.

8. Hudson, Charles, 1976, The Southeastern Indians, University of Tennessee Press, page 5.

9. Worth, Dr. John E., n. d., Before Creek and Cherokee: Georgia Indians during the Early Colonial Era, Fernbank Quarterly, Fernbank Museum of Natural History, page 24.

10. Winn, Bill, April 23, 1968, "The First Georgians No. 9 -- Fierce Tribe Turned Peaceful," Atlanta Journal, page 10A.

11. Smith, Marvin T., June, 1990, "Historic Period Indian Archaeology of Northern Georgia," Department of Anthropology, Georgia State University, page 21.

12. Smith, Marvin T., June, 1990, "Historic Period Indian Archaeology of Northern Georgia," Department of Anthropology, Georgia State University, page 28.

13. Winn, Bill, April 19, 1968, "The First Georgians No. 6 -- The Efforts for Conquest," Atlanta Journal, page 4A.

14. Smith, Martin T., June, 1990, "Historic Period Indian Archaeology of Northern Georgia," Department of Anthropology, Georgia State University, page 28.

15. Caughey, John Walton, 1938, McGillivray of the Creeks, Norman, University of Oklahoma Press, page 8.

16. Smith, Martin T., June, 1990, "Historic Period Indian Archaeology of Northern Georgia," Department of Anthropology, Georgia State University, page 28.

17. Winn, Bill, April, 19, 1968, "The First Georgians No. 6 -- The Efforts for Conquest," Atlanta Journal, page 4A.

18. Winn, Bill, April 19, 1968, "The First Georgians No. 6 -- The Efforts for Conquest, Atlanta Journal, page 4A.

19. Winn, Bill, April 18, 1968, "The First Georgians No. 5 -- DeSoto's Path Was Bloody," Atlanta Journal, page 16A.

20. Worth, Dr. John E., 1993, "Prelude to Abandonment: the Interior Provinces of Early 17th Century Georgia," Early Georgia, Vol. 21, No. 1, The Society for Georgia Archaeology, page 25.

21. Worth, Dr. John E., 1993, "Prelude to Abandonment: the Interior Provinces of Early 17th Century Georgia," Early Georgia, Vol. 21, No. 1, The Society for Georgia Archaeology, page 30.

22. Smith, Marvin T., June, 1990, "Historic Period Indian Archaeology of Northern Georgia," Department of Anthropology, Georgia State University, page 8.

Chapter 4

The changes that had beset Georgia were minor compared to what was to follow the landing of the first ship of settlers from England on February 12, 1733. The colonists encountered Indians who were for the most part friendly, willing to share both their land and their secrets to survival on it. In the coming century, that generosity would be sorely tested.

After almost 200 years of association with the white man, the Indians had reorganized their society into new tribes. The Cherokees were a single unified nation, occupying lands in north Georgia. Beyond their most recent migration from Tennessee, no one seems to know quite where the name Cherokee came from; they called themselves Aniyunwiga (The Principal People). [1]
The capital of the Cherokee nation was at New Echota in what is now Gordon County, Georgia.

The Creek Confederation, consisting of 47 tribes, [2] including Muskogees, Alabamas, Hitchitees (later called Seminoles) and Euchees, who spoke the Muskogean language, lived in middle and south Georgia and in Alabama. The capital city of the Creek Confederation was the home of the presiding chief of the annual meeting. Coweta and Cussita, on opposite sides of the Chattahoochee River at present-day Columbus, were considered important towns. [3]

Comparatively few historic period Indians lived in what today is DeKalb County. The land was considered a buffer zone between tribes and used as hunting grounds by all. [4]

Christopher Columbus, mistakenly thinking he had reached the East Indies, dubbed the people he found "Indians." The white man also bestowed the name "Creek" to the indigenous people they found living in a land crisscrossed by many large and small streams. "Creek" also may be a reference to the Ocheese Creek Indians. Ocheese Creek was an old name for the Ocmulgee River near which many of the Lower Creeks once lived. However incorrect they may be, these are the names that have endured. The Creek name for themselves was Muskogee (also spelled Muscogee or Muskhogee), which is derived from an Algonquian word meaning swamp or wet ground. [5]

That multiple spellings of Indian names that have survived to this day can be attributed to the fact that the Creek Indians had no written language; the written interpretation of a spoken word often differed from one writer to the next.

Only three months after the English colonists arrived in 1733, the Creek Indians ceded to the white settlers land between the Savannah and Altamah rivers "as far as the tide ebbed and flowed," except for their campground near Yamacraw Bluff and the islands of Sapelo, St. Catherine's and Ossabaw. [6] Although this cession could have been interpreted as giving the white man many thousands of acres, reaching to today's Yellow and South rivers in DeKalb County, the colonists at first claimed land only about 30 miles upstream.

Relations between the white man and the Indian remained peaceful for the next 50 years. Oglethorpe and the Yamacraw Indian chief Tomochichi led a delegation of Indians traveling to England to ratify their cession treaty with King George II in 1734. The town of Augusta, which would be connected to DeKalb County by an important Indian trail also was founded in that year. The town would become the largest fur trading center in the south. Georgia's founder Gen. James Edward Oglethorpe traveled without incident to Coweta, then the capitol of the Creek Confederation, on the Chattahoochee River, in the location of present-day Fort Benning.

Smallpox epidemics continued to ravage the Indians, reducing their population to as few as 7,560 (2,160 warriors) in 1761. [7] By the late 18th century the Creeks had fewer than 5,000 "gunmen" in western Georgia and northern Alabama. In comparison, "even the smallest American state had greater man power." [8]

William Bartram, the English naturalist who traveled in Georgia in 1765, described a "magnificent" land with grand forests, green knolls and glittering brooks. He noted oak trees generally with a girth of eleven feet measured at five feet above the ground, with some as large as 30 feet around. [9] He documented a vast variety of plant life from stately oak, sweet gum and beech trees, to fragrant magnolias and sweet shrubs to colorful dogwoods, rhododendrons and azaleas. Delphiniums, strawberries, monkshood and mallow bloomed in abundance.

He and his entourage ate huge fish speared with harpoons by Indians in his party. They were constantly on the lookout for venomous snakes and enjoyed concerts given by the "gay mock-bird." [10]

Although the buffalo already had disappeared from the Southeast, Bartram's journal tells of abundant deer, bear, wolves, wild cats and wild turkey. "Tygers," also called panthers, Bartram said, were yellow-brown in color, very strong and mischievous. Much larger than a dog, they preyed on calves and colts. [11] Undoubtedly these "tygers" were the panthers for which DeKalb's Panthersville is named.

The Indians Bartram encountered no longer subsisted by hunting alone. They had long ago forsaken the nomadic lifestyle and lived in well-established towns. Communities continued to be exclusively along the banks of rivers and streams, in close walking distance from that basic necessity, water. They planted communal gardens, growing corn, beans, sweet potatoes, squash and pumpkins. [12] Peaches and plums flourished in their well-cultivated orchards. [13]

The first white settlers in DeKalb would adopt agricultural and food preparation practices from the Indians. The basic staple of the Indian diet -- corn -- became essential in white households. Grits, cornbread, hoecake and hushpuppies all are derived from the Indian culture. Many a Southern soldier survived on "Confederate bullets," cornbread dough boiled in corn husks.

Indians taught white settlers to roast corn on the cob, to boil and dry vegetables and to roast meats over hickory coals.

Early DeKalb County doctors mixed their European science with Indian herbalism, using ginseng, wild cherry bark, persimmon bark, poplar bark, lady's-slipper, poke leaves, poke root, poke berries, sassafras, yellow root, chestnut leaves, boneset, pine needles, ferns, horsemint, peppermint, snakeroot, and pennyroyal. [14]

Although historians disagree on an exact number, there were 50-60 towns in the Creek Confederation, with Upper Creeks living in Alabama and Lower Creeks in Georgia. Some 15 Creek towns were situated in the fertile lands along the Chattahoochee River, the majority at or below the falls at present-day Columbus, Georgia. Towns above the falls changed hands periodically between the Creeks and Cherokees, until white settlers finally predominated.

The nature of Indian towns and homes depended entirely on whom you asked. Bartram found Indian homes to be large and neatly built, with walls consisting of a wooden frame, lathed and plastered with clay, giving the appearance of red brick. [15]

Each family had a cool summer house and a more tightly constructed house for wintertime, according to one writer. A prosperous family might have additional buildings for storing corn and animal hides.[16]

R. S. Cotterill wrote of log cabins with dirt floors that were dirty, uncomfortable and unsightly. Houses, he wrote, were simply a "point of departure" for the Indian. "The Southern Indian, being both Southern and Indian, regarded his house as a place in which to sleep at night and to find haven from inclement weather; he lived out of doors." [17]

Each town contained 25-30 houses (100 at most) in square compounds radiating from a central village where government business and ceremonies were conducted. An important feature of each town was a playing field. [18] The Creek Indians were fond of games, especially lacrosse and a form of lawn bowling known as chunky. The Creeks also were notorious gamblers, sometimes betting all of their personal possessions on a single ball game. [19]

Indian women worked harder than men, but no harder than the white farmer's wife. Women were the primary farmers and food preparers, and also tended small herds of cattle. Men were responsible for hunting, fishing and fighting. [20]

In short, the Creek and Cherokee Indians living, roaming or hunting in what would be DeKalb County were not much different than the white settlers who migrated to the rolling, wooded territory in the first decades of 19th century.

Where Creek, Cherokee and later white territory converged were two Indian settlements along the Chattahoochee River. One, by the name of Standing Peachtree, was located where Peachtree Creek flowed into the great river. The other was called Buzzard's Roost, later Sandtown, was located at the junction of Utoy Creek and the river. Sandtown was the northernmost wholly Creek town going upstream on the Chattahoochee. The Buzzard's Roost Island in the Chattahoochee River was at the boundary between the Creeks and Cherokees, with Cherokees to the north and Creeks to the south. [21]

Historians and mapmakers through the years frequently were confused as to the location and name of the town, which lay on the east side of the Chattahoochee below the mouth of Utoy Creek in now southwest Fulton County, near the intersection of Cascade Road and Boatrock Road. [22] Although the town never moved, it later would belong to four different political jurisdictions. Land District 14 was first located in Fayette County after the Creek Indian cession of 1821, then was included in to DeKalb County in 1822, to Campbell County in 1828 and finally to Fulton County in 1932. [23] Today vestiges of the old Sandtown community still can be found along Campbellton Road in southwest Atlanta, and Buzzard's Roost Island still is the point at which three jurisdictions (Cobb, Fulton and Douglas counties) converge.

Officially, the land that would become DeKalb County fell wholly within Creek Indian territory, the boundary being the Chattahoochee River, but the land and towns were used by both Creek and Cherokee.

Ancestors of the Creek Indians established a village in the deep bend of the Chattahoochee River at the confluence of Peachtree Creek around 1000 A.D. [24] The Creek name for the village, Pakanahuili, translates into the English, Standing Peachtree. "Pakana" may have been a reference to one of the tribes that became a part of the Creek Confederation, or simply to the fruit. "Huili" meant standing or upright, a reference to the nature of the peach tree, or could have meant that the tribe "stood" or stayed in one place. [25]

The Indians may have named the village for a large peach tree that is said to have grown there. In an interview on April 25, 1897, George Washington Collier said, "There was a great, huge mound of earth heaped up there -- big as this house, maybe bigger -- and right on top of it grew a big peach tree. It bore fruit and was a useful and beautiful tree." [72] [26]

With its strategic location, the village was an important center of trade and travel before 1800. It would survive until around 1842, [27] lending its name to a famous street and landmarks recognized around the world.

Standing Peachtree, the most important Indian town in the area, was considered a Cherokee town, although it lay in Creek country. [73] A nearby Cherokee village, Suwanee Old Town, would later

---

[72] George Washington (Wash) Collier (1813-1903) was Atlanta's first postmaster. He was the son of DeKalb County pioneers Meredith Collier and Elizabeth Gray. (Source: Garrett, Franklin M., 1954, 1969, Atlanta and Environs -- A Chronicle of Its People and Events, Vol. 1, page 59).

[73] In files of the Cherokees-East, of the Bureau of Indian Affairs in Washington, is the following copy of an affidavit, made by James Montgomery and sworn to before Samuel A. Wales, Commissioner, January 22, 1829, when testimony was being taken as to how far north the land ceded by the Creeks extended:
"Georgia
DeKalb County   James M. C. Montgomery saith on oath that he was superintendent of Artifices in the service of United States in the year 1814 and stationed at the Standing Peach tree on the Chattahoochee River for the purpose of erecting public boat to transport provisions down the Chattahoochee. That while in service at said place he understood from the Indians in that vicinity who were chiefly or entirely Cherokees, that the land on both sides of said River belonged to the Creeks -- and this deponent further saith that some years prior to 1814 he obtained a decree of the Cherokee nation against certain Cawdry who was then at the head of an Indian family -- that he was informed by the Cherokee Indians that said Cawdry run his property to the Standing peach tree, on enquiring whether then the land there was Creek or Cherokee, this

become a part of Gwinnett County. Together with Sandtown, the three villages would experience a remarkable transition period during which whites and Indians lived together before all the Indians were removed.

White traders were firmly established at Sandtown/Buzzard's Roost as early as 1767. On May 28 of that year, a delegation of Creek Indians led by Mad Dog of the Eutassies met with whites in Augusta to protest unfair practices employed by traders headquartered at Buzzard's Roost. The conference caused more strict trade laws to be approved. [28]

While DeKalb, of course, took no part in the American Revolution (1775-1781), the war presented an opportunity for Indians to conduct raids on whites living south of the Chattahoochee River. The Indians frequently switched their allegiance from one white government to another, seeking profitable trading partners and trying to stem the tide of land-hungry settlers. Whites, in turn, continued to pit tribes against each other in an attempt to lay claim to the land and gain strategic advantage over rival governments. [29]

The Indians continued to give up more territory, granting cessions periodically from 1763 through 1835. Millions of acres were surrendered to satisfy debts the Indians owed to "factories," frontier stores established by the newly formed American government to encourage them to spend beyond their ability to pay. Endorsed by Thomas Jefferson, the factory system encouraged the Indians "to run in debt beyond their individual means of paying; and whenever in that situation they will always cede land to rid themselves of debt." [30]

The Creek Indians continued to threaten white settlements after the Revolutionary War. Sandwiched between whites to the east and west, they fought to keep the land along the Chattahoochee. A letter dated May 27, 1782 from John Martin to Gen. Andrew Pickens of South Carolina relates information that a band of Coweta Indians, led by William McIntosh, was to rendezvous at the village of Standing Peachtree in preparation for an attack. In response, an observer, John Brandon, was sent to Standing Peachtree by the Executive Council of Georgia to spy on the Indians. [31] In his letter, Martin urged the general's speedy action: "...for God's sake exert yourself and come in to our timely aid, as delays are dangerous." [32] John Martin's letter is the first known mention of the village of Standing Peachtree.

Unbeknownst to participants at the time, events in the year 1790 would propel them into a legendary confrontation, one that would seal the fate of the Indians and establish Georgia the winner of a challenge to the authority of the federal government. In that year, Congress revoked the right of states to acquire Indian lands, giving that power exclusively to the federal government. [33]

---

deponent was informed by several who were leading men in the Cherokee nation that it belonged to the Creeks, and that any claim or title the Cherokees had to the lands there was by permission of the Creeks -- and that it was common for the two tribes being connected with each other by marriage, to occupy each others land, and this deponent further saith that the Standing peach tree is from ten to twelve miles above the buzzard roost the point from whence the temporary line between the two lines now starts and further this deponent saith that one John Woodall was permitted by the Cherokees to erect a Mill, etc., on the west side of the Chattahoochee immediately above the peach tree -- and that Rolly McIntosh at the head of a party of Creek Indians as this deponent understood came up and destroyed said Woodall's crop and mill, and this deponent has often seen the ruins of the same." (Source: Anderson, E. Katherine, December, 1937, "James McC. Montgomery of Standing Peachtree," Atlanta Historical Bulletin, No. 12, citing The Southern Recorder of Feb. 7, 1829.)

President George Washington summoned Indians to a treaty conference in New York in August of 1790. Marinus Willett was Washington's special envoy to the Indians. He promised that a treaty "as strong as the hills and lasting as the rivers" would be made to protect Indian lands from white encroachment.

Against the advice of many, Alexander McGillivray, [74] the famous son of a Scottish trader and an Creek mother, agreed to lead an Indian delegation to New York. Notice of the impending meeting went out to the Creeks through riders on horseback and through smoke signals from atop Stone Mountain. [34] The entourage must have formed a colorful pageant. From Alabama to New York, they traveled through the wilderness, past Stone Mountain. McGillivray rode on horseback and Willett in a sulky, while twenty-six other chiefs and warriors traveled in wagons. All along the way the delegation generated great interest, and prominent citizens hosted parties for McGillivray. [35]

One of the landmarks passed by the convoy was Stone Mountain. Willett recalled the visit in his personal journal:

"June 9, at 9 o'clock a.m. arrived at the Stony Mountain about 8 miles from where we encamped. Here we found the Cowetas and the Curates to the number of eleven waiting for us; lay by until 3 o'clock p.m. and then proceeded 8 miles and encamped by a large Creek of the Waters of Ockmulgee. Course in general nearly east, north east. Pleasant day, shower of rain after we encamped. While I was at Stony Mountain I ascended the summit. It is one solid rock of circular form, about one miles across. Many strange tales are told by the Indians of this Mountain. I have now passed all Indian settlements and shall only observe that the inhabitants of these countries appear very happy." [36]

Unfortunately, Willett did not relate any of the "strange tales" of Stone Mountain or any details of Indian life.

Georgians vehemently opposed the Treaty of New York, which guaranteed the Indians permanent possession of their lands. [37] The 1790 treaty established a boundary line between Indian and white settlements, a line that already had been crossed by many whites.

While there is documented evidence of thievery, kidnappings and killings [38] perpetrated by whites and Indians against each other in the years between the treaty-signing and the final removal, there are at least three examples of the two groups living peaceably together.

DeKalb County pioneers Dempsey Perkerson and his son-in-law David Waldrop both purchased land along the South River, which the Indians called Weelaunee. Perkerson and Waldrop tradition holds

---

[74] Alexander McGillivray was the son of Scottish trader Lachlan McGillivray and Sehoy Marchand of the Creek Indian Wind Clan, who was herself the daughter of a French army officer. Born in 1759, he was continuously plagued by debilitating illnesses until his untimely death in 1793. Educated by his cousin, a Presbyterian minister, in Charleston, he proved to be an extraordinary and charismatic leader. Although he signed the treaty of New York, McGillivray long opposed alliance with the Americans. His father, a Loyalist during the Revolution, was banished from the colonies and his property confiscated. Of Americans, McGillivray wrote in 1784: "The restlessness of the American frontiersman and their propensity for encroaching upon the land of the Indians was a most powerful argument against the United States." McGillivray also did not expect the new nation to last. "The whole Continent is in Confusion. Before long I expect to hear that the three kinds (of England, Spain and France) must Settle the matter by dividing America between them." (Source: Caughey, John Walton, 1938, McGillivray of the Creeks, University of Oklahoma Press, page 23)

that Cherokee Indians lived with the families. The Indians were sequestered by their white friends when the government canvassed DeKalb County during the removal of 1838. Several Cherokees are said to be buried in the Perkerson family cemetery on River Road.[39]

Cherokee Indians are said to have helped build the Solomon Goodwin house on what is now Peachtree Road in the Brookhaven community.[40] Cherokee Indians were said to have camped peacefully in woods along the Hightower Trail at the now intersection of Lawrenceville Highway in a spot where two small creeks came together to form a waterfall.[41]

One of DeKalb's first physicians, Dr. Chapman Powell,[75] treated Indians and whites alike at his cabin on the Shallow Ford Trail (now Clairmont Road). He is said to have earned the respect of the Cherokees by curing a chief's child. As a teenager, it was Powell's son John's job to ride across the Chattahoochee to trade gold for Indian herbal medicines.[42]

---

[75] Various documents and reference publications, including books written by his descendants, show Dr. Powell's given name spelled Chapmon.

Chapter 4 Notes

1. Cotterill, R. S., 1954, The Southern Indians -- The Story of the Civilized Tribes Before Removal, University of Oklahoma Press, page 5.

2. Cooper, Walter G., 1924, Official History of Fulton County, page 5.

3. Corkran, David H., 1967, The Creek Frontier, 1540-1783, University of Oklahoma Press, pages 4-5.

4. Worth, Dr. John E., anthropologist/educational coordinator, Fernbank Museum of Natural History, interview August 25, 1994.

5. Swanton, John R., 1922, "Early History of The Creek Indians and Their Neighbors," Government Printing Office, Smithsonian Institution, Bureau of American Ethnology, Bulletin 73 Ocheese Creek Indians, page 215.

6. Winn, Bill, April 21, 1968, "The First Georgians No. 7 -- Oglethorpe Found Creeks At Peace With Settlers," Atlanta Journal, page 22A.

7. Swanton, John R., 1922, "Early History of The Creek Indians and Their Neighbors," Government Printing Office, Smithsonian Institution, Bureau of American Ethnology, Bulletin 73 Ocheese Creek Indians, page 443.

8. Caughey, John Walton, 1938, McGillivray of the Creeks, Norman, University of Oklahoma Press, page 6.

9. Bartram, William, 1792, 1973, Travels Through North and South Carolina, Georgia, East and West Florida, Beehive Press, Savannah, Ga., page 37.

10. Bartram, William, 1792, 1973, Travels Through North and South Carolina, Georgia, East and West Florida, Beehive Press, Savannah, Ga., page 307.

11. Bartram, William, 1792, 1973, Travels Through North and South Carolina, Georgia, East and West Florida, Beehive Press, Savannah, Ga., page 46.

12. Hudson, Charles, 1976, The Southeastern Indians, University of Tennessee Press, page 498. Corkran, David H., 1967, The Creek Frontier, University of Oklahoma Press, page 9.

13. Cooper, Walter G., 1924, Official History of Fulton County, page 22.

14. Hudson, Charles, 1976, The Southeastern Indians, University of Tennessee Press, pages 498-499.

15. Bartram, William, 1792, 1973, Travels Through North and South Carolina, Georgia, East and West Florida, Beehive Press, Savannah, Ga., pages 385-392.

16. Winn, Bill, April 22, 1968, "The First Georgians No. 8 -- Creek Tribes Had Confederacy, Atlanta Journal, page 14A.

17. Cotterill, R. S., 1954, The Southern Indians -- The Story of the Civilized Tribes Before Removal, University of Oklahoma Press, pages 9-10.

18. Corkran, David H., 1967, The Creek Frontier, 1540-1783, University of Oklahoma Press, pages 8-9.

19. Winn, Bill, April 22, 1968, "The First Georgians No. 8 -- Creek Tribes Had Confederacy, Atlanta Journal, page 14A.

20. Reynolds, T. W., Cherokee and Creek, 1966, page 11. Mitchell, Eugene M., "The Indians Of Georgia," The Atlanta Historical Bulletin No. 11, September, 1937, pages 20-30. Cotterill, R. S., 1954, The Southern Indians -- The Story of the Civilized Tribes Before Removal, page 10.

21. Goff, John H., December, 1966, "The Sandtown Trail," Atlanta Historical Bulletin, Vol. XI No. 4, page 38. Mitchell, Eugene M., September, 1937, "The Indians of Georgia, Atlanta Historical Bulletin, No. 11, page 27.

22. Shadburn, Don L., 1989, Cherokee Planters in Georgia 1832-1838 -- Historical Essays on Eleven Counties in the Cherokee Nation of Georgia, Forsyth County Heritage Association, Cumming, Ga., page 93. Hemperley, Marion R., 1989, Historic Indian Trails of Georgia, The Garden Club of Georgia, page 43.

23. Shadburn, Don L., 1989, Cherokee Planters in Georgia 1832-1838 -- Historical Essays on Eleven Counties in the Cherokee Nation of Georgia, Forsyth County Heritage Association, Cumming, Ga., page 96.

24. Meier, Lawrence W., May 1973, "A Preliminary Report of Research at 9Co1, Standing Peach Tree Site, Cobb County, Georgia," The Profile Papers, Newsletter No. 6, The Society for Georgia Archaeology Special Publication No. 1 (the L. W. Meier Collection), page 2.

25. Thompson, Tim (cultural researcher, Muskogee Creek Nation, Okmulgee, Okla.), April 1, 1996, personal interview. Meier, Lawrence W., June 24, 1997, personal interview. Krakow, Kenneth K., 1975, Georgia Place-Names, Winship Press, page 216. Rozema, Vicki Rozema, n. d., Footsteps of the Cherokees -- A Guide to the Eastern Homelands of the Cherokee Nation, John F. Blair, publisher, Winston-Salem, N. C., page 336. Hemperley, Marion, memos, John Goff Collection, Georgia Department of Archives and History.

26. Patterson, Isabel Garrard, June 10, 1934, "'Standing Peach -- or Pitch -- Tree,' Atlanta's Forerunner; An Interesting Phase of the Unwritten History of Georgia," Atlanta Constitution.

27. Anderson, Katherine E., December 1937, "James McC. Montgomery of Standing Peachtree," The Atlanta Historical Bulletin No. 12. (Note: Katherine Anderson is the great-great granddaughter of James McC. Montgomery, patriarch of Standing Peachtree.)

28. Corkran, David H., The Creek Frontier, 1540-1783, University of Oklahoma Press, pages 260-261.

29. Winn, Bill, April 22, 1968, "The First Georgians No. 8 -- "Creek Tribes Had Confederacy," Atlanta Journal, page 14A. Caughey, John Walton, 1938, McGillivray of the Creeks, University of Oklahoma Press, Norman, page 10.

30. Winn, Bill, April 24, 1968, "The First Georgians No. 10 -- A Debt Scheme To Fleece Indians," Atlanta Journal, page 1A.

31. Forts Committee, Georgia Department of Archives and History, December 1966-January 1967, "Georgia Forts -- The Fort at Standing Peachtree," Georgia magazine. Patterson, Isabel Garrard, June 10, 1934, "'Standing Peach -- or Pitch -- Tree,' Atlanta's Forerunner; An Interesting Phase of Unwritten History of Georgia," Atlanta Constitution.

32. Kurtz, Wilbur G., fall 1950, "Standing Peach Tree," Early Georgia magazine, page 31.

33. Patterson, Isabel Garrard, March 22, 1936, "Many Treaties Marked Passing Of Georgia From Hands of Indians Into Possession of White Settlers," Atlanta Constitution, page 7K.

34. Miller, Dorothy Burke, 1952, "Creek Indians of DeKalb County," The Collections of the DeKalb Historical Society Vol. 1, The Yearbook, page 7.

35. Caughey, John Walton, 1938, McGillivray of the Creeks, University of Oklahoma Press, Norman, page 43. Mitchell, Eugene M., September 1937, "The Indians Of Georgia," The Atlanta Historical Bulletin No. 11, pages 23-24.

36. Willett, Marinus Col., A Narrative of the Military Actions of Marinus Willett.

37. Winn, Bill, April 24, 1968, "The First Georgians No. 10 -- A Debt Scheme To Fleece Indians," Atlanta Journal, page 1A.

38. Indian Depredation Claims, Georgia Department of Archives and History.

39. Butler, Mimi Jo Hill, July 28, 1995, personal correspondence.

40. Abercrombie, J. H., June 9, 1929, "House That Indians Helped Build," Atlanta Journal Magazine, page 6.

41. Author unknown, January 1, 1958, "Gwinnett, DeKalb Need Indians To Find Lost County Border," Atlanta Journal and Constitution, page 42 (Goff, Dr. John H., Collection, Emory University).

42. Weaver, J. Calvin, M. D., "100 Years of Medicine in DeKalb County -- 1822-1922," page 5.

Chapter 5

Georgia's burgeoning population could not be contained in its existing counties. White settlers formed an irresistible tide flowing from the coast into interior Georgia. Wilkes County, considered the frontier in 1790, was home to 32,000 of Georgia's 82,000 white population. [1] In the next 10 years, the state's white population would double. By comparison, the population of the entire Cherokee Nation was estimated to be only 15,000 in 1775. [2] The Creek Confederation represented a total population of approximately 16,500 in 1800. [3]

Georgia's campaign to banish the state's remaining Indians began to heat up in 1802. The state gave 100,000 square miles of land that would later become Alabama and Mississippi to the United States in return for $1,250,000 and a federal government promise to remove the Indians (an agreement that violated an earlier treaty guaranteeing the Indians title to the land). "The agreement was to cause federal government officials to wish they had never heard the name Georgia, and it further aggravated the already growing distrust, not to say hatred, which Georgians were developing of the United States." [4]

Meanwhile, the Creeks and Cherokees were developing separate strategies for dealing with the white man. The Cherokees, under the leadership of the great Sequoyah, were establishing written laws, a constitution and a legislative branch of government similar to that of the United States. Tecumseh, a Shawnee Indian whose mother was Creek, visited the Southern tribes, trying to united the Indians to drive out the white man. In 1811, the Creek Confederation officially banned further land cessions. [5]

The Creeks allied themselves with the British during the War of 1812, and incited by Tecumseh, caused trouble along the Georgia frontier. [6] Led by Gen. Andrew Jackson, the Americans, aided by their Cherokee Indian allies, defeated the British and the Creeks. Although the Cherokees had sided with Jackson and the Americans, their fate ultimately would be no better than that of the Creeks.

In 1813, Standing Peachtree was a good 30 miles within Creek Indian territory, located strategically where Peachtree Creek flowed into the Chattahoochee River. Once a Creek town, it was occupied by Cherokees who had been driven out of their ancestral homes to the north and, in turn, had pushed the

Creeks further south into Georgia. [76] In response to the Creek threat, the U. S. government established a chain of frontier outposts, one of which was at Standing Peachtree another at Hog Mountain in now Gwinnett County. [7] The forts were intended as part of a chain of communication and supply from Maj. Gen. Thomas Pinckney in Charleston, South Carolina to Brigadier Gen. John Floyd at Fort Mitchell at falls of the Chattahoochee and Gen. Jackson in Alabama, near now Columbus, Ga.

Given the command was George Rockingham Gilmer, a 23-year-old first lieutenant in the U. S. Infantry. The assignment would launch a successful career, which included Gilmer's election as U. S. representative from Georgia and governor of the state. [8] Playing a key role in the operation of the outpost was James McConnell Montgomery, who would later make his mark in many ways on DeKalb County.

Gilmer, who had never fired a musket and who knew nothing about fort-building, [9] assembled twenty two recruits, armed only with "a lot of old flint-locks that nobody else wanted, which had seen more service at the annual musters than on a firing line." [10] Their only ammunition was "some loose powder and a small quantity of unmolded lead" for bullets. [11]

The young soldiers were expected to protect Montgomery and his crew of boat-builders whose job it was to build supply boats and float them downriver to Fort Mitchell.

"It was an awkward business," Gilmer later wrote. "I had never seen a fort, and had no means of knowing how to obey the order but what I could get from Duane's Tactics," a book on military operations. Gilmer chose a site on a steep cliff overlooking the Chattahoochee, next to a large peach tree. [12]

"... In two months," Montgomery wrote, "(they) had built two large hew'd logg block houses, six dwelling houses, one fram'd store house, one Bridge half a mile from the Fort..." The compound was located on the east side of the Chattahoochee, with the fort on the north side of Peachtree Creek, and the boat yard on the south side of Peachtree Creek. [13] [77] Gilmer and Montgomery chose a location "on a commanding eminence below the mouth of a large creek which is navigable for several hundred

---

[76] "Georgia, DeKalb County
James M. C. Montgomery saith on oath that he was superintendent of Artifices in the service of the United States in the year 1814 and stationed at the Standing Peach tree on the Chattahoochee River for the purpose of erecting public boats to transport provisions down the Chattahoochee. That while in service at said place he understood from the Indians in that vicinity who were chiefly or entirely Cherokees, that the land on both sides of said River belonged to the Creeks -- and this deponent further saith that some years prior to 1814 he obtained a decree of the Cherokee nation against a certain Cawdry who was then at the head of an Indian family -- that he was informed by the Cherokee Indians that said Cawdry run his property to the Standing peach tree, on enquiring whether then the land there was Creek or Cherokee, this deponent was informed by several who were leading men in the Cherokee nation that it belonged to the Creeks, and that any claim or title the Cherokees had to the lands there was by permission of the Creeks -- and that it was common for the two tribes being connected with each other by marriage, to occupy each others land, and this deponent further saith that the Standing Peach Tree is from ten to twelve miles above the Buzzard Roost..." (Anderson, E. Katherine, December, 1937, "James McC. Montgomery of Standing Peachtree," The Atlanta Historical Bulletin, No. 12)

[77] The city of Atlanta's River Water Quality Control Center is now located on the Standing Peachtree site. As a 1976 Bicentennial project, employees of the water plant built a replica of Fort Peachtree. The exhibit is open to the public at no charge.

yards and makes an excellent convenient Harbour, and right opposite on a bend on the river where from the Gate of the Fort when built a view of the river can be had both up and down..." [14]

Having defeated the Creeks in a bloody battle at Auttose on Alabama's Tallapoosa River, Gen. Floyd withdrew to Fort Mitchell to await supplies. In January, 1814, a Maj. Burke, U. S. Deputy Quartermaster General, successfully experimented with floating supplies 150 miles down the Chattahoochee from Standing Peachtree to Fort Mitchell. Burke designated the Standing Peachtree location "Floydsville," a name now found only in military records. Burke is considered the first white resident of Standing Peachtree. [15]

James Montgomery had served as a teamster with the Quartermaster Department under Gen. Floyd and was cited for his courage. He was commissioned a major of the 52nd Battalion on March 19, 1808. On February 18, 1814, he accepted the assignment of director of the artificers who were to build the supply boats at Fort Peachtree. Montgomery recruited craftsmen back home in Jackson County, some sixty five miles northeast of Standing Peachtree. [16]

Montgomery and his builders were to report to "the Standing Peachtree on the Chatahoochy fifteen below the Cherokee line, at a place called Floydsville in the Creek Nation." His assignment, as he later wrote, was "to lay off the ground for a Fort and to superintend the building of ten boats for the purpose of transporting provisions and Forrage down the Chatahoochy..." [17]

The experiment was abandoned in May, 1814 after only five boats had been built, all of which were destroyed by rapids in the river. The troops at Fort Peachtree were never tested in battle. In fact, there were only two reported instances of hostility. [18]

The builders had yet to complete a stockade when Cherokees came at night, claiming that Creek warriors were nearby. Gilmer stationed men in the trench intended for stockade logs, but the enemy never came. [19] It was, Gilmer later wrote, an attempt to scare away the white men. Some of the artificers took the warning seriously and fled east. Only a fleet runner dispatched by Gilmer averted what could have been panic on the frontier.

The soldiers again took up defensive positions when shots were fired across the river from the fort. Enthusiastic braves were celebrating their participation in Jackson's victory at Horseshoe. The eighteen scalps they had claimed were displayed atop a pole around which the Indians danced all night. [20]

On his last day at the fort, Gilmer negotiated a stay of execution for two Creeks accused of killing the brother of a Cherokee man. The three factions had no way to know the key role Gilmer would play in the lives of the Indians more than 20 years later.

James Montgomery's stint at Fort Peachtree was only a matter of months, but he took a liking to the place he had once described to Gen. Andrew Jackson as "romantic."

"Floydsville Chatahuchee 20th March 1814
Genl Jackson

"Sir having completed a campaign under Genl Floyd on the last day of Feby, on the first of this Inst I accepted of an appointment in the United States Service, that of Superintendent of Artificers which appointment had been made on the 18th of Feby when I was at Fort Hull on the Calabee creek near the Tallipoosy, being notified by the proper Authority of my appointment I accepted of the same returned home to the up country (as I command most Frontier Battalion).

"I instantly organis'd a corpse of Artificers and with Lieut. Gilmore... took up our line of March for this place the Lieut. having twenty two Regulars though chiefly new recruits, and on the 14th the very respectable Lieut. A Mr. Bowman, Principle Boatright, Soldiers, artificers and myself arriv'd on the banks of the Chatahuchey at a place named as above, which place had been pitched on by Majr Burke one of the United States Deputy Quarter Master Genls. who in the month of Jany. last built, or had built a Boat in order to try the experiment of transporting Supplies from this place to Fort Mitchell the Experiment so far succeeded that Genl Pinkney has thought proper to order the building of ten Boats, which I am now stationed on the Chatahuchey in order to effect; It being left to my self to choose a site for the Fort and a place for a boat yard, I accordingly with Lieut Gilmer and Mr. Bowman the boatright pitched on a spot about a quarter and half quarter from where Majr Burke pitched on, on a commanding eminence below the mouth of a large creek which is navigable for several hundred yards and makes an excellent convenient Harbour, and right opposite a bend on the river from where the Gate of the Fort when built an view of the river can be had both up and down and renders the scene quite romantic, the boat yard may be either on the bank of the river or creek or both and can be commanded by the Fort.

As you will no doubt recollect me as we went to School together to old Mr. Stephenson on the Catabaw (Montgomery and Jackson were both born in Lancaster County, S. C., Jackson in 1767 and Montgomery three years later) and as we both suffered by the last Warr, I lost a brother and If I don't Mistake in addition to suffering yourself as a prisoner you lost one also and being both now engaged in the common cause, I should be much gratified to receive a few lines from you be each arrival as the line of expresses are now directed to pass this Station, you will no doubt recollect to have seen mention of my name in the foul fight on the Tallipoosey by Gen. Floyd. I had not an efficient command under the Gen. accept on that rout. I acted as Adjutant and even on the plains of Autose, I went as a private into the army but was early appointed to act in the Quarter masters department and as early as the 31st of October was appointed Special commissary the immoluments of which are nearly equal to that of Lieut. Colo., my appointment now about that (or nearly so) of a Major, but am within about sixty five miles of my family near the Standing Peach Tree.

"If you should not recollect me I am the son of James Montgomery brother to Robert who was prisoner and Wm. who died in the Service in the last Warr, a brother to John who was taken prisoner at the Hanging Rock battle who died a prisoner in Charlestown, you may recollect that I was in the Service in the year '92 in Cumberland when you acted as Comissary or contractor. That success may crown all your endeavours and that you may still continue cover yourself with Glory is the prayer of Sir your

                Obedient Servt &c
                J. McC. Montgomery S.U.S.A.

My best compliments to Doctor Philips If he is with you tell him I killed an Indian at Autausee with my sword..." [21]

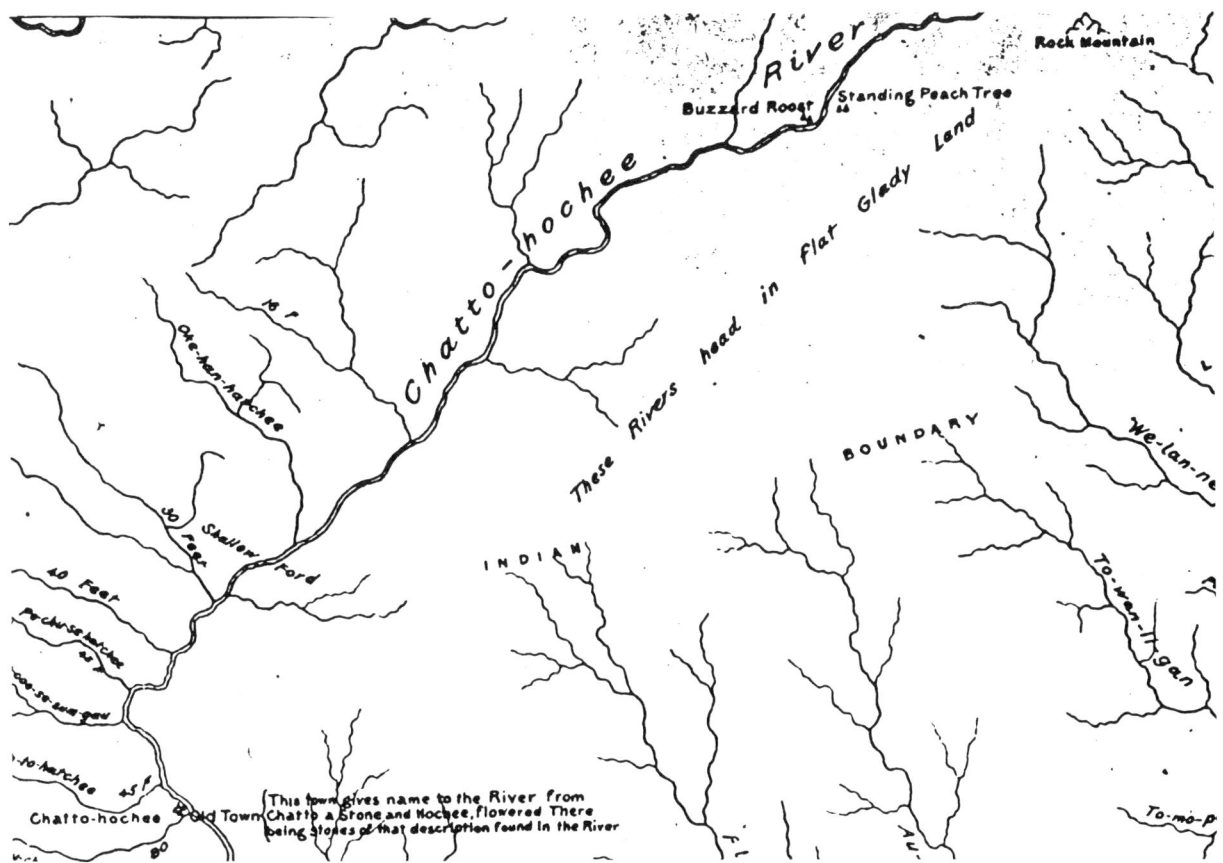

Eleazer Early's 1818 map shows "Rock Mountain," Buzzard's Roost and Standing Peachtree. A notation also accounts for one of the sources for the name, Chattahoochee: "chatto, a stone, and hoochee, flowered, there being stones of that description found in the river." (DeKalb Historical Society)

Montgomery later wrote to Jackson for help in getting paid for his service:

"...when the above were finished I was by Majr. Burke the D.Q.M. Gen'l. of the United States Army directed to discharge the Artificers and my Assistant and repair to Fort Hawkins (Macon) for a settlement of my accts; When I reach'd F. s. Majr. Burke had resign'd and Majr. Champlain could not settle without a possitive order from Genl Pinkney in every particular, I went on to Charlestown for the above purpose, but Genl. Pinkney was at Wilmington, N. C., his Aid Mr. Kinlough was present but could do nothing in my accts. which are about three thousand dollars, and I had only $744.00 advanc'd. However I left all my papers, with Majr. Irvin the Asst. Agt. Genl. to lay before the Genl. I have not heard from them since."

Montgomery did not get final payment until May 19, 1824, when the U. S. Congress passed "An Act for the relief of J. M. C. Montgomery." [22]

Faced with having to leave Standing Peachtree, Montgomery also asked Gen. Jackson to maintain a garrison at Fort Peachtree and to appoint him supply agent. He wrote on July 24, 1814: "I would just state to you that this is a nice place in the Creek country and will no doubt be a convenient place for a public Garsn. It is thought to be in the direction from Augusta and Milledgeville to Huntsville Ms and Colo Huger said would be kept up as a Sub. agency or something of that kind. It is no doubt a very

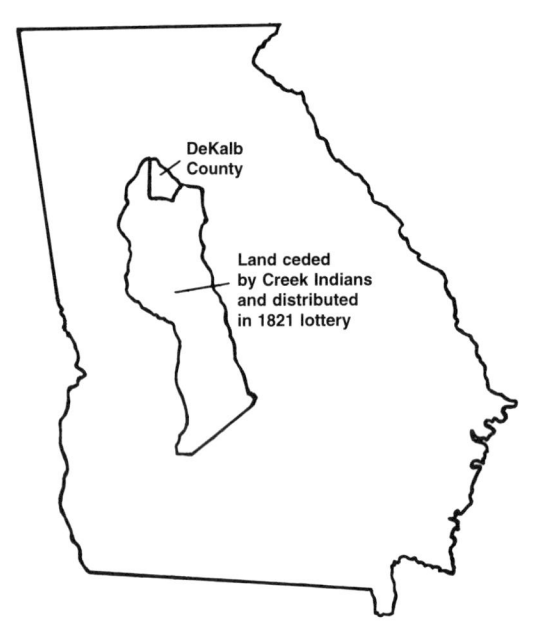

Map shows area of the 1821 Creek Indian cession, and the the location of DeKalb County within the ceded territory and the state of Georgia. (Map by Vivian Price)

healthy place and has cost the Government not less than five thousand dollars and it appears like a pity to abandon it. However, as all rests with you, you can do which you think best. If a public stand was made there such as an Agency, or Factory, I would be glad to have any appointment that you might think I merited at that place..." [1]

Montgomery never heard from Jackson. He went back to his farm and family in Jackson County and resumed his life as the county's sheriff, tax receiver, justice of the peace and mail carrier. But, Standing Peachtree was where he longed to be, and he would indeed return there while it was still Indian country.

In 1818 and 1819, the Creek Indians ceded to the state of Georgia a large tract of land that encompassed present day DeKalb County. The description of the territory includes landmarks still recognized today: "Beginning at the High Shoals on the Appalachee River [today's easternmost corner of Monroe County], the line ran along the High Tower Path to the Shallow Ford on the Chattahoochee River [a short distance down river from Roswell Road]; thence up the east bank of the Chattahoochee to Suwanee Old Town [now Gwinnett County]; thence along a direct line to the head of Appalachee, then down the river to the beginning point at High Shoals." [2]

The failure of the federal government to live up to its earlier agreements with the Creeks, the Cherokees and the Georgia government led to clashes between the Indians and white settlers. [3] For a while, the Cherokees found more support for their autonomy from the federal government than did the Creeks.

The federal government officially recognized the Cherokees as a sovereign nation and declared the territory in Georgia that lay north and east of the Chattahoochee River as foreign soil. On May 29, 1820, Gen. Andrew Jackson posted this notice at the Shallow Ford on the Chattahoochee: "Intruders on Cherokee lands, beware. I am required to remove all white men found trespassing on the Cherokee lands not having a written permit from the agent, Colo. R. J. Meigs. This duty I am about to perform. The Regulars and Light horse will be employed in performing this service, and any opposition will be promptly punished. All white men with there (sic) live stock found trespassing on the Indian land will be arrested and handed over to the civil authorities of the United States to be dealt with as the law directs, there (sic) families removed to U. S. land, there (sic) crops, houses and fences destroyed..."

Jackson later wrote to John C. Calhoun: "I found a great many intruders and those on the north of the Chatahoochey (sic) not only numerous but insolent and threatening resistance." [4]

The Creek Indians were back at the bargaining table on January 8, 1821 at Indian Springs near today's

Jackson in Butts County east of Griffin, Ga. The negotiations resulted in a huge cession. One concession on the part of the white government was agreeing to leave the Buzzard's Roost/Sandtown village one mile within Indian territory. [27]

Five large counties -- Dooly, Houston, Monroe, Henry and Fayette -- were created out of the 1821 cession. From these five counties came ten more new counties, including DeKalb. In addition, these five counties also gave portions of their land to seven more. [28]

Each of the new counties was divided into land districts nine miles square. Each district was divided into land lots of 202 1/2 acres each. "Fractional" lots were those left-over, odd-shaped lots caused by irregular topography. These "fractions" usually were auctioned by the state.

The Creek Indians ceded the last of their land in Georgia during negotiations in Indian Springs near Jackson, Ga. in January, 1825, but not without violence between the Lower and Upper Creeks. Signers of the Indian Springs Treaty were led by Lower Creek Chief William McIntosh, at whose tavern the negotiations were held. McIntosh's land in Butts County was exempt from the cession.

One of the most controversial figures in Georgia history, McIntosh was the son of a Tory Army officer and a Coweta Indian woman. His first cousin George M. Troup would be the Georgia governor who presided over the removal of the Cherokee Indians in 1838. [29]

Upper Creeks had vowed to kill any Creek Indian signing away more land to the whites. On May 1, 1825, they kept their promise. Setting fire to McIntosh's house in now Carroll County, they forced him out, then stabbed him and shot him 50 times, while wife Peggy and some of his children looked on. McIntosh was scalped, and his scalp suspended on a pole in the public square of the Octuskee village. McIntosh's son-in-law Sam Hawkins also was killed. The chief's son, Chilly McIntosh, escaped. [78] [30]

---

[78] William McIntosh's daughter Jane Hawkins, widow of Sam Hawkins who was killed with McIntosh, later wrote a letter to Col. Duncan G. Campbell and Maj. James Meriwether [both Georgians], the commissioners who represented the United States government in the 1825 treaty signing:

Line Creek, Fayette County, May 3, 1825
Col. Campbell and Major Meriwether:
   My dear friends I send you this paper, which will not tell you a lie, but if it had ten tongues, it could not tell you all the truth. On the morning of the 30th April at break of day my Father's house was surrounded by a party of hostile Indians to the number of several hundred who instantly fired his dwelling and murdered him and Thomas Tutunnuggee by shooting more than one hundred balls into them and took away the whole of father's money and property which they could not carry off and destroyed the rest, leaving the family no clothes (some not one rag) nor provision.
   Brother Chilly was at Father's and made his escape through a window under cover of a traveling white man who obtained leave for them to come out that way. It being not yet light, he was not discovered. While those hostiles were murdering my beloved father, they were tying my husband Col. Sam Hawkins with cords, to wait the arrival of Stockchunga Thloccocosconicco and Munnauca who were the commanders at Tatler to give orders for the other execution also which took place about three o'clock the same day, and these barbarous men, not content with spilling the blood of both my husband and father to attone for their constant friendship with your nation and our own, refused my hand the painful privilege of covering his body up in the very ground which he lately defended, against those hostile murderers, and drove me from my home, stript of my two best friends in one day, stript of all my property, my provision and my clothing with a more painful reflection than all these that the body of my poor murdered husband should remain unburied to be devoured by the birds, and the beast, was ever poor woman worse off than I?
   I have this moment arrived among our white friends, who altho they are very kind, have but little to bestow on me and my poor helpless infant, who must suffer before any aid can reach us from you but I can live a great while on very little, besides the confidence I have on you, and your government. For I know by your promise, you will aid and defend us as soon

The executioners refused Peggy's pleas to let her bury her husband. Eyewitnesses later disagreed as to the disposition of McIntosh's body. Some said it was buried near the burned-out house; others said it was thrown in the Chattahoochee River. [31]

Still others said it was carried to the town of Decatur for burial. [32]

White Georgians generally considered McIntosh a patriot. A marker on McIntosh Reserve in Carroll County, erected by the William McIntosh Chapter of the Daughters of the American Revolution of Jackson County in 1921, reads:

"1778-1825

To the memory and honor of Gen. William McIntosh

The distinguished and patriotic son of Georgia whose devotion was heroic, whose friendship was unselfish, and whose service was valiant, who negotiated the treaty between the Creek Indians and the State for all lands lying west of the Flint river, who sacrificed his life for his patriotism." [33]

As in 1821, those who were eligible -- adult men, widows and orphans -- flocked to their local general store to pull small slips of paper out of a barrel. Each was hoping to become a "fortunate drawer" of free land in one of the newly-created counties opened up by final Creek cession.

---

as you hear of from our situation. These murderers are the very same hostiles who treated the white 10 years ago as they have now treated my husband and father, who say they are determined to kill all who had any hand in selling the land and when they have completed the work of murdering, burning, plundering and destruction, they will send the president word that they have saved their land, and taken it back and that he and the white people never shall have it again which is the order of the heads of the nation, by the advice of the agent.

We expect that many of our best friends are already killed, but have not by reason of the water (Chattahoochee River) being too high for word to go quick, which is the only reason Col. Miller and others on his side of the river were not killed.

We are in a dreadful condition, and I don't think there will be one ear of corn made in this part of the nation, for the whole of the friendly party have fled to DeKalb and Fayette county, two (sic) much alarmed to return to their homes to get a little grain of what corn they left for themselves and their families to subsist on, much more to stay at home to make more and we fear every day that what little provision we left will be destroyed. I am afraid you wil think I make it worse, but how can that be? For it is worse of itself than any pen can write, my condition admits of no equal, and mock me when I try to speak of it, after I was stripped of my last frock but one humanity and duty called on me to pull it off and spread it over the body of my dead husband (which was allowed no other covering) which I did as a farewell witness of my affection. I was 25 miles fro many friend (but sister Catherine who was with me) and had to stay all night in the woods surrounded by a thousand hostile Indians who were constantly insulting and affrighting us. And now I am here with only one old coat to my back, and not a morsel of bread to save us from perishing, or a rag of a blanket to cover my poor little boy from the sun at noon or the dew at night, and I am a poor distracted orphan and widow.

Jane Hawkins

P. S. If you think properly I wish this to be published."

(Source: Garrett, Franklin M., 1954, 1969, Atlanta and Environs -- A Chronicle of Its People and Events, Vol. 1, pages 48-49)

Chapter 5 Notes

1. Clarke, Caroline McKinney, 1973, 1997, The Story of Decatur 1823-1899, page 4.

2. Cotterill, R. S., 1954, The Southern Indians -- The Story of the Civilized Tribes Before Removal, University of Oklahoma Press, page 9.

3. Caughey, John Walton, 1938, McGillivray of the Creeks, Norman, University of Oklahoma Press, page 6.

4. Winn, Bill Winn, April 24, 1968, "The First Georgians -- No. 10 "A Debt Scheme To Fleece Indians," Atlanta Journal, April 24, 1968, page A.

5. Patterson, Isabel Garrard, April 19, 1936, "Many Treaties Necessary Before All Georgia Was Finally Ceded to Whites by Indians," Atlanta Constitution, page 7B.

6. Patterson, Isabel Garrard, April 19, 1936, "Many Treaties Necessary Before All Georgia Was Finally Ceded to Whites by Indians," Atlanta Constitution, page 7B.

7. Forts Committee, Department of Archives and History, December, 1966-January, 1967, "Georgia Forts -- The Fort at Standing Peachtree," Georgia magazine, page 21.

8. Garrett, Franklin M., 1954, Atlanta and Environs -- A Chronicle of Its People and Events, Vol. 1, page 12.

9. Author unknown, April 22, 1923, "Indians First Chose Site Of Atlanta," page 21.

10. Kurtz, Wilbur G., Fall, 1950, "Standing Peach Tree," Early Georgia magazine, No. 2, page 31.

11. Gilmer, Gov. George Rockingham, 1989 (reprint), Georgians -- Sketches of Some of the First Settlers of Upper Georgia, of the Cherokees, and the Author, Mary Bondurant Warren, Heritage Papers, page 196.

12. Hudgins, Carl T., January 22, 1951, "DeKalb County Indian Trails," The Collections of the DeKalb Historical Society, Vol. 1, page 12-13. Author unknown, April 22, 1923, "Indians First Chose Site Of Atlanta, Atlanta Journal, page 21. Patterson, Isabel Garrard, June 10, 1934, "'Standing Peach -- or Pitch -- Tree,' Atlanta's Forerunner; An Interesting Phase of the Unwritten History of Georgia," Atlanta Constitution.

13. Kurtz, Wilbur G., Fall, 1950, "Standing Peach Tree," Early Georgia magazine, No. 2, page 31.

14. Forts Committee, Department of Archives and History, December, 1966-January, 1967, "Georgia Forts -- The Fort at Standing Peachtree," Georgia magazine, page 22.

15. Kurtz, Wilbur G., Fall, 1950, "Standing Peach Tree," Early Georgia magazine, No. 2, page 31.

16. Kurtz, Wilbur G., Fall, 1950, "Standing Peach Tree," Early Georgia magazine, No. 2, page 31. Anderson, E. Katherine, "James McC. Montgomery of Standing Peachtree," The Atlanta Historical Bulletin, No. 12.

17. Kurtz, Wilbur G., Fall, 1950, "Standing Peach Tree," Early Georgia magazine, No. 2, page 31.

18. Forts Committee, Department of Archives and History, December, 1966-January, 1967, "Georgia Forts -- The Fort at Standing Peachtree," Georgia magazine, page 22.

19. Gilmer, Gov. George Rockingham, 1989 (reprint), Georgians -- Sketches of Some of the First Settlers of Upper Georgia, of the Cherokees, and the Author, Mary Bondurant Warren, Heritage Papers, page 198. Kurtz, Wilbur G., Fall, 1950, "Standing Peach Tree," Early Georgia magazine, No. 2, page 31.

20. Gilmer, Gov. George Rockingham, 1989 (reprint), <u>Georgians -- Sketches of Some of the First Settlers of Upper Georgia, of the Cherokees, and the Author</u>, Mary Bondurant Warren, Heritage Papers, page 198.

21. Anderson, E. Katherine, December, 1937, "James McC. Montgomery of Standing Peachtree," The Atlanta Historical Bulletin No. 12.

22. Anderson, E. Katherine, "James McC. Montgomery of Standing Peachtree," The Atlanta Historical Bulletin, No. 12.

23. Anderson, E. Katherine, December, 1937, "James McC. Montgomery of Standing Peachtree," The Atlanta Historical Bulletin, No. 12. Kurtz, Wilbur G., Fall, 1950, "Standing Peach Tree," <u>Early Georgia</u> magazine, No. 2, page 31.

24. Garrett, Franklin M., 1954, <u>Atlanta and Environs -- A Chronicle of Its People and Events</u>, Vol. I, page 4.

25. Garrett, Franklin M., 1954, <u>Atlanta and Environs -- A Chronicle of Its People and Events</u>, Vol. I, page 5.

26. Garrett, Franklin M., 1954, <u>Atlanta and Environs -- A Chronicle of Its People and Events</u>, Vol. I, page 5.

27. Garrett, Franklin M., 1954, <u>Atlanta and Environs -- A Chronicle of Its People and Events</u>, Vol. I, page 7.

28. Garrett, Franklin M., 1954, <u>Atlanta and Environs -- A Chronicle of Its People and Events</u>, Vol. I, page 8.

29. Bonner, James C., 1958, Sketch of William McIntosh in <u>Georgians in Profile -- Historical Essays in Honor of Ellis Merton Coulter</u> edited by Horace Montgomery, University of Georgia Press, pages 114-140.

30. Garrett, Franklin M., 1954, 1969, <u>Atlanta and Environs -- A Chronicle of Its People and Events</u>, Vol. 1, pages 48.

31. Griffith Jr., Benjamin W., 1988, <u>McIntosh and Weatherford, Creek Indian Leaders</u>, The University of Alabama Press, Tuscaloosa and London, page 250.

32. Author unknown, June 7, 1931, "Indian War Near Five Points," <u>Atlanta Journal</u> Magazine, reproduced from the <u>Atlanta Daily New Era</u> Aug. 1, 1869.

33. Garrett, Franklin M., 1954, 1969, <u>Atlanta and Environs -- A Chronicle of Its People and Events</u>, Vol. 1, pages 48-49.

Chapter 6

𝒟eKalb County citizens today benefit from the experience gained by the Indians who had much more intimate knowledge of nature's landscape than do their modern counterparts. Many major highways and all the area's railroad lines follow the same routes taken by Indian trails hundreds of years ago. Despite the dense forest and tangled brush, the Indians invariably chose the highest ridges for their pathways in order to avoid crossing streams and swampy areas. White settlers found they could follow an Indian trail for miles without getting their feet wet. [1]

By the time of the 1821 Creek Indian cession that resulted in Henry and then DeKalb County, the area between the South and Chattahoochee rivers was crisscrossed with trails.

DeKalb's most famous Indian trail was the Hightower Trail, which became the county's eastern border, shared with Gwinnett, in 1822. Modern-day tourists sometimes seek the location of the "High Tower" for which they assume the trail must be named. The name actually is the white man's corruption of the Cherokee Indian word now spelled Etowah, and originally pronounced by the Indians: "I-ta-wa." [79] [2]

The trail followed a crooked, generally northwest-to-southeast path between two important river crossings at opposite ends of DeKalb County. The Shallow Ford on the Chattahoochee River was located two miles south of the present town of Roswell. A portion of the original route, now in north Fulton County, is still called Hightower Trail. The trail meandered some 20 miles to the Rock Bridge crossing on the Yellow River, so named because large protruding rocks in the river made crossing

---

[79] "This name, one can be certain, is a corruption of the Indian word Itawa which the white people also turned into the present `Etowah'... The really interesting point about the appellation, though, is the fact that the initial H of Hightower is a Cockney H that was long ago stuck on the word, probably by early Indian traders. In the years when we were closer to the British, it was common to use an H before place names beginning with a vowel... The H's were eventually dropped from such words, however, except in the case of `Hightower' and `Hiawassee.' The latter word is of Cherokee origin and should properly have been Ayuhwasi, meaning meadow or savannah. The significance of Itawa, or Etowah, is not known." (Source: Goff, Dr. John H., n. d., "Some Old Road Names in Georgia," publication unknown, Goff Collection, Emory University, pages 40-41; also "The Hightower Trail," June 23, 1952, The Collections of the DeKalb Historical Society, Vol. 1, pages 2-4.)

easy. At the Rock Bridge, the Hightower Trail merged with two branches of the Echota Trail, on their way from Standing Peachtree and Sandtown. [3]

To the east, the trails, known collectively as the Hightower Trail, followed the old route to Augusta, through Madison and Crawfordville, Camak and Dearing. Today, the old road has been replaced by I-20, but the route is virtually the same. [4]

Beyond DeKalb's borders to the north and west, the Hightower Trail ran through Roswell and Cobb County, to the Etowah River at Emerson in Bartow County. The Hightower Trail ended at the Sally Hughes's place near where U. S. Highway 41 today crosses the river in Bartow. This territory was considered by the Georgia government to be a portion of DeKalb County in 1830. [5] Other trails joined the Hightower at this point to lead the traveler to northern Alabama. [6] Portions of the old trail in Cobb are still called Shallowford Road.

Historical markers designate the places where the Hightower Trail crossed the Chattahoochee River, Buford Highway in Doraville and Lawrenceville Highway in Tucker. [7] A sign recently placed by local historian Jim Perkins marks the trail's location in Dunwoody, near the All Saints Catholic Church.

As white settlements began to spring up along the Hightower Trail, landmarks changed from natural to manmade. In southeast DeKalb, the Hightower Trail ran through the Anderson place, past a campsite favored by Cherokee Indians and near the home of Jake Chupp. Also along the way were the County Line Church and the Philadelphia Church, and an old track on the east side of Stone Mountain where Indians ran foot and horse races. [8] In north DeKalb, the trail ran a short distance to the east of the DeKalb waterworks plant. [9]

The Hightower Trail is one of the few in DeKalb which did not evolve into a larger road. As years went by, the trail was abandoned and began to disappear, but it remained the border between DeKalb and Gwinnett. Inability to conclusively locate the trail resulted in border disputes, causing friction between the two counties. As recently as 1958, Gwinnett County tax commissioner G. C. Montgomery said, "The trail is the official line, even if we don't know where it is." [10]

The two branches of the Echota Trail which departed from the Hightower at the Rock Bridge were known as the Stone Mountain-Sandtown Trail and the Stone Mountain-Standing Peachtree Trail. These trails connected DeKalb's two Indian towns with the all-important trading destination of Augusta. [11]

Today's commuters riding the MARTA rapid rail line from east DeKalb County into Atlanta travel along the Stone Mountain-Sandtown Trail. Mid-19th-century engineers seeking a route for the Georgia Railroad could find no better east-west path than the one the Indians had discovered years before.

The Echota Trail ran along a ridge which today includes Decatur's College Avenue and Atlanta's Decatur Street. The ridge forms a natural watershed. Rain falling north of the railroad tracks in Decatur flows into Peavine Creek, then into Peachtree Creek, the Chattahoochee River and flows into the Gulf of Mexico. Rainwater falling on the south side of the railroad ridge flows into Doolittle Creek, the South River and on to the Atlantic Ocean. [12]

In his essay on Indian trails, DeKalb historian Carl Hudgins wrote: "I believe it could be easily demonstrated that there is a building upon the Agnes Scott campus where a part of the water from the roof escapes in one direction and a part in another. It is the building nearest the corner of College Avenue and South McDonough Street. One might wonder if the Indians knew that right here, where several of their trails met, was such a natural watershed. I see no reason for doubting that they did know it."

In its entire length, the Echota Trail crossed only one stream, the Peavine in Decatur. [13]

From Five Points in Atlanta, the Stone Mountain-Sandtown Trail moved in a southwesterly direction to the Sandtown Indian village on the Chattahoochee River. Today's Cascade Road (formerly called Sandtown Road) follows the route of this trail. From Sandtown, the trail crossed the river and continued southwest to Douglasville, Villa Rica and Alabama. [14]

The Stone Mountain-Standing Peachtree Trail followed today's Rock Bridge and Nelson Ferry roads through what is now DeKalb County. In now Fulton, the path corresponded with today's Rock Springs, Montgomery Ferry and Collier roads. On its way to Standing Peachtree the trail skirted the edge of today's Piedmont Park. This early Indian trail later became the well-traveled stagecoach road between Decatur and Marietta. [15] Yet another trail, running along the banks of the Chattahoochee connected Standing Peachtree and Sandtown. [16]

There were several points in DeKalb where Indian trails crossed. Stone Mountain, Standing Peachtree and Atlanta's Five Points were prominent crossings. The Old Courthouse in Decatur stands today near the intersection of the Echota and the Shallowford trails.

From the courthouse the Shallowford Trail followed the path of today's Clairmont Road until it turned eastward along LaVista, Oak Grove and Briarcliff roads. A portion of the old path today is called Shallowford Road as it crosses the North Fork of Peachtree Creek, I-85 and Buford Highway. From Buford Highway, the trail crossed the Southern Railroad tracks and New Peachtree Road and by the Prosperity Presbyterian cemetery. The trail then followed today's North Shallowford and Chamblee-Dunwoody roads and Roberts Drive to connect with the Hightower Trail near the Northridge exit of the Georgia 400 highway. [17]

From today's Old Courthouse in Decatur southward, the trail continued but was called the Indian Springs Trail, with its destination the Butts County location of the 1821 treaty that lead to Chief McIntosh's death. The trail was later known as the McDonough Road. Yet another trail ran from the South River and the Soapstone Ridge area to Five Points in Atlanta along what is now Bouldercrest Road and Flat Shoals Avenue, connecting with the Stone Mountain-Sandtown Trail between the site of Fulton Bag and Cotton Mills and Five Points. [18]

PRINCIPAL INDIAN TRAILS
AND
EARLY ROADS
IN
DeKALB COUNTY
GEORGIA

Many of today's roads run along the same routes established by Creek and Cherokee Indians at least 200 years ago. The Indians were master engineers. Their trails followed the highest ridges and avoided streams or crossed them at at the easiest fording points, like the Shallow Ford on the Chattahoochee River near today's Roswell and the Rock Bridge on the Yellow River.

The east-west rail line of Atlanta's rapid transit system follows the path of the Stone Mountain-Sandtown Trail through the heart of Decatur. At one point near today's Agnes Scott College, the trail follows a natural watershed. Water that leaves the ridge from one direction flows eventually into the Gulf of Mexico; the other side of the ridge drains into the Atlantic Ocean.

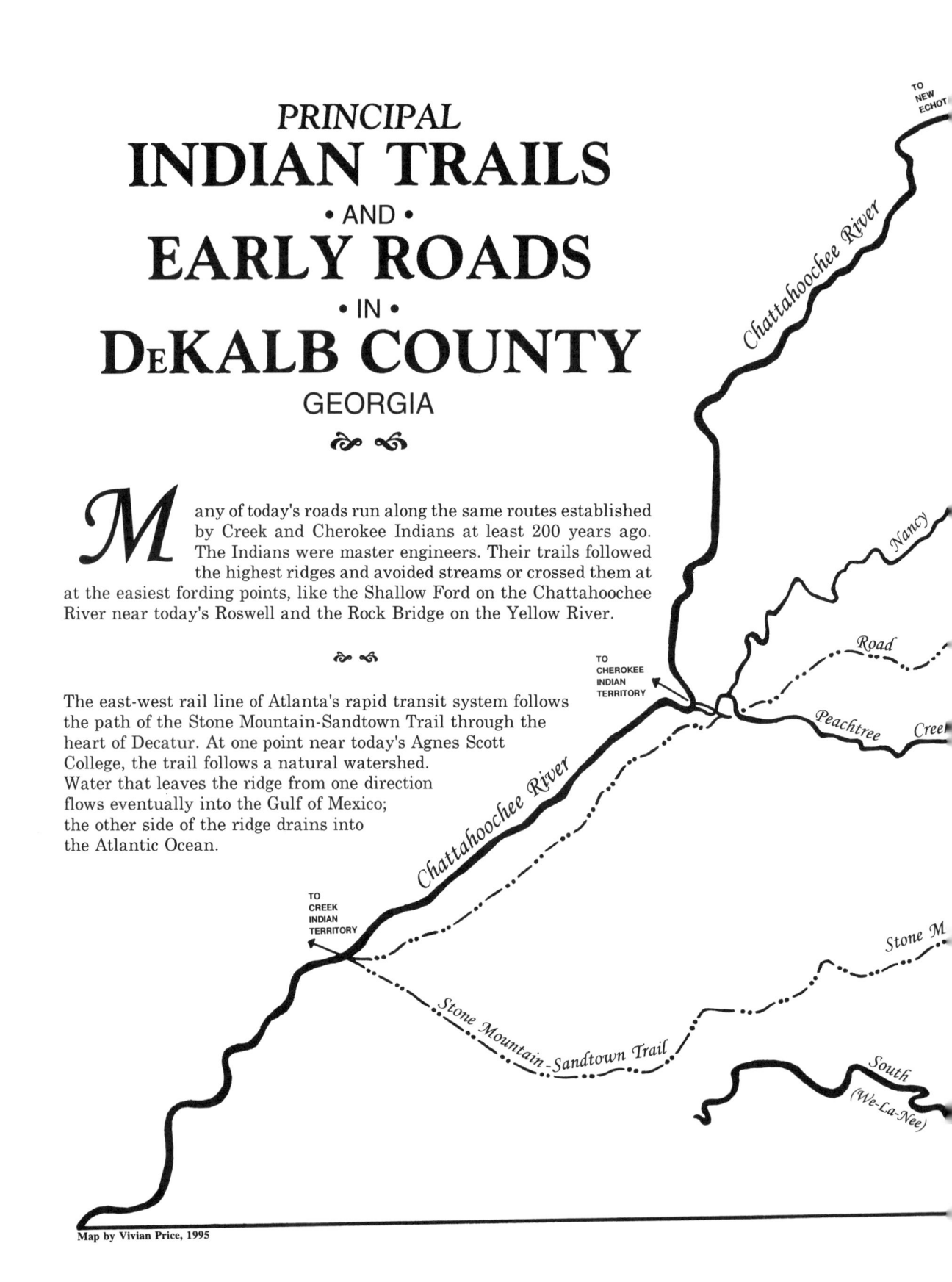

Map by Vivian Price, 1995

Many Indian trails crisscrossed DeKalb County, including the Hightower, or Etowah.

54   THE HISTORY OF DEKALB COUNTY, GA. 1822-1900 • CHAPTER 6

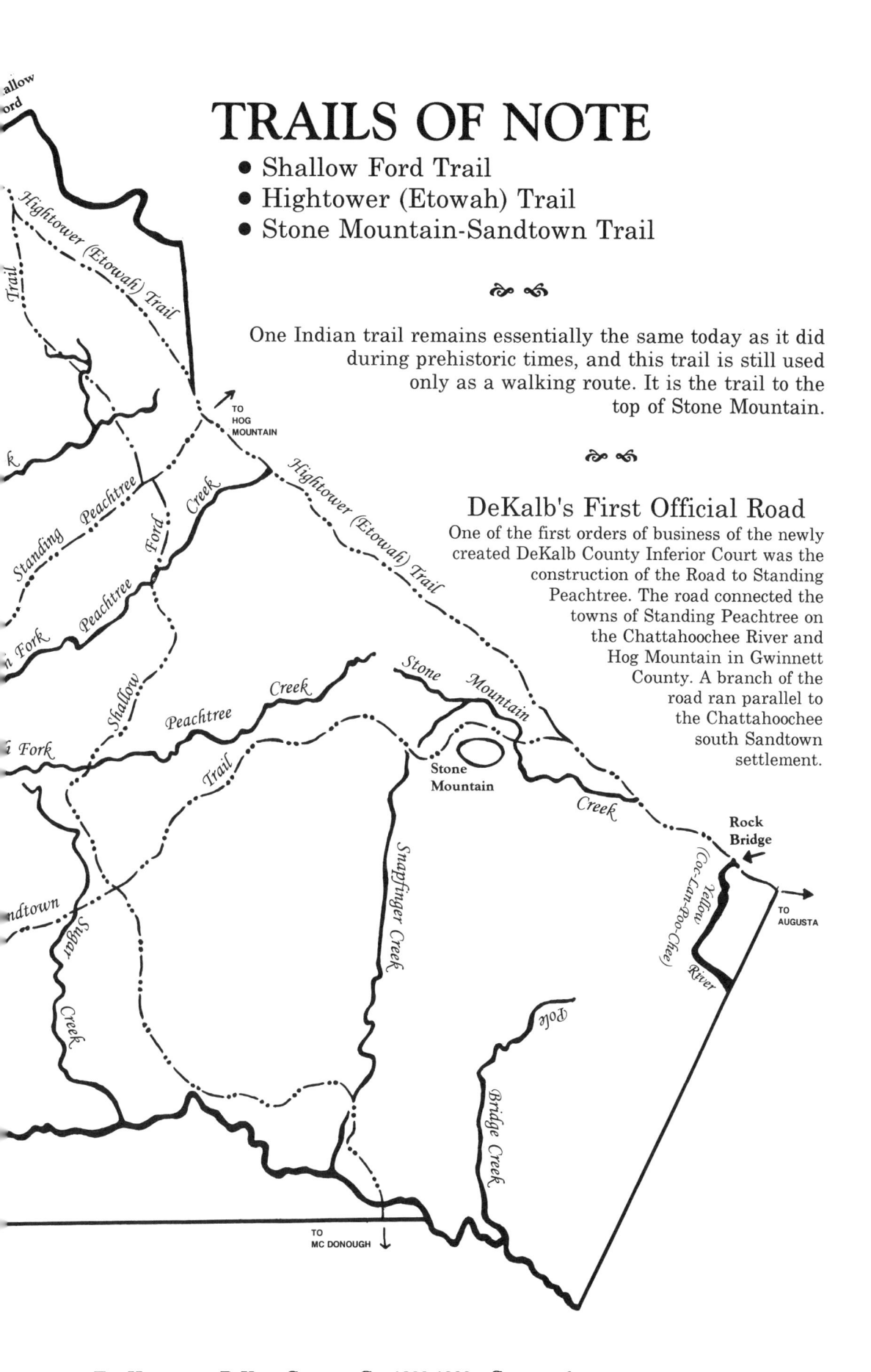

TRAILS OF NOTE
- Shallow Ford Trail
- Hightower (Etowah) Trail
- Stone Mountain-Sandtown Trail

߷

One Indian trail remains essentially the same today as it did during prehistoric times, and this trail is still used only as a walking route. It is the trail to the top of Stone Mountain.

߷

DeKalb's First Official Road

One of the first orders of business of the newly created DeKalb County Inferior Court was the construction of the Road to Standing Peachtree. The road connected the towns of Standing Peachtree on the Chattahoochee River and Hog Mountain in Gwinnett County. A branch of the road ran parallel to the Chattahoochee south Sandtown settlement.

THE HISTORY OF DEKALB COUNTY, GA. 1822-1900 • CHAPTER 6

The street that became synonymous with Atlanta began as an Indian path called the Peachtree Trail. Today's Southern Railway tracks through Atlanta, north DeKalb and east Gwinnett follow virtually the same route as the original Peachtree Trail. The trail forked in now Buckhead, with one branch following today's Paces Ferry and Moore's Mill roads to Standing Peachtree. [19]

In 1813, Lt. George R. Gilmer ordered that 30 miles of the Indian trail be improved to provide the Army better access between the newly-constructed Fort Gilmer at Standing Peachtree to Fort Daniel at Hog Mountain in then Jackson (later Gwinnett) County. Fort Daniel was located southeast of Buford, near the intersection of the modern-day Highway 124 and Highway 324. [20] William Nesbit supervised the road improvements. Workers were John Young, Lewis Lawly, John Lawly and an unnamed Negro man. Two young boys, Hiram Williams and Gustin Young, drove a cart, and Isham Williams and Bob Young, kept a look-out for marauding Indians. [21] Of the road-builders, only Gustin Young, son of Robert Young and Celia Strickland Young, later lived in DeKalb. He was a juror on the county's first Inferior Court. [22]

The famous Peachtree Road "is another instance where we find trained engineers adopting a route previously selected by the Indians. As did the Indians, they wanted to keep to the high ground. They wanted to avoid unnecessary cuts and fills and crossings of streams. They were unable to find any higher ridges than these the Indians had already appropriated." [23]

One Indian trail exists in DeKalb today virtually unchanged from the days before the white man came. Just as it was more than a century ago, the Indian path up the western slope of Stone Mountain is a trail used only for walking. [24]

As a project for a 1937 "City Improvement Contest" sponsored by the Atlanta Constitution, DeKalb County Camp Fire Girls researched area Indian Trails. Led by Mrs. J. Howell Green, the Camp Fire Girls created a simple map of trails in DeKalb. They were assisted by Lanier Billups, E. A. Minor, Wilbur G. Kurtz Sr., Mrs. A. B. Burrus, Ruth Blair and Stephens Mitchell. A plaque on the exterior of the Old Courthouse in Decatur commemorates their efforts. [25]

Chapter 6 Notes

1. Cotterill, R. S., 1954, The Southern Indians -- The Story of the Civilized Tribes Before Removal, University of Oklahoma Press, page 15.

2. Hemperley, Marion R., 1989, Historic Indian Trails of Georgia, The Garden Club of Georgia, pages 12 and 13.

3. Hemperley, Marion R., 1989, Historic Indian Trails of Georgia, The Garden Club of Georgia, page 12-13.

4. Goff, Dr. John H., June 23, 1952, "The Hightower Trail," The Collections of the DeKalb Historical Society, Vol. 1, pages 2-4; and the Goff Collection, Georgia Department of Archives and History. Hudgins, Carl T., January 22, 1951, "DeKalb County Indian Trails," The Collections of the DeKalb Historical Society, Vol. 1, page 12-13.

5. 1830 DeKalb County census.

6. Goff, John H. Dr., June 23,, 1952, "The Hightower Trail," The Collections of the DeKalb Historical Society, Vol. 1, page 4; and the Goff Collection, Georgia Department of Archives and History. Hemperley, Marion R., 1989, Historic Indian Trails of Georgia, The Garden Club of Georgia, page 68.

7. Hudgins, Carl T., January 22, 1951, DeKalb County Indian Trails, The Collections of the DeKalb Historical Society, Vol. 1, page 4.

8. Severinghaus, n. d., unpublished manuscript on the Hightower Trail, DeKalb Historical Society Scrapbook No. 1, page 240.

9. Goff, John Dr., June 23, 1952, "The Hightower Trail," The Collections of the DeKalb Historical Society, Vol. 1, page 3; and the Goff Collection, Georgia Department of Archives and History.

10. Author unknown, January 1, 1958, "Gwinnett, DeKalb Need Indians To Find Lost County Border," Atlanta Journal and Constitution, page 42 (Goff, Dr. John H., Collection, Emory University).

11. Hudgins, Carl T., January 22, 1951, "DeKalb County Indian Trails," The Collections of the DeKalb Historical Society, Vol. 1, page 4.

12. Hudgins, Carl T., January 22, 1951, "DeKalb County Indian Trails," The Collections of the DeKalb Historical Society, Vol. 1, page 3.

13. Hudgins, Carl T., January 22, 1951, "DeKalb County Indian Trails," The Collections of the DeKalb Historical Society, Vol. 1, page 3.

14. Hudgins, Carl T., January 22, 1951, "DeKalb County Indian Trails," The Collections of the DeKalb Historical Society, Vol. 1, page 4. Hemperley, Marion R., 1989, Historic Indian Trails of Georgia, The Garden Club of Georgia, pages 30-31.

15. Hudgins, Carl T., January 22, 1951, "DeKalb County Indian Trails," The Collections of the DeKalb Historical Society, Vol. 1, page 5. Hemperley, Marion R., 1989, Historic Indian Trails of Georgia, The Garden Club of Georgia, pages 30-31. Goff, Dr. John H., Collection, Georgia Department of Archives and History.

16. Author unknown, April, 1931, "Queer Place Names in Old Atlanta," The Atlanta Historical Bulletin, No. 5, page 27.

17. Hudgins, Carl T., January 22, 1951, "DeKalb County Indian Trails," The Collections of the DeKalb Historical Society, Vol. 1, page 7.

18. Hudgins, Carl T., January 22, 1951, "DeKalb County Indian Trails," The Collections of the DeKalb Historical Society, Vol. 1, pages 7-8.

19. Goff, Dr. John H., n. d., "Some Old Road Names in Georgia," publication unknown, Goff Collection, Emory University, page 27.

20. Flanigan, James C., 1943, 1995, History of Gwinnett County, Vol. 1, pages 9 and 15. Goff, Dr. John H., Collection, Georgia Department of Archives and History.

21. Flanigan, James C., 1943, 1995, History of Gwinnett County, Ga., 1818-1943, Vol. 1, page 17.

22. Garrett, Franklin M., 1954, 1969, Atlanta and Environs -- A Chronicle of Its People and Events, Vol. 1, page 17.

23. Hudgins, Carl T., January 22, 1951, "DeKalb County Indian Trails," The Collections of the DeKalb Historical Society, Vol. 1, pages 8-9, quoting Eugene Mitchell, co-founder of the Atlanta Historical Society and father of Gone With The Wind author Margaret Mitchell.

24. Hudgins, Carl T., January 22, 1951, "DeKalb County Indian Trails," The Collections of the DeKalb Historical Society, Vol. 1, page 12.

25. Hudgins, Carl T., January 22, 1951, "DeKalb County Indian Trails," The Collections of the DeKalb Historical Society, Vol. 1, page 13.

Chapter 7

The ink was barely dry on the Indian Springs treaty when the state of Georgia began doling out 202 1/2-acre plots through the 1821 land lottery. So many settlers streamed into Henry County that only one year later, in 1822, the Georgia General Assembly felt compelled to create another new county. At this same time, Masons were spearheading a drive to raise funds for a monument to a popular hero of the American Revolution, Baron Johann DeKalb. Of the three major heroes of the struggle for independence, DeKalb was the only one having no jurisdiction in Georgia named for him. The state already had counties named for George Washington and LaFayette.

Georgians, many of them Revolutionary War veterans and their families, carried with them a special fondness for the war hero whose personal background was so much like their own. Like Baron DeKalb, the down-to-earth pioneers of the new territory rose from humble beginnings through hard work, perseverance, belief in their own abilities and a deeply-felt spirit of independence.

DeKalb was no aristocrat. Born Johan Kalb on June 29, 1721 in Huttendorf Bavaria, Germany, he was a second son who stood to inherit nothing from his peasant father, not that there was much to inherit. His father owned only a quarter acre of rocky farmland. [1]

The teenaged son had little education; his only job before entering the military had been as a waiter. As a young man, he saw an opportunity to better his lot and he took it. [2] He left home to become a soldier of fortune. DeKalb decided to join the French army, because it was offering bonuses for tall enlistees. Young Johan was six foot five. [3]

Discovering that only noblemen could advance in rank and pay, he gave himself title of "baron." He was 42 years old before his military exploits earned the rank of lieutenant in the French infantry and the legitimate right to add the "de" to his name signifying his acquired title of baron. [4]

Only then did he feel secure enough to marry Anne Elizabeth Emelie van Robais, daughter of Peter van Robais, a French cloth and lace manufacturer. Only 16 years old, Anne brought to the marriage a substantial dowry. They were together nine years before DeKalb sailed for America. [5]

As a French agent assigned to judge the strength of the American freedom movement, DeKalb came to

Baron Johan de Kalb. (DeKalb Historical Society)

America on January 12, 1768, amidst excitement over the Stamp Act. Apparently impressed with American resolve, he wrote to his wife: "The women even discard tea and foreign sugar and we are constantly told of the use of the spinning wheels, which have been at work ever since the promulgation of the act to supersede the use of English linens." [6]

After reporting his findings to the French government, DeKalb returned to America with LaFayette. He wanted to be part of the fight for freedom. The baron sought a commission from the Continental Congress and was granted the rank of major general on October 4, 1777. [7]

With Gen. George Washington at Valley Forge, DeKalb was dismayed by the condition of the colonial army, said to be the poorest equipped, clothed and fed in the history of civilization. At Valley Forge, he wrote: "We are here going into winter quarters in the woods as usual. Since the beginning of the month we have been putting up shanties. But the severe frost greatly retards our work and does not even permit us to complete our chimneys. It may really be said that a foreign officer, who has served in America as long as I have under such adversities, must be either inspired with boundless enthusiasm for the liberties of the country, or possessed by the demons of fame and ambition, or inspired by an extraordinary zeal for the common cause of the King and his Confederates. I knew before I came that I should have put up with more than usual toils and privations, but I had no idea of their true extent. An iron constitution like mine is required to bear up under this sort of usage." [8]

Washington sent DeKalb and his Maryland and Delaware regiments to reinforce South Carolina troops who were trying to stop the British advance on Charleston. The fall of Charleston before DeKalb arrived caused Congress to appoint Horatio Gates as commander over DeKalb and his men. Outnumbered four to one, Gates launched an ill-advised attack against Cornwallis's troops at Camden, S. C. [9]

When American soldiers (including his commanding officer) were fleeing in fear, DeKalb stood fast with his Maryland and Delaware militiamen against the British in the doomed battle of Camden, S. C. on August 16, 1780. Bleeding from 11 wounds, his horse shot out from under him, DeKalb led his men on foot, through the most violent hand-to-hand bayonet fighting of the war. [10]

By the time the battle ended, Gates was 60 miles away, in Charlotte, N. C. The British general, Cornwallis, ordered that the courageous DeKalb be given the best of medical care, but he soon died. Consoled on his deathbed by a British soldier, DeKalb said, "I thank you for your generous sympathy; but I die the death I always prayed for -- the death of a soldier fighting for the rights of man." DeKalb's fellow Masons conducted the funeral ceremony, and the fallen hero was buried on the battlefield. [11]

Inspired by citizens of the state of South Carolina, Masons and Revolutionary veterans all over the country began to raise money for a suitable monument to DeKalb. The memorial campaign officially got underway at the same time the Georgia legislature was considering forming the new county that would come to bear the baron's name. The same Masons who had buried DeKalb 45 years earlier were called upon to locate the general's remains so he could receive a proper burial in front of the Presbyterian Church in Camden. Gen. LaFayette laid the cornerstone of the monument to his comrade. [80] [12]

The man for whom DeKalb County was named was the only Revolutionary War general to die on the battlefield, fighting in hand-to-hand combat, shoulder-to-shoulder with the average foot soldier. Of him, it was said: "A scruple on his part and the world would have gained another sturdy yeoman, but would have lost a hero." [13]

A bust of Baron DeKalb stands on the grounds of the Old Courthouse in Decatur, a gift from his native Germany. [14]

---

[80] Text of the monument to Baron DeKalb in Camden, S. C.: "Here lie the remains of Baron DeKalb, a German by birth, but in principle a citizen of the world. His love of liberty induced him to leave the Old World to aid the citizens of the New in this struggle for Independence. His distinguished talents and many virtues weighed with Congress to appoint him Major General in this Revolutionary Army. He was second in Command in the battle fought near Camden on the 16th of August 1780 between the British and Americans and there nobly fell covered with wounds while gallantly performing deeds of valour in rallying the friends and opposing the enemies of his adopted country. In gratitude for his zeal and services, the citizens of South Carolina have erected his monument." (Source: Kirkland, Thomas J., and Kennedy, Robert M., Historic Camden, Vol. 2, pages 80-81).

Chapter 7 Notes

1. Martin, Kirk, November 17, 1991, "Research Trip To Europe Tells Why Baron DeKalb Left Home," The DeKalb News/Sun, page 4C.

2. Newton, Maryellen Harvey, July 2, 1981, "Waiter, Courtier, Spy, General, deKalb Died Fighting For Freedom," DeKalb News/Sun "Heritage of DeKalb" special section, page 3E.

3. Pugh, Joe T. and Bryan T., October 24, 1985, "County's namesake fought with valor for American cause," Atlanta Journal, DeKalb Extra, page 4B. Martin, Kirk, November 27, 1981, "Research Trip To Europe Tells Why Baron DeKalb Left Home," DeKalb News/Sun, page 4C.

4. Newton, Maryellen Harvey, July 2, 1981, "Waiter, Courtier, Spy, General, deKalb Died Fighting For Freedom," DeKalb News/Sun "Heritage of DeKalb" special section, page 3E.

5. Newton, Maryellen Harvey, July 2, 1981, "Waiter, Courtier, Spy, General, deKalb Died Fighting For Freedom," DeKalb News/Sun "Heritage of DeKalb" special section, page 3E.

6. Newton, Maryellen Harvey, July 2, 1981, "Waiter, Courtier, Spy, General, deKalb Died Fighting For Freedom," DeKalb News/Sun "Heritage of DeKalb" special section, page 3E.

7. Newton, Maryellen Harvey, July 2, 1981, "Waiter, Courtier, Spy, General, deKalb Died Fighting For Freedom," DeKalb News/Sun "Heritage of DeKalb" special section, page 3E.

8. Newton, Maryellen Harvey, July 2, 1981, "Waiter, Courtier, Spy, General, deKalb Died Fighting For Freedom," DeKalb News/Sun "Heritage of DeKalb" special section, page 3E.

9. Morison, Samuel Eliot, 1965, The Oxford History of the American People, Oxford University Press, New York, pages 258, 259. Dupuy, R. Ernest and Trevor N., 1975, An Outline of the American Revolution, Harper and Row, page 158.

10. Morison, Samuel Eliot, 1965, The Oxford History of the American People, Oxford University Press, New York, pages 258, 259. Sherwood, Adiel, 1829, A Gazetteer of the State of Georgia, pages 197-198.

11. Kirkland, Thomas J. and Kennedy, Robert M., Historic Camden, Vol. 2, pages 80-81. Sherwood, Adiel, 1829, A Gazetteer of the State of Georgia, pages 197-198.

12. Kirkland, Thomas J. and Kennedy, Robert M., Historic Camden, Vol. 2, pages 80-81.

13. Newton, Maryellen Harvey, July 22, 1981, "Waiter, Courtier, Spy, General, deKalb Died Fighting For Freedom," DeKalb News/Sun, page 4E, (quoting Kapp, Frederick, author of Baron DeKalb).

14. Pugh, Joe T. and Bryan T., October 24, 1985, "County's namesake fought with valor for American cause," The Atlanta Journal, "DeKalb Extra," page 4B.

Chapter 8

Georgia Gov. John Clarke signed the original act creating DeKalb County on Dec. 9, 1822. The same session of the legislature created the counties of Bibb, Pike and Crawford counties from the larger counties of Houston, Twiggs, Monroe, Jones, Henry, Fayette and Gwinnett. DeKalb received most of its territory from Henry, with some coming from Gwinnett and Fayette. The original DeKalb County would include all or part of the eighth, 11th, 14th, 15th, 16th, 17th and 18th land districts.[1]

A second act, passed on December 29, 1822, provided for the organization of the new counties. The general assembly set the place for holding the Superior and Inferior Courts (today's county commissioners) and for the election of officers as the house of William Jackson.

Jackson's house, according to Charles Murphey Candler, writing in his Historic Address in 1922, "was on the McDonough Road, which at that time came into Decatur along the route of the present McDonough Street, on the left side of the road going from town."

In his history of Atlanta, Franklin M. Garrett states that the house was "on the east side of the old McDonough Road (now S. Chandler Street) a short distance south of Kirk Road, which would place it approximately one mile south of the DeKalb County Court House," in Land Lot 214 of the 15th land district. Garrett further writes that the marker at 250 South Chandler (sic), erected in 1945 by the Baron DeKalb Chapter of the Daughters of the American Revolution, is about a mile and a half too far south.[2]

In the same act of December 29, 1822, the Georgia legislature gave the surveyor of Fayette County the job of marking the boundaries between DeKalb and Gwinnett, with DeKalb picking up the tab for the survey.

The original DeKalb County was roughly twice as large as it is today, stretching all the way from the Hightower Trail and the South River on the east to the Chattahoochee River on the west, and from the Shallow Ford on the Chattahoochee on the north to Sandtown on the south.

The Georgia legislature's first attempt at describing the county boundaries must have proved incomprehensible to the surveyor. [3] A second attempt, in 1823, at describing the boundaries cleared up the "indefiniteness" and was found to be more acceptable: "Beginning at the Gwinnett corner on the Newton line, thence along the Hightower trail to where the peach tree road crosses said trail, from thence a direct line through Gwinnett county, to the lower corner of fractional lot on the Chatahoochie (sic) river, number three hundred and forty-four, in the sixth district of said county, thence down said river to the boundary line near Sandtown, thence along said boundary line to the district corner between districts number nine and fourteen, on the Chatahoochie river, thence a due east course along the district lines of thirteen and twelve to the corner of Newton county on the south Ocmulgee river, thence along the line of Newton county to the beginning corner on the Hightower trail." [4]

Thus, it was not until the early months of 1824 that the county was officially surveyed, and its boundaries distinguished from those established earlier for Henry, Fayette and Gwinnett counties. These territorial limits remained virtually unchanged until 1853 when the western half of DeKalb was cut off and became Fulton County. [5]

DeKalb proceeded under the same rules that had been established for Henry and Fayete counties the previous year. Elections were to be held for justices of the Inferior Court. When elected, the justices were to fix the site of the county town as near the center of the county as convenient. They were authorized to purchase as much land as they thought necessary for a courthouse and jail and to contract for their construction. The justices were required to hold countywide elections for sheriff, clerks of the Inferior and Superior courts, coroner, tax collector, tax receiver and surveyor, and for justices of the peace in each militia district. The responsibility for choosing petit and grand jurors through drawings also fell to the justices of the Inferior Court. [6]

The new county retained the numbered land districts (primarily districts numbered 14, 15, 16 and 18, plus portions of surrounding district). Land lots remained the same, as did the militia districts already designated for Henry, Gwinnett and Fayette counties. Justices of the Inferior Court and justices of the peace who had been chosen for Henry, Fayette and Gwinnett counties retained their offices. [7]

DeKalb's early militia districts were Diamond's (563), Lithonia (683), Evans (637), Phillips (487), Panthersville (536), Decatur (531), Browning's (572), Cross Keys (686) and Shallowford (524), which remained in DeKalb, and Cook's (469), Bryant's (479), Buckhead (722) and Blackhall (530), which were in the portion of DeKalb that later became Fulton County. [8]

DeKalb was attached to the Flint Judicial Circuit from its inception until December 1826. [9] Judge Eli S. Shorter presided over the Superior Court until 1825 when he was succeeded by Judge Charles J. McDonald. [10] James Hicks was the first county delegate to the state House of Representatives. James McC. Montgomery was the first state senator from DeKalb. [11]

Justices of the Inferior Court were required to "lay off" the county into Militia Districts, with captains assigned. As required by law, Justices of the peace were provided for elections of captains and subaltern officers. [12]

The house of Daniel E. Jackson (1796-1869) became well known in DeKalb for what it was not. The house was mistakenly labeled as the house of William Jackson. William Jackson's house was the first site of county government, before a county courthouse was built. Both houses were located on what is now Candler Street near Kirk Road. (DeKalb Historical Society; Vanishing Georgia Collection, Georgia Department of Archives and History)

The legislative act of December 23, 1822 authorized the justices of the Inferior Court to "fix on a public site for the Court House and jail to be as near the center of the county as convenience will admit." The commissioners also were authorized "to purchase for this purpose one square or lot of land, and to lay out a county town on said lot and dispose of lots under such rules and regulations as they may think most conducive to the interests of said County." [13]

More than six months later, on July 28, 1823, the commissioners reported that they had chosen a location for the new county town. Land Lot 246 in the 15th district. The commissioners ordered that the town be known by the name of Decatur and that "all public business should be held and done at the town of Decatur on and after the first Tuesday in September, 1823." [14] A legislative act, Dec. 10, 1823, made it official:

"AN ACT

"To make permanent the site of the public buildings in the County of DeKalb, at the town of Decatur, and to incorporate the same.

"Be it enacted by the Senate and House of Representatives of the State of Georgia, in General Assembly met, and it is hereby enacted by the authority of the same, that from and after the passing of

The city of Decatur was named for Commodore Stephen Decatur. (The Story of Decatur)

this act, the site of the public buildings for the county of DeKalb be and the same is hereby declared to be permanently fixed on lot number 246 in the fifteenth district, formerly Henry, now DeKalb, which said public site shall be called and known by the name of Decatur.

"Sec. 2. And be it further enacted, by the authority afore-said, that from and after the passing of this act that Reuben Cone, William Morris, William Gresham, James White, and Thomas A. Dobbs, be and they are hereby appointed Commissioners of the town of Decatur, in the County of DeKalb, and they, or a majority of them, shall have full power to convene at any time after the passage of this Act, and proceed to the appointment of a clerk, and such other officers as they may deem necessary to carry this act into execution.

"Sect. 3. And be it further enacted by the authority aforesaid, that the said commissioners shall hold their respective appointments hereby given them, until the first Monday in January, 1825, at which time, and on every subsequent year thereafter, the citizens of the said town of Decatur, entitled to vote for members of the General Assembly, shall choose by ballot, on the first Monday in January in every succeeding year, five persons to succeed them in office, as Commissioners of said town and they are hereby invested with full power and authority to make such by-laws and regulations, and to inflict such pains, penalties and forfeitures (sic) and do all other corporate acts as in their judgment shall be most conducive to the good order and government of the said town of Decatur; Provided, that such bye-laws and regulations be not repugnant to the laws and constitution of this state: And also provided, that no poll-tax shall exceed one dollar.

"Sec. 4. And be it further enacted, by the authority aforesaid, that any two or more justices of the peace, or justices of the Inferior Court for the County of DeKalb, not being themselves candidates, are hereby authorized and required to preside at such elections for commissioners as aforesaid: And provided, that nothing herein contained shall be construed so as to prevent the re-election of any commissioner pursuant to this act.

"Sec. 5. And be it further enacted by the Authority aforesaid, that should there be no election held on the day pointed out by this act, for that cause this act shall not be void, but an election may be held on any other day within three months, a justice of the peace, or justice of the Inferior Court, first advertising in said town ten days before said election.

"Sec. 6. And be it further enacted by the Authority aforesaid, that said commissioners shall have full power to extend the corporation laws over all the lots and land adjoining said town, agreeable to the plan of said town, which may be laid off for county purposes."

David Adams, Speaker of the House of Representatives
Thomas Stocks, President of the Senate
G. M. Troup, Governor
December 10, 1823 [1]

The new town was named in honor of Commodore Stephen Decatur (1779-1820), U. S. Naval hero, who commanded the U. S. S. Constitution, "Old Ironsides," and fought Barbary pirates at Tripoli. It was Decatur who said: "Our country! In her intercourse with foreign nations, may she always be in the right, but our country, right or wrong." He was killed in a duel with another naval officer. [16] [17]

James Diamond, a resident of the militia district that bore his name, north of the present-day town of Lithonia, was charged with surveying and establishing the boundaries of Decatur. [18] When the survey had been complete, town lots were sold at auction. [19]

A small log courthouse was built on the north (Clairemont Avenue) side of the present square. The exact date when the county ceased doing public business in William Jackson's living room has been lost to time. A short distance south of the square, on North McDonough Street, the county's first jail was built over a dungeon dug out of the earth. The dungeon, accessible only by a trap door in the floor of the jail building, served as a cell where prisoners were housed. This jail, which served the county's needs until 1842, proved quite sufficient to the task of holding prisoners securely. Stocks for punishment of minor offenses were located on the porch of the jail. [20]

Before the new county even had a chance to complete its first jail, it had to deal with its first criminal. Allen Burch was convicted of voluntary manslaughter in DeKalb Superior Court in April, 1823. The court ordered "the defendant be taken by the sheriff, from the bar of this court, to the Common Jail of Gwinnett County, there being no Safe Jail in DeKalb." Burch was pardoned by Gov. Clark and ordered to pay fines and court costs. [21]

DeKalb's original five Justices of Inferior Court all had been commissioned in other counties. Charles Gates Sr., Joseph D. Shumate and William Baker were installed February 6, 1822 in Fayette. Absalom Steward and Andrew Camp took their oaths of office in Henry in March 4, 1822. These commissioners are named in DeKalb's first Inferior Court Minute Book (1823-1867). This Inferior Court minute book and the 1836 Superior Court Minute Book are the only two record books that survived the courthouse fire of 1842. Superior Court Clerk John Glen and Inferior Court Clerk Elzey B. Reynolds can be thanked for saving these historic documents from the conflagration. Each had taken the books home to work on them. [22]

DeKalb County's first officers were sworn in Fayette County on March 18, 1822: John S. Welch, sheriff; Thomas A. Dobbs, clerk of Superior Court; Jonathan Dobbs, clerk of Inferior Court; John Calhoun, coroner; and James Adams, surveyor. All but Welch served until Jan. 15, 1824. The first sheriff resigned May 31, 1823, and was succeeded by Lochlin Johnson. Thomas Dobbs also was one of first commissioners of Decatur. [23]

Sheriff Welch was required to swear that they had not "since the first day of January, 1819, been engaged in a duel, either directly or indirectly, either as principal or second, or in any character whatsoever, in this State." [24]

DeKalb's first justices of the peace were Frederick Hilsback (Militia District 469), Daniel Gober and James Jett (Militia District 524), John Henry (Militia District 487), James Blackstock and Oliver

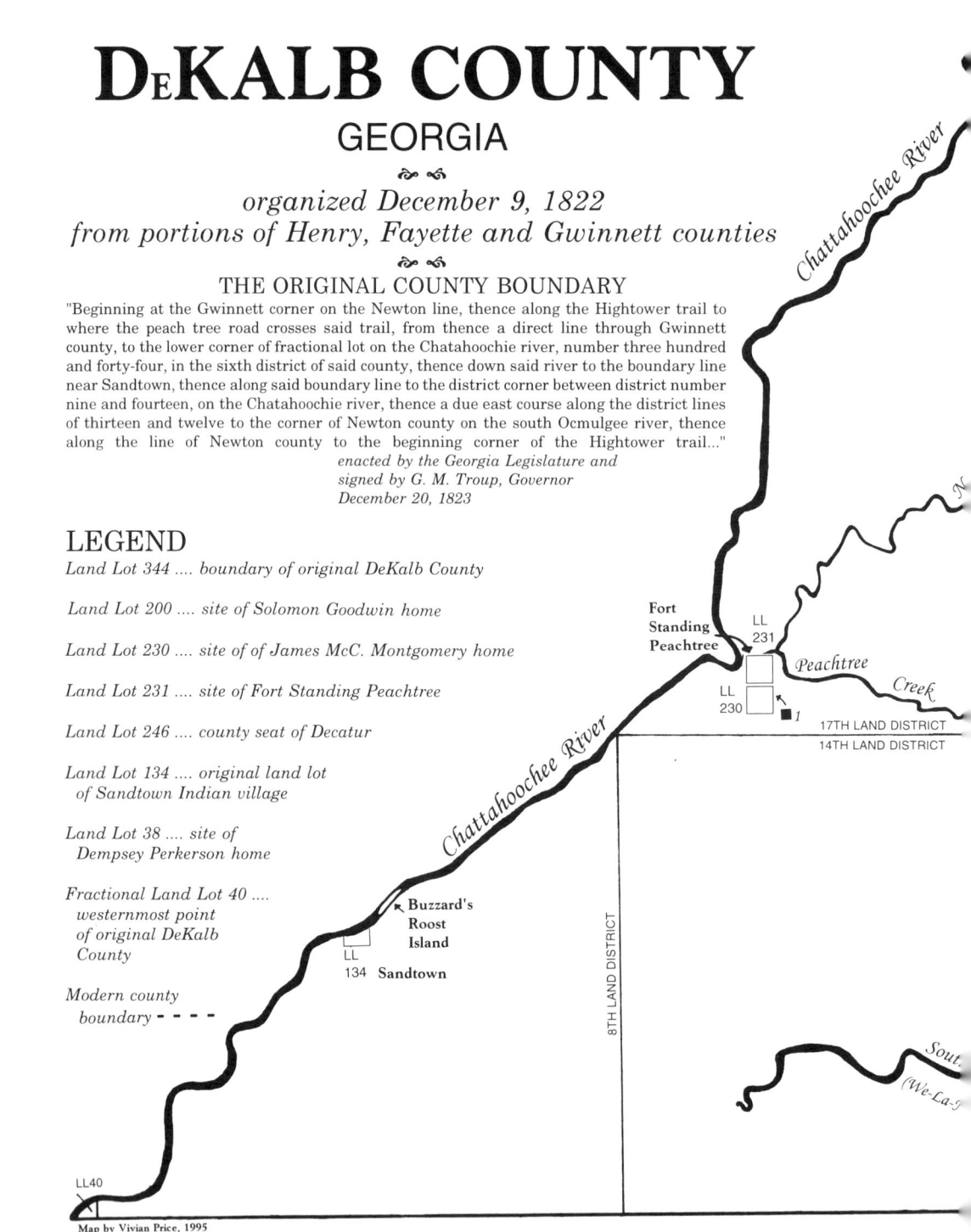

DeKALB COUNTY
GEORGIA

organized December 9, 1822
from portions of Henry, Fayette and Gwinnett counties

THE ORIGINAL COUNTY BOUNDARY

"Beginning at the Gwinnett corner on the Newton line, thence along the Hightower trail to where the peach tree road crosses said trail, from thence a direct line through Gwinnett county, to the lower corner of fractional lot on the Chatahoochie river, number three hundred and forty-four, in the sixth district of said county, thence down said river to the boundary line near Sandtown, thence along said boundary line to the district corner between district number nine and fourteen, on the Chatahoochie river, thence a due east course along the district lines of thirteen and twelve to the corner of Newton county on the south Ocmulgee river, thence along the line of Newton county to the beginning corner of the Hightower trail..."

enacted by the Georgia Legislature and
signed by G. M. Troup, Governor
December 20, 1823

LEGEND

Land Lot 344 .... boundary of original DeKalb County

Land Lot 200 .... site of Solomon Goodwin home

Land Lot 230 .... site of of James McC. Montgomery home

Land Lot 231 .... site of Fort Standing Peachtree

Land Lot 246 .... county seat of Decatur

Land Lot 134 .... original land lot of Sandtown Indian village

Land Lot 38 .... site of Dempsey Perkerson home

Fractional Land Lot 40 .... westernmost point of original DeKalb County

Modern county boundary - - - -

Map by Vivian Price, 1995

DeKalb County originally stretched all the way from the Chattahoochee River on the west to the Hightower Trail on the east. Map shows the original county boundary, as well as early towns and homes.

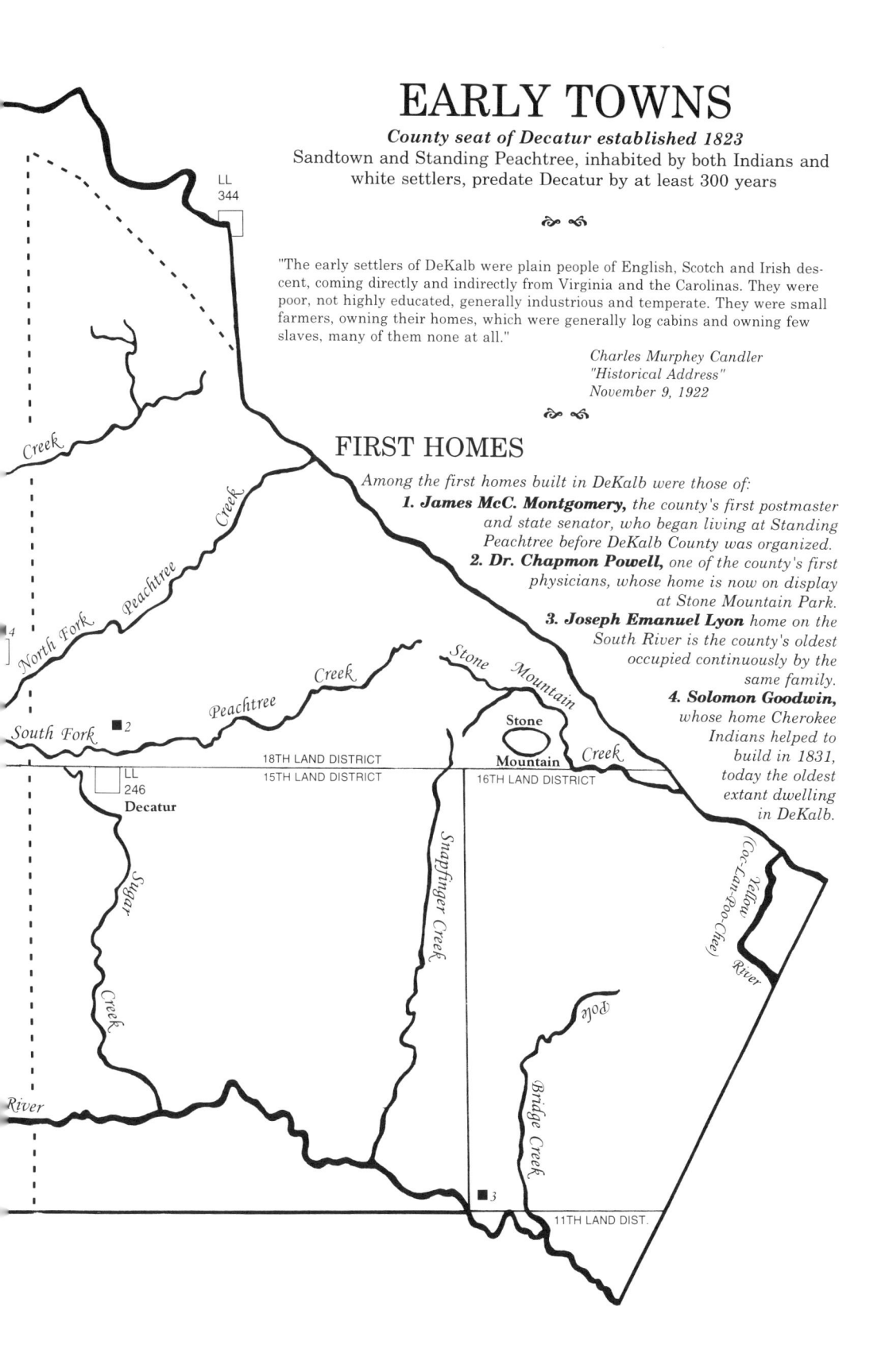

EARLY TOWNS
County seat of Decatur established 1823
Sandtown and Standing Peachtree, inhabited by both Indians and white settlers, predate Decatur by at least 300 years

❧ ☙

"The early settlers of DeKalb were plain people of English, Scotch and Irish descent, coming directly and indirectly from Virginia and the Carolinas. They were poor, not highly educated, generally industrious and temperate. They were small farmers, owning their homes, which were generally log cabins and owning few slaves, many of them none at all."

Charles Murphey Candler
"Historical Address"
November 9, 1922

❧ ☙

FIRST HOMES
Among the first homes built in DeKalb were those of:

1. James McC. Montgomery, the county's first postmaster and state senator, who began living at Standing Peachtree before DeKalb County was organized.

2. Dr. Chapmon Powell, one of the county's first physicians, whose home is now on display at Stone Mountain Park.

3. Joseph Emanuel Lyon home on the South River is the county's oldest occupied continuously by the same family.

4. Solomon Goodwin, whose home Cherokee Indians helped to build in 1831, today the oldest extant dwelling in DeKalb.

THE HISTORY OF DeKALB COUNTY, GA. • CHAPTER 8

Houston, (Militia District 530), Joseph Hubbard and Micajah Harris (Militia District 531), James Hendley (Militia District 563) and Matthew R. Grace (Militia District 487). [25]

DeKalb County's first Inferior Court jurors (county commissioners), chosen on July 29, 1823, were John Beasley, John Carter, William Carter, Loftin Fannin, Henry Grogin, Richard Grogin, William Hardman, William Heard, Thomas Hendrick, Joseph Hill, William Hill, William Hudspeth, Theofilus Jett, Nathan Jordan, Henry Logan, William McCarter, John McDaniel, John Morris, Davis Rollings, Britain Smith, Isaac Towers Jr., William Watts, William Wiley, Anson Williams and Augustine Young. [26]

The first order of business for the new county was creating and maintaining roads suitable for wagon traffic where once had only been single-file Indian trails. At their first meeting on May 20, 1823, the Inferior Court justices appointed road commissioners and issued two orders concerning roads.

James McC. Montgomery, Henry Logan and Ebenezer Pitts were appointed in the 17th District, and Samuel Prewett, T. A. Dobbs and James Hicks in the 14th District.

The justices designated the road from Standing Peachtree to Gwinnett, east of now Suwanee, known as the Hog Mountain Road, as a public road and ordered that it be maintained. This was the area's first road, having been cut in 1814 between the U. S. Army's two newly-built forts.

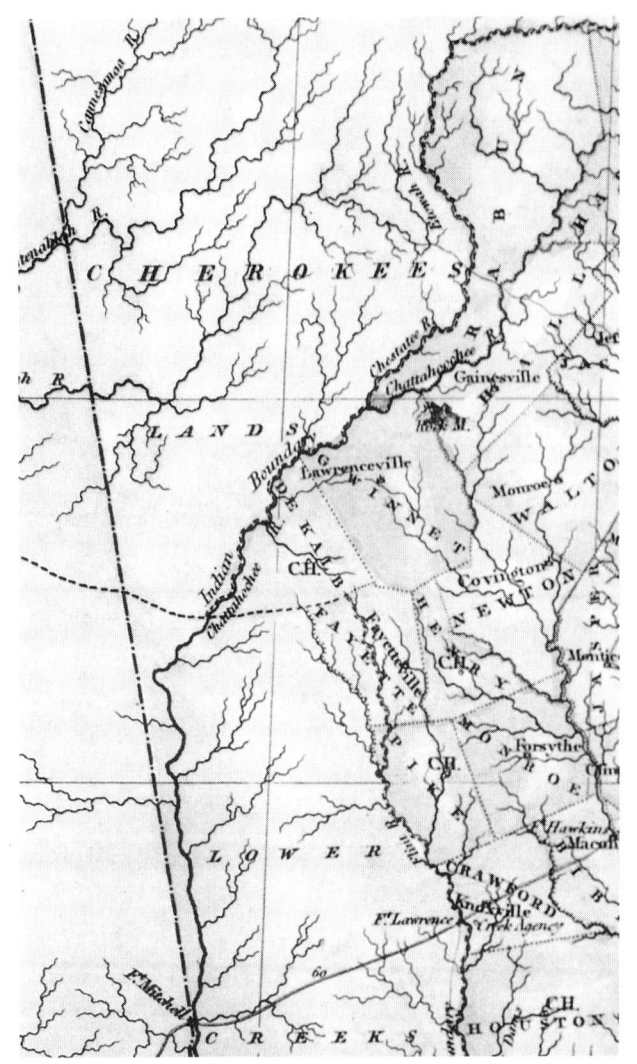

In 1824, DeKalb County was the farthest west the white man had ventured into north Georgia. The county was bounded on the northwest by the Cherokee Nation and on the south by Lower Creek Indian territory. Note the placement of Stone Mountain near Gainesville (Hall County) on the map. (Woodruff Library Special Collections, Emory University)

The justices also ordered a new road from "the Peachtree" by "the nearest and convenientest rout to intersect with the Boundary Line at or near Sandtown." [27]

The justices then, on May 25, 1823, created a new militia district with the following boundaries: "beginning at Thomas Carroll's on the Hightower trace thence a direct line to the nearest prong of Peachtree creek thence down said creek to Abraham Chandlers, thence a direct line to the mouth of long island Creek thence up the Chattahoochee to the dividing line between the counties of DeKalb and Gwinnett, thence along said line to the beginning, at Thomas Carroll's." This district included most all of what would soon become the Buckhead and Cross Keys districts. [28]

Justices Andrew Camp, Absalom Steward, William Baker and Joseph D. Shumate were present for the first Inferior Court meeting. [29]

The justices would not meet again until July 28, 1823, at which time they discussed access to the newly-created county seat of Decatur. The following order was approved: "Whereas there are many applicants to this court for new roads to be cut out from lot No. 246 in the 15th district of said county, the permanent site in and for DeKalb County, and as good roads attend greatly to facilitate the community at large and promote the interest of the public generally, we feel willing to grant the petitions of our citizens as far as appears reasonable. Therefore we have appointed several persons hereinafter named to view and designate the different routes on which roads are intended to pass if found to be of public utility agreeably to an Act of the General Assembly passed in the year 1818:

Joseph Hill, Britain Smith, Mathew Henry, Burrill Smith, and Joseph Hubbard -- from Rock Bridge to said lot 246.

Charles Harris, Joel Pritchett, Naman Hardman, Meredith Collier, and Joseph Morris -- from Standing Peach Tree to said lot.

D. R. Tillman, John Lawless, Abraham Gatehouse, Peter Brown, and James H. Knoll -- from said lot toward Fayetteville to the county line.

Naman Hardman, Silas McGrady, Greenville Pullin, James Galier, and William Anderson -- from the Shallowford to said lot.

Joel Swinney, David Telford, John Gunn, James Swinney, and John Townsend -- from said lot to intersect with the road leading from Covington, Newton County, to DeKalb court house at the dividing line between said counties.

William Jordan, Stephens Williams, John Morris, Reuben Braselton, and Thornton Ward -- from said lot to lot No. 10 in said district.

Joseph Woodall, William Stoker, Charles Anderson, Zachariah Jordan, and Evan Jenkins -- from said lot to intersect with the river road somewhere between the Utoy and Camp Creek. [30]

Portions of these first roads are still in use today, although in some cases the names have changed and the routes have been made obsolete by modern highways. Pioneer travelers could make their way from Gwinnett County to Standing Peachtree, crossing the South River and passing through Decatur, via Rockbridge Road and Ponce de Leon, and continuing westward along Montgomery Ferry Road. From the Shallow Ford on the Chattahoochee River, near Roswell, citizens with business in Decatur came along the Shallow Ford Road, now Clairmont, and could continue to Henry County along the Decatur-McDonough Road. This entire route today is State Road 155. Portions of the original Fayetteville Road still bear the name, and you can still get to Covington via East College Avenue and Covington Highway. [31]

Roads were not the only means of transportation to occupy the minds of lawmakers in 1823. The Georgia legislature had the authority to establish ferries across the Chattahoochee River. The first permit issued in DeKalb went to William Blake in 1823. Blake soon sold his ferry to a Mr. Nelson. Nelson's Ferry was located on fractional Land Lot 20 in the 14th District near the spot where Bankhead Highway crosses the river today. [32]

At the July 28, 1823 session of the DeKalb Inferior Court, the justices also authorized payment of $25.94 to former sheriff John Welch for transporting a prisoner by the name of John Campbell to the Gwinnett County jail, and $5.12 1/2 cents for arresting Samuel B. McClure on a state case. [33]

In addition, the justices appointed Abraham Chandler and John Morris as the county's first "overseers of the poor." [34]

Late in DeKalb County's first year of existence, the Georgia legislature appointed commissioners to establish an "academy" in the county. Although John B. Nelson, Zachariah Holloway, Jacob R. Brooks, Joseph Morris, Joseph D. Shumate, Reuben Cone and James Blackstock were appointed on November 18, 1823, no public school became a reality in DeKalb for a good many more years. [35]

Chapter 8 Notes

1. Candler, Charles Murphey, November 9, 1922, Historical Address, page 2.

2. Garrett, Franklin M., 1954, 1969, Atlanta and Environs -- A Chronicle of Its People and Events, Vol. I, page 35-36.

3. Acts of the General Assembly of the State of Georgia, 1823, page 56.

4. Acts of the General Assembly of the State of Georgia, 1823, page 56.

5. Candler, Charles Murphey, November 9, 1922, Historical Address, page 3.

6. Garrett, Franklin M., 1954, 1969, Atlanta and Environs -- A Chronicle of Its People and Events, Vol. I, pages 21 and 22.

7. Garrett, Franklin M., 1954, 1969, Atlanta and Environs -- A Chronicle of Its People and Events, Vol. I, page 24.

8. Humphries, December, 1947, "The Organization of DeKalb County," Atlanta Historical Bulletin, Vol. XXXII, page 1.

9. Humphries, December, 1947, "The Organization of DeKalb County," Atlanta Historical Bulletin, Vol. XXXII, page 1; Garrett, Franklin M., 1954, 1969, Atlanta and Environs -- A Chronicle of Its People and Events, Vol. I, page 137.

10. Garrett, Franklin M., 1954, 1969, Atlanta and Environs -- A Chronicle of Its People and Events, Vol. I, page 137; Candler, Charles Murphey, November 9, 1922, Historical Address, page 4.

11. Candler, Charles Murphey, November 9, 1922, Historical Address, page 4.

12. Humphries, December, 1947, "The Organization of DeKalb County," Atlanta Historical Bulletin, Vol. XXXII, page 2.

13. Candler, Charles Murphey, November 9, 1922, Historical Address, page 3.

14. Candler, Charles Murphey, November 9, 1922, Historical Address, page 3.

15. Garrett, Franklin M., 1954, 1969, Atlanta and Environs -- A Chronicle of Its People and Events, Vol. I, page 25-26; Georgia Laws 1823, pages 169-170.

16. Clarke, Caroline McKinney, 1973, 1997, The Story of Decatur 1823-1899, page 3.

17. Clarke, Caroline McKinney, 1973, 1996, The Story of Decatur 1823-1899, page 6.

18. Knight, Lucian Lamar, 1914, Georgia's Landmarks, Memorials and Legends, Vol. I, page 511.

19. Garrett, Franklin M., 1954, 1969, Atlanta and Environs -- A Chronicle of Its People and Events, Vol. I, page 26.

20. Clarke, Caroline McKinney, 1973, 1997, The Story of Decatur 1823-1899, page 7. Garrett, Franklin M., 1954, 1969, Atlanta and Environs -- A Chronicle of Its People and Events, Vol. I, page 26.

21. Garrett, Franklin M., 1954, 1969, Atlanta and Environs -- A Chronicle of Its People and Events, Vol. I, page 31, citing Executive Minutes for Friday, May 9, 1823, under the heading of Pardons by Governor Clark.

22. Garrett, Franklin M., 1954, 1969, Atlanta and Environs -- A Chronicle of Its People and Events, Vol. I, page 28.

23. Collins, L. Clyde, 1989, Findings Relating to the Hisory of the DeKalb County Sheriff's Department, Appendix page 1; Garrett, Franklin M., 1954, 1969, Atlanta and Environs -- A Chronicle of Its People and Events, Vol. I, page 38; Humphries, December, 1947, "The Organization of DeKalb County," Atlanta Historical Bulletin, Vol. XXXII, page 6.

24. Candler, Charles Murphey, November 9, 1922, Historical Address, page 4.

25. Garrett, Franklin M., 1954, 1969, Atlanta and Environs -- A Chronicle of Its People and Events, Vol. I, page 27.

26. DeKalb County Inferior Court Minutes, 1823; Garrett, Franklin M., 1954, 1969, Atlanta and Environs -- A Chronicle of Its People and Events, Vol. I, page 28.

27. DeKalb Inferior Court Minutes, 1823, page 1.

28. Humphries, December, 1947, "The Organization of DeKalb County," Atlanta Historical Bulletin, Vol. XXXII, page 4; Garrett, Franklin M., 1954, 1969, Atlanta and Environs -- A Chronicle of Its People and Events, Vol. I, page 29.

29. Humphries, December, 1947, "The Organization of DeKalb County," Atlanta Historical Bulletin, Vol. XXXII, page 6.

30. DeKalb Inferior Court Minutes, 1823; Garrett, Franklin M., 1954, 1969, Atlanta and Environs -- A Chronicle of Its People and Events, Vol. I, page 29-30; Humphries, December, 1947, "The Organization of DeKalb County," Atlanta Historical Bulletin, Vol. XXXII, page 4-5.

31. Garrett, Franklin M., 1954, 1969, Atlanta and Environs -- A Chronicle of Its People and Events, Vol. I, page 30.

32. Garrett, Franklin M., 1954, 1969, Atlanta and Environs -- A Chronicle of Its People and Events, Vol. I, page 30.

33. Humphries, December, 1947, "The Organization of DeKalb County," Atlanta Historical Bulletin, Vol. XXXII, page 4.

34. Minutes, Inferior Court; Garrett, Franklin M., 1954, 1969, Atlanta and Environs -- A Chronicle of Its People and Events, Vol. I, page 31.

35. Minutes, Inferior Court; Garrett, Franklin M., 1954, 1969, Atlanta and Environs -- A Chronicle of Its People and Events, Vol. I, page 31.

Chapter 9

*A*mong the estimated 2,500 original settlers of DeKalb County were many veterans of the American Revolution. Quite a few of these men and their families made significant contributions to the new county.

Among these was one who had fought with Baron DeKalb. The veteran of the Battle of Camden, S. C., John Fuller moved with his wife Mary and their nine children to DeKalb County in 1828. Their grandson William Allen Fuller, who died in 1905, worked for the Western and Atlantic Railroad, and was in the mercantile and real estate business in Atlanta. He is credited with having suggested the formation of the Atlanta Pioneer Citizens Society, forerunner of the Atlanta Historical Society. [1]

Twenty-one Revolutionary War veterans lived their last days and are buried in DeKalb (including that portion of the county that became Fulton County):

John Biffle	Jennings Hulsey	William B. Morris Sr.
Philip Terrel Burford	Edward Levell	William Reeve
Peter Cash	Joseph Emanuel Lyon	Lewis Stowers
Joel Chandler	John Maffett	William Suttles
Daniel Fones	James McNeil	William Terrell
William R. Gunnell	James McConnell	John Trimble
John Hayes	Montgomery	Graner Whitley
James Hooper		

Five of these graves have been identified and marked by the Baron DeKalb Chapter of the Daughters of the American Revolution. Veterans, cemeteries and dates markers were placed are as follows: John Hayes and John Maffett, Decatur Cemetery, 1920; William Morris, Cedar Grove Cemetery, 1927; Daniel Fones, Fellowship Cemetery, 1929; and James McNeil, Decatur Cemetery, 1950. The Baron DeKalb Chapter also marked in 1934 the grave of Thomas Gordon, who is buried near Snellville in Gwinnett County.

John Biffle, a native of Germany, was buried in an unmarked grave in the cemetery at Macedonia Baptist Church in southeast DeKalb. He served as a private in North Carolina, and married Sally Ingram, who is also buried at Macedonia. In addition to farming, Biffle was one of county's first real estate dealers, originally buying 800 acres and selling it in smaller parcels to incoming settlers. John's son, Leander Biffle, and his grandson, who was also named John, were prominent citizens in southeast DeKalb. [2]

The original Biffle home in DeKalb, a single-room log cabin, was moved to Adair Park in Decatur, and is being preserved for the public by the DeKalb Historical Society.

Also buried at Macedonia, in an unmarked grave, is Joseph Emanuel Lyon. Born February 13, 1754 in England, Lyon was a jeweler by trade. He came to the colonies as a British soldier. During fighting in Germantown, Penn. on October 4, 1777, he was captured. Obviously a pragmatic soul, he took the oath of allegiance and joined the Colonial Army. He was wounded at the Battle of Cowpens, S. C. on January 17, 1781.

Lyon family history holds that Joseph had been left for dead. "A passer-by saw that he was alive and carried water to him in his hat. He carried him to his home and cared for him until he recovered. He was ever after crippled and was a teacher..." While Lyon lay wounded, "it is said the wild hogs came from the woods to eat of the decaying flesh on the battlefield and he feared they would eat him alive. He did lose an arm as a result of his wounds. Right there he vowed never to eat hog meat again."

Joseph Emanuel Lyon married Mary Ann Marshbank about 1785 in South Carolina. Joseph died about 1830. Descendants of this couple still live on the same land along the South River where Joseph and Mary Ann first settled. Their house, much modified since Joseph built it, is still home to members of the Lyon clan. Lyons Road, off Browns Mill, is named for this family. [3]

Two Revolutionary War veterans -- William R. Gunnell and Joel Chandler -- are buried at Masters's Cemetery on Flakes Mill Road near the Henry County line. Joel Chandler served in the South Carolina Militia. [4]

Born in 1752, William R. Gunnell is listed as a pensioner in Campbell County in 1840. He fought in the Battles of Guilford Courthouse, Eutaw Springs, Cammelrake and White Bluff in South Carolina. Gunnell died on July 24, 1844; his widow later moved to Forsyth County. [5]

Four Revolutionary veterans found their last resting place at Fellowship Primitive Baptist Church Cemetery. Daniel Fones, Edward Levell, Peter Cash and Graner Whitley are buried at Fellowship, which is located off Lawrenceville Highway near Brockett Road in Tucker.

Born about 1764, Fones enlisted on April 5, 1777 and served until the end of the war, being promoted from corporal to sergeant along the way. His standard DAR tombstone reads:
"Sergt. Daniel Fones
1 R.I. Regt.
Rev. War."
The monument was shipped to Tucker from Washington, D. C. in 1914. Longtime Tucker resident Emmsy Thomas hauled the marker from the Tucker depot to the cemetery in a wagon. [6]

Large field stones with crudely carved letters, "E. L.," mark the grave of Edward Levell, who was born on July 16, 1756 in Newberry, S. C. and died on January 16, 1832. Levell's descendants still live in DeKalb County and elsewhere in the Atlanta area. [7]

Nothing beyond his burial place is known about Graner Whitley. [8] Peter Cash was born February 21, 1759 in Amherst or Albemarle County, Va., and served as a Minute Man in Amherst County. He is listed in the 1830 DeKalb County census, and applied for a pension in DeKalb in 1832. The husband of Ann Holiday, he died on November 15, 1832, and is buried in an unmarked grave at Fellowship. [9]

Three Revolutionary War veterans are buried in Decatur Cemetery, including Col. James McNeil, one of the most interesting characters in Decatur history. He was one of two veterans holding the rank of colonel.

From his unusual birth in 1757 aboard a ship in the Atlantic Ocean, McNeil was destined to live an uncommon life. McNeil's father was a colonel in the British Army. The family settled in North Carolina and supported England against the colonists. Young James sided with the rebels. He left his family and moved to Augusta, Ga. as a "refugee Patriot." He joined the colonial army and was soon promoted to the rank of colonel, commanding the 1st Battalion of the Georgia Militia in Richmond County. After the Revolution, he served in St. Paul's Parish as head of a commission charged with seizing property of persons disloyal to the new nation. He also was one of the state's ratifiers of the federal constitution.

McNeil was one of only nine courageous state representatives who voted against one of the state's biggest political scandals, the Yazoo Land Act of 1795. "Perhaps this act of his was the highlight of his career. It shows that he was put to the test of standing by his convictions, and the interest of the people, or betraying the people for a chance at enrichment of himself, and he did not yield to the temptation," said Mrs. Milton Scott, regent, Baron DeKalb DAR. Of McNeil's contributions, Atlanta historian Franklin M. Garrett said, "The influence of his foresighted statesmanship continues in the affairs of his state to the present day."

McNeil's public career had ended before he married his cousin Sarah McNeil in 1809. He was 52, she 19. They settled in Putnam County, but moved to DeKalb in 1830, having selected Decatur because of its educational opportunities. Their seven children were born in Putnam County. Their only son Daniel never married. The McNeils lived on the Shallow Ford Trail, now Clairmont Avenue, where he owned a saddle manufacturing business.

James McNeil died in 1853 at the age of 96; Sarah died in 1864. Both are buried in Decatur Cemetery. His simple tombstone is inscribed:
James McNeil
Colonel
Ga. Troops
Rev. War
1757-1853 [81]

---

[81] A ceremony for placing a marker on the grave of Col. James NcNeil were held Nov. 2, 1950 by the Baron DeKalb Chapter of the DAR. Participants in the ceremony included Mrs. Milton Scott, regent, Baron DeKalb Chapter; the Rev. Harry Tisdale, rector, Holy Trinity Church; Mrs. R. L. Paine, chaplain, Baron DeKalb Chapter; Mrs. Henry Newton; Carl Hudgins, past president, DeKalb Historical Society; Mrs. J. C. Peteet, historian, Baron DeKalb Chapter; Austin McNeill Ford, Richard Austin, Henry Shumate and Mary Virginia Shumate, descendants; and J. H. Owens, Decatur High musician.

Mrs. Harold A. Ford, a great-great granddaughter of James and Sarah McNeil, was active in the DeKalb Historical Society for many years. [10]

John Hayes, born on November 2, 1751, enlisted in the colonial army in North Carolina and applied for a pension in 1833 in DeKalb County. Hays died June 17, 1839. He and his wife Mary, who survived him by only two days, are buried in Decatur Cemetery. Near them is their son, Thomas, who died on January 7, 1831 at the age of 45. John Hayes's tombstone, placed by the Baron DeKalb Chapter of the DAR, is inscribed

>John Hayes
>Rev. Soldier. [11]

John Maffett (or Moffett) was born in 1742 in Virginia and served first as a captain and later as colonel in the Revolutionary War in South Carolina. Maffett died in 1829. The granite slab covering his grave is encompassed by a pipe railing, with stone posts at each end. His unusual tombstone inscription reads

>An old Revolutionary
>Supposed to be 87. [12]

Five Revolutionary War veterans are buried in small family cemeteries around DeKalb County.

Philip Terrel Burford is buried in the McCurdy family cemetery near Stone Mountain. Born June 29, 1763, he served as a lieutenant in North Carolina. He died in June 14, 1834. [13]

Jennings Hulsey, born in Kings Mountain, N. C. in 1765, is buried in the Hulsey family cemetery on the South River in south DeKalb County. He served as a private in the Battle of King's Mountain. Hulsey died December 16, 1850 in Henry County. He married Rebecca Pate in 1806. Children of Jennings and Rebecca grew up to marry children of other prominent DeKalb County families and made their mark on both DeKalb and Atlanta. [14]

Robert Lemon (or Lemmon/s) was born in 1768 County Atrim, Ireland and lived in the Pendleton District of South Carolina before moving to DeKalb in about 1822. He and his wife, Mary Anderson, had at least three children: James, John and Robert. Robert died in 1848 in DeKalb County, and Mary two years later. Both are buried in unknown locations in DeKalb.

Robert was a soldier in the Patriot Army during the American Revolution. He and his son James were early members of the Decatur Presbyterian Church, and both served as charter trustee and officer. James Lemon was born on June 3, 1794 in Anderson District, S. C. and died on March 6, 1849. He is buried in Mars Hill Cemetery in Acworth, Cobb County, Ga. James and his wife, Mary Brown Telford, had eight children: Louisa, Smith, George, Isabella, Sara Anne, William, Ann Maria and James Lile. [15]

James McConnell Montgomery, one of DeKalb's best-known pioneers, was born in Lancaster District, South Carolina on May 19, 1770. As a youngster, he accompanied his father, a second lieutenant, into battle in Burke County, Ga. A DAR biography states that Montgomery "though but a lad, followed his father to the field in the last campaign and bore his musket like a veteran." He was commissioned a major when he served in the War of 1812 at Fort Peachtree on the western edge of what would become DeKalb County. Montgomery and his wife, the former Nancy Farlow, moved their family of 14 children to Standing Peachtree from Jackson County, Ga. Montgomery died there on October 6, 1842. He and Nancy are buried in the Montgomery family cemetery near the Standing Peachtree homeplace. [16]

Lewis Stowers Sr., born in 1764 in Orange County, Va., is buried in the Stowers family cemetery south of the Klondike community near Lithonia. Stowers died on November 22, 1844. His wife, the former Joyce Shifflett, predeceased him by two years. [17]

North Carolinian William Terrell was born on July 6, 1760, but was a soldier in South Carolina. He was living in DeKalb by 1832, died in 1851, and is buried in the Terrell-Ford Family Cemetery near the intersection of Bouldercrest and Flat Shoals roads. [18]

James Hooper is buried in the Sandy Springs Cemetery, next to the Methodist Episcopal Church, in the portion of DeKalb that later became Fulton County. Born October 25, 1746, he enlisted in 1778 in Lunenburg County, Va. and served 12 months as a private. He died April 28, 1836. His widow, Elizabeth Chambers Hooper, applied for a pension in DeKalb on January 7, 1839, little more than one year before her death. [19]

William B. Morris Sr., who died in 1830, is buried in the Cedar Grove Cemetery. October 30, 1755, served as a private in North Carolina. His tombstone, inscribed
> NC Mil
> Rev War,

is one of those placed by the Baron DeKalb Chapter of the DAR. Sarah Terry Morris survived her husband by some six years. [20]

William Reeve was born April 5, 1756 in Virginia, where he served as a lieutenant. He died in 1842 and is buried in Nancy Creek Primitive Baptist Church cemetery near Chamblee. Married to the former Nettie White, Reeve wrote a will while living in Abbeville, S. C. His will lists 11 children, five sons and six daughters. He moved to DeKalb to live with his son James W. Reeve. [21]

William Suttles, born January 4, 1731, died January 23, 1839 at the age of 108. He is buried in the Utoy Primitive Baptist Church Cemetery in what is now south Fulton County. His grave was marked by the Daughters of the American Revolution. [22]

Born in 1756 in Mecklenburg County, N. C., John Trimble served in the militia in North and South Carolina. He was taken prisoner twice by the British. He and his wife Charity had at least nine children, several of whom settled in the Cross Keys District in north DeKalb. Trimble died in 1838 and is buried in an unknown location in DeKalb. [23]

From Deborah Gaudier's work, "Revolutionary War Soldiers and Widows of DeKalb County, Ga.," comes this list of other Revolutionary War veterans who lived a portion of their latter years in DeKalb:

Elijah Bankston	Meredith G. Brown	Samuel Cawly
William Beasley	William Bruce	John Childers
Humphrey Berditt		Richard Coleman
James Blackstock Sr.	Allen Cannon	Samuel Cone
Hugh Brewster	William Cash	Samuel Conn Sr.

William Copeland

John Dobbs
William Donaldson

Shadrick Ellis

William Fain Sr.
David Franklin

Thomas Garrett
William Gilbert
Robert Givens
John Goodwin
John Gresham

William Heard
Thomas House
Henry Huey

Dudley Jettar
Levi Johnston

Aaron Knight

John Landers

John Macomeson
John McCammon
Robert McDowell
Thomas Millican
John Murphy
Roger Murphey

Jeremiah Nesbit
Jacob New
William Nichols

William Oliver

Robert Patterson
Seamore Powell

John Sanders
John Sloan
William Spruill
Reuben Stephens

Bennett Tankersly
Isaac Towers

Benjamin Wadkins
Thomas P. Wagnon
Nathan Williford
Elliott Wood
John Woodall
Thomas Wooton
William Worthy

Forty-seven Revolutionary War veterans were living in DeKalb County at the time of the 1827 Georgia land lottery grants:

Robert Atkinson
Elijah Bankston
William Beasley
John Biffle
Hugh Brewster
Meredith Brown
William Bruce
Allen Cameron (Cannon)
William Carr
Ephraim Carson
John Chandler Sr.
Ezekiel Cloud
Samuel Colley (Cawly)
John Cook
William Coplin (Copeland)
John Dabbs

Thomas Dillon
William Donaldson
Isaac Durham
Thomas Duty
David Franklin
Joshua Gay
William Gilbert
Jacob Greathouse
William Gunnell
Benjamin Harris
John Hays
William Heard
Henry Huey
Aaron Knight
John Landers
James Martin

Thomas Millican
Jeremiah Nesbit
Jacob New
William Palmer
Thomas Slay
Reuben Stephens
William Suttles
Thomas Tanner
William Terrell
John Trimble
Benjamin Wadkins
Thomas P. Wagnon
George Watts
John Woodall
Thomas Wooten.[24]

Chapter 9 Notes

1. Garrett, Franklin M., Necrology, Roll 5, Frames 321-325, quoting biographical sketch written by William Allen Fuller.

2. Arnold, H. Ross Jr. and Burnham, H. Clifton, Georgia Revolutionary War Soldiers' Graves, page 172. Garrett, Franklin M., Necrology, Roll 1, Frame 474, and Roll 5, Frame 275. Hochim, Mrs. Eldred Martin, 1990, DAR Patriot Index Centennial Edition Part I, National Society of the DAR Centennial Administration, page 250.

3. Hochim, Mrs. Eldred Martin, 1990, DAR Patriot Index Centennial Edition Part I, National Society of the DAR Centennial Administration, page 431. Arnold Jr., H. Ross and Burnham, H. Clifton, Georgia Revolutionary War Soldiers' Graves, page 175. Johnson, Mr. and Mrs. J. Wallace, n. d., "Lyon Family History," unpublished manuscript. Porter, Phyllis, DAR Collection of Genealogical Records, Vol. 191, page 43.

4. Arnold Jr., H. Ross and Burnham, H. Clifton, Georgia Revolutionary War Soldiers' Graves, page 173. Moss, Bobby Gilmer, 1983, Roster of South Carolina Patriots in the American Revolution, page 162.

5. McCall, Mrs. Howard H., 1968, Roster of Revolutionary Soldiers in Georgia, Vol. III, Georgia Society of the Daughters of the American Revolution, page 322. Arnold Jr., H. Ross and Burnham, H. Clifton, Georgia Revolutionary War Soldiers' Graves, page 174. Abstracts of Revolutionary War Pension Files, page 1458.

6. Arnold, H. Ross and Burnham, H. Clifton, Georgia Revolutionary War Soldiers' Graves, page 174. Garrett, Franklin M., Necrology, Roll 1, Frame 492. Georgia Department of Archives and History. Tucker Eagle, 1964.

7. Arnold Jr., H. Ross and Burnham, H. Clifton, Georgia Revolutionary War Soldiers' Graves, page 175. Garrett, Franklin M., Necrology, Roll 1, Frame 492. Gaudier, Deborah, Revolutionary War Soldiers and Widows of DeKalb County, Ga., unpublished manuscript, page 49.

8. Arnold Jr., H. Ross and Burnham, H. Clifton, Georgia Revolutionary War Soldiers' Graves, page 179. Knight, Lucian Lamar, Georgia's Roster of the Revolution, page 466.

9. Gaudier, Deborah, Revolutionary War Soldiers and Widows of DeKalb County, Ga., page 12.

10. McCall, Mrs. Howard H., 1968, Roster of Revolutionary Soldiers in Georgia, Georgia Society of the Daughters of the American Revolution, Vol. III, pages 31, 32 and 307. Hochim, Mrs. Eldred Martin, 1990, DAR Patriot Index Centennial Edition Part I, National Society of the DAR Centennial Administration, page 1984. Arnold Jr., H. Ross and Burnham, H. Clifton, Georgia Revolutionary War Soldiers' Graves, page 176. Garrett, Franklin M., Roll 1, Frame 90. Histories of Georgia Revolutionary Soldiers, Vol. 372, page 74. Georgia Chapters, Daughters of the American Revolution, 1950-51, Genealogical Records, Vol. 82, pages 50-65. Garrett, Franklin M., 1954, 1969, Atlanta and Environs -- A Chronicle of Its People and Events, Vol. III, pages 577-578; Ford, Austin McNeill, 1952, "Extracts From Some Old Letters," The Collections of the DeKalb Historical Society, Vol. 1, pages 54-56.

11. McCall, Mrs. Howard H., 1968, Roster of Revolutionary Soldiers in Georgia, Vol. I, Georgia Society of the Daughters of the American Revolution, page 196. Arnold Jr., H. Ross, and Burnham, H. Clifton, Georgia Revolutionary War Soldiers' Graves, page 174. Garrett, Franklin M., Necrology, Roll 1, Frame 83. Knight, Lucian Lamar, Georgia's Roster of the Revolution, page 335. Knight, Lucian Lamar, Georgia's Landmarks, Memorials and Legends, Vol. 2, Section III, page 404.

12. McCall, Mrs. Howard H., 1968, Roster of Revolutionary Soldiers in Georgia, Vol. 1, Georgia Society of the Daughters of the American Revolution, page 200. Arnold Jr., H. Ross, and Burnham, H. Clifton, Georgia Revolutionary War Soldiers' Graves, page 176. Garrett, Franklin M., Necrology, Roll 1, Frame 125. Draper, Lyman C., 1881, 1954, King's Mountain and Its Heroes: History of the Battle of King's Mountain, Oct. 7, 1780 and the Events Which Led to It, page 465. Moss, Bobby Gilmer, 1983, Roster of South Carolina Patriots in the American Revolution, page 690. Knight, Lucian Lamar, Georgia's Landmarks, Memorials and Legends, Vol. 2, Section III, page 404.

13. Arnold Jr., H. Ross, and Burnham, H. Clifton, Georgia Revolutionary War Soldiers' Graves, page 173.

14. McCall, Mrs. Howard H., 1968, Roster of Revolutionary Soldiers in Georgia, Vol. 1, Georgia Society of the Daughters of the American Revolution, DAR, page 197. Hochim, Mrs. Eldred Martin, 1990, DAR Patriot Index Centennial Edition Part I, National Society of the DAR Centennial Administration, page 1532; Arnold Jr., H. Ross, and Burham, H. Clifton, Georgia Revolutionary War Soldiers' Graves, page 175; Rainer, Vessie Thrasher, 1871, Henry County -- Mother of All Counties, page 43.

15. Jones, John Carrol, 1997, personal collection.

16. McCall, Mrs. Howard H., 1968, Roster of Revolutionary Soldiers in Georgia, Georgia Society of the Daughters of American Revolution, page 225. Porter, Phyllis M., DAR Collection of Genealogical Records, Vol. 249, page 96. Hochim, Mrs. Eldred Martin, 1990, DAR Patriot Index Centennial Edition Part I, National Society of the DAR Centennial Administration, page 2055; Arnold Jr., H. Ross, and Burnham, H. Clifton, Georgia Revolutionary War Soldiers' Graves, page 176. Garrett, Franklin M., Necrology, Roll 1, Frame 125. Southern Genealogies, Georgia Society of the Daughters of the American Revolution, 1942-44, Vol. 78, page 138.

17. McCall, Mrs. Howard H., 1968, Roster of Revolutionary Soldiers in Georgia, Vol. 1, Georgia Society of the Daughters of the American Revolution, page 323. Porter, Phyllis M., DAR Collection of Genealogical Records, Vol. 137, Georgia Society of the Daughters of the American Revolution, page 188. Arnold Jr., H. Ross, and Burnham, H. Clifton, Georgia Revolutionary War Soldiers' Graves, page 177. Garrett, Franklin M., Necrology, Roll 1, Frame 430.

18. McCall, Mrs. Howard H., 1968, Roster of Revolutionary Soldiers in Georgia, Vol. 3, Georgia Society of the Daughters of the American Revolution, page 315. Arnold Jr., H. Ross, and Burnham, H. Clifton, Georgia Revolutionary War Soldiers' Graves, page 178. Garrett, Franklin M., Necrology, Roll 1, Frame 513. Knight, Lucian Lamar, Georgia's Roster of the Revolution, page 332. Abstracts of Revolutionary War Pension Files, page 3449. Moss, Bobby Gilmer, 1983, Roster of South Carolina Patriots in the American Revolution, page 922. Gaudier, Deborah, Revolutionary War Soldiers and Widows of DeKalb County, Ga., unpublished manuscript.

19. Arnold Jr., H. Ross, and Burnham, H. Clifton, Georgia Revolutionary War Soldiers' Graves, page 175. Garrett, Franklin M., Necrology, Roll 1, Frame 321. Knight, Lucian Lamar, Georgia's Roster of the Revolution, pages 418 and 441. Abstracts of Revolutionary War Pension Files, page 1700.

20. McCall, Mrs. Howard H., 1968, Roster of Revolutionary Soldiers in Georgia, Vol. 2, Georgia Society of the Daughters of the American Revolution, page 159. Hochim, Mrs. Eldred Martin, 1990, DAR Patriot Index Centennial Edition Part I, National Society of the DAR Centennial Administration, page 2082. Arnold Jr., H. Ross, and Burnham, H. Clifton, date?, Georgia Revolutionary War Soldiers' Graves, page 176. Garrett, Franklin M., Necrology, Roll 1, Frame 290. Histories of Revolutionary Soldiers, Vol. 326, 1986, Georgia Society of the Daughters of the American Revolution, page 158. Knight, Lucian Lamar, Georgia's Roster of the Revolution, page 443. Gaudier, Deborah, Revolutionary War Soldiers and Widows of DeKalb County, Ga., page 56.

21. Hochim, Mrs. Eldred Martin, 1990, DAR Patriot Index Centennial Edition Part I, National Society of the DAR Centennial Administration, page 2431. DAR Patriot Index, Vol. I, page 562. Arnold Jr., H. Ross, and Burnham, H. Clifton, Georgia Revolutionary War Soldiers' Graves, page 177. Knight, Lucian Lamar, Georgia's Roster of the Revolution, page 452. Abstracts of Revolutionary War Pension Files, page 2843. Gaudier, Deborah, Revolutionary War Soldiers and Widows of DeKalb County, Ga., page 66.

22. Gaudier, Deborah, Revolutionary War Soldiers and Widows of DeKalb County, Ga., page 75.

23. McCall, Mrs. Howard, 1968, Roster of Revolutionary Soldiers in Georgia, Vol. 3, Georgia Society of the Daughters of the American Revolution, page 302. Porter, Phyllis M., DAR Collection of Genealogical Records, Vol. 152, page 465. Hochim, Mrs. Eldred Martin, 1990, DAR Patriot Index Centennial Edition Part I, National Society of the DAR Centennial Administration, page 2975. Arnold Jr., H. Ross, and Burnham, H. Clifton, Georgia Revolutionary War Soldiers' Graves, page 178. Abstracts of Revolutionary War Pension Files, page 3538. Moss, Bobby Gilmer, 1983, Roster of South Carolina Patriots in the American Revolution, page 940. Gaudier, Deborah, Revolutionary War Soldiers and Widows of DeKalb County, Ga., page 79.

24. Hitz, Alex M., 1966, <u>Revolutionary War by the State of Georgia Taken from Official State Records in the Surveyor-General Department</u>, Georgia Department of Archives and History.

Chapter 10

The early settlers of DeKalb were plain people of English, Scotch and Irish descent, coming directly and indirectly from Virginia and the Carolinas. They were poor, not highly educated, generally industrious and temperate. They were small farmers, owning their homes, which were generally log cabins and owning few slaves, many of them none at all. I do not suppose there was in the entire county a single land and slave owner, who because of the size of his holdings or farm operations, could have been called a planter, such as were known in the older East and Middle Georgia counties."[1]

Charles Murphey Candler, whose description of DeKalb's pioneers was contained in his Historic Address of 1922, estimates that there were 2,500 hardy souls in the new county in 1822.

From his Historical Address comes a list of early male settlers:

William Akers	Fanning Brown	Jesse F. Cleveland
Thomas Akin	John Brown	James T. Cobb
Thomas Austin	Robert M. Brown Sr.	Lemuel Cobb
Dr. James C. Avary	John Bryce	John Collier
S. T. Bailey	G. B. Butler	Meredith Collier
William Baker	Dr. E. N. Calhoun	Merrill Collier
William Beauchamp	James M. Calhoun	Reuben Cone
Samuel Binion	Larkin Carlton	Alex Corry
James Blackstock	Benjamin Carr	James Crockett
E. J. Bond	J. M. Carroll	E. A. Davis
J. B. Bond	William Carson	Moses W. Davis
Dr. W. P. Bond	Tully Choice	Robert F. Davis
John W. Born	Jacob Chupp	James Diamond
William L. Born	Oliver Clark	T. A. Dobbs
Jacob R. Brooks	Rev. William H. Clark	Samuel Dodson

Charles Murphey Candler delivered the keynote address at DeKalb's centennial celebration in 1922. He is pictured here with his son, Milton, and dog, Bloxie. (Vanishing Georgia Collection, Georgia Department of Archives and History)

W. J. Donaldson	A. J. Goldsmith	William Hill
James R. Evans	James W. Goldsmith	Robert Hollingsworth
William Ezzard	William Goldsmith	Hines Holt
John Y. Flowers	Alston H. Green	John W. Hooper
Drury Fowler	William Gresham	Asa W. Howard
John W. Fowler	Rev. Josiah Grisham	Dr. P. F. Hoyle
Minty Fowler	Rev. Bedford Gunn	Eli J. Hulsey
Charles Gates	William Hairston	Hardy Ivy
Banks George	Zachariah Hallaway	William Jackson
Rev. James R. George	George K. Hamilton	John Jennings
J. W. George	Naman Hardman	Archibald Johnson
Tunstall B. George	Charles Harris	Daniel Johnson
Joseph W. Givens	George Heard	Gabe Johnson
Robert Givens	Charles C. Hicks	Lochlin Johnson
John Glen	James Hicks	William W. Johnson

John Jones
Robert Jones Sr.
Seaborn Jones
David Kiddoo
Alex Kirkpatrick
James H. Kirkpatrick
James W. Kirkpatrick
Watson Kittredge
Charles Latimer
H. B. Latimer
Drury Lee
James Lemon
Robert Lemon
James Ligon
John C. Maddox
John E. Maguire
Rev. James Mangum
Ezekiel Mason
William P. Mason
Samuel C. Masters
J. R. McAlister
John McCullough
Rev. John McElroy
Samuel McElroy Sr.
William McElroy
C. W. McGinnis
J. W. McLain
Malcolm McLeod
John W. McCurdy
P. B. McCurdy
Daniel McNeill
Robert McWilliams
John Meadow
W. H. Minor
J. Mc. Montgomery

Joseph Morgan
L. S. Morgan
Joe Morris
William Mosely
Charles Murphey
Moses Murphey
Robert Murphey
John B. Nelson
William New
Robert Ozmer
James Paden
Isaiah Parker
Rev. William Parks
William Pendley
Dempsey Perkerson
T. J. Perkerson
A. L. Pitts
Ebenezer Pitts
Joseph Pitts
Dr. Chapman Powell
Samuel Prewitt
Joel Pritchett
John C. Ragsdale
Leonard Randall
Thomas Ray
J. M. Riddling
William Rogers
William Scaife
Berryman D. Shumate
Mason D. Shumate
Asa Simmons
Simeon Smith
David R. Silliman
David M. Simpson
Leonard Simpson

G. K. Smith
Rev. John M. Smith
Robert H. Smith
William R. Smith
Benjamin Sprayberry
Harris Sprayberry
Rev. Uriah C. Sprayberry
Joel Starnes
Isaac Steele
M. A. Steele
John Stephens
John Stephenson
M. R. Stephenson
William Stephenson
Thomas Stevens
Elijah Steward
Joseph Stewart
Daniel Stone
John N. Swift
Asa Thompson
Dr. Joseph Thompson
Ebenezer Tilley
Stephen Tilley
Lewis Towers
William Towers
Walter Wadsworth
Joseph Walker
James White
Levi Willard
Ammi Williams
Jonathan B. Wilson
James J. Winn
William Wright. [2]

A good many of DeKalb's early residents came from Gwinnett County, as shown in the 1820 census of Gwinnett. Among the heads of households there were Green Baker, Jacob R. Brooks, Fanning Brown, Abraham Chandler, Meredith Collier, Levi Dempsey, James Diamond, Lindsey Ellsberry, John Evans, William Hairston, James Hicks, Richard Holt, Jennings Hulsey, William Jackson, James Jett, Dempsey Perkerson, Benjamin Plaster, Isaac Towers and William Towers. [3]

Although the days of the Creek and Cherokee Indians were numbered, it is unrealistic to assume that all the Indians had left before the white man moved in. In 1822, DeKalb County was frontier territory, only one year from belonging to the Creek Indians, and just across the Chattahoochee River from the Cherokee Nation and the remaining Creek lands. DeKalb remained adjacent to Indian territory officially until the last Creek Indian cession in 1835. The last of the Cherokees were removed three

The log cabin said to have been built by Revolutionary War veteran Joseph Emanuel Lyon in the 1820s is concealed inside this house in south DeKalb County. The house originally was one room, with a basement where slaves lived. The house has the distinction of being the oldest in the county occupied continuously by the same family. (Photo by Vivian Price)

years later. [4] Most of DeKalb's earliest settlers undoubtedly encountered Indians. The few remaining records of the era show that relations between Indians and white were peaceful for the most part. Occasionally, however, encounters could be scary and downright dangerous.

An 1869 newspaper article tells of an Indian confrontation in 1825 at Walton Spring near the intersection of Indian trails that became Five Points in downtown Atlanta. The Indian Springs treaty of 1825 and the subsequent killing of Chief William McIntosh caused bitter divisions among the Creek Indians who remained in DeKalb County. Two factions occupied enemy camps, one at Walton Springs, near what is now Spring Street and Carnegie Way, the other where the Union Station would be built.

In the summer of 1825, fueled by liquor they purchased with animals skins in Decatur, the two groups began trading insults and blows. The fighting progressed to knives, tomahawks and guns. "For more than two hours, the virgin forest rang with the clangor of arms and the demoniac yells of the drunken and infuriated savages."

The fight culminated in a battle in a grove of oak trees on Alabama, between Whitehall and Pryor. "The carnival of death went on until every actor in the tragic scene was disemboweled, or rendered utterly helpless, while in the adjacent thicket were scattered the dead and the dying who were engaged in the fight, the whole numbering not less than 50, which was probably the entire combative strength of the two factions." [5]

There is no existing record of any other violent conflict among Indians or between Indians and whites in DeKalb County. No "depredation" claims for property destroyed or stolen by Indians was ever filed from DeKalb County. [6]

Descendants of Joseph Emanuel Lyon, who settled on land along the South River, tell stories of their ancestors seeing Indians while doing their daily chores.

Elizabeth, one of the Lyon daughters, was responsible for bringing the cows home from the field. She would see Indians and, being afraid, would drive the cows home as fast as she could. Children of the Lyon family remembered their parents giving food to the Indians. Members of the Lyon family have found numerous artifacts on their property, including a beautifully polished gray stone pipe and many arrowheads. A grassy area near the Lyon home was called "Fortification Field," because an Indian battle was said to have been fought there. [7]

Some five miles upriver from the Lyon place, children in the Perkerson and Waldrop families played with Cherokee Indian children whose parents were friends with their parents. The Indians lived in "wigwams" near the river. Family history records that they were "not belligerent, but curious, and would peek in windows." [8] The family of Lochlin Johnson undoubtedly saw Indians on their plantation, which was located just west of the Perkerson place, near where Panthersville Road crosses the South River today. Johnson (1787-1861) was elected to almost every public office in DeKalb's early history. He was sheriff in 1823, state senator in 1824, road commissioner in 1826 and justice of the Inferior Court in 1837 and 1845.

The presence of Indians still in DeKalb County did not deter the white settlers. In the east Georgia counties, they loaded their possessions and their children onto horse-drawn wagons and oxcarts and headed for virgin territory, where roads were single-file tracks and cleared homesites nonexistent.

They camped in the open until they could cut down trees to build small log homes. They collected rocks to build huge stone fireplaces to accommodate large logs for cooking and heating. Like the Indians, they chose sites along creeks and streams. If they were among the most fortunate of the "fortunate drawers" in the land lottery, or made prudent purchases, they claimed the fertile bottom lands along the We-La-Nee (South) River, the Coc-lan-poo-chee (Yellow) River or the Chattahoochee.

Few of these early settlers owned more than one land lot (202 1/2 acres), and many did not own an entire lot, although settlers along the South River tended to be more prosperous than their counterparts in the interior of the county. They were primarily small farmers, usually working their own land with the help of only their family and neighbors. The man who owned a dozen slaves was rare. [9]

Life was not easy for these pioneers.

Campsites and homesteads always were located close to water. Water was dipped from streams and carried in buckets. Cooking was done in cast-iron pots and skillets over open fires. With the exception of coffee, salt and sugar, their food was home-grown. They grew the cotton, spun it into thread and dyed the thread with plants they cultivated or found growing wild. They wove the thread into cloth and sewed the cloth into pants and skirts and shirts. They raised livestock for food, fat, fur and hides to make clothing and shoes and harnesses, candles and soap. They made their own tools and wagons. One of the most important items DeKalb's pioneers brought from their former homes was a source of fire. Without matches, fire could only be "borrowed" from a neighbor, or started with flint, steel and dried kindling called "punk." [10]

One such family was that of George and Martha Thomas. They and their six children came from South Carolina by way of Jackson County, Ga. to south DeKalb in a covered wagon. A carefully-guarded cast iron pot in the back of the wagon contined hot coals. The Thomases settled on the Decatur-McDonough Road about half way between the two towns. George built a 20x30-foot log cabin with a field stone fireplace. Martha made mattresses stuffed with wheat straw. George fired a rifle shot through the cabin's front wall, making a peep-hole through which the family could see who might be coming down the road. [11] Called the Thomas-Barber Cabin, the pioneer dwelling now is part of the DeKalb Historical Society's Adair Park complex, which contains several historic structures.

The Hairstons were among the first settlers along Snapfinger and Barbashela creeks in the Redan area. Peter and Martha Baker Hairston had moved from the Abbeville District in South Carolina to Gwinnett County, where their son William married Lavinia Towers, eldest daughter of Isaac Towers, on May 6, 1819. Their son Albert Miles Hairston was born March 11, 1820 in Gwinnett County. He died December 23, 1901 in DeKalb and was buried in Wesley Chapel Cemetery. [82]

Albert Hairston wrote in 1901 that his parents came to "Boboshela Creek" with several of Lavinia's brothers and 10 months before DeKalb was officially organized. The Towers and Hairston families traveled to Georgia from South Carolina, along with the family of Thomas Mehaffey. In the spring of 1827, William Hairston "made a house raising and built a two story dwelling out of large hewn log." There were no sawmills in the area until William and his father-in-law, Isaac Towers, built one on Snapfinger Creek. That original Hairston home was just north of where Covington Highway now crosses Snapfinger Creek. [12]

The Towers and Hairston family names still linger on a number of roads, schools and other landmarks in the Redan area. In his 1901 sketches, Albert Hairston wrote that Snapfinger creek received its name "from one of the men who fell down and broke his finger when the surveyors were surveying the land." The story was told to a young Albert by his grandmother Elizabeth Akins Towers. Elizabeth and Isaac Towers lived on 500 acres of land along Snapfinger Creek that Isaac had purchased in 1821.

Isaac and his brother William "cleared some of the land... and made a crop on it that year. It was the first timber cut anywhere on Snapfinger creek. The virgin forest had been unbroken by the woodman's axe until then. Both creeks were fine ranges and were heavily timbered."

---

[82] Albert Miles Hairston married Nancy McLeon; their children were Rebecca Anna, Sara Caroline, William M. and Alice Priscilla. Sara Caroline Hairston married Hayes Adams Jolly; their children were Lawson E., Tom, Clem, Jesse, Alice, Mary Elizabeth, Carolina Adams and Kate. (Source: The Collections of the DeKalb Historical Society, Vol. 1, 1952, page 97).

Once the "house raising" was completed, the families were involved in raising sheep. "There was a large unbroken range. Sheep went where they pleased, coming home occasionally to be salted. At the time of the new moon in September our fathers would go to the forest and drive the sheep home and shear them, and our mothers would wash the wool and card and spin it, as there were no factories here in the twenties."

Thomas Mehaffey "was a wheelwright by trade, and made all the spinning wheels that were made in this county for the women who carded, spun and made their own ginghams at home, for themselves and their daughters. Everybody tried to excel her neighbor in making nice homespun dresses.

"We boys were pressed in spinning business also. Our mothers would have different kinds of bark brought in from the forest and dye the wool, some black and some brown, and if they wished to make a pair of grey jeans, they used white and black. To make a roan color they would mix brown and white." [13]

Mehaffey, his wife and several children are buried in a family cemetery, one of the oldest burial grounds in the county, "next to those occupied by the aborigines," in Land Lot 2 of the 16th District of DeKalb. There are no inscribed markers in the cemetery. [14]

Hairston also wrote about a number of other early settlers of southeast DeKalb.

1819. Their son Albert Miles Hairston was born March 11, 1820 in Gwinnett County. He died December 23, 1901 in DeKalb and was buried in Wesley Chapel Cemetery. [83]

Albert Hairston wrote in 1901 that his parents came to "Boboshela Creek" with several of Lavinia's brothers and 10 months before DeKalb was officially organized. The Towers and Hairston families traveled to Georgia from South Carolina, along with the family of Thomas Mehaffey. In the spring of 1827, William Hairston "made a house raising and built a two story dwelling out of large hewn log." There were no sawmills in the area until William and his father-in-law, Isaac Towers, built one on Snapfinger Creek. That original Hairston home was just north of where Covington Highway now crosses Snapfinger Creek. [15]

The Towers and Hairston family names still linger on a number of roads, schools and other landmarks in the Redan area. In his 1901 sketches, Albert Hairston wrote that Snapfinger creek received its name "from one of the men who fell down and broke his finger when the surveyors were surveying the land." The story was told to a young Albert by his grandmother Elizabeth Akins Towers. Elizabeth and Isaac Towers lived on 500 acres of land along Snapfinger Creek that Isaac had purchased in 1821.

Isaac and his brother William "cleared some of the land... and made a crop on it that year. It was the first timber cut anywhere on Snapfinger creek. The virgin forest had been unbroken by the woodman's axe until then. Both creeks were fine ranges and were heavily timbered."

---

[83] Albert Miles Hairston married Nancy McLeon; their children were Rebecca Anna, Sara Caroline, William M. and Alice Priscilla. Sara Caroline Hairston married Hayes Adams Jolly; their children were Lawson E., Tom, Clem, Jesse, Alice, Mary Elizabeth, Carolina Adams and Kate. (Source: The Collections of the DeKalb Historical Society, Vol. 1, 1952, page 97).

Once the "house raising" was completed, the families were involved in raising sheep. "There was a large unbroken range. Sheep went where they pleased, coming home occasionally to be salted. At the time of the new moon in September our fathers would go to the forest and drive the sheep home and shear them, and our mothers would wash the wool and card and spin it, as there were no factories here in the twenties."

Thomas Mehaffey "was a wheelwright by trade, and made all the spinning wheels that were made in this county for the women who carded, spun and made their own ginghams at home, for themselves and their daughters. Everybody tried to excel her neighbor in making nice homespun dresses.

"We boys were pressed in spinning business also. Our mothers would have different kinds of bark brought in from the forest and dye the wool, some black and some brown, and if they wished to make a pair of grey jeans, they used white and black. To make a roan color they would mix brown and white." [16]

The sign on Macedonia Baptist Church confirms its standing as the oldest church in DeKalb. (Photo by Vivian Price)

Mehaffey, his wife and several children are buried in a family cemetery, one of the oldest burial grounds in the county, "next to those occupied by the aborigines," in Land Lot 2 of the 16th District of DeKalb. There are no inscribed markers in the cemetery. [17]

Hairston also wrote about a number of other early settlers of southeast DeKalb.
Another South Carolinian, Elijah Bankston, came from Jackson County in 1822 and settled on Barbashela Creek. "He was an old Revolutionist -- went out at 16 in the war with Great Britain." The first justice of the peace in Evans's District, Elijah Bankston was the grandfather of Georgia Supreme Court Justice James Jackson, whose DeKalb County house Albert Hairston described as "the king's palace of Arabia." [18]

Young Hall and William and Dock Miller also settled in the area in 1822. William Miller's two sisters, known only by the initials, N. and E., were among DeKalb's first women business owners, having inherited his mill on Snapfinger Creek. [19]

Henry Watkins and Zachariah Holloway moved into the area as soon as it was opened to white settlement.

"Henry Watkins settled on the creek about the same time. He only lived three or four years and died,

A replica of the origial Macedonia Baptist Church building stands on the church grounds today. (Photo by Vivian Price)

The "new" Macedonia Baptist Church building was constructed in 1934. (Vivian Price, personal collection)

leaving his wife and three or four little children. He left her out of debt. She managed well and in a few years bought her a negro girl. She died before her children were hardly grown. Her eldest daughter soon married Leander Biffle, and they took care of the younger children.... The brother went to the Mexican war and died in 1847. [20]

"Zachariah Holloway built the third mill in DeKalb County. He was a `Bible Christian' minister and leaves many descendants, all Christians and living uprightly..."

Another Hairston neighbor was Merrill Collier who, with his twin brother Meredith, came to Georgia from North Carolina. They and their many descendants were to have a profound impact on the Atlanta area.

"Merrill Collier (and his wife Elizabeth Ward) raised a nice family of children, all girls except one. His daughter Charlotte married the Hon. Eli J. Hulsey, who brought up a family of noble children. Col. T. J. Flake married their daughter, Laura. They have brought up a family of bright noble children. This makes three generations of Merrill Collier's descendants brought up on the old Collier plantation, two miles south of Wesley Chapel and this place will be known for generations to come as the old `Collier Place.'"

Merrill Collier was a justice of the peace in the Panthersville District. His only son, Henry, was a physician. Henry married a Miss Wilson and had two children. Merrill Collier (May 10, 1782-June 9, 1855) and his son, Dr. Henry G. Collier (May 4, 1820-February 1, 1850), are both buried in Wesley Chapel Cemetery. [21]

Merrill Collier's twin brother, Meredith, settled in the area of the Chattahoochee River and Peachtree Creek, near Standing Peachtree. In addition to serving as a state senator himself, Meredith Collier had 15 children, several of whom were active in the development of the city of Atlanta. The children of Meredith and his wife, Elizabeth Gray, were Edwin G.; Nancy (Mrs. Green Hesterly), Merrill, Sarah (first Mrs. Miles Patey, second Mrs. John N. Bellinger), George Washington, John, Aaron, Francis Marion, Emily (Mrs. Mitchell Evins), James Madison, Wesley Gray, Elizabeth (Mrs. Haney Liddell), Andrew Jackson, Mary Ann (Mrs. Silas H. Donaldson) and Meredith Jr. Meredith Collier died on February 28, 1863 at his home on Peachtree Creek. He was buried on the Collier homeplace, now in the Sherwood Forest area. He and other family members were moved to West View Cemetery on July 2, 1913. Collier Road in Atlanta is named for this branch of the family. [22]

The brothers were said to be similar in personal appearance, but differed in politics, Merrill being a Whig, while Meredith was a Democrat, a difference which led to many friendly arguments. [23]

Another Revolutionary War veteran, Jennings Hulsey Sr., settled on land along the South River and was one of DeKalb County's first surveyors. He later moved to the Cross Roads community, which would become the town of Lithonia.

"He brought up a noble family of sons and daughters. The sons were William, Eli and Green. Green studied medicine and became a physician. Dr. (Hayden) Coe, of Panola, married one of his daughters. His first wife died and left six or seven children. He married a second wife and two children blessed this second marriage." [24]

In his later years, Jennings Hulsey held a public sale of some of his property. Albert Hairston attended the sale. "When they went to sell the horses he had them brought up to the yard fence. Then they helped him out to the fence, and he held up by the fence and cried like a child. It made him sad to part with his fine horses which he prized so highly. He knew that he could not live a great while and he seemed to want everything just to his notion while he lived. He was honest and upright in all his dealings. He was not uneducated. He would not allow a man to impose on him. It is said that he never passed any words with a man, for it was a word and a blow and the blow came first." [25]

Jennings Hulsey died December 16, 1850 at the age of 85. He is buried in the family cemetery on the north bank of the South River in Land Lot 48 of the 16th District of DeKalb. [26]

Dempsey Perkerson and his wife, Nancy Ward Perkerson, settled along the South River, where he became one of the few farmers who rightly could be called a planter. He owned all or part of six land lots in the area where Waldrop Road now crosses the South River. The Perkersons raised three sons -- John, Thomas Jefferson (Jeff) and Isaac W. Their daughter Martha married David Waldrop. Dempsey Perkerson died on July 28, 1875 at the age of 97, and is buried in the family cemetery on River Road. His obituary in the Atlanta Constitution said, "He died after a long career of usefulness, respected and loved by all who knew him." [27]

Rock Chapel in southeast DeKalb is said to have been the first community in DeKalb County. White settlers were beginning to encroach into Indian territory even before the land was ceded by the Creek Indians. Early in 1822, the federal government tried to discourage white settlers from crossing the Hightower Trail appropriating Indian lands.

In his autobiography, J. M. Griffin recalled the early years in Rock Chapel: "The people in the neighborhood were few and far between at first but every year added to the number, especially along the river and on the creek where was the best land. Indeed on some of the best of the creeks, white settlers called intruders had settled before the land was drawn and the county organized. Some of them lost crops by being cut down and destroyed by the United States authorities. Among those who thus suffered loss was James Diamond, a very prominent and worthy man. He had a crop cut down on Mountain Creek just across the line dividing the whites from the Indian country." [28]

James Diamond later moved into DeKalb and became one its leading citizens. He surveyed Land Lot 246 where town of Decatur was located. The district where he lived, north of Lithonia, was named for him. James Diamond and his wife, Nancy Cornwell, had nine children: Franklin Cornwell, Eli Matthew (Mat), Green B., John Roberson (Rob), Rebecca Ann, Catherine, James J., Nancy Jane, William Winfield, George Washington. Born in Virginia in 1781, James Diamond was described as "tall, over six feet, blonde, and ready to fight at the drop of a hat." Until his death in 1849, he was elected to many public offices in DeKalb, including state House of Representatives (1835) and state Senate (1840). He is buried in the Diamond family cemetery. [29]

Early Rock Chapel neighbors included the Lees, who were mill-builders, "Uncle Joe" Starnes, and the Reid, McGuffey, Carr, Stancil, Turner, Veal, Robinson, Parks, Bond, Patrick and Watts families. "Some distance up the river was Rockbridge. Here lived the Torries, Bill and John. John was a clean steady man, but Will was a reckless drunk and a rowdy. He kept a sort of wayside public house for the travelers at the bridge, which was a toll bridge, a small store and always plenty of liquor. This place... possessed attractions which drew to it from all sides; men of all classes, especially the fun lovers, the dissolute, the bullies among the fighters, the gamblers and the drunkards of which there were many. As the population increased, this place became a regular knock-down, drag-out, black eye and bloody nose resort, known and read of all men." [30]

Griffin vividly recalled Joseph B. Bond, whose descendant by the same name later would become the area's premier historian.

"The Bond family came from Hall County. Joseph B. Bond was a tall rather ill-shapen, bushy-headed man. Their land adoined the Griffins. He and his wife and daughter were Methodists. They were very plain, unpretentious people but added very materially to the vitality of the new (Methodist) movement. Joe was *the* leader." [31]

One of the first things the new settlers did was establish churches.

At a meeting of the Ocmulgee Association of the Baptist Church in 1823, 16 ministers volunteered to do "itinerant labor" among the settlements of the new counties, including DeKalb. The following year the Yellow River Association was formed with 13 member churches and seven more, including Macedonia and Nance's Creek from DeKalb -- petitioning for membership. [32] DeKalb's oldest church, Macedonia Baptist, was constituted as a Primitive Baptist [84] church on July 30, 1823 by the Rev. Luke Robinson and Rev. I. Parker. Among the charter members were John Biffle, James Phillips, Joseph Wootton, James R. George, Israel Hendon and John Stephenson. The Rev. Robinson was the first pastor, and Israel Hendon the first clerk. [33]

The original Macedonia church minutes, still in existence, include the church's Constitution and Rules

---

[84] The Yellow River Association did not refer to itself as "primitive" until 1867, but most of its member churches followed the theology and practices of the "primitive" or "old school" Baptist churches. "The Yellow River Association churches regarded missionary activities, Sunday schools, and other such practices as unnecessary interferences between the individual and God. Consistent with their intense individualism and emphasis on individual freedom of conscience, primitive Baptist churches were rigidly self-governing, recognizing the authority of no minister, association, or other congregation." Primitive Baptist ministers could be ordained by examination and laying on of hands, but no required training was necessary. Ministers were elected by the congregation. Foot-washing is a practice of the Primitive Baptist Church. (Source: Wells, Joel Dixon, and Cornell, Nancy Jones, June, 1984, "Nancy Creek Primitive Baptist Church Cemetery," prepared for the Metropolitan Atlanta Rapid Transit Authority). Macedonia Baptist Church today is not a Primitive Baptist congregation, while Nancy Creek is.

of Conduct. Church members were required to address each other as "Brother" and "Sister." No member could absent himself or herself from a conference or congregational meeting without leave of the moderator or pastor. Two such absences constituted cause for discipline. [34] Macedonia's original building still stands on Panola Road. The congregation's "new" building was constructed in 1938. [35] Burials are still conducted in the old Macedonia Baptist churchyard, where huge old cedar trees shade the graves of south DeKalb's original settlers.

Utoy Primitive Baptist Church was organized in August of 1824 in the extreme southwestern portion of the county. As in most churches of the era, discipline was strict. "Members were cited for non-attendance, for failure to commune, for drunkenness, fighting and other misconduct. Confessions of guilt and expression of regret were sufficient to receive foregiveness." One Utoy member was excluded for "moving into the Indian country and other misconduct; another for running race paths; another for failing to attend church conferences for 12 months." [36]

Wesley Chapel Methodist Church members, organized by a Rev. Kirby, met in a brush arbor in the Panthersville District until they built a log building shortly after DeKalb County was organized. Charter members included the Cobb, House, Gazaway, Crockett, Fowler, Hightower, Rogers, Boren, Burgess, Jackson, Hunter, Brown, Wilson, Watts, McGinnis, Bankston, Hairston, Duren, Pritchard and Bishop families. [37]

During the early years, a circuit preacher, the Rev. John Spier, conducted services once a month. The first church building was constructed on the Solly Mitchell place on Flakes Mill Road. Original trustees were Thomas W. Slaughter, George Hall, the Rev. Elijah Bird, the Rev. Uriah Sprayberry, James W. Givens, Gabe Johnson, Minty Fowler, William W. Johnson and Benjamin Sprayberry. The church later moved to the intersection of Wesley Chapel and Snapfinger after land was donated by a member of the Sprayberry family. The Wesley Chapel cemetery includes many prominent south DeKalb families, including Hairston, Flake, Tilly, Boring, Chandler and Fowler. Also buried there is J. W. Crockett, a cousin of Davy Crockett.

The church was not incorporated by the Georgia legislature until December 26, 1835 with these trustees: Thomas W. Slaughter, George Hall, the Rev. Elijah Bird, the Rev. Uriah Sprayberry, James W. Givens, Gabe Johnson, Minty Fowler, William W. Johnson and Benjamin Sprayberry. The church originally was called Wesley Chapel Camp Ground of the Methodist Episcopal Church of DeKalb County. [38]

Two dates of organization have been cited for Rock Chapel Methodist Church in Diamond's District, north of Lithonia. Charles Murphey Candler, in his "Historical Address" of 1922, said that the church was organized in 1825. Historian Franklin M. Garrett agrees with this date. J. M. Griffin in his "Reminiscences About His Life And Rock Chapel Methodist Church" puts the date at 1831. Griffin recalled that early preachers included John P. Carr, Levi Stancil and Luke Robinson. Property for the church in Land Lot 190 of the 16th District was given by Joseph Ballenger Bond to church commissioners Benjamin Carr and Joseph McGuffy in January of 1834. Rock Chapel was given the memorable nickname of Soap Factory, because an old ash hopper was found on the premises. A camp meeting, one of the most popular in north Georgia, was established in 1840 in connection with the church. Family names associated with the church were Bond, Diamond, Evans, Chupp, McGuffey, Griffin, Lee, Turner, Wellborn, Wesley, Marbut, Starnes, Johnson, Braswell, Cleland, Corley and Ragsdale. Rock Chapel sold its building to a black congregation in 1866; presumably some of the black congregation had been among the 61 slaves listed as members of Rock Chapel in 1858. Edmund

Lee donated yellow pine timber for the new Rock Chapel church building. Members David B. Chupp, Tandy Y. Nash, Easom J. Bond, Simeon Duncan and J. L. Chupp moved a sawmill to a pool near the new site to prepare the timber for building. [39] Griffin also said that W. J. Parks tried to organize a Baptist church in the Rock Chapel community as early as 1823, but that no church succeeded until Rockbridge Baptist Church begin services in 1830 or '31.

Cedar Grove Methodist Church, in southwestern DeKalb near the now Fulton County line, was established in 1828. It was first called Morris Church for the founding family, John B. Morris and four of his sons. Also instrumental in the church's organization were Allan J. Cook and John Moore. Property for the first log building was donated by Garret L. Morris. It was also a Morris who planted a grove of cedar trees near the church that eventually gave its name to the church and surrounding community. The first church building was unheated, in winter a bonfire was lighted outside where members could get warm. [40]

Also established in 1828 was Mt. Zion Methodist Church, located north of Hapeville in what is now south Fulton County. Organizers of Mt. Zion were the Rev. James Mangum, Aaron Knight, William Avery, Thomas Ward and John Evans. First services were conducted by Aaron Knight, and the Rev. Mangum became the first regular preacher. John Eaton gave the land for the church and cemetery. Both James Mangum and Aaron Knight are buried in the Mt. Zion Cemetery, along with William Mangum, William Avery, Elisha B. Burnham, Joseph Caldwell, Jeremiah S. Gilbert, Dr. Ely Griffin, Andrew P. McCool, Samuel G. Pegg, Richard and Edward M. Taliaferro, Thomas M. Poole, son of Adam, and Thomas Jefferson Perkerson and Angus M. Perkerson, son and grandson of Dempsey. Angus Perkerson was editor of the Atlanta Journal Sunday Magazine. [41]

Chapter 10 Notes

1. Candler, Charles Murphey, November 9, 1922, Historical Address, page 3.

2. Candler, Charles Murphey, November 9, 1922, Historical Address, pages 4-6.

3. Garrett, Franklin M., 1954, 1969, Atlanta and Environs -- A Chronicle of Its People and Events, Vol. 1, page 5.

4. Mitchell, Eugene M., September, 1937, "The Indians of Georgia," Atlanta Historical Bulletin, No. 11, page 27.

5. Author unknown, June 7, 1931, "Indian War Near Five Points," Atlanta Journal Magazine, page 27, reprinted from the Atlanta Daily New Era Aug. 1, 1869.

6. Georgia Department of Archives and History.

7. Johnson, Mrs. and Mrs. J. Wallace, n. d., Lyon Family History, unpublished manuscript, page B.

8. Author unknown, October 31, 1968, "Land Of Old DeKalb Pioneer Cost $1 An Acre In 1790s," DeKalb New Era, second front.

9. Garrett, Franklin M., 1954, 1969, Atlanta and Environs -- A Chronicle of Its People and Events, Vol. 1, page 31.

10. Garrett, Franklin M., 1954, 1969, Atlanta and Environs -- A Chronicle of Its People and Events, Vol. 1, page 32. Clarke, Caroline McKinney, 1973, 1997, The Story of Decatur 1823-1899, page 7.

11. Ordner, Helen, September 26, 1973, "100-Year Old Cabin Sits In South DeKalb, All That Remains Of Pioneer Travelers," DeKalb News/Sun, page 4C-South.

12. Hairston, Albert Miles, 1901, "Pioneers of DeKalb," The DeKalb Standard.

13. Hairston, Albert Miles, 1901, "Pioneers of DeKalb," The DeKalb Standard.

14. Hairston, Albert Miles, 1901, "Pioneers of DeKalb," The DeKalb Standard; Garrett, Franklin M., 1954, 1969, Atlanta and Environs -- A Chronicle of Its People and Events, page 37.

15. Hairston, Albert Miles, 1901, "Pioneers of DeKalb," The DeKalb Standard.

16. Hairston, Albert Miles, 1901, "Pioneers of DeKalb," The DeKalb Standard.

17. Hairston, Albert Miles, 1901, "Pioneers of DeKalb," The DeKalb Standard; Garrett, Franklin M., 1954, 1969, Atlanta and Environs -- A Chronicle of Its People and Events, page 37.

18. Hairston, Albert Miles, 1901, "Pioneers of DeKalb," The DeKalb Standard.

19. Hairston, Albert Miles, 1901, "Pioneers of DeKalb," The DeKalb Standard.

20. Hairston, Albert Miles, 1901, "Pioneers of DeKalb," The DeKalb Standard; Garrett, Franklin M., 1954, 1969, Atlanta and Environs -- A Chronicle of Its People and Events, page 37.

21. Hairston, Albert Miles, 1901, "Pioneers of DeKalb," The DeKalb Standard.

22. Garrett, Franklin M., 1954, 1969, Atlanta and Environs -- A Chronicle of Its People and Events, page 554. Evins genealogy files, DeKalb Historical Society.

23. Garrett, Franklin M., 1954, 1969, Atlanta and Environs -- A Chronicle of Its People and Events, page 395.

24. Hairston, Albert Miles, 1901, "Pioneers of DeKalb," The DeKalb Standard.

25. Hairston, Albert Miles, 1901, "Pioneers of DeKalb," The DeKalb Standard.

26. Hairston, Albert Miles, 1901, "Pioneers of DeKalb," The DeKalb Standard; Garrett, Franklin M., 1954, 1969, Atlanta and Environs -- A Chronicle of Its People and Events, page 34.

27. Poole, Joyce P., Gwinnett County Families 1818-1968, page 386. DeKalb Historical Society, title abstracts of Land Lots 38, 54, 74, 75, 85 and 86 of the 15th District.

28. Griffin, J. M., July 14, 1893, "J. M. Griffin Reminiscences About His Life and Rock Chapel Methodist Church (DeKalb County), abstracted from Autobiography of J. M.. Griffin by Mrs. E. P. Moody, page 1.

29. Garrett, Franklin M., 1954, 1969, Atlanta and Environs -- A Chronicle of Its People and Events, Vol. 1, page 26. Marbut, Laura P., 1970, James Diamond (1781-1849) And His Descendants.

30. Griffin, J. M., July 14, 1893, "J. M. Griffin Reminiscences About His Life and Rock Chapel Methodist Church (DeKalb County), abstracted from Autobiography of J. M.. Griffin by Mrs. E. P. Moody, page 2.

31. Griffin, J. M., July 14, 1893, "J. M. Griffin Reminiscences About His Life and Rock Chapel Methodist Church (DeKalb County), abstracted from Autobiography of J. M.. Griffin by Mrs. E. P. Moody, page 4.

32. Ford, Elizabeth Austin, 1952, "A Precis of DeKalb's Early Church History," The Collections of the DeKalb Historical Society, Vol. 1, pages 32-34.

33. Candler, Charles Murphey, November 9, 1922, Historical Address, page 12.

34. Garrett, Franklin M., 1954, 1969, Atlanta and Environs -- A Chronicle of Its People and Events, Vol. 1, page 46.

35. Faust, W. H. March, 1942, untitled article, publication unknown, Dorothy Nix Collection, DeKalb Historical Society.

36. Garrett, Franklin M., 1954, 1969, Atlanta and Environs -- A Chronicle of Its People and Events, Vol. 1, page 39.

37. Price, Vivian, September 13, 1978, "Jack Shipley Trying To Piece Together History Of Wesley Chapel Methodist Church," DeKalb News/Sun, page 7D South.

38. Candler, Charles Murphey, November 9, 1922, Historical Address.

39. Garrett, Franklin M., 1954, 1969, Atlanta and Environs -- A Chronicle of Its People and Events, Vol. 1, pages 51-52. Candler, Charles Murphey, November 9, 1922, Historical Address.

40. Nix, Dorothy, personal collection, DeKalb Historical Society.

41. Garrett, Franklin M., 1954, 1969, Atlanta and Environs -- A Chronicle of Its People and Events, Vol. 1, pages 57 and 69.

Chapter 11

At the opposite end of the county from the South River, other families were carving homes out of the wilderness along the Chattahoochee River.

After his military service at Standing Peachtree ended in May, 1814, Maj. James Montgomery returned to his home in Jackson County, Ga., but he never forgot the lush land he had grown to love. He sold his property in Jackson County and moved his family to the banks of the Chattahoochee. And quite a family it was.

James Montgomery Sr. was a Scottish immigrant who married Elizabeth McConnell in Lancaster District, S. C. It was in Lancaster County that their son Hugh Lawson Montgomery was born on January 8, 1769, followed by a second son, James McConnell Montgomery, who was born on May 19, 1770. After the death of Elizabeth, when his children were still quite young, James Montgomery Sr. married Susannah Strange. Additional children were born to this union, including Sarah (called Sally) and William Montgomery.

The family migrated to Hancock County, Ga., where the younger James Montgomery married Nancy Farlow on November 14, 1797. Their first child, a daughter named Adecia F. Montgomery, was born in Hancock County on April 4, 1799. The Montgomery family moved again, this time to Jackson County, Ga., where the elder James Montgomery died in 1808. Nine children were born to James and Nancy in Jackson County: Lucinda McConnell, Amelia S., Sophronia P., Ulysses McConnell, Tellemachus Farlow, Rhadamanthus J., James Floyd, Nunan (or Newman) Tarpley, William F. and Joseph Terrell Monroe. Rhoda Narcissa was the first Montgomery to be born in DeKalb, on March 22, 1822, followed by Hugh Brown Troup (called Troup) Montgomery and Rebecca Montgomery. Nunan Tarpley Montgomery died as an infant, and William F. Montgomery died in 1834 at the age of 17. [1]

The first four Montgomery children, all girls, married in Jackson County. Adecia married Samuel Pruitt Jr. (and later Elijah Wyatt in DeKalb). Dempsey J. Connally became the husband of Lucinda Montgomery. Amelia chose as her mate Joseph D. Shumate, who became one of the first justices of the Inferior Court of Fayette County and later DeKalb. Sophronia Montgomery, who married John

Franklin, died when their son, James Samuel Franklin, was born. James Samuel was then adopted by his grandparents. [2]

Thus, the Montgomery entourage that traveled to DeKalb about 1820 included the nine children of James and Nancy, who ranged in age from 21 to infancy, plus two of the children's spouses and at least one grandchild. Also accompanying the party were James's brother, Hugh, his wife, Margaret Barkley Montgomery, their children, and James and Hugh's step-sister and brother, Sally and William. James's daughter Lucinda and husband Dempsey Connally soon followed.

Sally Montgomery would marry Nathaniel Venable in DeKalb; their descendants are the Venables of Stone Mountain and Atlanta. Their son William Richard Venable married Cornelia Hoyt. [3]

Judge Samuel B. Hoyt, who would write a sketch of the family in 1886, first met James Montgomery in 1841. "When the ferry boat landed on the DeKalb, or south side of the Chattahoochee at the Montgomery ferry (later called Defoor's) about eight miles from Atlanta, the first person I saw was the major, standing on the bank. I went with him to his house, about half a mile south of the ferry, and stayed with him about six weeks."

Hoyt described Montgomery as "very jolly and good-natured, but well posted about the affairs of the country and very intelligent and well read. He was a strong `Troup' man [1] and Whig..."

Nancy Montgomery, Hoyt said, "was one of the noblest and best women I ever saw. She was the main stay of the little Methodist church near their residence. Often have I heard her make some of the best prayers I ever heard at the prayer meeting of her church. They seemed to come straight from her good heart. I never met a more harmonious and loving couple. He was a Presbyterian and she a Methodist, and yet there was never a jar. Even in the matter of family worship, he would give out the hymn, and then, in deference to her church, the whole family would rise and sing. At her death, he received a shock he never recovered from and died soon after."

Hoyt also called Nancy Montgomery "a notable housekeeper. For many years, travelers would stop over at their house. They never charged a preacher anything for their entertainment, and the poor and needy were never turned down from their door. There were few country houses better known in Georgia than theirs." As the Montgomery family compound, with its little trading post, was the only semblance of a town for miles around, overnight visitors probably were frequent. [4]

Montgomery had held several public posts in Jackson County, including sheriff, tax receiver, tax collector and census-taker in 1820, as well as being a trustee in the local Presbyterian church and a guardian to several orphans. It is not surprising to find him being the same kind of public-spirited citizen in his new home. He was appointed in 1821 one of the commissioners to superintend the election of the first Justices of Inferior Court for the newly-created Fayette County, the jurisdiction in which Standing Peachtree was first located. He collected rents for the county's fractional land lots at "Standing Peachtree, Fayette County." [5]

---

[1] Supportive of Gov. George M. Troup and his policies, including his fight to have the Cherokee Indians removed from Georgia.

The ink had hardly dried on the legal paperwork creating DeKalb County before James Montgomery had made himself almost indispensable. He quickly became a road commissioner, clerk of the Court of Ordinary, state senator, poor school commissioner, postmaster, census taker, justice of the peace, tax receiver and tax collector. These public jobs were in addition to his duties as farmer, saw mill, grist mill and ferry operator. [6]

The first order of the new DeKalb Inferior Court was to name James Montgomery one of the first county road commissioners. Montgomery kept records in 1823 for the Court of Ordinary in books he purchased himself until the Inferior Court appropriated $5 for that purpose. As commissioner of the Poor School in 1824, appointed by Gov. George M. Troup, he promised "to distribute whatever monies may come into my hands in such manner as, in my opinion, will most conduce to the education of poor children in my county."

With all his "firsts," however, James Montgomery was not the first postmaster of Standing Peachtree. That honor went to his son, Tellemachus, who was appointed in 1825 and served for two years. James Montgomery was the second Standing Peachtree postmaster, serving from 1827 until September 30, 1840, followed by James Floyd Montgomery, another son, who was postmaster until December 31, 1842 when the post office was renamed Bolton and moved to Cobb County. Even then the postmaster's job stayed in the family. The first Bolton postmaster was James A. Collins who married Cynthia Venable, daughter of James Montgomery's half sister Sally and her husband Nathaniel Venable. [7]

One of James Montgomery's several responsibilities as Indian Agent for the federal government was to keep whites from encroaching upon Cherokee Indian lands across the Chattahoochee River from Standing Peachtree. On May 29, 1820, Gen. Andrew Jackson posted the following notice at the Shallow Ford of the Chattahoochee:

"Intruders on Cherokee lands, beware. I am required to remove all white men found trespassing on the Cherokee lands not having a written permit from the agent, Colo. R. J. Meigs. This duty I am about to perform. The Regulars and Indian Light horse will be employed in performing this service, and any opposition will be promptly punished. All white men with there (sic) live stock found trespassing on the Indian land will be arrested and handed over to the civil authorities of the United States to be dealt with as the law directs, there (sic) families removed to U. S. land, there (sic) crops, houses and fences destroyed..." Less than one month later, Jackson wrote to John C. Calhoun: "I found a great many intruders and those on the north of the Chatahoochey (sic) not only numerous but insolent and threatening resistance." [8]

James Montgomery's brother, Hugh, also an Indian Agent, was stationed at the Cherokee Agency on the Tennessee-Georgia border. A letter dated August 26, 1826 from James at Standing Peachtree to Hugh in north Georgia details the difficulties of the job: "Between what some of the Indians themselves and what the white people steal from the poor honest Indians, I really think that in a little time there will not be a horse left in this side of the nation, and but few cattle and hogs, for the truth is that since there is a hiding place on the Tallepoosy there is scarcely a day but more or less is stealing."

In 1828, James Montgomery's son-in-law Dempsey Connally and four of Connally's hands at Standing

Peachtree were hired by the federal government to cut down corn and burn fences raised by white settlers on Cherokee Indian land. The government would attempt to banish intruders for a few more years as shown by this letter from James to Hugh:

"Georgia, Standing peach tree,
DeKalb County, 27 October 1830

"Dear Brother,
"This incloses an acct. of Owen H. Kennon for services rendered as stated in the amount. Mr. Connally has an acct to render as well as myself for the time and expenses which have occurred on and about the intolerable corn cutting business. We will in a few weeks send them on to you and hope you will exhibit them in such a way that we may be paid out of Uncle Sam as it is not reasonable that we should be put to trouble and expense without any fee or reward..."

In this letter James also reported on some of the tribulations the family endured in the 1830s. Nancy Farlow Montgomery suffered "delicate health" for at least two years, due to a tumor in her shoulder. Dr. N. N. Smith amputated Nancy's right arm at the shoulder on May 14, 1832, after which she made a remarkable recovery. In his sketch on the family, Judge Hoyt recalled Nancy Montgomery, in 1841, making good use of her remaining arm. "She wielded her little hoe with surprising vigor in the garden."

James also wrote Hugh: "We have just heard that the New College at Athens is destroyed by fire and expect we have lost at least one hundred dollars -- Tellemachus's bed furniture all his cloathes and books. Some of the students lost considerable money to pay off their Board, tuition, etc. However this was not the case with our son as we had none to send him." Tellemachus would go on to graduate from the University of Georgia in 1832. [9] Four of the Montgomery sons who survived to adulthood were college educated. [10]

James Floyd Montgomery, who was born while his father was in the Army in Alabama and named Floyd in honor of father's commander, was the only Montgomery son to settle near Standing Peachtree. He married Elizabeth Ann Young of Cobb County, and died in 1847, leaving five small children. His family moved to Marietta in 1852, where his son William R. Montgomery became the clerk of the Superior Court of Cobb County. [2]

Amelia and Joseph Shumate moved to Cobb County and later LaFayette, Ga. The eldest Montgomery son, Ulysses, married Elizabeth Humber in DeKalb, and died young, without children. Elizabeth later married Cornelius (Neal) McCarty Connally. Adecia Montgomery Wyatt and husband Elijah settled in Chattooga County, Ga.

Two of James and Nancy's sons, Tellemachus and Rhadamanthus, became Presbyterian ministers. Tellemachus moved to Florida. Rhadamanthus married Harriet N. Bogle of Blount County, Tenn. He died young without children. His widow married Jonathan Norcross, who would become mayor of Atlanta.

---

[2] William Rhadamanthus Montgomery, eldest son of James Floyd Montgomery, was the grandfather of Katherine Anderson, author of the sketch on James Montgomery and family.

Joseph and Troup Montgomery were both educated at Maryville College in Tennessee, and both became college professors. They founded the LaGrange Female College in Troup County, Ga. in 1843, and operated the school until 1856. Both married in Troup County, Joseph to Julia Cameron and Troup to Mary Broughton. Joseph later moved to Texas.

James Samuel Franklin, the grandson James and Nancy Montgomery adopted, died in the Mexican War. [11]

"Take them all in all, they were a noble family. Loving and devoted to each other, they were at the same time, generous, kind, religious, brainy and energetic. They were all church members, divided about half and half between the Presbyterian and Methodist churches." [12]

By 1840 the Standing Peachtree era in DeKalb County was drawing to a close.

Rhoda Narcissa Montgomery, who was born at Standing Peachtree, married Alfred B. Brown, a young railroad engineer. Alfred and their baby daughter died in August, 1840. Three years later Narcissa married Henry G. Dean. Lucinda Montgomery Connally and husband Dempsey, sold their Standing Peachtree land to brother-in-law Dean in 1846, and later moved to Texas. Narcissa and Henry sold the last of the family's Standing Peachtree land in 1853 and moved to Meriwether County, Ga. in the fall of 1854. After Henry's death, Narcissa went with her son to Arkansas.

Narcissa Montgomery Dean was the last Montgomery to live at Standing Peachtree. [13]

James Montgomery was described as "not wealthy," but a "good liver". There never was a better master. He was called in those days a "negro spoiler."

In his will, Montgomery left most of his land and property, including the saw mill, grist mill and ferry, to his daughter Narcissa Montgomery Brown and son Troup Montgomery. It was this land that was sold in 1853 to Martin DeFoor. The property included 1,000 acres in land lots 196, 219, 220, 230, 231, 244, 245 and 219, located on both sides of the Chattahoochee and on the south side of Peachtree Creek.

Aside from land, Montgomery's estate included 66 stock hogs, 24 fat pork hogs, a sow and eight pigs, three bee hives, three sheep, six head of geese, numerous steers, cows and calves, of all colors, 3 cedar churns, a "waffling iron," a bay horse named Bill and two other horses, a side saddle, a four wheeled carriage, an ox car, a brass clock, a book case and secretary, a library valued at $100 and a large atlas. A record of his estate sale listed a 12-volume encyclopedia, histories of England and Morocco, a dictionary, a gazetteer and numerous school and religious books. [14]

Nancy Farlow Montgomery died on July 27, 1842. Her husband of almost 45 years died scarcely three months later on October 6, 1842.

Nancy's obituary in The Southern Recorder of August 16, 1842 gave her credit for organizing the first religious meeting ever held in DeKalb.

James Montgomery's obituary was published in The Southern Recorder on October 25, 1842: "Died on the 6th of October at his residence `Standing Peachtree' in DeKalb County, in his 73rd year, Colonel

James M. C. Montgomery, after a long period of feeble health; following the recent death of his consort to whom he was devotedly attached, he sank rapidly. He was born in Lancaster Dist., S. C. At an early age he moved to Georgia and engaged in agricultural pursuits. He served in both civil and military capacities. He accompanied his father, a staunch Whig and military Captain in the Revolution. About the close of the Revolution, though but a lad, on a short expedition against the Tories. Later was a private in expeditions against the indians in East Tenn. in 1791-2. He commanded a battalion in the indian hostilities of 1813, and was Adjutant under General Floyd in the Battle of Autossee. He was a schoolmate and personal friend and for while army compatriot of General Jackson. He served as magistrate, collector of State and U. S. Revenues, State Senator, Agent of Indian Affairs, etc. He and his late wife were married for 45 years. Their home was the abode of hospitality and kindness. They had 13 children, one died in infancy. Eight are living. Members of the church 50 years. Funerals of both him and his wife were preached on the same day by different clergymen in the presence of a large concourse of friends and neighbors." [15]

James and Nancy Montgomery were buried in the Montgomery family cemetery, near the site of the old homeplace in land lot 230 in now Fulton County. Also buried there are four of their sons, Ulysses, James, Rhadamanthus and William, as well as Nancy E. Dean, daughter of Narcissa and Henry Dean, who died at the age of 10 months.

Between the graves of Montgomery and his wife is a stone obelisk inscribed: "Their children rise up and call them blessed; and erect this stone to their memory... They were lovely in their lives and in their death they were not divided. [16]

By 1837, 15 years after the county's founding, Standing Peachtree rated a small mention in Adiel Sherwood's Gazetteer of Georgia: "Standing Peach-tree is a noted crossing place over the Chattahoochee, in DeKalb county. Here are a few houses, and P. O.; on the great road to Cobb county. Mr. Montgomery resides at this place." With the heads of the leading family of Standing Peachtree gone, the little community began to disappear. Just two months after the death of James McConnell Montgomery, the Standing Peachtree Post Office was moved across the river and renamed Bolton.

Chapter 11 Notes

1. Porter, Phyllis M., DAR Collection of Genealogical Records, Vol. 249, page 96.

2. Anderson, E. Katherine, December, 1937, "James McC. Montgomery Of Standing Peachtree, Atlanta Historical Bulletin No. 12.

3. Garrett, Franklin M., Necrology, Roll 5, Frame 304.

4. Garrett, Franklin M., May 3, 1931, "Ancient Cemetery Marks Site of Fulton County's First Town," Atlanta Constitution, pages 12-13.

5. Anderson, E. Katherine, December, 1937, "James McC. Montgomery Of Standing Peachtree, Atlanta Historical Bulletin No. 12.

6. Garrett, Franklin M., 1954, 1969, Atlanta and Environs -- A Chronicle of Its People and Events, Vol. 1, page 197.

7. Garrett, Franklin M., 1954, 1969, Atlanta and Environs -- A Chronicle of Its People and Events, Vol. 1, page 28. Anderson, E. Katherine, December, 1937, "James McC. Montgomery Of Standing Peachtree, Atlanta Historical Bulletin No. 12.

8. Garrett, Franklin M., 1954, 1969, Atlanta and Environs -- A Chronicle of Its People and Events, Vol. 1, page 5.

9. Anderson, E. Katherine, December, 1937, "James McC. Montgomery Of Standing Peachtree, Atlanta Historical Bulletin No. 12.

10. Hoyt, Judge Samuel B., April 20, 1886, "The Montgomery Family An Interesting Sketch of One of the Pioneer Families of DeKalb County," Atlanta Constitution, typescript from newspaper article, DeKalb Historical Society files.

11. Anderson, E. Katherine, December, 1937, "James McC. Montgomery Of Standing Peachtree, Atlanta Historical Bulletin No. 12.

12. Hoyt, Judge Samuel B., April 20, 1886, "The Montgomery Family An Interesting Sketch of One of the Pioneer Families of DeKalb County," Atlanta Constitution, typescript from newspaper article, DeKalb Historical Society files.

13. Anderson, E. Katherine, December, 1937, "James McC. Montgomery Of Standing Peachtree, Atlanta Historical Bulletin No. 12. Hoyt, Judge Samuel B., April 20, 1886, "The Montgomery Family An Interesting Sketch of One of the Pioneer Families of DeKalb County," Atlanta Constitution, typescript from newspaper article, DeKalb Historical Society files.

14. Hoyt, Judge Samuel B., April 20, 1886, "The Montgomery Family An Interesting Sketch of One of the Pioneer Families of DeKalb County," Atlanta Constitution, typescript from newspaper article, DeKalb Historical Society files. Georgia Department of Archives and History.

15. Austin, Jeanette H., n. d., "Deaths of Revolutionary War Soldiers Who Died in Georgia."

16. Garrett, Franklin M., May 3, 1931, "Ancient Cemetery Marks Site of Fulton County's First Town," The Atlanta Constitution, pages 12-13. Garrett, Franklin M., 1954, 1969, Atlanta and Environs -- A Chronicle of Its People and Events, Vol. 1, page 197.

Chapter 12

*M*ore than 15 miles upriver from Standing Peachtree was the Shallow Ford, the main crossing on the Chattahoochee River, and the only place in DeKalb where wagons could safely negotiate the river. The point where the Hightower Trail met the Shallow Ford was the northernmost point of the original DeKalb County.

There the first ferry in DeKalb County was established in 1824. The Southern Recorder newspaper in Milledgeville ran an advertisement on May 18, 1824 to announce that Jacob R. Brooks had inaugurated ferry service. "Travelers from the Carolinas to Alabama coming by Augusta, Madison, Rockbridge &c will find it much the nearest and best route." Brooks's announcement asked the editors of the Augusta Chronicle, Columbia Telegraph and Raleigh Register to publish the ad three or four times and to "forward their accounts for payment." [1]

Jacob Brooks was one of the county's earliest residents, having come from Gwinnett County. Born in Wilkes County, Ga. in 1787, he served in the War of 1812. He would later become one of the commissioners of the DeKalb Academy, poor school commissioner and state representative from DeKalb in 1826 and 1827, before moving to Cobb and then Walker County. [2]

Other early residents of the north DeKalb area known as Cross Keys included the Johnston, Evins, Coker, Wells, Jarrell, Holbrook, Spruill, Goodwin and Flowers families. They settled on the fertile lands along the stream that originally was called Nancy's (or Nance's) Creek and has became known simply as Nancy Creek. The creek is said to have been named for Nancy Baugh Evins, wife of John Leroy (Jack) Evins. Jack knew his wife would rather be cooling her feet and fishing in the creek than cooking and cleaning. [3] Local tradition holds that these families settled along the creek about 1818, several years before the county was founded. Encounters with Indians were said to be commonplace, and not always friendly.

The church that took its name from the creek was organized July 3, 1824 with 18 members. By 1827, the congregation had grown to 57 members. William Johnston, one of the few Nancy Creek members considered to be wealthy, was the first recorded minister, called a "moderator." He also served as deacon. Josiah Gresham served as pastor of Nancy Creek from 1833-1852. Although he settled in the Tucker area, Gresham was pastor of Utoy (near Sandtown) and Hardman (north of Decatur), both

Primitive Baptist churches, as well as Nancy Creek. Gresham also had been pastor at Ozias in Henry County and Old Bethlehem in Gwinnett. [4]

Nancy Creek Primitive Baptist Church was at its inception, and still is, strictly Calvinistic. The church does not participate in missionary activities or Sunday school, but does practice foot-washing. The church began as a member of the Yellow River Baptist Association, which was organized the same year Nancy Creek was founded. [5]

The tiny church building, still in its original location at the southern edge of the Chamblee city limits, had no sewer system or gas or electric service until 1967. The church property, including its cemetery, has survived several dissections by automobile and railroads. Dr. John Yancey Flowers, who would become postmaster in Doraville, donated five acres of land for the church and cemetery. [6]

Nancy Evins, for whom Nancy Creek was named, is pictured at right with her daughter, Georgia Ann Evins. (DeKalb Historical Society)

Naomi, wife of Nancy Creek moderator William Johnston, one of the first people buried in Nancy Creek cemetery, died in 1844 at the age of 46. Naomi wrote in her will: "I desire my body to be buried in a christianlike manner by the side of my husband in the family burring ground and I wish out of money I may die possessed of to have my grave and that of my daughter (afflicted) Dorothy Ann Johnston fixed up in a decent and substantial manner." William Johnston died in 1855 at the age of 65. He is buried next to Naomi "in the same position they had taken at the marriage altar."

Also buried at Nancy Creek are children of William and Naomi: Jackson F., Nancy Elliott and Washington P. Two of the Johnston children married into another north DeKalb pioneer family, that of Jack and Nancy Evins. Jackson Johnston married Jack and Nancy's daughter, Susan Evins. Nancy Elliott Johnston married their son, William Crawford Evins.

Evins children made alliances with other prominent families in the mid-19th century, and continued to do so well into the 20th century. Georgia Ann Evins, daughter of Jack and Nancy, married Phillip House, one of Samuel House's seven sons. Thomas Mitchell (Mitch) Evins married Emiline (Emily) Collier, daughter of Meredith Collier, one of twin brothers who were pioneer settlers in DeKalb. Their son, Justinian Evins, was the well-known clerk of Corinth (Chamblee) Baptist Church and justice of the peace for 40 years. [7]

Geraldine (Gerry) Spruill, a three-great granddaughter of William Johnston of Nancy Creek and a Dunwoody resident today, is married to Hugh Spruill, a descendant of Stephen T. Spruill, progenitor of the large and prominent north DeKalb family. Stephen Spruill emigrated from North Carolina to

DeKalb shortly after the county was formed, and settled on Long Island Creek in what is now the Sandy Springs area of north Fulton County. [8]

Another child of William and Naomi Johnston, daughter Martha Maria, married Milton Charles Lively II, whose father, a Virginian by the same name, moved to the now Briarcliff Road area of DeKalb from Monroe County. Their many descendants include William Washington (Billy) Lively, who was a DeKalb County commissioner in the early 1900s. Current Doraville Mayor Gene Lively is descended from this line, as well as from John Y. Flowers and his wife Dicey Reeve and Nancy Creek church members George R. Jarrell and his wife Telephus Arendall. Daughters of William and Naomi Johnston also married into the Tilly and McElroy families from the Doraville area.

Nancy Creek Primitive Baptist Church cemetery was the last resting place for many early north DeKalb residents, many of whom were not members of the church. [9] Among the pioneers buried there are members of the House and Goodwin families, although the patriarchs of these families are not at Nancy Creek. Samuel House is said to have been buried in an unmarked grave at Prospect Methodist Church in Chamblee. Solomon Goodwin originally was buried at Nancy Creek, but was later moved to the Goodwin family cemetery on the grounds of the old homeplace on Peachtree Road in Brookhaven.

There were no Negro churches in DeKalb County before the Civil War. Slave-owners gave slaves religious instruction at home, with older children assigned to teaching the Bible and "simple catechism." Some white churches had separate seating for slaves, often in galleries. [10] Likewise separate areas generally were set aside for slaves in white cemeteries. Among the graves identified at Nancy Creek are those of Kitty, Rolly, Washington and Anthony, slaves of the House family, and Flowers family slaves Sam and Tilda. Blacks were barred from the cemetery in 1902 "owing to the want of vacant property in our cemetery." [11]

Nancy Baugh Evins died in November 1883, and is buried in an unmarked grave at Nancy Creek. [12] She was the mother of 11 children, 57 grandchildren and 93 great grandchildren. South Carolinians, Nancy and her husband Jack came to DeKalb from Gwinnett before the county was organized, and settled on what is now Windsor Parkway. Evins land covered the area of Peachtree Dunwoody, Osborne and House roads in now DeKalb and Fulton. [13]

Jack Evins is not buried at Nancy Creek, but in the vicinity of the Evins homeplace. Atlanta historian Franklin M. Garrett tells the story of trying to find Jack's burial site in 1931: "The home had disappeared but the site was easily discernible, being upon an elevation surrounded by fine old trees... A large cedar nearby seemed to indicate the presence of a family cemetery. An inspection disclosed what appeared to be one grave, but alas, no marker. Better luck was had some sixty feet away from the grave, for there, under the leaves and pine needles, lay some of the broken remains of a once handsome tomb box. Vandals had done their work. Enough fragments were located to piece together the sought for vital statistics. Expertly cut in deeply incised letters and numerals was the following inscription: `In Memory of John L. Evins Born March 23, 1794, Died August 8th, 1864.' Further investigation at the site led to the discovery that the side pieces of the tomb were serving as front doorstep and hearthstone of a small house nearby, while the lower half of the top slab, bearing the name of its maker, D. N. Judson, Atlanta, had been pressed into service as a back doorstep for the same house." [14]

That DeKalb County's first settlers were tough individuals is evidenced by family stories about Jack and Nancy Evins.

"Jack was a very rugged dominating old man, and Nancy was also hardy. They had to be to survive the pioneer hardships.

"The story goes that at one time Nancy was sitting in front of the fireplace. Jack commanded that she do something. She sat there, Jack picked up a shovel of hot coals and threw them into her lap, saying, `Now you will move.' Nancy sat there. Jack said, `you durn fool put the fire out.' She said, `I didn't put it there.' Jack got busy and put it out." [15]

Followers of the Primitive Baptist faith in the Dunwoody community founded the Ebenezer church in 1829 at what is now the intersection of Spalding Drive and Roberts Road. The first deacons were Henry Holcomb and Reuben Martin. The first pastor was Radford Gunn. Among the early members were Jane and Andrew Warnock, Peter Ball, Dicey Ball, Adam Jett, Reuben Martin, Larkin Martin, Henry and Priscilla Holcombe, Milly Martin, Catherine and Nancy Martin, Nancy Dooley, Elizabeth Burdett, Samuel Abernathy, Jesse Roberts, the Jordan family, the Adams family, the Dalrymple family and F. O. Carpenter and his son Ambrey. [16]

Margaret Malinda Tilly married William McElroy. She was an early member of Prospect Methodist Church, where she was known affectionately as "Granny McElroy." (Chamblee First United Methodist Church)

South Carolina provided north DeKalb County with three more families of solid pioneer citizens in the late 1820s.

After his wife Rebecca died in 1826, Stephen Tilly left the Pendleton District of South Carolina and made his way to DeKalb County with his seven children who ranged in age from 13 to an infant girl. Being the oldest daughter, Margaret Malinda Tilly, at the age of 11, took on the responsibility of helping raise her younger siblings. [17]

The Tillys arrived in DeKalb about 1827 and immediately became active in the newly-organized Prospect Methodist Church. Prospect, said to have constructed the first church building in DeKalb, was located where the Peachtree Indian trail and the Shallow Ford Trail intersected, where today the Chamblee and Doraville city boundaries meet. [18] Prospect's third sanctuary, built in 1885, is still standing at that location, adjacent to Prospect Cemetery, and is now occupied by an antiques shop. The church's first building, a log structure, was located behind the 1885 structure. At various times during its early history, the Prospect congregation may have met in the Stephen Tilly home and in the building of the Prosperity Presbyterian Church, which was located just north of Prospect, across the

Harwell Parks Tilly, his wife Amanda Beatrice (Beatrice) Bankson, son H. P. Jr. and daughters Olivia and Ella. (Donald S. Clarke)

Shallowford Trail. The earliest deed to Prospect land is dated 1851, when John Yancey Flowers, as executor of the estate of John W. Reeve, signed over two and one-half acres to Prospect trustees Samuel House, Stephen Tilly, Alfred J. H. Poole and Jabey (probably Jabez) M. Loyd. The land was in Land Lot 309 of the 18th District, the current location of the old sanctuary and the cemetery. [19]

Prospect Church was first assigned to the Decatur Circuit; then, as the church grew in numbers, was moved to the Norcross and Prospect Charge, sharing a minister with only one other church. "In the early history of Decatur Circuit, as well as all other circuits at that time, each Charge had quite a number of churches," historian McElroy wrote. "This caused the pastor, who was then called the circuit rider, to preach from four to six days in the week in order to get around once a month. Therefore, Prospect had a week-day preaching once a month by the pastor, Wednesday, I think, being the day. Nevertheless, we had services three Sundays in the month; preaching one Sunday by a local preacher, prayer meeting one Sunday, and class meeting one Sunday. The remaining Sunday we went where we chose, generally to Nancy's Creek." Early Prospect preachers remembered by McElroy were Noah Smith, David Ballenger, Henry Clark, Jimmie Williams, Elijah Byrd, a Dr. Fowler, Joe Huie, William Holbrook, S. H. Braswell and a Mr. Chandler. [20]

While no list of charter members exists, McElroy recalled some of the early families, including his own grandfather, Stephen Tilly, and Tilly's three sons, Ebenezer, Robert and Fletcher, and four daughters, Margaret, Adeline, Caroline and Jane. Other early members were David Ballenger, Dr. John Ballenger, John M. Ridling and Thomas Akins, along with their respective families. [21]

McElroy also named others involved in the early years of the church: Samuel House, a class leader "who was full of zeal and fervor and often so filled with the Holy Ghost that his cup would run over,"

Stephen Tilly McElroy. (H. Parks Tilly)

John William Fletcher (Uncle Fletcher) Tilly. (H. Parks Tilly)

and Elijah Boggs, who could not read, but knew hymns and scriptures from memory, as well as Jake Loyd, Joseph Elliott, Asa Braswell, George Gaddy, Alfred Peel and Francis Metcalf. [22]

Samuel House, another South Carolinian, came to DeKalb about 1829 with his wife, Elizabeth, and four sons. Three more sons would be born in DeKalb County. Samuel House's memory lives on in the stately white-columned home he built on Peachtree Road, now the clubhouse of the Peachtree Golf Club, one of DeKalb County's best examples of antebellum architecture. Born in about 1796, Samuel House died in August of 1873, "an old DeKalb County resident... full of years and honors." He is buried in an unmarked grave in Prospect Cemetery. [23]

Of the seven children of Stephen Tilly and Rebecca King Tilly, three remained in north DeKalb, and made significant contributions to the quality of life in their towns and their county. Many descendants of these three families still live in the area.

Eldest son Ebenezer Tilly married Martha Ballenger. Ebenezer and Martha named their only son, John William Fletcher Tilly, for Ebenezer's younger brother. Ebenezer's son was called Will, to avoid confusion with his uncle, who was called Fletcher. Yet another John William Fletcher Tilly was the son of Robert A. Tilly, middle son of Stephen and Rebecca. Ebenezer and Martha Tilly also had three daughters, Amanda Elmirah (Mandy), Sarah Ann R. J. and Martha W. Mandy Tilly married George Washington House, one of Samuel House's sons, and Sarah Ann Tilly married George Newton Flowers, son of John Yancey Flowers.

John William Fletcher Tilly, brother of Ebenezer, was called "Uncle Fletcher" in his later years. He married Susannah Elizabeth (Susan) Medlock of another prominent Gwinnett and DeKalb County family. Their children were John Stephen Albert (called Albert), Sarah Elizabeth Ann, Jane Susannah, Robert Ebenezer, Harwell Parks, Newdigate Owenby and William Fletcher. Four of their seven children died before the age of six. [24]

That Fletcher Tilly and his family were devoted Methodists and ardent supporters of Prospect Church is shown in many ways. Fletcher Tilly was single-handedly responsible for construction of a new sanctuary for Prospect's church. The clapboard building was placed directly in front of the old church, and was dedicated on the first Sunday in July, 1885. The "new" sanctuary was distinguished by the' traditional two doors. Men entered and sat together on the left side of the church, and women on the right. Babies and small children of both sexes sat with their mothers. Older boys sat with their fathers, while girls tended to stay with their mothers. The 1885 building, with many additions and modifications, served the congregation until the mid-1960s when the church changed its named to Chamblee First United Methodist and moved to Chamblee-Dunwoody Road. [25]

"Uncle Fletcher" Tilly's sanctuary dramatically increased the comfort level of its congregation. Steven Tilly McElroy, nephew of Fletcher Tilly, remembers the previous building as "a frame house, weather-boarded with rough boards, windows without sash, no ceiling inside, floor laid with undressed boards which left large cracks, no stove or heating device. It was comfortable in warm or pleasant weather, but colder in winter than being out in the sunshine." [26]

Two children of Fletcher and Susan were named for prominent Methodist preachers of the day. Harwell Parks Tilly, born October 27, 1856, was named for the Rev. Harwell H. Parks, a pioneer Methodist minister in Georgia and presiding elder of the Decatur Circuit, of which Prospect was a member. Newdigate Owenby Tilly, born December 11, 1859, was named for the Rev. Newdaygate B. Ousley, who was a preacher on the Decatur Circuit in 1858. The Rev. Ousley organized and was pastor of Briarwood Methodist Church on Candler Road south of Decatur. The church later changed its name to Ousley Methodist and has since moved to Panola Road in south DeKalb.

The Prospect Methodist Church made possible by the donations of Fletcher Tilly was built in 1885. Note the two doors, one for men and one for women. The building gained additions through the years, and now houses an antique shop. (Mr. and Mrs. J. David Chesnut)

As he passed through Cross Keys on his rounds, it is likely that the Rev. Ousley, like any other circuit riders, was a recipient of the generous hospitality offered by the Tillys. When Fletcher Tilly died on February 16, 1892 at the age of 68, the Wesleyan Christian Advocate published an obituary containing the following tribute: "The eyes of many itinerant preachers will grow dim with tears, and their hearts grow heavy with sadness to know that they can no longer feel the hearty grasp of welcome and enjoy the bountiful hospitality of `Uncle Fletcher Tilly' as he was called. As a worthy monument to his devotion to Christ, there stands today at `Old Prospect' (of which he was a member), a large, magnificent new church edifice, built through his effort, and largely with his money." [27]

Stephen Tilly's daughter, Margaret Malinda, the little girl who helped her father care for her siblings after her mother died, married William McElroy, one of three brothers to settle in the Chamblee-Doraville area. In 1830, Samuel McElroy Jr. was dead set on leaving South Carolina for the fertile opportunities of DeKalb County, Ga. At the age of 22, and newly married to wife Nancy, Samuel was considered by his family "too young to go into a new country alone." So, his brother, John, three years older, accompanied him. John and Samuel first rented land from a Mr. Tilly (probably Stephen Tilly), and later bought land in Land Lot 320 of the 18th District, from "Old Man Winters," who was said to have been sitting on a chest of gold when he moved to Mississippi. The brothers built a sturdy, story-and-a-half log house, and wrote the family back in South Carolina that life was good in Georgia. Apparently convinced, Samuel McElroy Sr. relocated the rest of the family, including William, age 19, to their new home. As the family branched out, Samuel McElroy Sr. continued to live in that first log cabin, which became known as "The Grandpap House." [28]

The McElroys brought with them Samuel's school math book, handmade and covered with homespun cloth and stitched together with cotton string. The book, dated May 25, 1827, contains problems and related useful information, written in McElroy's own hand, with his own spelling and punctuation. Samuel recorded the relative value of international money "as established by an act of Congress passed November 1792": pound sterling = $4.40, rubl (sic) of Russia = $0.66, rupee of Bengal = $0.55.5, gulder (sic) of the united Netherlands = $0.39.

"Single Rule of Three direct:
The golden rule hath places three
the first and third they must agree
Second by third multiply divide by you ingeniously
Then will your quotient shew the same
which you in second place did frame."

Hypothetical math questions pointed the way to solutions to everyday problems:
"If 48 men can build a road in 24 days how many men can do the same work in 92 days? If a staff 3 feet high cast a shadow 6 1/3 feet what is the hight (sic) of a steeple whose shadow extends 633 1/3 feet? What is the amount of $400.78 for 12 years at 6 per cent per anum?"

Scattered throughout the book were doodles and sayings written by Samuel and his brothers: "Samuel McElroy his hand and pen June 7th 1827... When this you see remember me John McElroy... State of Georgia Dekalb (sic) County waters of Nances (sic) Creek John McElroy May 7th 1830." With a drawing of an apple tree were the words: "In the beginning God created the heaven and the earth and made man after his own image in knowledge wisdom righteousness true holiness John McElroy." [29]

Samuel, William and John McElroy became progenitors of a large clan that eventually enfolded spouses from most of the well-known families in north DeKalb.

John McElroy married Margaret (Peggy) McDill on December 20, 1831, and soon after built her a frame house "with squared, hand-hewn log sills and half-hewn log sleepers." The house stood for more than 120 years in Doraville, and amazed latter-day historians. "The foundation stones of this chimney are so big that we wonder where they came from and how he hauled them." John quietly made his living as a farmer for almost 40 years, plowing with his favorite oxen, Billy and Buck, until they were stolen by Union soldiers.

Shortly after the war, John McElroy was elected to the state legislature. He bought a valise and clothes, but, not wishing to leave his wife and child, declined the office. When John McElroy died in 1886, The DeKalb Chronicle ran an obituary, signed "C.M.C." The eulogy said, in part: "Mr. McElroy in truth would have made a most excellent representative. He was well educated, studious and industrious. The service to the state of such men should be sought and insisted upon." Instead of going to Atlanta, John, in 1869, at the age of 64, embarked on a new career as a Presbyterian minister. As a circuit rider, he preached in homes, schoolhouses and churches of all denominations in DeKalb and surrounding counties. He traveled in a second-hand buggy, pulled by "Old Bones," a horse that had been abandoned by Union soldiers and was rescued from starvation by John.

John Calvin McElroy, only surviving child of John McElroy and Peggy McDill McElroy, remembered his father was "blessed with a jovial disposition. Often after performing a marriage ceremony he would kiss the bride and laughing heartily would say to the embarrassed groom, `Now, son, what you gonna do about it?'" [30]

Samuel McElroy Jr. and his wife, Nancy, had four children. Samuel Bryson McElroy was killed during the Civil War, and Mary McElroy, though married three times, had no children. John T. Pressley McElroy married Matilda Caroline Akins, and Nancy Martha McElroy became the second wife of Matilda's brother James Francis Akins. Matilda Caroline and James Francis were children of pioneer settler Thomas J. Akins and his wife, Elizabeth Ross.

The youngest brother, William McElroy, and Margaret Malinda Tilly became parents of Prospect Church historian Stephen Tilly McElroy, as well as Frances Rebecca McElroy, Mary Elizabeth McElroy, William Samuel McElroy and John Ebenezer McElroy. Three of the children lived to maturity, with only two spending time in DeKalb. Mary Elizabeth McElroy married N. M. Lankford and settled in Clarkston. [31]

Stephen Tilly McElroy, like several of his McElroy cousins, had a long and illustrious life. A Confederate soldier in Co. F of the 36th Georgia Regiment, he was wounded twice at the Battle of Baker's Creek, near Vicksburg, Miss. on May 16 1863. He had been back home in Chamblee only a few months when his father, William McElroy, died on October 11, 1864. Although a Presbyterian, William McElroy is the only one of the four original settlers, including Samuel McElroy Sr., who is buried in Prospect Methodist Churchyard. The other McElroy pioneers are buried in Prosperity Presbyterian Cemetery, a short distance north of the Methodist burying ground.

Stephen Tilly McElroy married four times, and fathered eight children by two of his wives. His first wife, Laura Ann N. Lively, was born on March 5, 1845; the couple married on February 27, 1866. Laura was was the daughter of Milton Charles Lively II and Martha Maria Johnston. Laura's paternal grandparents came to DeKalb between 1820 and 1830 from Morgan County and settled in what is now the Northlake area of the county. The children of Milton Charles Lively I and his wife, Mary, included Nancy Lena Lively, who married Wylie Jones; Elizabeth Ann Lively, the first wife of James Francis Akins; and Judith Matilda C. Lively, who married, first, Alfred J. H. Poole, and second, Jabez M. Loyd. Laura's maternal grandparents, William and Naomi Johnston, were early members of Nancy Creek Primitive Baptist Church.

Stephen and Laura had six children: Fannie Lenora, William Melton, Mattie Beatrice, Minnie Lee, Stephen Lovick and Ruby Lively. Laura died on July 17, 1883 at the age of 38. Stephen and his third wife, Mary Jane (Jennie) Dobbs of Bartow County, had two children: Newton Tilly, born in 1891, and Mary Elmina (Mina), born in 1893. Stephen's second wife was Mrs. Kate Elizabeth (Broddie) Farley, who lived only two years after they married in 1885. His fourth wife was Mrs. Ella Lowry, who survived him.

Although he moved to Norcross in Gwinnett County, and became a charter member of Norcross Methodist Church, he never severed his close relationship with Prospect Church. In Gwinnett, he organized two banks and served as mayor of the city of Norcross. Until his death on December 30, 1929, his annual birthday celebration in Norcross drew friends and family from miles around. [32]

Among largest family cemeteries in DeKalb are those of Akin(s) family on Shasta Way, near the

James Francis Akin (or Akins) was the eldest son of DeKalb pioneer Thomas J. Akins. Oak Grove United Methodist Church was built on James Akin's land. (Mr. and Mrs. J. David Chesnut)

intersection of Briarcliff and Shallowford roads, and the Lively cemetery on LaVista Road near the intersection of Briarcliff and Henderson Mill roads.

Thomas J. Akins, a tall, thin, big-boned man, came to DeKalb before 1830 from Bulloch County, Ga. with his wife, Elizabeth Ross, and several children. He served in several public offices, including state senator from DeKalb in 1826. [33]

James Francis Akins, eldest son of Thomas and Elizabeth, was born December 30, 1822 in Bulloch County. Thomas and Elizabeth Akins had 13 other children: Andrew J., Eliza Louisa, William G., Lewis L., Allen R., Thomas Berry, Henry M., Jefferson P. M., Harriet E., Matilda Caroline (wife of John T. Pressley McElroy), Samantha C., Martha and Jane. After his first wife's death in DeKalb, Thomas Akins married Lucinda A. Hairston in 1849; Lucinda died just two years later. Thomas Akins was 51 when he married his third wife, Sarah S. King, in 1852. Thomas and Sarah had two children: John M. S., and Daniel W. Akins, the last -- and 16th -- child born in 1856, when Thomas was 55 years old. Thomas J. Akins died on March 10, 1873 at the age of 72.

Some subsequent generations of Thomas J. Akins's descendants have dropped the final "s" from the surname.

The Lively name also was prominent in the early days of DeKalb County, where many descendants still live. Milton Charles Lively, a Virginian inherited land in DeKalb from Thomas Winston in 1826, and had moved from Morgan County, Ga. to DeKalb by 1830. Lively descendants lived on the same land near the intersection of now North Druid Hills and Briarcliff roads for seven generations. Children of Milton Charles Lively I and his wife, Mary, were Polly M., Nancy Lena, Emily G. (Milly), Lucinda, Jane F., Milton Charles II, Elizabeth Ann (wife of James F. Akins) and Judith Matilda C. (wife of Jabez Loyd).

Nancy Lena Lively married Wylie Jones, a native of Wales, who was in DeKalb by 1829, and who died the following year. Nancy Lively Jones never remarried, and raised three children: Frances Jane, Charles Melton and William L. Nancy's two eldest children married in DeKalb -- Frances Jane to Jacob G. House, son of north DeKalb pioneer Samuel House, and Charles to Sarah Frances Carroll.

Revolutionary veterans must have found Tucker a particularly congenial place to settle. Peter Cash, Daniel Fones, Edward Leavell (or Levell) and Graner Whitley and their extended families settled in the Browning's District, near what is now the town of Tucker.

The Cash and Leavell families helped organize Fellowship Primitive Baptist Church on August 15, 1829. Elder James Hale was moderator of the first church conference, with Jessie Wallis as church clerk. Charter members included seven received by letter: Robert D. Inzer, Elizabeth Inzer, Isaih (sic) Parker, Dicy Parker, Sarah Parker and Revolutionary War veteran Peter Cash and Peter's younger brother, James Cash. Received by voucher from Nancy Creek Primitive Baptist Church were Robert Carath, Green Ville (sic) Henderson, Nancy Henderson, Raihe Leavel (sic) and Jessie Wallis. James Cash wrote the Yellow River Baptist Association requesting membership in 1829.

The congregation originally built a log cabin with a dirt floor adjacent to the Fellowship Primitive Baptist Church Cemetery on Pine Valley Road, off Lawrenceville Highway, about a mile from the church's present site. Many other Tucker area pioneers are buried at Fellowship, including Andrew (Dad) Browning (for whom Browning's District is named), Isaiah Parker, Charles Whitlock, William Beauchamp, Aaron and John Goza, Larkin Nash and Martin Thompson. Tom Browning, a descendant of Andrew, is said to have been one of the area's most colorful characters. He owned a saloon and horserace track on Fellowship Road, and, wearing a high top hat, traveled throughout the community in a two-horse carriage with a Negro driver. [34]

Josiah Gresham drew Land Lot 308 in the 18th District of then Henry County in the 1821 land lottery. He moved from Morgan County shortly thereafter and paid $19 in fees for 202 1/2 acres of land near what is now the intersection of Chamblee Tucker Road and Norcross Tucker Road. Gresham's neighbors included Tucker pioneer Greenville Henderson, who lived on Henderson Mill Road, and Edward Leavell.

Leavell was the first of the Revolutionary veterans to settle in the area, arriving by 1825. Born on July 16, 1756 in South Carolina, he was the grandson of Jean LaVelle who came to Virginia from France in about 1715. With Edward came at least two of his children, John W. Leavell and Rachel M. Leavell. John, who was born in Newberry County, S. C. on November 4, 1804, had married Mary C. (Polly) Wood on January 16, 1825. Rachel married A. Henderson, a son of Greenville Henderson, on September 16, 1835.

Three of John Leavell's children married three of Josiah Gresham's children. Nancy E. Leavell was the second wife of William Collins Gresham. Margaret Kate Gresham married William Jasper Leavell, and Mary Howard Gresham married Francis Marion Leavell.

Josiah Gresham died in 1853, at the age of 61, and was the first person to be buried in Gresham-Weed Cemetery, adjacent to the Pleasant Hill Baptist Church, both of which are located on formerly Gresham land. [35]

Three Cash brothers -- Peter, William and James -- had moved from Virginia to DeKalb County by 1828. The Cash brothers were great grandsons of Scottish immigrant William Cash, and sons of Stephen Cash and his wife, Jamima Grining. Three of Stephen and Jamima's sons were Revolutionary soldiers. Five of his sons came to Georgia, three of them choosing the Browning's District of DeKalb County to put down roots.

On February 15, 1828, James Cash bought the western half (about 100 acres) of Land Lot 209 of the 18th District, now at the intersection of LaVista and Briarcliff roads, for $150. William purchased acreage in Land Lots 190, 191 and 164 in the area of now Montreal Road and the Seaboard Coastline Railroad (now CSX Railroad).

Peter Cash filed an application to receive a pension for his Revolutionary War service on November 5, 1832 in DeKalb, claiming four tours with the Virginia militia. John Hayes, himself a veteran living in Decatur, testified on Peter's behalf.

Peter and James both were married in their home county of Amherst in Virginia -- Peter to Anne Holliday and James to Nancy Wright. Both couples's children were born in Amherst County. Seven of their combined 15 children (seven for Peter, eight for James) accompanied their parents to DeKalb. Two of the first cousins -- Lucinda, daughter of Peter, and George Washington, son of James -- married on January 3, 1824 in Amherst County.

In addition, Howard, eldest son of James Cash and Nancy Wright, married Sally Proffitt; and Belinda, their eldest daughter, married John W. Campbell. Lewis L. Cash, second son of Peter Cash and Anne Holiday, married Mary (Polly) Mauze. Peter Cash Jr. married Catherine Campbell. Peter and Anne's daughter, Mary (Polly) Cash married Wesley Cash, whose parents are unknown.

The tradition of Cash cousins marrying repeated in the next generation when Oliver Perry Cash, born December 29, 1830 in DeKalb to Howard Cash and Sally Proffitt, married Amanda Jane Cash, born June 5, 1834 in DeKalb to Washington Cash and Lucinda Cash. Their wedding date was August 12, 1852.

The many descendants of the Peter, William and James Cash, Edward Leavell and Josiah Gresham soon spread out to several homeplaces from the area now around Lawrenceville Highway and I-285 to Briarlake and LaVista roads west of Northlake Mall. [36]

Chapter 12 Notes

1. Goff, John, personal collection, Georgia Department of Archives and History.

2. Garrett, Franklin M., 1954, 1969, Atlanta and Environs -- A Chronicle of Its People and Events, Vol. 1, pages 32, 41 and 43.

3. Price, Vivian, February 6, 1985, "Graves At Nancy Creek Cemetery Tell The Story Of 160 Years In North DeKalb," DeKalb News/Sun, page 8B North.

4. Flowers, Grace Gresham, 1987, The Cash, Leavell, Pylant, Gresham and Flowers Families of DeKalb County 1625-1987, 1987.

5. Price, Vivian, February 6, 1985, "Graves At Nancy Creek Cemetery Tell The Story Of 160 Years In North DeKalb," DeKalb News/Sun, page 8B North. Wells, Joel Dixon, and Cornell, Nancy Jones, June, 1984, "Nancy Creek Primitive Baptist Church Cemetery," prepared for the Metropolitan Atlanta Rapid Transit Authority.

6. Wells, Joel Dixon, and Cornell, Nancy Jones, June, 1984, "Nancy Creek Primitive Baptist Church Cemetery," prepared for the Metropolitan Atlanta Rapid Transit Authority.

7. Author unknown, 1875, A Century in North DeKalb -- The Story of the First Baptist Church of Chamblee, 1875-1975, page 20.

8. Davis, Elizabeth Lockhart, and Spruill, Ethel Warren, 1975, The Story of Dunwoody -- Its Heritage and Horizons 1821-1975.

9. Wells, Joel Dixon, and Cornell, Nancy Jones, June, 1984, "Nancy Creek Primitive Baptist Church Cemetery," prepared for the Metropolitan Atlanta Rapid Transit Authority.

10. Candler, Charles Murphey, November 9, 1922, Historical Address.

11. Wells, Joel Dixon, and Cornell, Nancy Jones, June, 1984, "Nancy Creek Primitive Baptist Church Cemetery," prepared for the Metropolitan Atlanta Rapid Transit Authority.

12. Wells, Joel Dixon, and Cornell, Nancy Jones, June, 1984, "Nancy Creek Primitive Baptist Church Cemetery," prepared for the Metropolitan Atlanta Rapid Transit Authority.

13. Dobbins, Beatrice, 1970, "With Love, Beatrice Dobbins," unpublished manuscript, DeKalb Historical Society.

14. Garrett, Franklin M., 1954, 1969, Atlanta and Environs -- A Chronicle of Its People and Events, Vol. 1, pages 42.

15. Dobbins, Beatrice, 1970, "With Love, Beatrice Dobbins," unpublished manuscript, DeKalb Historical Society.

16. Davis, Elizabeth Lockhart, and Spruill, Ethel Warren, 1975, The Story of Dunwoody, page 38.

17. Garrett, Franklin M., Necrology, citing obituary of Mrs. Margaret M. Tilly McElroy, Wesleyan Christian Advocate, March 16, 1916.

18. Nix, Dorothy, personal collection, DeKalb Historical Society.

19. First United Methodist Church, Chamblee, Georgia, 1826-1976, 1976, citing 1919 history written by S. T. McElroy. Tilly, Harwell Parks IV, 1993, Stephen and Rebecca (King) Tilly and Their Descendants 1782-1992.

20. First United Methodist Church, Chamblee, Georgia, 1826-1976, 1976, citing 1919 history written by S. T. McElroy.

21. <u>First United Methodist Church, Chamblee, Georgia, 1826-1976</u>, 1976, citing 1919 history written by S. T. McElroy.

22. <u>First United Methodist Church, Chamblee, Georgia, 1826-1976</u>, 1976, citing 1919 history written by S. T. McElroy.

23. Garrett, Franklin M., Garrett Necrology, citing Samuel House obituary in the <u>Atlanta Constitution</u>. Garrett, Franklin M., 1954, 1969, <u>Atlanta and Environs -- A Chronicle of Its People and Events</u>, Vol. 1. Cook, Tallulah House, May, 1935, personal correspondence. House, Dr. Fredrick Crissler, personal collection.

24. Tilly, Harwell Parks IV, 1993, <u>Stephen and Rebecca (King) Tilly and Their Descendants 1782-1992.</u>

25. <u>First United Methodist Church, Chamblee, Georgia, 1826-1976</u>, 1976, citing 1919 history written by S. T. McElroy.

26. <u>First United Methodist Church, Chamblee, Georgia, 1826-1976</u>, 1976, citing 1919 history written by S. T. McElroy.

27. Tilly, Harwell Parks IV, 1993, <u>Stephen and Rebecca (King) Tilly and Their Descendants 1782-1992.</u>

28. "Calvin McElroy Sr. Observes 99th Birthday on Thanksgiving," <u>DeKalb New Era</u>, November 19, 1951.

29. Chesnut, Mr. and Mrs. J. David, personal collection.

30. "Calvin McElroy Sr. Observes 99th Birthday on Thanksgiving," the <u>DeKalb New Era</u>, November 19, 1951.

31. Tilly, Harwell Parks IV, 1993, <u>Stephen and Rebecca (King) Tilly and Their Descendants 1782-1992.</u>

32. McCabe, Alice Smythe, 1980, <u>Gwinnett County, Ga. Families 1818-1968</u>, Gwinnett Historical Society. Tilly, Harwell Parks IV, 1993, <u>Stephen and Rebecca (King) Tilly and Their Descendants 1782-1992.</u>

33. Garrett, Franklin M., 1954, 1969, <u>Atlanta and Environs -- A Chronicle of Its People and Events</u>, Vol. 1, page 55.

34. Fellowship Primitive Baptist Church file, Georgia Department of Archives and History. Flowers, Grace Gresham, 1987, <u>The Cash, Leavell, Pylant, Gresham and Flowers Families of DeKalb County 1625-1987</u>, 1987. Garrett, Franklin M., 1954, 1969, <u>Atlanta and Environs -- A Chronicle of Its People and Events</u>, Vol. 1, page 78. <u>The Eagle</u>, Tucker Federal Savings and Loan Association, winter, 1978.

35. Flowers, Grace Gresham, 1987, <u>The Cash, Leavell, Pylant, Gresham and Flowers Families of DeKalb County 1625-1987</u>, 1987.

36. Flowers, Grace Gresham, 1987, <u>The Cash, Leavell, Pylant, Gresham and Flowers Families of DeKalb County 1625-1987</u>, 1987.

Chapter 13

*A*t the time the Georgia government was negotiating with the Creek Indians over their land between the Chattahoochee and South rivers, the place that would become the city of Decatur "could scarcely be dignified as a `settlement,' there being but a few shanties and an Indian lodge or two. It was a sort of trading post." The Etowah Trail was the primary transportation corridor, running from Decatur to what is now Five Points in downtown Atlanta. Now called DeKalb Avenue and Decatur Street, the path could only be traveled by foot or horse; it was not wide enough for wagons. [1]

The Etowah Trail continued westward to Sandtown on the Chattahoochee River, which at the time was considerably larger than the "settlement" at Decatur. Sandtown was as rough a town as the notorious "wild west" places like Dodge City. Gold had been discovered just across the Chattahoochee in Villa Rica, and fortune-hunters came in droves.

Contemporary "youth gangs" had nothing on the "Pony Boys" who headquartered at Sandtown. The Pony Boys spent their time "rustling cattle, pillaging and harassing the Indians who lived across the Chattahoochee River. The Indians complained to authorities, and claimed the Pony Boys came from DeKalb County. Catching the perpetrators proved difficult, since it was easy for them to escape by crossing the river, where the white man's government had no jurisdiction." [2]

Apparently, the Indians caused just as much trouble among the white population.

William W. White moved in 1824 from Franklin County, Ga. to what is now the West End section of Fulton County. He came "riding a lank horse, with his plowgear on the animal and a side of meat and various utensils tied up in a sack behind him. The "pilfering" Indians worried him and frightened his wife. They would come from Sandtown and "were forever peeping around the smokehouse and slyly picking up any useful articles lying around." Relations in the White household were further strained because William had put up their cabin hastily and had not sufficiently covered the cracks between the logs. "So when bears, wolves and panthers came prowling around the house at night, the lady refused to occupy the side of the bed next to the wall for fear that these wild animals would poke their noses through the openings and bite her." [3]

While they might have invited unwelcome advances from wildlife, unchinked spaces between logs in the interior of pioneer cabins provided valuable storage nooks for things like knitting, a corncob pipe or a child's rag doll. [4]

During the next few years Decatur would grow into a sizeable town, and Sandtown would disappear with the Indians.

The town of Decatur was incorporated on December 10, 1823. Reuben Cone, William Morris, William Gresham, James White and Thomas A. Dobbs were appointed by the General Assembly as the first commissioners of Decatur. [5]

By 1824 Decatur boasted a jail, an academy, about 50 houses and stores. That year, all of DeKalb County had a free white population of 3,569. [6]

The first slate of constitutional officers elected in and for DeKalb County took office on January 15, 1824. They were George Harris, sheriff; Thomas A. Dobbs, clerk of the Superior Court; Daniel Stone, clerk of the Inferior Court; Wileford Grogan, coroner; and Bennet Conine, surveyor. Dobbs was the only officer to have been re-elected. On November 1, 1824, the Inferior Court authorized clerk Daniel Stone to purchase an official county seal. [7]

State funds for the education of poor children in Georgia was distributed through Inferior Courts to superintendents in each county. Eligible for public funds to subsidize their education were children between the ages of eight and 18 with three years of schooling or less. [8]

Seven poor school superintendents were appointed in DeKalb on July 28, 1823: Jacob R. Brooks, Shallow Ford District; Joseph Morris, Captain Merritt's District; Samuel Prewitt, Captain Stagg's District; George Harris, Captain Hughy's District; James Blackstock, 14th District of formerly Henry County; James White, Captain Standifer's District; and David R. Pillam, Captain Jordan's District.

DeKalb County's first school, the DeKalb County Academy, was established by the General Assembly on November 10, 1823, and located in Decatur. Trustees were John B. Nelson, Zachariah Hollaway, Jacob R. Brooks, Joseph Morris, Joseph D. Shumate, Reuben Cone and James Blackstock. The Rev. Alexander Kirkpatrick, a Presbyterian minister, was the first principal, assisted by Watson Kittredge, a Massachusetts native. They were followed by David Kiddoo and E. A. Davis. The General Assembly on December 26, 1823 appointed S. T. Bailey, Alexander Corry, J. F. Cleveland, William Ezzard and Leonard Randall as commissioners to establish a lottery to raise $3,000 for use by the academy. [9]

In 1824, DeKalb received $319.65 in state poor school funds, or nine cents per resident, with $315 going to the DeKalb Academy. DeKalb Academy's share in 1825 was $236.67. In 1826 the Inferior Court ordered the county treasurer to pay half of the county's annual tax levy "to the commissioners of the poor for use by the poor." Trustees of poor schools appointed on March 28, 1826 were James McC. Montgomery, John Johnson and Silas McGrady. [10]

Levi Willard (1802-1884) came to Decatur on December 3, 1826 at the age of 22, having left his birthplace in Petersham, Mass. for a warmer climate. War in the Willard backyard caused him to move his family to Springfield, Ohio in the fall of 1864. A teacher and Presbyterian elder, Willard lived on West Court Square in Decatur where he also operated a store in partnership with his friend Oliver Clark. There he lived for 38 years, observing the daily life and townspeople in Decatur.

While in Springfield, he wrote a series of letters to the "Weekly News" in Decatur in 1879, which were reprinted in the DeKalb New Era in 1920. These articles told the story of Decatur in the early years. [11]

Willard remembered the Rev. Kirkpatrick, first principal of the DeKalb Academy, as "a warm-hearted Irishman," educated in Scotland, who came to DeKalb from South Carolina. He lived in a house on Lawrenceville Street, which was later known as the Scaife house, and still later as the James R. McAlister place. Kirkpatrick, Willard said, "was not a brilliant man, but an acceptable preacher." [12]

The Rev. Kirkpatrick provided some choice memories for Willard and doubtless many other early Decatur residents.

There was an embarrassing pause in the first marriage ceremony Kirkpatrick performed in the town. As the ceremony began, the couple handed the minister their marriage license. Being a South Carolinian, where no license was required, Kirkpatrick mistook the permit for a protest against the couple's union. Apparently to cover his confusion, Kirkpatrick spoke to the congregation about "popping the question." He remarked that he thought that young ladies "must have a presentment of what question was to be proposed to them, for if it were not so, he did not think Susan (his wife) would have known anything of what he meant when he asked her to marry him -- he did it in such a bungling way."

On another occasion, the Rev. Kirkpatrick tearfully, but mistakenly, informed his congregation that a popular minister, Dr. John S. Wilson of Gwinnett County, was dead. On his way to visit the bereaved family in Lawrenceville, he met Decatur lawyer Hines Holt who set Kirkpatrick straight, reassuring him that the minister had been ill, but was on the mend. "Well then," said Kirkpatrick, "I have told an egregious lie from the sacred desk, for I said he was dead." When Kirkpatrick reached Brother Wilson's bedside, he grasped his hand and said, "Die when you will, your funeral has been preached."

Kirkpatrick later returned to South Carolina. [13]

Willard also recalled the names of these early DeKalb County preachers: Telemachus F. Montgomery and Rhadamanthus J. Montgomery, sons of James McC. Montgomery of Standing Peachtree; Jonathan Norcross, later mayor of Atlanta; James J. Winn and two of his sons, Paul P. and Samuel K.; W. W. Brimm; and John M. Smith, a Methodist who also was tax collector, and who preached and collected taxes on same trip.

DeKalb had no lack of school teachers in the early 1820s. In addition to Kirkpatrick, Kittredge and Kiddoo in Decatur, Hiram Washburn taught at the Wade settlement, and Malcolm MacLeod down by the South River. Joseph Walker was considered the "patriarch of teachers," and also taught music. The favorite oath of teacher Fanning Brown was said to be "by Rip and Davy Jones." H. M. F. Lipford "prided himself on his excellent penmanship, and was rather conceited," according to Willard.

Lewis Towers also taught, and his wife was considered even a better teacher. The Rev. M. Dickson was the second rector of the academy, and George Anderson (not George D.) and his wife were in charge of the academy for a time. Edward D. Frost and P. M. Sheibly also were early Decatur teachers.

Female teachers were decidedly in the minority in the early days of DeKalb County. Miss Emily A. Cooley taught a classroom of girls who attended the male academy in 1834 and '35. Under Miss Cooley's guidance, students arranged themselves in the schoolyard as the sun and planets. Visitors were invited to question the students on particulars about the solar system. Miss Cooley moved to Massachusetts in June of 1835, but sent as her replacement Miss A. P. Hamilton. Miss Hamilton taught for one year, 1835-36, and is remembered for designing a circular bed of flowers at the academy with a mimosa tree in the center. Miss Frances S. Foster succeeded Miss Hamilton, and a Miss Dutton also taught for several years. [14]

Liquor seems to have flowed freely in early Decatur. There were nine or ten stores on or near the town square, and only one shopkeeper, William R. (Long Billy) Smith, refused to sell whiskey. William M. (Uncle Billy) Hill had no such misgivings. His was the first barroom (called a grocery) in Decatur. "In good demand at Hill's emporium were corn whiskey and peach and apple brandy." Hill moved to Atlanta, became an auctioneer and died in 1869. The Decatur entrepreneur with the dubious distinction is buried in an unmarked grave in Oakland Cemetery. [15]

Those who chose to get drunk and stay out late ran the risk of falling victim to Decatur's infamous "Wild Boys." In response to one of Levi Willard's newspaper articles, a self-proclaimed alumnus of the Wild Boys, who chose to remain anonymous, wrote this letter to the DeKalb New Era on November 11, 1920:

The Wild Boys of Decatur of 1825
"... (I) will, with your permission, tell you something of the wild boys of Decatur, as they were then called, used to coop and black old men, who came to Decatur and got tight. It was very common in 1824-1825-1826, to get up of a morning and find a crate swinging up to a horse-rack with one or two men in it, with their faces so black you could not tell who they were, or if not swung under the horse rack, the were under a crate or cart body, with perhaps a half cord of wood or rock piled on it so they could not get out. Some of those wild boys have scars now if they are living, from cuts they received in those days of `cooping' in Decatur. Many other such things would these wild boys do. One other memorable thing some of the old settlers remember. At court, the fall term, 1825, they went into Mr. R. Cone's horse lot and cut off one ear each of thirteen horses. Among them was Judge Shorter's and Solicitor General C. J. McDonald's (afterwards Judge and Governor of Georgia); and put a wagon on top of the court house. At the next court, in 1826, Mr. Cone by that time had built a good stable, and they entered that and cut a horse's ham-string and shoved three spokes out of a sulky. Many other things did the wild boys of Decatur in that time do.

"Well, I will not tell anything more on these wild boys. They have all that are now alive become gray-haired sires, and regret their wild days of the past, but by your indulgence, I will speak of some other things that Decatur may well be proud of, not mentioning any names. I know that she has furnished three solicitors general, six or seven judges of the superior court, four members of congress, one senator in congress and one governor of Georgia.

"They were all but one lawyers by profession. I could name many eminent physicians from Decatur. Decatur's merchants were from her earliest settlement until used up by Atlanta, equal to any country town in the State. The hotel keepers were equal to any in former days. Her mechanics in those days were not surpassed by any in the state. But being so near to Atlanta, Decatur has suffered very much in business and in improvements, but my prediction is that she is yet to be a considerable place. Her society, healthfulness and many other advantages, with some of the finest citizens you can find anywhere, will yet make her a delightful place to live and do business. I must not forget one thing about Decatur and her immediate neighborhood. She has furnished more good wives to her young men than almost any other town in Georgia. Having said this much and given what the wild boys used to do, I will say that Decatur has always maintained a good moral Christian character. Her citizens and her churches compare well with any town; her pubic officers and her members of the legislature will bear favorable comparison with any county in the state. This will do for one of the wild boys of Decatur fifty-four years, living away..."

Yours truly, ONE OF THE BOYS [16]

Willard responded with some comments of his own about mischief perpetrated by the "Wild Boys" in the early days of Decatur.

"I have heard old man Durham tell about sticking his knife blade into Bill's leg through the meshes, when the boys had him under the crate. That case put an end to the crate cooping, but not to blacking. In one case, they did not black the man, as he was a respectable citizen, otherwise than his intemperance. So they clipped off his whiskers on one side `in full force and virtue.' It cured him of his habit of staying till after dark in town.

"Col. Murphy's (sic) Joe, a black boy, was lying asleep and though not drunk, the boys thought him a fit subject for paint, so they painted him white. Looking in the glass he exclaimed: `Massa Charles, if they ain't blacked me!...'

"On one occasion, the boys annoyed the people of the village by ringing the academy bell at midnight.

"Some of the sober old men went to them to reprimand them, but they were met by the reply: `Pat Farrel has married the widow Scaife and we are giving them a serenade...

"In January 1826, after the result of the election of Daniel Stone and Charles Murphey as clerks of the court, the young men and some of the others had a jollification in the court house -- what they called a bull dance. Their bull dose had already been taken.

"David R. Silliven (not Sullivan) was elected sheriff, and John Brown was to be deputy. In the dance John Brown said that he and Billy Grisham would `be girls.'

"One of the young men (he is an old man now) said as they retired to their lodgings: `It is a shame to go to bed so drunk on such an occasion." [17]

Crime in early Decatur also took on a more serious nature. Blacksmith Nathan W. Wansley had part of his ear bitten off in a fight. The perpetrator, whose name in unknown, was found guilty of "mayhem" and sentenced to stand in the stocks. So as not to draw embarrassing attention to the criminal and his punishment, Sheriff George Harris hung a blanket in front of the stocks. [18]

John B. Nelson, one of the first DeKalb Academy trustees and proprietor of Nelson's Ferry on the Chattahoochee River, became the county's first known murder victim, killed in April of 1825 by John W. Davis. Gov. George M. Troup offered a $250 reward for the apprehension of Davis:

"Georgia:
"By his excellency George M. Troup Governor and Commander in Chief of the Army and Navy of this State and the militia thereof.
"It appearing by affidavit and Warrant in due form produced by the Deputy Sheriff of DeKalb County at the Executive Office, that on the second day of this present month, a certain John W. Davis had committed a murder on the body of John B. Nelson of the same County had fled from justice -- I have therefore thought property issue this my Proclamation hereby offering a reward of Two hundred and fifty dollars to any person of persons who may apprehend and deliver the said John W. Davis to the Sheriff or Jailor of the County aforesaid -- And I do moreover charge and require all officers civil and military to be vigilant in assisting to apprehend the said John W. Davis, that he may be brought to trial for the crime with which he has been charged.
"Given under my hand and the Great Seal of the State at the State House in Milledgeville this eighth day of April Eighteen hundred and twenty five.
G. M. Troup.
By the Governor,
Everard Hamilton,
Secretary of State
Note -- John W. Davis is between fifty and fifty six years of age, five feet six or seven inches high, stout built, round face, swarthy complexion, dark hair, a little grey with somewhat of baldness, and a shaking of his limbs at times as if affected by palsy."

Davis was caught, and incarcerated in the dungeon of the DeKalb County Jail. The DeKalb Inferior Court in its June, 1826 term "ordered that the sum of $35.12 1/2 be paid to William Carson or his order for guarding the jail while John W. Davis was a prisoner in said jail and the further sum of $1.25." [19]

Col. Samuel T. Bailey served as lead defense attorney for Davis. His fee was $200, plus a Negro boy named Jeff. Assisting Bailey were "a Judge Strong and a man named Warner from Monticello." Strong and Warner split the $200, and Bailey kept Jeff. [20]

There are no records of the outcome of Davis's trial, but on August 4, 1849, the DeKalb Inferior Court declared him a "pauper lunatic" and committed him to the state Lunatic Asylum in Milledgeville. [21]

DeKalb's first murder victim, John B. Nelson, was buried in his family cemetery, close to the old ferry landing, in now Fulton County. Nelson's daughter Mary J. E., born after his death, also is buried there. She became the wife of Frederic A. Williams, son of DeKalb pioneer Ammi Williams. Like her father, Mary was not destined for a long life; she died on November 16, 1845 at the age of 20 years and 18 days. [22]

The Rev. John S. Wilson organized Westminster (later Decatur) Presbyterian Church before moving on to Atlanta. (The Story of Decatur)

Being the county seat, Decatur naturally attracted more than its share of lawyers. While official courthouse records before 1842 may have burned, destroying forever the names of early attorneys in DeKalb, one memorable record survives. While spending time in the county jail in 1827 for a long-forgotten misdemeanor, William Stinsom, wrote this poem:

> "There is Bailey and Young
> With nimble tongue.
> Hooper and Colonel Ezzard,
> They all agree to take a fee,
> And call a terrapin a lizzard.
> In one slips whose name is Phipps,
> To keep a publick table,
> Where saint and sinner may get their dinner,
> If they are only able." [23]

One of the first lawyers in Decatur, William Ezzard was elected a state representative at the young age of 28. After serving as Superior Court judge in DeKalb, he moved to Atlanta where he was later elected mayor. Ezzard built a home where later the Piedmont Hotel would stand. Down the road from Decatur, where the Druid Hills Golf Club is today, lived another South Carolinian who was prominent in early DeKalb. James Paden, commissioned an Inferior Court Justice on October 29, 1827, was born in the Spartanburg District of South Carolina. He died in 1864 and is buried in an unmarked grave in Decatur Cemetery. [24]

Hines Holt, who launched his Decatur law practice in about 1827, was best remembered for his glib tongue. In a courtroom exchange, an exasperated Judge Walter T. Colquitt asked Holt, "Do you wish to argue me out of my senses?" Holt replied (in an undertone): "No, your honor, but rather the contrary." Later, the Inferior Court, acting as a Court of Ordinary, was called upon to set aside the marriage of a girl younger than 12. Holt was heard to remark that the session might be called a "court extraordinary." [25]

Holt soon came to need a lawyer of his own. In retaliation for being cursed by Martin Adams during an altercation on the square in Decatur, Holt hit Adams with his walking stick, splintering the stick, and stabbing Adams in the back with the dirk concealed in the stick. Holt was indicted, but found innocent of "stabbing with intent to murder." [26]

Charles J. McDonald was judge of the Superior Court in the Ocmulgee Circuit to which DeKalb first attached, and held the first Superior Court for the county in 1823. DeKalb was switched to the Coweta Circuit in 1826, where Walter T. Colquitt was the judge. Colquitt acted as his own chaplain and, kneeling on the judge's bench, opened court with prayer. "It has been remarked that Colquitt could preside in court, deliver a political speech at recess, and preach a sermon at night." [27]

Report of John B. Nelson's murder at the hands of John W. Davis was not the first published obituary from DeKalb County. That distinction goes to Jacobus Watts. The notice of his death was printed in the Southern Recorder at Milledgeville on June 14, 1825:

"Departed this life on the 20th of May, at his residence in the vicinity of the Standing Peachtree, in DeKalb County, Capt. Jacobus Watts, aged 53 years. He had been a citizen of Greene County and represented that county in legislature. Moved to Morgan County and became member of inferior court. A republican." [28]

The first sermon in Decatur is said to have been preached by a Father Knight of the Camp Creek.

Dr. John S. Wilson, alive and well, came to Decatur and organized the town's first church. Westminster Presbyterian Church was constituted on October 29, 1825, later changing its name to Decatur Presbyterian. Charter members were William Bryce and his wife Mary, James Lemon and wife Mary D., William Carson and wife Jane, Thomas Harris and Rebecca Luckie. The first Ruling Elders, elected October 30, 1825, were William Carson, James Lemon and Thomas Harris. [29]

The Georgia General Assembly approved the incorporation of the church on December 22, 1827, with trustees William Carson, Alexander Corry, James Lemon, Robert Lemon and Leonard Simpson. Robert Lemon (or Lemmon/s), father of James, was one of several Irish-born citizens of Decatur who made significant contributions to the character of the town. Father and son came to the area in 1821 while it was still Henry County. James Lemon, born 1794 in the Anderson District of South Carolina, moved to Cobb County in 1843. He died in 1849 and is buried in the Mars Hill Cemetery in Acworth.

Early members of Decatur Presbyterian Church had to obtain "tokens of good standing" in order to partake of communion. "As one came to the Communion table, he or she was required to surrender this token, a round piece of lead. Without its presentation no one was allowed to partake of the sacramental elements." Joseph D. Shumate, son-in-law of James Montgomery and one of the founders of Decatur Presbyterian, also was the first person disciplined by the church. "In 1826 all the streams of the county dried up from a drought. The people had to grind their grain in coffee mills, beat it in mortars and grate it, there being no water to run the mills. Shumate was a miller, and, upon the rain coming at last, ground for people on Sunday. That was the reason for the discipline but upon pleading the necessity of the people, he was unanimously exonerated." [30]

Dr. Wilson was well known in DeKalb, as well as in Gwinnett and later Fulton, although he did not move to Decatur until 1844 when he became pastor of Decatur Presbyterian Church. He is credited with organizing the Hannah Moore Institute for Girls in Decatur, as well as the First Presbyterian Church of Atlanta, where he was pastor from 1858 until his death in 1873. [31]

The Rev. Alexander Kirkpatrick, rector of the DeKalb Academy, also served as Decatur Presbyterian Church's first minister.

In 1825, the First Methodist Church became the first church to construct a building in Decatur. The church's current chapel building, pictured here in a drawing by Sarah Harbin, was built in 1897 of native granite. (DeKalb Historical Society)

Early members of the church were George D. Anderson, William U. Anderson, David Anderson, Samuel Anderson, Levi Willard and his wife and children, Joyce J. Word, her son, Robert C. Word, and four daughters, Eliza, Sarah, Elizabeth and Jane, Charles J. Hooper, William Latimer, Gary E. Adams, C. W. McGinnis, John McCullough and his wife, William Farrell and his wife, William Dickson and his wife, Sanders and David Dickson, Moses and Hardy Harris, Jonathan Hadden, Thomas B. McCrary, Mrs. Lucinda Cone, Daniel Stone and his wife, Joseph Pitts and his wife, Alexander Curry, Mason D. Shumate, his wife and children, Robert F., Moses E. and E. A. Davis, John Cullen, James Nichols, John McWilliams, Mrs. Elizabeth Bryce, Andrew Rogers, John Bryce, James H. Kirkpatrick and his wife and children, including James W. and the Rev. John L. Kirkpatrick, Mrs. Laura Williams, Frederic Williams, Ezekiel Mason, Joseph and L. S. Morgan and their children, Lochlin Johnson and his wife and children and Watson Kittredge.[32]

The exact date of the founding of Decatur Methodist Episcopal Church is unknown. The church is thought to have been organized between 1823 and 1826. It is known that the Inferior Court of Decatur gave Decatur Methodist a lot on what is now Sycamore Street, on which the church erected the first church building in Decatur in 1826.

According to the provisions included in the county's organization, the Inferior Court could give churches incorporating in Decatur a town lot on which to build. This practice was officially sanctioned by the legislature in 1832:

"Whereas the Inferior Court of DeKalb County, did on the first organization of the County, offer to the several religious societies each, a town lot on which to erect Churches for their accommodation; and, whereas, the Methodist Society did comply with said condition and erect a Church... Decatur's Presbyterians and Baptists also received town lots. [33]

No original deed for the Decatur Methodist property exists today. Church historian J. Howell Green wrote, "There is a tradition, which I remember hearing when I first came to Decatur, that the deed was in the custody of a member of the Church by the name of Diamond, who moved to Texas, and probably carried the deed with him." However, Green acknowledged, however, that the deed could have burned in a courthouse fire.

The Decatur Methodist Church building was used for several years for denominational and non-denominational religious meetings, as well as for classes of the DeKalb Academy. Decatur Methodist was incorporated by the Georgia legislature in 1830 with the following trustees: Jeptha V. George, Jesse P. Jones, Robert Ward, Larkin Carlton and Drury Fowler. [34]

Levi Willard recalled the story of J. V. George, a Decatur merchant and sometimes preacher. George was preaching at Decatur Methodist when he knocked over the building's only candlestick. The congregation was in darkness until someone went to a neighboring house and re-lit the candle. While waiting, George said: "It will be well, friends, if we never find ourselves in a darker place than this."

James R. Reid was an exhorter at Decatur Methodist, according to Willard, and Robert Ware a class leader. The Rev. Elijah Bird sometimes preached, Willard wrote, and was fond of using long, uncommon words. "Young men, rationate, I say, rationate." [35]

The DeKalb County Bible Society was organized in Decatur in 1826. Willard wrote "that the Society was formed for the purpose of supplying the destitute with a copy of the Holy Scriptures. The County was thoroughly canvassed at one time to ascertain what destitution there was. Some took offense at the inquiry as to whether they had Bibles, but generally answered with civility. The Society was revived three or four times, after almost dying out... Strange as it may appear, there were some who were opposed to the Bible Society. The reason was because some one may be making money by selling or printing the Bibles." [36]

Chapter 13 Notes

1. Author unknown, June 7, 1931, "Indian War Near Five Points," Atlanta Journal Magazine, reproduced from the Atlanta Daily New Era, page 6.

2. Goff, Dr. John, personal collection, Georgia Department of Archives and History.

3. Garrett, Franklin M., 1954, 1969, Atlanta and Environs -- A Chronicle of Its People and Events, Vol. 1, pages 43-44.

4. Garrett, Franklin M., 1954, 1969, Atlanta and Environs -- A Chronicle of Its People and Events, Vol. 1, pages 44.

5. Candler, Charles Murphey, November 9, 1922, Historical Address, page 4.

6. Garrett, Franklin M., 1954, 1969, Atlanta and Environs -- A Chronicle of Its People and Events, Vol. 1, page 38.

7. Garrett, Franklin M., 1954, 1969, Atlanta and Environs -- A Chronicle of Its People and Events, Vol. 1, page 39.

8. Garrett, Franklin M., 1954, 1969, Atlanta and Environs -- A Chronicle of Its People and Events, Vol. 1, page 41.

9. Candler, Charles Murphey, November 9, 1922, Historical Address, page 10.

10. Garrett, Franklin M., 1954, 1969, Atlanta and Environs -- A Chronicle of Its People and Events, Vol. 1, page 41.

11. Clarke, Caroline McKinney, 1973, 1997, The Story of Decatur 1823-1899, page 8. Nix, Dorothy, personal collection, DeKalb Historical Society. Garrett, Franklin M., 1954, 1969, Atlanta and Environs -- A Chronicle of Its People and Events, Vol. 1, page 59.

12. Willard, Levi, 1920, "The Early History of Decatur Written Many Years Ago," DeKalb New Era.

13. Willard, Levi, 1920, "The Early History of Decatur Written Many Years Ago," DeKalb New Era.

14. Willard, Levi, 1920, "The Early History of Decatur Written Many Years Ago," DeKalb New Era.

15. Clarke, Caroline McKinney, 1973, 1997, The Story of Decatur 1823-1899, page 8. Garrett, Franklin M., 1954, 1969, Atlanta and Environs -- A Chronicle of Its People and Events, Vol. 1, page 66.

16. Willard, Levi, 1920, "The Early History of Decatur Written Many Years Ago, DeKalb New Era.

17. Willard, Levi, 1920, "The Early History of Decatur Written Many Years Ago, DeKalb New Era.

18. Garrett, Franklin M., 1954, 1969, Atlanta and Environs -- A Chronicle of Its People and Events, Vol. 1, page 41.

19. Garrett, Franklin M., 1954, 1969, Atlanta and Environs -- A Chronicle of Its People and Events, Vol. 1, pages 51.

20. Willard, Levi, 1920, "The Early History of Decatur Written Many Years Ago, DeKalb New Era.

21. Garrett, Franklin M., 1954, 1969, Atlanta and Environs -- A Chronicle of Its People and Events, Vol. 1, page 51.

22. Garrett, Franklin M., 1954, 1969, Atlanta and Environs -- A Chronicle of Its People and Events, Vol. 1, page 51.

23. Willard, Levi, 1920, "The Early History of Decatur Written Many Years Ago, DeKalb New Era.

24. Garrett, Franklin M., 1954, 1969, Atlanta and Environs -- A Chronicle of Its People and Events, Vol. 1, page 63.

25. Willard, Levi, 1920, "The Early History of Decatur Written Many Years Ago, <u>DeKalb New Era</u>.

26. Willard, Levi, 1920, "The Early History of Decatur Written Many Years Ago, <u>DeKalb New Era</u>.

27. Willard, Levi, 1920, "The Early History of Decatur Written Many Years Ago, <u>DeKalb New Era</u>. Candler, Charles Murphey, November 9, 1922, Historical Address, page 4.

28. Garrett, Franklin M., 1954, 1969, <u>Atlanta and Environs -- A Chronicle of Its People and Events</u>, Vol. 1, page 53.

29. Candler, Charles Murphey, and Candler, Scott, October 29, 1950, <u>History of The Decatur Presbyterian Church, Decatur, Ga.</u>

30. Candler, Charles Murphey, November 9, 1922, Historical Address, page 13. Garrett, Franklin M., 1954, 1969, <u>Atlanta and Environs -- A Chronicle of Its People and Events</u>, Vol. 1, page 59.

31. Clarke, Caroline McKinney, 1973, 1997, <u>The Story of Decatur 1823-1899</u>, page 25.

32. Candler, Charles Murphey and Scott, October 29, 1950, "The History of The Decatur Presbyterian Church, Decatur, Ga.," page 6.

33. Green, J. Howell, August 1, 1920, "A Brief History of The Decatur Methodist Episcopal Church, South, and a Roll of Membership."

34. Green, J. Howell, August 1, 1920, "A Brief History of The Decatur Methodist Episcopal Church, South, and a Roll of Membership."

35. Willard, Levi, 1920, "The Early History of Decatur Written Many Years Ago, <u>DeKalb New Era</u>. Green, J. Howell August 1, 1920, "A Brief History of The Decatur Methodist Episcopal Church, South, and a Roll of Membership."

36. Garrett, Franklin M., 1954, 1969, <u>Atlanta and Environs -- A Chronicle of Its People and Events</u>, Vol. 1, page 59.

Chapter 14

A good many settlers who become prominent citizens of Decatur were already in the area while it was still Henry and Fayette counties.

Levi Willard remembers these: James McC. Montgomery, David Kiddoo, Watson Kittredge, Tully Choice, William Ezzard, Jesse F. Cleveland, Jonathan B. Wilson, Charles J. McDonald, Walter T. Colquitt, George Harris, Billy Grisham, Alexander Corry, Jesse Potter Jones, Ammi Williams, Reuben Cone, Mason D. Shumate, Lochlin Johnson and James H. Kirkpatrick.

Lochlin Johnson moved to Decatur so his children could attend the academy, at which Kiddo was an early instructor. During his almost 40 years of residence in the city of Decatur, Johnson held several positions of public responsibility. He died on July 17, 1861 and is buried in Decatur Cemetery. [1] Montgomery, Johnson, Choice, Ezzard, Cleveland and Wilson were early state senators from DeKalb, and Wilson "could make a good hat, either sugar-loaf or bellcrown."

Billy Grisham was one of the first in Decatur to open a store, located in a log cabin next above Billy Hill's grocery. Alexander Corry was a justice of peace in 1827; he beat Grisham by only two or three votes. Grisham also was later elected. Jesse Potter Jones was a jugmaker and had a shop and furnace in front of his house.

Merchant James Ligon came to December in 1826; his store occupied the corner of Broad and Lawrenceville streets. Thomas Dobbs built an office when he was clerk of court; the building was later occupied by Ligon's store. Still later, the building was moved by John Glen, but burned in 1846. Ligon was remembered for having built a new store eight feet out into the street. Adjacent property owners moved their fences up even with Ligon's building. The encroachment accounts for the narrowness of Lawrenceville Street for many years. [2]

John Glen was a clerk in Ligon's store and served as postmaster in Decatur. He also was clerk of DeKalb's Inferior and Superior courts, and worked as a Georgia Railroad agent. He moved to Atlanta where he was elected to the city council in 1854. [3]

Thomas Akins and William Gresham were the first merchants in Decatur and may have been the first to build a store. Gresham later moved to Cherokee County and died there in 1876. Historian Willard calls Akins "the patriarch of merchants," because he was in business longer than anyone else. Akins also had as his partner Shallow Ford ferry proprietor Jacob R. Brooks. Later Decatur postmaster Leonard Randall became Akins's business partner in a mercantile firm appropriately called Randall and Akins. Akins also was a state representative in 1826. Akins is said to have had a hearty laugh that could be heard across the square. Across the street from the Akins emporium was the Tully Choice store. Tully Choice was DeKalb's state senator in 1826. Nearby was Simeon Smith's store. Smith had come to DeKalb after drawing a lot in the 1821 land lottery. Once settled, he served in a variety of public capacities, including captain of the militia, tax collector and judge of the Inferior Court.

Col. R. M. Brown, although not an original settler, engaged in manufacturing in early Decatur, read law while he was clerk of the Superior Court, was a colonel in the militia, and later tanned leather for the Confederacy. Isaiah Parker was remembered as "a nursery and fruit man near Stone Mountain... and a Primitive Baptist."

Joseph Morgan had a chair factory. "He did his turning first at a mill in the neighborhood, but he soon exchanged water power for horse power." Joseph was joined in business by his brother, L. S. Morgan, who added cabinet furniture to the business. Joseph married Jane M., daughter of James H. Kirkpatrick, and L. S. married Martha J. McNeil, daughter of Revolutionary War veteran James McNeil. A third brother was named Enoch Morgan. Capt. John W. Fowler clerked in the store of Cleveland & Co. in 1826, then turned to farming and milling. He was a prominent member of Indian Creek Baptist Church, and held several county offices including sheriff. He was captain of a volunteer militia company in 1836, sent to collect Cherokees for removal. [4]

James Lemon, one of the charter members of Decatur Presbyterian Church, came to DeKalb from the Anderson District of South Carolina shortly after the county was organized. A partner in a mercantile firm of Lemon and Wilson, he is said to have built the first frame house in the town. Willard remembered that this house was called "the red corner," although he does not cite a reason for the intriguing name. Lemon was prominent in early DeKalb, holding several positions, including justice of the Inferior Court and state representative. He moved to Cobb County about 1839. [5]

Merchant John Reid was the original builder of Decatur's well-known "High House" on Covington Street, so named because it was one of the town's first two-story houses and sat on a slight rise. Reid bought goods from Bailey Goddard of Macon, but couldn't pay, so he sold the unfinished house to Goddard who completed it and sold it. It has been occupied through the years by several families, and today houses a business establishment at the corner of North Candler and Sycamore. [6]

Willard recalled that Ned Mullally had a grocery store on the corner between Simpson and Phipps's tavern and Alexander Corry's house, known later as the J. L. Williams house. Nathan Yarbrough clerked for a merchant named Smith. Green B. Butler had a store in 1827, and Thomas A. Sullivan clerked for him. Jesse Franklin Cleveland's fine two-story house later was the "temple" of the Free

Masons. Cleveland was the state senator from DeKalb in the early years, as well as postmaster. He was later elected U. S. representative from DeKalb. Cleveland married the daughter of James Smith of Clinton, Ga. and died at the young age of 37. [7]

Ezekiel Mason got his start in business clerking for G. W. Butler. He worked his way up to being Butler's partner, then struck out on his own. "He was from South Carolina and many old friends from that state patronized him." Not lacking in wealth, Mason owned farms and mills in DeKalb and was on the building committee of Decatur Presbyterian Church, contributing liberally to the fund. News was not always good for Mason, however. The early fire that started in Reuben Cone's hotel destroyed Mason's building and threatened a good part of Decatur before it was extinguished. Mason also was one of the incorporators of the ill-fated Atlanta Bank in 1852. [8]

Lemma Kirkley operated a hotel at his house; in 1826 he sold it to Simpson and Phipps for $1500, a large sum for those days. "They carried on business until the first of January 1827, when they caved in. James Simpson remained and paid the debts. John Phipps removed to the Creek nation and it was said married there." Simpson also ran a tavern and boarding house where hotel was. Later N. N. Smith bought the building as a residence. Still later it was the home of William Ezzard. George Tomlinson operated a boarding house next east of the Simpson-Smith-Ezzard house. [9]

Decatur's "High House," so called because of its location, is said to have been built in 1830. (DeKalb Historical Society)

James Hutchinson Kirkpatrick, thought to be the first native-born Irishman to settle in DeKalb, came from Morgan County, Ga. in 1827. At the time of his death in 1853, he had one of the largest estates in DeKalb County history, including thousands of acres west of Decatur that would come to be called the Kirkwood community. Kirkpatrick's estate was valued by appraisers Ezekiel Mason, Joseph Pitts, Joseph F. Clay and L. S. Morgan, at $11,157, excluding land, but including 11 slaves. Kirkpatrick and his wife, Jane Parks, had five sons: Hugh P., John L. (a preacher), William N, James W. and Thomas M., and a daughter, Jane, wife of Joseph Morgan. [10]

Reuben Cone, an early justice of the Inferior Court, built the first hotel in Decatur. Cone's parents and brothers also came to Decatur. The elder Cone was remembered by Willard as a Universalist who loved to argue and who owned two distinctive horses. One Cone claimed had been ridden by Gen. Packenham at the Battle of New Orleans in 1815. The other, named Spot, had sailed stormy seas and would rock back and forth in his stall during rain storms.

Mason D. Shumate rented and operated the hotel built by Reuben Cone, and was Decatur's first tavern-keeper. The fire on October 30, 1846 burned Cone's house, the hotel, Akins's store, the Chewning house and the corner post office, but Shumate's house was spared because the occupants placed wet blankets on the roof.[11] Judge Cone went on to marry Mason Shumate's oldest daughter, Lucinda, and moved to Atlanta where he and Ammi Williams owned much of the land on which the town would be built. A Connecticut native, Cone died in 1851. The Cones had one daughter, Harriett, who married Julius A. Hayden.[12]

Born in Fauquier County, Va. in 1764, Mason Shumate came to Decatur in 1824 with his wife, Nancy Gatewood, and their family. He later moved from town to a "plantation" a mile west of town. One of the founders of Decatur Presbyterian Church, he was considered an "intelligent, well read man in a day when the latter attribute was comparatively rare." He died on June 28, 1849 at the age of 85, and is buried in Decatur Cemetery.

The nine children of Mason and Nancy Shumate are "all worthy of note." Joseph D. Shumate married Amelia Montgomery, daughter of James McC. Montgomery of Standing Peachtree. Hariet Shumate married Judge Alexander Corry, another Decatur pioneer and early Atlantan. Berryman D. Shumate was an elder of the First Presbyterian Church of Atlanta. Sarah Shumate married Jesse C. Farrar. Cynthia Shumate married Daniel Stone, longtime clerk of the DeKalb Superior and Inferior courts. Elizabeth Shumate married E. G. Adams, an early Decatur merchant, who later moved his family to Mississippi. Benjamin Franklin Shumate was a substantial farmer in the Clarkston area. Eliza Shumate married John Glen; they moved to Atlanta where John worked for the Georgia Railroad and was mayor of the city in 1855.[13]

At the time of his death, Mason Shumate was a "moderately prosperous" citizen. His house and lot in Decatur, appraised at $420, was purchased on January 1, 1850 by James M. Calhoun for $520. His 16 slaves, more than most DeKalb citizens owned, were worth $7,162.

Shumate's estate was appraised on July 9, 1849 by Ezekiel Mason, William F. Chewning, T. B. George, Joseph A. Reeves and W. A. David.

Inventory

Cash found in hand, the property of deceased	$ 18.30
House and lot, late residence of deceased	420.00
Frances Sophia, a mulatto girl	505.00
Rosella, a Negro woman and her child, Savannah	650.00
Mary, a mulatto woman	620.00
Mary Emily, a black girl	230.00
Caroline, a mulatto girl	575.00
Elvira, a black girl	470.00
Minerva, a mulatto girl	430.00
Eli, a mulatto boy	590.00
Frances Isabella, a girl	371.00
Mary Loduska, a girl	261.00
Adaline and her child, John Albert	775.00
Felix, a mulatto boy	670.00
Emaline, a mulatto woman	560.00
Huldah, a girl	455.00
One yoke oxen	25.00
One cow and calf	10.00
One cow and calf	10.00

One sorrel filly	69.00
One lot stock hogs, 17 head	40.00
One small wagon	40.00
One lot kitchen furniture	6.50
One lot farming tools	7.00
One man's saddle	3.00
One spinning wheel and reel	3.00
3 featherbeds, 1 bedstead and bed furniture	30.00
1 Pattent (sic) clock	3.00
1 cupboard	3.00
1 lot crockery and glassware in the cupboard	1.00
1 pr. shovels and tongs and irons and candlesticks	.50
1 sideboard and chest and looking glass	3.00
1 walnut folding table	3.00
10 split bottom chairs @ 25 cents each	2.50
20 pieces bacon, 200 lbs.	13.00
1 Georgia hand loom	1.50

His estate also included promissory notes on several of his relatives and fellow Decatur citizens: B. F. Shumate, Mary A. Tipton, John Glen, William Roberts, Young Moore, Reuben Cone, James M. Holley, Jesse J. Jones, Moses W. Formwalt, Allison Nelson, Isham Cain, Joseph D. Shumate, C. W. McGinnis, J. V. Jones, Levi Simpson, James Grant and Allen Hardman. [14]

James Kirkpatrick was probably the first tanner in Decatur, according to Willard. Later came Walter Wadsworth. When Wadsworth first came to Decatur in 1827, he was employed by Eskew and Reece as a journeyman tinner (not tanner). During the Union army's occupation of Decatur during the Civil War, Willard recalled, "soldiers supplied themselves with what tin vessels they wanted, without money and without price." A native of Hartford Conn., Wadsworth was well known as a traveling salesman, whose kitchen utensils sold far and wide. Wadsworth's Tin Plant was located at the corner of now Ponce de Leon Avenue and Church Street. And, a Mr. Seay made stills by pounding sheet copper and annoyed the neighborhood "with a noise worse than hotel gongs." John and David M. Simpson made carriages in a shop on the northeast corner of the Square, but could not compete with northern manufacturers, so they closed up shop and moved to Atlanta. Joseph Shaw was Decatur's shoemaker; later Richard Gettins took over his clientele. [15]

George D. Anderson studied blacksmithing under the Rev. Alexander Kirkpatrick, but was not destined to remain a laborer. He later became a lawyer and solicitor general of the Coweta Circuit and judge of the Superior Court in the Cherokee Circuit.

Levi Willard recalled that young men, especially young lawyers, were plentiful in Decatur, while marriageable young women were scarce. If young men like William Ezzard, G. D. Anderson, Joseph Thompson and Charles Murphey wanted to go a-courtin', they had to ride out the Shallow Ford Trail or the Rock Bridge Road to the outlying communities.

Willard remembered these early marriages: William Ezzard and Sophia Lane, G. D. Anderson and Jane Dickson, Capt. Fowler and Harriet Towers, Judge Bryce and a Miss Heard, Judge John W. Hooper and Sarah Word, William Latimer and Elizabeth Word, C. J. Hooper and Jane Word, Col. Murphey and Eliza Word, Mary Word and a Col. Johnson from Cass County, Anne Kirkpatrick and a Mr. Shaw,

Robert Jones and a Miss McGinnis, Roxana Hodges and Allen Lovelace and Martha J. Cooper and Wilson Edwards.

Not all of the romantic outings had happy endings, however. Ann H. Stone was riding in a carriage with John C. White, when the horses "took fright and ran." The buggy's dashboard gave way, sending White to the ground, and he lost the reins. Stone was thrown (or jumped), her clothing caught, and she was dragged to the Square, where she died. Dr. Thomas W. Alexander also was killed when thrown from a carriage in Decatur. [16]

"The facilities for transporting goods from market were not so great as now," Willard wrote. "Augusta was our grocery market and goods were hauled in wagons. Freight varied according to the scarcity of wagons and the conditions of the roads, from $1.25 to $2 per hundred pounds. Not only were our freight facilities heavy and inconvenient, but our mail accommodations were calculated to exhaust our patience. Our northern mail came once a week and our southern mail the same way. There was a one-horse mail from Lawrenceville to Fayetteville once a week. To meet a bank note in Augusta, it was necessary to mail the money at least a week before it fell due.

He generally rode to Augusta on horseback, as there was no public conveyance, some two or three making it convenient to go together, taking our saddle bags -- one side for a change of clothing and the other for lunch and a flask of gin, rum or brandy; nor was it necessary to hide it, for it was considered a mark of disrespect to pass one by without offering. Ministers going to associations, would, like other travelers, supply themselves with ardent spirits for the journey.

"One company would start from Decatur after breakfast and travel all day with but little halting. As it was four days' ride the distance was divided into four equal parts as was practicable, generally reaching Todd's, seven miles below Covington, the first day. The second day would carry us three or four miles below Greensboro, to Ellison's or to Hart's, and the third day to old man Dursey's, a Quaker, who lived in Columbia County. We reached Augusta the fourth day. It was necessary to remain two or three days or more to make purchases and to load up wagons, and then we spent four days more in getting home.

"If anything should be wanting to make out a load, a few sacks of salt were put in, as salt was always worth the cost and freight.

"For the novelty of the affair," Willard said he once went from Augusta to Decatur with the wagons, sleeping on sacks of salt in the wagon, "but it was more tedious than on horseback.

"Goods were sold at a large per cent in Decatur, but on long credit. Fashions did not change so often as they do now. But few fine goods were in demand in 1826. Blue and white calico, red flannel and apron checks were in demand. Six or seven yards of calico made a dress, and no necessity for frills, ruffles, overskirts or trails. In 1834, I recollect that for a short space, and by a very few, shorty dresses -- not bloomers -- were worn. The reason I remember the date is that Miss Cooley, the teacher, wore a dress reaching nearly to the ankles and that was the year she taught. A boy who went to Augusta in 1830 said that he saw `a girl in Augusta with breeches on' -- having seen a miss wearing pantalets, not worn then in his neighborhood." [17]

Widening Indian trails into wagon roads and building new roads and bridges were at the top of the agenda for the DeKalb Inferior Court in the early days of the new county. Of particular priority was access to the new county town of Decatur.

In March, 1825, the Inferior Court ordered "that there be a bridge built across the South river where the Henry road cross #10 in 15th dist. (the Decatur-McDonough Road)." William Terry, Mathew Henry, Zachariah Lee, Augustin Young and Silas Poole were appointed "to view and mark line from from Newton County line on to John Pounds."

In May, the court ordered that a road be cut "from Decatur to Peachtree Creek in lot #56 and running through #57 crossing Peachtree on lot #102 thence on to William Bruce's, and a bridge to be made over Peachtree Creek (east of the Decatur water works in 1954)."

William A. Corry was authorized by the court on May 3, 1825 "to turn the road around their plantation on the nearest and most suitable ground intersecting the Ala. road at James B. Broughton provided they cut the new road as good as the old." [18]

John Morris was one of the county's "overseers of the poor" in 1825; in March, the Inferior Court ordered the court clerk to pay Morris $25 "for the use of the poor." [19]

DeKalb County supported John Clarke against George Troup, the "state's rights" candidate, in the 1825 governor's race. Although Troup won the statewide race, James Montomgery, a Troup supporter, was replaced by Lochlin Johnson, who was in Clarke's camp. Politics, dominated by the question of Indian removal, continued to be a hot topic for the remaining years of the 1820s. The county's next two state senators -- Tully Choice and William Ezzard -- were Troup men, followed by Jesse F. Cleveland and Jonathan B. Wilson, who sided with Clarke. [20]

The names of 26 DeKalb citizens were chosen to make up the 1825 DeKalb County jury list:

Joshua Broughton	Thomas Grogan	James D. Thompson
Elias Campbell	Thomas Harris	Ransom Thompson
Jonathan Childs	George Heard Jr.	Benjamin Waldrop
Joseph Crockett Sr.	George Heard Sr.	Jonathan Williams
John Davenport	John Lawson	Stephen Williams
Samuel Dobbs	William W. Maloney	William Williams
Alvin T. Foans	Richard G. Mayo	William Wilson
Brurill A. Gober	Benjamin Parrimore	Joseph Woodrough [21]
James Goodwin	Aaron Roberts	

With pioneer settlers building the county town literally from the ground up, carpenters and other craftsmen were in great demand in Decatur in the early years.

Robert Jones was considered the "patriarch of carpenters," and his father, Edward Jones, was a "respected citizen" who had held several offices in Baptist organizations and was president of the DeKalb County Bible Society. William Nimmons built the house that was later purchased by trustees from Isaac N. Johnson for the Decatur Female Academy. David Wright and Henry Mitchell built Clark and Willard's storehouse in 1827. Littleberry Harris and his brother-in-law, Charles Murphey, built the house next west of Dr. Durham's, which was known during the Civil War as Dr. Holmes' residence.

There were several practitioners of the medical arts in DeKalb during the county's first years. Sometimes, Willard recalled, their medicines could be worse than the disease they were supposed to cure. The most common ailments were malaria, bilious fever, pleurisy, pelagra, hookworm, yellow fever and smallpox. The average life span was 28 years. [22]

A Dr. Hopkins was Decatur's first physician, opening his practice in 1826, but he soon left town. Ormand L. Morgan succeeded Dr. Hopkins, but died suddenly in 1826. He was the second person buried in Decatur Cemetery, the first being a small child.

Dr. Ezekiel N. Calhoun opened a practice in 1826 or '27, with his partner, Dr. Joseph Thompson. Born in the Abbeville District of South Carolina, Calhoun rode on horseback from his home on the Savannah River to Philadelphia to attend Jefferson Medical School. He is thought to have graduated in 1823 from the University of Pennsylvania School of Medicine. He and his wife, Lucy B. Wellborn, raised nine children in Decatur: John C., twin daughters Georgia and Carolina, Virginia, Indiana, Missouri, Louisiana, Florida and Edward Pickens. Two daughters died in infancy. The family moved to Atlanta in 1854. Dr. Calhoun died in 1875 and is buried in Oakland Cemetery. He practiced almost 30 years in DeKalb. [23]

Decatur received a new citizen about this time in James M. Calhoun, 18, recently orphaned, who came from the Abbeville District of South Carolina to live with his older brother, the physician. After two years at the Decatur Academy, James studied law and was admitted to the bar. In 1832 he married Emma Eliza Dabney; they had eight children, one of whom, William Lowndes Calhoun, was mayor of Atlanta. Calhoun served as both a state representative and a state senator before moving to Atlanta in 1852. [24]

"Dr. Calhoun's practice was what might be called the heroic. It did not lack stamina," Willard said. "Calomel (mercury), quinine, capsicum (red pepper), camphor and opium combined, formed what he called `the black dose.' He gave me `the black dose' four nights in succession. I was prostrated, he said, by disease. I thought it was by medicine administered to break up typhus or typhoid fever. I was black-dosed, salivated, and had five blisters on me at once. The doctor was of the opinion that it took all of these medicines to cure me."

Joseph Thompson was no. 22 on the list of applicants to the Georgia Board of Physicians in Milledgeville in 1826. Once president of the Atlanta Medical College, he later became a hotel-keeper, and soon was "extensively and favorably known" for his Globe Hotel in Decatur and later his Atlanta Hotel. Born in the Greenville District of South Carolina on September 29, 1777, he moved to Decatur as a young man.

Thompson was a friend and admirer of Mary Ann Tomlinson Young, wife of David Young. Thompson treated Young, who was a victim of typhoid fever; Young died of the disease on September 8, 1828. Thompson later married the widow. The couple moved to Atlanta in 1845 where they raised several children. Among them were Mary Jane (Mrs. Richard Peters); George Harvey Thompson, first captain of the Gate City Guard of Atlanta; Julia Caroline (Mrs. William Priestley Orme); Joseph Thompson, Jr.; and Joan (Mrs. Thomas M. Clarke). Mary Ann Thompson died at the birth of her last child, a son, on April 23, 1849.

The Calhoun-Jones house was built on the Square in Decatur in the 1830s by Dr. Ezekiel N. Calhoun, one of DeKalb's first physicians. The house later became the home of the Hal C. Jones family. The house was torn down in 1905. (DeKalb Historical Society)

The unfortunate attorney, David Young, who was born on June 22, 1802, is buried in one of the oldest graves in Decatur Cemetery. [25]

Dr. Chapman Powell was said to be best-liked doctor in DeKalb County. "Many preferred his medicine because the first requisite was a gallon of whiskey in which to mix the pulverized roots and herbs, for Dr. Powell was bordering on the vegetarian scheme, so far as medicine was concerned."

Thomas Ray, called "The Lobelia Doctor," practiced medicine in addition to his job as a carpenter. He also was a justice of the Inferior Court in DeKalb. Ray lived on a hill on the Atlanta road where he cultivated a patch of lobelia to use in his treatments. Long after Ray had left Decatur, Preacher Singleton's wife gathered wild greens where the lobelia had grown. After eating the greens, she "sickened and died in great distress. Dr. E. N. Calhoun said the lobelia had caused her death." [26]

Drs. George B. Wood and Franklin Bache wrote in 1851 in The Dispensatory of the United States of America that lobelia was effective in the treatment of asthma and bronchitis, but should always be used with caution because of the serious effects of overdosing, described as "extreme prostratin, great anxiety and distress, and ultimately death preceded by convulsions." Neltje Blanchan, in Vol. 9 of the 1900 series, The Nature Library, is not nearly so restrained when commenting on Lobelia Inflata: "The most stupid of the lower animals knows enough to let this poisonous, acrid plant alone; but not so man, who formerly made a quack medicine from it in the days when a drug that set one's internal organism on fire was supposed to be especially beneficial. One taste of the plant gives a realizing sense of its value as an emetic."

Other early physicians in DeKalb were a Dr. Niles who practiced near Rockbridge, Dr. Avary in the Panthersville District, Dr. George K. Hamilton, Dr. P. F. Hoyle who was also a justice of the Inferior Court and master of the Pythagoras Lodge, Drs. Frank and N. S. Liddell, Dr. Hilliard J. Fowler and Dr. John Fall, a "root and herb practitioner" and son of Dr. Calvin J. Fall, who was considered a more scientific doctor. [27]

"The county was considered very healthy," Willard said, "until improvements began to be made, such as deadening trees to stand decaying, falling trees into the creeks to get rid of the trouble of cutting them up, raising mill ponds without clearing the ground of timber and other ways of obstructing the free course of the water. Thus malaria was produced, causing fevers of more or less malignity, according to the exposure.

"In 1838 there were cases of what was called bilious fever. Dr. Calhoun said it was the most insidious disease he had to treat. It sometimes commenced with a cough, sometimes with dysentery, with other patients it commenced with a slight pain in the back, with little appearance of fever. If cases of this kind were suffered to run without attention for two or three days, by the fifth or the sixth day the extremities became cold and death ensued almost without apprehension of danger. Others were in extreme agony before death." [28]

Doctors apparently tried almost any remedy at their disposal to try and cure bilious fever. Dr. Joseph G. Richardson, in the 1909 Home Health Society tome, "Health and Longevity," recommended a combination of antacids, purgatives and laxatives, including, but certainly not limited to, calomel, citrate of magnesia, quinine, balladonna and common lemon juice.

Dr. J. Calvin Weaver, author of a treatise entitled "A Preview of One Hundred Years of Medicine in DeKalb County," said that 84 physicians practiced in DeKalb during the county's first 100 years of existence.

Among the notables on Weaver's list were:

• Thomas Holley Chivers, who practiced medicine for two years at Crawfordville, Ga., before quitting to write poetry and moving to Decatur.

• Philip Burford, a North Carolina native who moved to Wilkes County, Ga. in the early 1800s, and then to DeKalb in about 1832. He was the great-grandfather of Dr. W. T. McCurdy of Stone Mountain, whose son Dr. Willis T. McCurdy practiced in Stone Mountain in 1952.

• Daniel Roscoe Chupp, one of triplets born in 1832 to Jacob and Betsy Chupp, who died in Lithonia on November 2, 1900. He and his wife, Mary King, who died in 1876, had six children.

• Chupp's friend W. P. Bond, also born in 1832, a farmer and state senator from DeKalb's District 34.

Bond read medicine under Dr. Reagan of Lithonia for two years, then attended Georgia Medical College in Augusta. While a senator, he helped pass a bill to enlarge and improve the state Hospital for the Insane in Milledgeville. He died on July 14, 1898 and is buried in Rock Chapel Methodist Church cemetery.

A Partial List of DeKalb County Doctors and Physicians -- 1822-1865

James F. Alexander, 1824
N. L. Angier, elected to Board of Health, Atlanta, 1848
Thomas Austin (1784-1852), owned the first brick dwelling in Atlanta
James C. Avery (1818-1875)
Addison Bell, licensed in 1853
Stephen Biggers
Benjamin F. Bomar
W. P. Bond
Augustus H. Brandley (1844-1934)
Philip H. Burford (1774-1862)
John Julius Byrd (1821-1844)
Andrew B. Calhoun, licensed in 1831
E. N. Calhoun (1799-1875)
Thomas Holley Chivers, 1858
Daniel Roscoe Chupp (1832-1900)
Henry G. Collier (1820-1850)
C. W. Crymes, licensed in 1829
Noel D'Alvigny
W. C. Daniel, 1861
---- Darnell, mentioned in 1826 records
Mathew Estes, licensed in 1829
Calvin J. Fall
John S. Fall, 1826
George Newton Flowers (1837-1917)
Hilliard J. Fowler
Joshua Gilbert, graduated in 1845
William Gilbert
J. L. Hamilton, Medical Association of Georgia, 1859
N. G. Hilburn
---- Hopkins
Peter F. Hoyle (1779-1864)
B. O. Jones
Frank Liddell
N. S. Liddell
F. Jeter Martin
Asbury Smith Mayson
W. C. Moor, Medical Association of Georgia, 1861
Ormond L. Morgan
---- Niles
Chapman Powell, 1826
---- Ray,
Bartrim M. Smith, licensed in 1851

George G. Smith, 1847
S. S. Smith
Joseph Thompson, 1826
---- Wildman, 1836
T. C. H. Wilson, 1849
James J. Winn, the youngest surgeon in the Confederate Army. [29]

Fees for doctors in 1829 was one of the topics in George Slappey's unpublished "History of DeKalb County," which he wrote in 1957:

Mileage in the day	$0.50
Visit	$1.00
Admonition	$1.00
Prescription	$1.00
Mileage in the night	$1.00
All doses of medicine	$0.25
Powders, per dozen	$1.00 to $2.00
Extracting a tooth	$1.00
In midwifery, presentations	$10.00 [30]

The Decatur City Cemetery has been used continuously since 1826, although it was not incorporated by the Georgia legislature until December 22, 1832. The first commissioners of "the Decatur Burial Ground" were James Anderson, James Lemon, Robert Jones, Thomas Stephens and Jonathan B. Wilson. [31]

The 7.5-acre cemetery contains the graves of Revolutionary War soldiers, Decatur pioneers and city and county government officials. The cemetery was the scene of a skirmish that was part of the Civil War Battle of Atlanta on July 22, 1864. Some 124 Confederate soldiers are buried throughout the cemetery. A plaque at the gate reads: "July 22, 1864. This cemetery was the scene of an engagement between 8th Confederate Cavalry, Col. J. S. Prather, commanding, and a large force of Federal troops. The latter were repulsed and 225 prisoners taken." The styles of markers vary from rough fieldstone to ornate Victorian cemetery art. A wooden wellhouse and fieldstone entry gates were built about 1881. The wellhouse has always been a popular trysting spot. "Young couples in the pre-automobile age would take Sunday afternoon walks in the cemetery and then without a thought of the hard wooden benches, gather at the Well House for congenial conversation." [32]

At first, the cemetery was not planned. "The first lots were on the high ground then, when these were filled, more lots were added by building circular roads around the sides of the hill. As a consequence the cemetery now has five irregular tiers of lots, each with retaining walls of Stone Mountain granite." The arrangement is haphazard, with narrow dirt roads and walkways, distinctive graves and monuments, and the numerous trees of oak, elm, holly, cedar, magnolia, dogwood and boxwood. [33]

Among those buried at Decatur are:
• Civil War heroine Mary A. H. Gay, her mother and her sister.

• Benjamin Franklin Swanton, Swanton's son John, John's wife, his spinster daughter and his daughter's beau from Macon, W. B. Moses, who died while visiting the Swantons.

• Donald Fraser, Decatur Presbyterian Church pastor, and one of the organizers of the Donald Fraser High School for boys.

• Ed Cox and Robert A. Alston, who fought duel over the state's convict labor system.

• Agnes Scott College benefactor and businessman George W. Scott and his wife, Rebecca. Their tombstones simply record their birth and death dates: February 22, 1829-October 3, 1903 (George) and May 20, 1834-July 12, 1899 (Rebecca).

• Charles M. Murphey, DeKalb's pro-Union delegate to the Secession Convention. Marble for his monument, described by some as the handsomest in the cemetery, ran the blockade during the Civil War. The inscription on the monument reads: "In memory of Hon. Charles Murphey. Born, May 9th, 1799. Died, January 16th, 1861. Wise as a legislator, conservative as a statesman, he won early in life the confidence of his countrymen, which he held uninterrupted and unshaken to the day of his death. Kind as a neighbor, honest and reliable as a counselor, he never failed to receive upon all occasions the warm support of a large majority of his fellow-citizens of DeKalb County. In the more intimate relations of parent and master, indulgent to a fault, he was loved almost to admiration. In affectionate remembrance of his many deeds of love and kindness, his only surviving daughter has placed this monument over his remains." Murphey is buried on the highest point of ground in the cemetery.

• Eliza Murphey Candler, Charles Murphey's only daughter, and Eliza's husband, Milton A. Candler, who also was a U. S. representative from DeKalb. Candler's stone is inscribed as follows: "Milton A. Candler. January 11, 1837. August 8, 1909. `And I heard a voice from heaven saying unto me, Write, Blessed are the dead which die in the Lord...' Rev. 14:13."

• Milton Candler Jr., son of Eliza and Milton Candler, and his wife, Nellie Scott, daughter of George W. Scott, and Charles Murphey Candler Sr., son of Eliza and Milton Candler, who married Nellie Scott's sister, Mary.

• "Bukumba, our little black pal of the white soul. Born Kasai District, Belgian Congo, Africa." Bakumba, the hunchback daughter of an African chief, had been employed in Africa by a missionary, Mrs. Motte Martin, as a nurse for Mrs. Martin's baby boy. Bakumba returned to Decatur with the Martin family, where she sang Presbyterian hymns in her native African language. Bakumba died in the influenza epidemic of 1920.

• Eleanor and Charles Latimer, parents of Rebecca Latimer Felton, the first female U. S. senator, adn Rebecca's sister Mary Latimer McLendon. [34]

• The oldest known birth date in the cemetery belongs to Ann Reynolds, consort of Francis Reynolds, who was born on April 28, 1750, and died on February 16, 1827. [35]

• Many familiar Decatur family names can be found there, including Adams, Anderson, Ansley, Barry, Blount, Bryce, Burgess, Clarke, Cofer, Guess, Houston, Howard, Kirkpatrick, McCoy, Marshall, Mason, Medlock, Morgan, Ramspeck, Sams, Scott, Shumate, Towers, Williams, Willard and Word.

In the "Orphan's Home Lot" there are 13 small unmarked graves, plus the last resting place for these children: May David, Comer Paine, Minnie Hughes, Madge Grice, Nettie Hickman, Mattie Cramers,

Effie Littleton, Andrew Hickman, Mary Benton, Ethel Hayes, Elizabeth Reed, Janie Parks, Pearl Malley, Willie Harris, Viola Harris and John Harris. [36]

The Decatur Cemetery Book, kept at Decatur City Hall, gives the names, ages, dates of burial and lot numbers of all burials since 1879. In addition, each entry records the cause of death.

Many women died as a result of pregnancy, during childbirth and miscarriages and due to other complications. "Countless babies and children are listed with the causes of death given as: croup, diptheria, grip, whooping cough, menengitis, measles, convulsions, teething (resulting in death from malnutrition), thrush (an ulcerous disease of the inner lining of the mouth, usually caused by lack of cleanliness, which could spread to the throat and esophagus and be fatal) and other troubles."

Adult deaths were caused by remittant fever, typhoid fever (especially the epidemic of 1884), brain fever, pneumonia, locked bowels, general debility, consumption (a frequent cause), "rising in the head," cancer, rheumatism, spasms, scrofula, paralysis, hives, nervous prostration, gradual emaciation, small pox, cholera morbus, "complications" and many others. "The diagnosis entitled, "complications," must have been most convenient to the good doctor of the day who was doing his best with practically no equipment and only a limited medical education." The Cemetery Book also lists "death by fire... drank poison by mistake... killed by railroad cars... stab wound in heart... suicide... drank laudanum through mistake... poisoned at guano mill... killed in riot of Dec. 8, 1889... killed in street car accident.... accidentally shot himself.... drank cold water while overheated... kicked by a horse... and alcoholic poison (bad liquor)."

Cemetery resident "Thomas Ford fell from the veranda of Mrs. Cox's at 2 1/2 o'clock in the night. Was afflicted with consumption, dropsy, heart disease and was a confirmed inebriate."

The body of a newborn child buried in the cemetery was found in a well. It is not known whether the infant was the same as the one belonging to "Laura B. On the night of Nov. 2, 1882, Laura B--- gave birth to an illegitimate child and she and her mother killed it the next morning. Both were indicted and tried in the DeKalb Superior Court." The fate of "Laura B." and her mother is unknown. [37]

Decatur Cemetery sexton O. M. Word was paid a salary of $5 month, plus $20 year for materials in 1881. Lots at that time were priced according to elevation. Lots on the first tier sold for 20 cents per "front foot," and were scaled down to 10 cents on fifth tier. Lots also were given by the city government "by prescription" to people who could not afford them.

"The most distinguished person found in the cemetery book," wrote Percy Plant, "is Thomas Holley Chivers, Decatur's remarkable poet, physician, inventor and portrait painter. He wrote wierd, mystical poetry and was a friend of Edgar Allen Poe. It has never been definitely determined whether Poe used Chivers' style and meter, whether Chivers plagarized Poe, or whether the friends exchanged ideas and thoughts along similar lines." The cause of death listed for Chivers is "died in the asylum." His marble box tomb is topped with a draped urn. The inscription reads: "here lie the remains of Thomas H. Chivers, M. D. Of his excellence as a lyric poet, his works will remain a monument for ages after this temporary tribute of love is in dust forgotten. This soul winged its flight Heavenward, December 19th, 1858. Aged 52 years." The poet-physician's wife, Harriett, who died in 1881, is buried nearby, as is their son, Thomas H. Chivers Jr., who died in 1892. [38]

Chapter 14 Notes

1. Garrett, Franklin M., 1954, 1969, Atlanta and Environs -- A Chronicle of Its People and Events, Vol. 1, pages 15-16.

2. Willard, Levi, 1920, "The Early History of Decatur Written Many Years Ago," DeKalb New Era.

3. Willard, Levi, 1920, "The Early History of Decatur Written Many Years Ago," DeKalb New Era. Garrett, Franklin M., 1954, 1969, Atlanta and Environs -- A Chronicle of Its People and Events, Vol. 1, page 372.

4. Willard, Levi, 1920, "The Early History of Decatur Written Many Years Ago," DeKalb New Era.

5. Jones, John Carrol, 1997, personal collection. Harris, Joel Chandler, Memoirs of Georgia, Vol. 1, 1895, page 505.

6. Willard, Levi, 1920, "The Early History of Decatur Written Many Years Ago," DeKalb New Era. Nix, Dorothy, Spring, 1980, "Some of Decatur's Lovely Old Homes," Georgia Life magazine.

7. Willard, Levi, 1920, "The Early History of Decatur Written Many Years Ago," DeKalb New Era.

8. Willard, Levi, 1920, "The Early History of Decatur Written Many Years Ago," DeKalb New Era. Garrett, Franklin M., 1954, 1969, Atlanta and Environs -- A Chronicle of Its People and Events, Vol. 1, page 346.

9. Willard, Levi, 1920, "The Early History of Decatur Written Many Years Ago," DeKalb New Era.

10. Willard, Levi, 1920, "The Early History of Decatur Written Many Years Ago," DeKalb New Era. Garrett, Franklin M., 1954, 1969, Atlanta and Environs -- A Chronicle of Its People and Events, Vol. 1, page 65.

11. Willard, Levi, 1920, "The Early History of Decatur Written Many Years Ago," DeKalb New Era.

12. Garrett, Franklin M., 1954, 1969, Atlanta and Environs -- A Chronicle of Its People and Events, Vol. 1, pages 335-336.

13. Garrett, Franklin M., 1954, 1969, Atlanta and Environs -- A Chronicle of Its People and Events, Vol. 1, pages 44-46.

14. Garrett, Franklin M., 1954, 1969, Atlanta and Environs -- A Chronicle of Its People and Events, Vol. 1, pages 45-46.

15. Willard, Levi, 1920, "The Early History of Decatur Written Many Years Ago," DeKalb New Era. Garrett, Franklin M., 1954, 1969, Atlanta and Environs -- A Chronicle of Its People and Events, Vol. 1, page 65. Hudgins, Carl T., 1952, "Mills and Other Early DeKalb County Industries (And Their Owners)," The Collections of the DeKalb Historical Society, Vol. 1, page 16.

16. Willard, Levi, 1920, "The Early History of Decatur Written Many Years Ago," DeKalb New Era.

17. Willard, Levi, 1920, "The Early History of Decatur Written Many Years Ago," DeKalb New Era.

18. Garrett, Franklin M., 1954, 1969, Atlanta and Environs -- A Chronicle of Its People and Events, Vol. 1, pages 52-53.

19. Garrett, Franklin M., 1954, 1969, Atlanta and Environs -- A Chronicle of Its People and Events, Vol. 1, page 53.

20. Garrett, Franklin M., 1954, 1969, Atlanta and Environs -- A Chronicle of Its People and Events, Vol. 1, page 65.

21. Garrett, Franklin M., 1954, 1969, Atlanta and Environs -- A Chronicle of Its People and Events, Vol. 1, page 53.

22. Clarke, Caroline McKinney, 1973, 1997, The Story of Decatur 1823-1899, page 10.

23. Weaver, J. Calvin, M. D., 1952, "A Preview of One Hundred Years of Medicine in DeKalb County, Georgia," The Collections of the DeKalb Historical Society -- the Yearbook, Vol. 1.

24. Garrett, Franklin M., 1954, 1969, Atlanta and Environs -- A Chronicle of Its People and Events, Vol. 1, page 77. Pioneer Citizens' History of Atlanta, pages 269-270, 289-291.

25. Weaver, J. Calvin, M. D., 1952, "A Preview of One Hundred Years of Medicine in DeKalb County, Georgia," The Collections of the DeKalb Historical Society -- the Yearbook, Vol. 1. Willard, Levi, 1920, "The Early History of Decatur Written Many Years Ago," DeKalb New Era. Garrett, Franklin M., 1954, 1969, Atlanta and Environs -- A Chronicle of Its People and Events, Vol. 1, pages 58, 66 and 110.

26. Willard, Levi, 1920, "The Early History of Decatur Written Many Years Ago," DeKalb New Era.

27. Willard, Levi, 1920, "The Early History of Decatur Written Many Years Ago," DeKalb New Era.

28. Willard, Levi, 1920, "The Early History of Decatur Written Many Years Ago," DeKalb New Era.

29. Weaver, J. Calvin, M. D., 1952, "A Preview of One Hundred Years of Medicine in DeKalb County, Georgia," The Collections of the DeKalb Historical Society -- the Yearbook, Vol. 1.

30. Nix, Dorothy, personal collection, DeKalb Historical Society.

31. Plant, Percy, January 3, 1963, "Decatur Cemetery Is Silent Recorder of History's March -- Fading Stones Recount Triumphs Trials of City," DeKalb New Era.

32. Sanders, Gayle, November 27, 1983, untitled, unpublished manuscript, DeKalb Historical Society. Plant, Percy, January 3, 1963, "Decatur Cemetery Is Silent Recorder of History's March -- Fading Stones Recount Triumphs Trials of City," DeKalb New Era.

33. Plant, Percy, January 3, 1963, "Decatur Cemetery Is Silent Recorder of History's March -- Fading Stones Recount Triumphs Trials of City," DeKalb New Era.

34. Plant, Percy, January 3, 1963, "Decatur Cemetery Is Silent Recorder Of History's March -- Fading Stones Recount Triumphs, Trials of City," DeKalb New Era. Knight, Lucian Lamar, Georgia's Landmarks, Memorials and Legends, Vol. 2, Section III, pages 404-407.

35. Garrett, Franklin M., 1954, 1969, Atlanta and Environs -- A Chronicle of Its People and Events, Vol. 1, page 110.

36. Plant, Percy, January 3, 1963, "Decatur Cemetery Is Silent Recorder Of History's March -- Fading Stones Recount Triumphs, Trials of City," DeKalb New Era.

37. Plant, Percy, August-September, 1961, "The Cemetery Book," Georgia magazine, pages 23 and 46.

38. Plant, Percy, August-September, 1961, "The Cemetery Book," Georgia magazine, pages 23 and 46. Knight, Lucian Lamar, Georgia's Landmarks, Memorials and Legends, Vol. 2, Section III.

Chapter 15

*A*mong the early citizens of DeKalb County were two families who figured quite prominently in county history and whose impact and influence stretch across at least eight generations to modern-day DeKalb. More than 150 years after the arrival of their ancestors in the new county, descendants of these pioneers still live in DeKalb and the Atlanta area.

The Powell and Houston Families

Chapman Powell, said to be the most popular and financially successful of the early doctors in DeKalb, was born in Wake County, N. C. on August 10, 1798 to Moses Powell Jr. and Nancy Pope Powell. His family moved to Clarke County, Ga. about 1803. [1]

Powell married Elizabeth (Betsy) Hardman, the daughter of Uriah Hardman and Frances Chandler, on April 7, 1824 in Oglethorpe County, Ga. Betsy Hardman was born on February 11, 1799. She was the sister of Naman Hardman and William Hardman, who had already moved to DeKalb County. Naman was married to Chapman Powell's cousin Joicy Smith. William married Chapman Powell's sister, Sylvia. Naman and William were in DeKalb by 1823, where William was appointed a member of the first Inferior Court jury on July 19, and Naman a road commissioner on July 28. Chapman and Betsy soon followed the Hardman brothers to DeKalb, and Chapman began buying land in the vicinity of where the Shallow Ford Indian trail crossed the South Fork of Peachtree Creek.

The Powells arrived in DeKalb and were settled on Land Lot 61 by January 12, 1825. The Hardmans settled nearby. Chapman Powell later acquired all or part of Land Lots 51, 52, 58, 59, 60, all of which are located along Clairmont Road, near the South Peachtree Creek. Chapman built a small log cabin for his bride on Land Lot 51; the cabin later was moved to Land Lot 61, near the current intersection of now Clairmont and North Decatur Road, on the west side of Clairmont and the south side of North Decatur, near where Powell Lane runs into Clairmont.

"It must have taken two stout hearts to begin married life in a log cabin almost in a wilderness with

Indians roaming all about," said Dr. J. Calvin Weaver in his treatise, "One Hundred Years of Medicine in DeKalb County." [2]

The original cabin measured 20 by 40 feet, with a large fireplace at one end and four windows and a door on the lower floor. On that main floor, Chapman and Betsy Powell had their sleeping quarters, as well as the family's combined living, cooking and dining area. Their children slept in a loft, reached by a narrow stairway, which had a window at each end. It was from these loft windows that the children watched for Amanda's friend, Martha Bulloch to come to visit from her home in Roswell. Mittie Bulloch would grow up to be the mother of President Theodore Roosevelt. "The Powells must have rated socially as they all married into families in the high social stratas. They also listed prominent families as their friends, particularly the Bullochs of Roswell... When the Bullochs were in the vicinity of the Powell home, a footman would blow a trumpet at the top of the rise near the home, announcing their approach." [3]

The cabin was commonly called "The Medicine House," because it is thought that Dr. Powell practiced his trade from the dwelling. Powell family historian, George T. Powell Jr., however, contends that the good doctor probably had a separate building for seeing patients. The building was moved to Stone Mountain Park in 1964, and is currently a part of the park's Antebellum Complex, where it is displayed as slave quarters rather than the home of pioneer settlers. Park officials had the cabin cut down in size to make it "look more like a slave cabin." Built between 1825 and 1833, the cabin may be the oldest building in DeKalb County. [3] During its almost 40 years on Clairmont Road, the cabin occupied several sites, always on the property of a Powell descendant. A bronze tablet embedded in a granite boulder marks its original location, near 1218 Clairmont Road. The monument was presented in 1928 to the Baron DeKalb Chapter of the Daughters of the American Revolution by these Powell grandchildren: Mrs. Laura L. Gibbs, Mrs. Alice F. Billups, Mrs. E. E. Ripley and Dr. W. J. (Wash) Houston, all of Decatur. Mrs. John Montgomery, a regent of the Baron DeKalb Chapter, also was a granddaughter of Powell. [4]

One of Chapman Powell's daughters once said that her father was "proud to say all his children were born in his cabin." The Powells raised eight children in the one-room home: William Alfred, born March 5 1825; James Oliver, born December 16, 1826; John Jefferson, born July 25, 1828; Martha Ann (Jincie), born August 6, 1830; Amanda Katherine (Katie), born October 17, 1832; Leonard

---

[3] The question of the oldest house in DeKalb County may never be answered. The designation of the Solomon Goodwin House as "the oldest extant house" in DeKalb County is literally cast in bronze on a plaque in front of the house. The plaque, placed by the Georgia Historical Commission, says the house was built in 1831. Research conducted by Albert Martin Jr., a Goodwin descendant, shows that Solomon Goodwin did not arrive in DeKalb until 1837. The first evidence of Goodwins in DeKalb is a letter written by one of Solomon's son, John Harris Goodwin, in 1835. If the house was built in 1831, it may have been built by John Dobbs, from whom Solomon purchased the land in 1838. Until 1961, the Goodwin house stood a few hundred feet closer to the intersection of Peachtree and North Druid Hills roads. The distinction of the oldest house may belong to the cabin of Dr. Chapmon Powell, which is said to have been built in 1825. The cabin was moved from its original location on Clairmont Road to the antebellum complex at Stone Mountain Park. The structure, now called "Mammy's Cabin," is somewhat smaller that its original size. The Lyon House in south DeKalb is the oldest house occupied continuously by the same family. Parrie King Lyon, age 91, widow of George O. Lyon, lives in the house today. George's great-great-grandfather, Revolutionary War veteran Joseph Emanuel Lyon, built the log cabin that is now the kitchen portion of the house when he first settled on the banks of the South River. Family tradition holds that he arrived when the area was still Henry County. Several other houses still standing in DeKalb were said to have been built in the early years of DeKalb's existence, including the Biffle Cabin, the Thomas-Barber Cabin and the Johns House near Tucker, as well as several others. No conclusive evidence exists to document the construction dates of any of these structures.

Chapman, born May 6, 1835; Mary Jane Elizabeth (Mollie), born September 24, 1837; and George Washington Lindsey, born February 16, 1840.

Naman Hardman donated land west of the intersection of Clairmont and North Decatur roads in 1825 for a church named the Primitive Baptist Church of Christ at Hardman's, which was constituted on November 19, 1825. The church's original Presbytery consisted of John Bankston, James Hale, Isaiah Parker and William McDonald. Charter members were John Johnson, Jacob Williams, Joicy Hardman, William Towers, Nancy Lunceford, Lucrecy Parker, Thurza Williams, Sarah Williams, Mary T. Williams, Mary Williams and Sarah Towers. The Rev. Bedford Gunn may have been the first pastor. While not charter members, Chapman and Betsy Powell were early church leaders. Naman and Joicy Hardman left the church and moved to Cobb County in 1842, after selling their property to Chapman Powell. [5]

William Towers reported on November 19, 1825 in the church's Book of Record: "After ballading it was unanomosly desided that Bro. John Bankston was their choice as pastor." On May 22, 1830, Towers continued, Isaac N. Johnson, James Jones, D. Stone, Namon Hardman, Chatmon (sic) Powell and S. D. Durham met to discuss a church building. The group agreed to give Patsey Johnson $3 "for taking cear of the meeting house."

Church members held conferences to discipline members. Thomas Ray was found guilty of fornication and excommunicated on July 18, 1834. Charges against three members were heard on December 27, 1834, although the verdicts were not recorded. Willis Robuck was charged with intemperance, and R. C. Todd with "being frequently intoxicated and shooting." Jeps Cox was charged with "leaving this county without having paid his just debts." Sister McOlister was excluded from the church on August 11, 1838 following "unfavorable reports against her."

The church forgave a member who "publicly denied one article of the altered Constitution of the Church (adopted in 1840)." He later "made an acknowledgement to the church for having gotten into a passion and speaking improperly in the conference."

The most unusual disciplinary case involved H. H. Embry, who came before the conference to charge himself "with having acted improperly by indirectly betting on an election." Embry had sold a horse to a man, who would only be required to pay for the animal if Van Buren was elected president. [6]

Meeting at Macedonia Primitive Baptist Church in 1838, 12 churches formed the Rock Mountain (later Stone Mountain) Association. Twelve of these churches had withdrawn from the Yellow River Association in a doctrinal dispute. Five from DeKalb were listed in the minutes: Coal Spring (Cool Spring), Hardman's Meeting House, Macedonia, Nance's Creek, Utie (Utoy) and Fellowship. Hardman church later moved south of Decatur on Glenwood Avenue, just west of Columbia Drive. Members of the church later were instrumental in organizing the Decatur Baptist and Indian Creek Baptist churches. [7]

Chapman Powell is reputed to have treated Indians and white settlers with respect. The Medicine House "was a haven of rest and cheer; and many a travelworn, footsore Cherokee found comfort in the medical skill and care of Dr. Powell, who was famed and loved for his kindness of heart." Stories about the Powells's relationship with the Indians abound. It is said that Powell once cured the baby of

Elizabeth and Chapman Powell raised their family in this cabin, which is now a part of Stone Mountain Park's Antebellum complex. Park officials shortened the building to fit the concept of a plantation slave cabin. The original structure had windows on either side of the front door. The cabin may be the oldest structure in DeKalb County. (Vivian Price, personal collection)

Front door hardware of the Powell cabin consisted of a simple iron ring. (Photo by Vivian Price)

an Indian chief, bringing him great favor with the Cherokees. Powell's daughter, Martha, knitted socks for Indian friends. It was the job of Martha's brother, John, when he was about 14 years of age, periodically to ride across the Chattahoochee into Cherokee country, "the western wilderness." His physician father would send with John a written order for roots and herbs. He would fill his saddlebags with gold with which to pay the Indians. "To their everlasting credit, they never once betrayed his trust and always delivered the orders to the letter and the day." [8]

Elizabeth Hardman Powell. (DeKalb Historical Society)

Dr. Chapman Powell. (DeKalb Historical Society)

A civic-minded citizen, Chapman Powell served in a variety of public offices. He was DeKalb County sheriff in 1833, a road commissioner in 1840 and grand jury foreman in 1851. He also was a 33rd degree Mason and member of Decatur's Pythagoras Lodge. [9]

As the delegate to the state House of Representatives from DeKalb in 1837, Powell strongly favored Decatur as the terminus for the new rail line being built across the Chattahoochee River from the northwest. He was opposed by fellow legislator James Calhoun as well as by a great many Decatur residents, who felt the railroad would be a detriment to their quiet community. Calhoun is said to have told Powell: "The terminus of that railroad will never be any more than an eating house." Powell responded: "True, and you will see the time when it will eat up Decatur." [10]

When Betsy Hardman Powell died on April 2, 1850, Chapman Powell's last secure tie with DeKalb County was broken. He moved to Atlanta and built the second house on Peachtree Street, at the intersection of Ellis. At one point, he owned all the land in what is now the Five Points area of downtown Atlanta. Although at the time, Chapman Powell was a relatively wealthy man, his new home was scarcely more pretentious than his original cabin. In Atlanta, Chapman Powell was elected a city councilman and was a member of the committee chosen to request removal of the state capital from Milledgeville to Atlanta. His office was located on the site where the Flat Iron Building later would be built in Atlanta. [11]

Chapman Powell was accompanied to Atlanta by his daughter, Martha (Jincie) who had married a

The home of James Oliver Powell on Clairmont Road was headquarters for Gen. William T. Sherman on July 19, 1864. This sketch by T. R. Davis shows soldiers on the porch, in the yard and at an operating table in front of the carriage house. Before the soldiers arrived, family furniture and valuables were hidden in a "secret room" in the eave of the house. Davis's sketch was published in Harper's Weekly on August 27, 1864. The site of the Powell house, on the west side of Clairmont between Peachtree Creek and North Decatur Road, has been marked by the Georgia Historical Commission. (DeKalb Historical Society)

cousin, Fielding Travis Powell. Travis Powell was also a physician. Children of Jincie and Travis were Frank Alexander, Ella May, Edward (Ned) and Henry Chapman. Ella, born on May 2, 1863, was an accomplished artist and well-known figure in Atlanta society. She completed her musical education in New York City and in Paris, and wrote several published novels, including Winona, A Story of To-Day, based on the Powell family, in 1891. Ella Powell made her musical debut at Carnegie Hall 1894, and, although she lived primarily in Atlanta, maintained a music studio in New York City. She died on January 25, 1955 in Washington, D. C.; her ashes were scattered over the graves of Betsy and Chapman Powell in DeKalb's Hardman Cemetery. She never married. In his 1996 book, Margaret Mitchell's Models in Gone With The Wind, Powell descendant Samuel J. Hardman claimed that Margaret Mitchell's novel was based on Ella Powell's book, Winona, and that the characters of Scarlet and Rhett were based on Chapman Powell's daughter, Amanda Katherine Powell Houston, and son-in-law Jett Willis Rucker. [12]

Chapman and Betsy's other children remained in DeKalb. Their eldest son, William Alfred Powell, married Louisa Ann Wilson, daughter of the Rev. Jonathan Wilson. James Oliver Powell married Sarah Carroll of Gwinnett County. John Jefferson Powell married Mary Simmons (first) and Elvaline Simmons (second). Amanda Katherine Powell married Washington Jackson Houston, and Mary Jane Elizabeth (Mollie) Powell married Jett Willis Rucker. Leonard Chapman Powell married Virginia Paden, and George Washington Lindsey Powell married Sebie Loutelia Turner. [13]

James Oliver Powell was sheriff of DeKalb County in 1862 and '66 and Inferior Court clerk in 1862. His home, located on Clairmont Road on a portion of the original Powell property, served as headquarters for Gen. Sherman on July 19, 1864. Sarah Carroll Powell "was standing in the door of her home and heard Sherman issue orders to destroy Atlanta." The famous directive officially was called "Special Field Orders, No. 39." The porch of the James Oliver Powell house also was used as a temporary Union hospital during the Battle of Decatur. [14]

James and Sarah had seven children: Thomas Riley, John Chapman, "Jennie" May, James Lindsey, Mary Parisade, William Houston and Winona. Their daughter, Mary, married John Allen Montgomery on February 17, 1892; they were the first couple to be married in the Decatur Presbyterian Church. Montgomery was mayor of Decatur from 1906 to 1913; he introduced President-elect William Howard Taft during a "whistle-stop" in Decatur in 1909. John Allen Montgomery was the son of Dr. William Allen Montgomery, who was pastor of the First Baptist Church of Decatur from 1897-1903. Montgomery, Mary Powell Montgomery, James Oliver Powell and Sarah Carroll Powell are buried in Decatur Cemetery. [15]

Washington Jackson Houston, who had married Amanda Katherine Powell on July 23, 1854, purchased the original homeplace from his father-in-law in 1860. There the couple raised three sons and seven daughters: Washington Jackson Jr., Anna Louisa (Lizzie), John Chapman, Eliza Katherine, Laura Lula, Mattie Bell, Alice Pharr, Sarah Amanda (Susie), Nanny and Appolonius Bohun (Lonnie). Amanda Powell Houston had a small chapel built on the property in 1905 for use by family and neighbors. The nondenominational chapel also housed a school, taught by Miss Mattie Tilly. Houston presided over services at the chapel. After the deaths of the senior Houstons, the chapel was moved and became the home of Ernest Moore, a black man who, with his wife, raised 14 of his 18 children in the small building. The land where the chapel had been was donated to Emory Presbyterian Church.[16]

Washington Houston was born on October 10, 1831 in the Abbeville District of South Carolina to Oswald Houston and Anna S. Shaw. The Houstons had moved from Savannah to Atlanta in 1846. Oswald Houston served as city treasurer for a number of years. At the age of 17, Washington Houston was a bank cashier and received the first deposit ever made in Atlanta. He later worked in various capacities for the Georgia, Atlanta and West Point and Atlanta and Charlotte Air Line railroads. As ticket agent on the Atlanta and Charlotte, he reduced fares to three cents per mile, "which created no inconsiderable stir in railway circles."

During the Civil War, Houston was transportation agent for the Confederate government. While he stayed in Atlanta, his family lived at the Powell homeplace on Clairmont Road. He was captured crossing enemy lines to reach his family on July 24, 1864, was convicted as a Confederate spy and sentenced to hang. Only his Masonic affiliation saved him from the death penalty. [17]

Although the Houstons lived in DeKalb, Washington Houston was active in Atlanta affairs. He was a charter member of Atlanta Fire Company No. 1, the first volunteer company in the city, which was chartered on February 23, 1850. The company was re-incorporated in 1854, with Houston as one of the incorporators. Houston wore the company uniform, a red flannel shirt embroidered with a black "1", black pants, fireman's hat with "Atlanta" and "1851" in raised letters.

A Presbyterian deacon and elder, Houston devoted many years service to the DeKalb Sunday School Association. With Milton A. Candler and William G. Whidby, he issued a call for a statewide Sunday school association.

In November, 1893, Washington Houston was appointed by U. S. Secretary of the Interior Hoke Smith as chairman of a commission to negotiate treaty with Yuma Indians of southern California and Arizona. More than half the money appropriated for the mission was returned to the federal government. The following year, Houston and his wife traveled to Oklahoma to complete a dangerous job for the U. S. government involving the Osage Indians. A state representative in 1894, Houston introduced a bill for the election of judges and solicitors by the people. "Here, as in every other position to which he was called, he proved to be one of the most faithful and hard-working of all members. Thoroughly posted, broad-minded, public-spirited and progressive, fully abreast with the advanced thought and methods of the times, and always at the post of assigned duty, it was not possible to exaggerate the value and efficiency of his services to his constituents and the State."

Later in life, Houston devoted himself to farming and raising Ayrshire cattle. He was president of the Decatur Electric Light Power and Water Company and installed the first electric lights in Decatur. [18]

Through remodeling and additions, the original Powell cabin eventually was completely concealed within a large home. Alice Pharr Houston Billups, and her son, Lanier Richardson Billups (Decatur postmaster and charter member of the DeKalb Historical Society), removed the cabin and gave it to Stone Mountain Park. [19]

Chapman Powell died on May 30, 1870, and is buried next to his wife in the Hardman Cemetery, which is now contained within the property of the University Apartments, on a hill overlooking South Peachtree Creek. To deter vandalism, the couple's obelisk monuments were later replaced with flat markers and moved to Decatur Cemetery.

Chapman Powell left an estate valued at $360,000. His Atlanta house was sold by his descendants to Atlanta Mayor John H. James for $14,000.

Many interesting items from the Powell estate have been donated to the DeKalb Historical Society and are preserved for public viewing in the society's museum. One of these artifacts is the still in which the doctor brewed the whiskey that made him so popular in early Decatur. [20]

Ironically, the land once owned by one of DeKalb County's first physicians, Dr. Chapman Powell, and later became part of the Walter Candler estate, is now home to the Veteran's Administration Hospital, Emory University Hospital and the Centers for Disease Control and Prevention.

The Murphey, Candler and Scott Families

Of the early settlers of DeKalb County, there was one family that, linked by marriage with two later-arriving clans, was to figure more prominently than any other.

Roger Murphey, who was born in North Carolina in 1767, and his wife, Nancy Wilson, came to DeKalb in 1823 from the Pendleton District of South Carolina. They built a home at the current intersection of Memorial and Indian Creek drives near Decatur. [4] Roger was received into the Hardman Primitive Baptist Church congregation on January 24, 1829, and Nancy on April 21, 1832.

---

[4] Scott Candler Sr. (1887-1973), two-great grandson of Roger and Nancy Murphey, had their original log cabin moved to his home on Candler Road. (Source: Clarke, Caroline McKinney, 1973, 1997, The Story of Decatur 1823-1899, page 234).

Nancy Murphey, who was described as "a great talker and very intelligent," also attended Macedonia Primitive Baptist Church near Lithonia.

Their eldest son, Charles, was born on May 9, 1799 in South Carolina. A disabled arm kept him from becoming a farmer like his father. Instead, he became a school teacher, plying his trade in Decatur in 1825. He was elected clerk of the Inferior Court in 1826 and immediately quit teaching. It was the beginning of a 35-year career in the public limelight. He was elected clerk of the Superior Court in 1832, state representative in 1839, state senator in 1842 and U. S. representative in 1851. [21]

Murphey "was considered a shrewd lawyer and had the faculty of drawing out opinions of others without disclosing his own." But, he had strong opinions and was not afraid to express them. An angry man once said to him: "If it were not for your lame arm, I would whip you." Murphey replied: "If it were not for my well arm, you might think of trying it."

Charles Murphey was an early member of Hardman Primitive Baptist Church, but later joined the Rev. William Henry Clarke's Methodist church at Wesley Chapel. Charles Murphey married Eliza Word, who died in 1838, nine months after the birth of their daughter, Eliza Caroline Murphey, on October 22, 1837. Roger and Nancy Murphey moved to Cass (later Bartow) County, where they are buried; Eliza Word Murphey also is buried in Cass County. As a child, Eliza Murphey was cared for by her grandmother, Sarah Joyce Word. [22]

Murphey was elected a delegate to the state's Secession Convention, which was scheduled to convene on January 16, 1861 in Milledgeville. Upon his arrival in the town, Murphey developed pneumonia, and died on opening day. In his 1922 "Historical Address," Charles Murphey Candler, grandson of Charles Murphey, said, "In speeches made throughout the county during the campaign my Grandfather frequently declared that he prayed that he would never live to see Georgia out of the Union. His prayer had been answered."

Charles Murphey's only daughter, Eliza, had married Milton Anthony Candler in Decatur on June 6, 1857. Candler, born on January 11, 1837 in Campbell County, Ga., was the eldest son of Samuel Charles Candler and Sarah Beall. The Candlers had 11 children, including seven sons: John S., Samuel Charles Jr., Asa Griggs, W. B., Warren A. and E. S. All were leaders in their chosen fields and communities. In addition to Milton, three of the sons lived in DeKalb. John S. Candler was a Georgia Supreme Court Justice (and raised prize Guernsey cattle). Asa Griggs Candler, of Coca-Cola fame, was responsible for development of the Druid Hills community (brother John built the first house there on the northeast corner of Ponce de Leon and Briarcliff), and for bringing the U. S. Army's Camp Gordon cantonment to Chamblee. Warren A. Candler was senior bishop of the Methodist Episcopal Church-South.

According to one account of the Candler family, "No more distinguished family has been produced by the South. It has taken a position of leadership in affairs of finance, law and religion."

Milton Anthony Candler practiced law in Decatur with his father-in-law, Charles Murphey. He served in the Confederate Army as a captain of a cavalry company. He was a state senator, 1868-72; state representative in 1893; and U. S. representative, 1875-79. Much of his governmental service was performed during the difficult days of Reconstruction. He was an elder of Decatur Presbyterian Church and superintendent of the Sunday school for 40 years, as well as a trustee of Oglethorpe and Agnes Scott colleges and Decatur's Donald Fraser School for Boys. He once remarked that he never belonged to anything but the Democratic Party and the Presbyterian Church. [23]

When their children were growing up, the M. A. Candlers lived on a 250-acre farm near the intersection of South Candler and Kirk Road. An avenue of mimosa trees lined the long drive to the house. Among the many distinguished visitors to their home was Confederate general and later governor, John B. Gordon, who rode there on horseback from his home in the Kirkwood area, to sit on the porch and talk politics. When Milton was elected to the U. S. House of Representatives in 1877, the men of Decatur held a torchlight parade from the town square to the Candler farm.

Of their 12 children, six reached maturity: Charles Murphey, Samuel Charles, Milton Anthony Jr., Florence, Claude and Ruth. Samuel Charles Candler married Jane Porter of Savannah, Florence married Clifford A. Cowles, and Ruth married Hunter Pope. Claude married Samuel Branch McKinney of Farmville, Va. Their daughter, Caroline McKinney Clarke, was the author of The Story of Decatur. Charles Murphey Candler (author of the Historical Address of 1922) married Mary Scott; Milton Anthony Candler Jr. married Mary's sister, Nellie.

Mary and Nellie were the daughters of George Washington Scott, who had settled in Decatur in 1877. Founder of Scottdale Mills and several other successful business ventures, Scott was the chief benefactor of the Decatur Female Seminary, the name of which was changed to Agnes Scott College, in honor of George's Irish immigrant mother. [24]

Charles Murphey Candler, born on March 17, 1858, continued in the tradition of his father, Milton Candler, becoming a lawyer, state representative, state senator and chairman of the state Public Service Commission. Perhaps his crowning achievement was an author of legislation ending the state's system of leasing prison convicts to work for private individuals.

Of the latter-day generations of this distinguished family, no single member had a larger impact on DeKalb County than George Scott Candler, son of Charles Murphey Candler and Mary Scott. Born on June 23, 1887, Scott Candler was mayor of Decatur from 1922-39, and DeKalb County Commissioner of Roads and Revenues beginning in 1939 and continuing through the post-war years of the county's most explosive growth. As manager of the Stone Mountain Authority from 1959-63, he laid the groundwork for final completion of the Confederate memorial carving. He was affectionately known as "Mr. DeKalb." [25]

When all but their two youngest daughters were grown, Milton and Eliza Candler moved in 1889 to a smaller home on Candler near Agnes Scott College. There Milton died on August 9, 1909, and Eliza on January 14, 1917. Claude and Samuel Branch McKinney, and later Caroline McKinney Clarke and her family, lived there. [26]

Milton Candler's 1909 obituary in The Atlanta Georgian newspaper tells as much about the emotion generated by the Reconstruction era in DeKalb County as it does about the deceased:

"One by one the men of strength who witnessed the iron days and who buried the thunderbolts of impassioned eloquence against the iniquitous measures of reconstruction are passing from life's din and turmoil to where beyond these voices there is peace.

"Milton A. Candler belonged to the Old Guard. The tocsin (sic) of war found him in the legislative halls at Milledgeville. But he was restless until he elbowed his way to the front of battle.

"On the field he won distinction for soldiership and courage.

"But he did not cease to make a bulwark of his bosom when the war ended. The days which really tried men's souls in this section were the days which followed the defeat at Appomattox. It was during the hideous carpetbag era, when the foundations of society were shaken and the nightmare of negro domination threatened an Anglo-Saxon civilization, that the hardy sinews of this man were tested. In the lexicon of his allegiance to Georgia there was no such word as fail; and, like the Iron Duke, he stood foursquare to every wind.

"For two consecutive terms he was honored by his constituents of this district with an election to congress. On retiring from the national arena he resumed the practice of law; and for more than fifty years he was one of the conspicuous figures in the court house. At the bar of DeKalb he was both Nestor and Achilles.

"Strong in his religious faith, he was for 40 years an authority on Presbyterian policy and doctrine and an honored elder of the kirk.

"One of the sturdiest representatives of the clan which has represented Georgia in almost every field of endeavor, he was respected by his fellow citizens for his robust traits of character and for his long career of public usefulness, and to multitudes in Georgia his memory will be fragrant when later blooms have faded." [27]

Chapter 15 Notes

1. Gheesling, Catherine Sams Bond, n. d., "Dr. Chapmon Powell 1798-1870." Powell, George T. Jr., 1985, The Virginians: Thomas Powell and John Hardman -- Their Descendants -- 1616-1985. Weaver, J. Calvin, M. D., 1952, "A Preview of One Hundred Years of Medicine in DeKalb County, Georgia," The Collections of the DeKalb Historical Society -- the Yearbook, Vol. 1.

2. Powell, George T. Jr., 1985, The Virginians: Thomas Powell and John Hardman -- Their Descendants -- 1616-1985. Ellis, Alfred C., 1997, personal correspondence.

3. Weaver, J. Calvin, M. D., 1952, "A Preview of One Hundred Years of Medicine in DeKalb County, Georgia," The Collections of the DeKalb Historical Society -- the Yearbook, Vol. 1.

4. Powell, George T. Jr., 1985, The Virginians: Thomas Powell and John Hardman -- Their Descendants -- 1616-1985. "A Romantic Cabin of Georgia's Long Ago, newspaper clipping, no date or publication, Houston genealogy file, DeKalb Historical Society. Gheesling, Catherine Sams Bond, August 21, 1985, "Dr. Chapmon Powell 1798-1870, unpublished manuscript, DeKalb Historical Society.

5. Nix, Dorothy, personal collection, DeKalb Historical Society. Atlanta Historical Bulletin, Vol. XI, No. 1, March, 1966, page 75. Candler, Charles Murphey, November 9, 1922, "Historical Address," DeKalb Historical Society.

6. Price, Vivian, July 22, 1981, "Hardeman (sic) Church Conference Dealt With Members' Sins," DeKalb News/Sun, page 2D.

7. Ford, Elizabeth Austin, 1952, "A Precis of DeKalb's Early Church History," The Collections of the DeKalb Historical Society -- The Yearbook, Vol. 1. Nix, Dorothy, personal collection, DeKalb Historical Society. Smith, R. Frank, August 1, 1922, "A Brief Historical Sketch of Indian Creek Missionary Baptist Church," unpublished manuscript.

8. "A Romantic Cabin of Georgia's Long Ago, newspaper clipping, no date or publication, Houston genealogy file, DeKalb Historical Society. Hamilton, Lucille, n. d., "Dr. Powell, Pioneer Physician and Friend of the Indians," publication unknown. Weaver, J. Calvin, M. D., 1952, "A Preview of One Hundred Years of Medicine in DeKalb County, Georgia," The Collections of the DeKalb Historical Society -- the Yearbook, Vol. 1.

9. Gheesling, Catherine Sams Bond, "Dr. Chapmon Powell 1798-1870," unpublished manuscript, DeKalb Historical Society. Weaver, J. Calvin, M. D., 1952, "A Preview of One Hundred Years of Medicine in DeKalb County, Georgia," The Collections of the DeKalb Historical Society -- the Yearbook, Vol. 1.

10. Hamilton, Lucille, n. d., "Dr. Powell, Pioneer Physician and Friend of the Indians," publication unknown, quoting a speech by Chapmon Powell's daughter, Martha, to the United Daughters of the Confederacy of Atlanta in 1914. Garrett, Franklin M., 1954, 1969, Atlanta and Environs -- A Chronicle of Its People and Events, Vol. 1, page 168.

11. Hamilton, Lucille, n. d., "Dr. Powell, Pioneer Physician and Friend of the Indians," publication unknown. Gheesling, Catherine Sams Bond, August 21, 1985, "Dr. Chapmon Powell 1798-1870, unpublished manuscript, DeKalb Historical Society. Powell, George T., correspondence in the Powell genealogy file, DeKalb Historical Society. The Collections of the DeKalb Historical Society -- 1952, Vol. 1, page 99.

12. Powell, George T., correspondence in the Powell genealogy file, DeKalb Historical Society. Hardman, Samuel J., 1997, timeline of Ella M. Powell and personal correspondence.

13. Powell, George T. Jr., 1985, The Virginians: Thomas Powell and John Hardman -- Their Descendants -- 1616-1985.

14. Hamilton, Lucille, n. d., "Dr. Powell, Pioneer Physician and Friend of the Indians," publication unknown. Garrett, Franklin M., 1954, 1969, Atlanta and Environs -- A Chronicle of Its People and Events, Vol. 1, pages 612 and 702.

15. Clarke, Caroline McKinney, 1973, 1997, The Story of Decatur 1823-1899, pages 228-229.

16. Gheesling, Catherine Sams Bond, 1985, "Washington Jackson Houston -- 1831-1911," unpublished manuscript, DeKalb Historical Society. Houston genealogy file, DeKalb Historical Society.

17. Gheesling, Catherine Sams Bond, 1985, "Washington Jackson Houston -- 1831-1911," unpublished manuscript, DeKalb Historical Society.

18. Harris, Joel Chandler, 1895, Memoirs of Georgia, Vol. 1., page 595. Gheesling, Catherine Sams Bond, 1985, "Washington Jackson Houston -- 1831-1911," unpublished manuscript, DeKalb Historical Society. Garrett, Franklin M., 1954, 1969, Atlanta and Environs -- A Chronicle of Its People and Events, Vol. 1, page 317.

19. Powell genealogy file, DeKalb Historical Society.

20. Gheesling, Catherine Sams Bond, "Dr. Chapmon Powell 1798-1870," unpublished manuscript, DeKalb Historical Society.

21. Garrett, Franklin M., 1954, 1969, Atlanta and Environs -- A Chronicle of Its People and Events, Vol. 1, page 55. Clarke, Caroline McKinney, 1973, 1997, The Story of Decatur 1823-1899, page 234.

22. Clarke, Caroline McKinney, 1973, 1997, The Story of Decatur 1823-1899. Willard, Levi, 1920, "The Early History of Decatur Written Many Years Ago," DeKalb New Era. Candler, Charles Murphey, November 9, 1922, Historical Address.

23. Clarke, Caroline McKinney, 1973, 1997, The Story of Decatur 1823-1899, page 234.

24. Park, Alice, December 21, 1987, "Kirk Road Landmark -- Candler's Civil War Era Homestead Giving Way To New Subdivision," DeKalb News/Sun. Clarke, Caroline McKinney, 1973, 1997, The Story of Decatur 1823-1899, page 234.

25. Shelton, Morris, 1971, Mr. DeKalb, page 19. Clarke, Caroline McKinney, 1973, 1997, The Story of Decatur 1823-1899, page 234.

26. Clarke, Caroline McKinney, 1973, 1997, The Story of Decatur 1823-1899, page 8. Chesnut, Mr. and Mrs. John David, personal collection. Shelton, Morris, 1971 Mr. DeKalb, page 39. Garrett, Franklin M., 1954, 1969, Atlanta and Environs -- A Chronicle of Its People and Events, Vol. 1, page 540.

27. Nix, Dorothy, personal collection, DeKalb Historical Society.

Chapter 16

*D*eKalb County may have been the edge of the wilderness in its early history, but its people had the resources and desire to provide en environment in which their children could grow into extraordinary citizens. One such citizen was Rebecca Latimer Felton.

William Latimer brought his wife, Rebecca Marshall, and family, including three boys -- William, Charles and Henry -- to Warren County, Ga. from Maryland in the early 1820s. The family settled on "the old Augusta Road," now Covington Highway, in a community called Belmont, near Snapfinger Creek, three miles west of the Cross Roads settlement that was later called Lythonia (now Lithonia).

The Latimer home also was the site of Latimer's Store, established April 26, 1832, and a post office by the same name, as well as a tavern (as roadside hotels were known in those days). Both William and Charles Latimer served as postmaster. The stagecoach line from Augusta changed horses there. "Prior to the building of the Georgia Railroad, Charleston and Augusta were the markets, in which the retail merchants of this section bought their merchandise. Merchants made about two or three trips a year to these cities, by horseback, buggy or stage as suited their convenience, sometimes, however, going on their wagon trains by which their purchases were brought back. The round trip, including the actual purchasing and packing while in Augusta, or sometimes Charleston, consumed from ten days to two weeks." Travelers were frequent guests in the Latimer home. [1]

The Latimer home was on the main road from Nashville, Tenn. to Augusta, 10 miles from Decatur and 20 miles from Covington. Rebecca remembered the stagecoaches as "ponderous affairs with a big leather boot on behind and a little bannister around the top to hold baggage. There were regular stage stands ten miles apart, where a relay of four horses were constantly stabled. About a mile away the stage driver's horn would be sounded so that the hostler would be ready with fresh horses on his arrival. They were also mail carriers. It cost ten cents a mile to travel on the stage coach and it required ten cents to send a letter." [2]

One by one, the brothers married: William to Elizabeth Furlow, Henry to the widow of Samuel L. Wilson and Charles to Eleanor Swift, daughter of Thomas Swift and Lucy Talbot, of Morgan County, Ga.

Two daughters were born to Charles and Eleanor Latimer: Rebecca Ann on June 10, 1835, and Mary in 1840. The family lived at Belmont for several years, then moved to Flat Shoals, then to Panola on the South River and later to the town of Decatur. [3]

From Notable American Women 1607-1950 comes this description of the Latimer family: "Eleanor Latimer was a woman of great vitality and something of a feminist. Her husband, a man of liberal, decided views, ardently Whig in politics, was the local postmaster and ran a tavern and general store as well as his farm. He encouraged his daughter's independent, competitive spirit, tomboyish ways, and love of books and music, and gave her the best education available to girls in the Georgia of her day."

Rebecca's earliest education came at a one-room school near her Belmont home. Her family later moved to Decatur, so that she and her sister could attend the Decatur Female Academy, under the direction of the Rev. John S. Wilson. At the age of 15, Rebecca started her tenure at the Madison Female College, where she gave the valedictorian address. The featured graduation speaker was Dr. William H. Felton, then a member of the state legislature, as well as a physician, minister and farmer. Little more than a year after meeting him at graduation, Rebecca climbed out a second story window and eloped with Dr. Felton; they were married on October 11, 1853. Her father had wished her to marry someone more successful. [4]

Following her marriage, the couple lived on the Felton farm in Bartow County. Rebecca went on to the most unusual and most distinguished career in politics and reform ever pursued by a Georgia woman. In an era when "nice ladies" stayed home, Rebecca Latimer Felton never hesitated to get involved in any issue she felt important and "would scrap with anybody, anywhere, on any issue about which she felt strongly." She was "easily the most versatile, and certainly the most remarkable woman the State has ever produced... the most powerful and influential woman in Georgia." [5]

She managed her husband's Congressional campaign in 1874, the first woman ever to do so. The campaign produced a win for the Feltons and launched the first of many editorials and cartoons in Georgia newspapers ridiculing Mrs. Felton's unprecedented behavior. She was William's secretary in Washington, D. C. until 1881. For the next 56 years, she campaigned for women's suffrage, temperance and educational opportunities for women. She and her husband crusaded against the convict lease system. She wrote a newspaper column and letters to the editor, many on the topic of political reform. "Sharp of tongue and facile of pen, she attacked wrong-doing wherever she saw it in the State. Many office holders unfolded their newspapers daily with fear and trepidation and often with shaking hands to see who Mrs. Felton had `landed on' last -- and if it were he." [6]

She was appointed on October 3, 1922, at the age of 87, by Gov. Thomas W. Hardwick to an interim term in the U. S. Senate. Sen. Thomas E. Watson had died in office, and Walter F. George had been elected his successor, but had yet to qualify. She occupied her seat on the floor of the Senate on November 21 and 22. Of her appointment, she later commented: "It meant that a woman reared in the sheltered security of an antebellum plantation was to be the first of her sex to sit in the United States Senate. It was hard to realize. I thought back through the years and decades and remembered the first time a woman had lifted her voice in public at our little country church in my girlhood. What a stir that had caused! Who in that day would have had the hardihood to predict that the time would come when Georgia women would hold public office?"

In her only speech from the floor of the U. S. Senate, Felton said in part: ""Let me say that when the women of this country come in and sit with you, though there may be but very few in the next few years, I pledge you that you will get ability, you will get integrity of purpose, you will get exalted patriotism and you will get unstinted usefulness." Women in the galleries cheered when she signed the book of senators. [7]

Her greatest contribution to DeKalb County history, however, are her chronicles of almost 100 years of life in Georgia. She published three important books: Country Life in Georgia in the Days of My Youth, My Memories of Georgia Politics and Romantic Story of Georgia's Women. She discussed cooking and courting, calico and coffins, "cipherin'" and cold sweet potatoes, giving readers an insight into the daily lives of early DeKalb countians found nowhere else.

"Except salt, iron, sugar and coffee, everything was raised by those early Georgia planters necessary for human comfort and sustenance," Rebecca wrote in Country Life. She paid particular attention to the many duties of a homemaker on an antebellum plantation. Pioneer women cultivated kitchen gardens, raised dairy cows, chickens, geese (for making feather beds) and pigs. They supervised a loom house, a meat house and a meal house "where there was always a super-abundance of supplies for white and colored." Woolen coverlets were woven at home, and "quilt making was never interrupted, winter or summer." Rebecca estimated that her mother, Eleanor Swift Latimer, made 50 quilts during first 10 years of her married life. Beds were maintained not only for the family but also for travelers who might drop in.

Rebecca Latimer Felton in a photo taken on the day she addressed the United States Senate, November 22, 1922. (DeKalb Historical Society)

Before the cotton gin, seed was picked from the lint by hand (and, cockleburs from wool). "The lint was then carded by hand, spun on home-made wheels, then reeled into what were called `hanks,' by use of home-made reels, then the warp was prepared for the home-made loom, by a variety of processes, all tedious and slow and all the work done by the house mother and her helpers... The family loom was kept going from Monday morning until Saturday night.

"In this slow, tedious, intricate and nerve-wracking and painstaking way all the wearing apparel of the masses was constructed. Well-to-do men generally contrived to get a broadcloth coat, maybe once in a lifetime. The rest had coats of plain jeans. Silk dresses were scarce and with scanty lengths and then were only worn occasionally, at weddings or brilliant occasions. A leghorn bonnet would last a woman a lifetime...

"The colored women were always busy and likewise the mistress. The daughters were taught to spin and weave, to knit and sew, and to overlook the dairy, etc., as the mother directed. There was plenty of work for all because a large slave family had to be clothed from that busy loom, and the cloth was to be cut out and made into garments as soon as woven, and that large house was to be kept in apple-pie order...

"I never saw a sewing machine until I was full grown and twenty one, but there was no lack of dainty finger work in those early homes... Homespun dresses were not to be despised by any means. Carefully spun and woven with indigo dyes and turkey red to form a pattern, they made admirable dress materials, washed well and endured mightily.

"Indigo, madder, turkey red and copperas were staple goods for dye purposes and the housewives of early Georgia went to meeting (church services) with every finger nail as blue as indigo mud would paint them. It was considered a badge of efficiency, experience and culture in cloth making. The wool dyes, made women's hands almost black with logwood and walnut leaves. Men's summer working breeches were copperas dyed and those plain men-folk were as yellow-legged as our choicest breeds of chickens."

Rebecca told of a neighbor's "industrious wife who spun and wove all their wearing apparel and who manufactured enough cloth to provide her husband with two strong, good shirts. When he returned at night from the hot corn and cotton plowing and his shirt was wet with perspiration she had always a clean, dry garment ready, for she did a bit of laundry work as regularly as she washed and dried her breakfast dishes, and this good woman's fame followed her down as an extraordinary manager and capable married woman. I was impressed as to her super-excellence, because the family washing in such plain homes was done once in seven days as a rule and where children were numerous they might take off their one garment and sit in their skin on hot days until a clean shirt or frock was ready for use."

Men might wear suspenders knitted by his wife or daughter, but he usually had professionally-made leather work boots. "The traveling shoemaker made periodic visits and one pair of shoes per annum was considered a liberal provision for grown-ups. Suffice to say the children as a rule all went barefooted summer and winter... Stumped toes in summer and cracked heels in winter were always in evidence with pupils during my school days."

Rebecca remembered her first store-bought bonnet, a gift when she was seven. The bottle green silk "was gathered in close rows on fine whale bone strips and shaped as a calash." The bonnet had a skirt, "and inside was a row of small pink rosebuds encircling the face.

"As a rule, in plain households, the mother purchased a nice calico dress with enough to make the little daughter one like it. If there were scraps left a bonnet was made for both and families could be identified by the flowers on the calico and the style of making. There were fine English and French calicoes and muslins and northern homespun came from the factories in New England fine and white, while our southern factory cloth was rough and unbleached after cotton mills were erected in Georgia... I had plaid woolen dresses at various times but generally my mother cut down her worn or out of date frocks for my use. My first silk dress was a made over. This descended to my small sister after I had outgrown it.

"When I reached the age of ten (1845) the fashionable wore voluminous skirts and many of them. The underskirts were starched as stiff as possible, and I remember hearing a friend of my mother say she had on at that time eight petticoats besides the outside frock made of balzarine (something like the voile of modern dress goods). As she came down the street she was like a ship in full sail. Her dress skirt was as wide as the sidewalk. The body to the dress was tight as beeswax and she was laced until her beaux could nearly span her waist with both hands."

Early DeKalb County farm families enjoyed an abundance of home-grown and homemade foods. Rebecca recalled that there were always milk, eggs, meat and poultry, breads made from home-grown wheat and white corn, sweet butter, beaten biscuits with rich red ham gravy, chicken and dumplings, cakes, "pot peach pie, smothered with cream and sugar" and watermelon in the summertime.

Peaches and honey from home orchards and hives were two farm products in generous supply. "It was a poor and thriftless domicile," Felton remembered, "that did not have dried peaches, apples, cherries and pears by the bushel, as well as preserves enough to last through the winter until the harvest came again."

Homemakers made starch from whole wheat or wheat bran, and soap from meat scraps and bones, cooked with lye and drained in ash-hoppers.

"Coffee was scarce and high, sometimes a Sunday morning luxury, and brown sugar was generally used, the exception being the beautiful loaf sugar brought from the North."

Cooking was done on a wide hearth before a huge fireplace hung with pots and kettles.

"Saturday and Sunday (church) meeting days always brought friends and neighbors for at least one meal, many to spend the night. My mother said it looked like a camp meeting when the kinspeople, the neighbors, the beaux and girl friends alighted from their horses and the crowd collected in the house. Servants carried the riding saddles into the harness room in the barn yard. The daughters prepared the Saturday big dinner while grandmother supervised the big Sunday dinner and the girls mounted the riding horses, wore their best dresses, and went to church, and, as was the custom of the time, there was a lot of courting going on when the beaux rode home with the girls they were inclined to marry... Every woman who rode horseback had a riding skirt made of substantial home weaving with a belt, but open to the hem. These riding skirts protected the dresses and were in universal use when my mother and grandmother were young."

Macedonia Baptist Church was the heart of social, as well as religious, life for early settlers in southeast DeKalb. Although younger than her teen-aged Belmont neighbors, Rebecca was allowed to tag along on outings, riding Pony, who was given to Charles Latimer in return for feed for stock belonging to a traveling horse trader, who was stranded at Latimer's Station, due to foul weather. Singing schools and revivals were popular events held at the church.

"It was three miles from our home to Macedonia meeting house where the whole neighborhood gathered for education in old fashioned round and square note books, and where we closed the exercises by marching around and singing, old and young, to the bent of our inclinations.

"We traveled along a leafy road, crossed two or three clear branches, and occasionally the big girls and boys raced their horses. This racing woke up in Pony's brain a remembrance of his Old Kentucky Home. Whenever I saw him lay back his shapely ears and arch his proud neck I always clutched the horn of the saddle to hold on. The race was all right for the rider and pony were in full accord in a frolic of that sort."

Rebecca's parents would attend, riding their matched pair of claybank (yellow) horses named Pompey and Caesar. "Hitched to a barouche they sped along in famous style, flinging white manes and tails to the breeze."

The entire community attended monthly services at Macedonia. "It was a great time with children, negro nurses and dogs. There was always a spring of good water close about. The mothers provided biscuit and teacakes for their hungry tribes. A quilt or shawl was spread on the church floor, the babies that could sit alone were thus made comfortable, and the preacher was in no wise disturbed by their various activities. The women occupied one half of the building. The men and larger boys kept to their own side of the house."

Courting at church often led straight up the aisle to the altar. The announcement of a couple's engagement launched a frenzy of preparation, not only for the wedding itself, but also to make many of the items necessary for the young couple to set up housekeeping.

"Weddings were sumptuous affairs. When my mother married there was a crowded wedding at night and three more days of festivities, with a different dress for each day. `Infairs' were popular, where the wedding spreads were transferred to the grooms's home. Everything good to eat was bountifully furnished, meats in abundance, all sorts of... concoctions topped off with pound-cake and syllabub. There was always a sideboard where gin, rum and peach brandy held distinction. Loaf sugar brought from Charleston and Augusta by wagons was uniformly present. I can remember with accurate recollection those beautiful snowy cones of white sugar encased in thick bluish-green papers, that were always in request when company came, and the sideboard drinks were set forth with generous array."

Preparations for one wedding, that of William Latimer to Elizabeth Furlow in November of 1833 was especially memorable because of a spectacular meteor shower clearly visible over DeKalb County.

The labor that went into the wedding and infair "was immense," with Rebecca's mother directing the arrangements. "They were working far into the night with some sewing for the children of that large family. There were blazing fires in the living room and candles on the sewing table. Going out on the back porch between midnight and day, for some wood to replenish the fire, my mother saw the falling stars. The negroes down at the quarter also witnessed the wonderful sight. They rushed to the big house in a panic of fear as the world was coming to an end. Soon everybody was up and wondering what would come next. Grandfather went out on the back porch and then discovered that no star ever rested on the ground. The star disappeared and its light went out, when it reached the dirt. He therefore quieted the frightened people but all hung around the big house until daylight came." [8]

Historian Levi Willard recalled that the meteor shower had lasting effects on man and nature. "A man from the country left town `rather full' and tied his horse to a sapling at the side of Fayetteville Road, lay down and fell asleep. On awaking, he said the stars were falling about him as thick as cotton bolls in the patch, and that he had to jump over them in running to his horse... The atmosphere was smoky for several days after, and the sun was like a ball of fire that might be looked upon with the naked eye."

Slave weddings also were festive occasions. Rebecca Latimer Felton told the story of the wedding of Ben, a miller, and Minerva, the housemaid: "They were to be given a house of their own, a plain cabin, but close and comfortable. Ben had a new suit of clothes for a bridal present. The bride got her outfit from we girls. There was a preacher to marry them and a good supper for the occasion. They were a happy couple, had a family of sprightly children and were a part of my sister's (Mary's) allotment after she married and had her own home.

"The surrender turned everything upside down and Ben went back to the old Panola home and secured a position as a miller. As the years rolled on Ben lost his wife and his boys married and he was lonely in his old age. He came back to his `Mis' Mary' and she gave him a house to live in, coal to burn, clothes to wear, was fed from her table at every meal and he swept the sidewalks and did errands for my sister as well as he could."

Corn-shuckings and quiltings also were popular social events in early DeKalb. Ripened corn was hauled to the barn lot and heaped on the ground outside the crib. The host family provided a huge meal, and neighbors -- both black and white -- would come. "It was a big time for everybody. Before the daylight came the shucked corn was safely housed. Everybody had a good time and all went home in the morning."

Women who attended quiltings would bring their own thimble and needles, "as needles were scarce and high. Along about midday the husbands began to come, some afoot, others on horseback. And the dinner was a spread that tested the skill and industry of the hostess to be sure. The tables groaned with everything that the mistress and her colored women could prepare. After dinner was over the farmers returned to their work and the women finished the quilt, even to binding the edges in first class style. And there were famous quilters abroad in the land in those industrious days."

Just as friends flocked to respond to a neighbor's party invitation, they rallied in support when the need arose. "When a farmer was very sick and unable to work and watch his crop his neighbors would go over on a day agreed upon, with all their forces, plow hands, horses and plows and before dark came the crop was in good order.

"In rural districts death always caught people at a disadvantage. Home-made coffins were clumsy. Shrouds were made around the dead body. Neighbors had to dig the graves and do all things else, as there were no bought things to help along. Crowds could be had to sit up with the dead. Silver coins were laid on eyelids to hold them down. When a person got so low down in reputation that he deserved the meanest that could be said, you would hear `He is mean enough to steal the silver on a dead man's eyes.' Graves had to be made nearby unless there was a meeting house within convenient distance. People were generally buried on their own land and enclosed like a tiny garden, with wooden palings."

Trips to Augusta and Charleston were both social and business. "Augusta was the great market place... Cotton and wheat were waggoned long distances to be sold in Augusta... The neighbors managed to go in large companies, camping out, with a supply of cooked victuals already prepared. After the produce was sold, salt, sugar and iron were purchased for the return trip. Store goods were bought in limited quantities for the women at home with an occasional bonnet and slippers. Nutmegs with other spices were hunted for in Augusta, brown sugar and black molasses were in demand."

Enterprising men brought back a surplus of goods to sell in small general stores. "My father had a country store," Rebecca said, "where he sold pins and needles, lute string ribbon and prunella shoes (upper portions made from heavy wool fabric) with on one counter and dealt out thick black molasses and kit mackerel within ten feet of the millinery."

Both English and American coins were acceptable as payment. "We had for small silver change thrips (three pences) and seven pences, value 6 1/3 cents and 12 1/2."

Rebecca and her sister were unusually-well educated for their time. Boys and girls generally received little schooling. "After these girl pupils were able to read fairly well and to write a little they vacated the school benches and went back home for the domestic duties that were imperative... Some of the finest business men at that early era had something less than three months schooling yet they were capable, wrote legibly and made headway in fortune-making and good living." Later in life, Rebecca frequently said that she felt that the public schools established in Georgia in the late 1800s did not provide near the quality of education she received in her early years. The state's first mistake, she said, was failing to require compulsory attendance. Testifying before the Georgia General Assembly, she said: "When Georgia legislators assumed the liberty to commandeer or conscript your tax money to educate my child it was only just, fair and equitable to compel me to send that child to school or know the reason why. I fully understand that public utilities are hard to manage, but I also agree with a level-headed old legislator who was `agin the whole business, because it is the easiest thing to do, spend other people's money.'"

Rebecca first attended a one-room community school, built on a site donated by Charles Latimer. The first teacher was the Rev. F. M. Haygood, who was paid by the parents. "It was readin', writin', and cipherin' from eight in the morning to five or six in the afternoon, and the big boys took their slates and worked sums out of doors and the girls had reading lessons in the school house part of the day, and the teacher taught the small ones every word of the lesson in the spelling book at his knee. All pupils when advanced to writing lessons took a spell at the high writing bench. All brought goose quills from home to fashion into pens, and the teacher occupied a good part of his teaching time cutting the goose quills into pen shape. There might have been some pencils in use, but the oak balls that fell from the oak tree limbs were plentiful. So the thrifty ones manufactured red ink in that way and the copy books were parti-colored on every page and almost every line. Slates and slate pencils were sold at my father's store, and I had a small slate on which I drew pictures of cows, cats and dogs and the large girls and boys made pictures of the teacher on the sly."

Occasionally, students were asked to shout their answers to spelling quizzes. "Just as loud as you please. You might spell baker or circumlocution or anything else and the people going along the road were happy to know that the children were getting their lessons, and that the teacher was earning his pay. When my first school term closed the entire neighborhood gathered to hear the boys speak, and listen to the girls as they read a page in the reading book."

After the community school burned, Rebecca, at the tender age of eight, was sent to school in Oxford, Newton County, where she boarded with a Rev. Simmons.

"In the rural schools of my earliest days nearly all of us wore a cord about our necks with a little wallet of brimstone or assafoetida [5] tied on as an itch preventive. And the warts. My! My! How to get rid of the itch and the warts on their hands occupied much of the general conversation at recess time."

Charles and Eleanor Latimer moved their family to Decatur in order for their daughters to attend the Hannah Moore Female Collegiate Institute, which was taught by Dr. John S. Wilson. The quality of education was among the finest available in northern Georgia at the time. The quality education went hand-in-hand with strict discipline. Among the many school rules were: no reading of fiction, no visiting except on Friday evening or Saturday afternoon and no dancing. [9]

"Dr. Wilson was unutterably opposed to dancing. His opposition became a serious matter when he forbade his scholars to attend dancing parties. For a while the controversy ran high. It put me in a panic because I loved to dance like I loved candy. My father liked to have me dance, he said it gave girls a graceful walk. My mother was not so much in favor of it. I was now very uneasy. There was always a big ball in Decatur at the principal hotel on Friday night of Superior Court week. Our judge was Hon. Edward Young Hill, one of the handsomest men I think I ever saw in my life. I looked forward to that ball with delight. I was just entering my teens and several times the judge would ask me to dance with him and he was a splendid dancer. I was quite sure at that time, that I was something extra on the light fantastic toe, but I am now satisfied that there were so many handsome belles fond of dancing that the judge evaded a choice by selecting an active little girl who cared only for the sport, just as he did. He and my father were great friends, both Whigs as I recollect, and it was the easiest way out to get a very harmless little dancing mate. Up and down inside the rows of partners or outside (as it happened) in the Virginia Reel, we kept our part of the business with joyful alacrity.

"But the opposition of Dr. Wilson grew apace. He became more and more aggressive and the school patrons were divided in their opinions. While some agreed others said it was none of his business. The crisis came. The time of the big ball was only a few days off. One morning after school opened, the stern old dominie shot his bolt. The fiat read this way: `Any girl that goes to a dancing party while in school attendance will be dismissed next day.' When he said a thing he said it with emphasis. We were up against it hard and fast.

"I told the story at home and my mother said `We'll wait until your father hears about it.' My heart was almost in my mouth when the case was laid before him. He was my dependence. I hoped he would assert his rights to govern his own household. But the case was decided against me. He finally said: `We keep up two establishments, one in town the other our river plantation, where I must stay from Monday until Saturday night, to give you school privileges. This is why I bought this house in town. Otherwise we would not be here.' He disliked to give me pain and he knew I loved to dance.

---

[5] Thought to ward off disease, ferula assafoetida (giant fennel) is a foul-smelling wild plant. It is not to be confused with garden fennel, which has a licorice scent.

Finally he jokingly said `Little girl, Dr. Wilson is trying to educate your mind and I must help him. After awhile there will be time a plenty to educate your heels.'"

Rebecca was delighted, however, when her parents gave her a dancing party at the end of the school term.

The Latimers spent five years in Decatur, while their daughters attended the Rev. Wilson's school. During that period, their education was interrupted for a time by the area's first smallpox epidemic. "The disease was brought into Atlanta by a guest at Thompson's hotel and spread panic all through that section... Vaccine matter was as scarce as hen's teeth. We refugeed to the river plantation."

Rebecca resumed attending a rural school. "I learned to play marbles and study Latin grammar and carried to school in a little basket a small bottle of molasses for use at lunch time. Nothing in later life has been more appetizing than those good biscuits with holes punched with my forefinger and then filled with molasses. We also ate hard-boiled eggs and cold sweet potatoes and green apples with salt without telling about the latter at home. We sat on hard benches ranged along the wall with books lying under us on the floor... At recess time we paddled in the spring branch occasionally with bare feet and the boys brought red apples and plums in their pockets for their favorite girls."

Rebecca attended college for two years in Madison, Ga., beginning when she was 15, studying piano, guitar, pencil drawing and French. At the age of 17, she received her diploma in July, 1852, and read the valedictory essay. It was in Madison that she met William Felton. Rebecca and William had five children, all but one died before adulthood. [10]

Rebecca Latimer Felton spoke at a luncheon at the DeKalb Courthouse sponsored by the Decatur Woman's Club on the occasion of her 90th birthday in 1925. "The goal of life is neither money nor fame," she said. "It is the battling against an obstruction, with the aim to conquering it and making it your own. Victory is the mind's elixir of youth. Brooding brings age, and I haven't had time to feel sorry for myself. Service is the secret of longevity."

Rebecca Latimer Felton died on January 24, 1930. The U. S. Senate held a special service in her memory two days later.

Chapter 16 Notes

1. Candler, Charles Murphey, November 9, 1922, Historical Address.

2. Trotti, Louise Haygood, "My Kinspeople," abstracted from Country Life in Georgia in the Days of My Youth, written by Rebecca Latimer Felton.

3. Willard, Levi, 1920, "The Early History of Decatur Written Many Years Ago, DeKalb New Era. Candler, Charles Murphey, November 9, 1922, Historical Address. Felton, Rebecca Latimer, genealogy file, DeKalb Historical Society.

4. Martin, Stiles A., 1952, "Mrs. William H. Felton," The Collections of the DeKalb Historical Society, Vol. 1, 1952, pages 60-65. Chapman, Ashton, May 21, 1933, "Felton Home to Be Restored -- The Historic Latimer Plantation at Flat Shoals, Fifteen Miles From Atlanta, Will Be Made Into a Memorial to Mrs. Rebecca Latimer Felton," Atlanta Journal.

5. Rogers, Evelyna Keadle, Summer, 1978, "Famous Georgia Women: Rebecca Latimer Felton," Georgia Life magazine. Martin, Stiles A., 1952, "Mrs. William H. Felton," The Collections of the DeKalb Historical Society, Vol. 1, pages 60-65. McCullar, Bernice, March 23, 1966, "First Woman in U. S. Senate Got Assist From George," Georgia Notebook.

6. Martin, Stiles A., 1952, "Mrs. William H. Felton," The Collections of the DeKalb Historical Society, Vol. 1, pages 60-65.

7. Martin, Stiles A., 1952, "Mrs. William H. Felton," The Collections of the DeKalb Historical Society, Vol. 1, pages 60-65. Felton, Rebecca Latimer, genealogy files, DeKalb Historical Society.

8. Clarke, Caroline McKinney, 1973, 1997, The Story of Decatur 1823-1899, page 13.

9. Clarke, Caroline McKinney, 1973, The Story of Decatur 1823-1899, page 16. Candler, Charles Murphey and Scott, Otober 29, 1950, "History of The Decatur Presbyterian Church, Decatur, Ga."

10. Trotti, Louise Haygood, "My Kinspeople," abstracted from Country Life in Georgia in the Days of My Youth, written by Rebecca Latimer Felton. Martin, Stiles A., 1952, "Mrs. William H. Felton," The Collections of the DeKalb Historical Society, Vol. 1, pages 60-65.

Chapter 17

*F*rom the time DeKalb County was organized, Stone Mountain has been what it is today -- a natural curiosity and a tourist attraction, an attractive location used primarily for recreation.

Prior to 1825, it was called Rock Mountain. The Rev. Adiel Sherwood, publisher of the Georgia Gazetteer, is credited with coining the "more euphonious" name, Stone Mountain. [1]

As early as the mid-1820s, the mountain was the most popular resort in Georgia. Climbing the mountain before dawn and watching the sun come up while eating breakfast at the Devil's Cross Roads was a popular activity. [2]

The Rev. Francis R. Goulding of Darien, Ga., then 12 years old, visited Stone Mountain on June 25, 1822, with his father, a cousin, a Cherokee guide named Kanooka and slave boy named Scipio. In later years, he recorded the approach to the mountain of the little party and his subsequent impressions:

"Twenty miles away to the southeast a vast prominence of rock loomed in lonely grandeur above the horizon. It was the great natural curiosity of the neighborhood, of which we had often heard and which we had resolved to visit at our first opportunity. That time had now come. Indeed, the fame of the great rock had extended to the Old Country, and had there excited interest through the representation of a British officer who had visited and described it as early as the year 1788.

"At the time of our visit the country around had barely passed into the hands of the white man, and there were few roads and fewer houses of accommodation. Our tent was pitched beside a spring near the mountain's base, around the north and west of which flows a pleasant stream. From this point the rock rose majestically, with an almost perpendicular face of a thousand feet. We enjoyed its rough grandeur almost as much by the soft light of the moon as we did by the red light of the setting sun.

"Taking an early breakfast the next morning we made our way first to the eastern side of the mountain. Here the view was stupendous. A bare, hemispherical mass of solid granite rose before us to the height of two or three thousand feet, striped along its side as if torn by lightning or `gullied' by the action of water through countless ages.

An 1845 engraving of Stone Mountain shows Cloud's Tower on the misty mountaintop. The original drawing by J. Smilie, from a sketch by T. Addison Richards, ran in Graham's Magazine. (DeKalb Historical Society)

"Our ascent was effected on the southwest side, where the slope is comparatively easy, and where the otherwise baldness of the rock is relieved by an occasional tuft of dwarfed cedars or stunted oaks, which find a root hold in the crevices. These trees, elevated a quarter of a mile above the surrounding level, seem to be a favorite resort for buzzards, many of which were wheeling in graceful flight in the air around, and a greater number which perched upon dead treetops, apparently resting from their labors and watching from the convenient height for objects on which they might feed in the level country below.

"We found the summit an irregularly flat oval about a furlong in length. The view from it was superb. Not another mountain could be seen in any direction within a distance of twenty-five or thirty miles. The country all around seemed to be an immense level, or rather a basin, the rim of which rose on all sides to meet the blue of the sky. To the east and south appeared a few clearings, but in every other direction the forest was unbroken." [3]

Early DeKalb County historian Levi Willard recalled that the mountain was a particularly popular place for couples. "Mountain visitors went to take the preliminary steps to such an issue (marriage)." Visits were usually made on horseback. "It is reported that matches were made on these little rides. It was easy to lag behind the company -- Sallie's saddle was turning and must be girted tighter, or the blanket was slipping out of place, or some other excuse for stopping a minute.

"This brings up fresh memories of old times, when we used to take rides to the Stone Mountain, each

By 1849, visitors were able to reach Stone Mountain by railroad. Pictured in the background is Andrew Johnson's Stone Mountain Hotel. (Woodruff Library Special Collections, Emory University)

young man and his ladylove coupled off together, as he waits `to get to pop the question.' Well does your humble correspondent remember those days, and how he tried to muster courage on those occasions to `pop the question,' but his heart failed him and he never could, nor did he get it out, but lost his lady. What happy reflections it revives of old times!"

Dr. R. J. Massey recalled: "As early as July 4, 1828, a number of visitors celebrated the day with a dinner on the top of this mountain. Along with other performances, a poem entitled `Spirits of '76' was delivered. Long after the completion of the Georgia Railroad to Atlanta, Stone Mountain retained its prominence as a pleasure resort and as a center of travel... At this time, in very important matters, Stone Mountain was a place of gathering, preferred even to Atlanta." [4]

"Thousands of people visited the place annually, some of them coming from remote parts of the State and some from distant sections of the South." [5]

Stone Mountain was the subject of an article in the Macon Telegraph on April 3, 1830:

"The Stone Mountain is a huge solid peak of solitary rock, three thousand feet in height, and six or

Legend has it that early owners of Stone Mountain would trade just about anything for the mountain because it was useless for farming. (Brooke Collection, DeKalb Historical Society)

seven miles in circumference. The finest view of this stupendous pyramid is obtained from the eastern side. Seen from this point at a distance, it has the appearance of a large dark cloud streaked with thunder and lightning. Approach it nearer, and its figure and consistence become distinguishable; you see the bold, naked rock, nearly globular in form, of a darkish gray colour. On climbing it, the shrubs and bushes are scattered so thinly over its sides among the crevices, that it appears nearly bald. About half way up to the right of your path is pointed out a small tuft of scrub cedars and oaks, designated as the Buzzard's Roost, from the number of those birds hovering about the spot.

"About a quarter of a mile from the top are seen the remains of a fortification that formerly extended around and defended every accessible point leading to the summit, the only entrance being through a natural passage under a large rock, where only one person could enter at a time, and that by crawling on all-fours. The whole length of the wall at first was probably a mile, breast high on the inside, and constructed of the loose fragments of the rocks. On reaching the summit, you have a beautiful and extensive view of the country. The top presents an uneven surface, nearly flat, of an oval shape, two or three hundred yards in width, and about twice that in length.

"Many hollows are observable in the winter and spring, filled with water, and occasionally little patches of soil, where various shrubs and herbs luxuriate. On the eastern side, some distance from the top, is a little grove called the Eagle's Nest. Adjoining it, among the broken fragments, are a number of frightful caverns, called the Lion's Den, the Panther's Hole, etc.

"From the summit you may ramble down the arch in any direction for several hundred yards, without danger.

"A pathetic story is told of a couple of hounds that a year or two ago followed their owners to the top of the mountain, and in performing their gambols around the edge of the precipice, had got too far down to be able to get back. One slid immediately over, and was dashed to pieces on the rocks below, not a whole bone being left in his skin; the other held to the rock for two days, howling piteously, but at last became exhausted, fell, and shared the fate of his companion." [6]

In 1838 Aaron Cloud, a Henry County resident, purchased from Andrew Johnson for $100 150 square feet at the apex of the mountain for a most unusual project. The Southern Recorder in Milledgeville reported on April 10, 1838: "Mr. Aaron Cloud, of McDonough, Ga., is now engaged in erecting a tower or observatory on the top of Stone Mountain in DeKalb County, and is determined to raise it to the height of 300 feet."

Appropriately called Cloud's Tower, the structure drew curious visitors from miles around, despite that its finished height was only slightly more than half what had been advertised. A popular dance hall and tavern occupied the ground floor. [7]

William C. Richards wrote about visiting the tower in an 1842 edition of Georgia Illustrated: "In the afternoon we ascended the mountain, accompanied by the owner of the tower. This singular edifice, resembling somewhat a lighthouse, is an octagonal pyramid, built entirely of wood. It stands upon the rock with no fastenings but its own gravity, and its height is 165 feet. It was built three years ago at a cost of $5,000. The erection of a lofty tower upon the summit of a high mountain is certainly a unique and curious exploit. The projector and proprietor is Mr. Aaron Cloud, of McDonough, and the work is commonly called Cloud's Tower. We ascended to the summit by nearly three hundred steps. The prospects we obtained were wide and beautiful, having the single fault of being rather too monotonous. The eyes rest upon a vast continuity of forest. The plantations and settlements appear small amid the sea of foliage. By the aid of good telescopes we distinguish five county towns. By way of parenthesis, I remark, that in 1847 I ascended this tower and took in view the surrounding territory. Among the towns I located was that of Atlanta, then a few straggling huts, just beyond Decatur. [8]

Rebecca Latimer Felton remembers visiting Cloud's Tower. "There was a tower on the mountain that I saw first when I was a small child. There was that day dancing galore in the lower hall of the tower. A candy vendor persuaded my father to buy for me a white candy dove with buckshot for its eyes. The first tower was blown down in a storm and its successor was erected on the highest point on the mountain. The second one, also, went to the discard." [9]

"Tradition holds that a small settlement was in existence prior to 1823, before a house was ever built in Decatur." [10] However, white settlement prior to the Creek Indian cession of 1821 and the subsequent state land lottery would have been quite unlikely.

Whenever it first appeared, the village at the base of the mountain was originally called New Gibraltar. By 1825 a stagecoach ran from Milledgeville to Stone Mountain with stops at Eatonton and Madison. In 1828 the route was expanded to Dahlonega, and stops added at Lawrenceville and Gainesville. The Rock Mountain Post Office was established on July 18, 1834, with William Cochran as the first postmaster, who served until January 13, 1835. He was succeeded by Andrew Browning. William Meadow was the first postmaster after the name was changed to Stone Mountain on June 9, 1836. Subsequent postmasters were Andrew Johnson, 1839-46; Drewry Lee, 1846-47; Alexander C. Fowler,

1847-48; George K. Smith, 1848-49; Samuel H. Dean, 1849-55; and Thompson A. Browning, 1855-65. [11]

The town of New Gibraltar (later called Stone Mountain) probably was located at the base of the mountain near the current location of Memorial Hall in Stone Mountain Park when it was incorporated by the Georgia General Assembly on December 21, 1839. First commissioners were Andrew Johnson, Isaiah Parker, Silas Pool, William Beauchamp and Drury Lee. The original city was all of Land Lot 89 in the 18th District. On December 28, 1843, the Georgia legislature enlarged the city limits to extend 600 yards in all directions from the house of Andrew Johnson. In addition, the 1843 act provided "that the citizens resident within the corporate limits of said town shall be exempt from road-duty -- provided, that nothing herein contained shall be so construed as to exempt said citizens from working on the streets and other public grounds in said town." [12]

The Stone Mountain Academy was incorporated one year before the town, on December 31, 1838. Tuition in 1840 was five and one-half cents per pupil per day. [13]

After the coming of the railroad in 1845, the town moved to its current location, with the depot becoming the central focus. The name of the town was changed to Stone Mountain on December 24, 1847. [14]

Although the land was not particularly good for farming, because of the frequent granite outcroppings, the area drew its share of early settlers. One was Absalom Steward, said to have been one of the first, if not the first, white settler in DeKalb. Steward was the son of William Stewart who was born in England in 1763 and ran away to sea at the age of 14. Absalom and his wife, Betty Cornwell, had two sons: Elijah Greene and Wilson. Elijah married Annie Alford; their John Barnett Steward married Mary Jane Dean. Absalom Steward was one of DeKalb County's first justices of the Inferior Court, originally commissioned in Henry County in 1822. [15]

Some early Stone Mountain landowners were Joel H. Stubbs, Aaron Cloud, S. H. Dean, Henry Dulley, J. B. Turner, William N. Pool, William B. Turner, William Roussom, Michael Winningham and Dr. J. L. Hamilton. The land where the town would spring up belonged to Andrew Johnson by the late 1830s, possibly sold to him by John William Beauchamp. [16]

Chapter 17 Notes

1. Eldridge, Leila Venable Mason, 1952, "Stone Mountain," The Collections of the DeKalb Historical Society, Vol. 1, pages 44-45.

2. Jones, Annie, May 22, 1950, "The First Things About DeKalb," DeKalb Historical Society.

3. Neal, Willard, 1963, "The Story of Stone Mountain."

4. Knight, Lucian Lamar, 1914, Georgia's Landmarks, Memorials and Legends, Vol. II, page 245-251.

5. Knight, Lucian Lamar, 1914, Georgia's Landmarks, Memorials and Legends, Vol. II, page 245-251.

6. Garrett, Franklin M., 1954, 1969, Atlanta and Environs -- A Chronicle of Its People and Events, Vol. 1, page 81.

7. Eldridge, Leila Venable Mason, 1952, "Stone Mountain," The Collections of the DeKalb Historical Society, Vol. 1, pages 44-45.

8. Knight, Lucian Lamar, 1914, Georgia's Landmarks, Memorials and Legends, Vol. II, page 245-251.

9. Trotti, Louise Haygood, "My Kinspeople," abstracted from Country Life in Georgia in the Days of My Youth, written by Rebecca Latimer Felton.

10. Joseph, J. W., and Kehoe, Lisa M., November 14, 1994, Historic Sites Survey, City of Stone Mountain DeKalb County, Georgia, New South Associates. Knight, Lucian Lamar, 1914, Georgia's Landmarks, Memorials and Legends, Vol. II, page 245-251.

11. Garrett, Franklin M., 1954, 1969, Atlanta and Environs -- A Chronicle of Its People and Events, Vol. 1, page 127.

12. Garrett, Franklin M., 1954, 1969, Atlanta and Environs -- A Chronicle of Its People and Events, Vol. 1, page 204.

13. Garrett, Franklin M., 1954, 1969, Atlanta and Environs -- A Chronicle of Its People and Events, Vol. 1, pages 127 and 159. Candler, Charles Murphey, November 9, 1922, Historical Address.

14. Joseph, J. W., and Kehoe, Lisa M., November 14, 1994, Historic Sites Survey, City of Stone Mountain DeKalb County, Georgia, New South Associates. Garrett, Franklin M., 1954, 1969, Atlanta and Environs -- A Chronicle of Its People and Events, Vol. 1, page 127.

15. The Collections of the DeKalb Historical Society, Vol. 1, 1952, page 99.

16. Joseph, J. W., and Kehoe, Lisa M., November 14, 1994, Historic Sites Survey, City of Stone Mountain DeKalb County, Georgia, New South Associates. Eldridge, Leila Venable Mason, 1952, "Stone Mountain," The Collections of the DeKalb Historical Society, Vol. 1, pages 44-45.

Chapter 18

In 1826 roads and bridges continued to be the primary topic of business before the DeKalb Inferior Court justices. Road commissioners John Beasley, Abraham Chandler, Benjamin Plaster and Charles Bonner reported to Magistrate Meredith Collier on January 23, 1826 that they had laid out a new road beginning at George Stitt's landing on the Chattahoochee River to Decatur. "We as commissioners in viewing the road believe that the road is practicable and on as good ground as the country will admit of." Stitt's Landing probably was somewhere between the Shallow Ford and Standing Peachtree. [1]

On February 14, 1826, the Inferior Court appointed the following new road commissioners: Thornton Ward, Dempsey Perkerson and Lochlin Johnson in Capt. Gettin's District; Samuel L. Wilson, Adam Poole and Daniel Childs in Capt. Scaif's District; and Meredith Collier and James Campbell in Capt. Merritt's Dist. [2]

Five months later, on July 3, 1826, the court ordered that the road leading from Fayetteville to Decatur (Fayetteville Road) "be turned so as to run from John Mitchell's or from the bridge on South River and to cross Intrenchment Creek at or near Meredith Brown's, thence the nearest and best way to Decatur." John Carter, James Corlee and Richard Respess were assigned the job of "turning" the road. [3]

One might naturally assume that Intrenchment Creek was named because of some Civil War activity there, but such is not the case. Intrenchment Creek was listed by District Surveyor John Kell in the original survey of then Henry County in 1821. Historian John Goff speculated that Kell "may have named it for an Indian mound or mounds that stood along the waterway; or, he may have applied the name because of some trenches the Indians had dug in quarrying soapstone in the vicinity of the stream... One clue intimates Intrenchment Creek may have derived its name from some sort of defensive structure. Mr. Wade H. Wright of the Georgia Power Company was reared on the lower side of South River, downstream from the mouth of the creek. He states on his father's farm there was a field which was traditionally known as the Fort Field because the Indians were said to have maintained a fort on the site." The field was closer to the mouth of Sugar Creek than Intrenchment Creek but presence of a fort in the community suggests there may have been some connection with the latter stream that is not now clear." [4]

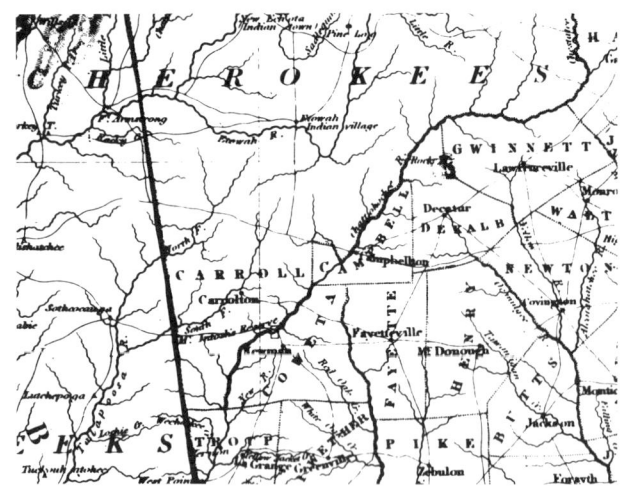

In 1829, DeKalb County no longer shared borders with the Cherokee and Creek Indians. Note the location of Stone Mountain at the northern boundary of DeKalb. (Woodruff Library Special Collections, Emory University)

The maintenance of James Montgomery's bridge over the Chattahoochee River was taken off his hands on November 26, 1826, when the Inferior Court ordered the bridge near Standing Peachtree "be received as a public bridge and taken into public patronage." Commissioners were appointed "to let or make a contract for a covering and banistering of said bridge and to see that it is kept in good order. Said covering and banistering not to exceed $30.00." Montgomery's bridge was probably located where the Moore's Mill Road bridge is now. [5]

In its final session in December, 1826 the sum of $24 was ordered to be paid to Joel Swinney out of county funds for building a bridge across Snapfinger Creek. The order was signed by Justices William Towers, John Reid and Reuben Cone. [6]

Other business before the Inferior Court in 1826 including payment of two citizens for services rendered to the county. On January 7, James Diamond was ordered to be paid $30 for surveying town lots in Decatur. Joseph D. Shumate was paid $10 for "an Inquest held on Utoy Creek over a person unknown." The order was approved on May 1. [7]

DeKalb County's second post office opened on May 23, 1826 in Decatur, with Ephraim McClean as the first Decatur postmaster. Following McClean were Jesse F. Cleveland, April 16, 1828; Barnett F. Cleveland, October 21, 1831; Jesse F. Cleveland, March 4, 1834; Thomas A. Sullivan, November 14, 1834; John Glen, March 29, 1839; Daniel Stone, February 3, 1848; Elijah Rosser, November 13, 1852; William A. Powell, January 24, 1856; James A. Bale, January 10, 1859; William W. Bradbury, December 2, 1859; and John N. Pate, December 6, 1865. [8]

Other citizens who moved to DeKalb about this time included John Johnson (1783-1850) who came from Clarke County in 1822 and raised a large family in the Cross Keys District. By his first wife, Permelia Mayne, he had four children. He sired 12 more children by his second wife, Mourning Britain. John Gerdine Johnson (1817-1883), son of John and Mourning, later owned much of the property now covered by the Druid Hills community.

South Carolinian James Donehoo came to DeKalb from Franklin County, Ga., where in 1817 he married Elizabeth, daughter of William Wilson. The Wilsons and Donehoos settled in western DeKalb. Brothers William, Richard, Benjamin F. and David Thurman came to Georgia from Chesterfield County, S. C. in 1826 and settled in what is now Ormewood Park and East Atlanta. [9]

Residents of western DeKalb County worried a little less about Indians in 1826, as the often-hostile Muskogee (Creek) Indians gave up the last of their land in Georgia to the state government on January 24. [10]

DeKalb County and the town of Decatur were described in 1827 by Rev. Adiel Sherwood in his

Georgia Gazetteer. The entire county had a population of only 3569 that year. Decatur, "the capital," contained a courthouse, jail, academy and 40 houses, stores and other structures. "Many buildings are now erecting," Sherwood said, "and it bids fair to be a large town." Two years later, in his 1829 Gazetteer, Sherwood said that the number of buildings had increased to 50. The DeKalb Academy had received $1267.05, and the Poor School Fund $639.30. Decatur, he said, was a "healthy spot, though it was visited for the first time by the bilious fever in 1828."

Sherwood also reported the figures from the 1825 Cherokee Indian census: 13,563 Cherokees in Georgia, all officially living just on the other side of the Chattahoochee River from DeKalb County, although several local family histories claim that Cherokee Indians were living in DeKalb. The census reported 147 white men married to Cherokee women and 73 white women married to Cherokee men. The Cherokees, the census said, owned 1,277 slaves.

On December 26, 1827, the state of Georgia gave DeKalb and Carroll counties criminal jurisdiction over portions of the Cherokee Nation.

"And be it further enacted by the Authority aforesaid, that all that portion of the unlocated territory of this State, lying north of the aforesaid line, and south of the Hightower Trail, be added to the County of DeKalb, for the purpose of criminal jurisdiction, and that all crimes and misdemeanors committed on any part of the aforesaid territory, by or against any citizen of this State, or of the United States, shall be cognizable and triable in the aforesaid County of DeKalb."

Thus, DeKalb County officials became involved in the case of a killing in Indian territory. John Goddard testified before DeKalb County justices of the Inferior Court on August 12, 1827 that he saw a Cherokee Indian named Old Man kill a white man named Dennis Mays. The following letter was sent to Gov. George M. Troup:

Sir
Your excellency will pleas (sic) Issue a proclamation sufficient as your Excellency in discretion may think proper for the apprehending and bringing to Justice said Indian and your humble petitioners as in duty bound will ever pray &c

Thomas Godard J.I.C.
John Godard
John W. Thompson
Isaac Howell
Joshua Brooks
Thomas Brown
Thomas Pettet
William Fain

Joseph C. Thompson
John W W dlf Thompson
James Adams
James D. Thompson
Isaac Calhoun
Randsom Thompson J. P.
W. T. Colquitt [11]

In legislation passed in 1828 and 1829, Georgia seized the Cherokee Nation, annexing its territory to Carroll, DeKalb, Gwinnett, Hall and Habersham counties. The legislation was signed by Gov. George R. Gilmer, who had been commanding officer at Fort Peachtree 15 years earlier. The Cherokees appealed to the U. S. Supreme Court for an injunction against the state, and Georgia, in turn, demanded that federal government comply with a promise it had made in 1802 to remove the Cherokees. [12]

The Supreme Court ruled that neither the federal, nor the state, government had any jurisdiction over the Cherokee Indian nation, with which the United States had signed a lawful treaty. Chief Justice John Marshall's opinion, delivered on March 3, 1832, declared Georgia's new laws unconstitutional. Marshall wrote: "The Cherokee Acts of the Georgia Legislature are repugnant to the constitution, laws ann treaties of the United States. They inferfere forcibly with the relations established between the United States and the Cherokee Nation. This controlling fact the laws of Georgia ignore. They violently disrupt the relations between the Indians and the United States; they are equally antagonistic to acts of Congress based upon these treaties..."

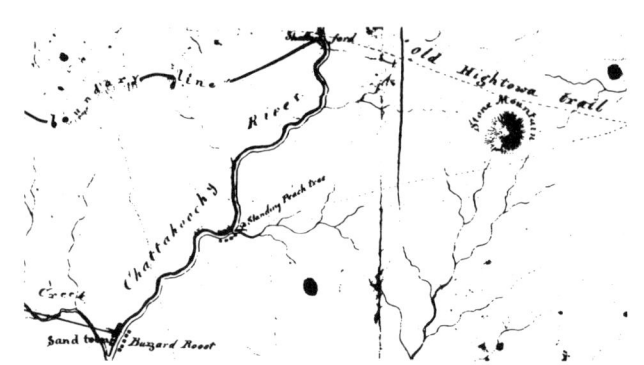

An 1829 map by John Coffee shows Sandtown, Buzzard's Roost, Standing Peachtree and the "Hightowa" Trail. (DeKalb Historical Society)

President Andrew Jackson gave his famous reply: "John Marshall has made his decision. Now let him enforce it!" Georgia had defied the federal government and won. The judgement did nothing to help the Cherokees. [13]

Gold was discovered in Dahlonega in 1829, and one year later 4,000 white prospectors had been lured deep into the Cherokee Nation. With money at stake, the drive to remove the Indians from north Georgia became even more urgent. In 1830, the Georgia legislature authorized a survey of all the land north and west of the Chattahoochee River and distribution of the land to white citizens through a lottery. Military guards were sent to protect surveyors and the territory's gold mines. [14]

The news of the gold strike spread as far away as Bath, Maine, where Benjamin Franklin Swanton his ship-building family had lived since the close of the 18th century. Swanton came to Georgia in 1828 to sell machinery to gold miners. Swanton sold his equipment and settled in Decatur, purchasing a home from Ammi Williams, shortly after Williams's daughter, Laura, was born there on February 4, 1844. The house, once described as the nicest in Decatur, was located on Atlanta Avenue. Swanton, and his wife, Sarah Fowle Hale, raised two children there: a daughter, Sarah Elizabeth, and son John Bowers. Swanton operated a steam and water powered gin, grist mill, machine shop, tanyard and brick kiln on nearby Peavine Creek. Sarah Elizabeth Swanton never married. John Swanton married Josephine Frances Woodbury in 1868; they had nine children. Their descendants lived in the house until the mid-1960s, when it was donated to the DeKalb Historical Society. The house was moved to Decatur's Adair Park historic complex and restored, and is now preserved for the public to visit.

"Gold fever" struck some of DeKalb's most prominent citizens. "Oliver Clarke, Reuben Cone, Alexander Corry, Jesse Fain, James White and William Ezzard formed what was known as the Decatur Gold Mining Company and went wild in looking for the precious metal. They brought to the county Kenneth Gillis, a much learned man, who could talk strata and substrata, of stars in the heavens and of things beneath the earth. It was never known who `salted' Avery's spring branch, but `salted' it was, and the Decatur Gold Mining Company went to pieces a much sadder, but a much wiser set of men than they were when Kenneth Gillis came among them." [15]

For most of DeKalb's citizens, however, it was business as usual in the county.

James Anderson was becoming useful Jack-of-all-trades in DeKalb. As county surveyor, he was paid $36.50 in June of 1827 "for running the line between DeKalb County and Newton County." He also received $7.50 for ironing during William Heard's "sundrie times while in the jail." On July 15, 1828, the Inferior Court "ordered that the County Treasurer of DeKalb County pay to James Anderson the sum of $6 for surveying a part of the town lot and mending jail lock out of county funds. Also $1.25 for arresting a woman out of any money arising from fines and forfeitures." [16]

Anderson was not the only public official in DeKalb to perform a variety of unrelated jobs. The Inferior Court, on April 28, 1827, reported that tax collector Jesse Sanford and treasurer Alexander Corry assisted coroner Larkin Carlton in an inquest held over the body of Samuel Davis.

More road business occupied the DeKalb Inferior Court in 1827:
• June 5, the court ordered "that a road be opened from the flat shoals on the South River to Swinney's Mill as has been marked by James Morris and John Gunn." Swinney's Mill was located on Snapfinger Creek near Covington Road.

• June 18, "Ordered that a road be cleared out and opened from or near the 7 mile post on Sandtown Road by Millally's (sic) store thence so as to touch the Fayette County line at lot #2 in 14 dist. at South line of lot 225, as has been marked out by James Blackstock, Joseph Stone and Thomas Higgins and kept up as public road of DeKalb County." This road was located in the southwest corner of DeKalb, west of present city of East Point.

• September 3, ordered "that Stephen Jett, James A. Davidson, Levi Dempsey and William Hardman be appointed to run and mark out a road leading from Decatur on by way of Harmony meeting house and on to the shoal where James Gober lives on the Chattahoochee."

• September 4, received "a petition was presented from a large and respectable number of the citizens requesting that a road may be established leading from Decatur to intersect the Peachtree Road at or near James Hooper's. Ordered that Silas McGrady, Varner Hardman, and James Hooper, Sr., are appointed to serve and mark out a road according to said petition and make a report to the next session of the Inferior Court." Hooper lived between the current towns of Chamblee and Doraville on Peachtree Road in the Cross Keys District. [17]

Road issues continued to occupy the Inferior Court in 1828. In March, the court ordered two new roads opened -- one "from the three mile post leading from Decatur towards Peachtree to Peachtree at or near James Hooper's on said Peachtree Road" and the other "leading from Decatur to the Shallow Ford on the Chattahoochee River as marked by Naman Hardman and Lindsey M. Post." On October 20, the court met in special session to appoint a replacement road commissioner for Adam Poole, who "refused to act as a Commissioner." Poole's job had been to lay out a road from Howell's Ferry on the Chattahoochee to Cross Roads or George's store (now Lithonia). Howell's Ferry Road is now Adamsville Road; the ferry was operated by Isaac Howell, great grandfather of Clark Howell, publisher of <u>The Atlanta Constitution</u>. [18]

The 1828 Georgia General Assembly added to DeKalb Land Lot 307 and fractional Land Lot 308 from the Sixth District of Gwinnett. The lot run along what is now Winters Chapel Road. DeKalb gained from Gwinnett an addition fractional land lot, no. 248, in 1829; small acreage lies at the intersection of the old Hightower Trail and Peachtree Road. The 1828 legislature created Campbell County in 1828 from parts of Carroll, Coweta, DeKalb and Fayette. The frontier Indian village of

Sandtown/Buzzard's Roost became part of the new county, and the mouth of Utoy Creek became DeKalb's southwestern border. [19]

Many early DeKalb names are found on the Inferior Court jury list drawn May 16, 1828:

James Adams	John Hesterly	Sidney Smith
William Baker	John B. Holbrooks	Ellis Swinney
Hiram Buckley	Lochlin Johnson	John Townsend
James Campbell	Robert Jones	Lodawick Tuggle
William Carr	William Lawson	Benjamin Vines
William Conn	J. V. Kilgore	Jordan Webb
Shadrick Farmer	James Millican	S. L. Wilson
W. P. Forster	J. McC. Montgomery	Elijah Williams
Daniel Furgerson	Newton Randal	Joseph Woodall
Nealy Goodwin	Willis Roberts	Jesse Williams
Williford Grogan	William Robertson	John Woodall
Naman Hardman	B. D. Shumate	
Edward C. Harris		

Because of his duties as postmaster and mail carrier at Standing Peachtree, James Montgomery was excused from serving.

On April 5, 1829, Lochlin Johnson, Lemuel Cobb and Aaron Starns (sic) certified to the Inferior Court: "We receive the bridge across South river on the road from Decatur to McDonough." On May 4, the court appointed Lewis Peacock, Thomas Smith and Thomas L. Thomas "to view and mark out a road from James Brewster on the road leading from Decatur to Coweta County on by the Methodist meeting house near John M. Smith's (Mt. Gilead near Ben Hill) through the corner of the 14th Dist. of originally Fayette now Campbell and DeKalb the nearest and best route on the line of Campbell and DeKalb counties." On July 14, Justices James Lemon, James Paden and Thomas Ray "ordered that the road leading through DeKalb from the line of Gwinnett County, known by the name of the Peachtree Road be opened and kept up as a public road of said county." On November 25, the court ordered the road marked out by Hiram Buckley, Wesley Martin and Lindsey Elsberry from Standing Peachtree to Leonard Hornsby's (in now East Point) be opened, cleared out and maintained as a public road. [20]

The court also approved on May 4, 1829 Reuben Martin's application to operate a ferry on the Chattahoochee River above the Shallow Ford. Martin was allowed to charge the following rates as toll: "for every road wagon loaded crossing .62; empty .50; cart or two horse wagon .37; for a gig or one horse carriage of any description .25; for a man and a single horse. 12. Footman or lead horse .06 1/4; cattle .04 a head; hogs and sheep .02 a head." Approval was contingent upon Martin posting a $1000 bond "for the keeping of a good flat" and his "faithful performance of the duties of ferryman." Martin's Ferry was located one-half mile upstream from the present Roswell Bridge. [21]

The Inferior Court appointed Samuel Rutledge and David Wright on May 27, 1827 "to view and value the extra work done in and about the court house and report on oath so far as respects the windows of said house which has been done by Harbour and King." The work was judged satisfactory, and the county treasurer ordered to pay Harbour and King $327.65. [22] This likely was the last work done on the county's first courthouse.

The county jury would continue to meet in the small log courthouse for two more years, until 1829, when "a neat brick building" was built at a cost of about $5,100. George Tomlinson was the contractor. This courthouse was built in the center of the public square. The courtroom was located on the first floor, with offices and the jury room on the second. The Inferior Court accepted the bid of contractor George Tomlinson on April 21, 1829. In March James Lemon was paid $10 to purchase materials for glazing, and Thomas Ray awarded $15 for making the steps to the front door. [23]

Levi Willard recalled that after the county abandoned the old log courthouse, it remained on the north side of the square and was occupied by "Uncle Joe Crockett" and used as a "grog shop." Later, the log building was moved across the street. At one it was known time known as Hodges House. [24]

Chapter 18 Notes

1. Garrett, Franklin M., 1954, 1969, Atlanta and Environs -- A Chronicle of Its People and Events, Vol. 1, page 56.

2. Garrett, Franklin M., 1954, 1969, Atlanta and Environs -- A Chronicle of Its People and Events, Vol. 1, page 56.

3. Garrett, Franklin M., 1954, 1969, Atlanta and Environs -- A Chronicle of Its People and Events, Vol. 1, page 56.

4. Goff, Dr. John H., Georgia Placenames, page 217.

5. Garrett, Franklin M., 1954, 1969, Atlanta and Environs -- A Chronicle of Its People and Events, Vol. 1, page 57.

6. Garrett, Franklin M., 1954, 1969, Atlanta and Environs -- A Chronicle of Its People and Events, Vol. 1, page 57.

7. Garrett, Franklin M., 1954, 1969, Atlanta and Environs -- A Chronicle of Its People and Events, Vol. 1, page 56.

8. Garrett, Franklin M., 1954, 1969, Atlanta and Environs -- A Chronicle of Its People and Events, Vol. 1, page 58.

9. Garrett, Franklin M., 1954, 1969, Atlanta and Environs -- A Chronicle of Its People and Events, Vol. 1, page 58.

10. Garrett, Franklin M., 1954, 1969, Atlanta and Environs -- A Chronicle of Its People and Events, Vol. 1, page 55.

11. Bryan, Mrs. Mary Givens, 1952, "Documents Related To Indian Affairs," The Collections of the DeKalb Historical Society, Vol. 1, pages 15-25.

12. Shadburn, Don L., 1989, Cherokee Planters in Georgia 1832-1838, page 201. Mitchell, Eugene M., September, 1937, "The Indians of Georgia," The Atlanta Historical Bulletin, No. 11, pages 20-30.

13. Garrett, Franklin M., 1954, 1969, Atlanta and Environs -- A Chronicle of Its People and Events, Vol. 1, page 106.

14. Shadburn, Don L., 1989, Cherokee Planters in Georgia 1832-1838, page 201. Mitchell, Eugene M., September, 1937, "The Indians of Georgia," The Atlanta Historical Bulletin, No. 11, pages 20-30.

15. Garrett, Franklin M., 1954, 1969, Atlanta and Environs -- A Chronicle of Its People and Events, Vol. 1, page 81.

16. Garrett, Franklin M., 1954, 1969, Atlanta and Environs -- A Chronicle of Its People and Events, Vol. 1, pages 63 and 69.

17. Garrett, Franklin M., 1954, 1969, Atlanta and Environs -- A Chronicle of Its People and Events, Vol. 1, pages 63 and 64.

18. Garrett, Franklin M., 1954, 1969, Atlanta and Environs -- A Chronicle of Its People and Events, Vol. 1, page 69.

19. Garrett, Franklin M., 1954, 1969, Atlanta and Environs -- A Chronicle of Its People and Events, Vol. 1, pages 71 and 76.

20. Garrett, Franklin M., 1954, 1969, Atlanta and Environs -- A Chronicle of Its People and Events, Vol. 1, pages 75 and 76.

21. Garrett, Franklin M., 1954, 1969, Atlanta and Environs -- A Chronicle of Its People and Events, Vol. 1, page 76.

22. Garrett, Franklin M., 1954, 1969, Atlanta and Environs -- A Chronicle of Its People and Events, Vol. 1, pages 63.

23. Willard, Levi, 1920, "The Early History of Decatur Written Many Years Ago," DeKalb New Era. Candler, Charles Murphey, November 9, 1922, Historical Address, page 6. Garrett, Franklin M., 1954, 1969, Atlanta and Environs -- A Chronicle of Its People and Events, Vol. 1, page 77.

24. Willard, Levi, 1920, "The Early History of Decatur Written Many Years Ago," DeKalb New Era.

Chapter 19

*I*t is likely that the murder trial of James Crowder was held in the county's new "neat brick" courthouse. Crowder was convicted of killing his wife and three children, and given the death penalty. In 1829, he became the first person ever hanged in the county.

In a story on September 22, 1883, The Atlanta Constitution discussed the case in a story entitled "Only 3 Men Have Been Hung in the History of DeKalb County":

"The first hanging in DeKalb occurred in 1829 when a white man by the name of Crowder paid the death penalty. He had murdered his wife and then set fire to his dwelling consuming the body of his murdered wife and his three young children. Crowder, after the commission of his crime, went to the back of his lot, cut his own throat with a razor and evidently thought thus to escape human justice. He was found, however, and lived. His crime was brought home to him in the most unmistakable manner and he was tried, convicted and hung. The occasion was one of great importance to the people of this section. It drew an immense crowd to Decatur and the above facts were given to the Constitution reported by a gentleman still living who was present at the hanging."

Although James Crowder's sentence is said to have been carried out in 1829, it was not until November 15, 1830 that the DeKalb Inferior Court "ordered that the County Treasurer of DeKalb County pay Thomas Kennedy the sum of $13.50 for holding an inquest over the body of James Crowder and Elizabeth Crowder, there being no Coroner at that time." The crime may have occurred in the Sandtown area, near the home of Thomas Kennedy. [1]

News of the hanging probably was carried in DeKalb's first newspaper, which began publication in 1830. Samuel Wright Miner moved from McDonough to Decatur and began publishing The DeKalb Gazette. Miner not only was publisher of the newspaper, he also was editor, typesetter, compositor, pressman and printer's devil. His printshop was on what is now Candler Street between Ponce de Leon and the entrance to Decatur Cemetery. The DeKalb Academy was located on the corner, and boys from the school reportedly heckled Miner until he left town. The Decatur Watchman soon replaced the Gazette, with John T. Riley as publisher, and George K. Smith as editor. [2]

Certainly the most historically important event in DeKalb in 1830 was the taking of the county's first census (the nation's fifth). Once again, the government called on its stalwart public servant, James McC. Montgomery, to do the important job. Montgomery reported a total population of 10,047, which would seem like a drastic increase from the 3569 total of 1824. But, because of the annexation of Cherokee Indian territory the previous year, Montgomery surveyed considerably more than the original limits of DeKalb County.

Montgomery described the census territory as follows: "The extent of my division which extends into the Cherokee Country agreeably to an act of the Legislature of Georgia commencing at the Buzzard Roost on the Chattahooche along an old indian trail which passes the Buffalow Fisher thence leaving Duk Scotts on the left hand thence by Jacksons (or Tarehonies) thence to the Missionaries on the Hightower waters by the indians call'd Etowa until the said trail (the direction of Sally Hughes's) intersects the road leading from Gates's Ferry to Duk Roes the distance forty miles from thence along the said Road to Gates ferry forty miles, thence with the meanders of the River down the same to the said Buzzard Roost on the Chattahooche River a distance from forty to fifty miles."

Montgomery's territory covered a good bit of what today is Cobb, Cherokee and Bartow counties -- a total of 400 square miles.

"Besides the Indians and the white men at the head of Indian families, there were legally settled in the Cherokee Country white families under permits from the Cherokee authorities, white families with permits from Col. Hugh Montgomery, to occupy (until further orders) plantations which had been abandoned by (Indian) emigrants from Georgia, the missionaries, and a few licensed traders and peddlers." [3]

On October 25, 1830, Montgomery reported these totals:

White males	4295
White females	4081
Total white population	8376
Male slaves	782
Female slaves	671
Free black males	9
Free black females	9 [1]

In 1831, the Georgia legislature organized Cherokee County from all the remaining Indian land in Georgia. In 1832, the one county was divided into 10: Cherokee, Cass (later Bartow), Cobb, Floyd, Forsyth, Gilmer, Lumpkin, Murray, Paulding and Union. Surveying was completed, and the lottery begun in 1832. The final Cherokee removal, however, would be another seven years away. [4]

On September 3, 1831, Montgomery received notification from U. S. Secretary of War Lewis Cass that he had been appointed by President Andrew Jackson an "appraiser to assess the value of the property, which may be abandoned by such of the Cherokee Indians, within the chartered limits of

---

[1] See Appendix 5 for 1830 census index.

Georgia, as may be disposed to migrate to the country west of the Mississippi." The pay was set at $1,000 per year.

Maj. Benjamin F. Currey had replaced Gov. William Carroll of Tennessee as Superintendent of Cherokee Removal. Gov. Carroll had said in his 1829 report:

"The advancement the Cherokees have made in morality, religion, general information, and agriculture astonishes me beyond measure. They have regular preachers in the churches; the use of spirituous liquors is in a great degree prohibited; their farms are worked much after the manner of the white people and are generally in good order. They are supplied with looms and spinning wheels, as well as farm implements. One of their gifted men, Sequoyah had invented an alphabet of eighty letters, which has been described as the most remarkable feat of its kind since Cadmus. At their capital, New Echota, they publish a newspaper, the Phoenix, in their own language. They insisted that they were a sovereign nation, over whom Georgia had no jurisdiction."

By the early 1830s, Cherokee homes had become indistinguishable from whites; when the Cherokees left, whites simply moved in. [5]

After pursuing his job as assessor for some months, Montgomery was convinced that the jobs of assessing the value of Cherokee property and enrolling Indians who wished to sell their property and move could be effectively combined. Following are extracts from a letter from James to Secretary Cass:

"Feb. 1832 Standing peachtree, Georgia, 18th (Saturday 10 o'clock P. M.)

"Sir Having been twenty-five days from home engaged in assessing the abandoned improvements by the Cherokees, I have this evening been gratified with the sight and enjoyment of my dear wife and family, nothing could have kept me so long from home at one time (and to have been so near too) as I was often within half a days ride of home, but the desire to discharge my duty to the War Department, and to the emigrants who are very anxious to get off, and here I would observe again, as I have done heretofore in a communication to you that this has been the coldest winter ever experienced in this country, at least for many years. Our labours have been of the most arduous kind, have never lay by a single day since we commenced neither for snow, nor rain... I would suggest that if it was so directed by the War Department, for the assessing agents to enroll as well as assess, I think from the present appearances of things and the success that we have had in the three weeks that the supt. has permitted us to enroll that we could perhaps enroll as fast as we could assess. This, I attribute to two causes, first the Indians seeing the assessment of those that have already enrolled, and believing that they get a fair price, or are to get for their improvements, it has a tendency to encourage them to enroll, but where the enrolling agents are far ahead of the assessors they know not what they will get for their improvements; a second reason I think is, that both Mr. Scudder and myself have been approved merchants, we both have dealt largely with them myself on the frontier and Mr. Scudder near the center of the Nation for many years... P.S. Excuse returns made out in part of the woods."

However, getting the Indians to agree to move, without benefit of payment for their property, proved to be difficult.

"...Every possible obstacle has been thrown in our way and the most unprincipled means resorted to by their chiefs and headmen to delude the Indians and prevent their enrolling for emigration... having to travel constantly among the Indians, in the woods over mountains and hills for days together, and being generally inconvenient to a post office has rendered it impracticable to forward you regular returns."

White settlers began moving into what had been Indian territory, taking up their lottery prizes, in 1833. Enrolling, which had been suspended, was restarted in 1834, with Montgomery and William M. Davis acting as "assistant appraisers." They were commended by Superintendent Currey: "Each appeared to manifest equal zeal in promoting emigration & I saw no disposition on the part of either to do injustice to those who preferred to remain. All their acts were open & fair & meritorious services of these gentlemen it is respectfully submitted whether their pay should not be equal at least to that allowed to enrolling agents from the 1st Decr."

Despite the praise, Montgomery lost his job, probably because he was known as a "Troup man," a supported Georgia Gov. Troup's efforts to rid Georgia of the Cherokees. This political position could not have set well with federal authorities. [6]

Settlers in 1831 in the Bouldercrest community in southwest DeKalb organized the Clifton (Methodist) Meeting House, named for Aaron Clifton, the first man to own the property where the church was built. [7]

Two new post offices were opened in DeKalb in 1831. Ulysses Montgomery, son of James Montgomery, became the postmaster of Clear Creek on November 4. He was succeeded by Meredith Collier on July 27, 1833. Aaron Collier, Meredith's son, took over on October 26, 1838 and served until the post office was discontinued on February 12, 1839. Clear Creek Post Office was probably located on the Collier plantation in today's Sherwood Forest subdivision in Atlanta. The Poolesville Post Office opened on November 18, with Ephraim M. Poole the first postmaster, succeeded by Thomas M. Poole and Jacob T. Cain until it was discontinued on March 13, 1827. Ephraim and Thomas Poole were sons of Adam Poole. The post office reopened on March 13, 1840 with James Caldwell, John Thrasher and Leonard H. Tomlinson as successive postmasters until the post office moved to Fayette County on April 5, 1847. [8]

Citizens of Decatur met at the Academy in June of 1831 and organized a Sunday School Union, offering classes to anyone from the town and county. The first superintendent was James Lemon, succeeded by Levi Willard, "one of the best men who ever walked the earth," who held the office for 25 years before moving to Ohio in 1864. B. T. Hunter succeeded Willard, followed by William A. Moore, then Milton A. Candler who held the office for 40 years until he died in 1909. Mrs. Catherine Winn joined the school the day it was organized, as a pupil, and continued as a member for more than 60 years. [9]

The DeKalb County Sunday School was later organized at Decatur Presbyterian Church by seven Sunday schools. First officers, chosen on July 14, 1866, were Z. R. Jones, Macedonia Sunday school, president; Dr. P. F. Hoyle, Decatur Union Sunday school, vice-president; B. Langford, Wesley Chapel Sunday school, vice-president; R. McWilliams, Corinth Sunday school, vice-president; and B. T. Hunter, Decatur Union Sunday school, secretary. The first Executive Committee was made up of

Joseph Walker, Indian Creek Sunday school; L. E. Jones, Mt. Vernon Sunday school; Milton A. Candler, Decatur Union Sunday school; J. J. Jones, Mt. Charlotte Sunday school; and Dr. T. T. Key, Corinth Sunday school. The first annual Sunday school celebration was held at Wesley Chapel on the first Saturday in September, 1866. [10]

On July 9, 1832, the Inferior Court of DeKalb County ordered Hardy Pace, Archibald Holland, Henry Wolfe, Benjamin Plaster and Charles Martin to mark a route for a road from the settlement of Hardy Pace on Nance's Creek to that of John A. D. Childress on Sand Town Road "and if you think said road to be a public utility report same to this court." [11]

On July 23 the court "ordered that a road be opened and kept as a public road commencing at Power's Ferry on the Chattahoochee River and intersecting the road leading from Lawrenceville at Robinson's as has been marked out by James Power, Samuel Henderson and William Worthy. "The road leading from Lawrenceville" may have been the present Mount Vernon Highway. [12]

Lodowick Tuggle, John McGinnis and James Hunt reported to the court on November 5: "We find that the new contemplated road (from Decatur to Swinney's) is the nearest and best, that is to say the Covington road from Decatur to the extreme corner of Captain Stephen Mays' plantation, thence leaving the same taking to the right along the road to James Hunt's plantation, thence to the left to the summit of the small hill in sight of Minty Fowler's plantation there entering the old road as before. Ordered established as a public road." Primarily in the Panthersville District, this road could have been what is now Wesley Chapel Road. [13]

The Georgia legislature in 1832 incorporated the DeKalb (Cotton) Manufacturing Company at the Flat Shoals on the South River. Commissioners of the enterprise were Thomas Stephens, Jesse F. Cleveland, Stephen Mays, James Morris and James Jones. The company never opened, but the Flat Shoals were later the location of the Oglethorpe Manufacturing Company, which made rope and warps, and the town of Panola. Robert M. Clarke was the head of both companies. [14]

DeKalb County's growth during the 1830s was evidenced by the number of new post offices opening. Cross Keys opened on March 12, 1832, with John Glenn postmaster, succeeded by James W. Reeve in 1839 and John Y. Flowers in 1852. The post office was located about where Ashford Dunwoody Road today crosses Nancy Creek. After the Civil War, the Cross Keys Post Office moved to Peachtree Road near Oglethorpe University. On April 26, 1832 a post office was established at Latimer's Store in the Belmont community. William M. Latimer was the first postmaster, succeeded in 1835 by his brother, Charles. Charles Latimer served until January 1845 when he was succeed by the Rev. William H. Clarke. Latimer's Store Post Office was moved to Lithonia in August, 1845. A post office called The Globe in the Cross Keys or Browning's District was opened on July 11, 1823, with John Rainey, postmaster until March 31, 1834. [15]

The county's four-year-old courthouse was in need of repairs in 1833. On April 29, the Inferior Court announced that it would accept sealed bids "for the repairing of the courthouse in DeKalb County... the work all to be done in a complete workmanlike manner. Ordered that the clerk send a copy of the above notice to the Georgia Telegraph and Federal Union and to put up a copy of said notice at the Crossroads, Cross Keys, and John A. D. Childress and two in Decatur."

Also on April 29, the court also ordered the county treasurer to pay Charles Murphey "the sum of $7.50 for the trees planted in the courthouse yard." On July 9, the county treasurer was ordered to pay James Paden $112 "for erecting and painting the railing around the Court House," and to pay Joseph Morgan 50 cents for repairing the county seal press.

On September 16, 1833, the court ordered paid "to E. N. Calhoun eleven dollars and seventy five cents for medical services rendered to one George Tooke an Indian from Murray County, lodged in jail on a charge of murder..." Concerning the same case, the county treasurer was ordered to pay DeKalb jailor M. Hillburn $94.38 1/2 "on accounty (sic) of George Tooke, an Indian from Murray County."

Concerning county roads in 1833:

• Green W. Baker, David Connally, John White, Thomas Kennedy and James Brewster were appointed commissioners on September 16 "to view a Rout (sic) for a Road, from Campbell county line at Rocky Ford on Utoy creek to run on the most practicable rout (sic) towards Macon by the way of Haynes Bridge on Flint River, and make their report to this Court, under oath of their actings and doings."

• John Simpson and Naman Hardman were ordered on June 4 to review the two roads, one crossing Peachtree creek at Robert Smith's and the other crossing said creek at Johnston's Mill and report to the Inferior Court on which road a bridge would be of most public utility." On July 1 the court ordered bridges to be built at both locations. On September 16 the county treasurer was ordered to pay James Guess $10 for building the bridge at Robert Smith's and John Johnson $40 for building the bridge at William Johnston's Mill (near where Briarcliff crosses the north fork of Peachtree Creek). Proprietor William Johnston (1789-1855) is buried at Nancy Creek Primitive Baptist Church Cemetery.

Robert H. Smith (1802-1875) was born in the Rutherford District of North Carolina and came to DeKalb shortly before 1830. Robert built the house where his great granddaughter Tullie Smith lived. The house was located at 2890 North Druid Hills Road until it was moved to the grounds of the Atlanta History Center. James Guess's bridge was probably between Briarcliff Road and Buford Highway on North Druid Hills Road, once was called the Decatur Road.

Decatur postmaster Barnett F. Cleveland reported taking in $225.34 for the year 1833, another sign of Decatur's continuing spirited growth. [16]

Repairs to the county jail were made in 1834. The Inferior Court issued orders on July 7 that Loveless and Jones be paid $3.85 for 27 1/2 lbs. of sheet iron to make repairs. Thomas C. Bradberry was paid $4.93 3/4 on July 14 for additional repairs, and $8 in September for making steps for the jail.

On March 18, the court ordered $10 to be paid toward building a bridge across Mountain Creek where the road from Decatur to Rockbridge crossed said creek. The neighborhood, the court said, would be required to make up any deficit incurred in building the bridge and guarantee it to stand for five years.

Thomas Farr, Isaiah Kirksey, John Harris, Dennis Hopkins and William P. Foster were appointed

The Tullie Smith House was moved from its original location on North Druid Hills Road and is now a part of the Atlanta History Center complex in Buckhead. (DeKalb Historical Society)

commissioners on May 5 "to let the building of a Bridge across Nancy's Creek at or near Hopkin's Mill on the Road to Pace's Ferry on the Chattahoochie (sic) River."

In November, 1834, William Fain Sr., John Patterson, Jesse Fain, Abel O. Embry and A. H. Green were appointed commissioners "to view the Road about Green's Mill, and see where the most suitable place will be to build a bridge across Utoy creek, and to make a report, etc..." [17]

For the first time, on November 3, 1834, the county Inferior Court abolished a road. "It appearing to the Court, that an order... was passed at the July term... to have a road opened and cleared out as a publick (sic) Road from Awtry's Mill on South River to the junction of the Rock Bridge & Lawrenceville Roads, as lately marked out by John Hambrick, William Parker, Lewis Stowers, and Abraham Housworth, and it also appearing by the petition of about two hundred persons residing near where said Road is to Run, that said Road will not be of publick (sic) utility but on the contrary, that it will be of but little advantage to a very small portion of said citizens: It is therefore ordered that said order for said Road be abolished..."

The Georgia legislature created the Coweta Circuit on December 16, 1833; the name was changed to the Atlanta Circuit in 1869. Superior Court judges in the Coweta Circuit from 1836-1869 were as follows: Hiram Warner, 1836-1840; William Ezzard, 1840-1844; Edward Young Hill, 1844-1853; Obediah Warner, 1853-1854; Orvill A. Bull, 1854-1864; Benjamin H. Bigham, 1864-66; Hiram Warner, 1866-1867; and John Collier, 1867-1869. [18]

The year 1835 began with the coldest weather experienced since the county was formed. Levi Willard recalled: "It is not common for the mercury to fall below zero in Georgia; but on the 17th of February, 1835, it stood at five below zero. The wind was high which made the weather harder to bear than several degrees colder in a still atmosphere."

Several new road commissioners were appointed on 4 Jan 1835:

Georgia Militia District 469 -- Justice of the Peace Moses Bibby, Richard C. Todd, and Dempsey J. Connally.
GMD 479 -- J. P. Nathaniel Mangum, Constantine Wood and John White.
GMD 487 -- J. P. Joseph D. McEver, John Jones and James A. Barr.
GMD 524 -- J. P. Josiah Power, Reuben Martin and John Isom.
GMD 530 -- J. P. Samuel L. Wilson, Charner Humphries and Edward White.
GMD 531 -- J. P. Robert Jones, William Jackson and James Paden.
GMD 536 -- J. P. John McGinnis, George L. Black and William Fowler.
GMD 563 -- J. P. James Diamond, John Hoyle and John P. Corr.
GMD 572 -- J. P. Willis Langston, John T. Dabney and Thomas J. Akins.
GMD 637 -- J. P. Ranson Seay, David D. Anderson and John W. Fowler.
GMD 683 -- J. P. Benjamin J. Camp, Charles Latimer and Josephus Harrison.
GMD 686 -- J. P. James W. Reeve, John L. Evins and Hastings D. Palmer.
GMD 722 -- J. P. Hardy Pace, John M. Harris and Isaac Reid. [19]

The DeKalb Inferior Court ordered on February 12, 1835 that the county treasurer pay $110 to E. B. Reynolds, Trustee of the Paupers, "for the benefit of said paupers." There is no record of how Reynolds dispersed the money.

Also on February 12, the court ordered "that Moses Bibby, Naman Hardman, James Paden, Angus Johnson & William Johnston are hereby appointed reviewers to view, that part of the Road, from Decatur to Pace's Ferry on the Chattahoochee, by the old Road at Garrison's Mill, to A. Chandler's, and the new Road that leaves the old Road at Garrison's Mill, and intersects the old Road again at Chandler's shop, and for said reviewers to report to the court as early as practicable, which of the two Routs will be of the most public utility." The commissioners reported on February 27: "We believe the Rout which goes around Mr. (Isaac) Steel's plantation, say leaving the head of the lane beyond Garrison's Mill, and intersecting the same Road near A. Chandler's Shop, to be considerably the best for carriages, and but little farther." Abraham Chandler, Isaac Steele and Matthias Garrison were neighbors in what is now the LaVista Road-Buford Highway corridor. [20]

On March 7, 1835, Philip H. Burford, Thomas Austin, Elijah Bird, Charles Latimer and Minty Fowler were appointed commissioners to let to lowest bidder the building of a bridge across Snapfinger Creek on the road from Decatur to Covington. Lochlin Johnson, John Morris, Josiah F. Cobb, James Jones and Dempsey Perkerson were appointed commissioners to contract for a bridge across the South River on the road from Decatur to McDonough at a place known as Clifton's Bridge.

Road commissioners were reminded of the serious nature of their jobs on December 9, 1835. The Inferior Court "ordered that a fine of Twenty Dollars be levied on each and every Commissioner of publick roads for neglect of duty, which may be remitted by their causing all the publick roads in their respective districts to be put in such order as required by the Road laws of this State by the Second Monday in January next."

The year 1835 saw a popular settlement spring up around the White Hall Tavern where the Decatur and Lawrenceville Road branched off from the Sandtown Road in what is now Atlanta's West End. Charner Humphries and his wife, Mary Darby, had come to DeKalb from the Chester District in South Carolina in the early 1830s. They built a two-story, whitewashed house that lent its name to the community, as well as later area landmarks. Across the road was a general store with a whiskey barrel in the back. It was "considered good etiquette for strangers or occasional visitors to leave a nickel or dime on the barrel after imbibing."

White Hall Tavern was a stagecoach stop and the site of an important annual event -- muster day. Militia companies, armed with their own guns, would drill for a few hours and participate in marksmanship contests, with a cow as the top prize. "Regardless of who won, the cow was offered up as a sacrifice to the collective appetites of the assemblage, for it was straightaway slaughtered, cooked and served, together with generous helpings from Charner's whiskey barrels... Muster day was usually topped off with not a few fist and dog fights, as the latter usually accompanied their masters."

White Hall was a post office from June 9, 1835 until October 14, 1840. Charner Humphries was the first postmaster, succeeded on July 19, 1839 by Samuel Lovejoy. [21]

Ebenezer Methodist Episcopal Church was incorporated on December 26, 1835 in the Belmont community in southeast DeKalb. The first trustees were the Rev. Jacob Lassiter, the Rev. Uriah C. Sprayberry, James W. Givens, Harris Sprayberry, Robert Givens, William W. Johnston and Joseph Harrison. [22]

John Ridge, on behalf of the Cherokee Indian Nation, signed a treaty on December 29, 1835 ceding all the land east of the Mississippi River in return for $5 million and land west of the Mississippi. The Indians were to be paid for their land and homes. The United States government was to pay for transportation and to furnish the Indians with needed supplies for one year after their removal. The treaty was ratified by the U. S. Senate on May 23, 1836 by one vote. The 16,542 Cherokees still living in Georgia were given until May, 1838 to get out. [23]

The year of 1835 was the first time there is documented evidence of the Solomon Goodwin family in DeKalb. The prominent north DeKalb pioneer may have visited the area in 1825, about the time of the first gold discovery in Georgia. [2] Two of his sons, Starling Goodwin and Harris Goodwin are found in Georgia in the 1820s and '30s. Solomon Goodwin Jr. married Elizabeth May Carter in Hall County in 1829. Harris Goodwin married Emily Dodgen in Forsyth County in 1834. A year later from DeKalb County, Harris Goodwin wrote to his father in South Carolina, suggesting that he, his mother, brother and two sisters join him in DeKalb.

Solomon Goodwin Sr.'s wife, Elizabeth, died in 1836 in South Carolina. The following year, Solomon, at the age of 73, sold his South Carolina land, packed his belongings and moved to DeKalb. Some of his children, their spouses and families followed later. In 1838, Solomon purchased adjoining land lots, Nos. 200 and 239 and half of Land Lot 238 in DeKalb's 18th District from John Dobbs. His land lay

---

[2] Solomon Goodwin Sr. would have been 61 years old in 1825. Albert Martin Jr., a Goodwin descendant and family researcher, believes that Solomon Goodwin, because of his relatively advanced age, did not visit Georgia in 1825.

The Solomon Goodwin House in Brookhaven was designated by the Georgia Historical Commission as the oldest extant house in DeKalb. (Photo by Vivian Price)

on both sides of the Peachtree (Echota) Indian trail and encompassed what today is the better part of the Brookhaven business district.

"The land, being on Peachtree Ridge, was not considered first-class farm land but Goodwin made a success of his farming operations and became an influential man in his neighborhood."[24] His home, however, is in sharp contrast with the one built by Goodwin's contemporary, Samuel House, just up the street. While Samuel House's federal brick mansion with its white Doric columns is the popular idea of an antebellum plantation home, Solomon Goodwin's low-ceilinged frame house is more typical of the dwellings of early DeKalb County settlers. The Goodwin House has only seven rooms, four on the ground floor and three reached by a narrow, steep staircase. The house was expanded to its present size in about 1840, and exterior weatherboarding was installed over the original logs.[25]

Said to have been built in 1831, the Goodwin House has the official distinction of being the "oldest extant house" in the county, although there are those who claim other dwellings in the county are older. Although still on the same lot, the house has been moved back from the intersection of Peachtree and North Druid Hills roads. The structure's pine logs were weathered-boarded on the exterior in about 1850, and covered with wide pine boards on the inside. The house originally had a separate kitchen and dining room connected by a covered walkway; construction of the Atlanta and

Charlotte Air Line Railroad (today Norfolk Southern Railway) forced demolition of the building in 1869. For many years "Goodwin's Station" appeared on railroad timetables. Solomon never gave up his hope of discovering gold, and sank several shafts on his property in search of the precious metal. [26]

Tradition holds that Cherokee Indians helped Solomon Goodwin build the house in the summer of 1831, and that he maintained friendly relations with the Cherokees. "He decided to live in peace with his Indian neighbors if it were possible to do so, and treated them with a kindness and consideration that unfortunately was not common on the frontier at that time... Mr. Goodwin's popularity with the Indians often caused consternation to his negro cook when Indians in large numbers and almost unlimited appetite would drop in unexpectedly about meal time, but the Goodwin hospitality never failed. [27]

"In the old days there was a long trough on the Peachtree Road side of the dwelling which was kept full of water from a nearby well so that all wayfarers could refresh their livestock. Afterward, the travelers, in the leisurely fashion of the day, would sit for a while upon the wide porch and discuss politics, crops and the weather with their host. Mindful of his standing orders, `Old Mitch,' the white-headed house servant, would soon appear with the requisite number of brandy toddies to lubricate the discussion." [28]

Solomon Goodwin and his wife, Elizabeth (Bessie) Saxton, had three sons and two daughters, all born in South Carolina: Starling, Solomon Jr., Harris, Sarah Elizabeth Catherine and Isabella A. Solomon was born in 1764 in Virginia, the son of a physician, Franklin Goodwin, and moved with his brother, Theophilus, to South Carolina in 1795. He died in DeKalb on December 18, 1849, possibly a victim of the smallpox epidemic that devastated the Atlanta area that year. He was buried in the Nancy Creek Primitive Baptist Church Cemetery, but was reinterred in 1966 in the Goodwin family cemetery in front of the Brookhaven home. [29]

Sarah Elizabeth Catherine Goodwin, daughter of Solomon and Bessie, married Hezekiah Cheshire, an Atlanta pioneer, who was 28 years her senior. They had nine children. Solomon Goodwin Jr. settled in the in the area that is now Executive Park, near Chantilly Drive. He is buried in a family cemetery there. Starling Goodwin and his wife, Elizabeth May Carter, were members of Nancy Creek Primitive Baptist Church; Starling was church clerk for 10 years around 1858. Harris Goodwin and his wife, Emily Dodgen, had 10 children: Janetta Ardella, Caroline Permelia, Charles H., Emily Frances Matilda, Lydia Ann Missouri, Sarah Jane, Augustine E., Elizabeth, Solomon Eli and Joicey E. Their only sons, 'Gustin and Charles were both killed during the Civil War. Charles was 16 and had enlisted only three weeks before his death. [30]

The house itself survived the war with only minor damage. The living room fireplace mantle bears scars from saber cuts made by Union soldiers. Two family stories are told about how the house was saved from the destruction that befell so many area homes during the war. One story says the house was spared because Solomon's Masonic apron was found in the house. Another story says a family slave, left behind by family members who refugeed to south Georgia, pleaded with soldiers not to burn the roof over his head. The house has passed out of family hands only one time, about the turn of the century. Alfred Martin, husband of Solomon Goodwin's great granddaughter, Naomi Childress, purchased the home in the name of the Goodwin Home Club, which was made up of family members who purchased shares in the property. [31]

Solomon Goodwin's house, now a tiny island of quiet historic significance, is completely surrounded by modern development. The small property is bounded on the front by Peachtree Road, now a five-lane highway, and the MARTA north-south rapid rail line just a few feet from its rear wall. Offices, retail stores, eateries and a motel are on either side and across the street.

Descendants of the north DeKalb pioneer recently established the Solomon Goodwin House Foundation with the goal of preserving the old dwelling and the family cemetery. Members of two generations of Goodwin descendants currently live within just a few miles of their ancestor's pioneer home.

Chapter 19 Notes

1. Garrett, Franklin M., 1954, 1969, Atlanta and Environs -- A Chronicle of Its People and Events, Vol. 1, page 81.

2. Willard, Levi, 1920, "The Early History of Decatur Written Many Years Ago," DeKalb New Era. Garrett, Franklin M., 1954, 1969, Atlanta and Environs -- A Chronicle of Its People and Events, Vol. 1, page 81.

3. Anderson, E. Katherine, December, 1937, "James McC. Montgomery of Standing Peachtree," The Atlanta Historical Bulletin No. 12.

4. Garrett, Franklin M., 1954, 1969, Atlanta and Environs -- A Chronicle of Its People and Events, Vol. 1, page 107.

5. Smith, Martin T., June, 1990, "Historic Period Indian Archaeology of Northern Georgia, Department of Anthropology, Georgia State University.

6. Anderson, E. Katherine, December, 1937, "James McC. Montgomery of Standing Peachtree," The Atlanta Historical Bulletin No. 12.

7. Nix, Dorothy, personal collection, DeKalb Historical Society.

8. Garrett, Franklin M., 1954, 1969, Atlanta and Environs -- A Chronicle of Its People and Events, Vol. 1, page 104.

9. Garrett, Franklin M., 1954, 1969, Atlanta and Environs -- A Chronicle of Its People and Events, Vol. 1, page 103. Candler, Charles Murphey, November 9, 1922, Historical Address.

10. Candler, Charles Murphey, November 9, 1922, Historical Address.

11. Garrett, Franklin M., 1954, 1969, Atlanta and Environs -- A Chronicle of Its People and Events, Vol. 1, page 108.

12. Garrett, Franklin M., 1954, 1969, Atlanta and Environs -- A Chronicle of Its People and Events, Vol. 1, page 109.

13. Garrett, Franklin M., 1954, 1969, Atlanta and Environs -- A Chronicle of Its People and Events, Vol. 1, page 110.

14. Garrett, Franklin M., 1954, 1969, Atlanta and Environs -- A Chronicle of Its People and Events, Vol. 1, page 111.

15. Garrett, Franklin M., 1954, 1969, Atlanta and Environs -- A Chronicle of Its People and Events, Vol. 1, page 112-113.

16. Garrett, Franklin M., 1954, 1969, Atlanta and Environs -- A Chronicle of Its People and Events, Vol. 1, pages 118-121.

17. Garrett, Franklin M., 1954, 1969, Atlanta and Environs -- A Chronicle of Its People and Events, Vol. 1, page 127.

18. Garrett, Franklin M., 1954, 1969, Atlanta and Environs -- A Chronicle of Its People and Events, Vol. 1, page 138.

19. Garrett, Franklin M., 1954, 1969, Atlanta and Environs -- A Chronicle of Its People and Events, Vol. 1, page 134.

20. Garrett, Franklin M., 1954, 1969, Atlanta and Environs -- A Chronicle of Its People and Events, Vol. 1, page 133.

21. Garrett, Franklin M., 1954, 1969, Atlanta and Environs -- A Chronicle of Its People and Events, Vol. 1, pages 129-130.

22. Candler, Charles Murphey, November 9, 1922, Historical Address.

23. Garrett, Franklin M., 1954, 1969, Atlanta and Environs -- A Chronicle of Its People and Events, Vol. 1, page 135.

24. Abercrombie, J. H., June 9, 1929, "House Indians Helped Build," Atlanta Journal Magazine, page 6.

25. Abercrombie, J. H., June 9, 1929, "House Indians Helped Build," <u>Atlanta Journal</u> Magazine, page 6.

26. Abercrombie, J. H., June 9, 1929, "House Indians Helped Build," <u>Atlanta Journal</u> Magazine, page 6.

27. Abercrombie, J. H., June 9, 1929, "House Indians Helped Build," <u>Atlanta Journal</u> Magazine, page 6.

28. Abercrombie, J. H., June 9, 1929, "House Indians Helped Build," <u>Atlanta Journal</u> Magazine, page 6.

29. Martin, Albert Jr., July 17, 1996, "A Guidebook to the Goodwin Family Cemetery."

30. Garrett, Franklin M., 1954, 1969, <u>Atlanta and Environs -- A Chronicle of Its People and Events</u>, Vol. 1, page 64.

31. Martin, Albert Jr., August 27,. 1996, personal interview.

Chapter 20

*I*n January of 1836, Alabama's Creek Indians, aided by the Seminoles of lower Alabama, began launching "lightning attacks" across the Chattahoochee River in Georgia. The county's militia organization, the DeKalb Light Infantry was ordered to be ready to march at a "moment's warning." The county's first company, the Light Infantry had been incorporated by the Georgia legislature on December 22, 1835. [1]

Ezekiel N. Calhoun, Decatur's well-known physician, was captain of the company. Judging from Calhoun's response to the company's marching orders, it would take considerably more than a moment's to get the DeKalb Light Infantry ready to march. Calhoun responded to the January 13 letter from Col. Bolling H. Robinson, Aide-de-Camp, at Headquarters, Milledgeville, Ga.:

"Decatur, DeKalb, Jan'ry 22nd, 1836
Col. B. H. Robinson:
On last night I received yours of the 13th Inst. requiring me to prepare my company (the DeKalb Light Infantry) to march at a moments warning if required, & also to report to Headquarters, etc. I will state to you that for the last two years, the company has abolished company Musters, and substituted in lieu thereof camp Musters, & since the last camp Muster the Emigration from our section of country has been so great, that at present after looking over the Roll, we have but 38 officers and privates left. Our uniform, is citizen's clothing. I find in town about 44 guns. There may be a few more. Persons moving off have deposited their Muskets in different places & as yet, I am unable to find them, but hope in the course of 8 or 10 days to get them. The orders I have received, I hope will be effectual in rousing immediately a necessary degree of military feeling so much so, as to keep us in a continual state of preparation. I have this day issued orders, for a company Muster on Wednesday the 27th Inst. at which time I will use my endeavours (sic) to reorganize the company & get them to adopt some uniform that would be suitable to such an occasion. The Musketts (sic) & accoutrements that we received from Milledgeville were very much out of repair. They seemed as though they had gone through, not only the last Indian war, but even the revolution. We have not any music, one thing that operates against us. I will give you the names of officers and privates at present belonging to the Company & after we have one or two Musters, which will be but a few days apart, I will report to you again, as it is likely we will be better off.
       E. N. Calhoun, Capt.

Calhoun's letter included a roster of the militia company's 37 officers and men:

E. N. Calhoun, Capt.	James R. Henry	John S. McGinnis
C. W. McGinnis, 1st Lieut.	Robert C. Anderson	R. A. Griffin
S. E. Binion, 2nd Lieut.	James D. Thompson	Robert F. Davis
John Jones, 1st Sergt.	Joseph R. White	Moses W. Davis
Joseph L. McGinnis, 2nd Sergt.	Milton B. Henry	Robert Watson
	John W. Fowler	J. B. Wilson
John L. Towers, 3rd Sergt.	Austin G. Steward	John T. Davney
A. Vaughn	Levi Hoyl	E. A. Davis
H. C. Roe	Royal Towers	E. B. Reynolds
S. J. Anderson	F. C. Diamond	John Glen
William Hawkins	E. M. Diamond	Moses Powell. [2]
J. A. Heard	A. B. Dabney	
John R. Bradford	Charles W. Griffin	
Jesse Warren	Reuben Pickens	

In less than one month, on February 12, Calhoun reported that his company was ready and eager: "The company seems to be in Suspense owing to their different occupations & situations, & therefore we would be glad to hear as quick as possible what were are to depend on..."

The company numbered 84 when it left Decatur in the spring of 1836, sporting banners made by women of the community. When it reached West Point, Ga., south of LaGrange, 10 men left the company "because they would not be mustered into the United States service." [3]

Ezekiel Calhoun resigned his command of the DeKalb Light Infantry and was replaced by John Jones on June 12, 1836. John L. Towers was named ensign.

Commissions were issued to the following on June 14, 1836 in West Point, Troup County, Ga.:
John Jones, captain
John L. Towers, ensign

E. H. Fleming	J. T. Bullock	A. Oliver
M. W. Davis	W. Argow	J. B. Turner
J. W. P. Johnson	J. B. Wilson	R. C. Anderson
M. B. Henry	R. Towers	J. Worbington
M. Webb	L. Calburt	John Jones
F. C. Dimond	M. H. Jones	Griffith Simpson
J. Choice	W. Dyre	T. A. Gaddy
R. Blair	L. Burnett	E. A. Davis
John Gillem	J. S. Cowen	John Bradford
James R. Henry	R. A. Griffin	W. Hays
R. Pickins	Moses Powell	C. W. Griffith
J. Herd	Thomas Edwards	J. Frost
B. Paramore	Andrew Jackson	Jordan Dixon
J. S. Wells	James Elom	W. Lester
J. E. Nash	H. C. Roe	S. E. Benson
Thomas J. Harris	E. M. Dimond	Samuel Edes
R. Pickins	James Rainey	L. S. Morgen

E. C. Simmons	A. C. Stewart	John Fowler
William Smith	H. P. Ivey	James D. Thompson. [4]
J. W. Fowler	B. F. Shewmate	
W. Hawkins	J. S. McGinnis	

On January 29, 1836, Capt. Charles D. Parr reported to Georgia Gov. William Schley that his cavalry company was in no better condition than Ezekiel Calhoun's infantry company had been on January 22.

Decatur 29th Jany 1836

Sir

In obedience to an order, requiring me to report to head quarters the number situation 26 of the company under my command -- I beg leave to submit the following statement, immediately after I received orders I caused my company to be notiv\fied to appear at this place on this day I have only been able to muster 28 including officers -- I have appointed a muster to be held on tommorrow week at which time I think I shall be enabled to increase the company to number of forty or thereabouts. We have no arms never having been furnished with any this is the principal reason why the company has dwindled down to its present size. Those who have been paraded today are ready for any service either in Florida or in this State if they should be required on the other page you have a list of the names of the officers and privates of the company.

Jefferson Evans was first lieutenant of this company, and Aaron Starnes, second lieutenant. Joseph J. Anderson was elected ensign. Sergeants were William L. Lyon, first; Thomas Harris, second; and John Fowler, third.

Members of the company were as follows:

William Burnet	Ephraim McDowell	Hon T. Jones
Titus Stavens	John Barnett	William Mason
F. Crow	Joseph Walker	Coleman Ford
Elish Landrum	William Jordan	W. T. Roberson
John R. Cook	James M. Calhoun	John B. McDaniel
Isaiah White	Miles Barnett	Benjamin Avery. [5]
Ralph Childs	James Eliotte	
William Turner		

James M. Calhoun, younger brother of Ezekiel, apparently reorganized the company later in the spring. He was elected captain of the DeKalb Cavalry on May 18, 1836, with Charles D. Parr as second lieutenant. James J. Evins was first lieutenant, and George W. Avery, third lieutenant. Calhoun reported to Georgia Gov. William Schley that the 65-man company was ready to march on June 4, 1836. The company later was involved in a battle with Indians near Fort McCrary in Stewart County in southwestern Georgia. Two company members were killed: John Willis, son of James Willis of the Snapfinger neighborhood, and Matthew J. Orr, son of Robert Orr, of Utoy Creek. [6]

These companies contained men from some of DeKalb's oldest families, including the Calhouns. Both Ezekiel and James moved to Atlanta in the 1850s, with James becoming the town's mayor during the Civil War. [7]

The men of DeKalb County continued to organize themselves into militia companies through 1836. All of DeKalb's militia companies were attached to the 54th Regiment of the Georgia Militia.

The Independent Volunteer Rifle Company was organized in DeKalb on June 16, 1836, with Thomas Skins elected captain. Other officers were Jessee C. Farrar, first lieutenant; Daniel Johnson, second lieutenant; Constantine Wood, third lieutenant; and William A. David, ensign. These officers and the following men were commissioned on June 23, 1836:

John Glenn	T. Petty	J. M. Wiggins
Joel Herring	John Merret	T. Jones
E. Yancy	O. D. Anderson	N. McLeod
H. Guess	J. Kennedy	D. Johnson
R. Ramsey	A. Johnson	C. R. Guen
G. Foote	Arch Johnson	R. Farris
H. Edwards	W. Allen	T. Gaddis
L. Carral	Thomas Akins	W. Hooper
J. J. Jeter	A. J. Walraven	J. M. Keller
S. Walker	J. C. Farrar	J. E. Walker
C. Thompson	W. L. Gumbles	H. Keller
E. A. Center	J. M. Simpson	J. Petty
J. Blalock	W. Swiney	C. Wood
H. Scott	Jesse Swiney	R. G. Gill
S. Goodman	K. Blackstock	J. McLeond
J. Godwin	M. Crawford	P. Carver
W. W. Levell	W. Hornsby	John McLeod Jun.
A. McDanel	J. Gaziway	N. Guiton
C. Ford	J. Martin	D. J. Conally
W. A. David	D. R. Weems	R. Orr.[8]
R. Griffin	John Power	
J. L. Cash	B. Bates	

William Ezzard was elected captain of the DeKalb Independent Guards on June 17, 1836. Cyrus Choice was elected first lieutenant; Henry B. Latimer, second lieutenant; and Alexander A. Heard, third lieutenant.

Members of the Independent Guards were as follows:

J. H. Dobbs	John E. Adams	James Farrell
C. R. Davis	C. Choice	G. Greenwood
G. B. Diamond	S. Crowley	A. B. Greenwood
S. Farmer	James Crowley	W. S. Grogen
James Farrell	H. J. Cureton	W. Garrison
G. Greenwood	J. T. S. Crawford	Thomas Gaddy
A. B. Greenwood	W. Craig	Charles J. Hooper
W. S. Grogen	W. Cash	J. B. Hardman
W. Garrison	T. Choice	R. F. Hilburn
Thomas Gaddy	J. H. Dobbs	W. Harrel
William A. Austin	C. R. Davis	Aaron Hightower
T. Atwood	G. B. Diamond	J. W. Bradberry
Joel Atkins	S. Farmer	John Bryce

C. Burton	John C. Johns	M. Nixon
R. Burdett	J. Jolly	W. Nixon
J. S. Binion	John G. Johnson	A. Reeves
J. A. Breedlove	Thomas M. Kemp	H. H. Southard
W. R. Brandon	A. Loveliss	D. M. Simpson
Robert Bryce	J. L. McGinnis	Joseph Stone
T. C. Bradberry	William Martin	William Sprewell
J. Brown	J. McLeod	R. Seay
T. Burdett	Moses Murphy	J. J. Smith
B. A. Burdett	J. D. McKeever	A. Smith
J. C. Hightower	J. G. McWilliams	A. Woodall
D. C. Hardman	N. McLeod	S. B. Wilson
J. Hambrick	Mc. McKee	T. D. Wilson
James Haynes	J. W. McLean	H. H. Williams
Charles Hilburn	J. J. Martin	A. Williams.[9]
John H. Hambrick	Andrew McLain	
Eli J. Hulsey	Holladay Moore	
H. H. Johnson	A. Neighbors	

Charles Latimer formed a militia company, of which he was captain, on June 17, 1836. Andrew Johnson was first lieutenant, and Lemuel Dean second lieutenant. Thomas Gardner was ensign. Sergeants were James Mize, first; William P. Turner, second; William Wright, third; and Alfred S. Waddle, fourth.

Company members were as follows:

Larken Austin	James W. Dodson	James Norton
Toliver L. Austin	Green B. Diamond	Samul Potts
Phillip Anderson	James Ferrel	John G. Power
John B. Austen	Asa Glore	William H. Pyson
Nelson Anderson	Hezekiah Harrison	James Richardson
James Askew	Asa W. Howard	Isac T. Rowe
James Burt	Edward Howard	Brantley Smith
Joseph Brantly	Joseph Hall	Brice M. Sprayberry
Leandrew Biffle	James Hall	Harvey J. Sprayberry
John Q. Bolton	James Harrison	Shubel Starnes
Edmund Burt	Nathaniel Howard	Holloway Sanders
Levi Betterton	James J. Howard	Mansfield Starns
Henry G. Borman	Vincent Jordan	James L. Sewell
James K. Cowan	Henry Z. Lasseter	Riley Smith
James W. Chandler	Thomas A. Lasseter	Chesley Thompson
John F. Cowan	Johnson Lyon	Silus Turner
Lewis Chandler	Wright Lee	Jefferson Tanner
Joshua L. Callehan	Michael Mackin	James J. Veal
William A. Callahan	James Miller	William W. Veal
Alexander Cockran	Archebal McElroy	Hamblition Ware
Moses B. Crawford	Francis M. Morris	Peter J. Waldraven.[10]
Joel Diggers	James M. McAlpine	

THE HISTORY OF DEKALB COUNTY, GA. 1822-1900 • CHAPTER 20

One trusty old weapon that was part of the arsenal of the DeKalb Light Infantry still rests on the grounds of the Old Courthouse in Decatur. The small cannon is said to have been left in DeKalb by Gen. Andrew Jackson who used it to preserve order when white men first began settling in the new county in 1821.

The cannon traveled to West Point with Capt. E. N. Calhoun's militia company, mounted on wheels and pulled by manpower. Calhoun is said to have had the cannon fired during drill muster on the square. The militiamen could not have been too popular with the town's people after cannonfire broke several windows.

After the Indian war of 1836, however, the cannon's function became purely ceremonial. It was used during the Civil War to salute soldiers passing on the railroad, until powder became scarce. Whigs from Gwinnett County borrowed it to celebrate a victory, but the Democrats stole it before it could be fired. It was said to have been taken to Stone Mountain to celebrate the victory of Grover Cleveland, the first Democratic president elected after Reconstruction.

It also was fired on the Fourth of July through the years and to salute couples at their weddings. [11]

Although DeKalb County certainly was legally authorized to convene a grand jury during the first years of its existence, the first recorded Grand Jury Presentments are from March, 1836, 14 years after the county's founding. The Grand Jury was scheduled to meet twice a year, in March and September, but terms sometimes were delayed as much as two months.

This grand jury commented on only two subjects, and handed down indictments against 11 citizens.

"We the Grand Jury sworn, chosen and selected for DeKalb County at March Term, 1836, having examined the tax collector's insolvent list, do agree to allow him $17.05 cts & 2 mills, in addition to what has already been allowed him for his insolvent list for the year 1835.

"We present as a grievance the bad situation of a great many of our public roads and bridges and do most earnestly urge upon the Justices of the Inferior Court the absolute necessity of their immediate and prompt enforcement of the Road laws, and that no excuse be received by them short of the same being cleared out and improved according to the strict letter of the law.

"In taking leave of his Honor Judge Iverson, we tender him our approbation for his able, prompt and impartial administration of the laws during the present Term of this Court.

"We tender to the Solicitor General our thanks for his polite attention to this body during said Term, and also for the faithful discharge of his duties.

      Hardy Pace, Foreman

James H. Kirkpatrick	Noah Hornsby	John Dabbs
James Guess	James Paden	Merrell Collier
Robert Crockett	Joel Farmer	Henry B. Latimer
Samuel McElroy	James Phillips	James Ligon
George Elam	Walter Wadsworth	Stephen Tilly
Edward Howard	John Stephenson	James Diamond
Benjamin Howard	James R. George	
Isaac Hughs	Thomas McGriff	

After Prosperity Presbyterian Church moved to the town of Doraville, the congregation first met in the Doraville School building at the intersection of what is now Central Avenue and Church Street. Prosperity changed its name to Doraville Presbyterian Church in 1890. The school burned before 1900. This photo was taken at Thanksgiving Day services in the 1890s. (City of Doraville)

"The Grand Jurors... Hardy Pace, Foreman... In the name and behalf of the citizens of Georgia, charge and accuse Ephriam M. Pool and Andrew Jackson with the offense of gaiming on the 25th day of March, 1836, for on that day and date the said Ephriam M. Pool and Andrew Jackson, of the County of DeKalb... did in a certain white house situate(d) in Decatur... known as the house of Matthias Hiburn, play at a certain game of cards called Brag alias Bluff alias Poker, contrary to the laws of said State, the good order, peace and dignity thereof.

"The Grand Jurors also charge and accuse Alfred B. Greenwood, Josiah Choice, John Townsen (of Henry County), Willis Cash, James Covington, Barnet Boling, Aaron Rapshir, Henry Stowers, and James N. Hodges, of DeKalb County, with the offence of gaming... on the 23rd day of March, 1836, at Decatur... that they did play and bet at a certain game of cards called Brag (alias Bluff) (alias Poker), contrary to the laws, etc."

All of the defendants were acquitted at the September, 1836 term of the Superior Court.

At the second term, September, 1836, the grand jury was complimentary to the work of county treasurer James Lemon.

"We have examined the fiscal concerns of the County and are happy to state that our County Treasurer, James Lemon, Esq., has discharged the duties of his office in a manner highly creditable to himself and satisfactory to us. We find in his hands $572.01 in Cash and a further sum of $2437.64 in Notes which we believe to be good.
       Thomas W. Slaughter, Foreman."

Presbyterians in north DeKalb County organized their first church on August 11, 1836. Prosperity Presbyterian Church was organized on Peachtree Road, near Prospect Methodist Church, by the Rev. Thomas Turner, pastor of the Hopewell Presbyterian Church in Newton County. The organizers, five families from a community called The Waxhaws in Mecklenburg County, N. C. and later from the Anderson District of South Carolina, met at the home of Samuel McElroy Sr., the "Grandpap House," at what is now the corner of Central Avenue and Buford Highway. [12]

The 12 charter members, in addition to McElroy and his wife Mary, were John Stevenson, Joseph Stewart and his wife Mary, Samuel McElroy Jr. and his wife Nancy M., John McElroy and his wife Margaret, William Stevenson and his wife Sarah, Elizabeth McElroy and her daughter Rachel, and William McElroy. Samuel McElroy Sr., Joseph Stewart and Samuel McElroy Jr. were ordained ruling elders, and William Stevenson and John McElroy were elected deacons.

On August 1, 1849, Stewart, whose home was in what is now the "old Chamblee" business district, gave the church a parcel of land "18 rods square." The original church building is thought to have been near the entrance to the present cemetery on Peachtree Road. Trustees were G. Chesley Campbell, William McElroy and Robert P. Jeffers. The second sanctuary, in the same location, had a wood stove which "furnished comfort, not only for the worshippers on Sabbath, but for the covered wagoners who used the church for an overnight camping place." [13]

The church moved to the corner of Central Avenue and Church Street in Doraville in 1871 on land donated by John Y. Flowers. The old church building later was sold to David Chesnut, who converted it into a cotton gin house. The name of the church was changed to Doraville Associate Reformed Presbyterian Church in 1890. From its inception until 1936, the church punished misconduct on the part of its members by barring them from communion until they "appeared before the congregation and declared repentance." Among the punishable infractions were fighting, use of profane language, intoxication and adultery.

Prosperity played a role in organizing two other Presbyterian churches in the area: New Hope in Dunwoody and Antioch, later Tucker, near Embry Hills. [14]

Several families allied with the organizers of Prosperity Presbyterian Church in Doraville were involved with beginning the Oak Grove Methodist Church in 1836. As was the case with many area churches, Oak Grove held services under a brush arbor until a log structure was built on Oak Grove Road. Original families were Akin, McElroy, Lively, Pennell, Jones, Loyd and Anderson. Alvin Dempsey, a circuit rider, was the first preacher. In 1888, James Francis Akins sold two and one-half acres of land on Oak Grove Road for $1 to church trustees J. M. Loyd, Jonathan Pennell, W. M. Henderson, J. M. Akins and W. B. Justice.

The church continued to meet in a one-room building until 1914. A curtain was hung around the walls to create space for Sunday school classes. The church's first full-time minister, James Weldon, went to work in the 1950s. [15]

Utoy Post Office opened on Sandtown, now Cascade, Road on March 9, 1836, with Daniel Stone as postmaster. Subsequent postmasters were Thomas A. Kennedy, Henry B. Latimer and Thomas A. Kennedy. The post office was discontinued on July 7, 1866.

The oldest DeKalb County will on record was filed in 1836 (and may have been refiled after the 1842 courthouse fire). The document contains the last wishes of Benjamin Plaster Sr. who died on November 25, 1836. He came to DeKalb in the early 1820s from Franklin County, Ga., having been born in Rowan County, N. C. in 1780. He and his family settled in the area that became the Peachtree District of Fulton County, near the intersection of Peachtree and Collier roads. Piedmont Road originally was called Plaster's Bridge Road.

The will not only tells about Benjamin Plaster, his family and his possessions, but also displays the manner in which wills of the day were written.

"In the name of God Amen I, Benjamin Plaster, of the State of Georgia and County of DeKalb, being sick and weak of body, but of perfect mind and memory, Knowing that it is appointed unto all men once to die, do make and ordain this, and this only, my last will and Testament. First and principally of all, I recommend my soul to God who gave it, and my body to the earth from whence it came, to be buried in decent Christian burial. At the discretion of after mentioned Executors as touching things of worldly estate, wherewith God has blessed me with, I give and bequeath and dispose of in the following manner and form.

"1st. I give and bequeath to my beloved wife Sally Plaster the lot of land whereon I now live, No. 58 in the 17th District of originally Henry, now DeKalb, three negroes, Gilber, Silva and Willis, two of the best feather beds and their furniture, three cows and calves, and all the hogs (except fifteen, ten of them to Edwin Plaster and five to Benjamin Plaster), together with all the cooking utensils, one of the choice horses, and one years support of the crop.

"2nd. I give and bequeath to my beloved Son-in-law John Williamson one dollar.

"3rd. I give and bequeath to my beloved daughter Dovey Daniel, two negroes Jesse and Orashe.

"4th. I give and bequeath to my beloved son Edwin Plaster the east part of lots of land No. 103 & 102 in the 17th dist. originally Henry now DeKalb County, the line dividing said lots commencing at Clear Creek, the creek to be the line to the mouth, thence a direct line from there to the middle of the east and west line of lot No. 102, also lot No. 57 in the same dist. and County, also two negroes, Crawford and Minty.

"5th. I give and bequeath to my beloved son Benjamin Plaster, the west part of the above divided lots of land No. 103 & 102, also lot No. 101 in the same district and County, and two negroes Elias and Winney.

"6th. I give and bequeath to my beloved daughter Elizabeth Gober, two negroes Nancy and Moses, also $4.00 in cash.

"7th. I give and bequeath to my beloved daughter Piety Plaster one half of lot of land No. 49. in the 17th district of originally Henry now DeKalb County, also half of lot no. 48 in the same district and County, and two negroes Lydia and Reuben.

"8th. I give and bequeath to my beloved grand daughter Sally Williamson, three negroes Jinkins, Leas and Sam. At the death of my beloved wife Sally Plaster, the lot of land whereon I now live is to be hers, one horse worth about fifty dollars, one feather bed and furniture, and one cow and calf. The balance of my negroes to be put into five lots, as follows, Bobb, Mariah in one lot, Tom and Molly in the 2nd lot, Daniel and Jerry to be in the 3rd lot, Cinda and Lauze in the 4th lot & Jiney in the fifth lot, and all the increase, should there be any, put with these five lots as near equal as possible. These five lots of negroes my five beloved Children is to have, Dovey Daniel, Edwin Plaster, Benjamin Plaster, Elizabeth Gober & Piety Plaster, they are to draw for them, and those of them that draws the valuablest lot they are to pay in proportion so as to make each lot of the same value.

"9th. The balance of my estate not specified consisting of Stock, Lands, Blacksmith Tools, Cotton Gin Threshing, and plantation tools to be sold at my death and equally divided between my five last named children. The three negroes that I bequeathed to my beloved wife, and their increase, should there be any, at her death to be sold and also equally divided between my five children Dovey Daniel, Edwin Plaster, Benjamin Plaster, Elizabeth Gober and Piety Plaster. It is also my will distinctly that my beloved son-in-law John Williamson and beloved grand daughter Sally Williamson is not to have any more than what I have bequeathed them individually in the 2nd and 8th bequeathing.

"10th. And in order that this my last will and Testament may be carried fully into effect, I do hereby constitute, ordain and appoint my beloved sons Edwin Plaster and Benjamin Plaster my Executors, and revoking all others & do hereby ratify and confirm this and this only my last will and Testament.

"In testimony whereof I have hereunto sett my hand and affixed my seal, this, the eighth day of November in the year of our lord one thousand eight hundred and thirty six. Signed, Sealed and acknowledged in presence of
                    Benj. Plaster (L.S.)"

The will was witnessed by Samuel Walker and Sarah and John N. Balenger (Bellinger). [16]

Gov. William Schley signed legislation on December 21, 1836 authorizing the state of Georgia to build a railroad "from some point on the Tennessee line near the Tennessee River, commencing at or near Rossville in the most direct practicable route to some point on the southeastern bank of the Chattahoochee River and which shall be most eligible for the extension of branch railroads thence to Athens, Madison, Milledgeville, Forsyth, and Columbus, and to any other points which may be designated by the engineer or engineers surveying the same as the most proper and practicable, and on which the Legislature may hereafter determine." [17]

Stephen Harriman Long was hired as chief engineer for the state's railroad project on May 12, 1837 to determine the best point for crossing the Chattahoochee and a point on the south side of the river where the railroads from Augusta, Macon, Columbus could meet. One of Long's associates, Abbott Hall Brisbane, wrote to Gov. Schley on September 10, 1837: "The result of the levels to the ridge near Decatur, DeKalb County, which you authorized me to run proved altogether flattering; the ascent to the main ridge, where we left a bench mark, is only two hundred eighty-five feet above the level of the Chattahoochee, which is to be reached with a distance of eight miles -- which at our assumed grades is attainable with ease. In fine, sir, nothing more is now required than to realize by physical ability that which intellectual enterprise has so handsomely planned. This I leave in your hands." [18]

On December 23, 1837, the Georgia legislature incorporated Long's findings into law. The spot chosen for the terminus, in Land Lot 78 of the 14th District, was owned in 1837 by Reuben Cone of Decatur. For $125 Cone granted the Western & Atlantic Railroad a 66-foot right-of-way through his property, including rights to use the timber and stone found there. Rights-of-way also were obtained from Hosea Maner, Cornelius M. Connally, T. E. Brown, Wesley Hudson, Josiah Long, Nathaniel Mangum, Solomon Sweat, Nathaniel Sweat, James McC. Montgomery, D. J. Connally and John Golden. Golden didn't give up his land without a fight. Having moved to DeKalb to get away from railroads, he was not happy when blasting threw "a boulder the size of a bed" within 100 feet of his house. Golden accused workmen of aiming rock at his house; in return, the workmen accused Golden of sabotaging their work by pushing rocks back into railroad cut.

Also at the 1837 session, the General Assembly approved plans by the Georgia Railroad and Banking Company to connect its line, which was progressing from the east, with the state rail line on the southeast bank of the Chattahoochee. [19]

Ammi Williams, along with Reuben Cone, would realize considerable financial gain from real estate dealings around the railroad terminus. Like Cone, Williams was a Connecticut native. He had passed through Decatur in 1830 on his way to hiring out his slaves to work in the Carroll County gold mines. He left his son Warren to supervise the workers while he "went North" for his family. In the meantime, Warren's mind "lost its balance and he became a lunatic." The Williams family lived for a short time at Sandtown before settling in Decatur in 1831. Williams purchased "the Garrison place" in 1837 where he lived until his death in 1864. Despite suffering from "nervous depression," Williams was financially successful, and was one of the backers of Atlanta as "an important place for business." He died at his home in Decatur on March 30, 1864. Both Cone and Williams are buried in Atlanta's Oakland Cemetery. Two Williams sons-in-law, Lemuel P. Grant and William H. Dabney, went on to prominence in Atlanta. [20]

The location of the railroad terminus was based purely on an engineering decision. Railroad and government officials and engineers probably paid little attention to the debate raging in Decatur over coming of the "iron horse." Although the point was moot, strong sentiment was expressed on both sides of the argument.

Historian Lucian Lamar Knight in 1914 described Decatur as "practically a suburb of Atlanta, from which bristling center of population it is only six miles distant. The beautiful thoroughfares which connect the towns are lined with elegant mansions. But the older city possesses a wealth of peculiar attractions. For years past it has been a favorite place of residence with professional and business men, who maintain offices in Atlanta but prefer to live in Decatur, where an atmosphere of refinement, unvexed by the feverish turmoil of commercialism, greets them at the close of the business hours. The little town of Decatur has always preferred culture to commerce. When the Georgia Railroad was built there was little hospitality extended to the newcomer. It was kept at a distance of more than half a mile from the court house, to avoid the disquieting effects; while Atlanta, on the other hand, true to her commercial instincts, greeted the swarthy stranger with open arms. Thus Decatur missed the opportunity of becoming a metropolis. She stepped aside in favor of her rival, content to pursue the even tenor of her way along the forest paths and to keep in touch with the fragrant memories and lofty ideals of the Old South." [21]

Decatur residents objected to the coming of the railroad because they thought the noise, smoke and dirt of the trains would disturb their tranquil community. Rebecca Latimer Felton recalled "distinctly" recalled how "the residents of Decatur protested against the invasion of the railway trains on the grounds that the smoke would ruin the paint on their homes." A history of the Georgia Railroad and Banking Company included this "interesting reprint" from the Atlanta Journal:

"The Georgia Road was built back about 1845. Decatur was at that time a proud, prosperous and aristocratic village. It is said that her inhabitants refused to allow the train to make its terminal there, claiming that the noise, smoke and general commotion that it created would prove a nuisance, in that the train would frighten the cows and chickens, thereby reducing the fine quality of milk, butter and eggs, as well as the quantity; and, last but not least, would disturb the early morning slumbers of its people. So the old Georgia Road was forced to make its terminal about six miles to the north,[3] which was the nearest stop Decatur would permit. The Atlanta of today is the result, and who can say that this metropolitan city and railroad center of the Southeast does not owe a debt to Decatur."

Charles Murphey Candler, in his 1922 "Historical Address," however, called the stories of Decatur's opposition "pure fiction.

"The selection of this point as the terminus of each of these railroads was not an accident of circumstance, nor was it because of the refusal or unwillingness of the town of Decatur to have a railroad terminus within its limits for fear smoke from the engines would blacken its houses, the noise of engines disturb its quietude or that it would bring undesirable citizens. This old story is pure fiction.

"More than this, the Georgia Railroad did not run through Decatur, but just outside its southern boundary, not because citizens objected, but solely for topographical reasons... The railroad in passing Decatur followed the backbone of the ridge dividing the waters running in the north to the Gulf, and in the South to the Atlantic, and avoided cutting through hills and crossing valleys as much as possible."

An anonymous Decatur citizen wrote to the editor of the Southern Recorder on July 24, 1839, calling the chosen terminus "unsuitable in every respect," and setting forth reasons to extend the railroad to Decatur:

"Mr. Editor: -- I must ask the use of your columns to make a few suggestions in regard to the propriety of extending the South-eastern end of the Western and Atlantic Railroad from its present terminus, to the town of Decatur, in DeKalb County. And here I will premise, that if this measure will interfere with the true interest and policy of the State, of any particular section, or of any Railroad company interest, then I would be silent on the subject. But so far from this, it can be easily illustrated, that at least the interest of the State and of the Georgia Railroad, would be particularly promoted by it, and no disadvantage whatever could accrue to the Monroe Railroad. If then the facts I

---

[3] The train station was located at the southern city limits of Decatur, less than one mile from the courthouse square.

have assumed be true, is it not highly improper that the terminus of this Road should be suffered to remain where it is, which most unquestionably would have the effect, from its vicinity to the town of Decatur, to destroy this town altogether. The citizens of Decatur who own property there, have purchased and improved it at an enormous expense, and now I appeal to every candid mind if it would not be an act of the grossest injustice, thus to inflict such an injury on those citizens, and to destroy one of the most flourishing villages in Georgia, when the same could be prevented in a manner so far from doing any interest any injury, that the interest of the State could be promoted by it.

"Before we proceed to advance any reason which the terminus should be removed to Decatur, may we not enquire why it should remain where it now is, more than at any other place. Men who are acquainted with the location of the terminus, may think that this place was selected on account of its being more suitable than any other place, without considering that its present location was as much the result of accident as design. The original law authorizing the construction of this Road, only provided for its extending to the South-eastern bank of the Chattahoochee river, which would have been a more unsuitable place, if possible, than the present, for the terminus, and for facilitating its connection with the branch Railroads. In 1837, the Legislature authorized the Road to be continued any distance not exceeding eight miles from the Chattahoochee river in a South-eastern direction. The object of which is nothing more than to remove the terminus from the bank of the river to some better place, which would be more practicable and convenient to effect a connection with the branch Roads. But I will venture to say that no one who is acquainted with the country, at the present terminus, ever seriously contemplated for a moment that this place would be the permanent terminus; a place so unsuitable in every respect -- the scarcity of water, the inaccessibility of wagon roads to this place, the poorness of the adjacent country, and, above all, the fact that the level of the Road will be somewhere between fifteen and twenty feet lower than the surface of the earth, are unfavorable circumstances to the terminus being at this place.

Again: If this place is not more suitable for the terminus than any other place, and the Road can be extended to Decatur without doing injury to any interest, and with but little expense, why not let it be taken there? The Legislature most certainly could have no wish to prostrate Decatur by building up a town at this terminus, which would, without doubt, have that effect, when in so doing it cannot benefit the State one cent, but on the contrary do it an injury. We have been led to believe that benefits instead of losses would result from the construction of this Road; but if this state of things is suffered to continue, the citizens of Decatur would be left in a far worse situation than before this Road was thought of. As I have before intimated, if the removal of the terminus to Decatur would affect the public interest, then I should remain quiescent upon the principle which I am very willing to admit, that private interest should yield to public interest. But I am persuaded, as I think all must be who are acquainted with the subject, that this measure would be favorable to the public interest. The distance from the terminus to Decatur is only a little upwards of five miles, and there is no place on the whole extent of the Road for so great a distance together that is more practicable for Railroading than between these points. The country is almost perfectly level, comparatively speaking, without any hills or vallies or rocks to obstruct the construction of a Railroad. Besides, Decatur is situated on the natural route to intersect the Georgia Railroad, and perhaps the Monroe Railroad, also. As regards the Georgia Railroad, three temporary routes have been surveyed preparatory to its location from Madison to the terminus of the Western and Atlantic Railroad, two of which pass directly through Decatur, and both of which are rationally considered infinitely preferable to the other route, and as regards the

Monroe Railroad, it is probable it could effect a connection at Decatur as well as at the present terminus, and even if it could not, it is difficult to conceive how the interest of that Road could not be affected; and the presumption is, that no objection to the contemplated removal of the terminus would come from that quarter...

"Decatur is a handsome, flourishing village, well improved, and for health and comfort is perhaps not surpassed by any in Georgia. It affords convenient and comfortable accommodations, good society, and most excellent schools. When our Railroads are completed, it will be a most commodious, comfortable, healthy, and convenient retreat for our citizens from sickness, from the lower and sickly regions of Georgia, and a most cheap, convenient and healthy place for the education of children..." [22]

The Georgia Railroad did come to DeKalb County in 1845, just to the south of the city limits of Decatur.

Historian Meta Barker wrote: "When the Georgia Railroad was completed, at last, through the eastern part of DeKalb County to Atlanta in 1845, the corporate limits of Decatur extended only a short distance in any direction from the courthouse square. To allow the track to run near the edge of the town, a quarter of a mile or so from the courthouse was obviously the only plan with `rhyme or reason' to recommend it -- the usual plan adopted by towns that preceded the age of steam transportation. From this circumstance arose, not improbably, a half-truth that took on all the proverbial color and blossomed into the legend that Decatur put to rout the iron horses upon their concerted invasion of DeKalb County more than a century ago." [23]

In March of 1837, the grand jury again was quite complimentary about the work of DeKalb County Treasurer James Lemon: "We as the Grand Inquest have with the strictest scrutiny examined the books of the County Treasurer James Lemon, and find with the greatest pleasure the greatest imaginable accuracy in his books. There is a neat undisbursed residue of money amounting to Eight hundred and twenty and 50/100 dollars and notes aggregating $2457.64/100."
Joseph Morgan [24]

In September, the Grand Jury had a bit more to say about the county's condition:

"The Grand Jury for the County of DeKalb with pleasure report that they have examined the books of the Treasurer of this County and find everything connected with the duty of that office in a condition highly satisfactory to us and creditable to himself. We find in favor of the County, cash, $367.78 and notes that we believe to be good, $2269.64/100.

"They have also examined the records of the clerks of the Superior and Inferior Courts and it affords us satisfaction, as the proper organs of the County to examine and report their condition, to say that they are kept in a style highly honorable to those officers.

"They have had under review the returns of the Tax Collection, and find the sum of $63.05 due unpaid and returned insolvent. From the fair showing of that officer in the discharge of his official duties, we all in his return, that amount to his credit.

"In some portions of our County we hear the situation of our roads complained of, and we are sorry to say not without just cause. The bridge across Peach Tree at Garrison's Mills unsafe. We therefore recommend to the Inferior Court early and efficient means for the remedy.

"They believe that a more rigid enforcement of the patrol law would produce salutary results in our slave population, and recommend especially to the (Decatur) Town Dist., to be vigilant in paying property attention to Houses occupied and controlled by slaves only.

"With regard to the morals of our citizens, it must be a subject of congratulation, that amid the changing scenes of fortune, our State docket us few subjects for capital offense as any other County in this State. We may ascribe this in a good degree to the just and prompt execution of her laws, and the ready obedience of her citizens to obey them.

"In taking leave of his Honor, Judge Warner, we individually tender to him our unqualified approbation for the able, impartial manner he has presided in administering the laws of the country (sic). Also we present to George D. Anderson, Esqr., Solicitor General, our thanks for his prompt and assiduous attention to his duty, and for the constant and kind attention paid to our body. We recommend that our presentments be published in the Federal Union and Georgia Journal."

Lochlin Johnson, Foreman

James Paden	John Rainy	Naman Hardman
William Johnson	John T. Savage	Edwin Johnson
John L. Bradley	John Morris	John G. Parker
Robert Crockett	William Jackson	William Smith
John Dabbs	Christopher Sewell	Charles D. Parr
William Morris	Meredith Collier	James Hall. [25]
Daniel Durham	William B. Anderson	
James M. Watson	Henry Grogan	

One of DeKalb County's oldest industries, Terry's Mill, was being operated by Thomas Simmons in 1837. The mill, which produced lumber and ground grain, was located on Sugar Creek in Land 174 of the 15th District, south of now Glenwood Avenue. Simmons's second wife, Mrs. Eleanor Terry, a Gwinnett County widow, had three children from her first marriage. One was Thomas Terry who took over operation of the mill after Simmons died in 1842. Thomas married Mary J. Thurman in 1849, and had six children: Ellen M. (1851-1880), Tom Jr., William M. (1854-1926), Sylvester J. (1856-1872), Newton Harrison (1858-1923) and Jasper (1861-1863). Ellen M. Terry was the first wife of Francis L. Guess, an early county surveyor. William M. Terry, a city of Atlanta merchant was the grandfather of Bill Terry, manager of the New York Giants baseball team. William Terry, who died in 1926, was the last family member to own the mill. [26]

Mills began to flourish along DeKalb County's rivers and creeks in the mid-1830s. Mills, including the huge wheels, usually were constructed by professional millwrights. Mill buildings were usually two stories high and raised above stream beds. They were substantially built, but rarely painted. Often, blacksmith shops and stores were located near the mills. The mill operator was not paid in money, but took a portion of the grain called a "toll." In the case of corn, the toll was one-eighth of the total grain ground. [27]

Two new post offices were opened in the county in 1837. Panthersville opened on July 27, with George L. Black as postmaster, succeeded by George S. Cobb, Hugh M. Boyd and Locklin Johnson, until the office was discontinued on August 9, 1856. The post office was re-opened on February 20, 1879, and functioned until April 30, 1901 when operations were transferred to Decatur. The South River Post Office was only open 10 days, August 2-10, 1837. The only postmaster, Nathaniel G. Hilburn, was later killed in one of Atlanta's "most sensational murder cases." [28]

Gov. George R. Gilmer signed legislation on December 25, 1837 authorizing James Montgomery, with whom he had worked at Fort Peachtree, to establish a ferry across the Chattahoochee River at Standing Peachtree. Montgomery showed cash receipts for operating the ferry between October 8 and December 30, 1842 of $72. [29]

Whatever the opinion of Decatur citizens generally, the DeKalb Grand Jury obviously was pleased with the coming of the railroad. In 1838, the panel reported:

"We congratulate our fellow citizens on the great subject of Internal improvement in our State and in our County with such vigor and industry which promises such benefits to our Section of the State. The Southern Terminus of the Western & Atlantic Rail Road being in our County, from which branches will connect the navigable waters of the west with the most of our Atlantic cities from which we must derive an invaluable trade."

Lochlin Johnson, Foreman

Jordan Webb	John T. Dabney	Thomas D. Harris
Hastings D. Palmer	Dempsey Perkerson	Leonard H. Tomlinson
Joel Herring	William Martin	Moses Murphey
Allen Hardman	John M. Harris	Benjamin B. Avery
Allen Crowley	James Millican	Lodowick Tuggle
Ransom Seay	James Guess	George Avery
James M. Holly	Green B. H. Terry	
John G. McWilliams	John Jennings	

At the September, 1838 term, the grand jury also commented on "the decayed condition of our Court House" and lined up a number of cases to be heard there. The jury indicted William Slay for the murder of his wife, Elizabeth, with John Ray as an accessory. Catharine (Catsey) Wright was indicted for "keeping a disorderly house," and William Heard for perjury in connection with a lawsuit involving "cutting and chopping of John Trimble's wagon." The Grand Jury indicted several citizens for gambling and expressed "regret to be under the necessity of finding so many True Bills for the violation of our law." [30]

On September 4, the Inferior Court ordered "that a Route for a Road as lately marked out by Hardy Ivy, Benjamin Little, Benjamin Thurman, and Hosea Maner, be opened out and kept up as one of the publick Roads of said County, said Road commencing on the Sandtown Road near the Southern Terminus of the Western & Atlantic Rail Road & intersecting the Nelson Ferry Road near Reid's Shantee" (near the present intersection of the railroad and Magnolia Street, formerly Nelson's Ferry Road). [31]

Henry Irby bought a land lot on December 18, 1838, and opened a tavern. The area, which was first called Irbyville, later became Buckhead. A post office opened there on October 5, 1841, with William W. Sentell as postmaster. The post office was discontinued on December 8, 1842, but was reinstated on August 28, 1855, with Riall B. Hicks, Irby's son-in-law, as postmaster. [32]

The final countdown began for the Cherokee Indians on April 6, 1838, when Gen. Winfield Scott was sent to Georgia to remove them. DeKalb's cavalry company commander, James M. Calhoun, surveyed conditions among the Indians and reported to Gov. George Gilmer:

"Decatur DeKalb County, Ga., Feb. 20th, 1838

His excellency, G. R. Gilmer,
"I saw Doct. Davidson today, who informed me that you wished me to write you the news from the Cherokee Country concerning the Indians, etc. I attended Cass Court last week & while there I made it my business to enquire a great deal about the conduct of the Indians, etc. & intended to write to you.

"From the enquiries I made, it appears that the people generally in that Country do not apprehend that there will be any hostilities. They seem to be pretty generally, so far as I could ascertain, of opinion that the Indians would leave without doing any mischief of consequence. Some think that perhaps a few desperate characters may revenge themselves upon son of the whites with whom they are unfriendly.

"For my own part, (judging from the Indian character & their previous conduct) I am afraid that the people in the Cherokee Country, have too much confidence in the Indians. I cannot see that the citizens there are making any preparations whatever to defend themselves -- except the companies, under the act of the last Legislature. They should bear in mind the condition of the white citizens in the Creek nation -- at the time of the breaking out of hostilities there. If hostilities should break out there, the same results would be experienced that were in the Creek Country.

"The citizens ought to make preparation, even if there be no danger. They have a direct interest in the preservation of their lives and property, and if difficulties should ensue, they will find it would have been preferable to have relied more on their own action, and not so much upon any immediate benefit to be derived from the military. Because they are more interested and their action would have been quicker.

If no previous preparation be made by the citizens themselves & hostilities should commence -- the consequence would be an abandonment of the Country -- at least for a time, which would give the enemy time to embody and do mischief -- as the whole country would be left in their possession except where the soldiers might be stationed. For it is natural to expect that the citizen would not remain and fight & leave his wife, children & property unprotected, to be massacred. The ties of nature & of interest would suggest that he should first put his family at least out of danger.

"It has been my opinion that though hostilities are not expected -- and are not probable, that it would be a prudent course in some of the Counties, having a dense Indian population, for the citizens to prepare forts at the villages, for the safety of their families, which could be guarded by a sufficient number while the balance of the citizens, with the assistance of the soldiers -- could apprehend the enemy.

"The act of the last session I am afraid, will have a bad effect, & I was so inclined to think at its passage. There is no doubt but what there are numbers of trifling individuals in that country, that would almost excite hostilities, in order to be mustered in to the service of the state, etc. They would at least put the country in a state of alarm and commotion -- by endeavoring to excite the fears of the people. Whereas as regards the protection of the Country they would be of no more benefit, when organized into companies & mustered into service, than to act upon the principle of self defence, as a body of citizens -- as all people are bound to do when they are directly invaded and attacked in their own homes.

"There seems to be no hostile preparations among the Indians that can be discovered. I saw a number of them at work on the Western & Atlantic Railroad. It is said they make very good hands at work. Those who are at work on the Road are making considerable progress. I am delighted with Cass County. You ought if you can spare time to visit the up Country in the summer. I think you would be very much pleased.
Yours with very great respect & esteem,
James M. Calhoun" [33]

On May 24, 1838, federal troops, assisted by two Georgia regiments, rounded up the Indians into four north Georgia camps called "removal forts." A volunteer company from DeKalb, led by Capt. John Fowler, participated in the removal effort. [34]

Some 15,000 Cherokees were forcibly removed in 1838; 4000 died en route to the west, some from sickness and the hardships of travel, "others simply of broken hearts." [35]

Seventeen years after DeKalb County's founding, in 1839, Decatur was a relatively sophisticated town. Thriving settlements existed at Cross Keys, Stone Mountain, Standing Peachtree and Rock Chapel. Plantations prospered along the South River. But, the "magnificent inland city" envisioned by Alexander Hamilton Stephens at the proposed railroad terminus location eight miles from the Chattahoochee River did not exist. [36]

In that year, 21-year-old John J. Thrasher moved to DeKalb from Newton County:

"When I arrived in this place, in 1839, the country was entirely covered by forest. There was but one house here at that time and that stood where the old post office was formerly located; it was built of logs and was occupied by an old woman and her daughter about 16 years of age. I found a man also, named (Benjamin F.) Thurman, living in the country nearby. I went to work building and fixing up, and built a store. First one moved in from the country and then another until we had a right smart little town. The people around here were very poor. There were a great many of the women wore no shoes at all. We had dirt floors to our houses. There was a man named Johnson with me in the store, and the firm was Johnson & Thrasher. That was the only store in the place at that time."

Thrasher, like many others who would follow, also worked on the railroad. Workmen and their families lived in "rude cabins made from roughly sawed timber. All of them had dirt floors. There was not a plank floor among them all," Thrasher said. The Atlanta pioneer recalled the town's first social event, Mrs. Mulligan's ball, which proved to be a turning point for the quality of housing.

"The first society of Atlanta was there, and it was a swell affair, or we thought it was..." It was the ball that allowed the women of the town to discover that the Mulligan home was the only one in town with a plank floor. "You know how women are about things," Thrasher said. "If one has something her neighbor wants it too. Well, sir, the day after the ball a delegation of the men came to me, and announced that their wives wanted plank floors in their shacks, and they declared if I didn't put them in the houses every blessed man of them would quit work. I had to send out to Collier's Mill and get a good many loads of puncheons to floor the other shacks."

Thrasher, Mulligan and the rest of the workmen were working at a feverish pace on the Monroe embankment, which is Atlanta's oldest man-made structure. The embankment formed the western base of the downtown railroad triangle, stretching from the north end of Terminal Station to the junction with the Western and Atlantic tracks at Foundry Street.

The coming of the railroad would revolutionize travel, which continued to be as slow in 1839 as it had when settlers first came to DeKalb. It took five weeks for Walter Walcott and his family to travel from Michigan to Decatur in the spring of 1839, by canal, river and wagon.

The DeKalb Grand Jury in March of 1839 apparently felt compelled to quash a rumor of a drinking problem in the county:

"... As no cause has been reported to this body by any of its members during the term against the laws and good order of this community we receive it as evidence that a favorable change has taken place with regard to the morals of our county. Therefore we congratulate our fellow citizens on the flattering prospects of an improvement in our moral condition generally. Therefore from the above the public can be able to judge whether the report that has gone forth to the world in public prints relative to the great amount of ardent Spirits consumed in the County is entitled to sufficient credit to be believed.

Robert Jones, Foreman

James W. Givens	Littleton Jackson	William Terry
John N. Bellenger	Francis War	John W. McGee
Malcolm McLeod	John McDaniel	Azmon R. Alman
Edwin Plaster	John Evans	Lawrence S. Morgan
John G. Parker	D. D. Anderson	Joseph Walker
William Johnston	James Caldwell	Thomas Akins. [37]
Stephen Martin	Shadrack Farmer	
John Hardman	Stephen Terry	

The September 1839 grand jury, with John Jennings as foreman, recommended to the commissioners of the town of Decatur that the "Publick Square and streets" be put "in good order."

Changes within the Primitive Baptist denomination were dramatic during 1838 and '39. The Yellow River Association at its annual meeting in 1838 had adopted the following resolution:

"Resolved, that the institutions of the day called benevolent societies, the Convention, Tract Society, Bible Society, Temperance Society, Abolition Society, Sunday School Union, Theological Seminary, and other institutions tributary to the mission plan, now existing in the United States, are unscriptural, and that we as an Association will not correspond with any Association that is united with them. Nor will we hold in our Union or fellowship, any church that is connected with them." [38]

Several churches withdrew from the Yellow River Association. The rift caused the formation of new churches in DeKalb County.

Hardman Primitive Baptist Church stayed in the association, but several of its members, led by Joseph Walker, left the congregation. On December 7, 1839, they organized a new church. The first presbytery consisted of the Rev. Luke Robinson, the Rev. T. U. Wilkes, the Rev. W. A. Callaway and Licentiate Lewis Towers. Charter members were Joseph and Jane Walker, William and Laura Towers, Deborah, Margaret and Mary Burdett, Sam Samuel, Seaborn Jones, Eliza and Sarah Crowley. The Rev. Callaway was the first pastor, and Joseph Walker the first clerk. Walker continued as clerk for 38 years, until 1877.

The new church adopted this resolution:

"Now, be it Known that we as a body are not connected with any of the societies above named (in the Resolution of the Association) and as for the Abolition Society, we spurn the thought of any Southern person, or body of persons, being such. But as for the balance of the societies, we contend that every person is at liberty to patronize them, and is not a matter than involves Fellowship. That if a brother sees fit to join a temperance or missionary society, no other brother should interfere." [39]

The church began services as Decatur Baptist Church on February 22, 1840; services were held in Decatur Presbyterian Church building. The church applied to the Rock Mountain Association for membership on October 24, 1840. Services were moved on November 13, 1841 to the Ensibia Academy, three miles east of Decatur on Rock Bridge Road. The church name was changed to Indian Creek Baptist Church on January 8, 1842. Church membership had grown to 140 by 1843.

The church was burned by Union soldiers in 1864, but was replaced with funds from an unusual source. Clerk Joseph Walker wrote of the church's destruction to a woman of his acquaintance in the north. Mrs. Theressa Seabrooks sent $325 to rebuild the church. [40]

Among those buried the Indian Creek cemetery are these DeKalb pioneers: W. R. Ayers, S. T. Corley, Lemuel Dean, William Doby, Richard H. Eskew, A. C. and John W. Fowler, A. M. Holcombe, W. P. Hudgins, James W. McClain, Mark H. Minor, P. M. Ray, Alexander Vaughn, Joseph Walker, James White and Benjamin Woodson. [41]

The Pace's Ferry Post Office opened on April 16, 1839, with Hardy Pace as postmaster. The office was later moved to Cobb County. [42]

Chapter 20 Notes

1. Miller, Dorothy Burke, 1952, "Creek Indians of DeKalb County," The Collections of the DeKalb Historical Society, Vol. 1, page 8.

2. Garrett, Franklin M., November, 1936, "DeKalb County During the Cherokee Troubles," The Atlanta Historical Bulletin, No. 9, pages 24-29.

3. Garrett, Franklin M., 1954, 1969, Atlanta and Environs -- A Chronicle of Its People and Events, Vol. 1, page 141.

4. Bryan, Mary Givens Mrs., 1952, "Documents Related To Indian Affairs," The Collections of the DeKalb Historical Society, Vol. 1, pages 15-25.

5. Bryan, Mary Givens Mrs., 1952, "Documents Related To Indian Affairs," The Collections of the DeKalb Historical Society, Vol. 1, pages 15-25.

6. Garrett, Franklin M., 1954, 1969, Atlanta and Environs -- A Chronicle of Its People and Events, Vol. 1, page 141. Bryan, Mary Givens Mrs., 1952, "Documents Related To Indian Affairs," The Collections of the DeKalb Historical Society, Vol. 1, pages 15-25. Pioneer Citizens' History of Atlanta.

7. Garrett, Franklin M., November, 1936, "DeKalb County During the Cherokee Troubles," The Atlanta Historical Bulletin, No. 9, pages 24-29.

8. Bryan, Mary Givens Mrs., 1952, "Documents Related To Indian Affairs," The Collections of the DeKalb Historical Society, Vol. 1, pages 15-25.

9. Bryan, Mary Givens Mrs., 1952, "Documents Related To Indian Affairs," The Collections of the DeKalb Historical Society, Vol. 1, pages 15-25.

10. Bryan, Mary Givens Mrs., 1952, "Documents Related To Indian Affairs," The Collections of the DeKalb Historical Society, Vol. 1, pages 15-25.

11. Nix, Dorothy, personal collection, DeKalb Historical Society.

12. Miller, Mrs. Flora McElroy, n. d., "History of Doraville Associate Reformed Presbyterian Church.

13. Miller, Mrs. Flora McElroy, n. d., "History of Doraville Associate Reformed Presbyterian Church.

14. Miller, Mrs. Flora McElroy, n. d., "History of Doraville Associate Reformed Presbyterian Church.

15. Lee, Rebecca Kirkland, February, 1996, talk at Oak Grove United Methodist Church. Nix, Dorothy, personal collection, DeKalb Historical Society.

16. Garrett, Franklin M., 1954, 1969, Atlanta and Environs -- A Chronicle of Its People and Events, Vol. 1, pages 141-142.

17. Garrett, Franklin M., 1954, 1969, Atlanta and Environs -- A Chronicle of Its People and Events, Vol. 1, page 144.

18. Garrett, Franklin M., 1954, 1969, Atlanta and Environs -- A Chronicle of Its People and Events, Vol. 1, page 148.

19. Garrett, Franklin M., 1954, 1969, Atlanta and Environs -- A Chronicle of Its People and Events, Vol. 1, pages 150 and 157.

20. Garrett, Franklin M., 1954, 1969, Atlanta and Environs -- A Chronicle of Its People and Events, Vol. 1, page 60. Willard, Levi, 1920, "The Early History of Decatur Written Many Years Ago," DeKalb New Era.

21. Knight, Lucian Lamar, 1914, <u>Georgia's Landmarks, Memorials and Legends</u>, Vol. 1, pages 508-509.

22. Barker, Meta, November, 1936, "How Decatur Escaped the Iron Horse," Atlanta Historical Bulletin, Vol. IX, pages 12-18.

23. Garrett, Franklin M., 1954, 1969, <u>Atlanta and Environs -- A Chronicle of Its People and Events</u>, Vol. 1, pages 168.

24. Garrett, Franklin M., 1954, 1969, <u>Atlanta and Environs -- A Chronicle of Its People and Events</u>, Vol. 1, page 151.

25. Garrett, Franklin M., 1954, 1969, <u>Atlanta and Environs -- A Chronicle of Its People and Events</u>, Vol. 1, page 152.

26. Hudgins, Carl T., 1952, "Mills and Other Early DeKalb County Industries (And Their Owners)," <u>The Collections of the DeKalb Historical Society</u>, Vol. 1, pages 6-7. Kurtz, Wilbur G., November, 1936, "The Murder of Tom Terry," The Atlanta Historical Bulletin, No. 9.

27. Hudgins, Carl T., 1952, "Mills and Other Early DeKalb County Industries (And Their Owners)," <u>The Collections of the DeKalb Historical Society</u>, Vol. 1, page 3.

28. Garrett, Franklin M., 1954, 1969, <u>Atlanta and Environs -- A Chronicle of Its People and Events</u>, Vol. 1, pages 152-153.

29. Anderson, E. Katherine, December, 1937, "James McC. Montgomery of Standing Peachtree," The Atlanta Historical Bulletin No. 12.

30. Garrett, Franklin M., 1954, 1969, <u>Atlanta and Environs -- A Chronicle of Its People and Events</u>, Vol. 1, page 158.

31. Garrett, Franklin M., 1954, 1969, <u>Atlanta and Environs -- A Chronicle of Its People and Events</u>, Vol. 1, page 159.

32. Garrett, Franklin M., 1954, 1969, <u>Atlanta and Environs -- A Chronicle of Its People and Events</u>, Vol. 1, page 159.

33. Garrett, Franklin M. November, 1936, "DeKalb County During the Cherokee Troubles," Atlanta Historical Bulletin, IX, page 24.

34. Garrett, Franklin M., 1954, 1969, <u>Atlanta and Environs -- A Chronicle of Its People and Events</u>, Vol. 1, page 162. DeKalb Historical society files.

35. Mitchell, Eugene M. September, 1937, "The Indians of Georgia," Atlanta Historical Bulletin, XI, page 29.

36. Garrett, Franklin M., 1954, 1969, <u>Atlanta and Environs -- A Chronicle of Its People and Events</u>, Vol. 1, page 164.

37. Garrett, Franklin M., 1954, 1969, <u>Atlanta and Environs -- A Chronicle of Its People and Events</u>, Vol. 1, page 170.

38. Candler, Charles Murphey, November 9, 1922, Historical Address. Smith, R. Frank, August 1, 1922, "A Brief Historical Sketch of Indian Creek Missionary Baptist Church."

39. Candler, Charles Murphey, November 9, 1922, Historical Address. Smith, R. Frank, August 1, 1922, "A Brief Historical Sketch of Indian Creek Missionary Baptist Church."

40. Ford, Elizabeth Austin, 1952, "A Precis of DeKalb's Early Church History," <u>The Collections of the DeKalb Historical Society</u>, Vol. 1, pages 32-34. Smith, R. Frank, August 1, 1922, "A Brief Historical Sketch of Indian Creek Missionary Baptist Church."

41. Garrett, Franklin M., 1954, 1969, <u>Atlanta and Environs -- A Chronicle of Its People and Events</u>, Vol. 1, page 170. Smith, R. Frank, August 1, 1922, "A Brief Historical Sketch of Indian Creek Missionary Baptist Church."

42. Garrett, Franklin M., 1954, 1969, <u>Atlanta and Environs -- A Chronicle of Its People and Events</u>, Vol. 1, page 170.

Chapter 21

*D*eKalb County's second census, taken in 1840, showed a total population of 10,466, only 424 persons more than 10 years before. Comparison is impossible, however. The Cherokee Indian territory north of the Chattahoochee that had been a portion of DeKalb in 1830 had since been removed from DeKalb and made into other counties. The DeKalb of 1840 was considerably smaller than the ground covered by James Montgomery in 1830.

DeKalb's 1840 census taker was Thomas C. Bolton of Diamond's District. Bolton reported:
 White males 4314 (126 older than 60, 916 younger than 5)
 White females 4142 (199 older than 60, 866 younger than 5)
 Male free persons of color 4
 Female free persons of color 2
 Male slaves 952 (2 more than 100)
 Female slaves 1,052 (3 older than 100)

According to the census, there were seven Revolutionary War veterans living in DeKalb in 1840:
 George Brooks, age 79
 William Copeland, 75
 John Macomson, 84
 William Reeve, 84
 Thomas Roberts, 95
 Lewis Stowers Sr., 76
 William Terrell, 84. [1]

The growing community of Panthersville where now Panthersville Road crosses the South River was designated an election district in 1840. The area had been known as the Panthersville District since the mid-1830s, and continues to be called Panthersville today. Originally, the district had been called Jordon's, then Perry's District.

In a letter dated December 20, 1939, DeKalb's Commissioner of Roads and Revenues, Scott Candler, explained the origin of the Panthersville name.

"I have been trying to find out some definite historical fact showing how the Panthersville District received its name. I know how local tradition accounts for the name. There was a family named Johnson (probably Lochlin) living on Blue Creek which flows north into South River. A son of this family lived in or near Decatur. About 1830, this son, his wife, and an infant child were returning to Decatur, when at the point now called Panthersville, they were chased by a panther. Family tradition says that the father urged that the baby be thrown out -- the mother insisted on continuing the race with the baby in the wagon.

"They reached Decatur. The baby was afterwards Mrs. James J. Winn, and became the mother of Mrs. George Bucher Scott, the Rev. Paul Winn (a missionary to Korea) and Mrs. Kate W. Kirkpatrick, who recently died in Decatur. I have heard this story all my life.

"I know of no better explanation of how Panthersville District secured its name.

"South of Panthersville District along South River there has always been an extensive swamp -- a part of which remains until this day. I imagine as the wild life was driven back from the rest of the territory in the county, an unusual number of panthers took refuge in this swamp."

Atlanta historian Franklin Garrett points out, however, that the birth date of Mrs. James J. Winn on her tombstone in the Decatur Cemetery is October 16, 1816, making her 14 years old in 1830. [2]

After last call at the local taverns, Decatur's midnight revelers apparently were taking their parties to the courthouse.

The DeKalb Grand Jury recommended at its March, 1840 term that the Inferior Court keep the Court House "closely locked during the night and prevent as far as possible the same being made use of for a dancing room and for disorderly collections in the night."

Zachariah Gholston, Foreman

John Evans	Angus Furgerson	Joseph Walker
Elijah Bird	John Morris	William Beauchamp
John N. Bellinger	Lemuel B. Edwards	Moses Murphey
Alexander Johnson	Edwin G. Collier	William Betts
Charles Whitlock	James McCurdy	John Rainey
John Huey	John Kile	Charles Inge. [3]
Robert Biggers	Daniel Durham	
Fanning Brown	John Mason	

Hornsby's Post Office opened January 17, 1840 in the area now west of East Point, and operated until July 18, 1844. Postmasters were Joseph Hornsby and James Blackstock. [4]

As construction of the railroad bed advanced into DeKalb County, John J. Thrasher sought more right-of-way on which to build. In the fall of 1840, he petitioned the DeKalb Superior Court for appointment of five commissioners to assess damages caused by the construction. Appointed were Palmer R. Phillips, county surveyor; James Diamond; William Jackson; Thomas J. Perkerson and Adam Poole. Each commissioner received $3 per day for his service, except Phillips who was given $4 per day, paid by the railroad company.

Only one property owner, Alexander Ratteree, was dissatisfied with his assessment. Ratteree appealed to a special jury and was awarded $350 in 1840. An owner of extensive lands in the area of now East Point and College Park, Ratteree spent considerable time in court during his lifetime, as both plaintiff and defendant. Nonetheless, he died in the Fulton County Alms House. [5]

James S. Williams succeeded Stephen Harriman Long as chief engineer of the Western and Atlantic project. Long had declined half interest in 200 acres in now downtown Atlanta, saying, "The terminus will be a good location for one tavern, a blacksmith shop, a grocery store, and nothing else."

A legislative act of December 22, 1840 designated three locations as elections districts: the house of Henry Irby in Buck Head, a place known as Steward's Store and the place known as Panthersville. [6]

New county road commissioners also were appointed in 1840:
Militia District 524 -- Josiah Power, John Bellinger and John Austin.
MD 469 -- Spencer B. Crow, James McCurdy and George Elliott.
MD 479 -- James Donehoo, Jacob Redwin and James Blackstock.
MD 487 -- Joseph D. McEver, Palmer R. Phillips and George Thomas.
MD 530 -- Thomas J. Perkerson, Charner Humphries and William Willis.
MD 531 -- Jonathan B. Wilson, Chapman Powell and John Bryce.
MD 536 -- Zachariah R. Jones, John H. Jones and Hugh M. Boyd.
MD 537 -- John Evans, Thomas Atwood and William Meadow.
MD 563 -- James Diamond, James R. Henry and Elijah Steward.
MD 572 -- James Milican, Thomas J. Akin and John Burns.
MD 683 -- James W. Givins, John Swift and William Miller.
MD 686 -- James W. Reeve, William Johnston and Hastings D. Palmer.
MD 722 -- Britton Sentell, Thomas Farr and Henry Irby. [7]

Plantation owners along the South River had their corn and wheat ground and their lumber sawed at Garr's Mill, later known as Flake's Mill, which was located in Land Lot 35 of the 15th District in 1840. Owner Russell W. Garr sold his property, including the mill, to Eli J. Hulsey in 1863. Hulsey, in 1884, sold 1,000 acres and the mill to T. J. Flake, who was a DeKalb County commissioner and grand jury member. The mill ceased operation in 1925 when "the U. S. government blasted out the shoals in the river in order to drain the government's Honor Farm at Panthersville."

Residents of the Rock Chapel community (later Lithonia) patronized Lee's Mill, built by Mrs. W. H. Lee on the Yellow River in about 1840. The mill dam may have been built even earlier by Zachary Lee. The mill's last owner was Jesse Baker. Jacob Chupp provided Mrs. Lee with a little competition when he opened his mill on the Yellow River about three miles from Lithonia in 1845. Chupp's Mill at first was powered by water; later steam power was introduced. In addition to grinding corn and wheat and sawing lumber, the business also included a cabinet shop. Later owners of the mill were D. B. Chupp, W. G. Griffith and Consolidated Quarries. [8]

Two men with the same surname died in 1840 in DeKalb. One, Peter Brown, born in 1778, lived to the relatively old age of 62. A farmer and blacksmith, he settled on Intrenchment Creek in what is now south Fulton County during the winter of 1822-23. He was the father of Killis, Meredith, William T., Joel and Edgefield Brown.

Alfred B. Brown, a railroad engineer, was only 26 years old when he died. His obituary in the <u>Southern Recorder</u> of September 8, 1840, read: "Died at Standing Peachtree, DeKalb County, Ga.,

August 29, 1840, at the house of Col. J. McC. Montgomery, his father-in-law, 26 years of age. Engaged in Engineering Department on the Western & Atlantic Railroad. Member and elder in Presbyterian Church. Columbus Enquirer requested to copy."

Alfred Brown was the first husband of Rhoda Narcissa Montgomery, youngest daughter of James and Nancy. Their infant child also died in August of 1840. Brown's tombstone in the Montgomery family cemetery bears the inscription:

In Memory Of Alfred B. Brown
A Civil Engineer in the Service of the State of Georgia,
Born April 1st 1813 died Aug. 29th 1840.

This tribute to his virtues is erected by the Engineer Corps of which he was a worthy member. Rhoda Narcissa Montgomery later married Henry G. Dean; she was the last Montgomery to live at Standing Peachtree, leaving in about 1854. [9]

An unfortunate incident occurred in Decatur on July 16, 1841 that served to cast a shadow on the grand jury's attempt two years earlier to establish DeKalb's reputation as a temperate community.

Thomas C. Hill, brother of William M. (Uncle Billy) Hill, proprietor of the first barroom in Decatur, was sleeping off a drunk, lying on his brother's store counter. A customer, Benjamin Stowers entered the store, "saw Hill asleep on the counter and decided to play a joke on him. Stowers put a hand on Hill's head, slapped his hand with the other and turned to walk out of the store. Hill awoke, grabbed an iron weight and threw it at Stowers, striking him behind left ear. Stowers, 50, died some five minutes later. In addition to Hill's brother, three witnesses -- James Farrel, James Farris and James W. Reeve -- saw the killing. Hill was convicted of manslaughter and spent time in the state penitentiary in Milledgeville. Upon his release, he moved to Atlanta and became a tailor. He died in the 1850s, survived by his wife, Lucinda Ivy Hill, daughter of Hardy Ivy. [10]

Money was tight all over the country in 1841, and in March, the DeKalb Grand Jury made an unprecedented request:

"In approaching anything of a public nature and expressing our opinion thereon, it is under a sense of duty we regret and deplore the embarrassed condition of the Country as concerns our Currency. As concerns the matters of our State affairs we call upon our members in the next legislature to use their efforts and influence to reduce the wages of the members of that body from five to three dollars per day, and while we have further to express our deepest expressions of regret in the frequent unsuccessful attempts to reduce the number of that body, we recommend that their influence be exerted to have biennial instead of annual sessions established.

"We recommend that a public meeting be had of the people in our County to consult on and adopt such measures and resolutions as relate to the foregoing subject and would say the fourth of July would be a proper day for such Meeting... We request that our representatives have the office of tax collector and receiver consolidated in our County... We request that these, our presentments, be published in the Southern Recorder & Federal Union."

Lodowick Tuggle, Foreman.

Merrell Collier	William H. Tanner	John McDaniel
John Perkerson	Benjamin Thurman	William W. White
John Reid	James W. Givens	William Avery
Christopher Connally	Dickson Jordan	Simeon Williams

William Goldsmith   Jesse L. Williams   John L. Evins
Samuel Lovejoy   Lemuel Dean   John Bird
Robert Orr   Charles W. McGinnis

The requested meeting was held on September 9. At the suggestion of Merrell Collier, William Jackson chaired the meeting, and Alexander Johnson served as secretary. Those at the meeting resolved "not to support anyone for legislature who is unfriendly to the reduction of all salaries and wages of public or State officers, to a property medium with the times; also for biennial sessions of the General Assembly of this State." [11]

Despite the poor state of the economy, road building continued to occupy the agenda of the Inferior Court in 1841. Six reviewers were appointed to "view and mark out a route for a Road from the Nelson Ferry Road on by Loving Martin's (near Montgomery's Ferry) to where the Stage Road intersects the Road from White Hall to Montgomery's Ferry." On October 1, reviewers assigned "to mark out a route for a road from Robert Lemon's to intersect the Road at or near the (Peachtree) creek between said Lemon's and Meredith Collier's make the following report, viz. We think the route as laid out by said Robert Lemon and used as said Montgomery Ferry road, for several years past, to be the best and most practical route." The reviewers were Joel Morton, S. B. Crow, W. Hudson and James McCurdy. On November 1, a new road was authorized: "... commencing at A. Browning's on Lawrenceville Road and running west so as to intersect the Peachtree Road at or near William's Gin" (possibly LaVista Road).

Chandler's Bridge across Peachtree Creek and Nelson Ferry Road apparently were in need of repair in September 1841, causing the Grand Jury to report: "... We present as a grievance the bad state of the bridge across the Peach Tree Creek generally known as Chandler's Bridge and recommend to the proper authorities to have the evil speedily remedied. We also present as a grievance the bad state of the road known as Nelson Ferry Road, leading by Thrasherville on the road from White Hall to Montgomery's Ferry on the Chattahoochee; also the road from the panther's branch passing by Awtry's Mills to Decatur. We therefore recommend to the proper Authorities to have the above roads forthwith put in good order..." Thrasherville, yet another name for the village that would become Atlanta, was the settlement around the Monroe embankment. James Diamond was the 1841 grand jury foreman. [12]

While roadbuilding went on steadily, the railroad was running out of money. After four years and $2.5 million, not a single rail had been laid. Work was suspended on December 4, 1841. [13]

The Log Cabin Post Office in Phillips's District opened on January 15, 1841, with Nathan Howard as postmaster. The office was discontinued one year later.

Two obituaries were written in 1841; one was that of a DeKalb pioneer, the other of a famous Georgian. Benjamin Chapman, 66, the broadaxe expert who made the sills for the Macedonia Baptist Church building, died on January 24, 1841, and was buried in Macedonia churchyard. Gen. Thomas Glascock II, the two-term U. S Representative who retired to Decatur, was thrown from a horse and killed on May 19, 1841 at the age of 51. A brigadier-general under Andrew Jackson, Glascock County was named for him. [14]

"What is more awfully frightful than the cry of fire! fire! in the dead of night, especially in a little village that is without a fire engine." These were the thoughts of Decatur's first historian, Levi Willard, remembering January 9, 1842, the night DeKalb's "neat brick" courthouse burned.

DeKalb's third courthouse was much the same in design as the one that burned in 1842. Completed in 1847, this courthouse featured the additions of exterior steps, a portico and columns. Conforming to tradition, the courthouse faced east, the direction from which settlers came to Georgia. (DeKalb Historical Society).

"The roaring of the fire awoke me as I was sleeping in my cottage on the west side of the square. Drawing aside the curtains, I saw volumes of smoke and flame issuing from the upper windows... All that could be done was to watch the flying sparks and burning cinders. Favorably, there was but little wind, and no other buildings were injured. The scarcity of long ladders to reach the roofs of exposed houses that night, caused many to supply themselves."

How the courthouse caught on fire "remains a mystery; whether designedly, as some supposed or to destroy court records, there being many suits in court, or through the carelessness of some card players at a late hour in the night, in one of the vacant rooms above." [15]

Only one record book -- the Minutes of the Inferior Court -- survived the fire, thanks to a diligent courthouse employee who had taken the volume home to complete some work. [16]

The rebuilt courthouse was essentially the same in design as the one recently burned, with the exception of an added portico, two columns and exterior steps. [17]

Three months later, at the conclusion of its first term in 1842, the Grand Jury said: "We deplore with all our fellow Citizens of this County the destruction of our fine Court House by fire which was in a good state of repair... we have examined the books of the Court of Ordinary and find in as good condition as circumstances will warrant as all the records of that office was burnt and we recommend that the Inferior Court furnish the proper books of that office so that a proper record may be kept... We further recommend to the proper authorities that part of the road in the Incorporation of Decatur and joining the Shallowford Road to be put upon such course and ground as to straighten the same and thereby remedy the difficulty of such sudden turn at that place..."
James Paden, Foreman [18]

Martha Lumpkin Compton, for whom Marthasville was named, lived in this house on Hillyer Street in Decatur. The house was torn down about 1965 during construction of the new Columbia-Clairemont Connector. (DeKalb Historical Society)

After much discussion, a new site, the northeast corner of Land Lot 77, was chosen for the meeting of the railroad lines. Samuel Mitchell of Pike County, owner of Land Lot 77 since 1822, conveyed five acres of the property on July 11, 1842. The spot later was the site of Union Station, between Pryor Street and Central Avenue. "Being actuated by patriotic motives ," Mitchell gave the property free of charge. Of course, he was left with the remainder of Land Lot 77, which he could, because of the railroad, expect to sell at a profit. [19]

For some still unknown reason, the terminal site was moved from Land Lot 78 to Land Lot 77, causing considerable inconvenience for those, including the Monroe Railroad, who already had made plans based on the original site. John J. Thrasher wrote in 1871: "That was my ruin. I bought 100 acres of land with the expectation that the Macon road would stop up by the State road shops and when I found that the road was going down there, I was very much enraged, and sold out half my interest in that 100 acres for $4 an acre, although it was about one-half of what I gave for it. I did not think the property would ever be worth anything out there, and I sold out and went to Griffin."

At the time, the entire western part of the county "was in a perfect state of nature -- a wild unmolested forest, not a fence or cabin to be seen anywhere in site of the location." Even though no town existed, the location began to be called Terminus. [20]

A new town was laid out around the train depot, and named Marthasville for Gov. Wilson Lumpkin's daughter. The Marthasville Post Office opened on December 22, 1842, with Frederick C. Arms the first postmaster. By the end of 1842 a plank depot had been constructed, and the iron rails laid. One year later, on December 23, 1843, Marthasville was incorporated. The town's first commissioners were L. V. Gannon, John Bailey, Willis Carlisle, John Kile Sr. and Patrick Quinn.

Samuel Mitchell had the remainder of his land surveyed and divided into town lots, which went on sale in 1844. [21]

The first train to arrive in the new town did not come under its own steam. Atlanta old-timers were fond of saying, "The railroad didn't start nowhere or go nowhere." The locomotive, named Florida, had to be loaded on a huge wagon and pulled by 16 mules from the end of the line in Madison, up the Covington Road through Decatur to the other end of the line in Marthasville. One passenger car, built at the state penitentiary at Milledgeville, and a freight car were hauled in similar fashion. Preparations were made for an inaugural excursion from Marthasville to Marietta on December 23, 1842. [22]

Atlanta historian Franklin Garrett called it "the most thoroughly witnessed event in DeKalb County up to that time. Indeed few people in north Georgia had ever seen a railroad train or locomotive... For days before the arrival of the Florida from Madison and its departure for Marietta, long lines of farm wagons began to converge upon Marthasville, some having traveled long distances to see the marvel of the century. The surrounding country was nearly depopulated and it is said that every man, woman, Negro and dog in Decatur came over to see the mechanical monster run. Marthasville took on a county fair atmosphere. A large ball had been arranged in Marietta, so as to properly greet the pioneer excursionists and commemorate the event. When departure time came the noise of the locomotive was drowned out by the deafening cheers of the spectators and the discharge of firearms, which many of the more exuberant had brought along for the occasion."

Rebecca Latimer Felton, then a child of seven, had been privy to conversations concerning the planning of the railroad, because one of the engineers lived in her home. The mule-drawn train stopped in front of her house on its way to Marthasville so the family could get a close-up look. Rebecca recalled the gala inaugural trip, on which she was a passenger:

"It was decided to celebrate the opening of the state road by an excursion to Marietta from Marthasville with a big ball at the latter place and considerable speech-making from the politicians. It was the first adventure of that sort in the Southern States and broke the ice for internal public improvements. My parents were invited by the civil engineers. I was included, a tot of seven years, and I could now paint scenes, if I was an artist, with distinct remembrance of what I saw on that great trip.

"The future Capital of Georgia then had one building, the rough plank depot, with a shed room equipped with a fireplace where all sorts of good liquor could be bought, etc.

"It was a cold day in the late fall and my father and mother, with my small self, reached Thompson's hotel in Decatur, where the excursionists assembled and where a fine dinner was provided. It was a six-mile drive to Marthasville and conveyances were in demand. We were delighted when Maria Gertrude Kyle took a seat in our barouche on my mother's invitation. She was a well-known authoress and poetess in our few Georgia papers... The supper was handed to us as the people sat on benches around the Marietta ball room. Some had syllabub strong with Madeira wine, but I had a wine glass of jelly and a spoon with which to dip it out.

"I soon had enough of the frolic and was put to sleep in a bed, already a foot deep with shawls, capes and bonnets. The joyful folks danced all night. There were relays of fiddlers to keep the tunes going...

"The trip homeward was as dull as the going had been hilarious, but I have always taken satisfaction in the thought that I was a trip passenger on the very first passenger train that ever left the Union Depot in the present city of Atlanta. Judge (Hiram) Warner was on board with his little daughter, now Ms. Hill. So far as we know she and I are the only two known to be living, and fellow travelers on that momentous occasion when a railroad was venturing into Cherokee Georgia, where the Cherokee Indians had been living only ten years before." [23]

Regular train service did not begin in Atlanta until three years later. [24] The DeKalb Grand Jury, at its September, 1842, term had much to deplore concerning citizens and civic duty:

"... Viewing the among of bill of indictment which have come before us, although it is with pain that we have to take notice to such an occurrence, as having been heretofore not to be complained of. We recommend too that all civil officers be vigilant in the discharge of their duties in the suppression of all of those petty matters that have to consume the time of grand juries and that of the court, resulting from personal broils...

"... We are apprised that former grand jurors of our county have before expressed their opinions with regard to the currency and the effects it has produced, and would recommend still as a proper course to pursue that the debtor class be vigilant, industrious and economical, and by pursuing this course those days of plenty which we so much lament will ere long return to our much distressed country. And also would recommend forbearance on the part of those who have it in their power to distress others, so far as is consistent with justice to themselves, their families and fellowmen...

"... This body have to regret that the repair of the court house of our county has been neglected until this late period, as it has been decided that if done in proper time it will save the great expense of making a new wall. And we now recommend to the Inferior Court forthwith to have the same put under contract for repair on as cheap and convenient a plan as will answer the purpose, and that they have contractors give sufficient bond so that additional trouble and expense not again devolve on this county, as our funds are entirely spent..."

Zachariah Gholston, Foreman.

James W. Givens	George Lyon	Charley Mason
Charles D. Parr	John L. Bradley	Joseph B. Bond
John C. Harris	Nathaniel Mangum	Malcolm McLeod
John Collier	Edwin Plaster	Hezekiah Cheshire
Thomas M. Poole	Handy Harris	Hazel Lovelace. [25]
Bois Edison	Benjamin Thurman	
George Thomas	Hiram H. Embry	

While completion of the railroad crept ever so slowly to Marthasville, the DeKalb Grand Jury considered wagon roads, public buildings, taxes, public officials, stray animals and persons of color living illegally in Decatur at its September, 1843, session.

"The roads in the 686 Dist. (Cross Keys), part of the roads in the 469 District (Cook's) particularly the road running by Esqr. Collier's; the roads in the 722 District (Buckhead), part of the roads in the 530 District (Blackhall); part of the Road in the Town District (Decatur), leading to Johnson's Mill on Peach Tree Creek are in such condition that the jury recommend the attention of the proper officers to be directed to their speedy improvement.

"We report that slaves and free persons of Color are permitted to reside in the Town of Decatur contrary to law, and if the people of the Town and citizens of the County have not yet felt the injury resulting from such open violation of law, this jury believe it their duty to guard them against the future evils and damage of its continuance, and recommend the subject to the Magistrate of the District and corporate authorities of the Town.

"We have examined the public buildings of the County and find that the platform and steps at the jail door need repair and we believe ourselves authorized to say that the Court House is not made of such materials nor the workmanship such as the County has a right to expect.

We recommend that the tax collector pay the extra tax levied in said County to the Judges of the Inferior Court to be applied to the purpose for which it was levied. We think this to be the true meaning of the law.

"We recommend to our Senators and Representatives in the next General Assembly the subject of a reduction of the numbers in said General Assembly, at least to one half their numbers; also to repeal the four months law respecting Justice's Courts and that the old law be renewed. Also to reduce the salaries of all County officers and to consolidate the office of Receiver and Collector of Tax for this County.

"We find from examination that some of the Justices of the Peace of this County are in default in making proper returns for Strays (livestock), and bring the subject to the attention in the general way that the error may be amended and the law complied with. In the event of this recommendation being neglected we especially recommend this subject to the Grand Jury of March Term, 1844.

"The Books of the Clerks of the Superior and Inferior Courts are kept in a style of neatness and correctness credible (sic) to each of these officers. The Books of the County Treasurer are honestly, but not neatly kept and recommend him to take more pains in keeping them neat. We find the accounts of the Treasurer of the poor school fund correctly and neatly kept and the money belonging to said fund disposed of according to the order of the Commissioners; $70.93 in his hands not yet appearing on his accounts, having very recently come into his hands.

"In taking leave of his honor Judge William Ezzard we express to him and our fellow citizens a decided approbation of the ability and industry manifested by him in the discharge of his official duties, and tender him our thanks for the polite attention he has bestowed on this body. To the

Solicitor General, Kinchin L. Haralson for his urbanity to this body and his vigilance as a prosecuting officer, we also tender our hearty thanks. Saturday Evening, September 23, 1843."

James H. Kirkpatrick, Foreman

Willis L. Wells	Thomas Kennedy	James W. Reeve
James F. Montgomery	Charner Humphries	Thomas C. Gober
Aaron Jones	John Dabbs	John Avery
George W. Foote	Joseph Willis	John McCullough
James Moore	Walter Wolcott	Josiah Power. [26]
William Gilbert	George Elliott	

Although Marthasville had been incorporated in 1843, its citizens resisted all attempts at any municipal structure. The city commission levied taxes for new streets; the townspeople refused to pay. Lawbreakers simply hid in the abundant forests to avoid capture. Most of the city's residents in 1844 were transient railroad workers.

The DeKalb Grand Jury of March, 1844 had no solutions: "... We have declined recommending to the Inferior Court the levy of an extra tax for the purpose of the poor school fund, as vice and immorality seems to be prevailing in our County, particularly on the line of the Rail Road. We recommend all officers whose duty it is to be vigilant in bringing offenders to justice..."

James Diamond, Foreman

Nonetheless, all areas of DeKalb began to lose citizens to the new town. J. M. and E. N. Calhoun, John Collier, Reuben Cone, Joseph Thomas, William Ezzard, George W. Adair and Green B. Butler were among the Decatur men who helped build Atlanta in the early days. Stephen Terry moved there from southeast DeKalb, and became the town's first real estate broker. Brothers-in-law James Loyd and James A. Collins moved from Boltonville (Standing Peachtree) on the Chattahoochee. Loyd, who was born in North Carolina in 1801, lived in Hall and Cobb counties before DeKalb. He married Mildred Collins, sister of James A. Collins, who was born in 1807 in North Carolina. James D. Collins (1846-1904), son of James A. Collins, longtime clerk of Fulton Superior Court, married Jennie Clarke, daughter of William Henry Clarke. [27]

At the September, 1844, term of the DeKalb Superior Court, naturalization certificates were issued to these Irish laborers: Patrick Dunahoo, John Bradley, Patrick Sullivan, Michael McCullough, William O'Neill, John Conner, Bernard Corby, John M. Doyle and Thomas Dunegan. [28]

Pythagoras Lodge No. 41, Free and Accepted Masons of Decatur, the oldest lodge in DeKalb County, was chartered on November 7, 1844, having received its official dispensation by the Grand Master of the Grand Lodge of Georgia on April 12 of that year. [29]

Original officers were Elzy B. Reynolds, Worshipful Master; George W. Reeves, Senior Warden; and John Evans, Junior Warden. Charter members were Elzy B. Reynolds, George W. Reeves, W. H. Graham, R. E. Mangum, John Evans, Thomas M. Darnell, Ezekiel Reeves, Nathaniel Mangum and Frederick Arms. Between April 12 and October 7, the lodge gained 12 new members: Leonard C. Simpson, W. M. Hill, Alexander Johnson, John Wadsworth, E. N. Calhoun, Michael O'Brien, Patrick Quinn, J. T. Slater, R. M. Brown, Lewis L. Ledbetter and James R. Henry.

A receipt dated July 17, 1844 shows that the first furniture for the lodge was purchased from J. and L. S. Morgan for $46 and included a lecture stand, three light stands, an altar, a ballot box, three squares, a rule and three trowels. The lodge paid William F. Chewning $7 on December 19, 1844 for engraving the first seal. While it is not known where the first meetings were held, the lodge built a two-story frame building in 1847, on the northeast corner of Ponce de Leon and Clairemont in Decatur. The frame building was used until 1900, when it was replaced by a brick structure. The granite Masonic Temple, standing today in the same location, was built in 1907. [30]

The DeKalb Grand Jury commented on a variety of subjects during its September, 1844, term: "We regret to find the roads and bridges in our county generally in a bad condition...

"We have examined the jail of our county by a committee appointed for that purpose, and find it sufficiently strong for ordinary purposes at this time... We recommend the Inferior Court to take measures for the preservation of the shade trees on the (Decatur) public square.

"We also recommend the Inferior Court to reserve one of the rooms in the court House for the use of the Grand Jury, and the balance of the rooms not necessary to be used as offices we recommend to be rented at public outcry to the highest bidder...

"We suggest to the Clerk of the Inferior Court the propriety of keeping a book for recording licenses and keeping an account of the pauper money.

"We have examined by our Committee the Tax Collector's books and make the following report:

The amount tax assessed for the present year is	$4,391.08
By amt. paid to the Inferior Court	$ 910.00
By amt. paid to the County Treasurer	$ 442.26
By amt. Tax Receiver's Commission	$ 149.47
	$1,501.73

Leaving in the hands of the Collector, unappropriated and not collected
$2,889.35

"...We have examined the County Treasurer's books and take pleasure in saying that his accounts are honestly and correctly kept, and the only exception that can be suggested is the style, which is not as neat and beautiful as we would desire.

"We recommend that the Justices of the Peace be requested to enforce with more rigidity the Patrol Laws."

Hastings D. Palmer, Foreman

Charles J. Cochran	William Barnett	John Huey
Hezekiah Cheshire	Boice Eidson	Edward Watts
William Miller	James Moore	John M. Boring
John Bellinger	Cornelius M. Connally	Peter Mitchell
Salathael Adams	Robert Orr	Lewis Towers
Thomas M. Evins	Marat Megee	John Patrick
Thomas C. Gober	Killis Brown	
Levi Betterton	Fanning Brown	

Both the Grand Jury and the DeKalb bar association commended William Ezzard, who retired in 1844 after four years as DeKalb Superior Court judge:

"As the official term of the Honorable William Ezzard, the presiding officer of the Superior Courts of the Coweta Circuit is rapidly hastening to a close, and as the last Court which he will hold in the County of DeKalb is about to adjourn, the undersigned members of the bar and officers of the Superior Court wish to pay him a tribute of respect and approbation..."

James M. Calhoun	Abram B. Fall
Leonard C. Simpson	William B. Stokes
Nathaniel Mangum	Kinchin L. Haralson
George Kerr Smith	John Glen, Clerk
John Collier	Spencer P. Wright, Shff.
Isham J. Wood	Thomas J. Perkerson, D. Shff.
Charles Murphey	John W. Fowler, Former Shff.
John N. Bellinger	John Jones, Former D. Shff. [31]
William H. Dabney	

In December 1844 a dramatic newcomer came to DeKalb from Morgan County. William Henry Clarke was the first full-time pastor at Ebenezer Methodist Church in the Belmont community of south DeKalb. Born on May 22, 1804 in Cumberland County, Va., Clarke was the only child of Lucy Ligon and her second husband, William Clarke Jr., who was killed in an altercation with Robert Armistead in 1805. After the death of her husband, Lucy moved to Clarke and later Morgan County, Ga., where she died in 1860 at the age of 92. William Henry Clarke was married for the first time on November 21, 1828 in Morgan County to Melinda Kirby, daughter of Francis Kirby and Mary Barry Lawson.

Elijah Henry Clarke, only surviving child of William Henry and Melinda Kirby Clarke was born on December 13, 1835 in Morgan County. Melinda died from measles on February 23, 1837. Two months later, William Henry married Melinda's sister, Alice Moore Kirby. The couple had four known children: Eugenia A., Albert Andrew, Robert Melville and Sarah Clarke, who died young. [32]

On December 3, 1844, William Henry Clarke purchased Charles Latimer's home, store, post office and stagecoach tavern located on 820 acres of land on the Covington Road, near now Panola Road. With the property he acquired the title of postmaster, which he held until August of 1845 when the post office moved to Lithonia. In 1847, he became Worshipful Master of the Pythagoras Lodge in Decatur.

Ebenezer Church disbanded in the mid-1850s, and Clarke began preaching at Wesley Chapel Methodist Church. By 1860, he had acquired 3,000 acres of land in area of now Covington Highway and Hairston Road. He owned more slaves, 69, than any other man in DeKalb County at that time. [33]

Clarke's second wife, Alice, died on August 8, 1863. Two years later he married a third Kirby sister, Julia Anne, who survived him, dying in 1905.

Elected to the Georgia House of Representatives in 1868, Clarke was a conservative Democrat who voted against the 14th and 15th amendments to the U. S. Constitution. Clarke purchased 200 acres of land on Columbia Drive in Decatur, and moved there a few years years before his death on May 1, 1872. He was buried in Decatur Cemetery. Five years later, Clarke's family sold the Columbia Drive property to the North Georgia Methodist Conference for a home for children orphaned by the war.

William Henry Clarke was known in the community as "a man of great force of character and of large influence in the civil and political affairs of the county as well as in its religious life." [34]

George W. Yarbrough, a minister who came to DeKalb as a boy, remembers Clarke as "a force, moral and muscular, against all evildoers throughout that country. A finer specimen of physical manhood I never saw. There was something of the lion's roar in the pulpit when he struck a den of evildoers. At Rock Chapel camp meeting a white man was caught playing cards with a negro. Mr. Clark, alone and on his own motion, arrested the man, collared him, led him through the camp ground, and delivered him to the presiding elder at the preacher's tent. The weapons of his warfare bordered on the `carnal' sometimes, but he was a tower of religious strength, a terror to evildoers, and a praise to them who did well." [35]

The Rev. William Henry Clarke (1804-1872) was described as a force "moral and muscular" against evildoers in DeKalb County. (Donald S. Clarke)

Eugenia A. (Jennie) Clarke, daughter of William Henry Clarke and Alice Moore Kirby, married Atlanta alderman James D. Collins. Collins Memorial Methodist Church in Atlanta is named for the couple, who donated stained glass windows in memory of William Henry Clarke and two of his wives, Alice and Julia. [36]

Elijah Henry Clarke, son of William Henry and Alice Moore Kirby Clarke, also was a land owner and slave holder in south DeKalb. He first married Mary Jane Burdette, daughter of Benjamin Burdette of DeKalb County, on February 19, 1857. Elijah and Mary Jane had five children: William Henry, Melinda M. (Minnie), Benjamin Burdette, Alice Moore and Albert Andrew. Mary Jane died in 1870, and Elijah married Martha America White on October 17, 1871. They had seven children: Nancy Pearl, Robert Melville, Charles Eugene, James David, Julia Ann, Ruth and Frank Kirby. Martha was the youngest child of Benjamin F. White of DeKalb, co-author of the popular Sacred Harp Hymnal" [37]

Elijah Clarke joined the Confederate Army as a private on March 4, 1862; he rose in rank to captain and commanded Co. D of the 42nd Regiment. After the war, he followed in his father's footsteps, becoming a deacon, elder and preacher at Wesley Chapel Methodist Church. In the 1880s, he operated a sawmill and is said to have built the communion rail for the new Wesley Chapel building. He died on June 12, 1898, and is buried at Wesley Chapel. His wife, Martha, who survived him by 38 years, also is buried at Wesley Chapel. Lovick Cobb, long time Wesley Chapel member and cemetery sexton said that Elijah Clarke "was such a preacher that you could wake him in the middle of the night and he could give you a sermon." [38]

The Georgia Railroad finally made its way to the connecting point with the Western and Atlantic in the fall of 1845. The first train, a freight, arrived on September 14, with the first passenger train coming the next day.

William F. Adair, a back-up engineer, did the honors of bringing the first Georgia Railroad train into Marthasville. His cargo was 10 cars of iron for the W&A from Augusta. In 1893, he recalled the run:

"While at Decatur my engineer, John Hopkins, was taken violently ill. My orders were positive. I must be in Marthasville that night. Nothing daunted I mounted my engine, the `Kentucky,' and pulled open the throttle. We rolled out of Decatur at 8 P.M. and I halted the engine right where the car shed now stands in Atlanta (the Old Union Depot, between Pryor and Central), a few minutes before 9 o'clock.

"The road being new and rough, I ran very slowly from Decatur to Marthasville. Having heard that the train would probably reach the town that day, a great many people had come down from the country above Marthasville to see the novel sight. Campfires were gleaming in the woods where the capitol now stands. My train was allowed to stand where I had stopped it all night. The W. & A. R. R., having a track laid one mile beyond the Chattahoochee, I ran my train out there and threw off the iron.

While I was out beyond the river, a passenger train came in from Augusta, with William Orme as conductor. I coupled on two cars containing stock and left for Augusta at 12 o'clock on the 15th and the passenger train followed me at 2 o'clock P.M., for the same destination." [39]

Jonathan Norcross recalled the event in an 1881 interview:

"...The coming of this train gave Atlanta her first `railroad boom,' and we thought then that we were fixed for good. The building of the State road had been recommenced, so that we had two roads. Then we had stage lines running to Griffin and beyond and to Newnan, LaGrange, Montgomery and New Orleans, under control of Dick Peters. The arrival of stages every evening in those primitive days was the great occasion of the day." [40]

Without headlights, nighttime train travel in 1845 was treacherous. Engineer William Hardman recalled:
"We couldn't see anything. We had no whistle, no cowcatcher, and what's more, no cab! The engineer stood on his platform without any shelter for any kind, without any light ahead of him, without any steam whistle to sound a note of warning... our brake was a long lever pole, working in the same way brakes are now used on large wagons. We had to bear down on the lever, stand on it altogether with the fireman, to stop the engine, and it locked only two wheels." [41]

In 1845, the train made its 171-mile run from Augusta to Atlanta, with stops at "Bell Air, Berzelia, Dearing, Thomson, Camak, Cumming, Crawfordville, Union Point, Greensborough, Buckhead,

Madison, Rutledge, Social Circle, Covington, Conyers, Lithonia, Stone Mountain and Decatur." Refreshments were served at Union Point each way. A train leaving Augusta at 8 p.m. got to Atlanta at 7:30 a.m. the next morning. The train left Atlanta at 4 p.m. and arrived at Augusta at 3:15 a.m. The first class fare from Augusta to Lithonia, Stone Mountain, Decatur or Atlanta was $7 per person, with children younger than 12 and Negroes riding at half price. Each passenger was allowed to bring 112 pounds of luggage.

Freight trains also left Augusta and Atlanta daily. Freight rates ranged from 15 cents per 100 pounds for iron to 30 cents per pound for "heavy merchandise such as sugar, salt and butter. Grain was hauled for eight cents per bushel, and dry goods for 60 cents per 100 pounds. No parcels taken for less than 25 cents. Horses could be hauled for $8 each, two-wheeled carriages for $6, and four-wheeled carriages for $10. [42]

In Decatur, the furor over the coming of the railroad must have died down. On July 9, 1845, two months before the railroad reached Marthasville, the DeKalb Inferior Court appointed commissioners to view and lay out a road from the Decatur town square to the new Georgia Rail Road depot. The commissioners made the following report, "that we met this morning and after viewing the ground situated between the publick Square and said depot, having located said Street, commencing at the South West corner of Green B. Butler's Stable (commencing said Street with the McDonough Street at that point) and running the North East line of said street straight through the South end of the Street, running by Doc Hamilton's Shop thence to said depot, distinguished by stakes and to be opened sixty feet throughout, south west of said line, as the most suitable ground for the accomplishment of the object so earnestly prayed for by the petitioners."
     J. B. Wilson, Commissioner
     E. Mason,   "
     John Collier,   "
     J. W. Kirkpatrick "
Today, the road from the square to the depot is known as Trinity Place. [43]

With rail transportation readily available to Marthasville from two directions, people began to flock to the town. The little village soon became just as rowdy as Sandtown had been 20 years earlier, after the area was opened to white settlers and gold was discovered just across the river. The coming of the railroad and out-of-town influence spurred Marthasville merchants into using "the Federal money system, cents, dimes, half dimes, etc." Heretofore, accounts were kept using fractions of cents. [44]

In 1845, the Georgia Supreme Court designated Decatur as one of nine cities where the court would meet. For its seventh term, the court met in Decatur in August of 1846 with 27 attorneys admitted to practice, including seven from Decatur: James M. Calhoun, Leonard C. Simpson, William Ezzard, William H. Dabney, John Collier, Isham J. Wood and Charles Murphey. Decatur was one of the Supreme Court's designated cities until December 22, 1855, when the sessions were moved to Atlanta.[45]

The DeKalb Grand Jury, in March of 1845, complimented its citizens on their moral character, while chastising railroad workers:

"We are gratified to find that our Superior Court has not been crowded with the usual number of Indictments for minor offences which has been frequently returned, and evinces a state of harmony and friendly feeling among our citizens, and shows an evident improvement in the moral condition of our community. Notwithstanding our County is not free of crime yet. The commission of offences are mostly confined to foreigners and other transient persons engaged on the Rail Roads.

"Our roads are generally in good order with the exception of those places where they are in contiguity with the Rail Road."
    Lochlin Johnson, Foreman

Some of the "foreigners" opted to stay. Naturalizations for that term included these Irishmen: Alexander McWilliams, James Burns and John Moore from County Antrim, Thomas Burke of County Armagh, Patrick Duffee of County Meath, John Fitzpatrick of County Limerick and Michael Nowland of County Cavan.

The supervision of slaves and the protection of trees occupied the thoughts of DeKalb Grand Jury members at the September, 1845, term:

"... We will not refrain from expressing our opinion that many of the evils complained or arise from the unlawful practice of some of our citizens leaving to their slaves their own time, and permitting them to live to themselves without the proper restraints from their owners. Their residences are not unfrequently the places for disorder and the hiding places of villany, and we hope the owners of all such slaves will discontinue to violate the law in this regard...

"The Grand Jury are impressed with the belief that too much indifference is felt on the subject of municipal regulations of the towns of Decatur and Marthasville, especially as it may affect the security of the public property in those Villages. The trees in the Court house square are liable to injury, and although an ornament to the Village, are left without proper security from wagons or horses..."
    Robert M. Brown, Foreman

Archibald Tomlinson	John Stephenson	Tunstal B. George
John Dabbs	William T. Beal	John Mason
William Gober	Henry Hollingsworth	John L. Bradley
William R. Brandon	John Simpson	John Bryce
Robert Hollingsworth	Thomas J. Stevens	Thomas J. Akins
George Thomas	Eli J. Hulsey	Shadrick Farmer. [46]
Berryman D. Shumate	Hiram H. Embry	

Toward the end of 1845, some Marthasvillians began to think their town needed a more sophisticated name. Georgia Railroad Superintendent Richard Peters was not satisfied with the name Marthasville and asked his friend, J. Edgar Thomson for ideas. Thomson replied: "Eureka -- Atlanta, the terminus of the Western and Atlantic Railroad -- Atlantic masculine, Atlanta feminine -- a coined word, and if you think it will suit, adopt it." Peters " delighted with the suggestion, and in a few days issued the circulars adopting the name, and had them very generally distributed throughout Georgia and Tennessee." The following year, the Georgia legislature made the change official. [47]

Jonathan Norcross, speaking at meeting of the Atlanta Pioneer and Historic Society in 1871, said:

"I recollect distinctly how the name of Atlanta was given to this city. It was formerly called Marthasville, and was also known throughout the State as Whitehall. I had a conversation with J. Edgar Thomson about it, and he said that he was going to call the depot Atlanta in connection with the Western and Atlantic Railroad. He said he did not care what they called the town, but he was going to call the depot Atlanta, and he did so, and the freight all came marked Atlanta, and very soon the town came to be known as Atlanta. It was not named after the goddess Atalanta, [1] and only the most ignorant people called it by that name. I recollect the matter distinctly. Atalanta had nothing to do with it." [48]

---

[1] Atalanta was not a goddess, but the daughter of Iasius, King of Arcadia. (Source: Bulfinch's Mythology.)

Chapter 21 Notes

1. Garrett, Franklin M., 1954, 1969, Atlanta and Environs -- A Chronicle of Its People and Events, Vol. 1, page 177.

2. Garrett, Franklin M., 1954, 1969, Atlanta and Environs -- A Chronicle of Its People and Events, Vol. 1, page 176.

3. Garrett, Franklin M., 1954, 1969, Atlanta and Environs -- A Chronicle of Its People and Events, Vol. 1, page 175.

4. Garrett, Franklin M., 1954, 1969, Atlanta and Environs -- A Chronicle of Its People and Events, Vol. 1, page 175.

5. Garrett, Franklin M., 1954, 1969, Atlanta and Environs -- A Chronicle of Its People and Events, Vol. 1, pages 171-172.

6. Garrett, Franklin M., 1954, 1969, Atlanta and Environs -- A Chronicle of Its People and Events, Vol. 1, page 175.

7. Garrett, Franklin M., 1954, 1969, Atlanta and Environs -- A Chronicle of Its People and Events, Vol. 1, page 176.

8. Hudgins, Carl T., 1952, "Mills and Other Early DeKalb County Industries (And Their Owners)," The Collections of the DeKalb Historical Society, Vol. 1, pages 13 and 17.

9. Garrett, Franklin M., 1954, 1969, Atlanta and Environs -- A Chronicle of Its People and Events, Vol. 1, page 177. Anderson, E. Katherine, December, 1937, "James McC. Montgomery of Standing Peachtree," The Atlanta Historical Bulletin No. 12.

10. Garrett, Franklin M., 1954, 1969, Atlanta and Environs -- A Chronicle of Its People and Events, Vol. 1, page 181.

11. Garrett, Franklin M., 1954, 1969, Atlanta and Environs -- A Chronicle of Its People and Events, Vol. 1, page 179.

12. Garrett, Franklin M., 1954, 1969, Atlanta and Environs -- A Chronicle of Its People and Events, Vol. 1, page 180.

13. Garrett, Franklin M., 1954, 1969, Atlanta and Environs -- A Chronicle of Its People and Events, Vol. 1, page 179.

14. Garrett, Franklin M., 1954, 1969, Atlanta and Environs -- A Chronicle of Its People and Events, Vol. 1, page 182.

15. Willard, Levi, 1920, "The Early History of Decatur Written Many Years Ago," DeKalb New Era.

16. Candler, Charles Murphey, November 9, 1922, Historical Address.

17. Willard, Levi, 1920, "The Early History of Decatur Written Many Years Ago," DeKalb New Era.

18. Garrett, Franklin M., 1954, 1969, Atlanta and Environs -- A Chronicle of Its People and Events, Vol. 1, page 193.

19. Garrett, Franklin M., 1954, 1969, Atlanta and Environs -- A Chronicle of Its People and Events, Vol. 1, pages 184 and 186.

20. Irvine, William Stafford, April, 1938, Atlanta Historical Bulletin, Vol. 3, No. 13.

21. Garrett, Franklin M., 1954, 1969, Atlanta and Environs -- A Chronicle of Its People and Events, Vol. 1, page 203.

22. Garrett, Franklin M., 1954, 1969, Atlanta and Environs -- A Chronicle of Its People and Events, Vol. 1, pages 189, 190 and 203.

23. Trotti, Louise Haygood, n. d., "My Kinspeople," abstracted from Country Life In Georgia in the Days of My Youth by Rebecca Latimer Felton.

24. Garrett, Franklin M., 1954, 1969, Atlanta and Environs -- A Chronicle of Its People and Events, Vol. 1, page 192.

25. Garrett, Franklin M., 1954, 1969, Atlanta and Environs -- A Chronicle of Its People and Events, Vol. 1, page 194.

26. Garrett, Franklin M., 1954, 1969, Atlanta and Environs -- A Chronicle of Its People and Events, Vol. 1, pages 201-202.

27. Garrett, Franklin M., 1954, 1969, Atlanta and Environs -- A Chronicle of Its People and Events, Vol. 1, pages 207 and 231. Candler, Charles Murphey, November 9, 1922, Historical Address.

28. Garrett, Franklin M., 1954, 1969, Atlanta and Environs -- A Chronicle of Its People and Events, Vol. 1, page 207.

29. Garrett, Franklin M., 1954, 1969, Atlanta and Environs -- A Chronicle of Its People and Events, Vol. 1, page 209. Clarke, Caroline McKinney, 1973, The Story of Decatur 1823-1899.

30. Garrett, Franklin M., 1954, 1969, Atlanta and Environs -- A Chronicle of Its People and Events, Vol. 1, page 209. Clarke, Caroline McKinney, 1973, The Story of Decatur 1823-1899.

31. Garrett, Franklin M., 1954, 1969, Atlanta and Environs -- A Chronicle of Its People and Events, Vol. 1, pages 210-211.

32. Clarke, Donald S., n. d., "The Reverends William Henry Clarke and Elijah Henry Clarke of Wesley Chapel Methodist Church."

33. Clarke, Donald S., n. d., "The Reverends William Henry Clarke and Elijah Henry Clarke of Wesley Chapel Methodist Church." 1860 DeKalb County, Ga. Slave Schedule.

34. Candler, Charles Murphey, November 9, 1922, Historical Address.

35. Yarbrough, George W., 1917, Boyhood and Other Days in Georgia, pages 137-145.

36. Clarke, Donald S., n. d., "The Reverends William Henry Clarke and Elijah Henry Clarke of Wesley Chapel Methodist Church."

37. Clarke, Donald S., n. d., "The Reverends William Henry Clarke and Elijah Henry Clarke of Wesley Chapel Methodist Church."

38. Clarke, Donald S., n. d., "The Reverends William Henry Clarke and Elijah Henry Clarke of Wesley Chapel Methodist Church."

39. Garrett, Franklin M., 1954, 1969, Atlanta and Environs -- A Chronicle of Its People and Events, Vol. 1, pages 218-219.

40. Garrett, Franklin M., 1954, 1969, Atlanta and Environs -- A Chronicle of Its People and Events, Vol. 1, page 219.

41. Garrett, Franklin M., 1954, 1969, Atlanta and Environs -- A Chronicle of Its People and Events, Vol. 1, page 221.

42. Cumming, Mary G., n. d., Georgia Railroad and Banking Company 1833-1945 -- An Historic Narrative, page 66.

43. Garrett, Franklin M., 1954, 1969, Atlanta and Environs -- A Chronicle of Its People and Events, Vol. 1, page 221.

44. Garrett, Franklin M., 1954, 1969, Atlanta and Environs -- A Chronicle of Its People and Events, Vol. 1, page 223.

45. Garrett, Franklin M., 1954, 1969, Atlanta and Environs -- A Chronicle of Its People and Events, Vol. 1, page 213. Candler, Charles Murphey, November 9, 1922, Historical Address.

46. Garrett, Franklin M., 1954, 1969, Atlanta and Environs -- A Chronicle of Its People and Events, Vol. 1, page 222.

47. Garrett, Franklin M., 1954, 1969, Atlanta and Environs -- A Chronicle of Its People and Events, Vol. 1, page 225.

48. Garrett, Franklin M., 1954, 1969, Atlanta and Environs -- A Chronicle of Its People and Events, Vol. 1, page 226.

Chapter 22

*G*eorgians gathered in Stone Mountain on August 1, 1846 for the first fair held by the new Southern Central Agricultural Society.

The idea for an agricultural fair resulted from a chance meeting between Newton County planter John W. Graves and Mark A. Cooper, a Cass County iron products manufacturer. Graves, owner of the land where the Stone Mountain Inn and the railroad depot were located, was looking for a way to promote the town of Stone Mountain, the region and the state of Georgia. Cooper suggested that the time and place might be right "to organize an agricultural and international improvement jubilee association," which had long been contemplated.

Cooper recalled in an 1852 letter that several attempts to establish such an association had been made "without marked success, owing, as I thought, to a lack of convenient transportation for persons and products, as well to a want of variety in agricultural products. That now the Rail Road had opened the rich valleys of Cherokee to Middle Georgia, the products of this farming region might meet the plantation products at the Stone Mountain, whilst the mass of intelligence from every section would diffuse itself and advance the general welfare."

A letter went out to prospective supporters of a state agricultural association:

"Agricultural Fair and Internal Improvement Jubilee.

The undersigned, believing that great good may result to the planting interests of Georgia, Carolina, Alabama and Tennessee, from a personal interchange of the results of the experience, accompanied (when convenient) by an exhibition of the products of their farms and plantations, suggest the propriety of those engaged in agricultural pursuits, and such others as may feel an interest in the subject, meeting at some central point in the up country for that purpose.

"As the several Rail Roads in Georgia will be finished by the 1st of August, at least from the Osstanaula (sic) to the seaboard, they would suggest the Stone Mountain in DeKalb County as the place most suitable for holding the meeting. This point will unite the attractions of nature with the facilities of access, ample accommodations and good fare, to a greater extent than the other.

"The connection of Georgia's splendid system of internal improvement will then be nearly completed -- a matter of sincere congratulation -- and all will have an opportunity of witnessing its operations and appreciating the incalculable benefits which it will confer upon the State at large, and agriculture in particular."

The letter was signed by George W. Crawford, C. J.McDonald, W. Lumpkin, Mark A. Cooper, Garnett Andrews, N. L. Hutchins, C. Dougherty, William C. Daniel, P. G. Morrow, R. M. Cleveland, Elijah E. Jones, A. F. Saffold, [2] William Jones, Junius Hillyer, A. J. Miller, Jacob Phinizy, B. H. Warren, William Dearing, John Cunningham, John H. Nelson, Asbury Hull, Carey Wood, John D. Watkins, Nathaniel Allen, H. J. Oglesby, D. Lyle, Ker Boyce, Matt Martin, George S. Myley, W. Cumming, John Phinizy, James Long, James Harper, J. M. Calhoun, D. McKenzie, E. R. Mills, J. C. Harrington, Thomas Flournoy, J. S. Richard, G. P. Cozart and Thomas Foster. [1]

The association was officially organized under a tree in front of the Stone Mountain Inn, with the secretary sitting on a stump, using his knee for a writing desk. Thomas Stocks of Greene County was elected president. Other officers were R. S. Hardwick of Hancock County, and J. A. Whitesides of Tennessee., vice presidents; Dr. Thomas Hamilton of Cass County, corresponding secretary; David W. Lewis of Hancock County, secretary, and William M. D'Antignac of Richmond County, treasurer.

Subscribers to the new association from DeKalb were Lewis Towers, James Diamond, John Bryce, William Johnson, John Evans, John W. Fowler, Leonard C. Simpson, Lemuel Dean, Isaiah Parker, Dr. James H. Davison, E. N. Calhoun, Weldon E. Wright, John Glen, Eli Hulsey, James M. Calhoun and Charles F. M. Garnett. In all, 61 members paid $1 each. The stated purpose of the annual event was "inquiring into the resources and facilities of agricultural pursuits, and the advancement of the arts and sciences connected therewith and into the best method of developing the one and illustrating the other." [2]

The only exhibits at the first fair were "a jack and ginnet [male and female donkey] with their groom, all the property of Mr. Graves."

The second fair, on August 11, 1847, was far bigger. Exhibits of livestock, agriculture products and "domestic manufactures" filled the ten pin alley in front of the Stone Mountain Inn. Ten cents admission was charged, and a few premiums were awarded. Banigan and Kelly's Caravan of Animals and side shows paid $10 to the county for a license to set up their carnival.

Exhibit highlights included:

• Miss Ezzard of Decatur received a $5 prize for the best example of tuft work, two "elegant specimens."

• Miss Lowe of DeKalb exhibited "tasteful and beautiful" tuft work, but apparently did not receive a premium.

---

[2] Through family genealogy research, the author believes "A. F. Saffold" was probably A. G. (Adam Goudyloch) Saffold (1784-1850) of Madison, Morgan County, Ga., who was a real estate speculator and a director of the Georgia Railroad and Banking Company in the 1840s.

• Mrs. Evans of DeKalb entered a "specimen of sewing silk, from the native mulberry, a good article."

• Miss Harden of DeKalb had "fine display of needlework."

• Miss Smith of DeKalb entered a pair of "very neat silk Pic Nic gloves."

• Mr. Sherman of DeKalb exhibited ten sides of leather, "superior articles."

• Miss Holden of Cass County exhibited "beautiful caskets" (jewelry boxes).

• Fine brooms from Cass County made in the vicinity of the iron works.

• Fine yarns from the Belville factory.

• Captain Hardwick's display of rough chaff wheat, weighing 66 pounds to the bushel and making 43 pounds of "super fine flour."

Several stallions, brood mares and colts were shown. Dr. Calhoun received a premium for his mare, named "Victoria." Dr. Calhoun's "John Stephen" was mentioned for high pedigree and "blood-like appearance," and he exhibited a high mettled Arab horse that was described as "blood-like." Dr. Wright's "John McGhee" was complimented for "bone, muscle, symmetry and weight, making him suitable for all work, and his pedigree giving him stamina and docility."

An estimated 3,000 people attended that year's fair. The writer of an article in the Savannah Georgian of August 16, 1847 said he slept in a room with 28 people. Hotels were filled to suffocation, the writer said. "Wagons, carriages, carts and pedestrians were arriving every moment." [3]

In her book, Country Life in Georgia, Rebecca Latimer Felton wrote:

"I remember well the coming together of the first state agriculture society ever organized in Georgia, at Stone Mountain, and the sensation created thereby in 1847 and also the crowds that went in 1848 when our household went along with all the neighbors who could be spared from home on that occasion. The little town had meagre hotel facilities and the visitors from Madison, Greensboro and as far down as Augusta, completely swamped their accommodations. I remember that day riding in a railroad box car, and sitting on a squash sent for exhibition that tipped the beam at eighty-two pounds. Some squash that, but I was weighed that same day and marked eighty-two pounds on the scales. My father remarked, `some girl and some squash.'

"The politicians were active at that early day and the defeated ones complained that the new agricultural society was only a political machine. History repeats itself and the society chaperoned several governors into the executive chair in later years."

The fairs of 1848 and '49 were even more spectacular, with attractions like P. T. Barnum's traveling circus, which featured Tipo Sultan, the largest elephant then in captivity.

DeKalb County citizens entered 50 articles in 1848, more than any other county. Some 250 entries

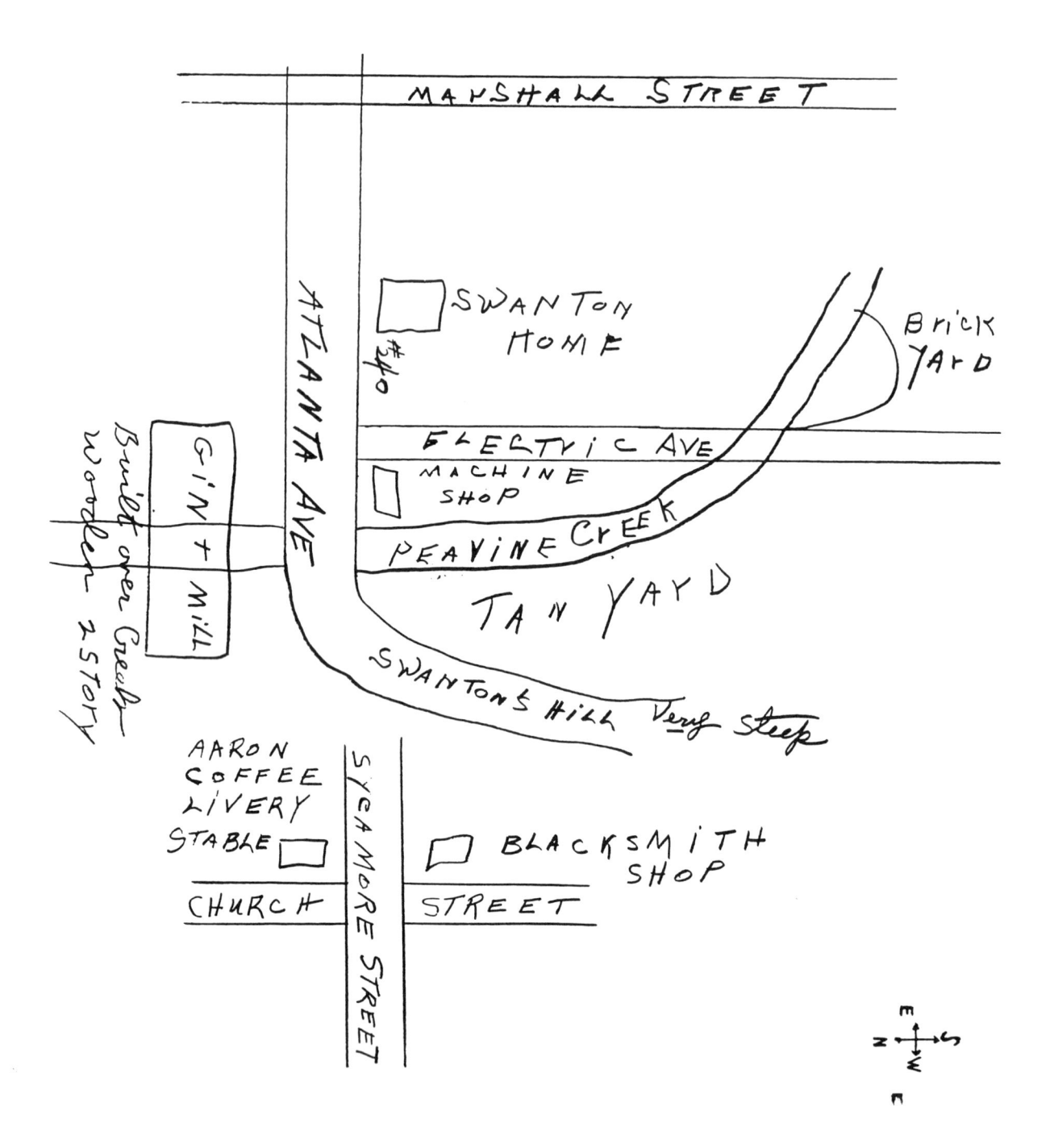

Benjamin Franklin Swanton, a shipbuilder from Maine, came to Georgia to sell mining equipment during the Georgia gold rush of the 1820s and '30s. He settled in Decatur, building a small industrial complex on Peavine Creek. This map, drawn by Mrs. Thurman Decatur Thompson in 1951, shows the location of Swanton's various enterprises. Information for the map was provided by Hamilton Weekes. (DeKalb Historical Society)

came from 30 Georgia counties, as well as Tennessee and South Carolina. A sampling of premiums presented in 1848 follows:

• William Ezzard of DeKalb for White Lane Corn, $3.
• Mrs. Kirkpatrick of DeKalb for 10 pounds of "the finest butter," $1.
• First place to John Evans of DeKalb for a basket of "Malakatoon" peaches, which sold for 10 cents each.
• J. W. Fowler, flour, $2.
• Laura C. Farrer of Decatur for Masonic apron, $2.
• Miss Sherman of DeKalb, painted Masonic apron, "an honor."
• Mrs. Evans of DeKalb, sewing silk made from native mulberry, $1.
• Hand Harris of Decatur, straw cutter, "an honor."
• B. F. Swanton of Decatur for "manufactures of Georgia furs, coonskins, buggy robes, shot pouches, etc., an honor."
• Mrs. Hayden of DeKalb, Mrs. Cone of Decatur each received an honor for a beaded bag.
• Mrs. Cone for "inlaid quilt," $2.
• Mrs. Martha Crowley of Decatur, an honor for her exhibit of gingham.
• Amanda Leigh, age 11, $2 for wax flowers.
• Virginia Chewning of Decatur and Mrs. Hayden of DeKalb, each "an honor" for ottoman covers.
• Mrs. Hayden, an honor for her embroidered scarf.
• Dr. Hoyle of DeKalb and William Nisbet of Unionville divided a $5 prize for their brood mares. [4]

In 1849, there were twice as many entries as the year before. Marie Schley was awarded $10 for her braided hair bracelet with a gold clasp and fancy stone. The bracelet was stolen at the fair, and a $25 reward offered for its return. J. M. Calhoun, Mr. Dean and Mr. Ezzard were appointed to investigate the theft, but the bracelet was never found.

DeKalb County exhibitors that year included:

• Mrs. Goldsmith and Mrs. L. A. Smith of Stone Mountain, preserves.

• Mrs. L. A. Trammell of DeKalb, first place, wax fruits and crystal basket.

• John Glenn of DeKalb, bag of flour

• Mrs. Mary Evans of Decatur, counterpane, an honor.

• Mrs. Mary Evans, $2 for sewing silk.

• A. E. Davis of DeKalb, two and one-half bushels of Red Flint wheat, weighing 66 pounds, first prize.

• Richard Peters of DeKalb, $3 for White Flint corn and an honor for Imperial Oats.

• John W. Fowler of DeKalb, three barrels of flour.

• Messrs. Barnes and Swift of DeKalb, one bag of flour, an honor.

- Miss Calhoun of Decatur, silk bag from silk she grew.

- Mrs. and Miss Ezzard of Decatur, mats; and Miss Ezzard, a purse, "articles showing taste and ingenuity."

- Mrs. S. D. Peak of Stone Mountain, an honor, black velvet embroidered cape.

- Mrs. D. G. Wear of Stone Mountain, an honor, embroidered miniature cottage.

- Mrs. Sherman of DeKalb, $2, two pairs of cotton stockings.

- Mrs. Emeline Harralson of DeKalb, $2, counterpane.

- Mrs. Emeline Peale of DeKalb, an honor, counterpane.

- Mrs. Henry and Miss Jackson of DeKalb, each an honor, patchwork quilt.

- Mrs. Crawley of DeKalb, an honor, Golden Flower Quilt. [5]

After the 1849 fair, a committee was appointed to choose a date and location for following year's fair. In his 1902 history of the agriculture association, Washington J. Houston wrote: "It was stated that this plan would place in the hands of disinterested people the selecting of the place of holding the next Fair, which would offer the most conveniences and facilities. Before this effort to move the fair from Stone Mountain had failed.

"Long and angry discussion had followed with members from a distance threatening to leave and form an association of their own."

A second association never materialized, and the 1850 fair was moved to Atlanta, and held at a site on the south side of now Fair Street. Several DeKalb County fair veterans were involved at the new location, including Richard Peters, William Ezzard and James M. Calhoun. Peters, it was said, "contributed more to the fast growth of diversified agriculture and stock raising than any other person in the state."

Several DeKalb County citizens won prizes at the 1850 fair:

- John Evans, a silver cup for a horse named Queen; also three varieties of native apples "of rare excellence;" also apple brandy "pronounced to be very superior by competent judges."

- J. H. Kirkpatrick, specimens of wheat, all over 64 pounds, several as high as 68, "remarkable because the last season had been unfavorable to the wheat crop."

- Mrs. Kirkpatrick, $5 for best butter.

- J. Morgan, $10 for a bedstead, dressing bureau and specimens of native walnut furniture, "in style and finish equal to that in the best warehouse of New York."

- Dr. Joseph Baker, $1 for Upland Rice, "wonderful height, valuable for mowing."

• W. H. Haven, $5 for his invention, a cast iron adjusting head block for saw mills.

Richard Peters beat out William Ezzard for the best White Flint corn. Ezzard won second place in 1850; he had won the top prize the previous two years.

D. N. B. D'Alvigny exhibited five oil paintings by an Italian artist named Orgali, and John Billups of Athens delivered the annual oration.

The 1851 fair was held in Macon. The fair later returned to Atlanta, and was the forerunner of the popular Southeastern Fair held at the Lakewood Fairgrounds.

The county's fiances concerned the Grand Jury in March of 1846, and its roads were problematic for jurors in September of that year:

"We regret an unusually large delinquent tax list, which is owning to the large amount of tranchant (sic) persons thrown in the County last year in consequence of the publick (sic) works, a large number of them being returned by the receiver of defaulters."
John Jones, Foreman

Jesse L. Jones	Christopher Connally	Zachariah R. Jones
William Hazelett	John W. Fowler	Simeon Smith
Thomas C. Bolton	John Elam	Ezekiel Reeve
Edward Talliaferro	James Phillips	Joel Herring
Edwin Plaster	William Akers	Handy Harris
James F. Montgomery	Moses W. Davis	Samuel Burdett. [6]
William A. David	Abraham Housworth	
John McDonald		

"As to the public roads in some parts of the County are in very bad condition -- in Dean's District, and the roads towards Campbellton South West of Atlanta, and we would recommend the proper authorities to have them put in better condition immediately."
Charles Latimer, Foreman

Some of the county's money was being spent to provide relief to paupers. "Qualifications for relief were considerably more strict and recipients included only the aged and infirm, the mentally deficient and the physically impaired. No tax money went to the indolent or lazy, or to the jobless by choice."

E. B. Reynolds, Overseer of the Poor, presented a list of the county's paupers in 1845 and '46, and the amount paid to each, to his successor, John M. Smith:

1845			
Roanah Wamble	$ 4.00	John Bookout	7.00
Sarah Biffle	4.50	John Ewings	7.00
Elizabeth Gant	7.50	Sucky Breedlove	
Rachel Wates	6.50	(to S. House)	0.00
Sarah Wiggins	10.00		$73.50
Judy Moore	10.00		
Wineford Golding	10.00	**1846**	
William McEver	7.00	Roanah Wamble	$18.00

THE HISTORY OF DEKALB COUNTY, GA. 1822-1900 • CHAPTER 22

Sarah Biffle	18.00	Sucky Breedlove	
Elizabeth Gant	13.00	(S. House)	100.00
Rachel Wates	15.00	Esther Cash	10.00
Sarah Wiggins	15.00	Alsey Lagget	9.00
Judy Moore	14.00	Jincey Sprayberry	3.00
Wineford Golding	15.00		
William McEver	13.00		------
John Bookout	13.00		$264.00
John Ewings	8.00		

Direct payments were made to paupers, or citizens could lease them in return for their room and board, with the county contributing funds for their upkeep.

Samuel House of the Cross Keys District in north DeKalb came to aid of Sucky Breedlove, a blind black woman. "Suky House," age 100, is found in Samuel House's household in the 1850 DeKalb County census.

Inferior Court records detail Sucky Breedlove's fate:

"Georgia
DeKalb County
By verbal order of the Inferior Court, `Old Suck,' commonly called Sucky Breedlove, was on the first Tuesday (7th day) of April, 1846, let to the lowest bidder at public outcry until 25th of December next, and was bid off by Samuel House at Five Dollars Eighty--seven and a Half Cents per month, to be fed and clothed and care taken of her -- this April 7th, 1846.
        H. B. Latimer, C. I. C."

House bid for Breedlove again in 1849:
"Blind Sookey, a pauper of DeKalb County, was let to the lowest bidder on the Second day of January, 1849, for the year 1849 and was bid off by Samuel House for $3.75 per month, by order of the Inferior Court. Registered 3rd day of January, 1849." [7]

The Mexican War began in May of 1846, and Georgia sent one regiment, 910 men; no companies were raised in DeKalb, although L. B. Nelson of Decatur and his son-in-law, Alston H. Green, served as officers in one company. The regiment served for one year and was never in battle. However, 145 men were killed by disease, and more than 315 discharged because of illness. DeKalb's only casualty was William McLeod, son of Malcolm McLeod, an original DeKalb settler, who died in New Orleans on the way home and is buried there. [8]

The Central of Georgia Railroad, formerly the Macon and Western, was completed into Atlanta in the summer of 1846. The completion gave Atlanta its "second railroad boom," according to Jonathan Norcross in an 1881 interview, "and it was tremendous, I can tell you. This was the time that the first railroad whistle was ever heard in Atlanta. The engines on the Georgia and State roads were little fellows without any whistles. But the engine on the Macon road had a real whistle, and it made a great stir when it was first heard in Atlanta... I shall never forget it. It was a clear, calm night, and the whistle commenced blowing way out by the Whitehall. I lived near where the West Point depot now stands and the minute I heard it I started on a full run for uptown, waving my hat above my head and shouting. Lord! It just lifted us out of our boots. It was a good large whistle -- none of these little penny pipes -- and it could be heard everywhere. When I got to the depot I found everybody in town was on hand, and there was more enthusiasm than I ever saw in Atlanta. The engineer blew the whistle for all who wanted to hear it, and it was late before the crowd dispersed.

"I believe that the real growth of Atlanta began right then. For the first time people began to have confidence in our judgment about it." Among those confident new Atlanta citizens were Decatur pioneers Lemuel Grant, Reuben Cone, Ammi Williams and William Ezzard, as well as George Washington Collier, son of Meredith. [9]

Collier bought land at what is now Five Points, then the northeast corner of Decatur and Peachtree streets, where he built a one-story frame building housing a grocery store and a post office. Reuben Cone moved built a house nearby, on the north side of Marietta Street between Fairlie and Cone. "The original and normal width of Marietta Street did not enable the Judge of obtain an unobstructed view of the post office from his front veranda. Being a man of means and years as well as the owner of the intervening property, he simply had the road widened so as to effectuate a clear view. This enabled him merely to step out upon the veranda at mail time and, by pre-arranged signal with Postmaster Collier, ascertain if he had any mail, thereby saving many unnecessary steps." [10]

Trains brought visitors to the town, and two hotels opened in 1846 to accommodate them. The Atlanta, owned by Dr. Joseph Thompson who had moved from Decatur, was the first brick building in Atlanta. Washington Hall was built by James Loyd in late 1846, and leased to H. C. Holcombe and Z. A. Rice in 1847.

In an 1871 interview, Holcombe recalled: "In October, 1847, I leased Washington Hall and kept that hotel until two years from that time. I boarded persons for $12.50 per month. I bought chickens from 6 1/4 to 10 cents per pair; butter from 8 to 10 cents per pound; eggs from 6 1/2 to 10 cents per dozen. I have bought good beef for 2 1/2 cents per pound; and the first time I paid 6 cents a pound for beef was during a fair held at Stone Mountain. There was not room enough at Stone Mountain, and we had to provide for a good many at Atlanta." [11]

The summer of 1846 saw the first newspapers published in Atlanta, but The Luminary, The Tribune and The Enterprise didn't stay in business long. The Rev. Joseph S. Baker and his partner, Thomas Wilson, launched The Luminary on July 14 Jul 1846, printing four pages weekly. Baker and Wilson sold the paper on December 9, 1846 to Joseph B. Clapp and Frederick W. Bartlett. Clapp sold in 1848 to Charles L. Wheeler who changed name of the paper to The Tribune; Wheeler closed his doors that same year. W. H. Royal and C. H. Yarbrough started The Enterprise, a Whig weekly, in August of 1846; they sold the paper to C. R. Hanleiter, and it folded in 1847. [12]

Bartlett was a friend of Decatur poet Thomas Holley Chivers and may have published some of his work. Chivers shared his poems with poet Edgar Allen Poe, and later accused him of plagiarism. On February 21, 1847, Chivers wrote to Poe:

"I sent you a tale sometime ago, entitled, I believe, `The Return from the Dead.' I wish you to look over it and correct any errors you may see in it, and envelope it as at first, and direct it to Frederick W. Bartlett Esq., Atlanta, Georgia... He is a great friend of mine and the Editor of the Atlanta Luminary." [13]

Born in Wilkes County, Ga., the son of a wealthy planter, Chivers had been educated as a doctor at Transylvania University in Kentucky, but turned to writing poetry. He also was an inventor, having devised a machine for unwinding silk cocoons, and a talented portrait painter. Chivers came to Decatur sometime before 1850 with his wife, a New England woman, and children: Thomas H. Jr., Emma Isadore and Fannie Isobel. They lived in a two-story house called "Villa Allegra" on East College Avenue. [14]

Chivers used extravagant, weird, mystical language in his works. Poe once commented: "Dr. Thomas Holley Chivers is at the same time one of the best and one of the worst poets in America... Even his worst nonsense (and some of it is horrible) has an indefinite charm of sentiment and melody. We can never be sure there is any meaning in his words, yet neither is there any meaning in some of our finest musical airs, but the effect is the same in both." Poe later apologized, and the two became friends.

Chivers claimed that Poe's famous poem, The Raven," was patterned on his poem,
"To Allegra Florence in Heaven:"

> "Then he cried out broken hearted,
> Ever true to his departed --
> In this desert world deserted,
> Are we not to meet, dear maiden?
> And the voice of that sweet maiden,
> From the jasper reeds of Aiden,
> With her lily-lips love-laden,
> Answered, `Yes -- forevermore.'"

Poe denied the allegations. The debate was never settled. [15]

Chivers died one hour after midnight on December 18, 1858. In his will, written only hours before, he requested that his body "be buried on this place wherein I now live, that my grave be made in some quiet spot where my children can daily visit it; I also desire that my wife, Harriette, shall visit my last resting place and I wish her to carry my children there." Some years later, Villa Allegra was sold, and the purchaser requested that the grave be moved. Chivers was reinterred in Decatur Cemetery. Thomas Holley Chivers Jr. became a merchant in Decatur, and died on January 7, 1892 at the age of 38. Harriett Chivers died on March 25, 1888. The poet's wife and son also are buried in Decatur Cemetery. [16]

In 1846, the Diocese of Georgia of the Protestant Episcopal Church of the United States appointed the Rev. John J. Hunt of Athens to be missionary to the mission stations in the Atlanta area. The first Episcopalian service was held on November 1, 1846 at the home of Samuel G. Jones, at the corner of Forsyth and Mitchell streets. St. Philip's Episcopal Church, the first of its denomination in the area, opened in 1849, with the Rev. Hunt as its clergyman. Since it would be some years until an Episcopal church was organized in Decatur, it is likely that followers of the denomination began attending services in Atlanta. The first vestrymen of St. Philip's were Dr. Needom L. Angier, Samuel G. Jones, Wilson P. Jones, Richard Peters, J. Edgar Thomson and Guy L. Warren. The first Catholic service was held in Atlanta in late 1845 or early 1846. The Church of the Immaculate Conception was built in 1848. [17]

Stone Mountain Baptist Church was constituted on September 2, 1846, with these charter members: William Loveless, Charles H. Rice, John Garrett, A. J. Holt, Daniel N. Pittman, John Shackleford,

Poet Thomas Holly Chivers. (DeKalb Historical Society)

"Villa Allegra," the home of Thomas Holly Chivers, was located at 339 College Avenue in Decatur. It was demolished in 1952. (DeKalb Historical Society)

Aaron Cloud, Thomas K. Guess and William Johnson, along with the women members of their families. The Rev. A. R. Almand was the first pastor. [18]

Decatur Presbyterian Church replaced its original log building with a brick structure, with a gallery for slaves, in 1846. The lumber from the old church was sold for use in building stores in Atlanta. Daniel Killian won the contract to build the brick church at a cost of $1,800, excluding pulpit and pews. However, Killian failed to deliver on the contract, and the church trustees built the sanctuary themselves, with help from a hired brick mason, B. D. Shumate. Shumate, son of Decatur pioneer, Mason D. Shumate, was a ruling elder in the church, as well as a choir member and Sunday school teacher. Joseph and L. S. Morgan, brothers and furniture manufacturers, donated the pulpit for the new church. The final cost of the new building was $2200.

The brick church was built on the lot originally given to the church by DeKalb's Justices of the Inferior Court. The lot was bounded on the east by the Lawrenceville Road (now Church Street) and on the west by the Shallow Ford Road (now Clairmont). The building was used until 1892, when the church sold both building and lot to the Donald Fraser High School for Boys, which was named for Decatur Presbyterian's pastor. [19]

Many religious revivals were held in Decatur during the 1840s, most notably a Methodist meeting led by the Rev. Alexander Means, Bishop James C. Andrew and Judge Longstreet. Services were held daily and nightly. [20]

The Georgia legislature created a new militia district in DeKalb County in December of 1846:

"The undersigned, who were appointed commissioners to take into consideration the propriety of creating a new Militia District in said County including the Town of Atlanta, beg leave to report that they have considered the matter and report that they have selected a line running three ranges off the fourteenth and fifteenth (land districts) to the seventeenth and eighteenth, then taking the line between the seventeenth and eighteenth running north to the Peachtree Creek, down said creek to (land lot) number 111 in the 17th Dist., taking five ranges in the 17th and including No. 111, then taking that line and running South to the present district line between the 14th and 17th, thence East to the beginning. All of which is respectfully submitted.
Atlanta, Decr. 26th, 1846."
    T. J. Perkerson
    James A. Collins
    Meredith Collier

It was later discovered that the boundary lines did not put Atlanta in center of new district as intended:

"It appears to the Court that it is necessary to change the lines of the newly established district in said County so as to include the Town of Atlanta in the centre of said district. It is therefore ordered by the Court that James Loyd of the newly established district, and Edwin Plaster of the same district, and C. M. Connally of the 469th Dist., the same being the districts between which the change of lines is proposed to be made, be and they are hereby appointed commissioners to lay out said lines so as t include Atlanta as aforesaid..."

The new district was assigned the number, 1026. Road commissioners for the new district were Edwin G. Collier (eldest son of pioneer settler Meredith Collier), Joseph H. Mead, Alexander F. Luckie and Willis Buell. [21]

Five years after the DeKalb Courthouse burned in 1842, government workers still had not been able to move into the new building. The Inferior Court had not found the work of contractors G. V. Margerum and W. H. Graham of Marietta acceptable, and the dispute had gone to a two-man board of arbitration.

The arbitrators submitted a report to the Inferior Court on February 24, 1847: "Whereas we John Stidham (mason) and Martin Colley (carpenter) being chosen as referees in a matter pending between said Court of the one part, and Margerum and Graham, of the other part, contractors for Rebuilding the Court House in Decatur. We having examined the contract and specifications hereby beg leave to Report. We believe that the manner in which the several branches of the work is executed is up to the contract, with the following exceptions, 1st, the plastering of the rooms on the lower story we consider to be subject to a deduction of $70. Sash in windows in lower story, $15, for lumber not well seasoned upstairs, $20, Total, $105. We also further beg leave to report that we find the following which exceeds the contract. An addition of the Portico, which we consider quite an ornament to the building, $20. Four hearth stones at $6 each, $24. Additional stone steps $10. All of which is respectfully submitted."
    John Stidman
    Martin Cooley
    Referees
Registerd the 24th day of Feb. 1847.   H. B. Latimer, C. I. C.

The difference of $51 was settled, and the courthouse officially accepted in February of 1847. Apparently there was never any question about the quality of the painting, which was done by J. and L. S. Morgan. In September, the Grand jury commented:

"We are gratified to say to the Citizens of this County that our court house is now paid for, and that of the money raised for that purpose, there is some left after paying for said Court House."
       Samuel Walker, Foreman.

John Hardman	William H. Tanner	James Smith
George W. Avery	Leandrew Biffle	Eli J. Hulsey
Joseph Willis	James A. Jett	Robert Ozmer
Ezekiel A. Davis	Simeon Smith	John Carpenter
Green V. Almond	Handy Harris	Thomas C. Gober
William P. Mason	James B. Robertson	Josiah Power
Jesse Wood	Lemuel Dean	
James Burns	John Cochran	

This second of the county's "neat brick" courthouses served for 51 years, until it was torn down in 1898 to make way for a larger structure. [22]

Two new roads opened in 1847. On June 1, the Inferior Court appointed Marat Megee, Claiborn Hawes and Alston H. Green commissioners "to view and mark out a new Road, commencing at Green and Nelson's Ferry and to intersect the Sand Town Road at or near Higgin's Shop on said Sand Town Road." On August 3, the Inferior Court appointed Killis Brown, James Burns and James J. Cowan commissioners "to view and mark out a new Road commencing at Atlanta crossing South River at Killis Brown's, thence to the line of Henry County near Thomas Moore's Mills." The first road became Fairburn Road; the second covers portions of now Capitol Avenue and McDonough Road to Conley. [23]

The Inferior Court in 1847 accepted the recommendation of area road commissioners to abandon Nelson's Ferry west of Decatur as a public road:

"Georgia, DeKalb County
531st District, G. M.
We, the commissioners of this District believe it be our duty to petition your honorable body to take into consideration the Nelson's Ferry Road. We as commissioners believe it entirely nugatory and idle to keep up said Road and we therefore pray your assistance.
  Daniel Johnson   Ezekiel A. Davis
  P. F. Hoyle   Joseph Pitts

Ordered, that said Road be recognized as a Settlement Road and be kept open as such.
      March 1, 1847."

The court also authorized William R. Roswell on December 30, 1847 to build a bridge across Nancy Creek on the Pace's Ferry Road, to be paid $99.75 for the job, provided he kept the road in repair for five years from time of completion. [24]

A small nondenominational church and schoolhouse was constructed in Atlanta in 1847, in the triangle now formed by Peachtree, Pryor and Houston streets. The first sermon is said to have been delivered by Rev. John S. Wilson of Decatur Presbyterian Church. The Rev. Wilson officially organized the First Presbyterian Church of Atlanta on January 8, 1848. The church was dedicated on July 4, 1852. Reuben Cone had donated a lot for the building, but did not live to see it completed. Wilson was pastor there from 1858 until his death in 1873. Charter members of the new church included a number of former members of Decatur Presbyterian, as well as Oswald and Anna Shaw Houston, parents of Washington J. Houston. [25]

Atlanta also got a Masonic lodge, a bank, two new newspapers and several schools in 1847. John F. Mims, an agent at the Georgia Railroad depot, opened a bank in 1847. A second was opened in 1848 by Scott, Carhart and Co. of Macon, who hired U. L. Wright as manager and W. J. Houston as cashier. Houston, then 17, would later marry Amanda Catherine Powell, daughter of DeKalb's Dr. Chapman Powell.

Atlanta's third newspaper, The Democrat, lasted only three months, edited and published by Dr. William Henry Fonerden. The Democrat was followed by The Southern Miscellany, founded in Madison in 1842, and edited by Cornelius R. Hanleiter. A "weekly family newspaper," it was "devoted to literature, education, agriculture, mechanic arts, news, humor and politics." [26]

Local merchants advertised goods and services in the issue of December 4, 1847:

Washington Hall,
Atlanta, Georgia.
By H. C. Holcombe & Z. A. Rice.
The undersigned have leased the above establishment for a term of years and take this method to acquaint their friends and the traveling public, that they will spare neither pains or expense to render ALL comfortable who may favor them with a call. The Hall is convenient to the Depot, where servants will be in readiness, on the arrival of the various trains, to take charge of baggage, &c. A share of patronage is respectfully solicited.
Passengers per the Georgia train from Augusta are invited to try ours as a Breakfast house, there being ample time allowed for that purpose before the departure of other trains.
                      Holcombe & Rice.

New Store and New Goods!
The subscriber has just opened a fine assortment of Goods, recently purchased in New York, consisting in part of
Gunny and Kentucky Bagging, Rope, Twine, Coffee, Salt, Crushed, Loaf and Brown Sugars, Molasses, Swedes Iron, Cast Steel, Nails, Train and Linseed Oil, Blankets, Homespuns, Ladies' and gentlemen's Saddles, Boots and Shoes.
Yarns, Kerseys, Sole Leather, Horse Collars, Riding and blind Bridles.
Trace and Fifth Chains.
Powder, Lead, Shot, Spice, Pepper, Ginger, Indigo.
Madder, Copperass, Saleratus, Blue Stone, Saltpetre, Pearl Starch, Wool and Fur Hats, Caps.
A choice lot of Ready made Clothing.
Gentlemen's fine Cloaks, fine and common Trunks, and a limited but well selected stock of Dry Goods, all of which he will sell low for cash, or exchange for Country Produce, viz: Cotton, Corn, Meal, Flour, Wheat, &c. He solicits a call from ALL.
                      Al Dulin
Near the stand of J. Norcross, Atlanta, Nov. 20 1847.

New and Desirable Goods!
Just the Kinds Wanted!
Everybody Come and See -- Come and See!
Don't go near those Houses whose proprietors are too stingy to Advertise, (Good advice -- Editor), or whose goods will not bear recommendation, and who have no pity on the poor Printer (Handsomely expressed -- Ed.). Come where you will find the best assortment in town -- consisting of Buggy Springs, Axels, and all other kinds of Iron and Trimmings necessary for Buggies; Cutlery and Hardware of every description; Groceries, Dry Goods, and a great variety of other articles too numerous to mention, making the best assortment in town -- all of which were selected with great care in the City of New York, and paid for in cash -- except what was bought on credit! Come, and take a look, if you don't buy. It will make you feel good to look at good, handsome and cheap articles.

J. Norcross

Atlanta, October 30, 1847 [27]

Dr. William N. White, recently graduated from Hamilton College in New York, came to Atlanta in 1847 in the hope of opening a school. White estimated that 187 buildings were built in the town during summer of 1847. He wrote in his diary:

"The woods all around are full of shanties, and the merchants live in them until they can find time to build. The streets are still full of stumps and roots; large chestnut and oak logs are scattered about, -- but the streets are alive with people and the stores full of trade and bustle. Not a church has yet been built, though the Baptists, Methodists and Episcopalians each have one ready to raise in a short time. Preaching is held in the railroad depot, and in the school-houses or `academies' -- as they are called.

"... Nearly half the population are northern men. Board is cheap, only $8 a month, and three scholars in the higher branches would board me for a year. There are lots of children, who I am assured would go to a school worth patronizing, and from what I can see I am sure with a good building, in a very short time I could make a thousand dollars a year. But there is the difficulty, the only building I can get is a miserable shell of a thing without ceiling, and it cannot be finished this winter. I have been to all prominent men of the place, who promise their influence, and those who have children, their patronage...

"There are several beautiful springs in the village and the water is good; -- the land is rolling. There are not 100 negroes in the place, and white men black their own shoes, and dust their own clothes, as independently as in the north... Carpenters get but ten shillings a day here, and labor commands about the same price as at the north. Tuition is $12, $16, $24 and $32 a year, according to what they study. I have only been here two days and am becoming quite an old settler. The people here bow and shake hands with everybody they meet, as there are so many coming in all the time that they cannot remember with whom they are acquainted..." [28]

White also recalled that Atlanta was a rowdy place before a charter was obtained from the Georgia legislature in 1847:

"Sunday, October 24th. We have in Atlanta as yet no city law or charter. The nights are full of noise and commotion which a city government would easily repress. Last night I was very much disturbed by these noises. No preaching here today. It does not seem like the Sabbath, except that the stores are closed.

"Saturday, October 30th. Was present this evening at the meeting of the citizens of Atlanta to petition for a City Government. Captain (James) Loyd was in the chair. Mr. (Frederick) Bartlett, the printer, was the secretary. A committee of Colonel (John) Collier, Dr. (Benjamin F.) Bomar, Dr. (George G.) Smith, Jonathan Norcross, and (William H.) Thurmond were appointed to draft a bill of incorporation for the city. Atlanta now contains 2000 inhabitants, yet everyone does what is right in his own eyes. There is no government and it is wonderful that they are as steady as they are at present; no minister, no church and little preaching; a Sabbath school is in successful operation and that is almost the only religious privilege that is enjoyed." [29]

Atlanta's city charter had been drawn by John Collier, 32, who had moved to Atlanta from Decatur that year. It was approved by the legislature and signed by Gov. George W. Towns on December 29, 1847. [30]

Several miles north of the lawlessness in Atlanta, Peachtree Baptist Church was organized in 1847 with 41 members. The first building was constructed at the corner of now Briarcliff and LaVista Roads. Its name derives from its location, midway between the north and south forks of Peachtree Creek. Notable pioneer families buried in its cemetery include those of Akins, Almand, Brownlee, Cheek, Evans, Haynie, Hopkins, Ivy, Jones, Lively, Medlock, Stephens, Tuggle and Wallace. [31]

One of DeKalb County's wealthiest men, Alston Hunter Green, died in June of 1847, leaving the largest estate ever administered in the county. The estate, appraised on December 29, 1847 by Thomas J. Perkerson, Charner Humphries and Nathaniel Knight, at nearly $24,000, included 37 slaves, many town lots in Atlanta and a plantation made up of several entire land lots along the Chattahoochee River between now Bankhead Highway and the Adamsville or Garrett Bridge Road.

In December of 1847, a new family came to Decatur with a boy whose later recollections would paint a colorful picture of the town and its inhabitants.

"My father's carriage and the two-horse wagon containing our goods and chattels halted a little before sundown on the north side of the public square of Decatur, Georgia, near a large two-story building used for a drug store and Free Mason purposes," recalled George W. Yarbrough in his 1917 book, Boyhood and Other Days in Georgia.

Yarbrough's father was a Methodist minister on a new assignment, but parsonages were scarce. There was not a single vacant house in Decatur.

The senior Yarbrough also was a Mason, and the family was allowed to live in the Masonic Lodge until they found more suitable quarters. George recalled the mysterious nighttime Masonic activities:

"There were times when it appeared to me that all of them were on the `goat' at the same time, with a full purpose to stay there, and the `goat' as fully determined that they should not. Aroused from my sleep, anywhere about midnight, I would shudder and ask myself the question, `Will any of them ever get out of there again alive and see their wives and little children?' Bang! bang! Rattle! rattle! rattle! Then a twist at something like rolling logs, the handspikes slipping out of their hands at times! ~Surely they will be on crutches to-morrow, lots of them,' I would say. Then again after somebody, over chairs, tables, spittoons, nothing standing in the way, windowpanes rattling, all hands, it seemed about to break through the floor, and that, too, just over where I lay! It would die out for a few minutes, and then it would come to again. The `goat,' seeming to have taken fresh courage, made another stand reenforced by additional horns and hoofs, and all set on making another mount; and I, there in that little room by myself, with my head under the cover and wishing I was back in old Coweta, where I came from, with Charlie McKinley and Bolton and George Anderson and `Billy' Martin! The Masons would look as nice and complacent the next day as if nothing had happened..."

When he first arrived in Decatur, young George saw that the square was "full of romping boys." They would later be identified to him as William Ezzard, Green Berry Butler, Will Green, Lowndes Calhoun, Ned Calhoun, Pickens Calhoun, William McCoy and John McCoy.

George learned that the houses fronting the square were, as he wrote: "Col. Charles Murphey's, Mr. (Levi) Willard's, Mr. (Ezekiel) Mason's, Mr. Reaves's, Col. James Calhoun's, Mr. George's, Judge William Ezzard's, Mr. Butler's, Dr. E. N. Calhoun's, and Mr. William (familiarly called `Billy') Hill's." Businesses on the square in the late 1840s were Woodall's tan yard, Mr. Wilson's wool hat plant, Billy Hill's grocery, Wadsworth's tin ware shop, Mr. Willard's dry goods and grocery, a drug store, Paden's grist mill, Dr. Aleck Johnson's blacksmith shop, Mr. Mason's dry goods store, Mr. Powell's dry goods store, Mr. Aiken's grocery, the Morgan brothers's cabinet shop, Mr. Reaves's dry good store, Mr. McNeil's saddlery, Washington Kirkpatrick's dry goods and general merchandise store, Mr. Gregory's and Mr. Rosser's stores, Mr. Clemons's cigar store and the Globe Hotel. "There was a large gilt globe in an iron frame, suspended in front of it. The same kind of advertisement stood in front of the hotel on the north side.

"I come now to a name and business that must be eternally embalmed in our hearts and memories. Aunt Seney Douglass was a tall, fat old negro woman, of gingercake color, with a big soul, exuberant with cheerfulness, and a big chest always supplied with ginger-cakes and a little keg of persimmon beer, sitting by (if 'simmons were ripe, if not corn beer). Aunt Seney knew, to the minute almost, when Mr. Frost's school would be out on Friday evening (earlier than any other day) and she would be ready for us as we would call on our way out to Dr. Hoyle's saw mill pond for going in swimming, we would lay aside our `thrips' through the week, to be ready for the treats on Friday evening."

George Kirkpatrick was the town marshal. "Dr. Calhoun stood guard over the health department, and he practiced for the town and the surrounding country."

The town had two teachers: Mr. Frost, a northern man, the teacher for boys, and Dr. John S. Wilson, for girls. Dr. Wilson, called "Parson Wilson," lived a mile out of town on a high hill, and walked to the academy. "He was broadly and thoroughly educated, commanding in person, not unlike the Duke of Wellington in this respect..." "Young ladies," said Parson Wilson to his school one day, "I understand that there is to be a ball in town to-night. No young lady can attend that ball and remain in this school." One went, and there was one less on his roll.

There were six stores -- two groceries, a cabinet shop, tanyard, tinnery and a hattery, a blacksmith shop or two and a saddle shop in Decatur in 1847. There were two churches and one Sunday school union. Mr. Willard, a Presbyterian, was the superintendent of the Sunday school union.

The Decatur Circuit of the Methodist church covered territory between Lithonia and Mayson's Ferry on Chattahoochee River. Preachers in charge in 1848 were George's father, John W. Yarbrough, and James W. Hinton. The Methodists had three campgrounds, Mount Gilead in the extreme western portion of the Circuit, Rock Chapel in the extreme east, and Wesley Chapel, six miles south of Decatur. The Presbyterian campground was two and one half miles east of Decatur.

Temperance rallies were sources of entertainment during the 1840s. George recalled that a state rally in 1847 drew thousands to Atlanta. Judge William Ezzard presided over Decatur's temperance rallies, organized by a group called The Washingtonian Society. "These were great temperance times, and the old courthouse was the rallying place on Friday nights monthly. They were stirring occasions -- powerful speaking, and earnest exhortations to sign the pledge. In those days Decatur was not `wet,' but a little damp, particularly during court weeks, militia muster days, and Fourth of July. I never saw a resident of Decatur drunk on the streets. Some took their drams regularly, but they did it as gentlemanly as the thing could be done."

"One bright moonlight night the monthly meeting was on in Decatur, and the orators were at their best; but there was too much of it for the boys of the town, especially as it was Friday night. Thinking that they had plenty of time ahead to devote to the temperance question, they quietly retired to the public square for a round of fun and very soon were disturbing the audience. Marshal Kirkpatrick understood a boy through and through; and as to those Decatur boys, he could be at home at night and know what they were up to. He followed them to the courthouse; and when they got fairly down to business, he was among them, taking down their names for imprisonment in jail the next morning. `Our Saturday in jail!' said the boys among themselves. The next morning, by a little after sunrise, every boy in Decatur was at Hoyle's mill pond, about two miles out, and the town had rest. The marshal really had his eye on that."

George recalled that he learned how to swim at Hoyle's mill pond. "The big boys would make a raft of puncheons, put the small boys on it, take out to middle of pond and sink it." George said he tried to find the pond some years later. "The old mineral spring was there, with some beautiful marble masonry around it; but the majestic poplar and the deep, dark grove that shaded it when we were boys, the little rail fence we jumped over getting to its delicious waters, the climbing vines the smiling flowers, the calamus root -- all were gone. In 1848 it was the boys' paradise on Saturday all around there. Atlanta, six miles off, was enjoying her fresh incorporation by the legislature and had begun to put on airs, but we would not have given that spring and mill pond for all of Atlanta. `Big Ben' Avery, George recalled, was the best swimmer, and Ralph Badger the best diver. [3]

George's schoolmates and playfellows included Larkin Farrar, Bob Farrar, the Brown boys, the McCulloch boys, Josiah Willard, Scott Wilson, Clem Green, Young Thompson, James Thompson, a Buchanan boy and Vol Dunning.

George recalled that a tree in front of the courthouse was associated with a tragic death. A man who

---

[3] Carl T. Hudgins, in his 1952, essay, "Mills and Other Early DeKalb County Industries," said the exact location of Hoyle's millpond is unknown. Owner Dr. Peter F. Hoyle lived on what is now McDonough Street in Decatur, about 400 yards south of the Georgia Railroad. Creeks converge near the lowest point of McDonough, one flowing from behind Agnes Scott College, and one from the Oakhurst area.

had been attending a horse race in town returned intoxicated, and was thrown against the tree from his sulky by his frightened horse. His neck was broken.

The dead man had been involved in another Decatur tragedy. He had argued in the state legislature against a pardon for a man named Johnson. Mr. Johnson, who was a Methodist preacher and once a member of the legislature, had been tried and convicted of murdering a little girl, although he claimed to be innocent. He was sentenced to death and hanged. The legislature refused to overturn the conviction. Later another man confessed to the crime. The judge who presided over the case committed suicide, and nearly every member of the jury "came to an unnatural death."

A killing frost, on April 16, George remembered, devastated crops around Decatur. "The farmers of Georgia raised their wheat in those days, and it was in the boot when the frost fell. Corn was up and doing well, having been well plowed. The leaves of the woods were almost full-grown. Everything of the kind hung in mourning. An offensive odor filled the air. It really looked like a premature burial of 1849. The snap was followed by intensely hot weather.

"Rev. Henry Clark gave my father a load of corn and fodder, and I had the honor of going for it with a wagon and yoke of steers. The steers were hot and seemed to be after water, and nothing else, all the route. They would take near cuts with me through the woods to get to water and hang my wagon on stumps and logs and against saplings.

"Being a lightweight, I was unable to cope with so formidable an adversary, and have never been able to tell how I got through; but this I know, I have not been caught behind a yoke of steers since, and it is now 1898, and I proposed to have nothing more to do with steers in hot weather and fly time." [32]

DeKalb got another Baptist congregation on February 26, 1848, when the Lithonia Baptist Church was constituted. The original church, located at the corner of Main Street and Stone Mountain Street, was constructed by slaves from granite field stones. J. M. Born donated the lot. James R. George was the first pastor. A vestibule and belfry were added in 1894. It was said that the bell could be heard for five miles around. [33]

Chapter 22 Notes

1. Garrett, Franklin M., 1954, 1969, <u>Atlanta and Environs -- A Chronicle of Its People and Events</u>, Vol. 1, page 177. Houston, Washington J., 1902, Agricultural Fair at Stone Mountain, <u>Pioneer Citizens' History of Atlanta 1833-1902</u>, pages 228-233.

2. Garrett, Franklin M., 1954, 1969, <u>Atlanta and Environs -- A Chronicle of Its People and Events</u>, Vol. 1, page 177. Houston, Washington J., 1902, Agricultural Fair at Stone Mountain, <u>Pioneer Citizens' History of Atlanta 1833-1902</u>, pages 228-233.

3. Houston, Washington J., 1902, Agricultural Fair at Stone Mountain, <u>Pioneer Citizens' History of Atlanta 1833-1902</u>, pages 228-233.

4. Houston, Washington J., 1902, Agricultural Fair at Stone Mountain, <u>Pioneer Citizens' History of Atlanta 1833-1902</u>, pages 228-233. Garrett, Franklin M., 1954, 1969, <u>Atlanta and Environs -- A Chronicle of Its People and Events</u>, Vol. 1, page 318.

5. Houston, Washington J., 1902, Agricultural Fair at Stone Mountain, <u>Pioneer Citizens' History of Atlanta 1833-1902</u>, pages 228-233.

6. Garrett, Franklin M., 1954, 1969, <u>Atlanta and Environs -- A Chronicle of Its People and Events</u>, Vol. 1, page 231.

7. Garrett, Franklin M., 1954, 1969, <u>Atlanta and Environs -- A Chronicle of Its People and Events</u>, Vol. 1, page 233. Candler, Charles Murphey, November 9, 1922, Historical Address.

8. Garrett, Franklin M., 1954, 1969, <u>Atlanta and Environs -- A Chronicle of Its People and Events</u>, Vol. 1, page 230-231. Candler, Charles Murphey, November 9, 1922, Historic Address.

9. Garrett, Franklin M., 1954, 1969, <u>Atlanta and Environs -- A Chronicle of Its People and Events</u>, Vol. 1, page 235-236.

10. Garrett, Franklin M., 1954, 1969, <u>Atlanta and Environs -- A Chronicle of Its People and Events</u>, Vol. 1, pages 237-238.

11. Garrett, Franklin M., 1954, 1969, <u>Atlanta and Environs -- A Chronicle of Its People and Events</u>, Vol. 1, pages 236-237.

12. Garrett, Franklin M., 1954, 1969, <u>Atlanta and Environs -- A Chronicle of Its People and Events</u>, Vol. 1, page 234.

13. Garrett, Franklin M., 1954, 1969, <u>Atlanta and Environs -- A Chronicle of Its People and Events</u>, Vol. 1, page 234.

14. Clarke, Caroline McKinney, 1973, <u>The Story of Decatur 1823-1899</u>, pages 42-43. Nix, Dorothy, personal collection, DeKalb Historical Society.

15. Plant, Percy, August-September, 1961, "The Cemetery Book," <u>Georgia</u> magazine, pages 23 and 46.

16. Clarke, Caroline McKinney, 1973, <u>The Story of Decatur 1823-1899</u>, pages 42-43. Garrett, Franklin M., 1954, 1969, <u>Atlanta and Environs -- A Chronicle of Its People and Events</u>, Vol. 1, pages 443-444.

17. Garrett, Franklin M., 1954, 1969, <u>Atlanta and Environs -- A Chronicle of Its People and Events</u>, Vol. 1, pages 240 and 247. Ford, Elizabeth Austin, 1952, "A Precis of DeKalb's Early Church History, <u>The Collections of the DeKalb Historical Society</u>, Vol. 1, pages 32-34.

18. Ford, Elizabeth Austin, 1952, "A Precis of DeKalb's Early Church History, <u>The Collections of the DeKalb Historical Society</u>, Vol. 1, pages 32-34.

19. Candler, Charles Murphey and Scott, October 29, 1950, "History of The Decatur Presbyterian Church, Decatur, Ga.," pages 3 and 4.

20. Trotti, Louise Haygood, "My Kinspeople," abstracted from Country Life in Georgia in the Days of My Youth" by Rebecca Latimer Felton.

21. Garrett, Franklin M., 1954, 1969, Atlanta and Environs -- A Chronicle of Its People and Events, Vol. 1, page 241.

22. Garrett, Franklin M., 1954, 1969, Atlanta and Environs -- A Chronicle of Its People and Events, Vol. 1, page 244. Candler, Charles Murphey, November 9, 1922, Historical Address.

23. Garrett, Franklin M., 1954, 1969, Atlanta and Environs -- A Chronicle of Its People and Events, Vol. 1, page 245.

24. Garrett, Franklin M., 1954, 1969, Atlanta and Environs -- A Chronicle of Its People and Events, Vol. 1, page 247.

25. Candler, Charles Murphey and Scott, October 29, 1950, "History of the Decatur Presbyterian Church, Decatur, Ga., page 2. Garrett, Franklin M., 1954, 1969, Atlanta and Environs -- A Chronicle of Its People and Events, Vol. 1, pages 247, 270 and 347.

26. Garrett, Franklin M., 1954, 1969, Atlanta and Environs -- A Chronicle of Its People and Events, Vol. 1, page 251.

27. Garrett, Franklin M., 1954, 1969, Atlanta and Environs -- A Chronicle of Its People and Events, Vol. 1, pages 252-253.

28. Garrett, Franklin M., 1954, 1969, Atlanta and Environs -- A Chronicle of Its People and Events, Vol. 1, page 249.

29. Garrett, Franklin M., 1954, 1969, Atlanta and Environs -- A Chronicle of Its People and Events, Vol. 1, page 259.

30. Garrett, Franklin M., 1954, 1969, Atlanta and Environs -- A Chronicle of Its People and Events, Vol. 1, page 259.

31. Georgia Division, Daughters of the American Revolution, 1958, Cemetery, Church and Family Records, Vol. 94, pages 185-192 and 272-288. Garrett, Franklin M., 1954, 1969, Atlanta and Environs -- A Chronicle of Its People and Events, Vol. 1, page 347.

32. Yarbrough, George M., 1917, Boyhood and Other Days in Georgia, pages 137-145. Yarbrough, George W., November 3, 1911, "Reminiscences of Decatur, Ga. -- Address Delivered on Home Coming Day," October 12, 1911, printed in the Wesleyan Christian Advocate.

33. Nix, Dorothy, personal collection, DeKalb Historical Society. Lithonia Baptist Church file, Georgia Department of Archives and History.

Chapter 23

Atlanta held its first election on January 29, 1848. The single polling place, Thomas Kile's grocery at now Five Points, saw 215 citizens cast ballots for two mayoral candidates -- Moses W. Formwalt and Jonathan Norcross. Formwalt was elected mayor; councilmen were Jonas S. Smith, Benjamin F. Bomar, Robert W. Bullard, James A. Collins, Anderson W. Walton and Leonard C. Simpson. The first justice of the peace was Edwin G. Collier, another son of DeKalb pioneer Meredith Collier. Oswald Houston, father of the young bank clerk, Washington J. Houston, was elected treasurer.

Taming the town was not going to be easy for Mayor Formwalt and the other new officials. Atlanta was described as "tough." Drinking and gambling houses and brothels were operated with impunity. "Headquarters of the rowdy element was the block of Decatur Street beginning back of Collier's grocery and Formwalt's tin shop and running east to Pryor Street. The locality was known as Murrel's Row, as a salute to the notorious outlaw John A. Murrel, whose exploits were a favorite theme of conversation among the semi-outlaws of that quarter.

"Their chief amusement was cock-fighting. There were several cock-pits in the rear of the block, and some of the fights therein attracted hundreds of spectators. The low wooden shanties of the quarter, many of them built of rough slabs, harbored all kinds of games of chance, and some of them were downright robbers' dens. Nearly every other building was a groggery, in which drunken rows were of almost hourly occurrence. On Saturday nights it was common to have free-for-all fights that assumed the proportions of riots.

"Meanwhile two other tenderloin districts had developed on the outskirts of town. One of these was the nondescript cluster of bark-covered cabins erected by the very poor to whom Jonathan Norcross had generously given slabs from his sawmill a few years before. The locality, around the present intersection of Decatur and Pratt streets, came to be known as Slabtown. It was noted more for poverty than lawlessness.

"The other was on a par with Murrel's Row and was, if anything, more degraded. Known as Snake Nation, it was a settlement devoted almost entirely to the criminal and immoral element, and was sprawled along the old Whitehall Road (later Peters Street) from the railroad crossing to about where

Fair Street now crosses. Several murders occurred in the Snake Nation before the section was cleaned out by the law-abiding element in the early 1850s." [1]

The DeKalb Grand Jury was kept quite busy trying to deal with the lawlessness. The March, 1848, jury, with Charles Latimer as foreman, indicted William Chapman, Black Johnson, Washington Stegall, James Carlton, Rolly White and Irbin Powell for the offense of gambling, "which offense occurred April 5, 1848, and involved `playing cards, the game of Bluff for money and other valuable things.'

The grand jury of September, 1848, indicted Lud Edmonson and Hut Robinson for operating a Faro Table on August 28, 1848, "for the purpose of playing and betting money, and permitting persons to assemble at said table, etc."

The DeKalb County jail was too far away and too small to be of much use incarcerating so many lawbreakers. The city's first jail was built in 1848 on the southwest corner of Pryor and Alabama, a short distance out of town. It was constructed of hewn timbers, three logs thick, and had a large wooden lock with a brass key.

But the builders of the Atlanta jail would have done well to copy the design of the DeKalb jail. The bastille in Decatur was firmly planted over a cell dug deep into the earth, accessible only through a trap door in the log floor. It served the county for many years without a single reported jail break. Atlanta's jail was similarly constructed, but without the dungeon. Single prisoners burrowed out. If more than one lawbreaker was incarcerated, they would tip the building over. Friends of prisoners could easily lift the jail off its foundation, allowing their buddies to crawl out.

By September, 1848, however, the DeKalb Grand Jury found the 25-year-old county jail "altogether deficient," and recommended that a tax be levied to build a new one. [2]

With new businesses opening daily in Atlanta, the county tax base continued to grow. The DeKalb County tax receiver reported in 1848: "I do certify that Three Thousand Five Hundred and Thirty Six Dollars and Eighty Eight cents and Six Mills is the Fair Aggregate of the Tax of DeKalb County for the year 1848, this 27th Day June, 1848. Given under my Hand this Day.
     John Hawkins, R. T. R."
The tax returns for 1849 grew by $300 to $3824.41.

John Collier and J. Norcross were appointed commissioners in 1848 "for the purpose of examining the ground for a public road from the City of Atlanta to intersect the Nelson Ferry Road near Mr. Coursey's and running a westerly direction from the City of Atlanta by John Colliers, James A. Jett and Simeon Akridge and thence to said Coursey's."

Commissioners appointed "to review the ground for a road from Panther Ville to Atlanta recommend the clearing and establishing a road recently cut and leaving the McDonough Road at Thos. M. Darnall's, from thence to William Morris' saw mill, thence to Atlanta."
    Thos. M. Darnall
    Zachariah R. Jones
    Wm. Morris
    Commrs. [3]

The September, 1848, Grand Jury, found fault with some of DeKalb's roads.

"The publick Roads & bridges are reported to be in good order except the bridge over Snapfinger Creek at Fowler's Mill. Also the bridge of Peach Tree Creek at Chandler's old place; also various bridges over the Rail Road. The Roads in Panthersville District are reported in bad order except the one leading from Decatur by Doc. T. M. Darnall's to the bridge on South River. Also the road running from Collier's Mill to Montgomery Ferry is reported to be in bad order to which the attention of the property authorities is directed."

                    Jonathan B. Wilson, Foreman

Martin De Foor	Robert Orr	James Kennedy
Thomas Akin	Edwin G. Collier	Cornelius M. Connally
Berry Ragsdale	Silas Poole	James F. Stubbs
Charles H. Wood	Samuel Potts	William H. Pyron
Peter Mitchell	Tunstal B. George	Robert Hollingsworth
Patterson M. Hodge	John Reid	William Terry. [4]
Thomas Barnes	Thomas H. Griffis	
Zachariah R. Jones	William Beauchamp	

The 1848 presidential campaign between Whig Zachary Taylor (with his running mate, Millard Fillmore) and Democrat Lewis Cass was hotly debated in DeKalb and Atlanta. "Indeed, the zeal of some was so strong that, when fortified by white corn liquor a fisticuff occurred nearly every day during the fall, between citizens of contrary political beliefs." A September political rally at Walton Spring drew a crowd from 50 miles around to eat barbecue and hear the oratory. Among those attending were James McWilliams and William Terrell, both about 21 years old and both from old DeKalb families. Terrell was a Cass supporter; McWilliams favored Taylor. The two swapped harsh words during the day, as their ancestors may have done over the course of the past 70 years. One young man's grandfather had fought under Gates at the Battle of Camden, the other's commanding officer was Baron DeKalb.

B y nightfall the men and their companions were full of fervor for their candidates and stumping on Decatur Street. They met in front of the home of John Kile Jr. (near the now intersection of Central Avenue). Insults and blows were traded. Terrell called McWilliams "a Tory and a coward" and stabbed him. McWilliams died the next day at the Kile home. Terrell and his friend, William Henson, escaped to Randolph County, Ala., where Terrell was later caught. He was tried and found guilty of voluntary manslaughter at the March, 1850, term of the DeKalb Superior Court. Judge E. Y. Hill sentenced Terrell to four years of hard labor in the state penitentiary. Davidson G. Waldrup was the jury foreman. The Supreme Court later denied a request for a new trial. [5]

George Gilman Smith, D. D. (1836-1913), Methodist minister and historian, lived in Atlanta between 1847 and 1855 with his parents. His recollections of early Atlanta, including the political rally of 1848, were published in the Atlanta Journal from 1909-1910.

"This was the year of the great Taylor and Fillmore campaign and there was great excitement, and a mass meeting and barbecue was held at Walton Spring. I recall little save about the great barbecue, where whole hogs and oxen were roasted, and the viands spread on long tables, and the wild rush of the hungry crowds to snatch the smoking food. I remember the torchlight procession and the transparencies and the great crowds of strangers."

Political fervor resulted in a second act of violence, this between Judge Francis H. Cone and Alexander H. Stephens on September 3, 1848. Smith recalled that Judge Cone, a northern man (native of East Haddam, Conn.) and a Democrat, had said that "if Mr. Stephens favored the Clayton Compomise, he was a traitor to the South.

"The fiery little commoner said that if Judge Cone said that to him he would strike him in the mouth. As bad fortune would have it, as Judge Cone stood paring his nails on the steps of Dr. Thompson's hotel, Mr. Stephens walked briskly up from the car shed. He saw Judge Cone, and at once asked him if he said `he was a traitor.' Judge Cone said he did and Little Aleck struck him. The infuriated Judge stuck the knife in hand and knocked Mr. Stephens to the floor and stabbed him repeatedly. He escaped the fury of the mob by a quick flight. Then gave himself up and stood his trial in Decatur and was fined.

"As soon as he was able to be moved, Mr. John F. Mims, the first agent of the Georgia Railroad & Banking Company, had him taken to his house where the Constitution Building is now. When the convention came the horses were taken from the carriage and men drew it by long ropes to the scene of the speaking. I remember the pale face of the little man as he sat in the carriage." [6]

Merchant James Bell Sr. died in Atlanta on April 30, 1848. He was the progenitor of a large family with historic connections to both DeKalb County and Atlanta. Bell and his wife, Susan Bell Key, had 10 children: Eugene M., Adison A., Jasper M., Marcus Aurelius, Marianne E., Jedediah F., Lycurgus M. Margenius A., James Eugene and Henry B. Bell. Marcus Aurelius Bell (1828-1885) married Mary Jane Hulsey, daughter of Eli J. Hulsey and granddaughter of Merrell Collier. Piromis Hulsey Bell, son of Marcus and Mary Jane and a prominent Atlanta lawyer, lived on part of the old Merrell Collier plantation near the South River. [7]

Stone Mountain tax collector and Justice of the Peace Robert McCurdy of Stone Mountain died on May 7, 1848, at the relatively young age of 43, leaving a wife and eight young children. Descended from Scottish immigrants, Robert, the son of John McCurdy and Elizabeth Groves, had come to DeKalb County about 1830. Robert's wife, Clarissa Burford, was the daughter of Philip H. Burford and Agnes Bulloch of Oglethorpe County, Ga. The Burfords had preceeded the McCurdys to DeKalb.

All of Robert and Clarissa's children were born in DeKalb County, when the family lived on the road between Decatur and Covington, near the Charles Latimers. Shortly before Robert's death, the family moved to Stone Mountain. Two of their sons, Stephen Cicero McCurdy and James Robert McCurdy, were killed during the Civil War. A third son, John Wilson McCurdy, fought in the war and was discharged to Yellow River, Ga., a refugee camp south of Stone Mountain.

John McCurdy married Sarah Jane (Sally) Carter while on furlough in 1863. Sally was the sister of Celia Ann Carter, who married John's brother Philip Burford McCurdy.

Several descendants of Robert and Clarissa McCurdy were involved in the granite industry. Ida

Several members of the McCurdy family have served as DeKalb County sheriff or deputy sheriff through the years. Until 1925, the sheriff was required to live at the jail. Julius Augustus McCurdy and his family lived in this jail from 1913-1928. The jail stood at the corner of McDonough and Herring streets until it was torn down in 1948. The tower was where hangings were conducted. (DeKalb Historical Society)

Jackson McCurdy, daughter of John Wilson and Sally Carter McCurdy, married Carl T. Wells in 1887. Wells was a stonecutter and quarry owner, who supplied the granite to build the county courthouse in 1898. William Tarlton (Dr. Bill) McCurdy, son of John and Sally, married Mary Pinckney Tuggle and practiced medicine and kept fox hounds in Stone Mountain.

Philip Burford McCurdy was a stone contractor, as well as a Baptist minister who preached at Stone Mountain Baptist Church from 1881-1897. A story has been handed down through generations of the family about the Sunday morning the Rev. McCurdy was preaching at Tucker Baptist Church:

"Evidently, some of his sons were not as religious as he was. It seemed that there was only one good suit in the family, and he appropriated it for the Sunday morning service. As he began to wax eloquent, approaching the climax of his sermon, perspiration developed and he reached in his pocket for a handkerchief. Pulling it out, a deck of cards spilled out on the pulpit. He is reported to have calmly explained that one of his boys had worn that suit on the previous night, and then he had proceeded to complete the sermon. What happened to the son after the sermon has never been known."

Philip McCurdy's wife, Celia Ann, apparently was not as strict about card playing as her husband. One of her neighbors once called her to task for not respecting her husband's views, because she permitted dancing in their home and playing cards on Saturday nights. Her reply was: "Phil is not raising these children, -- I am, -- and I would much rather have them at home playing cards than out behind the barn or in the cornfields drinking and gambling."

One of those sons was Julius Augustus McCurdy Sr., who was born on July 12, 1876, and married Leomie B. Goldsmith in 1900. A stonecutter, who worked in the Venable Quarries, McCurdy was elected DeKalb County sheriff in 1913. As sheriff, he and his family were required to live in the jail. The brick jail that was their home had a tower in which those who received the death penalty were hung. McCurdy never was called upon to perform a hanging. He held the office until his death on April 22, 1928.

Julius Augustus McCurdy Jr., son of Gus and Leomie McCurdy, was an attorney and founder of Decatur Building and Loan Association (later Decatur Federal Savings and Loan Association) in 1926. Julius McCurdy's brother, Walter McCurdy Sr., also was a prominent Decatur attorney.

McCurdys have held a variety of public offices through the years -- from state representative to mayor of Stone Mountain -- and many public jobs -- from prison camp warden to county attorney. Many descendants of Robert and Clarissa are still prominent citizens of DeKalb County today. [8]

DeKalb County's new jail was well on its way to completion early in 1849. The grand jury reported in March:

"... We find a new Jale (sic) in progress of erection in the hands of an efficient and energetic contractor, which we are happy to learn will be completed in the course of the present year, the plan of which we highly approve..."

The Inferior Court had, on January 2, 1849, accepted a proposal from James R. Evins, son of north DeKalb pioneer, John L. Evins, to build the new jail at a cost of $5,500. Evins, his father and their associate, Thomas Akin, did not finish the job, however, and were released on May 16, 1849. The bond and contract were assumed by John Bryce and Lemuel Dean.

The new two-story granite jail was completed in 1850, but, in the meantime, dangerous prisoners were housed outside the county.

The Inferior Court, on August 23, 1849, reported: "Whereas the jail in Decatur being insufficient for the safekeeping of persons charged with Capital Offences, it is therefore ordered by the Court that Robert Jones, jailer, convey to the jail in Marietta, Franklin Lee, who is now in jail charged with the crime of murder, and safely deliver him to the jailer of Cobb County for safe keeping."

        L. S. Morgan
        J. A. Hayden
        J. N. Bellinger. [9]

The DeKalb Grand Jury, in 1849, asked that the county place a higher priority to the education of its poor children: "... We strictly enjoin upon the justices of the peace of said County to be more particular in returning the children as entitled (to participate in the poor school fund) and that they be more vigilant in returning those who are entitled. Considering it the highest moral, political, social, as well as religious duty that we owe to ourselves, our county, society, and the rising generation to apted (sic) in the education of the poor and indigent of our County, we therefore earnestly recommend that the Inferior Court levy a tax of twelve and a half percent on the state to be applied to the poor scoul (sic) fund of said County."

In addition, the jury recommended that the roads be "kept in good order, particularly the roads leading from Atlanta to the Chattahoochee River and towards the counties of Coweta, Fayette and Henry that are traveled so much..."

        Charles Latimer, Foreman

Henry Brockman	William Hazelet	William F. Connally
James Diamond	A. W. Wheat	William M. Hulsey
Thomas Kennedy	Ezekiel A. Davis	William Avery
James L. Mayson	John Y. Flowers	Robert F. Davis
Joseph T. Bellinger	Hiram Casey	James R. McAllister
Thomas W. Connally	James R. George	John Holcomb. [10]
Alexander F. Luckie	William New	

The Inferior Court, in 1849, created the Stone Mountain (1045th) Militia District. The new district comprised parts of Diamond's, Evans and Browning's Districts and included the Stone Mountain Depot. The original district lines were as follows: "Commencing at the line of the Decatur District where the Rock Bridge Road crosses said District line, and running on said road until it crosses the road leading from Lawrenceville to McDonough, thence up the said Lawrenceville Road until it reaches the old Hightower Trail; thence up said Trail to where an old road called the old Towers Road crosses said Trail, it being on fraction of Land (Lot) Number 219 on the Northwest corner of said fraction; thence along said Towers old road until it crosses Stone Mountain Creek; thence along a new road called the Parker road, leading from his farm on said creek to his house, until it strikes the Geo. Rail Road; then up said Rail Road, until it crosses said Decatur District line, thence along said District line to the beginning."

The California gold rush lured several DeKalb County "prospectors" to the west coast in 1849. Among them was Jett W. Rucker, son-in-law of Dr. Chapman Powell, who soon returned. [11]

The smallpox epidemic, in the spring of 1849, caused C. R. Hanleiter to suspend publication of the Southern Miscellany. He later sold his presses and type to Jonathan Norcross, Ira O. McDaniel, Benjamin F. Bomar and Zachariah A. Rice, who changed the name of the newspaper to the Weekly Atlanta Intelligencer. Atlanta's first daily newspaper was the Daily Examiner, founded in July of 1854, followed by The Atlanta Daily Intelligencer, published by W. B. Ruggles, which opened on February 1, 1856. The Examiner and Intelligencer combined in 1857. [12]

The editor of the Atlanta Daily Intelligencer was Thomas Coke Howard (1817-1893), an attorney, who had come to Atlanta in the 1840s. T. C. Howard and his fourth wife, Susan Harris of Savannah, were the parents of William Schley Howard Sr. of Decatur, who served in the U. S. House of Representatives from 1907-1917. William Schley Howard Sr. (1875-1953) and his wife, Lucia Augusta duVinage, were the parents of William Schley Howard Jr., who was a member of the Decatur City Commission. W. S. Howard Jr. and his wife, Nelle Sherwood Chamlee, were the parents of Pierre duVinage Howard Sr., state representative from DeKalb and county attorney, and the grandparents of Pierre duVinage Howard Jr., the current lieutenant governor of Georgia. [13]

George Gilman Smith, who came to Atlanta as a boy, recalled being frightened at first by the disorderly behavior of some of the town's early citizens.

"The first night (in 1847) we spent in the little house near Whitehall which was to shelter us for awhile. I was alarmed by the yelling of the drunken wagoners, who, after selling their cotton and loading up the goods they were to carry to the west, proceeded to fill up themselves. There was no marshal or policeman to say them nay, and they had a free and easy time. The next day I began my tour of exploration. Whitehall was then the chief street of the town. It was pretty well built up with wooden houses to what is now Mitchell. Many of these houses had rooms above the stores, in which the families made their homes.

I have a pretty accurate recollection of the business houses. Going out to West End from the railroad, the first house was the new grocery of John and James Lynch, two of as clever Irishmen as ever left the Green Isle. They did a large grocery trade and bought cotton. Across Alabama Street, Smith, Jones & Johnson had a general supply store. Jonas S. Smith was the manager. He was a warm hearted kindly man, who was postmaster after George Collier lost his place for being a Democrat. The Enterprise was published above the next store. Cooper Holliday had a barroom a little up the street. (Robert M.) Clarke & (Thomas F.) Grubb had a general supply store at or near that time, and they packed a very large amount of bacon. Dr. Bomar had a general grocery store. The dry goods store of Dr. Angier was on that side, and a large supply store of (Larkin H.) Davis & Lewis (probably Wade H. Lester) was on the corner of Hunter and Whitehall. On the side beyond Hunter and on the right was an almost unbroken row of small store houses to Mitchell, where the store houses ended. On the other side (east) Scott, Carhart & Co. had a very large grocery on the (southeast) corner of Alabama. Their managing partner, U. L. Wright, was a great cotton buyer. The Sternberger Brothers, with Jett Rucker, afterward of Maddox, Rucker & Co., clerk, was next; then (John J.) Thrasher and Scaife (Thrasher's brother-in-law), who had a large variety store; then old Billy Mann, the Irishman, for whom John H. James was clerk, and then Terrence Doonan, an Irishman and a great cotton buyer, who had a large grocery store.

"On the (northeast) corner of Hunter and Whitehall was the only brick store in the town, occupied by (Ira O.) McDaniel, (Alexander Weldon) Mitchell & (Eli J.) Hulsey. Before coming to them was the large dry goods and clothing store of Jacob Haas & Bro., for whom John Silvey and Calvin Hunnicutt were clerks. On the south side of Hunter on Whitehall was J. T. Doane & Co. Mr. Doane was a northern man, as was his partner, Mr. Robinson. They sold everything the country trade wanted, and next door to them in aftertime was the bookstore of James McPherson & Co., in which I was the boy clerk in 1848. I do not remember any other stores until the corner of Mitchell and Whitehall, where Mr. Davis had a grocery. I cannot be accurate in dates, but in a few years then a brick hotel, a range of brick buildings on Mitchell, a brick block near Hunter on the west side, but it required several fires to clear off the uncomely wooden buildings from the lower street.

"From our little home towards the railroad there were no houses, and in front of us only one cabin in a scrubby wood. This was occupied by old Mr. Durham, who made ginger cakes for Bill, his son, to peddle. They were good cakes, too, as I can testify, for I have eaten none for these fifty years with such relish. There were no streets as such, but a few. There was the Newnan Road, the Sandtown Road, the Green's Ferry Road, the McDonough Road on the south side; and the Forsyth Road, the Marietta Road and the Decatur Road on the north side.

The heavy timber had been cut off, as had been all the saplings large enough for wood and the roots and little stumps gave fine gleaning for we little trash gathers to get wood for the kitchen fires. Beyond Mitchell Street all along the Newnan Road, was now and then a building. Mr. (Richard) Peters had already bought the lot on which for so many years, was his home. It was a commodious and highly improved plat, covering several acres in after time, while his large barn and stables were about where the Terminus (sic) Hotel [4] is now. [5]

"Along the Whitehall or Sandtown Road were a few straggling houses and Mr. (Jesse) Clark's cabinet shop. On Pryor Street, south, there were sundry buildings. Eli Hulsey, I. R. Black, Ira O. McDaniel, Dr. Cheek and some others had houses and large lots, but nearly all that part of the new thickly settled city was an unbroken forest. There was at that time a large spring on the west side, and a little school house near it. All along what is now Peters Street were small log and frame houses, with now and then one of greater pretensions. This was `Snake Nation,' and was the tenderloin district of the young town for many years. I was taught to give it a wide berth when I went out to my grandmother's who lived beyond Whitehall.

Smith continued his tour from the corner of Forsyth and Marietta streets. "Taking the Norcross corner for a starting point, going down Decatur Street on the right side was Dr. Thompson's garden. Then the railway buildings and yards. On the left was Murrel's Row, where every house was a groggery and gambling house, except a few small stores, until Ivy Street was reached. On the corner of Ivy and Decatur was a large boarding house of a Mrs. Wells. In this house, a few years afterward Elijah Bird cut to death Dr. Hilburn, who was one of the first dentists in Atlanta. Then came Slabtown, a long row of small houses built on slabs and logs, with now and then one more pretentious. Dr. S. T. Biggers, the botanic physician, lived in a two-story building and had an office on a commodious lot in the midst of Slabtown. There were scattered homes over the hills looking toward Decatur, but the lots were mostly unimproved.

---

[4] Terminal Hotel.

[5] Richard Peters (1810-1889) boarded at Dr. Joseph Thompson's Atlanta Hotel when he arrived in 1846. Two years later, he married Thompson's eldest daughter, Mary Jane. All of their children were born while they lived in the house at the corner of Mitchell and Forsyth. (Source: Garrett, Franklin M., 1954, 1969, <u>Atlanta and Environs -- A Chronicle of Its People and Events</u>, Vol. 1, page 255).

"The business man Jonathan Norcross, who had a large department store and a large country trade; George Collier had a post office on the corner of Decatur and Peachtree, and the Kile's drinking shop on Peachtree, while just off from that street Moses Formwalt had his tin shop. Addison Dulin had a general supply store where the Empire Building is now, and on the corner where the new skyscraper of John Grant is to be, was a warehouse occupied in the front by L. W. Walton, and in the rear by my father and Dr. (F. Jeter) Martin, who had moved their doctor's office from the corner of Alabama and Pryor.

"There were but a few buildings of any pretensions along Marietta Street or Peachtree at that time. Going out Marietta Street there were a number of small uncomely houses, and near Squire (Edwin) Payne's, a little hamlet with a few small houses and then came his home. He lived at that time in a double log house, and was just building his imposing 8-room house, in which he died. Beyond him was the handsome home, for those days, of Neil (Cornelius M.) Connally. All these places have long been absorbed by the city.

There had been built a handsome residence, at that time the handsomest in the city, of Judge Reuben Cone, who had removed from Decatur. He owned much property in Atlanta in unimproved lots, which I remember were divided into a quarter of an acre each and sold for $150. Judge Julius A. Hayden, who had come originally from Connecticut, was his son-in-law. I remember Judge Cone had the first door bell in Atlanta, and the first I ever saw. Dr. (Joshua) Gilbert had a home opposite ours, and Dr. (Nathaniel) Austin was building a handsome brick just opposite us on the north side of the street.

"During the year there was a Negro hanged for murder in Lawrenceville, and Dr. Austin fell heir to the dead man's body. It was brought to Atlanta to be dissected by the few doctors, and as my father was one, he took his two sons to the dissecting room to show them how fearfully and wonderfully we were made. I remember the ghastly vision to this day.

"Along the railroad going east on the north side were quite a number of four and five room cottages, in one of which lived William Thuston, the English machinist; boys of the Georgia shops, and James A. Collins who had married the widow Bolton, and was step-father of the beautiful Julia. There was a famous blacksmith shop further down -- the first in town -- owned by a Mr. Martin. Rev. (David) Thurman, another blacksmith and a Methodist preacher, had a somewhat pretentious 2-story house, next to him on the hill. There were scattered cabins and cottages all through the section between Wheat and Decatur, and along Pryor and Ivy.

"Much the larger part of the infant city, or rather the city in prospect, was a forest. The young timber had been cut out for wood and the pines for lumber, and the beautiful oaks formed a great park. The limits of the city were defined as one mile in every direction from the Union Station, or as it was then called, the car shed...

"On the west side, out of the limits, was Charner Humphries, who owned White Hall, and whose straggling house was a stage stand and a tavern before the railroads were built. He was a man of large wealth for those times. A Mr. (Wiley G.) Marchman had a farm adjoining, out of which West View Cemetery was formed. A Mr. (Henry T.) McDaniel was his neighbor. A Mr. (James A.) Jett had a large farm on the same side...

"On the north side Samuel Walker owned all the land in the Piedmont Park tract, and much beside. A Mrs. (Sarah) Ivy, a staunch old lady with a fine family of boys came up to the city's edge on the east side...

"The City of Atlanta, early in 1848, was in prospect. The legislature had granted the charter, but for the early months of the year all things continued as they were.

"My mother opened the first female school in the town in January 1848. She had limited her number to 25, charged $25 per year, and took only girls, not even her own sons being admitted. I remember some of her pupils. Dr. Thompson sent his two daughters, Julia, afterward Mrs. (William P.) Orme, and Joan, later Mrs. (Thomas. M.) Clarke. Captain Loyd sent his two daughters. James A. Collins sent Julia Bolton, his step-daughter and Sallie Collins, his own child. Squire Payne sent his daughter Letitia, afterward Mrs. Calvin Hunnicutt. A. B. Forsyth, his daughter Fannie, afterward Mrs. (William J.) McDaniel. There were several Haynes girls, daughters of Reuben Haynes, and doubtless a few others whose names I cannot now recall. At the same time Dr. Fonerdon and his wife had a mixed school at the academy. There was also a mixed school on the west side, but I do not remember the name of the teacher.

Mr. (L. W.) Walton and I were great friends and I had the position of a general office boy, and was used to measure grain, and I am sorry to say to measure liquids made from grain. My only connection with the liquor trade was that year. I never drank, but I drew liquor for the up country folks who did. When a man came in with a load of corn, the first thing to do was to load him up with corn. Sometimes his wife was with him, and she was always invited to take a little something, which she generally did, and I noticed it was always rum.

"The Irish famine was on and much corn was being shipped from Atlanta to Charleston, and thence to Ireland. The corn was generally on the cob when it was sold. The first corn shellers I ever saw were used by Jonathan Norcross to shell the grain and a dozen boys were employed to sew up the sacks. I remember their wage was 20 cents a day and they boarded themselves. These two stores and Addison Dulin's were the only stores of any size on Marietta above Pryor. I do not remember one below Pryor but that of James Bell. All the rest were drinking shops and gambling rooms.

Smith waxed poetic when remembering Atlanta in the spring of 1848. "I never saw more beauty than there was in the springtime in the groves all over Atlanta. All the undergrowth except the azalias and dogwoods had been cut out. The sward was covered with the fairest woodland flowers, floxes, lilies, trilliums, violets, pink roots, primroses -- a fairer vision than any garden of exotics show now. Honeysuckles of every beautiful hue, deep red, pink, golden, white were in lavish luxuriance. The white dogwood was everywhere; the red woodbine and now and then a yellow jessamine climbed on the trees. When a stream was found it was clear as crystal...

"The Methodist church was covered and floored, and I think the windows were in. My father got some loads of puncheons from the mill, and with the aid of hands sent by Edwin Payne and Samuel Walker, some backless benches were made, and regular services were held. Every two weeks the circuit preachers came and in the intervals the local preachers filled the pulpit. On the sides of the house were wooden candle holders, and in the center was a frame to hold half a dozen. My brother and I were the unpaid sextons. The Rev. John W. Yarbrough (of Decatur) was our preacher and Dr. John W. Hinton was the junior preacher. My father and James W. Collins were the only two Methodists in the town who could house the preacher. The other brethren were in the country. The puncheon benches did not continue very long, for my father raised $60 by public subscription of one dollar each, and put in better seats...

Smith recalled that in the lawless days of early Atlanta the town drunks pursued their day's work unmolested by the constables and sheriffs. "Old Painter Smith came from his cabin on McDonough street, neatly dressed by his good old wife, and proceeded at once to tank up and make things lively. `Smell of my neck,' he used to shout out defiantly. `I hain't afraid of nobody sens I killed them two men.' `You are a fool and I am a fool; I am a fool to do as I do; you are a fool for want of sense.' One day I saw John White, who was being `cussed out' by Cole Brown, leap off Claiborn Powell's porch on his vituperator and hurl him to the earth, and heard Brown say just as he fell, `Nuff, nuff, take him off.' [6] Just below this groggery I saw the only chicken fight with gaffs I ever saw, and a disgusting sight it was.

"When the first election took place I cannot exactly say, but sometime during that year Jonathan Norcross and Moses Formwalt were candidates. Jonathan was known to be uncompromising in his hatred to liquor and disorder, and Formwalt was one of the boys. He was elected. It was said that day there were 60 fights. I remember when Stephen Terry, who was also a candidate, standing by me, was being soundly berated by old Painter. His patience ceased to be a virtue, and good Methodist as he was, he seized old Painter by the collar and wore the stick to a frazzle on his back.

"That year was a year of conventions. The Temperance people, the old Washingtonians had one. Joseph Henry Lumpkin was present and Judge Robert M. Charlton was the orator...

"That fall... I know the street gang was put to work to dig up the stumps in the main streets, and that we had a marshal, German Lester, and a deputy, Ben Williford, and that eggs sold at 8 cents a dozen, and butter at 10 cents per pound, and corn at 40 cents a bushel, and sweet potatoes at 15 cents a bushel, and wood at 50 cents a load. I have seen venison sold at 25 cents a ham and fine apples at 40 cents a bushel. Coffee was to 12 1/2 cents a pound, and sugar, always brown, at from 6 to 10 cents a pound.

"In glancing back over my first days in Atlanta, I recall the first lawsuit I ever attended. It was evidently a distress warrant case, and was tried before Justice (Willis) Buell. He was a New Englander and the very impersonation of dignity. He sat in his judicial seat with his law books and a ginger cake before him. The lawyers were Christopher Simpson on one side and Squire (John N.) Bellinger on the other. I remember nothing of the case except that before it was finished I was on both sides. Old Squire Buell, was, I think, the first judicial officer in the town. He was an old bachelor of somewhat bibulous habits, but of very dignified ways, drunk or sober.

"The next case I remember was a somewhat more serious one. A man named Crawford, who lived in

---

[6] Following publication of his reminiscences, Smith received a letter from a descendant of Mr. Painter, who apparently chastised him for his portrayal, and reported that Painter had "reformed, joined the church and died in peace. Smith responded, calling Painter a "quaint old man of whom I never heard any harm. I regret any pain my mention of him gave. Drink was his curse, as it was the curse of many who had not his quaintness."

Snake Nation, in connection with another, had driven a wagon to the back of a store on Whitehall Street and looted the store. He was arrested and committed to jail, and I was at the commitment trial, which was held in the basement room of an old tavern on the corner of Decatur and Loyd streets.

"In 1849... the smallpox came to Atlanta. A merchant from Florida had gone to New York, and when on his return he found himself quite sick and in Atlanta, he sent for Dr. Gilbert. The doctor could not exactly decide what was the matter with him, and called in my father. As soon as my father saw him he told him that it was a violent case of confluent smallpox. To this verdict the doctors assented, and then came the panic. He offered to pay any price to stay at the hotel, but that could not be thought of. The city authorities hastily had a shanty knocked up, and he, with Pat Hodge, as nurse, was housed into it. Such a panic Atlanta has never had since, not even during the war, as that one case of smallpox produced. Business was almost at an end; schools were closed and churches not opened. The poor fellow died and poor Pat had an attack, and after weeks of excitement was over, and there were no more cases.

"The old swimming pool of Whitcomb Riley may have been more picturesque, but it certainly was not more popular than a great rain water pond... which was made by the Georgia R. R. embankment below Oakland Cemetery... We had no bathing suits in those times and were `in puris naturalibus' when the cars swept by.

The most popular place on (Mitchell) street was a little house next door to the store in which I clerked, the drinking house of Dock (R. U.) Hightower. Dock was a very popular man, especially with the country folk. He generally managed to have a country fiddler on hand, and `Billy In the Low Grounds' and the `Arkansas Traveler,' and such like melodies, with now and then a country jig thrown in, made our neighborhood lively enough. Immediately opposite our store was the store of a mysterious shopkeeper named Beecham. If he ever had a customer I never saw him, except when I went in to buy a thri' pence worth of raisins. He had a little Negro and a little pony. He fed the pony somewhat economically. As the wagons came in the cows raided them for fodder, and snatched a bundle and ran; then Beecham's nigger ran after the cow and captured the fodder and fed it to the pony.

"The young city was a center for shows. The legerdemain men reaped quite a harvest with their tricks. The magic lantern men with their dissolving views, and the mesmerists with their wonderful exhibitions. I remember one who said he could mesmerize anybody, but especially Ike (Isaac B., Atlanta printer) Pilgrim. Ike did just as the lecturer wished him to do. He slept and woke and dance and fished; but one time I think Ike a little overdid his part. He had a pole in his hand, and a line and hook, and was very solemnly fishing in an imaginary pond `Now,' said the lecturer, `you have got a bite; ah, you have caught him; jerk him out.' `Yes,' said Ike, `I've got a cat.' Then Ike overdid it.

"Once we had a scientific lecture and were told all about electricity and galvanism, and laughing gas. I stepped forward at the invitation of the lecturer and inhaled to intoxication, and spouted out loudly:
> `Goliath was a man of might
> And challenged Israel all to fight;
> Now David was not great or high,
> But thought the giant he would try,
> He took his little stone and...'

"Here I awoke to find the audience in a roar, and to find I had been speaking a little speech my father had taught me years ago.

"The newspapers in the town were the Enterprise and the Luminary. Then came the Miscellany, Colonel Hanleiter's paper. My father wrote the carrier's address for my venerable old friend, W. (William) R. Hanleiter, of Griffin, to carry around and sell. He sent me a copy years ago, which I am sorry I lost. I remember one part of it. It said:

> `Atlanta, the greatest spot in all the nation,
> The greatest place for legislation
> Or any other occupation
> The very center of creation.'

"Despite the building of the new (rail) roads which cut off the wagon trade, Atlanta continued to grow... The board walks were removed and brick pavements were laid on Whitehall, and new streets were laid out...

"Near this time, 1850, there was the first considerable fire in the young city. The Wheat Brothers had a large wooden building where Mr. (Frank E.) Block's candy factory is now, and one night about midnight it was found on fire. It was the first large fire I had ever seen. It burned the block but did no other damage...

There were some improvements in the architecture of the private homes, but what was a palace then, would be a mere cottage now. Near this time Aaron Alexander moved from Charleston and opened a drug store in which he installed a soda fountain, the first soft drink place in the city. He was the first man to bring a carload of ice to the city...

"McPherson's book store (opened in 1848) was the only one in the up country, and had a pretty good supply of books and fancy goods. Among our visitors, for I was the only clerk, were many fine people. One was a dignified gentleman who came in his carriage with two bright little girls. One of these was Mrs. (W. H.) Felton, the other her sister, Mrs. McLendon. Their father was Mr. Charles Latimer. Among our most regular visitors was Miss Ellen Peters, who generally brought with her a gentle little girl, now Mrs. (Nellie Peters) Black. One of the books which was in constant demand was the Sacred Harp, [7] which is still popular after fifty years.

"Atlanta was now an overgrown town with none of the marks of a city. Its streets were unpaved and such a thing as a sewer was unheard of. One marshal and his assistant were the police force, and I think the mayor's salary was $250 (actually $200). But with sublime confidence in itself the city was moving forward.

"... The city of Atlanta was never laid out except in spots. Several persons owned the land on which it was built. If I remember correctly the first owners (not original grantees from the state) were Samuel

---

[7] The Sacred Harp Hymnal was written by Benjamin F. White of DeKalb and E. J. King. (Source: Clarke, Donald S., The Reverends William Henry Clarke and Elijah Henry Clarke of Wesley Chapel Methodist Church.)

Mitchell (Land Lot 77), who owned all the land contiguous to the railroads... Judge Reuben Cone (Land Lot 78) had another lot; Ammi Williams, father-in-law of L. P. Grant, a large body on the southeast side; the Ivy estate (Land Lot 51), a large body on the northeast side...

"Whitehall Street was named for the old tavern of Charner Humphries in which is now West End; Forsyth named for A. B. Forsyth; Pryor for Col. (Allen) Pryor, a surveyor; Washington named in honor of the truthful George; Loyd, for Capt. James Loyd; Decatur, for the town to which it led; Collins for James A. Collins. Alabama was so named because the Alabama wagons followed it on their way west; Hunter after a civil engineer; Peters, after Richard Peters; Garnett, after Colonel (C. F. M.) Garnett, and Walton after A. W. Walton. I think these were all the streets then marked out.

I think there were no other streets then laid out, but numberless pathways from the cabins to the woods. There were long rows of cheap houses along the Alabama Road and the McDonough Road, where no streets were as yet laid out. The first work of the city was to clear the streets of stumps, which was by no means an easy job. No pavements had been heard of. In front of the stores on Whitehall were wooden platforms raised a foot or more from the surface. Crossing the streets were quite a task. All the men wore boots in those days, and with their pants legs in their boots they defied the mud.

Smith was on the street when "the conquering heroes" from the Mexican War came through on their way north. "They were hungry for news and one of them asked me to find him a New York paper. The Miscellany office was nearby and I got him one for which he offered to pay, but I was too patriotic for that. He insisted, and paid several times its worth. Others called for papers and while I broke up the Miscellany's collection, I could not meet the demand. So I was the first newsboy in Atlanta. We were not stuck up in those days.

"The western trade was pretty well lost, but a profitable business had sprung up with Tennessee, and the young city had much trade from North Georgia. Atlanta was no longer so great a cotton and grocery market, but was a distributing point for western produce. It came down the Tennessee to London,[8] where it met the East Tennessee & Virginia road and thence shipped to Atlanta, and sold to the cotton belt.

"James E. Williams did a large business with East Tennessee. So did Seago and Abbott, Clark and Grubb, and sundry others, who sold immense quantities of bacon and corn to the planters in middle Georgia.

"Atlanta continued to grow; new streets were opened and old streets were extended. the city government had been a mere government in name. Snake Nation was given over to iniquity, and Murrel's Row nobly deserved its name. The license for whiskey dens was small and they had things their own way. Boys met in billiard rooms and threw their coins into a pool, and feared no man. Faro

---

[8] Should read Loudon. The railroad from Loudon, Tenn. to Dalton, Ga. was the East Tennessee and Georgia Railroad. The East Tennessee and Virginia Railroad extended from Knoxville to Bristol. The roads were consolidated in 1869 and later became part of the Southern Railway. (Source: Bogle, James G., August 27, 1997, personal correspondence).

banks held an almost open session, and vile women visited their paramours in the daytime without shame. There was only one marshal and a deputy, and there was a city of two miles in diameter to oversee.

"But when Jonathan Norcross was elected (mayor in 1851) against the will of the rowdies, the battle was gained. I was in the store where I clerked, on Whitehall Street, when the marshal, William McConnell, came hurriedly to the door and said to Mr. McPherson, `I summon you to go to Decatur Street to suppress a riot.' There was open war. One of the gamblers had defied arrest. At last a brave fellow walked up to him and he surrendered. He was put in the calaboose. The rowdies got together and prized up the logs and let him out. Then they got the old cannon and loaded it with powder and bellowed defiance at the authorities. The leading spirit was arrested and a night session of the mayor's court was held. He was ordered to prison but whipped out a bowie knife and struck at the daring Jonathan across the table. `Then such a getting downstairs you never did see,' as the old song has it, but the prisoner went to prison nevertheless and he did not get out. The next day was Sunday, but a mayor's court was called at Davis Hall and the rioters were all fined. A vigilance committee was organized, headed by a young Virginia teacher, Mr. (Alexander N.) Wilson, and the gentlemen of the green table subsided, though I think the faro bank still clicked over the barroom on Alabama Street.

That summer, I think, the agricultural fair was held in Atlanta. A large lot was secured on the outskirts of the city and plain houses were built after which the fair was opened. It would be considered a very tame thing now, but it was agricultural and mechanical and educational. There were addresses every day and the exhibits were very creditable for those times. It was, in its moral features, vastly beyond any we have lately had in Georgia, or are likely to have..." [14]

George White, in his Statistics of Georgia, described DeKalb County as it approached the new decade of 1850:

"The Chattahoochee is the chief stream. One of the head branches of the Ocmulgee is in this county. Nancy's, Peachtree, Utoy and Camp creeks empty into the Chattahoochee. Shoal, Snap Finger, and Pole Bridge, empty into South River.

"Decatur is the seat of justice. It is a pretty village situated on a ridge, dividing the waters of the Chattahoochee and South rivers... The place is proverbially healthy. The court-house is a neat brick edifice, and cost $5100. A jail constructed of granite is under contract. There are two churches, Presbyterian and Methodist; the former is built of brick and is a handsome structure. It has two hotels, two flourishing schools, several stores, etc. Population 600. Amount of business done in Decatur is not great as formerly.

"Atlanta is a new place, formerly called Marthasville... The population may be put down at 2500, and this number is constantly augmenting. Atlanta is situated on a high ridge,... and is the point at which the Western and Atlantic, the Macon and Western, and the Georgia Railroads connect. This has made Atlanta a place of bustle and business. At this time there are four churches and another will be erected in the course of the year; six schools, about twenty dry goods and grocery stores, etc. Immense quantities of produce pass through Atlanta. Amount of business done is over 200,000 dollars.

"Stone Mountain, formerly called New Gibraltar, is a very thriving place; has four hotels, eight stores and several mechanics. Population 300. A stage from Gainesville comes to this village three times a week.

"The face of the country is undulating. Much of the soil will hardly repay the labour of cultivation. The rich lands are on the Chattahoochee and South rivers, Peach Tree, Nancy's and Utoy creeks, and have been known to produce 1000 to 1500 pounds of cotton per acre, and from 8 to 12 barrels of corn per acre. Wheat is rather an uncertain crop. The gray lands will produce from 500 to 700 pounds of cotton per acre, from 5 to 8 barrels of corn, and from 15 to 25 bushels of wheat. Lands of the first quality are worth from 20 to 25 dollars per acre; the other lands from 3 to 10 dollars per acre.

"Some gold has been found in the vicinity of Rock bridge, near Yellow river, and on Nancy's creek; asbestos in large quantities at the plantation of John Evans, Esq.; granite in quantities sufficient to supply the State of Georgia for a century to come; tourmaline, quartz, iron, etc.

"Manufacturers, etc. -- Two wool-carding mills, about 25 saw-mills, 35 grist-mills, 2 merchant-mills and 2 distilleries.

"The roads and bridges are not kept in the state which the comfort and convenience of the citizens require.

"Religion -- Education. Methodists, Presbyterians, Baptists, Catholics, Episcopalians and Christians. In Atlanta and Decatur are good schools. The subject of education begins to be more fully appreciated than formerly.

"We hazard nothing in saying that the citizens of this county are generally industrious and temperate. The farms are not kept with that neatness which could be wished. Some improvements in agricultural implements is much wanted.

"Mountain -- The Stone or Rock mountain, as it is sometimes called, is one of the greatest curiosities which can be found in this or any other country. It is said to be 2,226 feet above the creek, and is seven miles in circumference. This wonder of nature is visited by thousands during the summer season. " [15]

Chapter 23 Notes

1. Garrett, Franklin M., 1954, 1969, Atlanta and Environs -- A Chronicle of Its People and Events, Vol. 1, page 265-266.

2. Garrett, Franklin M., 1954, 1969, Atlanta and Environs -- A Chronicle of Its People and Events, Vol. 1, page 266-267.

3. Garrett, Franklin M., 1954, 1969, Atlanta and Environs -- A Chronicle of Its People and Events, Vol. 1, page 267.

4. Garrett, Franklin M., 1954, 1969, Atlanta and Environs -- A Chronicle of Its People and Events, Vol. 1, page 268.

5. Garrett, Franklin M., 1954, 1969, Atlanta and Environs -- A Chronicle of Its People and Events, Vol. 1, pages 273-274.

6. Garrett, Franklin M., 1954, 1969, Atlanta and Environs -- A Chronicle of Its People and Events, Vol. 1, pages 286-299.

7. Garrett, Franklin M., 1954, 1969, Atlanta and Environs -- A Chronicle of Its People and Events, Vol. 1, page 274.

8. McCurdy, Julius Augustus, 1979, The Stone Mountain McCurdys.

9. Garrett, Franklin M., 1954, 1969, Atlanta and Environs -- A Chronicle of Its People and Events, Vol. 1, page 284. Park, Alice, n. d., "DeKalb's 1830 Victorian-style Jail Housed All 35 Prisoners," DeKalb News/Sun.

10. Garrett, Franklin M., 1954, 1969, Atlanta and Environs -- A Chronicle of Its People and Events, Vol. 1, page 284.

11. Garrett, Franklin M., 1954, 1969, Atlanta and Environs -- A Chronicle of Its People and Events, Vol. 1, page 277.

12. Garrett, Franklin M., 1954, 1969, Atlanta and Environs -- A Chronicle of Its People and Events, Vol. 1, pages 278-279.

13. Clarke, Caroline McKinney, 1973, The Story of Decatur 1823-1899, pages 206-207.

14. Garrett, Franklin M., 1954, 1969, Atlanta and Environs -- A Chronicle of Its People and Events, Vol. 1, pages 286-299.

15. White, George, 1849, Statistics of the State of Georgia, pages 204-207.

Chapter 24

DeKalb County's third census, in 1850, showed the county with a total of 14,398 inhabitants, 3932 more than enumerated in the 1840 census. The 25.6 per cent growth rate was slightly less than that of the country as a whole. The United States had a population of 23,191,876 people in 1850, compared to 17,069,453 in 1840. DeKalb County's slave population grew from 2004 in 1840 to 2994 in 1850, a growth rate of 33 percent. The category of largest increase was free black females, growing from two to 23.

White males	5704
White females	5668
Free black males	9
Free black females	23
Slaves	2994
Total	14,398

In addition to Georgia, South Carolina and North Carolina, DeKalb residents listed 13 states as birthplaces: Alabama, Connecticut, Delaware, Kentucky, Maine, Maryland, Massachusetts, New Hampshire, New York, Tennessee, Vermont and Virginia. Other birthplaces were Germany, England, Ireland, Bavaria, Holland, Europe and "at sea." DeKalb had 1792 dwellings in 1850, occupied by 1794 families. Students numbered 322, and there were 435 white citizens older than the age of 20 who were listed as illiterate. Farming was by far the most numerous occupation. In addition to farming, DeKalb citizens had a variety of other occupations:

attending mill	city marshal	hatter
baggage master	city mayor	innkeeper
bar keeper	clergyman	iron foundry
bootmaker	clerk	keeping wood station
brick maker	conductor	laborer
brick mason	dentist	lawyer
butcher	engineer	livery stable
cabinet maker	ferryman	machinist
carpenter	grocer	mail coach driver
carriage maker	gunsmith	marketing

mail agent	road repairer	timber hewer
mechanic	sailor	tin and coppersmith
merchant	sawyer	tin plate worker
miller	sheriff	track repairer
millwright	silversmith	trading
overseeing	stone cutter	turner
painter	stone mason	waggoner
physician	superintendent of plank road	well digger
plasterer	tailor	wheelwright
printer	teacher	wool carding [1]
railroad engineer	teamster	
railroad worker	telegraph operator	

The total value of real estate in the county was $1,669,810, and the total value of personal property (including slaves) was $1,721,560.

Seven Revolutionary pensioners lived in the county. Four of DeKalb's white citizens were blind, and six were listed as insane. Two black citizens were blind.

William Goldsberry, the county's assistant marshal, was the 1850 census taker. [2]

The town of Decatur contained 86 households in 1850. The average age of a Decatur head of household in 1850 was 43, with the oldest being Revolutionary War veteran James McNeal (McNeil) at 72 and the youngest, John B. Holly, 21. There were nine heads of households younger than 25 years of age, and three older than 70. Nine heads of household were women. Heads of households were primarily Georgia natives, followed closely by those born in South Carolina and North Carolina. The town had 11 merchants, eight farmers, five carpenters, four cabinet/chair makers and four wagon/carriage makers, as well as two lawyers, two doctors and two clergymen and other assorted occupations.

The ages, occupations and birthplaces of those men and women residing in the county seat present a microcosm of DeKalb's total population in 1850:

Head	**Age**	**Occupation**	**Birthplace**
1. William Hill	52	merchant	Va.
2. James Ferrell	56	none	Ireland
3. J. W. Kirkpatrick	31	merchant	Ga.
4. H. T. Hall	50	blank	blank
5. William A. David	49	carpenter	Ga.
6. Willis Browning	64	none	N. C.
7. Jane Pendley	51	blank	Ga.
8. R. C. Buchanan	24	tanning	Ga.
9. John B. Holly	21	wagonmaker	Ga.
10. Allen Woodall	43	farming	S. C.
11. Jesse Farrar	44	none	Va.
12. Berryman D. Shumate	50	bricklayer	S. C.
13. John Durham	37	saddlery	S. C.
14. Lucinda Scott	39	blank	Ga.
15. J. M. Holly	52	carriagemaker	N. C.

16. Hiram J. Holly	23	chairmaker	Ga.
17. Merrill Humphries	40	shoemaker	S. C.
18. Samuel H. Wilson	48	attend mill	S. C.
19. Hiram R. Delay	43	cabinetmaker	S. C.
20. Thomas F. Hall	46	carriagemaker	Ga.
21. Thomas Austin	66	farmer	N. C.
22. William Veal	71	farmer	Va.
23. Ezekiel Mason	51	merchant	S. C.
24. John Simpson	54	none	S. C.
25. William A. Powell	25	merchant	Ga.
26. Alexander Johnson	35	blank	Ga.
27. Robert M. Brown	37	blank	N. C.
28. Daniel Adams	23	tin plate work	Ga.
29. J. B. Wilson	48	hatter	N. C.
30. William Ezzard	51	lawyer	Ga.
31. Gardner Adams	25	merchant	Mass.
32. John N. Swift	34	merchant	Ga.
33. Elijah Rosser	25	merchant	Ga.
34. Nancy McCrary	49	blank	S. C.
35. Isaac Rosser	71	P. M. Clergy	N. C.
36. Jane E. Bowie	40	blank	S. C.
37. Nancy Cameron	55	blank	S. C.
38. James McGinnis	24	mechanic	N. C.
39. Robert Davis	50	farming	S. C.
40. Jesse Anderson	51	laborer	N. C.
41. Lavena Robinson	32	blank	S. C.
42. Robert Jones	51	blank	N. C.
43. Joseph A. Reeves	48	merchant	Ga.
44. James McNeal	72	saddlery	blank
45. Riley M. Willingham	41	carpenter	blank
46. James Blackstock	30	tailor	Tenn.
47. Elizabeth A. Butler	35	blank	Ga.
48. Elizabeth Wilkerson	60	blank	N. C.
49. Eliza Nisbet	47	blank	S. C.
50. Thomas Reynolds	25	cabinet work	Ga.
51. David Floyd	50	laborer	S. C.
52. D. S. Floyd	25	? maker	Tenn.
53. E. N. Calhoun	50	physician	Ga.
54. Levi Willard	47	merchant	Mass.
55. Walter Wadsworth	49	tin plate worker	Conn.
56. Jesse L. Williams	35	merchant	N. C.
57. John S. Wilson	53	Pres. clergyman	N. C.
58. James R. McAllister	29	tailor	N. J.
59. W. F. Chewning	47	farmer	Ga.
60. Ammi Williams	60	none	Conn.
61. John J. Williams	31	R. R. repairs	Ga.
62. James M. Calhoun	39	lawyer	S. C.
63. James B. Buchanan	51	carpenter	S. C.

64. Wesley Tilley	45	well digger	N. C.
65. Eli Holsomback	22	painting	S. C.
66. J. Morgan	50	cabinet and chair maker	Mass.
67. L. S. Morgan	45	cabinet and chair maker	Mass.
68. Charles Murphey	51	lawyer	S. C.
69. Peter F. Hoyle	39	physician	N. C.
70. Daniel Stone	49	R. R. agent	N. C.
71. Lemuel P. Grant	32	R. R. engineer	Maine
72. Thena Douglass	50	blank	Ga.
73. T. B. George	50	innkeeper	Ga.
74. Cullin Linsey	50	laborer	S. C.
75. Elijah L. Bird	22	carriagemaker	Ga.
76. Thomas P. Ivy	30	blacksmith	S. C.
77. Henry A. Dorsey	24	blacksmith	Ga.
78. Nathaniel Johnson	25	farmer	S. C.
79. William Dearing	65	farmer	Va.
80. Henry B. Hill	54	innkeeper	N. C.
81. Thomas Rape	37	carpenter	N. C.
82. Jeremiah Waits	56	farmer	N. C.
83. Thomas Knight	32	chair maker	S. C.
84. Thomas Wallace	35	blank	Ga.
85. A. Alexander	48	merchant	Ga.
86. Jesse Robinson	48	carpenter	Ga. [3]

The coming to Decatur of one widow with three children probably was not widely noticed in 1850. Indeed, the lives of Mary Stokes and her children would have been rather unremarkable had it not been for the contributions of her elder daughter, Mary Ann Harris Gay.

Mary Stevens, daughter of Decatur pioneer Thomas Stevens, married William Gay in 1828 in Jones County, Ga. Their daughter, Mary, was born on March 19, 1829 in Jones County. Gay died while Mary was still a baby. When she was four, her mother married Decatur lawyer Joseph Stokes. The couple had two children, a son named Thomas J. Stokes, born in 1837, and a daughter, Missouri Horton Stokes, born one year later. Thomas Stevens died in 1840 while the Stokes family was living in Cass County. The family later moved to Marietta, where Joseph Stokes died. Mary Stokes and her three children, ages 21, 13 and 12, relocated to property she had inherited from her father in Decatur. [4]

When she was 16, while the family was living in Cobb County, Mary Gay's first poem, "My Valley Home," was published anonymously. Her writing career began to flourish after they reached Decatur. Her first book, Prose and Poetry, was published anonymously in 1858. The book contained several poems about lost love, inspired by Mary's breakup with her fiance who had renounced Christianity. Prose and Poetry was reprinted 10 times over the course of the next 23 years by the Southern Methodist Publishing House in Nashville, Tenn. The final edition contained a complimentary letter from William McAdoo, later a member of Woodrow Wilson's cabinet, who requested that Mary Gay's biography be included in a dictionary of southern authors. Her final published literary work was a novel set in the Mississippi lowlands during the antebellum years. Titled The Transplanted, it was written in 1907 when Mary Gay was 78 years old.

Mark Twain included some of Mary Gay's work in Chapter 21 of Tom Sawyer in 1876, with the note:

"The pretended `compositions' quoted in this chapter area taken without alteration, from a volume entitled `Prose and Poetry, by a Western Lady' -- but they are exactly and precisely after the schoolgirl pattern, and hence are much happier than any mere imitations could be."

Mary Gay responded with this notice published in the December, 1879 edition of the Christian Index: "Mark Twain is accused of plagiarism by Miss Mary Gay of Georgia, who will bring out a new edition of her book to prove the assertions. The public will be curious to see this proof. Mark Twain is a wealthy man of humor and if it is true that he stole from a lady it would be a very remarkable instance of literary kleptomania."

In the 11th edition of Prose and Poetry, published in 1881, she commented that "unprincipled aspirants for literary distinction" had plagiarized her work.

Only one of Mary Gay's books remains in print today. Life In Dixie During The War, a non-fiction account of the Civil War years in Decatur, Atlanta and north Georgia, was first published in 1892, and there were three subsequent editions in 1984, 1897 and 1901. [9] The book has been a source for many authors who have written about the war, including Margaret Mitchell, author of Gone With The Wind. Joel Chandler Harris wrote the original introduction to Life In Dixie: "Here indeed, is one of the sources from which history must get its supplies, and it is informed with a simplicity which history can never hope to attain."

The home where Mary Gay lived with her mother and siblings was headquarters for Union soldiers during the occupation of Decatur in 1864. In search of food, for her family and other women and children who remained in the town, Mary evaded pickets to enter Atlanta while the city was under siege. After the troops left Atlanta, she acquired a lame army horse and constructed a wagon for trips to Social Circle and Augusta, the closest likely sources for supplies. Long before the horse dropped dead, Mary had begun to make the trips on foot, saving the beast's strength for pulling the wagon.

After the war, Mary Gay devoted herself to philanthropic projects. She traveled all over the South, collecting nickels and dimes to start a Baptist church in Decatur. In Texas, she raised money to place an iron fence around the cemetery in Franklin, Tenn., where her brother died. She was a charter member and first recording secretary of the Agnes Lee Chapter of the United Daughters of the Confederacy. She and her sister, Missouri, were active in the Women's Christian Temperance Union. The home Mary and Missouri shared "became a center for women active in the early progressive movement." That home was moved from its original location on Marshall Street to Decatur's Adair Park historic complex, and is now headquarters for DeKalb County's Junior League.

A neighbor, Wesley Hamilton Weekes, remembered Mary Gay as a tiny woman who always wore black. In her later years, "she lived in a haunted solitude." Some in Decatur shunned her, interpreting her willingness to accept food offered by Union soldiers during the war as being "friendly" with the Yankees. She lived alone, except for visits from her widowed sister. "The components of her past, whether of her doing or undoing, were combining to crush the fragile Mary Gay, yet, the

---

[9] The DeKalb Historical Society reprinted the fourth edition in 1979. (Source, Bogle, James G., August 27, 1997, personal correspondence).

vindictiveness of the townspeople persisted with a smoldering fury." Mary Gay died in the state sanitarium in Milledgeville on November 21, 1918, shortly before her 90th birthday. She is buried next to her sister and mother at Decatur Cemetery. With her death, the "vindictiveness" apparently passed. At her funeral, it is said that "members of the group of mourners stood up in the pews and recounted story after amazing story of the little lady's courage, strength, and ingenuity."

Mary Ann Harris Gay was named a Woman of Achievement in Georgia in 1997, 79 years after her death.

Outside the town of Decatur, grist mills and sawmills were the primary industries in DeKalb County in the 1850s. Every stream large enough to generate water power sufficient to turn a mill wheel accommodated a small mill. Many a farmer subsidized his farm income by turning his neighbor's grain into flour and trees into lumber.

Greenville Henderson began operating his corn and wheat grist mill in 1851 on what is now Henderson Mill Road, about one mile north of the intersection of LaVista Road. The mill at one time was owned by Michael A. Steele.

White's Mill on Doolittle Creek, near the area of the intersection of now Flat Shoals and Whites Mill roads, was owed by the White family for more than 100 years. The first recorded owner was J. P. White, who willed the mill to his wife, Sarah, in 1857. John W. White deeded one-half interest in the mill to A. L. Pitts in 1870, and Pitts conveyed his half to John's wife, Susan A. White, in 1878. In 1897, Susan, then a widow, deeded the sawmill, grist mill, ginhouse and machinery to James M. White. James M. White built a house near the mill, where he died in 1928, survived by 15 children. The mill burned in 1942, but was rebuilt. One of James M. White's sons, Howell, was still operating the water-powered mill in 1951.

DeKalb County pioneer Thomas J. Akins operated a mill on the North Fork of Peachtree Creek, one quarter mile north of the old Shallow Ford Road. This portion of the old road is still called Shallowford Road today. The mill was located near what is now the intersection of the I-85 freeway. Akins's property had been the old William McElroy plantation. Akins sold the land and mill to John W. Miller in 1855. The mill closed in 1910.

William W. McAfee's mill was on Shoal Creek where it crosses what is now McAfee Road, midway between now Candler Road and Columbia Drive. The earliest recorded deed, dated 1859, showed the sale of the mill and 12 acres of land by DeKalb County Sheriff William Wright to William Ezzard. The deed identified the property as the former location of a sawmill owned by Joel C. Hinsen. Early maps of the area also identified the property as the location of Wadsworth's Mill. Ezzard deeded the land and mill to Walter Wadsworth on July 2, 1863. In 1870 Wadsworth sold it to Robert K. Wilson. Wilson, in 1875, deeded it to William R. Shelverton of Wilkes County, Ga. In 1877, the mill came full circle, when Shelverton deeded it back to William McAfee. Through all these changes of ownership, a man named Ragsdale is said to have operated the mill and lived there. [5]

The DeKalb County Grand Jury found the new jail almost completed in September, 1850, and the courthouse in need of some repairs.

"... We have, through a committee, examined our public buildings. We find that the new jail is not yet completed, but learn that it will be done in a few days, and we find the work neatly and substantially done, highly creditable to our Inferior Court; Mr. (John) Bryce, the contractor and Judge (L. S.) Morgan, superintendent of the work.

"The Court House we find in good repair except windows, and recommend the proper authorities to have them repaired, and attend more strictly to have the blinds fastened, either when open or shut. We have examined the old jail and find it kept in a manner highly creditable to the Jailor, Mr. (Robert) Jones.

The grand jury gave no explanation of what might have precipitated its remarks concerning slaves or the county treasury:

"We also recommend the citizens of our County owning Slaves to prohibit them from attending public meetings of any kind, except going to church under the supervision of white persons, as we believe such a course has a tendency to injure the slave and consequently the owner, at these times of excitement, particularly in the South.

"From the number of criminal cases which have come before this body, we are sorry to say there has not been that improvement in the morals of a portion of our citizens that we would have wished, and unless some beneficial changes, lament the condition of our County Treasury."
                    Peter F. Hoyle, Foreman

Andrew Johnson	William A David	Samuel House
Richard E. Eskew	Elijah Steward	Thomas Farr
John K. Landers	Charles W. McGinnis	Edwin Payne
Simeon Smith	Robert McWilliams	Berryman D. Shumate
Moses W. Davis	William W. Sentell	Henry G. Dean
William C. Austin	Ezekiel Mason	Samuel H. Wilson. [6]
James Robinson	James M. Holley	
Robert Crockett	Edwin Plaster	

The DeKalb Grand Jury handed down several indictments during the March, 1850, term:

William J. Mann, a well-known Atlanta merchant, was indicted "... for buying of a Negro man slave by the name of Asa, belonging to Lewis Peacock, 4 bushels of corn meal of value exceeding one dollar, without having written permission from the owner, overseer or employer of said slave, authorizing slave to dispose of said corn meal."

William G. (Buck) Heard and William M. Beasley were indicted "for stealing, on January 4, 1850, a sorrel horse of the female sex, belonging to Thomas Farr and valued at $50." Beasley plead guilty and was sentenced to three years at hard labor in penitentiary at Milledgeville. [7]

Several immigrants who would become well-known in DeKalb and Atlanta, took their oaths of citizenship before the DeKalb Superior Court in 1850. They were Michael McShaffery, age 26, Charles Savage, 27, Patrick Lynch, 30, Timothy Kirby, 24, and Edward Cornwell, 27, all from Ireland; and John Erminger, 26, Christian Kontz, 32, and Carston Brockhan, 37, who came from were Germany.

A young man who would later have a great impact on the town of Decatur spent one night there in teh fall of 1850. George Washington Scott, 21, wrote in his diary for October 30, 1850: "Arrived Decatur about 5:00 in the evening... Stopped at Dr. Calhoun's hotel. Read Isaiah 14." The following day, Scott wrote: "Left Decatur about half past seven. Arrived in Atlanta about 8:00 -- very warm and pleasant. Stopped at the Atlanta Hotel. This is the most stirring place of the size that I have ever seen. I suppose I saw between two and three hundred wagons in the town today, principally all hauling cotton. Some were drawn by horses, some by mules, and a great many by oxen... Read Isaiah 15."

Scott remained in Atlanta until November 5. It would be 27 years before he would return to DeKalb County. [8]

Roswell Road got its start on March 4, 1850, when the DeKalb County Inferior Court authorized John Isom, William C. Austin and William W. Sentell "to mark and lay out a road in DeKalb County commencing at the Shallowford Court Ground and running by the way of Peter Ball's, by A. Waits', by Sandy Springs Church, by the Bruce's Bridge on Nancy's Creek, intersecting with the Decatur and Atlanta Road at Buckhead." On December 26, 1850, the Inferior Court granted a charter to the Atlanta and Dahlonega Plank Road Company "for the purpose of constructing a Plank Graded or Macadamized road from Atlanta by Cumming through the County of Forsyth to Dahlonega." Principals in the company were Jonathan Norcross, Julius A. Hayden, Barrington King, Clark Howell, Ira R. Foster, Noah Strong and William Martin. [9]

DeKalb County's second city cemetery originated on June 6, 1850 when the county purchased six acres of land southeast of the town limits of Atlanta. The land was purchased from Alfred W. Wooding at a cost of $75 per acre. The cemetery was called Atlanta Cemetery or City Cemetery, but the name was later changed to Oakland. Oliver Hazard Perry Conant, the first sexton, began work the next year. The first burial, that of a young doctor James Nissen who became ill while visiting the city, was said to have been in the fall of 1850. As was the custom, Dr. Noel D'Alvigny severed the man's jugular vein, a precaution against being buried alive. [10]

The city of Atlanta conveyed to the Southern Central Agricultural Association a lot on the south side of Fair Street (now Memorial Drive) for the 1850 fair. David W. Lewis continued as association secretary after the fair was moved from Stone Mountain the previous year. The 1850 fair was held the week of August 14.

Lewis, along with Mark A. Cooper, Richard Peters, William Ezzard and James M. Calhoun formed the committee that cataloged entries.

Participants were asked to submit a report on the condition of agriculture in their counties for publication by the association. The ambitious goal of the 1850 fair was to exhibit items "embracing everything that is ingenious or useful in business or art." Citizens of all the southeastern states were invited to exhibit "stock, mechanics, agricultural implements, and valuable improvements or inventions, garden products, fruits, flowers, paintings, needle-work, etc."

As it had been in previous years, the annual oration was given by Col. John Billups of Athens.

All the railroad lines ran trains twice a day to Atlanta from various spots in Georgia.

Moving the fair did not discourage DeKalb County residents from entering. Many, including some familiar names from previous years' fairs, won premiums:

William Ezzard again won a prize for his White Flint Corn, and Richard Peters for his Imperial Oats. Dr. Joseph Baker's Upland Rice was worthy of a $1 premium. Peters also won $5 for his Red heifer named "Jenny Lind" and $3 for his red bull calf named "DeKalb."

John Evans continued to make the "competent judges" happy with his apple brandy. The reputation of Morgan brothers furniture was further enhanced when J. Morgan won a $10 prize for his bedstead and dressing bureau made of native walnut.

Other DeKalb County premium winners were a Miss Guthrie (monochromatic drawings), Mrs. V. Foster (India ink drawings), Mrs. E. Gordon (counterpane), Mrs. J. J. Peoples (patch quilt), Mrs. Mary Daniel (rag hearth rug) and Sarah Jane Corry (raised work picture).

The fair committee was impressed with an invention presented by DeKalb's James L. Mayson. The combination cultivator and scraper was considered "a very useful and economical implement in the culture of cotton."

Apparently Washington J. Houston felt that the first fairs were of a much higher caliber than the ones that were to follow. Writing in 1902, he said: "After disclaiming any intention to reflect on the methods of conducting fairs of the present day, I will add that the exhibits of the forties and fifties were solely conducted for the elevation of mankind and the development of our mechanical, agricultural and educational interests and did not embrace many features of the present that are prominently displayed on the boards as leading attractions. Such things as pool rooms, midways, beer gardens and gambling devices were unknown on the grounds." [11]

While it certainly was a popular novelty, rail travel in first few years after the train made its way to Atlanta was not considered a faster, safer or more comfortable means of public transportation than the stagecoach. Dr. Henry C. Hornady, who was pastor of the First Baptist Church of Atlanta from 1861-67, first arrived in Atlanta by train. He recalled:

"The railroads then running into Atlanta were laid with flat bars of iron, upon long pieces of timber, called stringers, and were by no means considered safe. Sometimes the end of a bar would break loose from its fastenings, and rise up a foot or more above the stringer, and such disjointings were called `snake heads,' from supposed resemblance to these reptiles. When the train would approach one of these `snake head,' the wheels would run under, and rip it up from its further fastenings, until it would pierce the bottom of some car, greatly endangering the lives of the passengers. On the very trip now under consideration, Rev. Jesse H. Campbell narrowly escaped by having just left his seat, when a `snake head' was thrust through it, doing it some damage and overturning the car.

"This occurred on the Macon and Western road somewhere between Macon and Forsyth, but the train was making such poor speed that a good trotter would have distanced it. Not much harm was done, only some of the passengers were shaken up, and others frightened nearly out of their sanity by the shock. This was the writer's trial trip on rail, and although thirty years have passed since then, he well remembers his feelings and impressions as he was whirled along at what he then thought a reckless rate of speed, and he inwardly blamed the managers for sacrificing the safety of the passengers for a foolish desire for rapid going, covering from ten to twelve miles an hour. He would look out and see the trees doing the Fisher's Hornpipe, or the Highland Fling, and then think, suppose this thing were to jump the track. Whew! would there not be destruction, and then he would shut his eyes, and abandon himself to the inevitable."

"When we boarded the train at Marietta, on our return trip (from a convention), the writer's nerves were not in first rate condition, he being somewhat dyspeptic, from too free indulgence in Convention fare, and he could not avoid a cold shiver, when told that it was down grade to the Chattahoochee river, and when the engineer said he was behind time fifteen minutes, and he was bound to run into Atlanta on time, or run the thing off its wheels. I found myself clutching tightly the back of the seat in front, and preparing, as a prudent man should do, if there should come a sudden shock and crash which would tear things to splinters; nor was I reassured when holding my watch in full view I found that we were rushing along at the rate of fifteen miles and hour, and that the car was swaying from side to side like a ship in a billowy sea. Every nerve was wrought up to its utmost tension, and when we ran into the car-shed at Atlanta, and I found myself still together, I breathed a sigh of relief, and immediately thanked God for escape from such dreadful peril." [12]

The city of Atlanta almost did not survive to see its fourth birthday. The criminal element from Murrel's Row and Snake Nation controlled the town, and neither the Atlanta nor the DeKalb County government seemed to be able to do a thing about it.

One of two grand juries that met in March of 1851 hinted that DeKalb might prefer that Atlanta handled its own crime problems:

"... In view of the vast accumulated business on our criminal docket originating in the City of Atlanta, and the difficulty of reaching cases and meating (sic) out justice to offenders against law, we would present the propriety of instructing our Legislators at the next session to obtain for the City of Atlanta jurisdiction over her own criminals by the establishments of a court in the aforesaid city with power to try and punish all offences not embracing capital punishment or confinement in the penitentiary. We would present as a grievance the prevalence of the practice, among our youth assembling at tippling and other houses to play at the game of Ken, or to be and becoming thereby only initiated into the corrupting vice of gambling, and beg our Legislature would prohibit the same under penalty against those who encourage it in their houses...

"We would present as a grievance the administration of Wyllys Buell, Esq., as magistrate in the City of Atlanta in defeating the ends of justice by leniency in offenses of aggravated carictur (sic), insufficient bonds as to amount, and allowing irresponsible securities on such bonds... We would desire to express our commendation of the Marshals of the City of Atlanta for the vigilance they have exhibited in the discharge of their duties..."
   Henry B. Latimer, Foreman [13]

The turning point for Atlanta proved to be the 1851 city elections, which pitted Jonathan Norcross of the Moral Party against Leonard C. Simpson, a former councilman, representing the Free and Rowdy Party. Norcross was elected.

Mayor Norcross's first test was the trial of a "tough" before a room filled with spectators, many of whom were not law-and-order supporters. The defendant, having been found guilty, did not go quietly, but pulled a knife, threatening all in the room, especially the mayor. The unarmed mayor defended himself with a chair. The man was subdued by former DeKalb Sheriff Allen E. Johnson, with the help of his "stout hickory cane" and some of the on-lookers. The episode was far from finished, however. There was talk of the need for a vigilance committee on one side and expectations of a bloody riot on the other.

Under cover of the following night, some of Atlanta's ruffians crept into Decatur and stole the War of 1812 cannon from the courthouse grounds. The cannon was planted in front of Mayor Norcross's store. Warning blasts, loads of sand and gravel, were fired, accompanied by a note demanding that the mayor resign, or have his business smashed blown up.

Mayor Norcross and the council issued a proclamation calling upon all law-abiding citizens to organize. Led by Alexander Weldon Mitchell, the volunteer police force marched at midnight on the Rowdy Party headquarters at the northeast corner of Decatur and Ivy streets. The riot that had been predicted never materialized. The Rowdy Party abandoned its previous courageous show and "dissolved like frost in the sunshine."

The "rowdies" were rounded up, arrested, tried and convicted. Mayor Norcross continued to be threatened; the volunteer police force continued to maintain order and protect the town's chief executive. With the Murrel's Row inhabitants behind bars or run out of town, Snake Nation was the next target. "Finally, with a determination to eradicate this den of iniquity, a large body of disguised Atlantans raided the Snake Nation by night. The men found in the filthy huts were whipped by the `White Caps' and warned to leave town, while the abandoned creatures of the other sex were hauled nearly to Decatur, where they were allowed to go with a similar warning. The shanties of both Snake Nation and Slabtown were destroyed by fire so completely that neither rose again." [14]

New council members and city officers were elected on January 24, 1851. Council members were Julius A. Hayden, John T. Humphries, Daniel McSheffrey, William W. Roark, John Jones and Paschal House. Officers were William McConnell, marshal; Benjamin N. Williford, deputy marshal; Adam Jones, clerk and tax receiver and collector; and Oswald Houston, treasurer. [15]

The year that began with the theft of DeKalb's cannon, courtroom violence and the Snake Nation raid ended with a sensational murder involving one of the county's most prominent families.

John Bird began acquiring land along the South River in the mid-1830s. By 1851, his was possibly the richest plantation owner in the county. John's daughter, Martha, married Dr. Nathaniel G. Hilburn, an Atlanta dentist. In 1849, John Bird purchased a lot at the corner of Decatur and Ivy streets in Atlanta and gave it to his daughter. The Hilburns made their home there.

There was no love lost between Hilburn and his in-laws, particularly Martha's brother, Elijah, and their mother, Mrs. John Bird, whom Hilburn had accused of interfering in his business.

At midday on Monday, December 1, 1851, John Bird and his wife drove from their plantation to the

Hilburn home. Mrs. Bird remained in the carriage, while Mr. Bird went inside. After some two hours, Hilburn stormed out of the house with an axe, threatening to cut off the top of the Bird carriage. He gave the buggy a mighty chop. Mrs. Bird and Hilburn's daughters managed to talk him into surrendering the axe, whereupon Mrs. Bird took the offensive and struck him with his own walking stick. Hilburn's chief adversary, Elijah Bird, arrived at that moment and stabbed Hilburn in the neck with a 50-cent double-blade buckhorn handled pocket knife. Hilburn died a short time later. Elijah Bird was arrested by Atlanta Marshal William McConnell. He was indicted in April of 1852 by a DeKalb grand jury, led by foreman Jonathan B. Wilson. The trial was held one year later, with Judge Edward Young Hill presiding, and Solicitor General M. M. Tidwell prosecuting. Elijah Bird was represented by four of DeKalb County's most prestigious, and expensive, attorneys: William Ezzard, James M. Calhoun, Thomas A. Latham and Charles Murphey. Prominent citizens testified for the prosecution and the defense. A "guilty" verdict was delivered on April 14, 1853.

Sentencing was anxiously awaited by courtroom spectators, as well as citizens all over the county. Jury foreman Henry H. Bolton read the panel's recommendation:

"The defendant, Elijah Bird, having been convicted by a jury of the offense of murder, and he having been called on by the Court to show cause if any he had why the judgment of the law should not be pronounced in said case, and he having failed to show any cause, It is therefore considered, ordered, adjudged and sentenced by the Court, that he the said Elijah Bird be taken from the bar of this Court to the common Jail of said County of DeKalb and there kept in safe and close custody until Friday the tenth day of June next, and that he then be taken from said Jail by the Sheriff of said County or his deputy to a suitable gallows to be erected near and at a convenient place from the Court House in DeKalb County, Georgia, and then and there on said day between the hours of ten o'clock in the forenoon and two o'clock in the afternoon of said day to be hung (sic) by the next to said gallows by the Sheriff of said County, or his deputy until he is dead, dead, dead, and may God have mercy on his soul.
April 21st, 1853."
    M. M. Tidwell
    So. Gen.

The case was appealed all the way to the Supreme Court of Georgia, where Associate Justice Eugenius A. Nisbet affirmed the lower court ruling. DeKalb Superior Court Judge David Irwin again pronounced the death penalty in October, 1853.

A wealthy and well-connected man, John Bird had a bill for his son's pardon introduced in Georgia legislature in November, 1853. The <u>Columbus Times and Sentinel</u> newspaper reported on November 25, 1853:

"House of Representatives
    Milledgeville, Nov. 22.
Afternoon Session
The day was mainly consumed in discussing the bill for the pardon of Elijah Bird. The discussion was opened by Mr. (George K.) Smith of DeKalb, against the bill, in a lucid and impressive address, which commanded the attention of the House. He was replied to by Mr. McDougald, of Muscogee, at great length, in support of the bill. He was ingenious, at times eloquent, and always interesting. The House adjourned after he closed his argument. The case will probably consume the whole of tomorrow. Bird will, in all probability, be pardoned."

The Southern Recorder of Milledgeville ran a short announcement on December 20, 1853:
"Pardon of Elijah Bird
A bill has passed the Legislature pardoning this individual, who was condemned to be hanged for murder. There being a tie, on its passage through the Senate, the President cast a vote in favor of a pardon. The bill is passed."

The pardon of Elijah Bird enraged many DeKalb and Atlanta citizens. The Columbus Times and Sentinel, on January 3, 1854, quoted from The Atlanta Intelligencer:
"Town Meeting -- The citizens of Atlanta and vicinity are requested to meet at Parr's Hall on Friday night, the 23rd inst., to make some expression of public feeling in regard to the pardon of Elijah Bird, and take such other action as may be deemed necessary for the future enforcement of the laws of the land.
Many Citizens."

Whether as a result of public indignation or not, it was made a condition of Elijah Bird's parole that he leave Georgia. He moved to Louisiana where he acquired a plantation. A few years later he was murdered by a hired man who bashed his head in with a hoe. The killer was never caught.

Elijah Bird's death was not the end of the story. John Bird spent all of his wealth defending his son, and sold his plantation to pay his creditors. William H. Sprayberry later purchased the Bird plantation and was living there in 1910.

Some time before his death, Sprayberry had erected for himself in Wesley Chapel Cemetery a large imposing monument with the following inscription:
W. H. Sprayberry
son of Bengman (sic) Sprayberry
was born in N. Car., Feb. 14, 1821
moved to DeKalb Co., Ga. in 1825
reared on this lot of land
first married Martha Price, daughter of Peland Price, June 2, 1842. She departed this life February 17, 1847. Next married M. A. Crane, daughter of James Crane, August 7, 1849.
As you pass me by remember that I
once lived as well as you. This is
to commemorate me for all time to come.

But, Mr. Sprayberry is not buried under the monument. No one is. Mr. Sprayberry and his wife were murdered, victims of drinking poisoned coffee. They are buried in unmarked graves in the Master's Cemetery on Flake's Mill Road in south DeKalb.

No one was ever prosecuted for the murders, although there was a confession. John H. Ozmer, a prominent and wealthy DeKalb man, and Dr. B. F. Sprayberry were indicted for the murder. Sprayberry confessed, later recanted, and then died about six months after the indictment. Charges against Ozmer were dropped in 1911, when DeKalb Superior Court Judge Charles Whitefoord Smith ruled there was not enough evidence for prosecution. Ozmer's attorneys were Supreme Court Justice John S. Candler and Leslie J. Steele, who later would be elected to the U. S. House of Representatives. [16]

The 1851 DeKalb Grand Jury, with Henry Latimer as foreman, dealt with several road worries:

"We present the condition of the road through this county toward Fayetteville as requiring repair; also the road from Atlanta toward Green's Ferry by White Hall; also the road from Atlanta by White Hall to Rough & Ready; also the road in Elijah Donehoo's or Casey District, in which we are informed there are no commissioners. We also present the bridge on Snapfinger Creek near the widow Autry's mills as impassible without danger."

A second grand jury met in March, 1851, under the watchful eye of Foreman Chapman Powell:

"... By our Committees we have examined the new Jail and find it completely ready for the reception of prisoners. 'Tis a safe, substantial building, kept in good order by the Jailor, Mr. Robert Jones. The cement floor in the upper story we find to be a failure and would recommend a substitute to be made for either by plank floor or otherwise. We are unable to find by reference to the records of Court the actual cost of the new Jail, or the receipts and disbursements of the Jail fund. We have been informed that the old Jail building has been sold for twenty five dollars, but find no record of it. We recommend that said proceeds be paid over to the County Treasurer...

"... We find by our Committee the sum of $79.57 for Retail License, which amount has been paid over to the Treasurer. Considerable complaint has been made in regard to selling liquors without license. We hope the grand jury of next week will examine and enquire into this matter particularly. Also ferret out if possible all persons traficking (sic) with slaves in an unlawful manner..." [17]

On November 3, 1851 the DeKalb Inferior Court appointed Robert H. Smith, Starling Goodwin and William Johnston to review "that part of the road known as Power's Ferry Road from where it crosses the old Peachtree Road at L. Arendall's to where it intersects with the Shallowford Road leading to William Johnston's Mill on Peachtree Creek about 4 miles from Decatur -- also that part of the Public Road below Harris Goodwin's between the two last mentioned points by Lemuel Lunceford's." [10] [18]

The concept of a free education for poor children, and ultimately for all children, began to be discussed seriously all over Georgia in the 1850s, with DeKalb participating in the debate. It would be many years before public education became a reality in Georgia. Concerned about the quality of education, the DeKalb Grand Jury, at its September, 1851, term, suggested a competency examination for teachers:

"... We have had under consideration the subject of Education of the Poor, and think it is worthy of more interest than is generally manifested. Our system, we think is defective, and could be greatly remedied by compelling teachers, before they take charge of schools, to appear before trustees appointed for that purpose, and undergo an examination as to their competency to teach. We would therefore respectfully call the attention of the next Legislature to this subject in order that proper laws may be enacted that will correct this great public abuse.

"The youthful mind, from its tenderness and flexibility is too often made susceptible of incorrect

---

[10] Power's Ferry Road from Decatur to ferry included parts of now Roxboro Road and most of Wieuca Road. Laughlin Arendall's house was on or about present northwest intersection of Peachtree and Wieuca. Harris Goodwin's house (called the Solomon Goodwin House) is still standing on Peachtree Road in Brookhaven.

impressions from an injudicious course of instruction, which can alone be remedied by compelling those who attempt to instruct, first to be qualified themselves. We fully concur in opinion with his Honor that the females as well as the males should be educated to feel this importance. We have but to refer to the character and prospect of the rising generation. We all know that children are ignorant and need instruction, and the mother, being the first instructress, how important is it that she should know the parts in which to lead the precious trust committed to her care. Then let the Mothers be educated; let them be enabled to instill into the minds of their offspring, correct notions and virtuous principles, and as a people and a nation we will ever have a proper Safe Guard against foreign damages or internal disturbances..."

Spencer P. Wright, Foreman

Thomas D. Johnson	Joseph Stewart	James Moore
Robert E. Mangum	Jesse J. Jones	William Crowell
James M. Holly	James Robinson	William A. Powell
Berryman D. Shumate	Benjamin F. Shumate	William Goldsberry
Meredith Brown	Samuel Fee	John K. Landers
George K. Hamilton	John N. Swift	Clark R. Waddail. [19]
William C. Parker	Edwin Plaster	
Ebenezer Tilley	David D. Anderson	

DeKalb pioneer Reuben Cone, one of the original commissioners of the town of Decatur, died on April 10, 1851 at the age of 63. He had lived in Decatur 20 years before moving to Atlanta in the mid-1840s. He and his wife, Lucinda Shumate, had one daughter, Harriett, who became the wife of Julius A. Hayden, first president of Atlanta Gas Light Company. Cone donated land for Atlanta's First Baptist and First Presbyterian churches. Atlanta's third mayor, William Buell, a bachelor, also died in 1851. Cone and Buell were both Connecticut natives. [20]

Alexander Johnson became DeKalb's first ordinary on January 27, 1852, in addition to his duties as clerk of the Inferior Court. The new Court of Ordinary (later Probate Court) had been created in 1851 to register wills, grant letters of administration and issue marriage licenses, jobs that previously had been handled by the Inferior Court in each Georgia county.

The DeKalb Grand Jury reported in April of 1852 that the new county jail had cost $6,887.28, $1,387.28 over budget. The grand jury also handed down indictments for "keeping a tippling house open on the Sabbath day," "selling spirituous liquors to negro man slaves" and "selling liquor without a license." [21]

At its October, 1852, session, the grand jury criticized the state legislature for its failure to provide quality public education. The lack of education, combined with the availability of alcoholic beverages, the jurors said, was responsible for the rise in crime in DeKalb and Atlanta:

"We concur with his Honor on the Subject of Education, but regret that we are not able to offer something more worthy of consideration on the subject. We are satisfied, as remarked by his Honor, that the different religious denominations have taken the subject of Education into consideration, and are doing much good in the way of colleges and high schools. We would recommend our Legislature to adopt some general system different from our present, as the amount raised is not sufficient and teachers are not competent. We would recommend a System of free Schools, sustained and supported by the State, in which the rudiments of an Education are thoroughly taught, and the Youth of our Country fitted for the practical duties of life.

"It is a burning shame and disgrace to the Legislature of our State when we come to examine and see from our Census returns, the number of person who cannot read and write. It is truly a reproach, and should not exist. We deem it far better that we be taxed to educate our children, than to support the idle and dissolute in alms houses and prisons, which we deem a natural consequence in the absence of Education.

"As a body we can but deplore the alarming increase of crime in our county, and in casting about for the cause, the conviction is irresistibly forced upon us, from the facts which have been developed by our investigations, that it is attributable mainly to the excessive intemperate use of ardent spirits. Nor indeed is this to be wondered at when we reflect that it deprives man of his reason; influences and excites to action all the grocer (sic) and animal passions of his nature, and thereby fits and qualifies him for the perpetration of the most degrading and atrocious crimes.

"Neither can we hope for any amendment in this particular while this bane of human life and destroyer of human happiness is so abundant and so easy to be obtained. We are therefore of opinion that no plan which has been suggested for the suppression of this evil can be looked to with any hope of success which stops short of an absolute prohibition of the retail of intoxicating drinks.

"We would therefore desire to bring this subject before the public mind, with a view that our fellow citizens would give to it that calm and sober reflection which its importance demands, and determine for themselves whether they are willing to be taxed annually the Enormous sum of fifteen hundred or two thousand dollars for the support of pauper criminals with which our jail is crowded, for the sole benefit of a few licensed retail grocery keepers who are no advantage to the community, and whose business is production of only evil, and that continually.

"We feel satisfied that when this subject is viewed in all its bearings by an intelligent community, that there is but little doubt as to the nature of the verdict which will be pronounced. Therefore, acting under a deep sense of the importance of the subject, and of their high obligations to the community, we cheerfully unite with our fellow jurors of the first week of this Court, and with the Grand Juries of Floyd, Cass, Gwinnett and other counties who have spoken on the subject, in recommending to the next Legislature the passage of such laws, as in their wisdom, will most effectually suppress the retail of intoxicating drinks."

The jurors also urged DeKalb citizens to contribute to the fund to build a monument to President George Washington:

"In accordance with the action of several States of the Union we deem it a debt of gratitude we owe the father of this Country in the perpetuation of his memory, by the erection of the Washington Monument. For the promotion of this great object we recommend that the Managers of Elections at each precinct throughout the County be provided with a small box into which each voter may cast his mite, and that the sum so collected be paid to the County Treasurer and the same be forwarded to the Treasurer of the monument."

                Ludowick Tuggle, Foreman

John C. Harris	James W. Kirkpatrick	Benjamin Crowley
Robert Jones	Alfred J. H. Poole	James W. Crockett

William R. Ayres
Larkin Nash
John McCullough
William A. David
Cammilus A. Haralson
Bartley M. Smith

Alexander Vaughn
Daniel McNeil
Robert M. Clarke
Ebenezer Tilley
Edward D. Wood
Harris Crowley

John N. Swift
Hilliard J. Fowler
William W. Roark
James J. Winn

A few of the jurors apparently felt that it was not the government's place to restrict alcohol consumption:

"We, the undersigned members of the Grand Jury, regret that the evil of intemperance exists in our community, and hope that all good men and worthy citizens will use their influence to suppress same evil by the force of moral example. But believing as we do that any Legislative action on this subject to be improper and impolitic, therefore we beg leave to enter our protest against that portion of the general presentments of this Body."

James W. Crockett
William A. David
Larkin Nash

Robert Jones
John C. Harris

Alfred J. H. Poole. [22]

Jonathan Norcross survived his term as mayor of Atlanta, and was succeeded by Dr. Thomas Fortson Gibbs in 1852. New councilmen were Stephen Terry, Ira O. McDaniel, Jonathan Norcross, William T. Gunby, Leonard C. Simpson and Robert E. Mangum. Former Atlanta Mayor Moses Formwalt was serving as a deputy sheriff in May of 1852, when he was stabbed to death by a prisoner. Formwalt was buried in an unmarked grave in Oakland Cemetery. His grave was moved within the cemetery in 1916, and a monument erected. [23]

The commissioners of roads in east DeKalb found themselves in trouble with the Inferior Court in December of 1852:

"In appearing to the Court that the Public Road leading from Decatur by John W. Fowler's Mill, called the Rock Bridge Road, and also the Road leading from the Rock Bridge Road near Indian Creek Church to Stone Mountain are in such bad condition as to be impassible. It is therefore ordered that the commissioners on said Roads be fined the sum of twenty dollars each for their neglect of duty, unless they cause said Roads to be put in good order within thirty days from this date." [24]

Although several prominent citizens signed on as incorporators of the Atlanta Bank in 1852, the institution lasted only three years. Incorporators were John F. Mims, William Ezzard, E. W. Holland, I. O. McDaniel, Clark Howell, Jonathan Norcross, Benjamin O. Jones, J. A. Hayden, Richard Peters, William M. Butt, L. P. Grant, Ezekiel Mason, James A. Collins, Joseph Winship, Barrington King, Willis P. Menifee, C. W. Arnold, John D. Stell, T. M. Jones, N. L. Angier, J. T. Humphries, Stephen Terry, Joseph Thompson and James Loyd. [25]

DeKalb began to lose some of its pioneer citizens in the early 1850s. Innkeeper Andrew Johnson and William Goldsmith, both of Stone Mountain, died in 1852. Both are buried in a family cemetery on Memorial Drive west of town. James W. Reeve of Cross Keys, owner of north DeKalb's most extensive real estate holdings, died in 1851 or '52. He is buried in Nancy Creek Primitive Baptist Church cemetery.

John Nelson Bellinger, an early member of the DeKalb bar, died during the summer of 1853. Bellinger was a member of the Prospect Methodist Church in the Cross Keys District, and is buried in an unmarked grave in the Prospect cemetery. The Superior Court minutes contained this tribute:

"The `fell destroyer' has again assaulted our ranks. One of our members has fallen beneath his waving shaft. Our Brother, the Hon. John N. Bellinger, is no more. We mourn, but not as those without hope. The Citizens of DeKalb County again and again demanded his services in the State Legislature. That confidence was not misplaced. As a Legislator he was wise and patriotic. For more than twelve years he was a Justice of the Inferior Court. In this office he showed himself capable, honest, impartial and In his death the Masonic Fraternity has lost a Corinthian column of Wisdom, Beauty and Strength. The Methodist Church, of which he was a member for more than twenty years, an humble, faithful, consistent, prayerful, hoping and loving Brother. The Bar an intelligent, well informed, courteous and polite member.

"The Halls of Legislature will again glow with the eloquence of others; the doors of the Hall of the mystic tie will again be thronged with votaries; the Bench will have its incumbent; the banner of the Cross will be sustained by other hands, and the charmed circle of the Coweta
Bar will once again be crowded by brotherly love. But Oh! what can we say to the widow and six orphans? Who will again preside at the family altar, who read the Bible, who train the children? Our tongues are silent. Our hearts swell and pray to the God of the widow and the father of the orphans in their behalf."
                James M. Calhoun,
                John Collier,
                B. H. Overby,
                Charles Murphey,
                Thomas L. Cooper,
                    Committee [26]

John F. Mims was elected mayor of Atlanta on January 17, 1853, but resigned and was succeeded in November by William Markham. Councilmen were Julius A. Hayden, Jonathan Norcross, Leonard C. Simpson, Jared I. Whitaker, William M. Butt, Ira O. McDaniel and Joseph Winship. The new council's first order of business was to hire a chief of police and two constables, who at first only worked at night. E. T. Hunnicutt was named chief, and J. A. Medlin and James M. Lester his two assistant assistants. The city's first board of health in 1853 ordered that slaughter houses be moved outside the city limits, and the city's first hospital opened in July at the fair grounds, in response a smallpox threat. [27]

Edmund W. Holland opened the city's first free public school, offering spelling, reading, writing, arithmetic, geography free, and more advanced higher subjects for a fee. Teacher A. W. Owen was paid by the city council.

The move earned the city praise from the April, 1853, DeKalb Grand Jury, which also made recommendations on jail improvements:

"... We would recommend the Inferior Court to have the apertures in the grates of the windows (of the jail) lessened, as bottles and other articles can be and are drawn or handed up and into the prisoners.

"We feel deeply interested in the morality and prosperity of our young and thriving City of Atlanta, and regard with satisfaction the firm stand taken and maintained by his Honor the Mayor, Council and officers in the administration of the ordinances made for the promotion of morals and good order. We cannot close our presentments without mentioning in terms of commendation the generous public spirit of the City authorities of Atlanta and Mr. E. W. Holland in founding a free school for the education of the poor. We take pleasure in stating that it is in successful operation under the management of Mr. Owen, with from 80 to 100 pupils."

George W. Humphries, Foreman.

Allen E. Johnson	William Goldsberry	Killis Brown
Jesse Wood	John M. Hawkins	William Avery
John F. Bellinger	William Barnett	Eli J. Hulsey
Cicero H. Strong	Richard Owens	Joseph Pitts
Garland D. Black	Benjamin Burdett	Augustus L. Pitts
James Smith	Tunstal B. George	Samuel G. Pegg. [28]
Edward A. Turner	William A. Miller	
Edmund W. Holland	Robert Baxter	

Crime and alcohol abuse continued to worry the grand juries in 1853:

"... When we reflect that this traffic is the most fruitful source of ruin to our slave population, as well as crime among the white population, and lastly that the evil falls most heavily on innocent women and children whose claims and rights to protection are as sacred as any. We find that it is not the retailer or hard drinker, but the sober and temperate classes whose rights are infringed, whose time and money is consumed by this nefarious practice, and that it is they who have a just claim for relief from intolerable burdens as to the free trade contended for by the advocates of liquor, which lays our Fathers and Brothers and children, and sometimes our Mothers and Sisters in the ditch with the brute. We would say deliver us from such and give us that which arises from clear intellects and sober heads, acting as we think we do on the principles of reason and justice. This is the view of the question we would present to the County at large..."

Jonathan Norcross, Foreman

"... We had hoped the time had arrived when the commission of crime would be less frequent, but we must say we are disappointed, that notwithstanding the strong arm of the law, has and is being enforced against all offenders, that crime still stalks abroad. The perpetration of crime are like the plagues sent upon Egypt. When one is removed from jail to be hanged or sent to the penitentiary, there is another ready to step in. Are these things to continue? Is the County of DeKalb to be pointed at from all parts of the State and elsewhere as the county famous for the commission of crime?"

James Paden, Foreman [29]

It seems that DeKalb had just as much trouble keeping its livestock corralled as it did keeping criminals off the streets. The 1853 grand jury criticized justices of the peace:

"... We also find the Estray Books properly kept but regret to find several delinquent Justices of the Peace. There are no returns of the disposition made of the following Estrays: One Bull posted 10th Dec. 1852, before A. P. McColl, J. P.; one mule posted 25th Sept. 1852 before William Goldsberry, J. P.; Cow and calf and one hog posted in 1852, one sow and sow and pigs posted in 1851, and one ox posted in 1850, all before H. Casey, J. P. We desire to call especial attention of the Justices of the Inferior Court to these delinquencies and to urge on them <u>strongly</u> the <u>necessity</u> of <u>adopting prompt measures</u> to <u>correct</u> these evils."

      Ira O. McDaniel, Foreman [30]

Georgia citizens read about the murder of Elisha Tiller by John R. Humphries as far away as Columbus. The city's <u>Tri-Weekly Times and Sentinel</u> reported on January 29, 1853:

"MURDER -- An awful murder was committed in Atlanta on last Friday night 21st inst. by John R. Humphries. It seems, from what we have heard of the case, that Humphries had heard that Elisha Tiller had threatened to kill him. They met on the above mentioned evening at James Kile's grocery, when Humphries asked Tiller if he intended to kill him. He answered that he did not, nor had he anything against him. Humphries then requested him to look towards him, and as he turned to look, he shot him with a double barreled shot gun. Tiller was killed so dead as not even to kick after he fell. Humphries burst the cap of the other barrel at Kile, the grocer, but the gun missed fire."

Humphries was the son of Charner Humpries of White Hall. He was later involved in another murder with his brother, Asa, and others.

Only one murder of a master by a slave was ever reported in DeKalb County. William H. Graham of Stone Mountain, who was blind, was "a notorious Negro trader and had the reputation of being a hard master." Graham's slave, named Frank, was buying his freedom, working at the Atlanta Hotel. Frank fell behind in his payments and was ordered to return to Graham. On the night of June 15, 1853, Frank walked from Atlanta to Stone Mountain along the Georgia railroad tracks. He found Graham asleep at the Diamond home where the slave master boarded. Frank struck the sleeping Graham with an axe handle; Graham died nine days later. Frank confessed his crime, was tried and found guilt on July 13, 1853. He was later hanged, one of only three men ever hung in the history of DeKalb County. [31]

Atlanta in the early 1850s was a bustling place with 57 stores (excluding retail liquor), four large cotton warehouses, a steam flour mill, an iron foundry and machine shop, three carriage and wheelwright shops, two large tanneries and a large shoemaking establishment. [32]

DeKalb County's territory was cut in half on December 20, 1853, when the state legislature passed, and Gov. Herschel V. Johnson approved, a bill creating Fulton County. Atlanta, then a city of 6,000 residents, far more than the city of Decatur, became the county seat. Among those participating in the legislative discussions were DeKalb's state senator, John Collier, an Atlanta resident; and Greenville Henderson of the Browning's district and George K. Smith of Stone Mountain, DeKalb's state representatives.

The boundary of the new county were defined as follows:

"Beginning on the north boundary of Fayette and Henry counties, at a point dividing said counties, running thence due north until it strikes Cobb County, making the line between the 14th, 15th, 17th and 18th districts of the original survey, the line; thence along the line of DeKalb and Cobb, till it strikes Campbell County; thence along the line that divides Campbell from DeKalb county til it strikes

Fayette county; thence along the northern boundary of Fayette County to the starting point." [33]

The act creating Fulton County included the provision "that the County site of DeKalb County shall not be removed, or the public buildings transferred from the town of Decatur, the present County Site of said county, to any other place on account of laying out of said new county, but that the county site of said county, with the public buildings, be, and the same are hereby declared to be permanently and perpetually located at the town of Decatur, the present county site." The stipulation would become key to stopping an attempt to move the county seat from Decatur to Stone Mountain in 1896. [34]

Today's Dunwoody Baptist Church had its roots in the Providence Baptist Church, which was founded in 1853. The first preacher was the Rev. W. G. Aiken, and the first church was built on his land near the present site of the New Hope Cemetery on Chamblee Dunwoody Road. Providence had nine charter members in addition to the Rev. Aiken and his wife: W. M. Johnson, W. C. Johnston, Joseph E. Walker, Samuel Johnson, Elizabeth Johnson, Nancy Johnston, Mary Walker, Harriet Densmore and Mary Reeves. After the Civil War, the church reorganized in a brush arbor in Sandy Springs; a small building was constructed in 1878. In 1886, Providence gave 11 of its members "letters of authority" to start Dunwoody Baptist Church. Among Dunwoody's charter members were Bunyan Cheek and his sisters, Myra Cheek and Lizzie Cheek Newhard. Myra later married Will Martin, and the couple gave land on Chamblee Dunwoody Road in 1903 for a Dunwoody Baptist Church building. [35]

Stone Mountain Methodist Church was organized in 1854. The church's first building was constructed in 1870, and torn down in 1909, with the lumber used to build a parsonage. The present granite building was dedicated in 1926. [36]

A small Baptist church that was destined to become the largest congregation in DeKalb County was constituted on August 5, 1854. The first meeting of Rehoboth Baptist Church was held in the J. B. Johns' schoolhouse, behind the church's current location on Lawrenceville Highway.

John Bolen Johns came to DeKalb from Wilkes County, Ga. in 1823, and began a settlement midway between Decatur and now Tucker. The community originally was called Pea Ridge.

At that first meeting, the Rev. S. B. Churchhill preached and organized a Presbytery composed of the Revs. Samuel Bryant, William H. Roberts and James H. Weaver. Charter members of Rehoboth were Ezekiel Reeves, John Cooper, Zephenia Estes, John Bagwell, Green Woodson, John B. Johns, Isaac Towers, Mary Reeves, Amanda Cooper, Emeline Bagwell, Elizabeth Bagwell and Temperance Towers.

Within one month of organizing, the church had conducted 21 baptisms, including two slaves: Ed, the slave of S. P. Cash; and Samuel, the slave of S. Cochran. Betsy, the slave of S. P. Wright, joined the church by letter. By the end of August, church membership numbered 36.

On October 21, 1854, church trustees John Bagwell, Joe Britt, S. Burdette and Ezekiel Reeves contracted with their host, J. B. Johns, to construct a church building. Johns also was a trustee. The original contract still is owned by the church. It calls for the building to be 40 feet long and 30 feet wide, with four "batten doors," each six and one-half feet high and three and one-half feet broad, 12 side windows and an additional window behind the pulpit. The cost was set at $119. The contract

A singing group from Rehoboth Baptist Church is pictured at the turn of the century. (DeKalb Historical Society)

specified that "the house shall be bilt (sic) in a workmanlike manner." The contracted delivery date was January 1, 1855, but Johns completed the building on December 20, 1854.

Rehoboth's first recorded preacher was the Rev. P. A. Hughes who started in 1857. He was paid $17.50 for the year. Hughes later was pastor at the First Baptist Church of Decatur. The next recorded minutes still in existence showed the Rev. R. T. Ayers as pastor in 1888, with T. E. Chewning clerk. Ayers was succeeded by the Rev. H. F. Buchanan in 1889, the year the congregation moved to a larger building.

Rehoboth was a member of the Stone Mountain Association until 1894, then moved to the new South River Association, which showed the church with a membership of 88 in 1897. The Rev. John B. Spivey was pastor from 1911-1943. Spivey baptized Lester Buice in 1933. Buice grew up in the Rehoboth community and became the church's pastor in 1947.

John B. Jones married Elizabeth Tuggle on December 26, 1799 in Wilkes County. Their descendants still live on a portion of the original Johns property near Rehoboth Baptist Church, in one of the oldest houses in DeKalb County. The family still has the receipt for 81 1/4 cents John Johns paid in taxes on his 202 1/2 acre farm in 1829.

The J. B. Johns School was renamed Rehoboth School in 1854. When a larger school was needed in 1912, J. A. Frazier donated land adjacent to his home at the corner of Lawrenceville Highway and Frazier Road, a short distance south of the first location. He also donated land where the church grew cotton to sell to help meet expenses. Rehoboth School today is still operating in this same location. [37]

A few housekeeping measures were required in 1854 to complete the split between DeKalb band Fulton counties.

The DeKalb Superior Court transferred 28 cases to the new Fulton court. Fifteen of DeKalb's 29 paupers were delivered into Fulton's care. The Fulton Grand Jury met for the first time in April, 1854, and said: "Good faith requires us to pay our proportionate share of the outstanding debts of DeKalb County at the time of the division of said County. We therefore recommend the Justices of the Inferior Court to levy in the usual way, such additional taxes as may be necessary to pay this debt, to build a jail, and to defray other necessary county expenses." [38]

Coincidental with the split of the counties was an apparent drop in the crime rate. The DeKalb Grand Jury of April, 1854, commented:

"We are highly gratified to see such a reformation among the people of DeKalb County. Most all seem to be at peace. Harmony seems to exist. For several years past we have had several presentments each term of the Court. We think there has been less the present term than since DeKalb County was organized. We hope the time is fast approaching when we will have none; that we as good citizens, will be like man to man and Brother to Brother."

John M. Born, Foreman

Thomas J. Dean	Simeon Smith	Seaborn Cochran
William Shepard	John Huey	Thomas L. Robertson
George Lyon	James M. Blackstock	William Crowell
John M. Ridling	John Bryce	Thomas Barnes
George W. Crowley	Edwin A. Center	George K. Hamilton
John Holcomb	Berry Ragsdale	John J. Maxey. [39]
Jonathan Hadden	James F. Stubbs	
John Y. Flowers	James Moore	

The hiatus lasted only through the summer. In September, 1854, two pairs of brothers were involved in an altercation at a church revival. David and George Armistead and Wesley and James Veal were attending the revival at the Rock Chapel Camp Ground near Lithonia. On September 30, 1854, at dusk, Joseph Bond gave out the hymn to be sung, and was leading prayer.

George Armistead was heard to say, "I expect some lady has cut my horse loose." The Veal brothers, who were passing by, said they did not do it. Armistead replied, "I did not say you did it, but you are none too good to do it."

"I could do it if I wanted to," said Wesley Veal. "If you do I'll whip you," Armistead retorted. "Do it if you want to," the Veals challenged.

George Armistead tried to appeal to his brother, David, "Don't let us have any fuss here." Wesley said to his brother, James: "Come along, they are nothing but a pack of damn dogs no how."

Wesley Veal and George Armstead began to fight with sticks. The brothers joined in. David then stabbed James Veal in the stomach; he died the following day.

Both Armistead brothers were indicted by the DeKalb Grand Jury in October, 1854. David Armistead was convicted in April, 1855, and sentenced to hang June 22, 1855. His conviction was later overturned by the Georgia Supreme Court. [40]

The Atlanta Medical College was chartered on February 14, 1854, with trustees L. C. Simpson, Jared I. Whitaker, John Collier, Hubbard W. Cozart, Daniel Hook, John L. Harris, William Herring, Green B. Haygood and James M. Calhoun. [41]

The opening of classes for prospective physicians caused problems in DeKalb County.

"The Atlanta Medical College, later to become part of Emory University Medical School, was started about 1854. Students were expected to furnish their own cadavers for anatomy studies, and had been robbing graves in the city cemeteries until local police were alerted." Members of Prosperity Presbyterian Church placed a lighted lantern on each new grave "every night for two weeks while members of the Session took turns watching the site from inside the small session house." [42]

Former President Millard Fillmore visited with John Pendleton Kennedy, former Secretary of the Navy, in Georgia in May of 1854. They made two stops in DeKalb. The Macon Journal and Messenger reported on May 10, 1854: "At... Stone Mountain and Decatur, numerous bodies of citizens were assembled, who were introduced, as far as time allowed, and exchanged cordial greetings with the ex-president. [43]

Fulton County apparently was slow to fulfill its promise to pay its share of county debts. The DeKalb Grand Jury in April, 1855, recommended:

"We ask our next Legislature to pass an Act compelling the County of Fulton to pay its pro-rata share of the old original debt of DeKalb County by a certain specified time, as we are credibly informed they have made no provision as yet for the payment of said debt."

Reacting to the Elijah Bird case, the 1855 grand jury also recommended that the legislature amend the state constitution in order to restrict its pardoning power.

Daniel Johnson, Foreman

Moses W. Davis	John G. McWilliams	John M. Phillips
James Moore	Asa W. Howard	Joseph Stewart
Ezekiel Reeves	Harris S. Norman	Thomas J. Dean
Berry Ragsdale	William Crowell	William Mosely
John C. Austin	H. J. Fowler	Willis L. Wells
Harris Crowley	William Shepherd	Paschal C. Phillips. [44]
Benjamin F. Veal	James Burns	
Thomas L. Robertson	Starling Goodwin	

By 1856, crime in DeKalb had become almost nonexistent, as witnessed by the October grand jury presentments:

"It is a source of extreme pleasure for us to be able to congratulate our fellow citizens on the almost entire absence of criminal business before our body, as a favorable index to the character of our people as good citizens and law abiding men, loving virtue and despising crime."

J. B. Wilson, Foreman

James Burns	Henry Sherman	James Smith Sr.
John Holcombe	James C. Avary	David M. Shepherd
George Key	John C. Maddox	James R. McAllister
John C. Roe	Alexander Chestnut	James Millican
James W. McClain	William R. Ayers	Spencer P. Wright. [45]
Thomas Thompson	Ebenezer Tilly	
John Y. Flowers	Benjamin Woodson	

The city of Lithonia was chartered by the Georgia General Assembly on March 5, 1856. The Cross Roads settlement, around the intersection of the Lawrenceville-McDonough Road and the Decatur-Augusta Road, had existed for several years, but the community began to grow in 1845 when the Georgia Railroad reached the area. The original city limits extended one-half mile in all directions from the railroad depot. The name, Lithonia, is a combination of two Greek words, "lithos" meaning stone, and "onia" meaning place. The name is said to have been given to the town by a teacher at a one-room schoolhouse who also was a Greek scholar.

Henry George was Lithonia's first mayor. First commissioners were William Pendley, J. H. Rozan, John C. Maddox, William L. Born and John W. Born. Early settlers of the Cross Roads community included the families of Almand, Anderson, Argo, Bond, Born, Braswell, Cagle, Chapman, Chupp, George, Hollingsworth, Marbut, Nash, Norton, Pendley, Phillips, Reagan, Swift and Wesley. Lithonia had 250 inhabitants at the time it was chartered.

A letter from B. M. Johnson in the DeKalb Standard newspaper on May 10, 1901, gives insight into the history of Lithonia:

"Mr. Editor: I noticed a piece in the Standard from Mr. J. S. Mills telling about the great rock quarries round and about Lithonia, so I will name some of the old patriots around Lithonia. I will first mention Dave Longshore, who lived on the east side of town just over the branch, and ran a public blacksmith shop near his house. He did all the work for the people in the country. Dave was a great possum hunter and generally kept the town supplied with possums in the fall of the year. Everybody thought well of Dave, although he kept his books with a piece of charcoal.

And there was Hamp Braswell, who kept a store just below the depot. He sold goods and kept everything straight as a shingle. He kept so busy that he missed his dinner fifty times a year. And then I see Colonel (John N.) Swift setting (sic) over in his veranda, cracking off jokes on everybody that passes by. Everybody liked the Colonel. And there was old Uncle Andy Wells, who for years kept the hotel in town and was a great Sunday school man. He gave a great many talks in Sunday schools and at prayer meetings. Everybody loved Uncle Andy and his wife.

"And there was old Uncle Johnnie (John P.) Marbut, who lived up the railroad and always kept a fine saddle horse. He took great pride in riding his horse down town about once or twice every day. I very often met him down at Dave Longshore's shop, and always liked to hear him talk about his clover patches and grass lots. I could mention many more of the old citizens who lived around Lithonia at that time (circa 1860) and will do so in my next."

The granite industry has always been the backbone of Lithonia's economy. The first quarry opened in 1879, and workmen flocked to the area from Scotland, Wales and Italy. Many, including the Davidson family from Scotland, have been in the Lithonia area for several generations. John Keay Davidson Sr. incorporated Davidson Granite Company in 1919. The company was later owned by his sons: John Keay Davidson Jr., Norton A. Davidson, Charles L. Davidson and Wheeler Davidson.

Granite is as common a building material in Lithonia as wood and brick are in other parts of DeKalb. Granite construction is said to have saved Lithonia from destruction by Union soldiers in 1864. [46]

DeKalb County lost another pioneer, when John Fisher Adair died on April 16, 1856. He was the father of George W. Adair and the Rev. Thomas Owen Adair, two early Atlanta settlers. Born in the Laurens District of South Carolina in 1785, he moved to DeKalb in 1825 from Morgan County, Ga. He settled along the South River, and was a wagon maker by trade. He is buried in a family cemetery in the Panthersville District. [47]

The Georgia General Assembly incorporated the Hannah Moore Female Collegiate Institute on December 22, 1857. Located in Decatur, this first female institution of higher learning in DeKalb was founded by the Rev. John S. Wilson. Its most famous student was Rebecca Latimer Felton, the first female United States senator. [48]

Decatur mourned the passing of Mrs. James H. Kirkpatrick in 1857. She is said to have ridden horseback to Decatur Presbyterian Church, and never missed a Sunday. [49]

Milton County was formed by the Georgia General Assembly on December 18, 1857. Located north of DeKalb, Milton's boundaries were defined as follows:

"Beginning at the (Chattahoochee) river where Fulton and DeKalb counties corner, and running the line between said counties to the ridge or Martin Ferry Road, near the house of James Ball, thence along said road to the ford where said road crosses Crooked Creek, thence down said creek to the Chattahoochee River, the line between Gwinnett and Milton counties; and the territory embraced within said lines shall be hereafter in the County of Milton." [50]

County roads and the county jail occupied the attention of the DeKalb Grand Jury at its October, 1857, term:

"...We find the roads generally in good order, with the exception of the roads in Decatur District leading from Decatur to Stone Mountain, Covington and Fayetteville; also the road leading from the Lawrenceville Road to the old Peachtree Road leading by Henderson's Mill. We especially call the attention of the proper authorities to the same. We have examined the Jail and finding no one therein, are in hopes there will be no further use for it, the same not being a safe one.

"We further recommend to the proper authorities to notice that portion of the road leading from Decatur to Flat Shoals, where it crosses the Rail Road near the Depot, the same being obstructed by wood and otherwise. Also the different Public Roads of this County to be furnished with Mile posts and sign Boards..."

James W. Crockett, Foreman

Samuel C. Clay	William D. Wright	Starling Goodwin
William R. Brandon	James J. Ragan	Floyd F. McAlpin
Asa W. Howard	James F. Stubbs	John Jett
Charles W. McGinnis	Solomon E. Jordan	John G. McWilliams
John M. Ridling	William Mosely	Zachariah R. Jones
William Crowell	Benjamin Crowley	Daniel McNeill. [51]
Robert Baxter	John W. Scruggs, Sec.	
Rufus A. Henderson	Micajah Hamby	

A new law passed by the Georgia General Assembly in 1857 authorized each county's ordinary to require justices of the peace to furnish by January 1 a list, by district, of poor children between the ages of six and 18. The ordinary was authorized to judge the legitimacy of invoices submitted by teachers and whether or not funds were available to pay them.

The DeKalb Grand Jury for the April, 1858 term asked the legislature to require qualifications for teachers and to restrict the amount of free education a child could receive:

"... We also request our Senator and Representative to procure an amendment of the Poor School law passed at the last session of the Legislature, authorizing the Judges of the Inferior Court to appoint a committee of suitable persons whose duty it shall be to examine the qualification of Teachers and grant certificates. And that no Teacher be permitted to draw pay as teachers of Poor Children without such certificate. We further request an amendment that no child participating in such funds be permitted to advance in any branch of study higher than Reading, Writing and Arithmetic through simple Interest..."

Joseph Walker, Foreman

Joseph T. Bond	Robert H. Smith	James M. McAlpin
Samuel House	Albert M. Hairston	David Chupp
William L. Williams	James L. Wilson	John Nash
James J. Winn	Tunstal B George	Russel W. Gaar
Reuben B. Perkins	John G. Snead	William L. Wood. [52]
James M. Smith	Daniel E. Jackson	
Nathan Center	Thomas J. Akins	
Giles F. Humphries	James W. McClain	

Several Georgia counties, including DeKalb, agreed with Gov. Joseph E. Brown that all "free, white" children should have the benefit of taxpayer-funded schools. Although DeKalb began making plans for a public school system in 1858, those plans were interrupted by the Civil War. [53]

Atlanta got its first black professional man in 1859 (much to the distaste of some white Atlanta citizens), with the assistance of Dr. Joshua B. Badger of south DeKalb. Roderick D. Badger was a slave of Dr. Badger, who taught him to do dental work. He was still a slave when he began practicing dentistry in Atlanta. White dentists registered this complaint with the Atlanta City Council on July 15: "We feel aggrieved, as Southern citizens, that your honorable body tolerates a negro dentist in our midst, and in justice to ourselves and the community it ought to be abated. We, the residents of Atlanta, appeal to you for justice."

The city council apparently did not agree with the white dentists. Badger continued to practice in the city until his death in 1891.

Dr. Joshua Badger, a South Carolina native, was a very wealthy man. He built a three-story brick mansion near Wesley Chapel, elegantly furnished with mahogany, crystal and brass. The landscaped grounds featured rose gardens, marble tables and vine-covered summer houses. The doctor was described as a cultured gentleman, with courtly manners and a genial disposition. He died on May 25, 1859 in Florida, leaving a widow and children, then living in Atlanta. [54]

The Literary and Temperance Crusader started printing in Atlanta in January 1859, having moved from Penfield, Ga. John H. Seals was editor, and William G. Whidby, local editor. Mrs. Mary E. Bryan, a resident of the area that would become Clarkston in DeKalb County, was the literary editor. The Temperance Crusader only published a few issues before the Civil War forced its suspension.

The DeKalb Grand Jury, at its October, 1859, session, investigated a variety of subjects:

"We, through a committee have furnished the Court of Ordinary with a list of all the children in our County between the ages of 8 and 18, and have marked all those which in our opinion are entitled to a participation in the poor school fund, as our County has not been surveyed off into school districts.

"Through a committee we have examined the books and vouchers of the County Treasurer, and take pleasure in saying that we find his books correct, and that he has exhibited proper vouchers for all moneys disbursed by him....

"We notice that one of our public wells is in bad condition, and therefore recommend the proper authorities to have said well put in good substantial repair forthwith.

"We notice that a portion of Power's Ferry Road from the fork on Shallowford Road until the Powers Ferry Road intersects the Atlanta road, is in bad repair, and recommend the proper authorities to have it worked out immediately. We recommend that a portion of the Nelson's Ferry Road from some 20 or 3 miles (from Decatur) be worked out as soon as practicable.

"We recommend to those having the care of the Court House rooms keep them in better order so far as ashes and dirt is concerned.

"We are happy to say at the close of this term of our Superior Court that there has been no presentments brought before our body, and that our jail is empty, which speaks well for the morals of our County.

      John McElroy, Foreman

Green B. Clay	E. M. Kittredge	John Carpenter
John M. Born	J. C. Austin	John T. Alford
James J. Winn	Solomon Goodwin	Thomas L. Robertson
E. G. Allen	Nathan Center	Richard Gittens
W. W. Wells	J. B. Walker	James Ball
Harris Crowley	W R. Randon	Bennett H. Tuggle
J. E. George	G. B. Hudson	Seaborn Cochran. [55]
Harris Goodwin		

Chapter 24 Notes

1. 1850 DeKalb County, Ga. census records.

2. Garrett, Franklin M., 1954, 1969, <u>Atlanta and Environs -- A Chronicle of Its People and Events</u>, Vol. 1, pages 304-305. 1850 DeKalb County, Ga. census records.

3. 1850 DeKalb County, Ga. census reports. Garrett, Franklin M., 1954, 1969, <u>Atlanta and Environs -- A Chronicle of Its People and Events</u>, Vol. 1, pages 308-309.

4. Midgette, Gordon, 1979, "Mary Gay, A Brief Sketch of Her Life and Literary Career." Hoehling, A. A., 1958, <u>Last Train From Atlanta</u>, pages 541-543. DeKalb Historical Society files.

5. Hudgins, Carl T., 1952, "Mills and Other Early DeKalb County Industries (and Their Owners)," <u>The Collections of the DeKalb Historical Society</u>, Vol. 1.

6. Garrett, Franklin M., 1954, 1969, <u>Atlanta and Environs -- A Chronicle of Its People and Events</u>, Vol. 1, pages 310.

7. Garrett, Franklin M., 1954, 1969, <u>Atlanta and Environs -- A Chronicle of Its People and Events</u>, Vol. 1, page 311.

8. Clarke, Caroline McKinney, 1973, 1997, <u>The Story of Decatur 1823-1899</u>. Austin, Dr. Wallace M., "Colonel George Washington Scott."

9. Garrett, Franklin M., 1954, 1969, <u>Atlanta and Environs -- A Chronicle of Its People and Events</u>, Vol. 1, page 312.

10. Garrett, Franklin M., 1954, 1969, <u>Atlanta and Environs -- A Chronicle of Its People and Events</u>, Vol. 1, page 317.

11. Garrett, Franklin M., 1954, 1969, <u>Atlanta and Environs -- A Chronicle of Its People and Events</u>, Vol. 1, pages 318-322.

12. Garrett, Franklin M., 1954, 1969, <u>Atlanta and Environs -- A Chronicle of Its People and Events</u>, Vol. 1, page 325.

13. Garrett, Franklin M., 1954, 1969, <u>Atlanta and Environs -- A Chronicle of Its People and Events</u>, Vol. 1, pages 328-329.

14. Garrett, Franklin M., 1954, 1969, <u>Atlanta and Environs -- A Chronicle of Its People and Events</u>, Vol. 1, pages 329-31.

15. Garrett, Franklin M., 1954, 1969, <u>Atlanta and Environs -- A Chronicle of Its People and Events</u>, Vol. 1, page 331.

16. Garrett, Franklin M., 1954, 1969, <u>Atlanta and Environs -- A Chronicle of Its People and Events</u>, Vol. 1, pages 336-337. Potter, Pat, n. d., "Great Plantations, Murder Are Part of South DeKalb's Past." Bird and Sprayberry genealogy files, DeKalb Historical Society.

17. Garrett, Franklin M., 1954, 1969, <u>Atlanta and Environs -- A Chronicle of Its People and Events</u>, Vol. 1, pages 328-329.

18. Garrett, Franklin M., 1954, 1969, <u>Atlanta and Environs -- A Chronicle of Its People and Events</u>, Vol. 1, page 333.

19. Garrett, Franklin M., 1954, 1969, <u>Atlanta and Environs -- A Chronicle of Its People and Events</u>, Vol. 1, page 335.

20. Garrett, Franklin M., 1954, 1969, <u>Atlanta and Environs -- A Chronicle of Its People and Events</u>, Vol. 1, pages 335-336.

21. Garrett, Franklin M., 1954, 1969, <u>Atlanta and Environs -- A Chronicle of Its People and Events</u>, Vol. 1, page 340.

22. Garrett, Franklin M., 1954, 1969, <u>Atlanta and Environs -- A Chronicle of Its People and Events</u>, Vol. 1, pages 341-342.

23. Garrett, Franklin M., 1954, 1969, <u>Atlanta and Environs -- A Chronicle of Its People and Events</u>, Vol. 1, page 342 and 347.

24. Garrett, Franklin M., 1954, 1969, <u>Atlanta and Environs -- A Chronicle of Its People and Events</u>, Vol. 1, page 343.

25. Garrett, Franklin M., 1954, 1969, <u>Atlanta and Environs -- A Chronicle of Its People and Events</u>, Vol. 1, page 347.

26. Garrett, Franklin M., 1954, 1969, <u>Atlanta and Environs -- A Chronicle of Its People and Events</u>, Vol. 1, pages 349 and 360-61. <u>First United Methodist Church, Chamblee, Georgia, 1826-1976</u>, 1976, citing 1919 history written by S. T. McElroy.

27. Garrett, Franklin M., 1954, 1969, <u>Atlanta and Environs -- A Chronicle of Its People and Events</u>, Vol. 1, page 355.

28. Garrett, Franklin M., 1954, 1969, <u>Atlanta and Environs -- A Chronicle of Its People and Events</u>, Vol. 1, page 357.

29. Garrett, Franklin M., 1954, 1969, <u>Atlanta and Environs -- A Chronicle of Its People and Events</u>, Vol. 1, pages 357-358.

30. Garrett, Franklin M., 1954, 1969, <u>Atlanta and Environs -- A Chronicle of Its People and Events</u>, Vol. 1, page 359.

31. Garrett, Franklin M., 1954, 1969, <u>Atlanta and Environs -- A Chronicle of Its People and Events</u>, Vol. 1, page 359.

32. Garrett, Franklin M., 1954, 1969, <u>Atlanta and Environs -- A Chronicle of Its People and Events</u>, Vol. 1, pages 359-360.

33. Garrett, Franklin M., 1954, 1969, <u>Atlanta and Environs -- A Chronicle of Its People and Events</u>, Vol. 1, page 363.

34. Garrett, Franklin M., 1954, 1969, <u>Atlanta and Environs -- A Chronicle of Its People and Events</u>, Vol. 1, pages 361-362.

35. Davis, Elizabeth Lockhart, and Spruill, Ethel Warren, 1975, <u>The Story of Dunwoody</u>, pages 38-39.

36. Nix, Dorothy, personal collection, DeKalb Historical Society.

37. "Centennial Celebration -- Rehoboth Baptist -- 1854-1954. Rehoboth Baptist Church files, DeKalb Historical Society and Georgia Department of Archives and History. Nix, Dorothy, personal collection, DeKalb Historical Society. Johns genealogy file, DeKalb Historical Society.

38. Garrett, Franklin M., 1954, 1969, <u>Atlanta and Environs -- A Chronicle of Its People and Events</u>, Vol. 1, pages 368-369.

39. Garrett, Franklin M., 1954, 1969, <u>Atlanta and Environs -- A Chronicle of Its People and Events</u>, Vol. 1, page 371.

40. Garrett, Franklin M., 1954, 1969, <u>Atlanta and Environs -- A Chronicle of Its People and Events</u>, Vol. 1, pages 371-372.

41. Garrett, Franklin M., 1954, 1969, <u>Atlanta and Environs -- A Chronicle of Its People and Events</u>, Vol. 1, page 376.

42. Miller, Mrs. Flora McElroy, n. d., "History of Doraville Associate Reformed Presbyterian Church."

43. Garrett, Franklin M., 1954, 1969, <u>Atlanta and Environs -- A Chronicle of Its People and Events</u>, Vol. 1, page 376.

44. Garrett, Franklin M., 1954, 1969, <u>Atlanta and Environs -- A Chronicle of Its People and Events</u>, Vol. 1, page 392.

45. Garrett, Franklin M., 1954, 1969, <u>Atlanta and Environs -- A Chronicle of Its People and Events</u>, Vol. 1, page 415.

46. City of Lithonia files, DeKalb Historical Society. Garrett, Franklin M., 1954, 1969, <u>Atlanta and Environs -- A Chronicle of Its People and Events</u>, Vol. 1, page 414.

47. Garrett, Franklin M., 1954, 1969, <u>Atlanta and Environs -- A Chronicle of Its People and Events</u>, Vol. 1, pages 420-421.

48. Candler, Charles Murphey, November 9, 1922, Historical Address. Clarke, Caroline McKinney, 1973, The Story of Decatur 1823-1899.

49. Candler, Charles Murphey, November 9, 1922, Historical Address.

50. Garrett, Franklin M., 1954, 1969, Atlanta and Environs -- A Chronicle of Its People and Events, Vol. 1, page 424.

51. Garrett, Franklin M., 1954, 1969, Atlanta and Environs -- A Chronicle of Its People and Events, Vol. 1, page 430.

52. Garrett, Franklin M., 1954, 1969, Atlanta and Environs -- A Chronicle of Its People and Events, Vol. 1, pages 447.

53. Garrett, Franklin M., 1954, 1969, Atlanta and Environs -- A Chronicle of Its People and Events, Vol. 1, pages 446.

54. Garrett, Franklin M., 1954, 1969, Atlanta and Environs -- A Chronicle of Its People and Events, Vol. 1, pages 453-454.

55. Garrett, Franklin M., 1954, 1969, Atlanta and Environs -- A Chronicle of Its People and Events, Vol. 1, pages 459-460.

Chapter 25

*I*n 1860, at the beginning of the most catastrophic decade in DeKalb County's history, the census showed the county with a total white population of 5854. Census taker James S. Elliott of Cross Keys, an assistant DeKalb County marshall, recorded 2850 white male residents and 3004 white females. The county's white population represented almost 75 percent of its total. By comparison, whites in Fulton, Milton, Campbell and Gwinnett were more than 75 percent of the total population in those counties. Slavery was more prevalent in Clayton, Henry and Newton counties, where whites made up only 50-60 percent of total. The census reported eight free Negroes living in DeKalb: one farmer in Stone Mountain, six in the Panthersville District and one in Decatur, Preston Webb, a horse trainer who lived with the John N. Pate family. [1]

Atlanta had rapidly overtaken DeKalb in population. The city had 7741 residents in 1860. Fulton County had more than double the number of people of DeKalb, with 11,572. [2]

The 1860 census was poorer for its lack of several members of one valuable DeKalb County family. A wagon train made up of almost all of the Diamond family left Stone Mountain for Texas in 1858. Six of the children of pioneer settler James Diamond, along with their spouses and children, moved in 1858. State Rep. James J. Diamond resigned his House seat the following year and left for Texas, along with another brother, William Winfield (Will) Diamond and his family. Only Rebecca Diamond, wife of Young Marbut and later Euclidus (Clide) Marbut, and Franklin Diamond remained in Georgia, having moved to Floyd County.

The next few years would not be kind to the Diamond family, in Texas or in Georgia. Within five years after the Civil War, 25 members of the Diamond family would be dead -- many of them from the Yellow Fever epidemic in Houston, Texas in 1867. Among the Texas dead was Nancy Cornwell Diamond, widow of James Diamond who had died in DeKalb in 1849. The few survivors scattered, some staying in Texas, some returning to Georgia and some settling in Alabama. None of James Diamond's descendants ever again lived in DeKalb County. [3]

In October, 1860, Charles Latimer was reprimanded by the DeKalb Grand Jury over his maintenance of a South River crossing:

"... We recommend that the Inferior Court require Charles Latimer to build a new bridge across South River at Flat Shoals in this county, or remove the obstructions out of the ford at that place, or enforce the laws against him, the said Latimer, in case of failure to remove said obstructions..."

    Robert McWilliams, Foreman

	William R. Pendley	John K. McCarter
Leonard Sims	J. I. Whitlow	J. L. Morris
Harris Goodwin	Killis Brown	Seaborn Crowley
W. A. Shields	J. M. Evans	Augustus L. Pitts
James Moore	Ebenezer Tilley	J. W. F. Tilley
Benjamin Burdett	Laban Sturgess	Jabez Lord. [4]
J. L. Kilgore	William McElroy	
David Chupp	Michael A. Steele	

Marcus Aurelius Bell and his wife, Mary Jane Hulsey, completed construction of one of Atlanta's most unusual houses in 1860. Calico House, located at the corner of Wheat and Collins streets (now Auburn Avenue and Courtland Street) was three stories tall and cost $25,000, an enormous sum for those days. It contained 12 rooms, each 22 feet square. The exterior of house was covered with a thin coating of plaster, "marbleized" with pastel blue, yellow and red paint.

During the Civil War, Calico House was used as a hospital and headquarters for supply distribution and storage for the Confederate Army. Asa G. Candler bought the house in 1904 for $17,500, and made it the first home of Wesley Memorial, now Emory University Hospital. The hospital moved to the Emory University campus in December, 1922. Mary Jane Hulsey was the daughter of one south DeKalb pioneer, Jennings Hulsey, and the granddaughter of another, Merrill Collier. [5]

Two mills of note opened in north DeKalb County in 1860. Jabez M. Loyd built his grist mill on Little Peachtree Creek in what is now Chamblee. Little Peachtree Creek once ran along the portion of Chamblee Tucker Road that was known as Carroll Avenue. The mill closed when Loyd died in 1890. Dr. C. C. Hart, who lived on Peachtree Road in the Brookhaven community built a corn mill on Nancy Creek near the current intersection of Harts Mill and Ashford Dunwoody roads. Harts Mill also closed upon Dr. Hart's death in 1890. [6]

Lithonia Methodist Church was the only church organized in DeKalb in 1860. The congregation first met on October 14 in a small building on Church Street near the home of Mrs. J. J. (Margaret) Summers. The church's present building was built in 1910, designed by John Parks Almand. [7]

Tension over growing animosities between the North and South continued to keep DeKalb County citizens on edge through the year of 1860. Anxiety increased with the election of Abraham Lincoln as president in November, and the secession of South Carolina from the Union on December 20.

Locally, elections were held on January 2, 1861 to choose delegates to a Georgia Secession Convention. Fulton County citizens chose secession candidates. After a "lively contest," DeKalb chose two union candidates: Charles Murphey of Decatur and George K. Smith of Stone Mountain, both of whom were lawyers by trade.

"From its organization DeKalb had always been a Union County, that is, its people supported all measures and leaders favorable to the preservation of the Union under the Constitution and opposition to secession and disruption as not demanded by then existing political conditions. A majority of its citizens favored further efforts, before secession, to end sectional prejudice and bring about a peaceful solution of the grave problems confronting the Union and the States." [8]

A slight earthquake felt in DeKalb on January 3, 1861 was seen by some as an omen of the man-made cataclysm to come.

Georgia's Secession Convention opened on January 16, 1861, in Milledgeville, without one of DeKalb's delegates. Charles Murphey, who had said he hoped he died before he ever saw the state secede, did die of pneumonia on opening day. In his 1922 Historical Address, Charles Murphey Candler, grandson of Charles Murphey, said, "His prayer had been answered." A special election to replace Murphey was won by Dr. Peter F. Hoyle, a Decatur physician. Hoyle took his seat in Milledgeville on January 25, after the votes had been taken. [9]

Piromis Hulsey Bell, son of Marcus Aurelius Bell and Mary Jane Hulsey, was born on March 19, 1858 at Calico House. This photo was taken on Christmas Day, 1864. (DeKalb Historical Society)

The initial resolution to secede was adopted by a close vote, 166 to 130. An ordinance of secession was then written by a convention committee and approved by a vote of 208-89, with 44 delegates yielding to the inevitable. DeKalb's only delegate voted against both the resolution and the ordinance. All the delegates, including Hoyle, were "required to sign the ordinance as a pledge of united determination." Six signed under protest. Georgia was the fourth of 11 states to secede. [10]

Peter Hoyle went home to be sworn in as a Inferior Court justice. [11] Dr. W. C. Daniel left Decatur for Kentucky, as a commissioner appointed by the secession convention to urge Kentucky to secede. Daniel's mission was unsuccessful; Kentucky remained a border state. [12]

The news from Milledgeville of Georgia's secession spread quickly to DeKalb by way of the telegraph. "Guns were fired and orators spoke in burning words. The die was cast for war." [13] "DeKalb men, union and secession, alike, promptly responded to their state's call for volunteers. Secession declared, they were as one in defense of her rights." [14]

Edward L. Morton soon raised the first Confederate flag in DeKalb, atop a poplar tree near Williams's Mill on Peachtree Creek a few miles from Decatur. The flag had been made by Mrs. Morton, Mrs. James Hunter and other ladies of the community. During the occupation of Decatur in 1864, the Morton family would care for a dying Union soldier. Upon his death, they sent to his family in Ohio a lock of his hair and some verses written by one of the Morton daughters. In return for the family's kindness, a Union guard was stationed at the Morton home during the worst of the fight in Decatur. In yet another ironic turn of events of the Morton family, Union soldiers later accused one daughter of providing information that resulted in the capture of a wagon train. The Mortons moved to Mississippi. A popular local story tells the fate of the flag, although through the course of time, the poplar tree became a willow tree. The story goes that the tree had grown from a willow riding switch that belonged to Leslie J. Steele's grandmother. She had stuck the switch into the ground when she came to DeKalb in about 1823. The Confederate flag stayed in tree, "frazzled and weather-beaten" until Sherman came, and the Yankees cut down the tree in order to destroy the flag. Thirteen sprouts are said to have grown from the stump of the tree. [15]

The DeKalb Grand Jury met in April, 1861, apparently after April 12, when shots were fired at Fort Sumter, S. C., starting the Civil War. The jury gave brief attention to roads and the jail, and called county citizens to arms:

"We are happy to say no prisoners are now confined in our County Jail, and that our public roads are in tolerably good condition...

"In view of the present war which has been forced upon us, we urge upon our citizens the propriety of a thorough organization of the militia. We recommend that all persons having the good of their country at heart, to organize themselves in companies and vigilant committees and arm themselves the best they can to meet the emergencies that may come..."

Zachariah R. Jones, Foreman

Ezekiel Reeve	J. T. Alford	E. A. Turner
Robert Cagle	J. T. Willingham	A. J. H. Poole
William Moseley	J. M. Hambrick	James B. Robertson
S. E. Brown	Simeon Smith	James H. Born, Clerk
Nelson Anderson	Ichabod Williams	George Key
A. T. Fowler	L. B. Underwood	P. H. Hightower. [16]
J. C. Austin	J. H. Young	
Jacob Chupp	E. A. Center	

Men all over the county began to form themselves into military companies, inspired by the popular new song, "Dixie."

"It is marvelous with what wild-fire rapidity this tune of `Dixie' has spread over the whole South... it now bids fair to become the musical symbol of a new nationality, and we shall be fortunate if it does not impose its very name on our country," wrote Henry Hotze, a Confederate propaganda agent in London, on May 5, 1861. "Dixie" had been written in April of 1859, by a Northerner, Daniel Decatur Emmett, for Bryant's Minstrels. The tune originally was an advertising ditty, a "hooray song" that could be sung through streets to advertise the minstrel show. [17]

Minutes of Pythagoras Lodge No. 41 on May 11, 1861, recorded a resolution: "that we give to the brethren who join during the war and go into active service with the present company now about to leave, the amount of $20." [18]

The first volunteers from Decatur were James L. George, Hardy Randall, L. J. Winn and Beattie Wilson who joined the Atlanta Grays (Co. F of the 8th Regiment, Georgia Volunteer Infantry) in May of 1861. J. M. C. Hulsey was first sergeant of this company, and William A. Powell, son of Chapman Powell, was fourth sergeant.

The DeKalb Light Infantry, Co. E of the 7th Regiment, Georgia Volunteer Infantry, was the first company to leave DeKalb, mustered into service in Atlanta. Under Captain John W. Fowler, the company left for Virginia on June 1, 1861. Members of the company wore uniforms handmade by the women of Decatur, led by Mrs. Jonathan B. Wilson, Mrs. Jane Morgan, Mrs. Ezekiel Mason, Mrs. Levi Willard, Anna Davis, Mrs. James McCulloch and Lou Fowler. The home of Ezekiel Mason on the north side of the square was headquarters for the seamstresses. The company marched and fought under a silk banner also made by women in Decatur. Mollie G. Brown gave the address at the banner presentation ceremony. [19]

The second company from DeKalb, the Stephens Rifles, became a part of Cobb's Legion in August of 1861. L. J. Glenn was the captain. Frank Herron, Norman Adams, John McCulloch, John J. McKoy and others from Decatur were in this company.

DeKalb delegate Charles Murphey died on opening day of the Georgia Secession Convention on January 16, 1861. (The Story of Decatur)

Co. A of the 38th Regiment was organized by Captain John Y. Fowler in north DeKalb, and named the Murphey Guards in memory of Charles Murphey, the secession convention delegate who died on opening day of the session. The Murphey Guards were the third company to leave DeKalb. Their uniforms were provided by people in the county, with a large share contributed by Mr. and Mrs. Milton A. Candler, Mr. and Mrs. Ezekiel Mason. Eliza Murphey Candler, only child of Charles Murphey, gave the banner inscribed, "The God of Jacob is with us."

DeKalb's fourth company was the Bartow Avengers, Co. K of the 38th Regiment, Georgia Volunteer Infantry. William Wright was captain of this company from the South River area of the county. Missouri Stokes presented a banner to this company in September of 1861. This company would sustain the highest number of casualties of any DeKalb company in the war. Of the 118 members, 46 were killed, including three captains.

The McCullough Rifles, Co. D of the 38th Regiment, Georgia Volunteer Infantry, was the fifth company to leave DeKalb. John G. Rankin was captain of this company from Stone Mountain.

E. L. Morton was captain of DeKalb's 6th company, Co. F of the 36th Regiment, Georgia Volunteer Infantry. The seventh company to leave DeKalb was Co. D of the 42nd Regiment, Georgia Volunteer

Infantry, the Fowler Guards. Nathan Clay was captain. They left DeKalb under a banner made by Anna E. Davis and presented by Georgia Hoyle.

Several companies were organized at a "camp of instruction" near Decatur.[11] Moses L. Brown was captain of Co. E of the 66th Regiment, Georgia Volunteer Infantry. L. D. Belisle was captain of Co. H of the 66th Regiment. In addition, many soldiers from DeKalb enlisted in other towns, wherever they happened to be when war was declared. Dr. James J. Winn joined the Barker Greys in Clayton, Ala. Winn later became the youngest surgeon in the army. John C. Kirkpatrick enlisted in the Oglethorpe Infantry, along with his cousin, William Dabney, and his friend, Frank Stone. Others who enlisted outside Decatur included John B. Swanton, Henry, Daniel and Joseph Morgan, Jesse Chewning and Samuel Mann. Still others enlisted in the cavalry and artillery service in the regular army.

Those who were physically unable to fight often were assigned to other jobs. Because he was nearsighted, Josiah Willard, only son of Levi Willard, was assigned to the commissary department at Camp Randolph near Decatur. He later moved with the department to Macon, where he stayed until the surrender.

In 1863, Georgia raised companies of troops called State Guards to defend the state in the event of invasion. Milton A. Candler was captain of Co. A of the 10th Cavalry Regiment of the Georgia State Guards. Paul P. Winn, then 18 years old, joined the 45th Georgia Regiment in April, 1863.[20]

DeKalb was jubilant in July of 1861. The Confederate Army had won the First Battle of Manassas, and most were certain that the South would make short work of defeating the Union army. DeKalb lost three of its sons as a result of the fighting in Virginia. Sgt. James S. (Jimmie) George of the Atlanta Grays (8th Georgia Regiment) was a young lawyer practicing in Atlanta before enlistment. Lt. Bartley M. Smith, also of the Atlanta Grays, the son of Simeon Smith, was a promising physician who had married the eldest daughter of William Ezzard. Billy Morgan was wounded at Manassas and died soon after; his brother, DeWitt Morgan, was killed during the battle of Vicksburg, Miss.[21]

Green J. Foreacre, an Atlanta realtor and railroad man, who had come to DeKalb in the early 1850s. After his return from the battlefield, he was assigned by the Confederate government to supervise the recently built Sugar Creek Paper Mills in south DeKalb. He built a home on nearby McDonough (now Bouldercrest) Road. The Sugar Creek mill was built by William McNaught, James Ormond, Thomas Scrutchins and Thomas F. Scully. Ormond later built another mill on Entrenchment Creek, called the Atlanta Paper Mill. The name was changed to Glendale Paper Mill with new ownership. A second mill was built on Sugar Creek, with both being run by William McNaught and later Thomas Scully. All three had ceased operation by 1900.[22]

Just as there were heroes on the battlefield, there were those back home who performed heroic deeds.

---

[11] The exact location of the recruit camp, called Camp Randolph, is disputed. Some sources place it on the north side of the Georgia Railroad, on or near the Kirkpatrick property; it is also said to have been where the Sears store on Ponce de Leon Avenue in Atlanta later stood. (Sources: Garrett, Franklin M., 1954, 1969, <u>Atlanta and Environs -- A Chronicle of Its People and Events</u>, Vol. 1, page 552. Gay, Mary A. H., 1879, 1979, <u>Life In Dixie During The War</u>.

Decatur postmaster, William Bradbury enlisted in the DeKalb Light Infantry in 1861, leaving his job to Hiram J. Williams, age 14, who was said to be "small for his age and quiet in temperament." The quantity of mail during the war years was enormous, but Hiram carried on his job with "unwearied attention to the business before him, unvarying courtesy, beautiful modesty, calm unbroken serenity of manner, and an unswerving honesty."

Decatur's depot agent, John N. Pate, was appointed postmaster in 1862, but his only contribution to the delivery effort was to carry the bundles of mail from the depot to Hiram at the post office on the square. During the war there were few functioning post offices. People just sent their mail to Decatur, and expected it to be delivered. Soldiers, "unless writing to young ladies," rarely put postage on their mail. Postage had to be collected from the recipients, and accounted for on post office reports. Hiram also answered letters for people whose writing skills were less than acceptable. Sometimes Hiram got help from his teenaged friend, John Bowie.

The post office closed for several months during the Union occupation of Decatur in the summer of 1864. After the war, Hiram went into the mercantile business with Willard and McKoy, then opened his own store. He finally got the official nod for the postmaster's job in 1867, and served until 1880. He also served as clerk of the Superior Court from 1869 until 1884. He later worked for the G. W. Scott Manufacturing Company. Hiram became a deacon of Decatur Presbyterian Church and secretary-treasurer of the Agnes Scott Institute. He was married twice, to Jennie Hugh and Belle Steward, and lived on Sycamore Street. [23]

Mary Ann Harris Gay (1829-1918) was Decatur's heroine of the Civil War, providing supplies for Confederate soldiers and helping her neighbors survive the town's occupation by Union soldiers. After the war, she raised funds for the construction of the Decatur Baptist Church. (DeKalb Historical Society)

Mary Gay, one of the many DeKalb women who supported the war effort, "became a veritable knitting machine... At the midnight hour the weird click of knitting needles chasing each other round and round in the formation of these useful garments for the nether limbs of `our boys,' was no unusual sound; and tears and orisons blended with woof and warp and melancholy sighs." Mary would make a dozen pair, then sent them to their destinations, one pair to a package. With each pair went a necktie, gloves and a handkerchief, in addition to a letter, with encouragement to the soldier to respond. Twelve packages went into a bundle, addressed to an officer who was asked to distribute them.

Mary wrote letters to soldiers she had never met "for their spiritual edification, their mental improvement and their amusement." Her letters always included short poems and sayings:

Love thy neighbor as thyself.
If in the early morn of life,
You give yourself to God,
He'll stand by you 'mid earthly strife,
And spare the chast'ning rod.

P. S. Roses are red and violets are blue,
Sugar is sweet and so are you. -- M.

May ever joy that earth can give
Around thee brightly shine;
Remote from sorrow may you live,
And all of heaven be thine.

P. S. -- Remember me when this you see,
Though many miles apart we be. -- M.

Remember now thy Creator in the days of thy youth.
Love worketh no ill to his neighbor; therefore love is the fulfillment of the law.

This above all -- to thine own self be true,
And it must follow as night the day,
Thou canst not then be false to any one.

P. S. -- Sure as the vine twines round the stump,
You are my darling sugar lump. -- M.

Blessed are the peacemakers; for they shall be called the children of God.

The harp that once through Tara's halls
The soul of music shed
Now hangs as mute on Tara's wall,
As if that soul were fled.
So sleeps the pride of former days,
So glory's thrill is o'er;
And hearts that once beat high for praise
Now feel that pulse no more
No more to chiefs and ladies bright
The harp of Tara swells;
The chord alone that breaks at night
Its tale of ruin tells.
Thus Freedom, now so seldom wakes,
the only throb she gives
Is when some heart indignant breaks
To show that still she lives.

P. S. -- My love for you will ever flow,
Like water down a cotton row. -- M. [24]

With ports blockaded and the Confederacy ill equipped to produce munitions on an adequate scale, Georgia Gov. Joseph E. Brown concocted the idea of arming Confederate soldiers with pikes. Atlanta's railroad shops were equipped to make the blades -- 16 inches long with three-inch spurs on each side -- but had no machinery to turn the staffs. J. C. Peck of Decatur was the only craftsman who agreed to try and make the six-foot rods. His planing mill on Decatur Street in Atlanta turned out 10,000 pike handles in 1861. [25]

In early August of 1861, the attention of DeKalb citizens was turned from the war to a shocking murder at home. Thomas Terry, a popular southwest DeKalb grist and sawmill owner, was murdered in broad daylight near the corner of Bell and Decatur streets in Atlanta. Terry's Mill was located on Sugar Creek in what is now East Atlanta, south of Glenwood Avenue, near Sylvester Church. Tom Terry's mother, Eleanor Terry Simmons, had inherited the property from her second husband, Thomas Simmons, who died in 1842. Eleanor, a nurse by profession, had met Simmons while caring for his ailing first wife, who later died.

In 1859 Terry hired Walton (Watt) Wilson to work for him at the mill, and gave him a house nearby for the duration of his employment. Walton enlisted in Captain G. T. Foreacre's 7th Georgia Regiment, and was sent to Virginia. His wife and children continued to live in the house Terry had provided. Wilson had many relatives in the area, including an uncle named John, and a cousin, James, who lived in the Reynoldstown section of Atlanta. James had sent his children to a school taught by Terry's sister, but had refused to pay the tuition. When Terry tried to get James Wilson to pay, Wilson became infuriated and threatened Terry with a gun. The Wilsons' feud with Tom Terry simmered, with the Wilsons trying unsuccessfully to draw Walton Wilson's wife and children into the fray. John and James Wilson, father and son, began to haunt Flat Shoals Road and Decatur Street, hoping to meet Terry and take what they proudly called their revenge. They were not secretive about it; soon it was the talk of Atlanta.

On Saturday morning, August 3, 1861 Terry planted potato slips in the morning at his DeKalb County farm before riding his mule into Atlanta. On Flat Shoals Road, he stopped to see his sister, Nancy (Mrs. James Brown), who warned him that the Wilsons were gunning for him.

Tom went ahead to Five Points, and stopped at the shop of bootmaker W. A. Kennedy with a stirrup, the strap of which he needed to have repaired. Kennedy happily shared a letter he had just received from his son who had survived the Battle of Manassas. Back on the street, Terry was met with a blow above the right eye from the fist of John Wilson. Terry tried to retaliate by swinging the stirrup. James Wilson then hit Terry on the left side of the head with a liquor bottle. Terry fell to the ground, and John rained blows to Terry's face. Kennedy tried to break it up, while a bystander went for the doctor. Dr. Joshua Gilbert was hampered in trying to minster to Terry by rocks thrown by yet another member of the Wilson clan. Gilbert subdued the new assailant with a solid punch and a boot on his neck. Two more doctors, Solomon S. Beach and H. W. Brown, arrived, but Terry's skull had been fractured. He was placed on a mattress on Kennedy's porch and died at 2:15 a.m. on August 4. His last words were "I want to go home."

The three Wilsons were held in the Fulton County jail until a preliminary hearing could be held. "The absence of all reasonable motive or extenuating circumstance -- the presence of nothing but brutal stupidity and savagery, so aroused the citizenry of the town, that, but for sane and persuasive counsel from the law-abiding element, a lynching was narrowly averted."

The trial was held on October 12, 1861 in Atlanta. John Wilson was found guilty of manslaughter sentenced to three years in the state penitentiary. James Wilson was convicted of murder and sentenced to hang on December 13, 1861. The case was appealed, the appeal denied and James resentenced to hang on June 6, 1862.

But James Wilson was never hanged. He was still in prison in Milledgeville in 1864 when Gov. Joe Brown ordered all prisoners be inducted into the state militia. Not surprisingly, Wilson disappeared.

Thomas Terry died a few weeks short of his 38th birthday. He was buried in the Sylvester Church cemetery. His wife died on September 4, 1903, and was buried beside her husband. [26]

The Rev. Isaiah Parker, the prominent Primitive Baptist Church preacher, also died in 1861, and was buried in an unmarked grave in Fellowship Primitive Baptist Church cemetery. The Rev. Isaac Rosser, a Methodist minister, also died in 1861, at the age of 80, just four months after he had married his second wife. DeKalb lost three other pioneer citizens in 1861. A native of Ireland, John McCullough had lived in Decatur for 30 years. Lochlin Johnson, who had been instrumental in the county's early growth, died on July 17. Oswald Houston, city treasurer and father of DeKalb's Washington Jackson Houston, died on June 11, 1861.

In October of 1861, the DeKalb Grand Jury sought help from the state legislature to stop wartime speculators who charged exorbitant prices for necessary goods:

"In view of the present condition of our Country, the result of the unnatural and placable war waged against us by the North, the scarcity of money, and the enormous high price of the necessaries of life produced by the closing of usual channels of trade, a large class of our community must necessarily suffer for many things which are essential to their comfort and welfare in life. And while this state of things has been brought upon us to a great extent by enemies without, still we regret to say it has been considerably enhanced by enemies within. We mean those capitalists who are using their means to speculate and reap immense profits upon the necessaries of life. And we earnestly hope that our Legislature, now shortly to meet, will take this subject in hand and check so far as it can, this spirit of speculation, which is so rife in our suffering Country."
Moses W. Davis, Foreman [27]

The DeKalb County elections of 1862 produced a county first. At the age of 35, James Oliver Powell, second son of DeKalb's pioneer physician Chapman Powell, was elected sheriff and clerk of the Inferior Court. It was the first time someone held two county offices simultaneously.

With the worst of the war yet to come, the county's fund for needy families of soldiers was already almost empty. The April 1862 grand jury addressed the problem:

"... Fund for the benefit of Soldiers' families about exhausted...

"We recommend the Inferior Court to take the present Grand Jury fund and make it a part and parcel

Photo above shows a boyish Elijah Henry Clarke in 1862. Photo at right was taken just three years later. (Donald S. Clarke; Vanishing Georgia Collection, Georgia Department of Archives and History)

Elijah Henry Clarke, son of the Rev. William Henry Clarke enlisted in Co. D of the 42nd Regiment in 1862 at the age of 27. He was captured at Vicksburg in 1863, later released, and served until the end of the war. (Donald S. Clarke)

of the fund for the support of indigent soldiers' families, and recommend the raising of no Grand Jury Fund for the future, till the present war is ended. We also recommend the Inferior Court to levy such a

tax upon the State Tax, as they in their judgment think will be sufficient for the various County purposes. No poor school fund is recommended. We further recommend the Inferior Court to levy such a tax upon the State as will be sufficient to raise the sun of $3000 for the benefit of the indigent soldiers' families of this County for the present year.

"We would call the attention of the proper authorities to the very bad condition of the public roads in the County. We do not expect them to be well worked under the present circumstances, but think they should be kept passable. We are opposed to the Inferior Court paying physicians' bills out of the fund raised for the use of Soldiers' families..."

John W. Fowler, Foreman [28]

By early in 1862 Atlanta was already a hospital and relief center for Confederate soldiers, as well as a transportation hub, military command post and the site of many industries producing war materials.

Private shops made a variety of products, including buttons, belt buckles, spurs, saddlery, canteens, tents, railroad cars, revolvers, bowie knives, cannon, gun carriages and cartridges for the Confederacy. The Atlanta Rolling Mill made metal plates to cover gunboats for the Confederate Navy. The Confederate Army's Quartermaster's Department was located in Atlanta, making tents and clothing. Atlanta's railroads transported supplies, as well as soldiers -- living, wounded and dead.

By the spring of 1862 every daily paper in Atlanta carried on its front page, under the heading "The Dead," a list of soldiers who had died at Atlanta hospitals. Women from miles around traveled to the city to care for the sick, and to distribute clothing and food. [29]

DeKalb County women cooked biscuits and chicken and took baskets of food, coffee and blackberry wine to the Fair Ground and Empire hospitals. Toby, one of the Stokes family servants, brought water and bathed wounded soldiers. Mary Gay recalled her experience of trying to locate a Catholic priest for a soldier who was dying. The soldier already had paid others to find a priest, but they had taken his money and never returned. Mary went to the Catholic parsonage on Hunter Street. The priest told her he would not come before he had eaten and napped. Mary later wrote that she told him, "O, sir, you don't realize the importance of haste. Please let me remain in your sitting room until you have eaten your luncheon, and then I know you will go with me." The priest went with Mary and heard the soldier's last confession. He died the next day. [30]

The pressure to enlist on men in the area who had not already volunteered to fight was increased through a notice from D. C. Smith, Enrolling Officer for the Eighth Congressional District: "I hereby, in most solemn and emphatic manner, warn all delinquents and skulkers of their peril in attempting to evade the high and overruling obligation of coming up to their duty on this occasion..." [31]

Some in DeKalb, however, were not enthusiastic about joining the Confederate Army.

At a Civil War claims hearing on February 27, 1878 at the home of Ambrose Chewning near Tucker, George Washington Cash, then 77, testified: "I had been on the Union side all the time, never any other way. I was opposed to the Confederacy and did what I was allowed to do against the war. I voted against secession. I went with the U. S., but not with Georgia... My son, James Ellis Cash, was also a Union man...

"My son, James Ellis Cash, was in the Confederate Army, drafted. He was over 36 years old when he entered the army. I advised him to keep out till he was obliged to go and he did. I contributed nothing to his outfit or support while he was in the service...

"I harbored men to keep them out of the Rebel Service. One was my son and the other was my son-in-law (Oliver P. Cash). I kept them out in this way some time, from the time the army came in to the time they left Atlanta. The time I was doing this, the Rebels were raiding and taking all they could get and killing people who would not go. They shot at Randolph Payton because he would not go about this time."

James Cash testified: "I was conscripted August 12, 1862... I stayed on duty at Calhoun, Ga. and when we moved to Decatur. I stayed on duty until just before the Yankees came. I came home and didn't go back. My father told me not to go back, and that he would help keep me out of the way, so I did hide out and at the same time was doing the same with Oliver P. Cash, his son-in-law, who was with me. My father would go out during the day and hear what he could and come to where we were and let us know at night. He said he did not want us to fight the Yankees because the Union should not be broken up, that it would ruin the country. Those conversations were when we were hiding out. My father helped no others except his kinfolks that I know of."

Payton corroborated George Cash's testimony: "He (George Cash) talked very much against secession and lamented the war and said that he was mighty sorry for it, that it was breaking up the country. Always he talked and advocated the Union cause throughout the war. We had a few Union men here and among them he was thought to be a loyal man to the Union cause. I was in danger from the Rebels when I talked with him, and there ain't the shadow of a doubt but that they would have put us to death if they could have caught us. I never had no conversation with him in the presence of Rebels. Union men could not talk publicly about here during the war. John and Joel Morris both Union men up above here 4 or 5 miles were killed on account of their talk against the Rebels."

In the Tucker community, John B. Johns, Ambrose Chewning, Abram Benino and Billy Johnson also were Union men. Johns testified that he had visited a camp where local Union men hid, in order to avoid entering the Confederate Army. [32]

If the war had been seen as a gallant adventure in 1861, death brought grim reality home in 1862. DeKalb County lost at least 28 young men from a single company that year. Co. K of the 38th Georgia served for the entire length of the war, losing almost 40 percent of its original members to fighting or disease. Following Co. K through the war, the folks back home were learning a gruesome geography lesson through battle sites: Cold Harbor, Malvern Hill, Second Manassas, Sharpsburg, Fredericksburg, Chancellorsville, Winchester, Gettysburg, The Wilderness, Spottsylvania Courthouse, Mechanicsville, Fisher's Hill, Cedar Creek, Louise Courthouse, High Bridge. Nine DeKalb soldiers died at the Battle of Cold Harbor, Va. on June 27, 1862, four at the Second Battle of Manassas in August, five at Sharpsburg, Md. on September 17, 1862.

Killed at Cold Harbor were J. M. Dowis, David N. Fair, Charles H. Goodwin, J. L. Henry, H. H. Hornbuckle, R. F. Jones, John W. Phillips, J. S. Richardson and Jordan Wilson. John H. Akers, John W. Chandler, F. M. Gassaway and E. H. C. Morris died at Manassas. James E. Chandler, Gideon Grogan, J. D. Grogan, Joshua Hammond and E. W. Wiggins were killed at Sharpsburg.

The roster of DeKalb's dead for 1862 also included Henry Bibb Bell, Pickens Noble Calhoun, James Collier, James L. Davis, A. M. Gentry, Julius J. Gober, Augustine E. Goodwin, Eli W. Hoyle, J. M. C. Hulsey, John S. Johnston, Robert F. Jones, James W. McCulloch, Samuel Bryson McElroy, John W. Nash, D. D. Richardson, John D. B. Weed and James H. Young. Also killed in 1862 was William Nicholas Chamblee, son of John William Chamblee of Gwinnett County, who had joined DeKalb's Co. E, 7th Regiment.

'Gustin Goodwin, one of two sons of Harris and Emily Dodgen Goodwin to be killed in 1862, was also one of three captains of Co. K to be killed during the war. George W. Stubbs and R. H. Fletcher also were killed. "In nearly ever instance, promotion in this company meant death upon the battlefield," wrote Mary Gay. [33]

Long before the war was over, families buried their dead and went about the painful process of providing for the continuance of the living. Samuel McElroy served as administrator for the estate of his son, Samuel Bryson McElroy. The younger McElroy left a widow and five minor children. The father of the slain Confederate soldier petitioned DeKalb County Ordinary J. B. Milson twice in early 1864, once to allow his daughter-in-law and grandchildren to continue to live rent free on McElroy land. In the second petition, McElroy said "it would be to the Interest of said estate to keep half Lot of Land No. 296 in the 18th District of said County, belonging to said estate whereon the widow resides for the purpose of cultivating the same for the benefit of the widow and five minor children of the said deceased, And also the Interest of money due the children, during the present year 1864, which support is to include Boarding, clothing & Schooling the said children as such parts of the year they may goe (sic) to School, all free of charge to the Administrator, Samuel McElroy." Both petitions were granted. [34]

Women continued throughout the years of 1862 and '63 to sew uniforms and underwear, and assemble packets for soldiers at the front. They also raised money by staging benefits like this one:

GRAND MUSICAL ENTERTAINMENT!
RELIEF FUND
FOR OUR SOLDIERS
THURSDAY, MAY 15, 1862
AT THE COURTHOUSE.

By the ladies of Decatur, Georgia, assisted by William H. Barnes, Colonel Thomas F. Lowe, Professor Hanlon, W. A. Haynes, R. O. Haynes, Dr. Geutebruck and Dr. Warmouth, of Atlanta

PROGRAMME.
Part I.

1. Opening Chorus -- Company.
2. Piano Duet -- "March from Norma" -- Miss Georgia Hoyle and Miss Missouri Stokes.
3. Solo -- "Roy Neil" -- Mrs. Robert Alston.
4. Quartette -- Atlanta Amateurs.
5. "Tell Me, Ye Winged Winds" -- Company.
6. "Our Way Across the Sea" -- Miss G. Hoyle and Professor Hanlon.
7. March -- Piano Duet -- Miss Laura Williams and Miss Fredonia Hoyle.
8. Solo -- Professor Hanlon.
9. Comic Song -- W. H. Barnes.
10. Violin Solo -- Colonel Thomas F. Lowe.
11. Solo -- Dr Warmouth.
12. "When Night Comes O'er the Plain" -- Miss M. Stokes and Professor Hanlon.
13. "The Mother's Farewell" -- Mrs. Maggie Benedict.

PART II

1. Chorus -- "Way to the Prairie" -- Company.
2. Piano Solo -- Miss G. Hoyle.
3. Song -- Atlanta Amateurs.
4. Coquette Polka -- Misses Hoyle and Stokes.
5. Chorus -- "Let us Live with a Hope" -- Company
6. "Mountain Bugle" -- Miss M. Stokes and Company.
7. "Mazurke des Traineaux" -- Piano Duet -- Misses Hoyle and Stokes.
8. Shiloh Retreat -- Violin -- Colonel Thomas F. Lowe.

Concluding with the Battle Song: "Cheer, Boys, Cheer" -- W. H. Barnes.

Tickets, 50¢. Children and Servants, half price.
Doors open 7:30 o'clock. Commence at 8:15 o'clock.

Martial law was declared in Atlanta on May 23, 1862, with former Decatur resident James M. Calhoun appointed "civil governor." Strict regulations were instituted by the Confederate army. Visitors to the city had to carry passes approved by the military.

On April 10, 1863, Confederate President Jefferson Davis issued a proclamation urging farmers in the Confederate States to plant corn, beans, peas and other food crops, instead of cotton and tobacco. The entreaty apparently had little effect in DeKalb. In October of 1862, the DeKalb Grand Jury urged the Georgia legislature to limit the amount of cotton that could be planted in the county:

"In looking to the condition of the various Roads in our County, we are constrained to make complaint against the Commissioners whose duty it is to have them in good order. We return the Snapfinger bridge on the Covington Road especially, as being almost impassable.

"In regards to the planting of cotton in our County for the next year -- if planted to any great extent we cannot but regard it as a fatal step towards the destruction of the Confederacy. We respectfully recommend to our Senator and Representative from this County to use their influence in the passage of a law limiting the planting of cotton to one half acre to each hand over fourteen years old. We would also ask of them to use their influence in the passage of such a law as will prevent the distillation of grain.

"In conclusion, we most respectfully return our thanks to his honor Judge Bull, and the Solicitor-General for their courtesy towards us during this short term, hoping to meet them at the next term of our Court under more favorable auspices, when this beloved Confederacy shall record her name among the nations of the earth a separate and independent Republic."

        Joseph Walker, Foreman

Franklin H. Gay	David Chestnut	Archibald McElroy
John T. Meador	Eli O. Estes	William O. Hightower
Alexander Vaughan	Joseph T. Henry	James M. Beaty
Robert H. Smith	Winston H. Cash	William L. McClain
James M. Reeve	Jeptha R. Adkins	Eli T. Chapman. [35]
John W. Stewart	Benjamin F. Shumate	
William Sheppard	John W. Miller	

DeKalb County government slowed to a halt. The grand jury may not have met again until after the war; no presentments were recorded until April, 1865. No juries were empaneled in 1863. A grand jury was chosen on April 25, 1864, with John Bryce as foreman, but no presentments were recorded.

George Lyon, a DeKalb County pioneer and son of Revolutionary soldier Joseph Emanuel Lyon, died on January 12, 1862 at the age of 74. A South Carolina native, he had lived in DeKalb for 40 years. He and his wife, Elizabeth Howard, had 13 children. He is buried in the Macedonia Primitive Baptist Church cemetery. [36]

Lawrence Sterne Morgan, one of Decatur's three brothers, died on June 14, 1862 at the age of 56. He and his brothers, Joseph (1800-1854) and Enoch (1804-1843) were born in Brimfield, Mass. Joseph and Lawrence became well-know makers of cabinetry and fine furniture. Lawrence Morgan was married to Martha Jane McNeil, daughter of Revolutionary soldier James McNeil. Joseph Morgan married Jane Kirkpatrick, daughter of James H. Kirkpatrick. Enoch never married. The brothers are buried in Decatur Cemetery.

The year of 1863 was filled with tragic and momentous occasions. One of the Confederacy's best generals, Thomas J. (Stonewall) Jackson, was accidentally shot by his own men in Chancellorsville, Va. in May. In November, Lincoln delivered his famous Gettysburg address, and Georgia Gov. Joseph E. Brown was elected to an unprecedented fourth term. The fall of Vicksburg, Miss. to the Union army on July 4, 1863, after a six-month siege, caused some to predict the same for Atlanta. But, Vicksburg made at least one DeKalb citizen even more determined than ever. Confederate soldier Robert Alston wrote: "... even should Lee's army be destroyed and every town in the South burned, the rebellion would be unsubdued. There are a hundred thousand men in the South who feel as I do, that they would rather an earthquake should swallow the whole country than yield to our oppressors. Men will retire to the mountains and live on acorns, and crawl on their bellies to shoot an invader wherever they see one." [37]

Smallpox hit Atlanta and the surrounding communities hard in early 1863, causing military authorities to seize 155 acres belonging to William Markham between the current communities of Grant Park and Ormewood Park, for construction of a hospital. Markham sued unsuccessfully to recover his property. The hospital was hardly in operation before the Battle of Chickamauga on September 19 and 20, 1863, sent hundreds of wounded to Atlanta. The city requested that private citizens send their carriages to help moved wounded from trains to hospitals. Along with the wounded came hundreds of uniformed federal prisoners, the first Atlanta had seen. [38]

President Lincoln's Emancipation Proclamation on January 1, 1863 had little effect on slave traffic in the Atlanta area. Robert M. Clarke, son of DeKalb minister, William Henry Clarke, ran this advertisement in an The Atlanta Intelligencer on June 10:

SLAVE YARD
On the west side of Whitehall Street, who has a commodious, well arranged Yard, with every convenience for the health and comfort of slaves. Constantly kept on hand for sale a large number of

Mechanics,
    Coachmen,
        Cooks,
           House Servants
              and Field Hands
BUYS AND SELLS ON COMMISSION
By close personal attention to business he hopes to receive a liberal patronage. [39]

The war progressed, and more Confederate soldiers were removed from the battlefield. From his headquarters in Atlanta, Gen. Howell Cobb, commander of the state troops, ordered all companies to be ready for active service by November 1, 1863. [40]

DeKalb lost three young men (James E. Ball, W. F. Goodwin and J. H. Wilson) at Gettysburg, Penn. in July of 1863. Others killed in 1863 included W. B. Chandler, S. J. Summey and B. L. Wilson. Capt. Alfred J. H. Poole, one of earliest settlers of Browning's District, was an accidental victim of the war in 1863. In January, on Alabama Street in Atlanta, Poole was helping unload rifles that had been captured at Murfreesboro, Tenn. One of the rifles accidentally discharged, hitting Poole, who died the next day at the home of Oliver H. Jones. He is buried in his in-laws's Lively Cemetery on Briarcliff Road. His widow, Judith Matilda C. Lively Poole, later married Jabez M. Loyd. [41]

Many more of DeKalb's young men were wounded in 1862 and '63. Stephen Tilly McElroy of Cross Keys was 18 when he enlisted in Company F of the 36th Georgia Regiment. During the battle of Baker's Creek, May 16, 1863, he was twice wounded, first with a gunshot wound through the left side, then through the left leg. His leg was amputated halfway between the knee and ankle. He was hospitalized in Clinton, Miss.

McElroy takes up his story in his autobiography:

"After I got to be on crutches just a little, a good Virginia lady by the name of Mrs. Lungher, who lived two miles out from the hospital, carried me to her home in Georgia. The treatment I received at the hands of this extraordinarily fine family was such that words will not do it justice. They did for me all that was possible for anyone to do, regardless of favor, reward or the hope thereof, and they did it because I was a Confederate soldier. The memory of such people lingers with us old veterans, and each thought of them sets our heartstrings quivering to a sweeter tune.

"I arrived at home, that is to say in Atlanta, on the 4th day of July. When I got off the train in Atlanta I allowed my detail nurse to go on to his home in Marietta, taking the chances on getting out to my father's home in the country, 12 miles distant. I went to a merchant whom my father and kinspeople had been trading with for years, and asked him to send me out to a friend's house where I could spend the night. He declined to do it, but consented to send me the next morning if I could not do any better. I had to accept that as I had no money, and he was the only man there that I knew to whom I could go. I went to the Wayside Home, a place kept for passing soldiers to stop over, and spent the night. It was a miserable place.

The next morning I went to this man's store (for the purposes of this paper it is not necessary that his name be given) and awaited the arrival of his conveyance. It was Sunday morning. Finally his negro drayman drove up with a dray that he hauled goods on, and carried me out to Mr. Medlock's (John W. Medlock, kin by marriage to the Tilly family). When I got *there* I was surely in the hands of *friends*. His daughter, of whom I thought quite a lot, met me at the gate and helped me up the steps into the house. The contrast between my treatment there and that of this should-be friend in Atlanta, was very striking. Mr. Medlock had his carriage hitched up and sent me to my father's home.

Just how I was received at home by the family and even by the old watch-dog, words fail to correctly tell. I was very weak, and thought then that I was ruined for life; that I never could accomplish anything; would never be able to do anything, and that I would be an object of charity to my family for the balance of my life. But I quickly regained the health and flesh I had lost, and circumstances soon forced me into the world to take a man's place there, for my father died the next year, leaving my mother, sister and brother in my care. The surrender came in 1865, finding us and our country in devastated condition. We had neither meat nor bread, and just how we lived that year it would be difficult to tell." [42]

As the war dragged on through the year of 1863, more DeKalb soldiers found themselves prisoners of war. While the no longer had to endure the dangers of the battlefield, the prison camps held horrors of their own.

John McKoy of Decatur had enlisted in the Stephens Rifles in August of 1861. After two years away from home, he returned in order to marry Laura Williams, daughter of Ammi Williams. After this joyous respite, McKoy re-enlisted. He was captured in July of 1864, and sent to Fort Delaware, where he remained for the duration of the war. He was one of 34 at the prison camp who refused to take the oath of nonaggression against the United States. [43]

Called the "Andersonville of the North," Fort Delaware held 12,000 Confederate prisoners in a facility built for 7,000. "Ditches of scummy water and human waste were the only washing water for the thousands of wretched inmates." Cholera, smallpox, malnutrition and exposure killed every fourth man in the winter of 1863. [44]

Meanwhile, Mary Stokes and her daughters, Missouri Stokes and Mary Gay, anxiously awaited a visit from their son and brother, Thomas J. (Thomie) Stokes, with the 10th Texas Infantry, who was a prisoner at Camp Chase, Ohio. Thomie wrote:

"I have learned that the soldiers of the 10th Texas Infantry will be exchanged for the United States troops very soon, perhaps tomorrow; and then, what happiness will be mine! I can scarcely wait its realization. A visit home, a mother's embrace and kiss, the heart-felt manifestations of the love of two sisters, and the joy and glad expression of faithful servants. I may bring several friends with me, whom I know you will welcome, both for my sake and theirs -- they are valiant defenders of the cause we love. Adieu, dear mother, and sisters, until I see you at home, `home, sweet home.'"

Thomie arrived in Decatur on May 16, 1863. His sister, Mary Gay, recalled:

"As we stood upon the platform of the Decatur depot, and saw him step from the train, which we had been told by telegram would bring him to us, our hearts were filled with consternation and pity, and tears unbidden coursed down our cheeks, as we looked upon the brave and gallant brother, who had now given three years of his manhood to a cause rendered dear by inheritance and the highest principles of patriotism, and, in doing so, had himself become a physical wreck. He was lean to emaciation and in his pale face not a suggestion of the ruddy color he had carried away. A constant cough, which he tried in vain to repress, betrayed the deep inroads which prison life had made upon his system; and in this respect he represented his friends -- in describing his appearance, we leave nothing untold about theirs. In war-torn pants and faded grey coats, they presented a spectacle never to be forgotten."

During the spring and summer of 1863, Missouri Stokes wrote in her diary: "Our fallen braves, how numerous! Among our generals, Zollicoffer, Ben McCulloch, Albert Sidney Johnston, and the saintly, dauntless Stonewall Jackson, are numbered with the dead; while scarcely a household in our land does not mourn the loss of a brave husband and father, son or brother." [45]

While most eyes were turned toward loved ones in the war, death continued to claim older citizens at home. The Rev. James Mangum, a North Carolina native who came to DeKalb about 1824, died on March 3, 1863 at the age of 81. He and his younger brother, William, settled in the area that would become south Atlanta, where they became well-known for growing the "Mangum apple." [46]

Chapter 25 Notes

1. Garrett, Franklin M., 1954, 1969, <u>Atlanta and Environs -- A Chronicle of Its People and Events</u>, Vol. 1, page 740.

2. Garrett, Franklin M., 1954, 1969, <u>Atlanta and Environs -- A Chronicle of Its People and Events</u>, Vol. 1, pages 488-489.

3. Marbut, Laura P., 1970, <u>James Diamond (1781-1849) And His Descendants</u>.

4. Garrett, Franklin M., 1954, 1969, <u>Atlanta and Environs -- A Chronicle of Its People and Events</u>, Vol. 1, pages 479-480.

5. Garrett, Franklin M., 1954, 1969, <u>Atlanta and Environs -- A Chronicle of Its People and Events</u>, Vol. 1, pages 481-482 and 556.

6. Hudgins, Carl T., 1952, "Mills and Other Early DeKalb County Industries (And Their Owners)," <u>The Collections of the DeKalb Historical Society</u>, Vol. 1.

7. Nix, Dorothy, personal collection, DeKalb Historical Society.

8. Candler, Charles Murphey, November 9, 1922, Historical Address.

9. Garrett, Franklin M., 1954, 1969, <u>Atlanta and Environs -- A Chronicle of Its People and Events</u>, Vol. 1, page 494.

10. Garrett, Franklin M., 1954, 1969, <u>Atlanta and Environs -- A Chronicle of Its People and Events</u>, Vol. 1, page 495.

11. Garrett, Franklin M., 1954, 1969, <u>Atlanta and Environs -- A Chronicle of Its People and Events</u>, Vol. 1, page 495.

12. Nix, Dorothy, personal collection, DeKalb Historical Society ("A History of DeKalb County" by Charles Murphey Candler Sr.).

13. Knight, Lucian Lamar, <u>Georgia's Landmarks, Memorials and Legends</u>, Vol. 2, page 570.

14. Nix, Dorothy, personal collection, DeKalb Historical Society ("A History of DeKalb County" by Charles Murphey Candler Sr.).

15. Nix, Dorothy, personal collection, DeKalb Historical Society. Gay, Mary A. H., 1879, 1979, <u>Life In Dixie During The War</u>.

16. Garrett, Franklin M., 1954, 1969, <u>Atlanta and Environs -- A Chronicle of Its People and Events</u>, Vol. 1, page 499.

17. Harwell, Richard B., 1950, <u>Confederate Music</u>, pages 41-43.

18. Nix, Dorothy, personal collection, DeKalb Historical Society.

19. Plant, Percy, 1957, "Historic Decatur." Gay, Mary A. H., 1879, 1979, <u>Life In Dixie During The War</u>.

20. Gay, Mary A. H., 1879, 1979, <u>Life In Dixie During The War</u>, page 24. Plant, Percy, 1957, "Historic Decatur." Garrett, Franklin M., 1954, 1969, <u>Atlanta and Environs -- A Chronicle of Its People and Events</u>, Vol. 1, pages 505-507. Henderson, Lillian, <u>Roster of the Confederate Soldiers of Georgia 1861-1865</u>, compiled for the State of Georgia. Candler, Charles Murphey, November 9, 1922, "Historical Address." Confederate muster rolls and service records, Georgia Department of Archives and History.

21. Garrett, Franklin M., 1954, 1969, <u>Atlanta and Environs -- A Chronicle of Its People and Events</u>, Vol. 1, pages 516-517. Gay, Mary A. H., 1879, 1979, <u>Life In Dixie During The War</u>, page 25.

22. Garrett, Franklin M., 1954, 1969, Atlanta and Environs -- A Chronicle of Its People and Events, Vol. 1, pages 486-487. DeKalb County Chamber of Commerce, July 1976, "DeKalb County History."

23. Gay, Mary A. H., 1879, 1979, Life In Dixie During The War, page 25.

24. Gay, Mary A. H., 1879, 1979, Life In Dixie During The War, page 45.

25. Gay, Mary A. H., 1879, 1979, Life In Dixie During The War.

26. Kurtz, Wilbur G., November, 1936, "The Murder of Tom Terry," The Atlanta Historical Bulletin, No. 9. Garrett, Franklin M., 1954, 1969, Atlanta and Environs -- A Chronicle of Its People and Events, Vol. 1, pages 514-515. Hudgins, Carl T., 1952, "Mills and Other Early DeKalb County Industries (And Their Owners)," The Collections of the DeKalb Historical Society, Vol. 1.

27. Garrett, Franklin M., 1954, 1969, Atlanta and Environs -- A Chronicle of Its People and Events, Vol. 1, page 514.

28. Garrett, Franklin M., 1954, 1969, Atlanta and Environs -- A Chronicle of Its People and Events, Vol. 1, page 529.

29. Garrett, Franklin M., 1954, 1969, Atlanta and Environs -- A Chronicle of Its People and Events, Vol. 1, page 531.

30. Gay, Mary A. H., 1879, 1979, Life In Dixie During The War, page 48.

31. Garrett, Franklin M., 1954, 1969, Atlanta and Environs -- A Chronicle of Its People and Events, Vol. 1, page 530 and 532-533.

32. Flowers, Grace Gresham, 1987, The Cash, Leavell, Pylant, Gresham and Flowers Families of DeKalb County 1625-1987.

33. Gay, Mary A. H., 1879, 1979, Life In Dixie During The War, page 30. McElroy genealogy file, DeKalb Historical Society. Flowers, Grace Gresham, 1987, The Cash, Leavell, Pylant, Gresham and Flowers Families of DeKalb County 1625-1987. Garrett, Franklin M., 1954, 1969, Atlanta and Environs -- A Chronicle of Its People and Events, Vol. 1, page 555.

34. Chesnut, Mr. and Mrs. J. David, personal collection.

35. Garrett, Franklin M., 1954, 1969, Atlanta and Environs -- A Chronicle of Its People and Events, Vol. 1, pages 536 and 548.

36. Garrett, Franklin M., 1954, 1969, Atlanta and Environs -- A Chronicle of Its People and Events, Vol. 1, page 541. Johnson, Mr. and Mrs. J. Wallace, n. d., "Lyon Family History."

37. Garrett, Franklin M., 1954, 1969, Atlanta and Environs -- A Chronicle of Its People and Events, Vol. 1, pages 545 and 549. DeKalb Historical Society Bulletin, Vol. 1, No. 1., Christmas, 1976.

38. Garrett, Franklin M., 1954, 1969, Atlanta and Environs -- A Chronicle of Its People and Events, Vol. 1, pages 548 and 551.

39. Garrett, Franklin M., 1954, 1969, Atlanta and Environs -- A Chronicle of Its People and Events, Vol. 1, page 553.

40. Garrett, Franklin M., 1954, 1969, Atlanta and Environs -- A Chronicle of Its People and Events, Vol. 1, page 551.

41. Garrett, Franklin M., 1954, 1969, Atlanta and Environs -- A Chronicle of Its People and Events, Vol. 1, page 555. Wells, Joel Dixon, and Cornell, Nancy Jones, June, 1984, "Nancy Creek Primitive Baptist Church Cemetery," prepared for the Metropolitan Atlanta Rapid Transit Authority.

42. Tilly, Harwell Parks IV, 1993, Stephen and Rebecca (King) Tilly and Their Descendants 1782-1992).

43. Gay, Mary A. H., 1879, 1979, Life In Dixie During The War, page 28.

44. Clarke, Caroline McKinney, 1973, 1996, The Story of Decatur 1823-1899.

45. Gay, Mary A. H., 1879, 1979, Life In Dixie During The War, page 71.

46. Garrett, Franklin M., 1954, 1969, Atlanta and Environs -- A Chronicle of Its People and Events, Vol. 1, page 554.

Chapter 26

January, 1864 brought daytime temperatures of 8 degrees. Atlanta was "throbbing with all the manifold activities of an industrial center in a wartime economy." Some war-related business was enjoyed by DeKalb's mills, but with far fewer industries than Atlanta, the county had much less to gain. [1]

Thomas Stokes's unit returned to Georgia in February, and by April was camped near Dalton. He and his comrades were living on salty bacon and hardtack (hard biscuits made of unsalted flour and water). Mary Gay and her family sent supplies to Dalton, but they disappeared. Typically, Mary took matters into her own hands and made two trips by train to Dalton, taking jugs of sorghum syrup, bread, pies, cakes, potatoes, onions and peppers.

Like Mary, many family members, including small children, went by train to see husbands and fathers "for, perhaps, the last time on earth." Travel by any means was slow. Railroads were commandeered by the military. Roads were crowded with wagons and carriages carrying refugees and their possessions away from the area that was soon to be a target of the Union army. "In those days the depot was a favorite resort with ladies and children of Decatur," Mary wrote. The agent was the only man in town who might have recent news from the front. The depot also was the first stop in town for the mail delivery. Decatur got mail twice a day -- once from west and once from east. [2]

One old Decatur citizen did not live to see his home and Atlanta, a town he helped build, invaded by the Union army. Ammi Williams died on March 30, 1864 at his home in Decatur. Born in Connecticut in 1780, he had come to Georgia lured by the discovery of gold in north Georgia in the 1830s. Williams was survived by his wife, Laura Loomis, and several children. He was buried in Oakland Cemetery. [3]

When Confederate troops began to move out of northwest Georgia toward Atlanta, Thomas Stokes wrote and asked Mary to store things, like overcoats and blankets, that he and his comrades would not need until the July heat gave way to winter cold. "Consider well the proposition before you consent," Thomie wrote." Should they be found in your possession, by the enemy, then our home might be demolished, and you perhaps imprisoned, or killed upon the spot." When the items came by train to Atlanta, Mary had them transferred to the Decatur train, then hired a wagon and horses from Ezekiel

Gen. William T. Sherman set up his headquarters at the home of Samuel House on July 18, 1864. The House family had fled to Hall County to escape the Union army. The house, built from bricks made on the property, is now the clubhouse for the Peachtree Golf Club. (Hayes Collection, DeKalb Historical Society)

Mason to take the nine boxes the last few blocks to her home.

The home folks shared the horrors of battle through letters like the one Thomie wrote from the Battle of New Hope Church in northwest Georgia on May 27:

"I saw a tall, muscular Federal lying dead and the moonlight shining in his face. I could not help but shudder... I went out again to see if I could do anything for their wounded. Soon found one with his leg shot through whom I told we would take care of. Another, shot in the head, was crying out continually; `Oh, my God! O, my God!!' I asked him if we could do anything for him, but he replied that it would be of no use. I told him God would have mercy upon him, but his mind seemed to be wandering. I could not have him taken care of that night, and, poor fellow, there he lay all night.

"The next morning I had the privilege of walking over the whole ground, and such a scene! Here lay the wounded, the dying, and the dead, hundreds upon hundreds, in every conceivable position; some with contorted features, showing the agony of death, others as if quietly sleeping. I noticed some soft beardless faces which ill comported with the savage warfare in which they had been engaged. Hundreds of letters from mothers, sisters and friends were found upon them, and ambroytypes, taken singly and in groups. Though they had been my enemies, my heart bled at the sickening scene."

Thomas Stokes was spared fighting in the Battles of Decatur and Atlanta. In July 1864 he was sent to a hospital in Macon due to illness, later transferred to Augusta, then to the home of a cousin, Mrs. T. J. Hillsman, daughter of the Rev. William H. Stokes, where Missouri Stokes had refugeed. [4]

On Friday, June 10, 1864, Confederate President Jefferson Davis proclaimed a day of fasting and prayer. The Confederacy was running out of men and bullets with which to meet the enemy.

In the spring of 1864, Atlanta began fortifying the city with redoubts, wood and earthen walls, and trenches. A circular barrier 10 miles long was constructed one mile out from the center of the city. Meanwhile, on May 1, 1864, Union Gen. William Tecumseh Sherman amassed 100,000 men at Chattanooga, Tenn. in preparation for an assault on the city. By comparison, Confederate Gen. Joseph E. Johnston at Dalton, 34 miles southeast of Chattanooga, could only assemble 60,000 men. On May 23, Atlanta Mayor James M. Calhoun issued a proclamation requiring all male citizens capable of bearing arms to rally in defense of the city. On May 27 the first sounds of battle reached Atlanta from New Hope Church, 25 miles to the west. [5]

The town of Roswell just across the Chattahoochee River from north DeKalb County, was captured by Sherman's soldiers on July 6, 1864. Two cotton mills and one woolen mill were burned. One of the mills had housed machinery worth more than $1 million, and had employed 400 women. The mill operators, men and women, were transported to northern states by the Union army. [6]

The Union army began crossing the Chattahoochee River into DeKalb and Fulton counties on July 9. On her way to the post office "one morning in the sultry month of July, 1864," Mary Gay was told by a Negro blacksmith named "Uncle Mack" that the Yankees had crossed the river. [7]

I t was time to hide the clothing entrusted to her by her brother and his fellow soldiers. Mary thought their servant, Toby, might not keep the secret, so her mother took him to the depot under the pretense of seeking news. With the help of another servant, Telitha, Mary placed a chair on top of the dining room table, and with a hammer and chisel removed the plaster and the supporting laths from the ceiling. She laid the lids from the boxes across the joists, making a floor upon which to lay the goods. The laths she replaced. She and Telitha pounded the large pieces of plaster into small pieces, filled every vessel and basket in the house. "I then went out and walked very leisurely over the yard and lot, and lingered over every lowly flower that sweetened the atmosphere with its fragrance, and when I was fully persuaded that no spy was lurking nigh I re-entered the house. Picking up the largest vessel and motioning Telitha to follow suit, I led the way through a back door to a huge old ash hopper, and emptied the pulverized plastering into it. In this way we soon had every trace of it removed from the floor. The dust that had settled upon everything was not so easily removed, but the frequent use of dusting brushes and flannel cloths disposed of most of it." [8]

On July 17, 1864, Confederate Gen. Joseph E. Johnston was replaced by Gen. John Bell Hood, a move that some said was a mistake that cost the Confederacy Atlanta. [9]

The Union command remained stable. On that same day, July 17, from his headquarters on what is now Powers Ferry Road, Sherman outlined his plans for the following day in Special Field Order No. 36.

"The operations of the army for tomorrow, the 18th of July, will be as follows:

I. Major-General (George H.) Thomas will move forward, occupy Buck Head and the ridge between Nancy's Creek and Peach-Tree, also all the roads toward Atlanta, as far as Peach-Tree Creek.

II. Major-General (John M.) Schofield will pass through Cross Keys and occupy the Peach-Tree road where intersected by the road from Cross Keys to Decatur.

III. Major-General (James B.) McPherson will move toward Stone Mountain to secure strong ground within four miles of General Schofield's position, and push Brigadier-General Garrard's cavalry to the railroad, and destroy some section of the road, and then resume position to the front and left of General McPherson..." [10]

Sherman spent the next night, that of July 18, at the home of Samuel House, at the intersection of Peachtree and Old Cross Keys Road (now Ashford Dunwoody. The House family had refugeed to Hall County. [11]

From there, Sherman wrote to Gen. McPherson:

"Hdqrs. Military Division of the Mississippi
In the Field, on Peach-Tree Road, July 18, 1864

General McPherson:
I am at Sam. House's, a brick house well known, and near Old Cross Keys. A sick negro, the only human being left on the premises, says we are eleven miles from Atlanta, five from Buck Head, and a sign board says ten miles to McAfee's Bridge and eleven to Roswell Factory. At this place the main Buck Head and Atlanta road is strongly marked and forks, the right-hand looking north going to McAfee's, and the left to Roswell Factory. This left-hand road forks one mile from here, at Old Cross Keys, the main road going to Roswell and left-hand to Johnson's Ferry. The latter is the road traveled by us. I suppose all of Thomas' troops are at Buck Head, with advance guard down to Peach Tree Creek. I think I will move Schofield one mile and a half toward Buck Head, where the negro represents a road to Decatur and forward on that road a mile or so. I think Sam. House's is not far from the northwest corner of lot 273, and if I move him as contemplated he will be to-night about 202, 203. On our map a road comes from the direction of McAfee's toward Decatur, and if you can find position about 192, 191 it would best fulfill my purpose, but be careful to order Garrard to break the road to-day or to-night and report result. I will stay here or down at the forks of the road to-night. Schofield encountered nothing but cavalry, about 500, according to the negro's report, and all retreated toward Atlanta. Tell Garrard that it will be much easier to break the telegraph and road to-day and night than if he waits longer. This negro says there is a road leading to Stone Mountain from Mr. Lively's, on the Decatur road, on which I suppose you to be. At any rate I will be here till evening and would like to hear from you.
                        Yours,
                        W. T. Sherman,
                        Major-General." [12]

From Samuel House's house, Sherman telegraphed Maj. Gen. Halleck, Gen. Ulysses S. Grant's chief-of-staff, that by 7 p.m. on July 18 McPherson had destroyed five miles of Georgia Railroad track near what is now Clarkston ("seven miles east of Decatur and four miles from Stone Mountain").

"Thus far we have encountered only cavalry with light resistance, and tomorrow will move on Decatur and Atlanta," Sherman reported.

Decatur historian Robert M. Ervin wrote in 1951: "As a matter of fact, virtually no local resistance was encountered because there were no able-bodied men left to resist. From Decatur and immediate vicinity alone, 136 officers and 1,220 men had marched forth to serve the Confederate cause. This was from a county which in 1860 had a total population of little more than 7,000. Since May, 1864, boys of 16, and younger, and men up to 65, had been called into the State Militia. Most of this state guard force, to the number of about 10,000, was assigned to the fortifications around Atlanta. By July, 1864, Decatur's population had fallen to just a few more than 600. Women, children, a few men over 65, sick or wounded veterans incapable of further military service, and a few Negro slaves, were all that remained." The few Confederate troops who could be spared from the defense of Atlanta "failed to present a serious obstacle in the path of the federal troops." [13]

Nonetheless, it took Sherman six weeks to conquer the city of Atlanta. He had thought he would be in possession of the city within 48 hours. [14]

On the evening of July 18, Sherman issued Special Field Order No. 37, detailing his orders for the following day.

"HDQRS. MIL. DIV. OF THE MISS.
In the Field, near Cross Keys, Ga. July 18, 1864.
The movements of the army tomorrow, July 19, will be as follows:

I. Major-General Thomas will press down from the north on Atlanta, holding in strength the line of Peachtree (Creek), but crossing and threatening the enemy at all accessible points to hold him there, and also taking advantage of any ground gained, especially on the extreme right.

II. Major-General Schofield will move direct on Decatur and gain a footing on the railroad holding it, and breaking the railroad and telegraph wire.

III. Major-General McPherson will move along the railroad toward Decatur and break the telegraph wires and the railroad. In case of the sounds of serious battle he will close in on General Schofield, but otherwise will keep every man of his command at work in destroying the railroad by tearing up track, burning the ties and iron and twisting the bars when hot. Officers should be instructed that bars simply bent may be used again, but if when red hot they are twisted out of line, they cannot be used again. Pile the ties into shape for a bonfire, put the rails across and when red hot in the middle, let a man at each end twist the bar so that its surface becomes a spiral. [12] General McPherson will dispatch General Garrard's cavalry eastward along the line of the railroad to continue the destruction as far as deemed prudent.

IV. All the troops should be in motion at 5 a.m., and should not lose a moment's time until night, when the lines should be closed on General Schofield about Pea Vine and Decatur.

By order of Maj.-Gen. W. T. Sherman:
L. M. Dayton, Aide-de-Camp." [15]

From Samuel House's home, Sherman traveled the Old Shallow Ford Road (now Clairmont) and commandeered the James Oliver Powell home just south of the South Fork of Peachtree Creek as his

---

[12] These twisted sections of railroad track were called "Sherman's Neckties."

new headquarters. James's wife, Sarah Carroll Powell, was on hand to hear Sherman "issue the orders to destroy Atlanta." Sherman's troops camped on the Powell property, and the home's front porch was used as a field hospital. [16]

Sherman's famous directive concerning the conquering of Atlanta were contained in Special Field Order, No. 39.

Written "in the field, near Decatur, Ga., July 19, 1864," the injunction directs the entire contingent of Union troops "to move on Atlanta by the most direct roads tomorrow, July 20, beginning at 5 a.m." Thomas was to proceed "from the direction of Buck Head, his left to connect with General Schofield's right about two miles northeast of Atlanta." Schofield was ordered to move "by the road leading from Dr. Powell's to Atlanta." McPherson's troops were to "follow one or more roads direct from Decatur to Atlanta, following substantially the railroad."

Special Field Order No. 39 concludes: "Each army commander will accept battle on anything like fair terms, but if the army reach within cannon-range of the city without receiving artillery or musket fire he will halt, form a strong line, with batteries in position and await orders. If fired on from the forts or buildings in Atlanta no consideration must be paid to the fact that they are occupied by families but the place must be cannonaded without the formality of a demand."

Erwin, writing in 1951, said he had "never seen an explanation of Sherman's expression: `forts or buildings... occupied by families.' Had he, at this point, become unusually wary of walking into a trap? Or is this double talk of the nature of some of his subsequent orders, by which he gave to the officers and men of his command the opportunity to commit the most atrocious depredations, while the general sought to safeguard his military reputation and to absolve himself from future charges of unusual cruelty and inhumanity? After all, `forts occupied by families' or even `buildings occupied by families' with sufficient heavy weapons to direct cannon fire upon Sherman's men, must, at the very least have been exceedingly rare in Atlanta in 1864." [17]

While Sherman was issuing orders permitting his troops to fire on homes, his soldiers were coming to the aid of Sarah Carroll Powell, whose child was desperately ill. The family, in whose home the soldiers were headquartered, was treated with care and courtesy. Up the road just a few hundred yards, Sarah's brother-in-law Washington Jackson Houston had a close call with the Union troops. Houston's duties as Transportation Agent of the Confederate government kept him in Atlanta during the summer of '64. He got home to see his family as often as he could. One day he got as far as the Avary farm when he spotted enemy soldiers.

Mrs. Avary said to him, "Major Houston, run hide in the collard patch. There never has been a Yankee who would get near collards." The soldiers did not see Houston hiding in the collards but caught him as he slipped through the woods near the cemetery. They were going to shoot him for a spy until he gave the Masonic distress signal. When they found he was a Mason, the soldiers escorted him home. [18]

While half of McPherson's troops struck the Georgia railroad near Clarkston on July 19, the town of Decatur was occupied by the other half. Maj. Gen. Schofield's soldiers swarmed over the town and

Gen. Sherman spent his second night in DeKalb County at the home of James Oliver Powell home on Clairmont Road. From here he issued his famous Special Field Order No. 39, allowing his troops to fire on residences. (DeKalb Historical Society)

pushed through to a line just south of the Georgia Railroad. Here they immediately dug in along two sides of the town.

An L-shaped line of entrenchments to south and east of Decatur began at point 50 yards south of College Avenue and a few yards east of Adams Street. The earthworks extended to within a few yards of the present Commerce Drive, roughly parallel to the railroad. Here the line turned north, almost at a right angle, and crossed the tracks. The trenches then followed Commerce, across now Ponce de Leon Avenue to spot beyond northeast corner of the town, a few yards west of now Glendale Avenue.[19]

Charles Murphey Candler described the fortifications in his 1922 address: The hastily-constructed line of earth entrenchments ran "on the south and eastern limits of the town along the ridge where Rebeckah Scott Hall and the Main Hall of Agnes Scott College now stand, across South Candler Street... crossing the Georgia Railroad about Oak Street (now Commerce Drive), bending thence a little eastward and crossing Sycamore Street... and thence on in a northerly direction, protecting the old cemetery in which were parked (Union) wagon trains."

Additional trenches were dug around court square as secondary line of defense. [20]

While Union troops were converging on Decatur, Mary Gay and Toby loaded several trunks filled with quilts, blankets, bedding, family papers and relics and took them on the train to Atlanta to be stored with friends. They hurried back to the depot to catch the next train to Decatur. "Imagine our consternation," Mary wrote, "on learning that the Yankees had dashed in and torn up the Georgia Railroad track from Atlanta to Decatur, and were pursuing their destructive work towards Augusta. Neither for love nor money could a seat on any kind of vehicle going in that direction be obtained, nor were I and my attendant the only ones thus cut off from home; and I soon discovered that a spirit of independence pervaded the crowd. Many were proud possessors of elegant spans of `little white ponies' which they did not deem too good to propel them homeward. Seeking to infuse a little more life and animation into Toby, I said:

`Well, my boy, what do you think of bringing out your little black ponies and running a race with my white ones to Decatur? Do you think you can beat (me) in the race?'"

Mary and Toby followed the Georgia Railroad tracks, and at twilight, were overtaken by what seemed to be "an interminable line of soldiery" that was Maj. Gen. Joseph Wheeler's Confederate cavalry, headed for Decatur. The "spectre-like band" disappeared, but Mary and Toby caught up with them again when they neared Decatur. "They were lying on the ground, asleep, all over the place; and in most instances their horses were lying by them, sleeping too. And I noticed that the soldiers, even though asleep, never released their hold upon the bridles...

"The distant roar of cannon and sharp retort of musketry spoke in language unmistakable the approach of the enemy, and the rapidity of that approach was becoming fearfully alarming."

Mary and Toby arrived home to find Decatur occupied by Union troops. From the destruction that followed, Mary wrote that she was certain that "every species of criminals ever incarcerated in the prisons of the Northern States of America (had) swooped down upon us, and every species of deviltry followed in their footsteps." Soldiers broke through locked doors at the Stokes home, and "everything of value they could get their hands upon they stole." Much that was not stolen was smashed. "Outside the marauders had killed every chicken and other fowl upon the place, except one setting hen. A fine cow, and two calves, and twelve hogs shared a similar fate... Outrages and indignities too revolting to mention met the eye at every turn. And the state of affairs in the parlor baffle description. Not an article had escaped the destroyer's touch but the piano, and circumstances which followed proved that was regarded as a trophy and only waited removal."

The destructive soldiers proved to be Union Gen. Schofield's advance troops. Later Brig. Gen. Kenner Garrard's cavalry chose the Stokes homeplace for its headquarters.

Less than two hours after their arrival, the barn had been demolished, and the wood used to support tents occupied by hundreds of privates and non-commissioned officers. A long rope was attached to the balusters of the portico and other portions of house, on which to tether horses and mules. Soldiers took drawers from bureaus and wardrobes in the Stokes house, as well as wash stands, to use as horse

A closet in the eaves of the Swanton House was a prison for a Union soldier held captive by a woman and 10 little girls during the occupation of Decatur in 1864. The house originally was a one and one-half-story cottage. A dormer, added later, was removed when the house was restored. The house was moved from its original Decatur location and placed in the Adair Park historic complex. The house is maintained by the DeKalb Historical Society. (DeKalb Historical Society)

troughs. Tables, chairs and lamps were taken from the house, and hundreds of soldiers settled down to play card games and drink whiskey.

A Maj. Campbell of Gen. Schofield's staff later visited Mary Gay and her family, apologizing for the destruction caused by his troops. He brought food and medicine for Toby, who had come down with the measles. "That tray on its humane mission, having found its way into our house, more than once opportunely reappeared. We enjoyed the repast thus furnished, although briny tears were mingled with it." [21]

Nearby, a widow, Mrs. Johnson, and 10 little girls, hers and her deceased brother's, had leased the Decatur house of Benjamin Franklin Swanton. The Swantons refugeed out of town. Mrs. Johnson surprised a Union soldier snooping in the closet of the upstairs bedroom and managed to lock him in. The closet ran the length of the house under the roof eaves, and was accessible via a door at each end. Mrs. Johnson and her young charges kept the soldier prisoner, placing his food just inside one door, while he was made to stand at the other. When Confederate soldiers camped nearby, Mrs. Johnson made the prisoner undress and led him at the point of gun to the Confederates and turned him in.

After the war, the Swantons returned, and the story unfolded bit by bit. The Union soldier's uniform was found in the upstairs closet in 1909. It was not until 1925 that one of the little girls who had lived in the house during the war returned to Decatur in 1925 that the Swantons heard the entire tale.

When Union soldiers arrived in Decatur, the Swanton house became headquarters for Ohio's Brig. Gen. Thomas W. Sweeny. During the Battle of Decatur, the Swanton cellar was considered one of the few safe places in town. Walter Alonzo Sexton, whose family was friends with the Swantons, later recalled:

"When cannon balls began to strike our house and go through it my father said to my mother: `Our only hope is to try to make it over to Swanton's house and get in his cellar. You carry the baby (which was me), and I will carry your mother (who was very feeble and blind). A cannon ball passed through our house and struck my cradle and knocked it into fragments. A few days after that we left Decatur and I did not return until 20 years later when I went back on a visit."

The Swanton house, described as one of the nicest houses in Decatur, was in the thick of the fighting. The first time it was re-roofed after the war, a dishpan full of minie balls was removed from the roof and walls of the house. [22]

While Decatur was occupied by Union troops, Mary got permission to read northern newspapers. On the day she received a letter from a sick relative, she conceived a plan for delivering the potentially valuable newspapers to the Confederate army. She lined her petticoats and stuffed her bustle with the Cincinnati Enquirer, the New York Daily Times, the Cincinnati Commercial Gazette and the Philadelphia Evening Ledger. Armed with permission from the provost marshal to visit Atlanta, she set out to visit her ailing kin and to find friendly soldiers. Mary successfully completed both her missions.[23]

Although most of Sherman's troops were busy in what today is Atlanta's eastern suburbs, the primary target remained the city itself. "Since early May, Sherman's army starting at Dalton, had sought to reach Atlanta, a railroad, communications and manufacturing center, vital to the life of the Confederacy. Sherman was well aware that as long as Atlanta remained in the hands of the Confederacy, war material could be supplied by the city's factories to the Army of Northern Virginia and to the other Southern armies resisting invasion. He knew too, that Atlanta was the key to the rich agricultural region of Middle Georgia, without whose foodstuffs the South would starve." The conquest of Decatur and the Georgia Railroad was the first step in cutting off supply lines. [24]

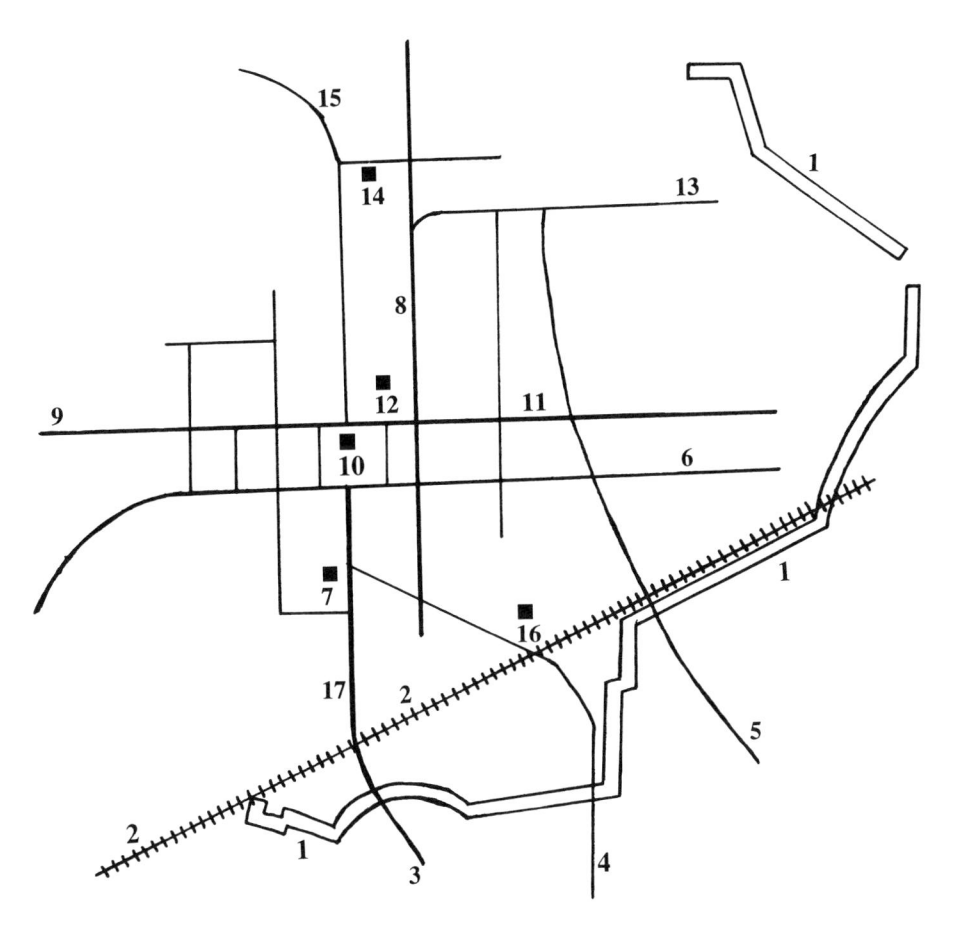

1. Union Entrenchments
2. Georgia Railroad
3. S. McDonough/Fayetteville Road
4. McDonough Road/S. Candler Street
5. Columbia Drive
6. Sycamore Street
7. Jail
8. Church Street
9. W. Ponce de Leon
10. Courthouse
11. E. Ponce de Leon
12. Mary Gay House/Garrard's headquarters
13. Decatur Cemetery
14. Old Presbyterian Church
15. Old Shallowford Road/Clairmont
16. Railroad Depot
17. N. McDonough Street

BATTLE OF DECATUR
July 22, 1864

The left wing of General Sherman's Union army, commanded by Maj. Gen. James B. McPherson, had crossed the Chattahoochee River at the Shallow Ford and moved toward Decatur on the Shallow Ford Road. Half of the troops intended to strike the Georgia Railroad near Clarkston, while the other half, commanded by Maj. Gen. J. M. Schofield, occupied Decatur. The soldiers built earth entrenchments along the ridge near the railroad tracks. They parked their supply trains in the Decatur cemetery. Thousands of soldiers filled the city, and camped along the railway for several miles toward Atlanta.

The Confederate Army had only a small force with which to try and repel the attack. Under 27-year-old Gen. Joseph Wheeler, the Confederates fought hand-to-hand through dense underbrush. The initial battle was won by Wheeler's troops, but the Confederates could not press the advantage, and Decatur was later surrendered. The fighting moved west from Decatur along the railroad corridor, culminating in the infamous Battle of Atlanta, which was not fought in the city of Atlanta, but in DeKalb County, at a point halfway between Decatur and Atlanta.

On July 20 Sherman ordered that more Georgia Railroad track between Lithonia and Covington be destroyed and the Yellow River bridge west of Covington be burned. Thus, Union soldiers first invaded at Thomas Maguire's "Promised Land" plantation near Rockbridge. Maguire wrote in his diary on July 21: "At 12 or 1 o'clock at night the Yankees came here in force. Knocked us up. The house was soon filled with thieving Yankees -- robbed us of nearly everything they could carry off. Broke open all our trunks, drawers, etc. & carried off the keys. They must have practiced roguery from their childhood up, so well they appeared to know the art." [25]

From a tent at the intersection of North Decatur and Briarcliff (then Williams Mill Road), Sherman directed the Battle of Peachtree Creek on July 20, 1864. Casualties were heavy, with 4796 Confederates killed, while the Union army lost 1710 men. It was an inauspicious start for Confederate Gen. Hood in his defense of Atlanta. [26]

By July 20, McPherson's troops, following the Georgia Railroad, had yet to reach the DeKalb-Fulton County line at Moreland Avenue, but were strung out on both sides of the railroad between Decatur and Atlanta. The head of the line of soldiers was beyond the Kirkwood railroad crossing, while the rear was still in Decatur with the heavily-guarded wagon train loaded with supplies. [27]

McPherson spent his last night, that of July 21, in a house at now Winter Avenue and College, on the Sisson Plantation.

Having fought the previous day in the Battle of Peachtree Creek, Confederate soldiers, led by Lt. Gen. William J. Hardee, were ordered to march through the night of July 21 to confront McPherson's legion. Hardee's corps proceeded south and east from Peachtree Creek almost to the South River before turning north toward Decatur. By dawn they had come no farther than East McDonough (now Bouldercrest) Road. Hampered by poor roads and heavily wooded terrain, and without maps, the Confederates hired a local guide. Against the advice of the guide, Maj. Gen. W. H. T. Walker chose to detour farther east. Walker was to pay dearly for his mistake. The troops became lost on the south side of Thomas Terry's mill pond and stuck in the pond's notorious swamp. Walker was killed there by a federal picket. After a forced-march, they arrived exhausted at Decatur at midday on July 22, considerably behind Wheeler's cavalry.

The morning of July 22 found Sherman gazing out a second story window of the home of Augustus F. Hurt. Called Copenhill, the house commanded a good view of the fortifications of Atlanta. McPherson made a morning inspection of his lines, met with Sherman at the Hurt house and returned to his lines, stopping for lunch with his staff at the railroad. Hearing rifle fire in the Sugar Creek valley, McPherson rode off to investigate, inadvertently stumbling into a group of Confederate soldiers, who ordered him to surrender. Instead, the general turned to flee and was shot. McPherson's body taken to the Hurt House, where it was laid on a door, removed from its hinges, and draped with an American flag. [28]

Meanwhile, in the heart of Decatur, Wheeler's men "drove the federal troops from the entrenchments in hand-to-hand fighting... swept the enemy before them through the town and beyond the old limits to the north."

This DeKalb County jail held Union soldiers captured by Joseph Wheeler's Confederate troops during the Battle of Decatur. (DeKalb Historical Society)

The 27-year-old Wheeler later reported: "Seeing the strength of the position in front, I threw a force upon his right flank and rear right, with the right of my line covering the enemy's front. From these positions simultaneous charges were made upon the enemy, the troops bearing upon the enemy's right being somewhat the more advanced. At first, the galling fire made the most exposed portion of my line waver, but quickly rallying, the onset was renewed and with a triumphant shout the entire line of works was carried. Some 225 prisoners, a large number of small arms, one 12-pounder gun, one forge, one battery wagon, one caisson, and six wagons and teams, together with the captain of the battery and most of his men were captured and brought off. We also captured his camp equipage, stores and hospitals." [29]

Mary Gay recalled the scene at her home just prior to Wheeler's attack:

"Garrard and his staff officers were in our parlor -- their parlor pro tem -- holding a council; the teamsters and army followers were lounging about promiscuously, cursing and swearing and playing cards, and seeming not to notice the approaching artillery until their attention was called to it, and then they contended that it was their men firing off blank cartridges...

"A signal, long, loud, and shrill, awakened the drowsy, and scattered to the four winds of heaven cards, books and papers; and, in a few minutes, horses and mules were hitched to wagons, and the mules, wagons and men were fairly flying from the approach of the Confederates. Women and children came pouring in from every direction, and the house was soon filled. Before Garrard's wagon train was three hundred yards away, our yard was full of our men -- our own dear `Johnnie Rebs.'"

The Stokes home was between the Confederate and Union battle lines. Mary Gay recalled:

"Shot and shell flew in all direction, and the shingles on the roof were following suit, and the leaves, and the limbs, and the bark of the trees were descending in showers so heavy as almost to obscure the view of the contending forces. The roaring of cannon and the sound of musketry blended in harmony so full and so grand, and the scene was so absorbing, that I thought not of personal danger, and more than once found myself outside of the portals ready to rush into the conflict...

"Mine was, no doubt, the only feminine eye that witnessed the complete rout of the Federals on that occasion. At first I could not realize what they were doing, and feared some strategic movement; but the `rebel yell' and the flying blue-coats brought me to a full realization of the situation, and I too joined in the loud acclaim of victory. And the women and children, until now panic-stricken and silent as death, joined in the rejoicing. All the discouragement of the past few weeks fled from me, and hope revived, and I was happy, oh, so happy! I had seen a splendidly equipped army, Schofield's division, I think, ignominiously flee from a little band of lean, lank, hungry, poorly-clad Confederate soldiers."

The victorious occasion was marred on the same day by the death of Toby. The women "laid him out." Robert Jones Sr. made a coffin. As soon as the shells stopped flying, Uncle Mack and Henry Oliver dug the grave. Mary, her mother, Telitha and three other slaves were pallbearers. Uncle Mack presided at the service.

The Confederates later lost the advantage they had gained, and surrendered Decatur to the Union army.

Wheeler wrote: "Just as I was pursuing the enemy beyond the town three of General Hardee's staff officers came to me in rapid succession, directing that I should re-enforce Gen. Hardee as quickly as possible. The pursuit was stopped and all my available troops moved at a gallop to Gen. Hardees' position."

Jason Lester Hudson of Huron, Ohio climbed the flag pole in Decatur's square, and took down the Confederate flag. A private in Maj. Gen. Joseph Hooker's 20th Army Corps immortalized the combat in a song called "Battle of Decata, Near Atlanta, July 20, 1864." The parody was sung to the tune of "The Bonnie Blue Flag." [13] [30]

The loss of Decatur meant the loss of the railroad and, ultimately, of Atlanta. "The people of Decatur can and should take pride in the fact that they live in a city where brave Americans fought, bled and

---

[13] In seeking the lyrics to this song, the writer has been in communication with a number of experts on Civil War music, who have suggested that the town name is misspelled. The writer is certain the town name is spelled just like the soldier heard it from the lips of native-born Southerners.

died, not only in defense of their homes, but for principles in which they believed so firmly that they were willing to die for them, if need be. Decatur people should feel inspired when they realize that upon this hallowed ground was performed the kind of deeds from which America draws its strength..."[31]

Meanwhile the Battle of Atlanta raged on in DeKalb County, just east of Atlanta. A spot called Leggett's Hill was "a seething inferno of carnage." Late in the day, the battled moved to the north side of the railroad, around the partially-built brick home of George M. Troup Hurt (older brother of Augustus) on the eastern edge of what is now the Inman Park neighborhood. By nightfall on July 22, 1864 7,000 Confederate soldiers had been killed. The tally was 2,000 Union dead. Each side had lost a general. [32]

Fighting in and around Atlanta lasted from July 20 to August 9 "during which period the citizens went about their daily affairs with little precaution against the ever present danger, though the prudent kept away from the railroads, church spires and tall chimneys, all of which served as prime targets for the federal gunners." Many did have "dugout" shelters in their yards in which they hid during particularly heavy periods of bombardment. [33]

Then came August 10, "that red day in August, when the fires of hell, and all the thunders of the universe seemed to be blazing and roaring over Atlanta... Great volumes of sulphurous smoke rolled over the town, trailing down to the ground, and through this stifling gloom the sun glared down like a great red eye peering through a bronze colored cloud." There were many civilian casualties. Confederate Gen. Hood protested Sherman's bombardment of a town full of civilians. Sherman was unmoved, responding that one of the objectives of war was "devastating the enemy's country, rendering it unfit for human habitation. [34]

The siege of Atlanta was suddenly lifted on August 25, 1864. Casualties were horrendous 34,979 Confederate soldiers and 31,687 Union troops. The Atlanta totals, amazingly, were not as great as other battles of the same year.

The Confederate troops pulled out of Atlanta on August 31. Before leaving, Hood's troops set fire to the ammunition trains, which exploded with a terrific din, and destroyed anything thought to be of value to the enemy, including the rolling mill. [35]

Mary Gay wrote: "Hark! Hark! An explosion! An earthquake? The angry bellowing sound rises in deafening grandeur, and reverberates along the far-off valleys and distant hilltops. What is it? This mighty thunder that never ceases? The earth is ablaze -- what can it be? This illumination that reveals minutest objects? With blanched face and tearful eye, the soldier said: `Atlanta has surrendered to the enemy. The mighty reports are occasioned by the blowing up of the magazines and arsenals.' Dumbfounded we stood, trying to realize the crushing fact." [36]

On the morning of September 2, 1864, "Atlanta, worn out and shattered by the storm of war, lay stranded between two flags, under the protection of neither, abandoned by one, and with little hope of mercy from the other." Atlanta Mayor James M. Calhoun, who lived in Decatur as a young man, formally surrendered the city to Col. John Colburn, commander of the 20th U. S. Army Corps. Five days later, on September 7, Sherman ordered all non-combatants out of Atlanta. [37]

THE BATTLE OF ATLANTA
July 22, 1864

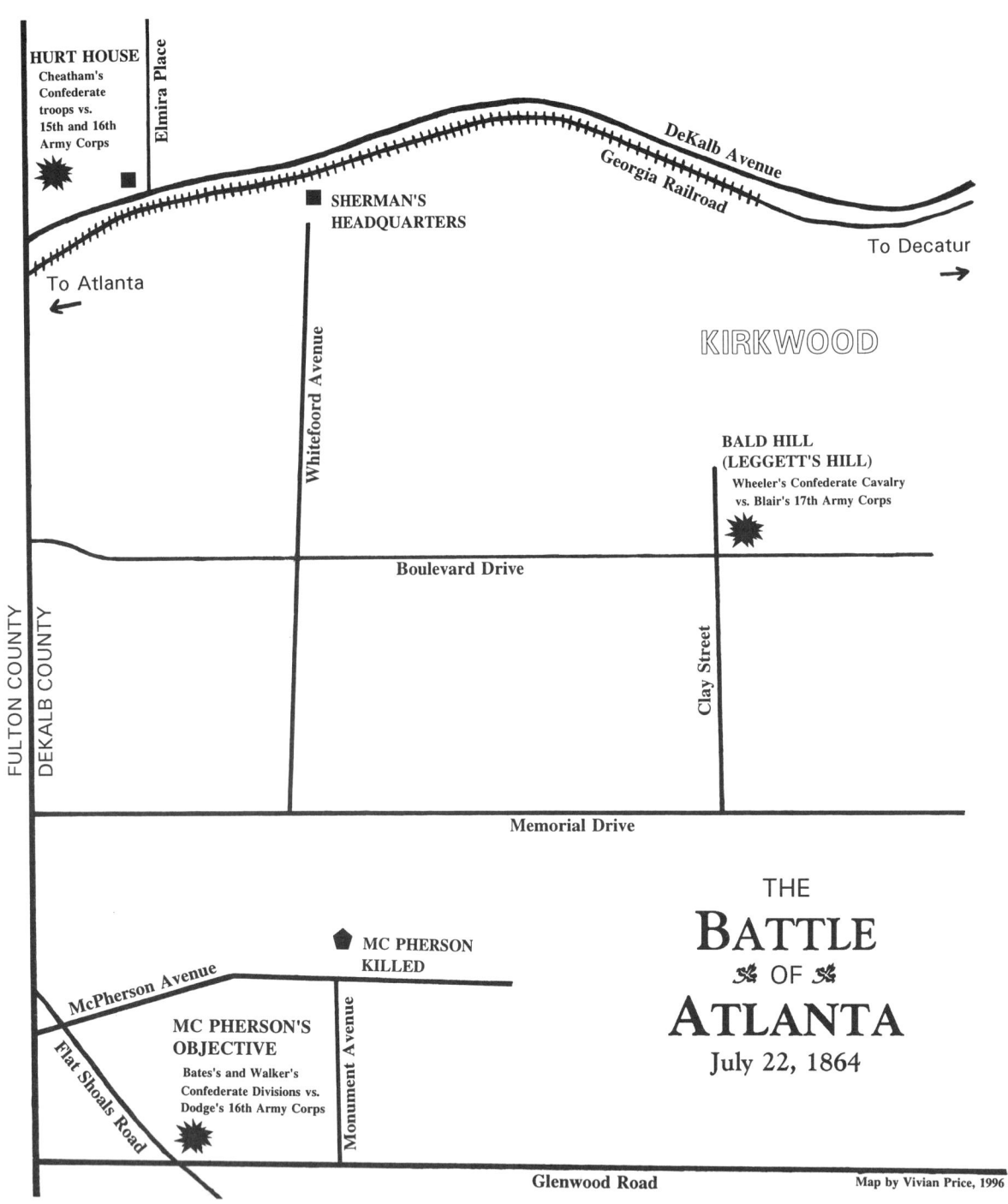

Map by Vivian Price, 1996

What would become known as the Battle of Atlanta actually started in DeKalb County, along the Georgia Railroad west of Decatur in the community of Kirkwood. The Hurt House, featured prominently in Atlanta's famous Cyclorama painting, also was in DeKalb. Gen. Sherman commanded the Union Army from his headquarters in a two-story frame house on Whitefoord Avenue, where he lunched with Maj. Gen. James B. McPherson that day. McPherson later set out on horseback to check on his troops who were engaged in a fierce battle to the south. Along the way he was mortally wounded while trying to escape a band of Confederate soldiers under the command of Capt. Richard Beard. A monument marks the spot of the death of the general said to be the union army's most capable general.

Residents remaining in Decatur also considered leaving. If they left, their homes would be declared abandoned property "and furnish material for a bonfire for Nero to fiddle by." If they stayed, there was no assurance they would be able to feed and protect themselves. Among those who stayed, some, like Mrs. Ammi Williams, whose son Frederick was paralyzed, had little choice. Among those who left was Decatur's pioneer historian, Levi Willard, who moved to Springfield, Ohio.

Another was Eliza Murphey Candler, 25-year-old wife of Milton A. Candler and mother of four children ages six years to seven months. The eldest of the children, Charles Murphey Candler, wrote in 1922: "Household goods, supplies and other impediments had been loaded on wagons for days in anticipation of the probable fall of Atlanta. The news of Hoods's withdrawal, confirmed by the brilliant illumination of the country for miles around caused by the destruction of hundreds of tons of ammunition and the burning city, reached her in the night time, and with her little family about her in the family carriage, at the head of a refugee train, composed of slaves, horses, wagons, and cattle and hogs on foot, she started out somewhere, anywhere to the south, hoping to get beyond the Federal raiders... The second day after leaving home, a squad of Andrews' federal cavalry came upon them, destroyed every wagon and piece of furniture, killed the hogs and the cattle, and took away captive with them the slaves and the horses. Eliza escaped because she, the children, the nurse, and the driver had gone on ahead several miles and were not followed.

"After the war the family returned to the old home to find only the two Negro cabins left standing. The house itself had been destroyed. The family lived in one cabin, and the Negroes, who were still with them, in the other while the home was being rebuilt on the foundations of the one which had been destroyed." [38]

In order to try and feed her family and neighbors, Mary Gay requested permission to come and go. She received from Gen. Schofield's aide a letter:
"Decatur, Ga., Sept. 1, 1864.
Miss Gay -- It was hard for me to reconcile my conscience to giving the enclosed recommendation to one whose sentiments I cannot approve, but if I have committed an error it has been on the side of mercy, and I hope I'll be forgiven. Hereafter I hope you will not think of Yankees as all being bad, and beyond the pale of redemption.

"To-morrow I leave for my own home in the `frozen North,' and when I return it will be to fight for my country, and against your friends, so that I suppose I shall not have the pleasure of again meeting you.
      Very respectfully,
      J. W. Campbell"
Campbell had provided the requested permission:
"Headquarters, Army of Ohio
Decatur, Ga., Sept. 14, 1864.

To Colonel J. C. Parkhurst,
Pro. Mar. Gen., Army of the Cumberland
My Dear Colonel -- I have the honor to introduce Miss Mary A. H. Gay, of this village, and I

recommend her case to your favorable consideration. I do not know exactly what orders are now in force, but if you think you can grant her desires without detriment to the public service, I am confident the indulgence will not be abused.
Very respectfully your obedient servant,
   J. W. Campbell."

Mary's first trip was to Jonesboro where she had heard her brother was stationed. While in Atlanta waiting on a train, she saw "wagons filled with pianos and fine furniture waiting to be shipped north." In Jonesboro, she found exiled Atlantans "dumped out upon the cold ground without shelter and without any of the comforts of home, and an autumnal mist or drizzle slowly but surely saturating every article of clothing upon them; and pulmonary diseases in all stages of admonishing them of the danger of such exposure. Aged grandmothers tottering upon the verge of the grave, and tender maidens in the first bloom of young womanhood, and little babes not three days old in the arms of sick mothers, driven from their homes, were all out upon the cold charity of the world."

After visiting with her brother in Jonesboro, Mary left with a terrible premonition that she would never see him again. She then set off on the first of her own foraging trips. She paid "an enormous sum" to hire a rickety wagon, pulled by two oxen. "Out of compassion for the oxen" she walked alongside the wagon.

"The long tramp to Stone Mountain was very lonely. Not a living thing overtook or passed us, and we soon crossed over the line and entered a war-stricken section of country where stood chimneys only, where lately were pretty homes and prosperity, now departed." The chimneys, called Sherman's Sentinels, "seemed to be keeping guard over those scenes of desolation. The very birds of the air and beasts of the field had fled to other sections." [39]

Mary arrived in Stone Mountain some time during the next night, and was given shelter at the hotel, but not a place to sleep, since all the beds were occupied.

"Early in the morning, hungry and footsore, I started all alone walking to Decatur. The solitude was terrific, and the feeling of awe was so intense that I was startled by the breaking of a twig, or the gruesome sound of my own footsteps. Constantly reminded by ruined homes, I realized that I was indeed within the arbitrary lines of a cruel, merciless foe, and but for my lonely mother, anxiously awaiting my return, I should have turned and run for dear life until again within the boundaries of Dixie."

The entire trip had netted her a large yam and a piece of sausage.

Back in Decatur, Mary, her mother and Telitha spent a day picking grains of corn off the ground and from the crevices of bureau drawers and other improvised troughs for federal horses. "In this diligent and persevering work, about a half bushel was obtained from the now deserted camping ground of Garrard's cavalry." The corn was washed and dried and carried to the only area mill that survived burning, to be ground into coarse meal. The women found a cooking pot abandoned on the campground, and cooked cornmeal mush and hoecakes. [40]

Those living outside of Atlanta had come to fear foraging parties of Union soldiers, for whom such aids seemingly were carried not so much out of necessity as to hunt for things worth stealing. A letter from a 5th Connecticut Volunteers, dated October 22, 1864, described the "plunder:"

"Dear Folks at Home... Just now foraging or raiding parties are all the rage with us, in fact it was a necessity for the mules were dying fast. Week before last we sent a Brigade of Infty from each of the 3 Divisions of our Corps and 2 Batteries & a Battalion of Cavalry with 500 wagons. They went about 25 miles, were gone 4 days & brought back every wagon full of corn or sweet potatoes, as well as any number of sheep, calves, pigs, fowls, etc. The men lived high off the country and brought back lots of plunder.

"Last Sunday another similar party went out a little further and Tom went with them. Our Regt wagon went too and brought back a calf, goose, 2 chickens, 2 pumpkins & a bushel of sweet potatoes for our mess of three.

"He (Tom) came in Wednesday and since then we've lived on the fat of the land and have a goose and rooster fattening yet. It makes me feel like a countryman again to be woke up in the morning by goose gabble and rooster crowing. I enjoy it hugely. It may seem barbarous to you to rob henroosts but Hood cut off our R. R. communication and forced us to forage for corn & of course we don't refuse to accept any thing better that offers. All is fair in war you know." [41]

Amanda (Katie) Powell Houston refused to comply with a Union soldier's order to dig potatoes. Instead she struck the soldier with a shovel. (The Story of Decatur)

Not every citizen submitted passively to the wishes of the foraging parties. Amanda Powell Houston, daughter of pioneer physician Chapman Powell and wife of Washington Jackson Houston Sr., was one who refused to surrender. Katie, as she was called was living with her children at the Powell homeplace, near the current intersection of Clairmont and North Decatur roads, while her husband was performing his duties as transportation agent for the Confederacy. She had gone to the fields and dug up some potatoes, when a Yankee soldier appeared and demanded the potatoes she had already dug. When he stooped over to pick up the potatoes, she struck him a blow with the shovel -- "such a hard blow that the invader was definitely inhibited from further depredations and arrogant demands." [42]

Families tried to hide what they could from the marauding soldiers, as well as from roving bands of poor whites. At the Promised Land, Thomas Maguire wrote in his diary:

Oct. 19 -- This day devoted to hiding our wheat, two boxes in the farmer field, 80 bushels. Little hands pulling fodder of syrup-cane in the patches. Will put out some barrels of syrup this day making preparation for the evil time coming should it come...

"Oct. 22 -- Yankees at Lithonia and may be here today or tomorrow. Are getting things put away from them... With sheep and cattle being out of the way, we are now ready to stand a trial with the Yankees.

"Oct. 27 -- At 10 1/2 o'clock some 30 Yankees rode up. Took Phillip's wagon and two horses, all our meal and flour, one keg of syrup and several articles from the house that I do not know of, one bu. grain the last we had. They stayed some 15 or 20 minutes and put back over the (Yellow) river. They also took John E's saddlebags and a large tin cup.

"Nov. 2 -- Hands gathering up corn and some trifling folks at it too, but this is war time and maybe worse is coming, but we must try and bear it as best we can.

"Nov. 3 -- What will become of us. God only knows."

On November 14, Sherman's soldiers set fire to what remained of Atlanta and began their March of the Sea, cutting a swath of destruction along the way. [43]

Thomas Maguire wrote in his journal:

"Nov. 14 -- 5 soldiers at dinner here today -- smoke considerable at Atlanta.

"Nov. 16 -- Up last night nearly all night. News that Yankees were coming this way after burning Atlanta, Decatur and some houses at Stone Mountain. Hid out box tools, horse, buggy and other things. Mr. Anderson left after breakfast. We are now waiting for the worst to come, still hoping they will not come this way. If they are coming they will be here at 9 o'clock. It is now 7. I went to see Mr. Anderson and while I was gone the Yankees came sure enough. I did not like to go back home so I stayed with David. A little after ten the Yankees were here and coming. Slocum's corps came and camped all around the house. At every side hogs and sheep are being shot down and skinned to regale the Yankee palates. Mr. Anderson and I slept in the woods all night, not very pleasant for either body or mind not knowing what was going on at home.

Nov. 17 -- Still in the woods. Slept but little, was dodging about in the woods trying to see the Yankees from our hiding place. The Yankees all gone about 11 o'clock. I came home at 2 tired enough and sleepy but glad to find that home folks were not abused although there was great destruction of property. Gin house and screw burned, stables and barn all in ashes, fencing burned and destruction visible all around. The carriage and big wagon burned up, corn and potatoes gone, horses and steers gone, sheep, chickens and geese, also syrup boiler damaged, one barrel of syrup burned, saddles and bridles in the same fix. Now engaged in gathering up the fragments of the spoils. It is useless to try to record the destruction of property, still I hope we can live. I think we have plenty of corn & wheat & syrup hid out. There was some 20 bushels of wheat burned in the ginhouse of our own, some of Mr. Minor's and others. Had much to do to save the corn cribs, gin house still burning and the straw piles, also three bales of cotton burned and the other cut open to make beds for the soldiers, all belonging to Mr. Ed Turner. The gin thrash and fan burned, the castings laying to cog wheel and other parts of machinery in ruins; the destruction of Jerusalem on a small scale.

"Nov. 18 -- Roving around trying to save something from the grasp of plundering neighbors around who are here in droves. Still we are all cheerful and hopeful that the worst is passed and the Yankees gone. I hope forever. Several dead horses, and mules lying around. We have one horse that was left, one of his hoofs nearly off. We are trying to doctor him up. Several people still prowling around here and the Yankees' camp and taking any and everything they can find no matter who the owner may be. No news from where the Yankees are.

"Nov. 19 -- Lots of folks still hunting around here for plunder.

"Dec. 19 -- Whipped three negroes after dinner -- viz, Francis, Phillis and Dick -- so much for stealing. I hope this will be the last for some time.

"Dec. 24 -- Little or no preparation for Christmas is being made.

"Dec. 25 -- Not much fuss this morning by the little ones about Christmas. Not like it used to be in other years." [14] [44]

In the fall of 1864, one of Mary Gay's neighbors, Maggie Benedict, asked for Mary's help in moving with her three children to her sister's home in Madison, 50 miles to the east of Decatur. In a cane-break, Mary found a sick horse with a "U.S." brand. Uncle Mack improvised "the most grotesque vehicle ever dignified by the name of wagon," and they secured it to the horse by ropes and pieces of crocus sack, contriving a "pathetic and amusing" conveyance. Mary called the horse Yankee. With Maggie and her three children in the wagon, and Mary walking alongside, they followed in the footsteps of Sherman's March. Mary "contemplated the devastation and ruin on every side. Not a vestige of anything remained to mark the sites of the pretty homes which had dotted this fair country before the destroyer came, except, perhaps a standing chimney now and then." By dark on the first day, "not an animate thing had we seen since we left Decatur, not even a bird..." The spent the night in a cabin, where the gracious hostess fed them yams and let them sleep in chairs and on the floor. After another day of traveling, they were able to catch a train at Social Circle and ride the remaining 10 miles into Madison. On her way back home, Mary bought what food she could in Social Circle, flour, sorghum syrup, butter and meat. Along the road between Social Circle and Decatur, she ate muscadine grapes she found growing wild.

Mary had planned to stop at the home of the Rev. William Henry Clarke along the way. When she arrived at the site, she "stood amazed, bewildered... Elegant rosewood and mahogany furniture, broken into a thousand fragments, covered the face of the ground as far as I could see; and china and glass looked as if it had been sown. And the house, what of that? Alas! it too had been scattered to the four winds of heaven in the form of smoke and ashes. Not even a chimney stood to mark its site."

The slave cabins were not burned, and the slaves were still there. "Men, women and children stalked about in restless uncertainty, and in surly indifference. They had been led to believe that the country would be apportioned to them, but they had sense enough to know that such a mighty revolution involved trouble and delay, and they were supinely waiting developments. Neither man, woman nor child approached me. There was mutual distrust and mutual avoidance."

---

[14] The Promised Land homeplace is still standing, 133 years after the last Union soldiers passed through.

Night was coming. Mary had no place to go. And, Yankee simply laid down in the road. "I knelt by his side and told him the true state of affairs, and implored him not to desert me in this terrible crisis." Mary stayed that night with the Negroes. They shared Mary's food, and she read to them from the Rev. Clarke's theological books that she found in the cabins. She slept on two cedar chests set side by side and covered with Clarke family linens. The next morning, she paid for her night's accommodations, as well as for a steer to pull the wagon, to which the hapless Yankee was tied." [45]

Union soldiers had passed over William Henry Clarke's land three times, in August, October and November of 1864. In October, soldiers took 900 loads of forage and provisions from farms and plantations from five miles around, and left the Clarke house in flaming ruins. [46]
"In due time Decatur appeared in sight, and then there ensued a scene which for pathos defies description. Matron and maiden, mother and child, each with a tin can, picked up off the enemy's camping-ground, ran after me and begged for just a little something to eat -- just enough to keep them from starving. Not an applicant was refused, and by the time the poor, rickety, cumbersome wagon reached its destination, its contents had been greatly diminished. But there was yet enough left to last for some time the patient, loving mother, the faithful Telitha, and myself."

Yankee, now called Johnny Reb, and Mary made other trips to Social Circle to purchase food for the people of Decatur. Mary had no choice but to accept the highly inflated prices for corn, apples, butter, sweet potatoes and syrup, but was relieved that merchants allowed her, time after time, to pay for her purchases with nearly worthless Confederate money.

That generosity would come to an end, and the situation for DeKalb County citizens became desperate. Mary wrote: "In vain did I look round for relief. There was nothing left in the country to eat... Every larder was empty, and those with thousands and tens of thousands of dollars, were as poor as the poorest, and as hungry. Packing trunks, in every house to which refugees had returned, contained large amounts of Confederate money. We had invested all we possessed except our home, and land and negroes, in Confederate bonds, and these were now inefficient for purchasing purposes. Gold and silver had we none." [47]

By the end of 1864, another list of DeKalb County soldiers was added to the growing number of dead: George W. Stubbs, J. A. Maddox, A. W. Allman, J. C. Wiggins and Amos Wheeler. On November 30, 1864, Mary Gay's brother, Thomie, was killed in Franklin, Tenn. Mary Stokes never recovered from the shock of her son's death, and she died on April 1, 1866 at the age of 59.

Even before the war ended, refugees began coming back to DeKalb: J. W. Kirkpatrick, Ezekiel Mason, Capt. Milton A. Candler, Dr. W. W. Durham, Dr. P. F. Hoyle, Mrs. Jane Morgan, Mrs. Cynthia Stone, James Winn, Benjamin Swanton, Jonathan Wilson and J. N. Pate, to name a few. John Kirkpatrick, a war veteran at the age of 21, undertook the rebuilding of Decatur Presbyterian Church, including making seats to replace the pews that had been stolen. The only piece of church furnishings ever recovered after the war was a melodeon (American organ) preserved by a Negro woman named Rosella Stone.

The stalwart people of Decatur never suspended church or Sunday school services or school sessions, even when the Decatur Presbyterian Church building was occupied by the Union army and used as a storage house for ammunition. Meetings were held in the homes of different members; sometimes the only attendees were women and old men. [48] Lizzie Mortin (sic) continued to teach school in the summer of 1864 for the children of the few families who had chosen to remain in town. The school was held on the second floor of the Masonic building; the family of John M. Hawkins lived on the first floor. Cynthia Brown, Mrs. T. H. Chivers, Mrs. Eddleman, Lizzie Morton and Lizzie McCrary organized a Sunday school, which met in the Hawkins home.

The Sunday school later met in the courthouse, but moved back to the Hawkins home when soldiers commandeered the government building. Students were Charley, Guss and Lizzie Hawkins; their cousins John, Sam, Ellen and Lizzie Hawkins; the children of R. J. Cooper and Mrs. Eddleman, Mrs. Chivers, Ed Morton and others.

One student remembered: "We were a peculiarly dressed lot. I had a stand-by suit, the skirt made of a blanket shawl; with this I wore one of my brother's white shirts and a red flannel jacket. I had grown so fast that I was taller than my mother, and there was literally nothing large enough in our house or circle of friends to make me a whole suit. One of the ladies wore a gray plaid silk, a pair of brown jeans shoes, and a woven straw bonnet. She had nothing else to wear. Many of the children were rigged on in clothes made from thrown-away uniforms, picked up, washed, and cut down by the mothers." [49]

The winter of 1864 was particularly cold, with rain and sleet. Stores in Atlanta re-opened and were trading food for munitions. Mary Gay raised a company of women, girls and boys to gather minie balls, despite fingers which bled from the cold. They swapped the lead for sugar, coffee, meal, lard, flour and meat. [50]

A letter dated December 2, 1864 from a young woman to her brother describes the conditions that winter. Elizabeth (Lizzie) Perkerson was the daughter of Thomas Perkerson, once the sheriff of DeKalb, and the granddaughter of Dempsey Perkerson, a pioneer settler of the Panthersville District of DeKalb. The letter was written to her brother, Angus M. Perkerson, then a soldier in the Confederate Army in Virginia.

Lizzie wrote: "The Yankees took pretty near all they could get from grandpa. They got all his horses, mules, cows and oxen. Pa will start down there Monday to help grandpa haul his corn. He sent word if Pa would come haul it he would give him part of it, so he will go, as corn is an object just at the moment." [51]

Lizzie's letter, more than 5,000 words long, written on "enormous sheets of an army hospital muster roll" scavenged from a federal camp after the soldiers left, never reached her brother. In 1944, the letter was delivered to Angus Perkerson, Sunday Magazine editor of the Atlanta Journal, son of the Angus to whom it originally was addressed. In 1864 the letter had been rescued from a heap of mail dumped on the floor of the railway depot in Charleston, S. C. and taken to Ohio by a federal soldier, Samuel A. Wildman, later Judge Wildman of Norwalk, Ohio. The letter reposed in the collection of the Western Reserve Historical Association of Cleveland for many years. In 1944, Wildman's daughter, Mrs. J. A. Fenner of Cleveland, decided the letter should go to Angus's family. She entrusted it to Mrs. Harvey Kurz who was going to visit Atlanta. Mrs. Kurz delivered it to the only likely name she found in the Atlanta telephone directory.

"We are cut off from the world as yet, but I hope we will be all right soon... Atlanta is a perfect mass of ruins. All the public buildings are gone except the City Hall... We are making our calculations to live rather hard next year. But if we can live at all, I am not afraid that we will perish." [52]

The Atlanta area, in the fall of 1864, was threatened by a new kind of predator created by the war -- abandoned pets gone wild.

Sarah Huff recalled: "The sound seemed to start a long way off and first came to us from the northeast or the direction of Peachtree Creek. Mother said it sounded to her like the moaning of doves. But no doves or other birds were heard, even when the springtime came. The bluebirds were missed for three years. No, it was not the sound of doves, but the distant baying of dogs, dangerous dogs... The baying of these animals in unison was the only sound to break the profound silence..." Ravenous felines grew bold and entered homes, "glaring, ready to devour the scanty food before anybody could scare them away from the pot, the skillet, or the half-canteen tin plates on the table." [53]

Christmas was a grim affair in DeKalb County in 1864.

Tallulah House Cook was the daughter of Philip H. House and Georgia Ann Evins, the granddaughter of Samuel House and north DeKalb pioneer John L. Evins. Her House grandfather's brick home on Peachtree Road served as Sherman's headquarters in 1864. In a 1935 letter, Tallulah wrote:

"I remember a lot about the hard times we went through the last years of the war between the states. My mother refugeed with Uncle William Palmer who was a cripple and couldn't go to the war, and his family. They took their slaves, horses, mules, and some milk cows. My mother had many hogs and cattle that she could not take, so she had them driven into a lot and before leaving we all went out and looked at them. I guess we did it to tell them goodbye since we didn't even see them again.

"We went somewhere in Hall County and rented cabins from a Mr. Turk and I remember we got so short of food that my mother was killing her milk cows to feed us and when he found us so short of food he went home and sent us a two-horses wagon load of provisions by an old slave, Ceb. On returning from Hall County we go to the home of Grandmother Evins on Christmas Eve and spent the night; times were so hard that no one noticed that it was Christmas and the children did not hang their stockings that night. It was very cold and there was a shortage of bed covers since the Yankees had stolen a great deal from my grandmother, so they took the six little girls, three Palmer girls and three House girls, and put them in the same bed, three at the head of the bed and three at the foot of the bed and covered them with a few bed (covers). None of us smothered and two out of the six are now living.

"While we were staying in the cabins in Hall County we had a big snow and the cabins were very open so my mother took counterpanes and stretched them over the top of the four poster bed in order to keep the greatest part of the snow off us while we slept."

Chapter 26 Notes

1. Garrett, Franklin M., 1954, 1969, Atlanta and Environs -- A Chronicle of Its People and Events, Vol. 1, page 562.

2. Gay, Mary A. H., 1879, 1979, Life In Dixie During The War, pages 91 and 104.

3. Garrett, Franklin M., 1954, 1969, Atlanta and Environs -- A Chronicle of Its People and Events, Vol. 1, page 662.

4. Gay, Mary A. H., 1879, 1979, Life In Dixie During The War, page 93.

5. Garrett, Franklin M., 1954, 1969, Atlanta and Environs -- A Chronicle of Its People and Events, Vol. 1, pages 568-590.

6. Garrett, Franklin M., 1954, 1969, Atlanta and Environs -- A Chronicle of Its People and Events, Vol. 1, pages 595-597.

7. Garrett, Franklin M., 1954, 1969, Atlanta and Environs -- A Chronicle of Its People and Events, Vol. 1, page 597. Gay, Mary A. H., 1879, 1979, Life In Dixie During The War.

8. Gay, Mary A. H., 1879, 1979, Life In Dixie During The War, pages 105 and 117.

9. Ervin, Robert M., July 19, 1951, "Decatur's Role In The Battle For Atlanta," DeKalb New Era, page 11.

10. Garrett, Franklin M., 1954, 1969, Atlanta and Environs -- A Chronicle of Its People and Events, Vol. 1, pages 606-607.

11. Cook, Tallulah House, May, 1935, "Reminiscences of the House and Evins Families."

12. Atlanta Campaign, Official Records of the Union and Confederate Armies, Series I, Volume XXXVIII, Part V, pages 175-176.

13. Ervin, Robert M., July 19, 1951, "Decatur's Role In The Battle For Atlanta," The DeKalb New Era, page 11. Ervin, Robert M., August 16, 1951, "Battle of Decatur Was A Fierce Struggle," DeKalb New Era, page 10.

14. Ervin, Robert M., July 19, 1951, "Decatur's Role In The Battle For Atlanta," DeKalb New Era, page 11.

15. Ervin, Robert M., July 19, 1951, "Decatur's Role In The Battle For Atlanta," DeKalb New Era, page 11.

16. Ervin, Robert M., July 19, 1951, "Decatur's Role In The Battle For Atlanta," The DeKalb New Era, page 11. Ervin, Robert M., August 16, 1951, "Battle of Decatur Was A Fierce Struggle," DeKalb New Era, page 10. Garrett, Franklin M., 1954, 1969, Atlanta and Environs -- A Chronicle of Its People and Events, Vol. 1, page 612. Powell genealogy files, DeKalb Historical Society.

17. Ervin, Robert M., July 19, 1951, "Decatur's Role In The Battle For Atlanta," DeKalb New Era, page 11.

18. Bond, Lula Sams, February 23, 1967, comments contained in a talk about her grandfather, Washington Jackson Houston, DeKalb Historical Society. Clarke, Caroline McKinney, 1973, 1996, The Story of Decatur.

19. Ervin, Robert M., July 19, 1951, "Decatur's Role In The Battle For Atlanta," The DeKalb New Era, page 11. Ervin, Robert M., August 16, 1951, "Battle of Decatur Was A Fierce Struggle," DeKalb New Era, page 10.

20. Ervin, Robert M., July 19, 1951, "Decatur's Role In The Battle For Atlanta," DeKalb New Era, page 11.

21. Gay, Mary A. H., 1879, 1979, Life In Dixie During The War, pages 129-130.

22. Swanton House files, DeKalb Historical Society.

23. Gay, Mary A. H., 1879, 1979, Life In Dixie During The War, page 158.

24. Ervin, Robert M., July 19, 1951, "Decatur's Role In The Battle For Atlanta," The DeKalb New Era, page 11. Ervin, Robert M., August 16, 1951, "Battle of Decatur Was A Fierce Struggle," DeKalb New Era, page 10.

25. Garrett, Franklin M., 1954, 1969, Atlanta and Environs -- A Chronicle of Its People and Events, Vol. 1, page 609.

26. Garrett, Franklin M., 1954, 1969, Atlanta and Environs -- A Chronicle of Its People and Events, Vol. 1, pages 612-614.

27. Garrett, Franklin M., 1954, 1969, Atlanta and Environs -- A Chronicle of Its People and Events, Vol. 1, page 610. Ervin, Robert M., July 19, 1951, "Decatur's Role In The Battle For Atlanta," DeKalb New Era, page 11.

28. Ervin, Robert M., July 19, 1951, "Decatur's Role In The Battle For Atlanta," The DeKalb New Era, page 11. Ervin, Robert M., August 16, 1951, "Battle of Decatur Was A Fierce Struggle," DeKalb New Era, page 10.

29. Ervin, Robert M., July 19, 1951, "Decatur's Role In The Battle For Atlanta," The DeKalb New Era, page 11. Ervin, Robert M., August 16, 1951, "Battle of Decatur Was A Fierce Struggle," DeKalb New Era, page 10.

30. Nix, Dorothy, personal collection, DeKalb Historical Society. Ervin, Robert M., August 16, 1951, "Battle of Decatur Was A Fierce Struggle," DeKalb New Era, page 10, citing an article entitled "Lincoln and Dixie: The Yankee Conversion of Some Southern Songs" by Richard Barksdale Harwell.

31. Ervin, Robert M., July 19, 1951, "Decatur's Role In The Battle For Atlanta," The DeKalb New Era, page 11. Ervin, Robert M., August 16, 1951, "Battle of Decatur Was A Fierce Struggle," DeKalb New Era, page 10. Garrett, Franklin M., 1954, 1969, Atlanta and Environs -- A Chronicle of Its People and Events, Vol. 1, pages 618-619.

32. Garrett, Franklin M., 1954, 1969, Atlanta and Environs -- A Chronicle of Its People and Events, Vol. 1, pages 619-621.

33. Garrett, Franklin M., 1954, 1969, Atlanta and Environs -- A Chronicle of Its People and Events, Vol. 1, page 626.

34. Garrett, Franklin M., 1954, 1969, Atlanta and Environs -- A Chronicle of Its People and Events, Vol. 1, pages 627-629.

35. Garrett, Franklin M., 1954, 1969, Atlanta and Environs -- A Chronicle of Its People and Events, Vol. 1, pages 631-635.

36. Gay, Mary A. H., 1879, 1979, Life In Dixie During The War, page 166.

37. Garrett, Franklin M., 1954, 1969, Atlanta and Environs -- A Chronicle of Its People and Events, Vol. 1, pages 634, 640.

38. Gay, Mary A. H., 1879, 1979, Life In Dixie During The War, page 208. Clarke, Caroline McKinney, 1973, 1997, The Story of Decatur 1823-1899. Candler, Charles Murphey, November 9, 1922, Historical Address.

39. Gay, Mary A. H., 1879, 1979, Life In Dixie During The War, page 205.

40. Gay, Mary A. H., 1879, 1979, Life In Dixie During The War, page 207.

41. Garrett, Franklin M., 1954, 1969, Atlanta and Environs -- A Chronicle of Its People and Events, Vol. 1, page 647.

42. Nix, Dorothy, personal collection, DeKalb Historical Society.

43. Garrett, Franklin M., 1954, 1969, Atlanta and Environs -- A Chronicle of Its People and Events, Vol. 1, page 650.

44. Price, Vivian, July 17, 1991, "Lithonia Man's Journal Tells Of War-Time Hardships," DeKalb News/Sun, page 4A.

45. Gay, Mary A. H., 1879, 1979, Life In Dixie During The War, page 222.

46. Clarke, Donald S., n. d., "The Reverends William Henry Clarke and Elijah Henry Clarke of Wesley Chapel Methodist Church."

47. Gay, Mary A. H., 1879, 1979, Life In Dixie During The War, page 255.

48. Gay, Mary A. H., 1897, 1979, Life In Dixie During The War, page 280. Candler, Charles Murphey and Scott, October 29, 1950, "History of The Decatur Presbyterian Church, Decatur, Ga."

49. Gay, Mary A. H., 1897, 1979, Life In Dixie During The War, page 291.

50. Gay, Mary A. H., 1879, 1979, Life In Dixie During The War, page 260.

51. Garrett, Franklin M., 1954, 1969, Atlanta and Environs -- A Chronicle of Its People and Events, Vol. 1, page 660.

52. Perkerson, Medora Field, 1952, White Columns in Georgia, pages 332-339.

53. Perkerson, Medora Field, 1952, White Columns in Georgia, pages 332-339. Garrett, Franklin M., 1954, 1969, Atlanta and Environs -- A Chronicle of Its People and Events, Vol. 1, page 661.

Chapter 27

Confederate Gen. Robert E. Lee surrendered at Appomattox, Va. on April 9, 1865. Many in DeKalb did not consider the Confederacy defeated until Gen. Joseph E. Johnston gave up on April 26, 1865 in Raleigh, N. C. Between the two surrender dates, President Abraham Lincoln was assassinated on April 14. [1]

"Our entire people were to begin life over again in the midst of poverty, uncertainty, and under the watchful eye of the conqueror. The war was over, but military rule was not." [2]

DeKalb County's government had begun to function again in late 1864; by early the following year the Inferior Court had been reconstituted. The first post-war justices were E. J. Bailey, Zachariah R. Jones, R. J. Cooper, J. M. Smith and Michael Winningham. [3]

With Confederate money worthless, and lives in chaos, there was little work the government could do. There is no record that DeKalb County went into debt after the war, as the city of Atlanta did. Work was simply deferred. [4]

The April, 1865, grand jury found that there were no records of county finances on hand for the jurors to peruse. The 1865 presentments were the first since October of 1862:

"On account of the presence of the enemy in this County the officers of the County found it necessary to send off the Books and Public Records in order to secure them, and they have not yet been returned except the County Treasure (sic) Books. We are informed that the other Books and Records of the County are all safe and we commend the conduct of the officers in their efforts to secure them. The Books and Records not being present we cannot make further report in regard to them that are not present. We suggest that they be brought back at the earliest practicable manner consistent with their safety and security.

"We have through a committee examined the County Jail and Court House and consider the Jail safe with the exception of the locks to the outer doors. We respectfully call the attention of the proper authorities to them and recommend the necessary repairs be made as soon as practicable. We examined the County Treasury, and find that Levi Willard, former Treasurer paid over to the Clerk of the

Superior Court $230, balance on hand on the 15th of Sept. 1864. The present County Treasurer informed the committee that he has not received any funds in his hands, therefore has made no entry.

"We recommend that the officers of this county use their best efforts in the suppressing of crime and all immoral conduct. We tender our thanks as a body to the Judge for his courtesy returned to us. Also to the Solicitor General for his kindness to us."

      Henry P. Wooten, Foreman

Robert Cable	John T. Alford	Benjamin F. Veal
Simeon Smith	Mark H. Minor	Abraham Martin
Lodowick Tuggle	James Smith	William R. Ayers
Elijah Steward	Elijah Stevenson	Edmond J. Bailey
Stephen Martin	Esom J. Bond	James M. Smith. [5]
John McElroy	Edmond A. Turner	

As soon as the war was over, exiled DeKalb citizens returned to what was left of their homes, and assumed lifestyles vastly different from the ones they had left. In many ways, life became as it had been in pioneer days, with small farmers scratching out a living with the help only of their family and neighbors. [6]

"Destitution and stark poverty" marked the second half of the 1860s, especially in areas like DeKalb, where many were penniless and had no way of making a living."

The <u>Atlanta Daily Intelligencer</u> of September 13, 1865 wrote:

"There is a population in and on the suburbs of this city whose condition is such as to enlist the sympathies of all good people, and for whom something should be done. It is larger than a casual observer would imagine, and is entitled to more consideration than in times like these is usually accorded to the destitute. It consists of families who have been stripped of everything, and whose male members went into the war and have never returned. On the blackened ruins of their once happy homes, under sheds and tents that furnish but little protection from the storm, they simply exist, and such an existence. With barely food sufficient to keep soul and body together, and no assurance that even so small a pittance as that may long be reckoned upon, they live from day to day in an almost hopeless state of destitution. We have heard recounted from the lips of many, of these stories of their wants and sufferings, of hopes vanished, and of longings for rescue from their unhappy condition, that would melt the sternest of hearts to pity..."

The <u>Intelligencer</u> was less sympathetic toward the plight of the Negro during the years immediately following the war:

"Another class, larger and increasing, somewhat entitled to our pity and commiseration, are huddled together in most abject wretchedness everywhere, and living in idleness, vice and profligacy. Having brought upon their own heads the unhappy condition in which they are found, our feelings are not so keenly aroused in their behalf. We allude to the recently liberated slaves who are able-bodied and can be made useful if the proper steps were taken to put them to labor. As now found in persistent idleness, life to them -- and more especially a life of freedom -- is a curse. Nothing short of the strong arm of the law can ameliorate their condition, and we hope soon to see that now dormant element of usefulness made to subserve some good end.

"An hour's stroll on the suburbs of Atlanta will reveal much that requires Christian intervention on the part of the benevolent, as well as the application of civil or military regulations. Of the two, the former appeals loudly to our hearts; of the latter it may be said that the good of society, and the abatement of crime, demand interference, and that speedily!" [7]

Many former slaves flocked to Atlanta, some drawn by a rumor that at Christmastime in 1865, the United States government would confiscate property and give each Negro 40 acres and a mule. With no means of support from their former owners or paying jobs, many resorted to stealing from gardens and chicken houses. The Freedmen's Bureau, organized in the fall of 1865, provided some support. Before January 15, 1866, bureau policy allowed Negroes to enter into work contracts with whomever they chose; after that date, the bureau began assigning job situations. [8]

Confederate veteran John Barnett Steward (1833-1893) survived the battlefield only to find another kind of war for survival awaited him at home. Trained as a lawyer, he went to work scavaging lumber to rebuild an Atlanta foundry. The lifelong Stone Mountain area resident and former lawyer wrote:

"In September, 1861, I went into the service of the Confederate Government and served up to the surrender in 1865, being with the Western Army all the time, and under Johnston in North Carolina, and in command of Company I, in the 42nd Georgia Regiment.

When I arrived home my wife and two lovely little daughters met me to say that they had nothing to welcome me to but their loving embrace, which was all that I could ask in those dark and gloomy days. Our first three days' meals were made of what I had brought home, to-wit: hard tack, bacon and coffee. I had one dollar in silver which had been given to me by the General commanding the Confederate Army, that noble and grand hero, Joseph E. Johnston, who had no superior.

"With all the dark and murky clouds hanging over and around me, I shouldered my ax and walked two miles at early dawn and returned late at night, and worked hard getting out boards to cover what was known as the Hoge and Mills Foundry in Atlanta, at 75 cents per day, until I had earned $18. Then with my old tattered `Joe Brown Suit,' I marched to the U. S. Commissary and expended the full sum for bacon, flour and coffee.

"Then, without means, but with an iron will, I began the building of a steam saw mill, and with close management and hard work and hard living, in three months I was sawing lumber at the rate of five to six thousand feet per day and selling it at the rate of $3.50 to $5.50 per hundred. With this, I was still sleeping on a blanket in the corner of the fence, doing my own cooking, and visiting my family twice a week, Wednesday and Saturday nights."

Steward later was able to practice law again, and was elected solicitor-general, ordinary, state representative from DeKalb. [9]

With so much to rebuild, one good way to make a living in post-war DeKalb was to operate a sawmill that could be moved to the jobsite. Some who operated these steam-powered itinerant sawmills were Cash, Chewning, Cheek, Dunnahoo, Fincher, Johns, Jones, Lively, Mason, McElroy, McWilliams, Metcalf, Morris, Steele, Tilly, Talton and Wallace.

One of first to establish himself was Michael A. Steele. Steele lived two miles from Decatur on what is now Medlock Road. Together with J. A. Mason, Steele operated a mill based on Hunter's Branch near the currently location of the Decatur swimming pool on Church Street. One of the most active DeKalb sawmillers was Thomas H. Fincher who lived on McDonough Road just south of the South River. At various times after the war, Fincher owned and operated 11 mills. Fincher "was a man of fine temperament, friendly disposition, and pleasing personality. He was fastidious in his tastes, and nearly always wore a Prince Albert coat." William W. Lively, who lived on Briarcliff Road near the intersection of Shallowford Road (now Oak Grove), operated a mill that was later run by his son, C. M. Lively. "William W. Lively was in every sense -- in his appearance, in his dress, in his speech, in the discharge of his duties as a citizen, a typical Southerner of the old school." Lively was a member of the DeKalb Board of Commissioners in the early 1900s when board had several members. [10]

The sawmills were especially busy in DeKalb in 1866. They supplied lumber to a new chair factory on the northeast corner of Sycamore Street and East Court Square. William Mosely and W. H. Minor bought lumber to rebuild the Indian Creek Baptist Church which had been burned by Sherman's soldiers on June 8, 1863. The Rev. H. T. Buchanan conducted the first services in the new church building. Ben Veal of Stone Mountain built his grist mill on Mountain Creek, one of the business ventures that made him one of the wealthiest men in east DeKalb. The mill operated until about 1884.[11]

In those desperate times, job opportunities sometimes were not completely legitimate. Coal for heating was scarce after the war, and wood was in demand. Enterprising small businessmen simply cut trees without getting permission from property owners. [12]

Less than six months after Sherman's departure, a different kind of siege was in store for the governments of Atlanta and Georgia. On May 3, 1865, a military government was installed where a civilian mayor and governor already ruled. [13]

Thomas Maguire of Rockbridge wrote in May and June, 1865:
"May 3 -- Everything is now in confusion as regards government.

"May 5 -- Lithonia... conferred three (Masonic) degrees... the times are out of joint... I fear we will have bad times, but we must take them as they come.

"May 8 -- Some 30 Yanks passed at 11 o'clock on their way to Covington. They left an advertisement offering a reward of $100,000 in gold for the apprehension of Jefferson Davis. I hope they will not find him.

"May 10 -- Some Yanks passed this morning. They wanted corn but got none. The dark hour is coming.

"May 13 -- I have no mind to do anything. A few Yanks passed today. Wish they were all in Heaven.

"May 14 -- Sunday... the family all well and we still have a little to eat. It is said there are more Yankees coming this way. It may well be so. I did not get to meeting (at church). I now think I will put away some more corn. If the Yanks should come they will take all I have. If I hide it they may

After the war, Elijah Henry Clarke operated an itinerant sawmill. Clarke is pictured in the foreground of this photo taken in the late 1880s. Note the man standing behind the oxen, holding a whip. The term, "Georgia Cracker," described the teamster who controlled his oxen with loud cracks of his whip. (Donald S. Clarke; Vanishing Georgia Collection, Georgia Department of Archives and History)

not find it, but if they do I will be no worse off than if I leave it in the crib... What a country we have at the present time! We have nothing that we can call our own. The vile Yankees take everything they please and go where they please. We are a powerless people, but by no means a conquered people. I have lost hope of yet gaining our independence.

"May 19 -- John E. and James H. C., came home from Atlanta. Got their paroles... John E. brought today's paper. From it we are back in the Union, but how I do not know and do not much care. I look for nothing but hard times for the balance of my life. What will become of my family it is hard to say. I had hoped for better things, but hoped in vain, so I will try and put up with my lot as best I can. I have no heart to do anything. All is dark and gloomy. I could weep, but that would do no good, so I will stop writing on this painful subject.

"May 28 -- Sunday. Would like to know the state of our country, more particularly our situation as a people, whether we have a government or not. What is to become of us as a people. I fear we will have bad times, but some think otherwise, and some think we will be treated kindly by the Yankee government, but I am not of this opinion. I have no faith in the Yankees, nor in their love for us. They have treated me so badly I can never forget their meanness and dishonesty -- as a people I look upon them as rogues and swindlers.

"June 4 -- Three or four of Mr. Lee's negroes went off this morning to the Yankees.

"June 5 -- Andrew gone to the Yankees with the Lee negroes.

"June 6 -- Nearly all the talk now is of the negroes going to the Yankees. They will see a hard time before long. Some of mine may go. It will be a disadvantage to me and a great misfortune to them...

"June 18 -- Report said our negroes would leave last night, but I did not believe it -- Dick is at his post this morning. I think the excitement of the negroes going to the Yankees is nearly over. The poor negroes will be sorry enough after they realize the effects of this, to them, great revolution. The race, I think will be exterminated in a few years. The negroes will be like the Indians, but in a far worse condition. They are now of little profit to their owners, and they cannot make out by themselves. Work they will not, still they must live. The whites will kill them in self-defense..."

Gov. Joseph E. Brown discovered early on who was in charge in Georgia. On May 22, 1865 he issued a call for the General Assembly to meet. The military authorities not only countermanded his call, but arrested the governor, as well as Alexander H. Stephens, Howell Cobb, Benjamin H. Hill and other prominent leaders. After his release, Brown would move to Atlanta, where he would live the remainder of his life.

James Johnson of Columbus was appointed provisional governor of Georgia. A statewide election was held on November 15 resulted in Charles J. Jenkins being the new governor. Oliver Winningham of Stone Mountain was elected state representative from DeKalb County. [14]

Sadly, DeKalb had yet to see the last of killing associated with the war. James T. Jones, a 22-year-old Confederate veteran, was killed by "a drunken Yankee" in Decatur in August of 1865. In retaliation, James's brother, John, killed seven Union soldiers, stuffed their bodies in beer barrels and dumped them in Peachtree Creek. "Not surprisingly, John had to leave Decatur for a while." [15]

The final war-related death was that of an innocent civilian. Sarah (Sallie) Durham, 17, and her family had just returned to their Sycamore Street home after waiting out the war at her grandmother's home. Sallie was the daughter of Dr. William H. Durham and the late Sarah Lowe. Durham had come to Decatur in 1859 with his second wife, Georgia A. Allen (Wood), and his four children, including Sallie's brothers, John and William, and sister, Catherine.

Sallie was making breakfast on the morning of September 1, 1865 at the rear of the Durham home, which faced the ruins of the burned Decatur depot, about 350 yards away. Hearing an incoming train, Sallie went to dining room window to watch. While standing at the window, she was hit in the chest by a bullet fired recklessly by a Union soldier from a train window. Sallie managed to walk to her father and say, "Oh, father, the Yankees have killed me!" She died a week later.

A Gen. Stephenson, in command of the federal post at Atlanta, refused to believe that Sallie had even been shot, much less that she had been shot by one of his soldiers. In the course of his investigation, he visited the Durham home. "In full uniform, with spur and sabre rattling upon the bare floor, he advanced to the bed where the dying girl lay, and threw back the covering to see if she had really been shot. This intrusion almost threw her into a spasm..." Nothing was ever done about finding or punishing the errant soldier.

"For years a great stain of blood remained upon the floor, as a grim and silent reminder of this most awful tragedy..."

One Decatur citizen remembered Sallie: "One of the most vivid pictures of the past in my memory is that of Sallie Durham emptying her pail of blackberries into the hands of Federal prisoners on a train that had just stopped for a moment at Decatur, in 1863. We had all been gathering berries at Moss's Hill, and stopped on our way home for the train to pass." [16]

Apparently, the U. S. government saw no reason to establish military rule in DeKalb. The grand jury in October of 1865 found the government in disarray:

"... We find in the hands of the Ordinary the amount of $860.64 1/2 in Confederate States funds, the same being the balance of school fund not disbursed; also that no funds have been received since November 25, 1862. On examination we find the sheriff's book in a neat condition... but one entry having been made on the docket since October term of Court, 1862. We find that the County Treasurer has not received any monies, but we find in the hands of the Inferior Court notes amounting to $212.98, and the further sum of eleven dollars in currency belonging to the county. We further find that the amount of $230 in Confederate money was turned over by Levi Willard, the former County Treasurer, to J. M. Hawkins, clerk of the Superior Court.

In a hasty examination of the books of the clerk of the Superior and Inferior Court we find no entries of the amount of monies received by the latter from the State for distribution to the needy of the county, nor the amount of money that has been distributed by the agents of the Court. We further find that there have been two mules, one wagon and a lot of sacks advertised for sale, but cannot find what disposition was made of them, and consequently request the Inferior Court to investigate the matter and lay it before the people of the county.

"We have examined the Jail and Court House and find them both very much out of repair. All the inner doors of the jail need repairing; also one of the cells and part of the stone steps. The windows of the Court House are in a very bad condition, the sash being broken and the lights out; the walls are defaced and the locks off of some of the doors, altogether rendering the Court House uncomfortable and the jail insecure. We would respectfully recommend the Inferior Court to have them repaired as soon as the funds of the county will allow it. We find that the roads and bridges in the different parts of the county need repairs and we request the Inferior Court to take such steps as are necessary to put them in good order.

"We request the Legislature to relieve the County from the State Tax for the year 1866..."

E. A. Davis, Foreman [17]

Although surely many citizens had come to accept the defeat of the Confederacy, many more harbored a stubborn resentment toward the federal government and a smoldering hatred of those who had caused such massive devastation to their lives and homes.

One year after Sherman's March to the Sea, on November 15, 1865, Martha Amanda Qullin (1838-1913), later Mrs. Thomas Hanby Mitchell, daughter of the Rev. and Mrs. William Quillin wrote to her cousin Sarah E. Quillin in Ipava, Ill.

"Near Decatur, Georgia,
Nov. 15, 1865.

"Dear Cousin Sallie:
"Yours of Sept. 25 was duly received and should have been promptly answered had not sickness prevented...

"I wrote you in '61, indeed it seems a long time since we have heard from you; true I wrote your Father a line or two a year ago, and committed it to the care of the most reasonable man I found in all Sherman's army. I received his reply in January. It had been inspected and came to me by flag of truce from Savannah. I do not remember anything I wrote your Father, but the circumstances under which it was written can *never be forgotten*. Heaven grant I may *never* pass another such day. Could you have looked in upon us but for a moment, you would have thought in impossible for life and reason to survive the torture to which mind and body were that day subjected. But that day had an end, and in safety we welcomed the much needed repose that night alone brought us. But the act of dating my letter brings forcibly to my mind the fact that this day one year ago was the most miserable of all my life. Sherman's troops were then passing us on their way to Savannah.

Their orders were positive to *burn* and *destroy everything* on their march, and well they executed this most *christian* order of his *most christian majesty*. All day and all night one continual stream of wagons and guards poured by. As darkness came on the work of burning commenced, from Atlanta to Rockbridge, a distance of twenty miles, we in the center. On every side, as far as the eye could reach, the lurid flames of burning buildings lit up the heavens and dissipated the darkness of night. I could stand out on the verandah, and for two or three miles watch them as they came on. I could mark when they reached the residence of each and every friend on the road. I could see the first building fired, and then the torch carried round and round until I knew that everything on the premises was wrapped in flames; then hear the wild shout they raised, as torch in hand, they started for the next house. The night was cold, but I never once left my post. With my sisters and others I stood from dark until daylight, and watched their onward progress. Calmly I calculated the distance they travelled in a given time; how long it took to fire such a number of buildings, and ascertained almost to the very minute when the torch would be set to our house. As the flames rolled on I could hear, or fancy that I heard, above the oaths, the yells, the eternal gab of the Yankee army, the screams of the frightened neighbors as the fire swallowed up the labors of a life time. Thus the night rolled on. The Academy, the Church (Indian Creek), in two or three hundred yards of us, were laid in ashes. The torch several times brought fire to our house, but each time it was extinguished. The sitting room was Headquarters and full of officers who must not be disturbed. Consequently an order had been given to burn nothing on the place. I knew nothing of it. I looked abroad upon the smoldering ruins, the smoke almost suffocated me. I knew it was not long until daylight -- but had no reason to hope that we would have a change of clothing, a mouthful of bread or a roof to shelter us. If it was sin may Heaven forgive me if I prayed that I might never see the destruction, the deep distress, the morn would reveal to me.

"That, too, has all passed and lives only in memory; but no one, I hope, will ever expect me to love Yankees. They tell us the war has ended, and some cry lustily, *peace peace*. I have peered into the deep gloom that surrounds us and can scarce see a glimmer of that welcome visitant. The shadow of a great sorrow has darkened our land. He, who a short time since, was the pride of our Confederacy, the pure statesman, the christian gentleman, the accomplished scholar, our beloved President Jefferson

Davis, now ekes out a miserable existence in a Yankee bastille. In proportion as his sufferings increase, our sympathy for him and hatred of his oppressors increase also. One thing in the past few weeks has cheered us a little and that is the return to his home of A. H. Stephens from his long confinement in a Yankee prison. He comes back to us with his head as white as the eternal snows of winter, and we hope, before a great while, to know all that he suffered while there...

"We are not sorry for anything we have done down here, are not repenting, are not whipped or subjugated, or anything of that kind. True, we were with numbers overpowered, but we battled upon our own soil, and for that soil we contended for every principle of honor and justice, and for the most sacred rights -- for the sanctity of home, for self government, for the truths of God's word. The North fought for no principle and no right -- her sole aim was to subjugate the South.

"We expected to go back to our home in LaFayette when the war ended, but our house and everything there has been burned, and we have nothing to go to. This is now the poorest country in the world, and we are homeless wanderers through the desert. We had nothing left us and nothing to buy with, so I send you a scrap of our dresses we have been making. The cotton grew here and every thread of it was manufactured in the family. I wove it myself. We call it Dixie silk." [18]

As soon as the war was over, and the realization of freedom settled on DeKalb's former slaves, they began to organize churches of their own. Although the actual organization date is unknown, the first black church in DeKalb apparently was Mt. Pleasant Baptist Church. Joseph Walker, a former slave owner, fostered organization of the church. Walker gave land for the church and a cemetery, as well as a church building. Walker also preached until a black minister for the church was found. On August 17, 1869, Walker deeded two and one-half aces of land on the north side of Land Lot 229 in the 15th District of DeKalb to church deacons Jacob Austin, James Howard, Robert Fowler and Jasper Howard. Mt. Pleasant was located off Covington Road, east of Decatur, and is located today on Porter Road. [19]

F lat Rock Methodist Church also was organized by the black community in Lithonia about this time. Founders were Sam Ford, Yoke McKnight, Alex Henderson, Edmond and Nathan Bryant and members of Reed and Holt families. In 1870 church leaders bought land on Panola Road; the congregation later moved to Flat Rock Road in Lithonia.

Mary Gay recalled that a black Sunday school was organized at Decatur Presbyterian Church. Shortly thereafter, an African Methodist Episcopal Church and a Negro Baptist Church were formed in Decatur.

Ben T. Hunter was superintendent of Decatur's Sunday school after the war, and John J. McKoy was the treasurer. Josiah Willard, son of Levi Willard, returned to Decatur from Ohio, and became the Sunday school librarian, replacing John C. Kirkpatrick, who moved to Atlanta. Post-war teachers were J. W. Kirkpatrick, Dr. P. F. Hoyle, the Rev. A. T. Holmes, W. W. Brimm, Milton A. Candler, George A. Ramspeck (later Sunday School treasurer for 27 years), Dr. John L. Hardman, H. H. Puckett, W. A. Moore (later superintendent), Cynthia Brown, Mrs. T. H. Chivers, Mrs. Eddleman, Mrs. Catharine Winn, Mrs. Jane Morgan, Lizzie Swanton, Mrs. E. A. Mason, Mrs. Valeria A. Hawkins, Mrs. J. J. McKoy and Miss Lee Moore. Music leaders were the Rev. J. D. Burkhead, Mrs. Mary Jane Wood, Joseph Morgan and Mrs. Martha Morgan.

Milton Candler recalled his years as a teacher: "I taught my pupils, a class of little boys, to read from the `blue-back speller,' and, when that lesson was over, read to them from the Bible, explaining it to them as best I could in all humility." Candler later was Sunday school superintendent.

Dr. (Peter) Holmes preached Decatur's first service after the war on August 27, 1865 in the Presbyterian sanctuary. The Rev. William Henry Clarke preached the first service in the Decatur Methodist Church after the war. [20]

President Andrew Johnson proclaimed the Civil War officially ended in April of 1866, but the "war of malice" against southern states by Congress was just beginning. The Civil Rights bill of 1866, including the 14th Amendment to the U. S. Constitution, which declared all persons born in the United States citizens, denied the right to vote to all citizens who had held office in a Southern state before the war or who had fought for the Confederacy. Further, the bill provided that disenfranchised persons did not count toward representation in Congress. Johnson vetoed the measure, but was overridden. [21]

The Atlanta area was struck with yet another smallpox epidemic in late 1865 and early '66. [22]

Sarah Jemison Ware Medlock, wife of John Williams Medlock, wrote to her daughter, Martha Medlock Terry in Texas, on March 12, 1866:

"... The small pox is more common that you ever knew the measles, yes is five times as much. I believe there has been thousands of cases. There is and has been more negroes died around here than belong to the place before the war. The Yanks is throwing them out. (No) blacks is with us except Jude and Mary... We left home in July '64 the 12th day. We left our furniture. We took a few chairs and bedding, the best or the most of our clothes -- our cattle we sold to the government except three cows and calves. We have one cow and calf is all the stock except two mules. We lost our hogs and horses. We refugeed to Washington County (Sandersville, Ga.), stayed there September '64 until November '65 (with John Williams Medlock's brother, Lewis Henry Medlock). The fighting was mostly from Peachtree Road around to Decatur. Our houses burned, our timber cut down on the home lot our shade trees -- pretty well all of our fruit trees.

"There has been thousands of pounds of lead picked up on our land. People supported their family picking up lead. They got 50 cents a pound before the surrender. The bombshells is plenty, many with the load in them.

"... I also told you about the boys, they are all at home except Thomas (Medlock),... his body lies in the nearest grave yard to his house. He was wounded in the 7 days fight before Richmond in '62... John (Medlock) came unhurt, only his constitution somewhat impaired. B. F. W. is alright at home, W. P. (William Parks Medlock) badly hurt, has lost his left hand and fore finger on his right hand neither amputated. Robert (Medlock) is also at home, has bad health. E. W. (Eli Wren Medlock) is living in Troop (sic) County. Was wounded at Sharpsburg, hurt badly but has, I learn got over it. I have not seem him since the surrender. Fletcher Tilly and Albert (Tilly) was both wounded, not serious." [23]

Georgia's first Confederate Memorial Day was celebrated on April 26, 1866 at Oakland Cemetery. Graves of the Confederate dead were decorated with flowers and boughs of cedar brought from Stone

Mountain. Federal military officials prohibited any oratory during the observance. A few days later the Atlanta Ladies Memorial Association was formed. The women took on the gruesome job of removing the bodies of dead Confederate soldiers that had lain in trenches and battlefields for more than a year. Proper burials were arranged for all soldiers recovered from sites within 10 miles of Atlanta. [24]

The DeKalb Grand Jury was concerned about the post-war influx of new people in April 1866:

"It is gratifying to us, and we feel that it is so to every good citizen, that the country is again restored to peace, with the Union of the States unimpaired, and we hope that the efforts of the people will be to perpetuate that Union and build up and restore our desolated country, and make that paramount to building up political parties. This alone can be done by encouraging proper emigration, and all the labor in the various branches that are induced by the fertility to our soil, genial climate, and the many advantages bestowed upon us by a kind Providence...

"We feel unwilling under present circumstances to recommend any appropriation for educational purposes at present, thinking the people will be sufficiently taxed without..."
        Joseph Walker, Foreman [25]

Once again, in 1866, the Georgia legislature took up the issue of public schools, this time passing a law establishing a statewide public school system, offering free instruction to white citizens between the ages of 16 and 21 and to any disabled and indigent soldier younger than 30. The system was to be supported by taxes collected by each county, and was to begin in January of 1868. The legislature's target date proved to be overly optimistic. No public school system materialized in Georgia until 1873. Likewise, the Atlanta Street Railroad Company, the forerunner of today's rapid transit system, was incorporated in 1866, but was unable to get underway. [26]

Unlike Decatur, school was interrupted for most DeKalb students in 1864. Gradually, private schools, like the one taught in north DeKalb by Jim Miller, began to reopen. Miller's school was located on what was later the Bob Bolton property in the summer of 1865. Among those attending were Billy Hardeman, the Melt Jones boys, the Morris boys (Emory, Andrew, John and Gid) and Parks and Albert Tilly. This school may have been the forerunner of the Doraville School which opened in what is now Flowers Park. The school was started by John Y. Flowers, and had one teacher. Parents provided wood for heating. Doraville School remained open for the next 106 years. The well once used by the school still sites on Church Street as a reminder of days gone by. [27]

A few new endeavors were launched successfully in 1866. An announcement ran in The Atlanta Daily Intelligencer for a new business in Stone Mountain:
        NEW GEORGIA RAILROAD
        EATING HOUSE
        At Stone Mountain

        Blue Front

The undersigned, proprietors of this New Eating House, take pleasure in notifying the traveling public, by railroad or otherwise, that it is now open for their accommodation. The best the country affords will always be on their table, and served up in the best style. A first-rate cook, and attentive servants are employed. The traveling public are invited to call and judge for themselves.

Pleasure Parties to the "Stone Mountain" will be accommodated at short notice with lunch or meals, and a hall provided them for the "dance," should they desire to indulge in it.

The undersigned, determined to please, only ask for a trial.

Don't forget the House with the Blue Front!
                    M. D. Lee & Co. Proprietors [28]

The U. S. Army stopped dispensing food to needy Atlanta citizens in 1866. To pick up the slack, the Atlanta city government borrowed money from the city of Louisville, Ky. to buy rations. The city of Decatur, Ill. also donated food. Theft in the city was at epidemic proportions. [29]

DeKalb apparently was faring better than its neighbors to the west, and thus escaped the crime that accompanied the food shortage. The grand jury of October, 1866, reported:

"We congratulate our fellow citizens upon the improved conditions of the morals of our county, and confiding as we do in the honesty and integrity of our neighbors, we trust the day will soon come when good citizens will be protected by law in all their rights and privileges and bad men punished for their misdeeds... The Treasurer's books, which are neatly kept, show that he has received the sum of $14.50, and that he has paid out the same upon the proper vouchers.

"The jail we find repaired with the exception of the debtors' room, but as there is no present use for that room, we do not recommend any work to be done upon it. The Court-House is now undergoing repairs..."
                    James Polk, Foreman.

John W. F. Tilly	Henry P. Wooten	John J. Whitlow
Alfred S. Fowler	John W. Fowler, Sr.	Eli J. Hulsey
James T. Cobb	John G. McWilliams	David Chestnut
Benjamin F. Veal	George A. Ramspeck	Ezekiel A. Davis
Augustus L. Pitts	John R. Mahaffey	Charles W. McGinnis
Garrett L. Morris	John W. Scruggs	Josiah J. Willard (son of
Thomas N. Paden	Benjamin F. Chapman	Levi) [30]
William G. Ham	John C. Ragsdale	

At the end of 1866, the Georgia government was at a loss to deal with a serious crisis. The state prison was overflowing with ex-slaves and outlaws who had come to Georgia from other parts of the country. There simply was no place to incarcerate any more lawbreakers, and state treasury was empty. The solution, however expedient in the beginning, would cause Georgia grief for many years to come.

The Georgia General Assembly passed an act "to regulate the manner in which the Penitentiary shall be managed, and to provide for farming out the same... The Governor shall cause to be advertised, for sixty days, in two or more newspapers in the State of Georgia, for proposals to farm out the Penitentiary; and the same shall be farmed out to such persons as shall take it on the best terms, and give such bond as the Governor may require to secure the comfort and security of the prisoners." Prisoners could be put to any work the lessee desired, and no lease could last longer than five years.

The first convicts, 100 Negroes, were leased in 1868 to work on the Georgia and Alabama Railroad for one year. The state received $2500. The Atlanta railroad-building firm of Grant, Alexander and Co. contracted with the state for the services of the all 393 inmates in the penitentiary in 1869. The fee was simply the expense of caring for the prisoners. By 1875, the state penitentiary had 926 convicts -- 90 white males, 805 black males, 30 black females and one white female. By leasing the prisoners, the state received $10,756.48 that year. What had been a state dilemma had turned into a profit-making enterprise. [31]

The DeKalb County Sunday School Association was organized by seven county Sunday schools on July 14, 1866 at Decatur Presbyterian Church. Z. R. Jones of Macedonia Baptist Church was the first president. Other first officers were Dr. P. F. Hoyle, Decatur Union Sunday school, vice president; B. Langford, Wesley Chapel Sunday school, vice president; R. McWilliams, Corinth Sunday school, vice president; and B. T. Hunter, Decatur Union Sunday school, secretary. The executive committee consisted of Joseph Walker, Indian Creek Sunday school; L. E. Jones, Mt. Vernon; Milton A. Candler, Decatur Union; J. J. Jones, Mt. Charlotte; and Dr. T. T. Key, Corinth.

The association held its first annual celebration at Wesley Chapel on the first Saturday in September. Esquire C. W. McGinnis was the association's marshal for many years. He wore a bright red sash across his chest in the manner of a marshal of the French empire. "His well remembered cry of `Order, gentlemen, order,' coming as it frequently did in the midst of a set speech by some noted orator for the occasion, not only stifled the audience, but momentarily distracted the speaker." [32]

Decatur Methodist Church also organized a Sunday School after the war. V. R. Tommey, a newcomer to Decatur, was the first superintendent, followed by W. F. Pattillo, J. Howell Green and George M. Napier. [33]

Congressional radicals succeeded in passing, over President Johnson's veto, the Reconstruction Act of 1867. Military government resumed in Georgia. The U. S. Army came once again to Georgia, this time to register the voters Congress deemed qualified and to arrange for election of delegates to a convention to draw up a new state constitution which would provide for Negro suffrage. The state legislature already had rejected the 14th Amendment. If such a constitution were approved, military rule would be withdrawn and Georgia readmitted to the Union. [34]

I. W. Avery wrote: "It was an amazing piece of statesmanship to disenfranchise our intelligence and make the hereditary slaves of two centuries rulers of our political destiny. It degraded, alarmed and exasperated our people. We had the whole argument of the case on our side. They had the might. Our reconstructors had excelled themselves in this last fantastic art of national restoration. Our people were angered to white heat, and they entered upon an uncompromising fight against the astounding project." Many Georgians were ready to secede again. [35]

Maj. Gen. John Pope was appointed commander of Third Military District, which included Georgia, Alabama and Florida. First on Pope's agenda was organizing boards of voter registration in each senatorial district, each consisting of two white men and one Negro. Registrars apparently did not consider their job to educate former slaves on the voting process or to regulate registration. Negroes brought baskets and bucket, because they thought they were going to receive some free commodity.

Many registered two and three times. Despite the resentment and confusion, the constitutional convention got underway on December 9, 1867 and lasted until March 11, 1868. There were 169 delegates to the convention. The majority, 111, were white Georgia reconstructionists known as Scalawags. There were 37 Negroes, 12 conservative whites and nine Carpetbaggers, white newcomers from Northern states.

Among the Negroes were two notables who were distinct opposites. Aaron Alpeoria Bradley's background included a prison sentence in New York and losing his license to practice law in Massachusetts. He was expelled from the convention for "malicious mouthing." Henry M. Turner had been chaplain of a Negro unit in the Union Army and served in the Georgia legislature in 1868. He later became a bishop of the African Methodist Episcopal Church.

The session was popularly called "The Menagerie Convention," a great show which accomplished little except to spend $2000 per day. One significant and lasting change made by the convention was moving the state capital from Milledgeville to Atlanta. [36]

In August of 1867, Pope decreed that Negroes would serve on juries. Judge Augustus Reece of Ocmulgee Circuit refused to carry out the mandate and was removed from office. [37]

The DeKalb Grand Jury was concerned about public roads and buildings in April of 1867:

"We recommend the Inferior Court to have all Public Roads thoroughly worked after crops are made.

"We have examined the Public buildings and find they need repairing to some extent, but on account of the pecuniary embarrassment of the County, we do not recommend any funds being appropriated for that purpose.

"In taking into consideration the moral condition of the country we have but little cause to complain, but hope the day is not far distant when Society will become more refined; our morals more elevated, and good citizens will be protected in all their rights and privilege, and bad men punished for their transgressions.

"In taking leave of his Honor, Judge Hiram Warner, we unanimously approve the able, efficient and dignified manner in which he has presided, and we flatter ourselves that we can assure our fellow citizens, that when and where he presides, he will use his best endeavors to enforce law and order."
William Wright, Foreman.

James L. Kilgore	Harris Crowley	Edward M. Kittridge
John T. Alford	Harris Goodwin	Thomas T. Key
Marcus L. Minor	Charles M. Jones	William W. Veal
William S. McLain	John F. Brown	Hilliard J. Fowler
Martin C. McKee	James J. Cowan	Daniel S. Jones
John W. Weekes	Paschal C. Phillips	Seaborn Crowley. [38]
Job J. Marbut	Lewis Ethridge	
William P. Bond	James C. Chupp	

While several schools for Negro children had opened in the Atlanta area in 1867, thanks to the

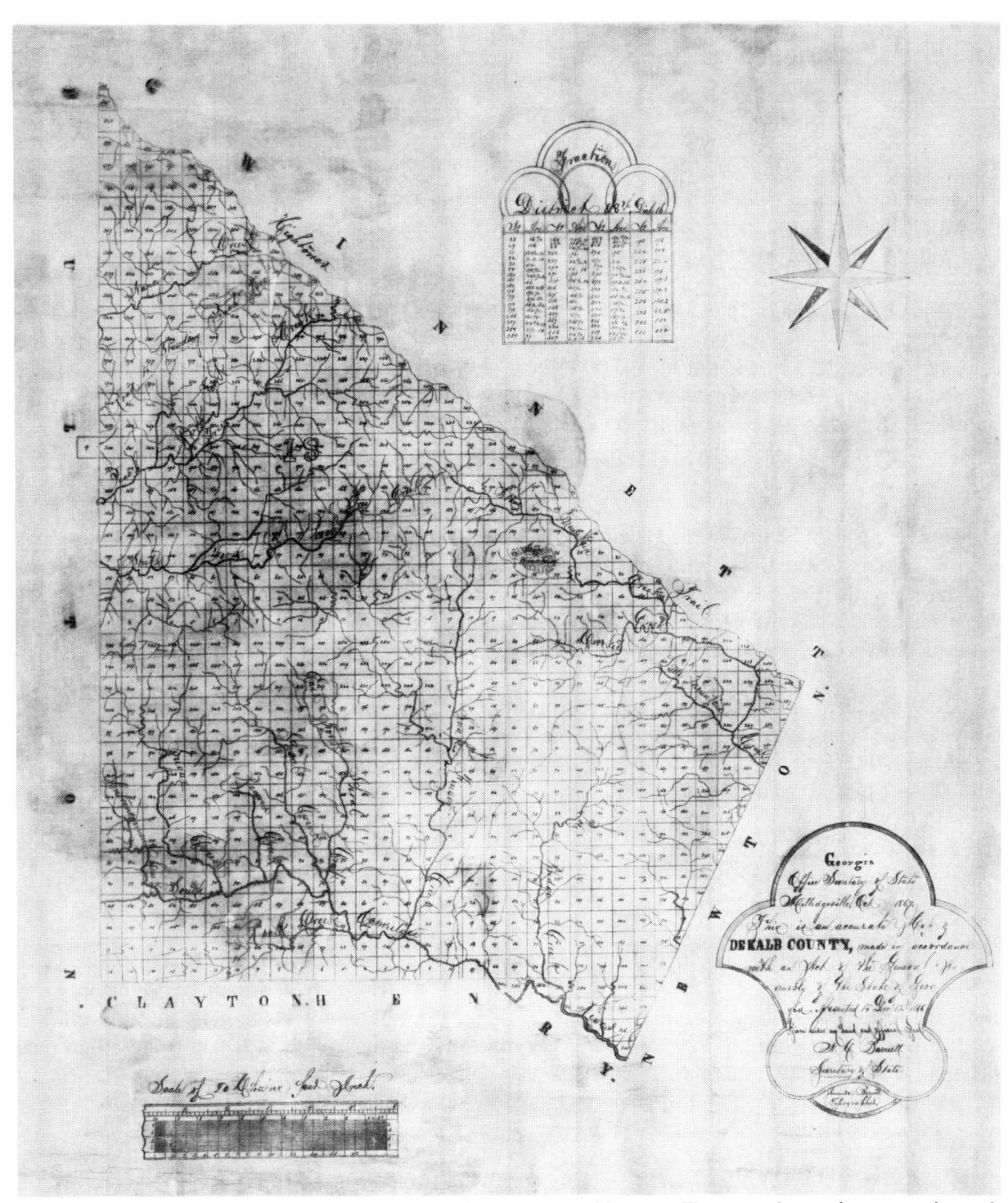

The oldest DeKalb County map in existence is this one, created in 1867. The map shows rivers, creeks and land lots. (DeKalb Historical Society)

Freedmen's Bureau and private philanthropic efforts, new efforts to establish public schools for white children again were unsuccessful. Several notable endeavors were launched in Atlanta in 1867. A lottery was established to raise money for war widows and orphans. The Young Men's Library

THE HISTORY OF DEKALB COUNTY, GA. 1822-1900 • CHAPTER 27 387

Association of the City of Atlanta was formed. Commuter rail service was launched between Atlanta and West End. Rich's department store opened its doors, and patrons sampled a new taste treat at the area's first soda fountain. [39]

One of DeKalb's many well-known Irish natives, John McWilliams, died in January of 1867. Born in Ireland in 1780, he came to the Panthersville District on Christmas Eve, 1827. The Pythagoras Lodge conducted the funeral; he is buried in an unmarked grave in the Clifton Methodist Church cemetery in the Mills District. McWilliams had six sons: John G., Alexander, Robert, Samuel, David and James, who was the victim of Atlanta's first homicide in 1848. [40]

Gen. Pope left Georgia early in 1868 after an undistinguished tenure as the state's military commander of Georgia, and was replaced by Maj. Gen. George Gordon Meade. Members of the constitutional convention demanded an additional $40,000 to pay for its expenses. State treasurer John Jones and Gov. Jenkins refused to pay. Meade removed both from office, replacing them with Brevet Brig. Gen. Thomas H. Ruger as governor and Brevet Capt. Charles F. Rockwell as treasurer. Meanwhile, Gov. Jenkins went to Washington, D. C., taking with him for safekeeping the state seal and $400,000. [41]

Meade also disqualified two Democratic (Conservative) candidates for governor before allowing Gen. John B. Gordon to run against the Republican nominee, Rufus Brown Bullock, a New York native who served in the Confederate Army, in the April, 1868, elections. After a bitter campaign, Bullock was elected and a surprisingly progressive constitution approved. The newly formed Ku Klux Klan made its presence felt for the first time, intimidating Negroes into staying away from the polls. [42]

Milton A. Candler was elected to the state senate from the 34th District, which included DeKalb, Gwinnett and Henry counties. The Rev. William Henry Clarke was chosen to represent DeKalb in the state House. The 1868 legislature, convened on July 4 in crowded quarters at the Atlanta City Hall, ratified the 14th Amendment, but handed Gov. Bullock a defeat by choosing as U. S. senators Joshua Hill and Dr. Homer Virgil Milton Miller over the governor's candidates, former Gov. Joseph E. Brown and Foster Blodgett. [43]

Georgia was once again allowed representation in the U. S. Congress, and military authority was withdrawn, although Meade remained in command. As temperatures rose in the summer of 1868, the political climate also got hotter. Georgia Democrats flocked to a huge political rally, called the "Bush Arbor Meeting," on July 23 to hear fiery rhetoric and the strains of "Dixie" for the first time since the war. To make matters worse, in September, 1868, however, the Georgia legislature expelled all its Negro members, 25 from the House and three from the Senate. Democratic presidential electors were chosen for the upcoming election. Congress was not pleased. [44]

In the November, 1868, presidential election, DeKalb voters chose Democrats Horatio Seymour of New York and Frank P. Blair of St. Louis over Republicans Ulysses S. Grant and Schuyler Colfax. Again the effect of the Ku Klux Klan on the Negro turn-out was evident. [45]

The Georgia legislature abolished Inferior Courts in 1868; the functions of the courts in each counties were thereafter taken over by ordinaries.[46]

Though the DeKalb Grand Jury of October, 1868, admitted that county finances were still in poor condition, the jurors demanded that roads and bridges be repaired and that they be paid for their time:

"1st. In Committee of the whole we have examined the Jail of the County and find it to be in a very unsafe condition. We recommend that the Court House be whitewashed on the inside and any other repairs that area absolutely necessary to be done.

"2nd. In regard to the Roads, we regret to say that we have to report them in very *Bad Condition* over the County and would recommend that the proper authorities have the laws *rigidly* enforced. We also recommend that hands be placed upon the Fayetteville road and they be required to work the same and put it in good order.

"3rd. We also report the following Bridges to be in bad, and some of them in a dangerous condition, viz: The Bridges on Snapfinger Creek on the Covington Road. Also McWilliams' Bridge over South River and the Bridge over Shoal Creek. All need repairs very much.

"4th. Through a Committee selected from our Body we have, as far as our limited time and opportunity would admit, examined the books of the Sheriff, Ordinary, Clerk and Treasurer, and find them kept in a neat condition.

"5th. Under the charge of His Honor to the jury it became necessary for our body to fix the per diem for our services. Therefore we recommend that the Jurors receive Two Dollars per day.

"6th. We regret to report that the present condition of our County is not flourishing and satisfactory as could be wished. The pecuniary affairs, together with the short crops of the present season would seem almost sufficient cause to the more timid to despair. Yet under all these trying circumstances we would counsel our Fellow Citizens to persevere, use the most strict economy and prudence in all our dealings, and hope a brighter day may soon dawn upon our unfortunate and unhappy country.

"7th. In taking leave of His Honor J. D Pope we would return our thanks for the kind, courteous and prompt manner in which he has discharged the various duties of his office. We also tender our thanks to Solicitor General Adams for his prompt and courteous attention to our Body."

      John Ragsdale, Foreman.

Isaiah C. Stewart	Edwin A. Turner	William R. Pendley
Robert Cagle	Martin C. McKee	Angus McLeod
Michael A. Steele	Ezekiel A. Davis	Alexander C. Tuggle
James R. McAllister	William T. Cobb	James G. Laird
Harris Crowley	Charles H. Spear	William S. McLain.[47]
James T. Cobb	Benjamin F. Chapman	
John W. Tuggle	James C. Chupp	
John J. Cowan	Benjamin Crowley	

The Antioch African Methodist Episcopal Church was organized in 1868 at the home of Louise Bratcher on Electric Avenue in Decatur. First ministers were Henry Anderson, Jethro Brooks, William Howard, Van Ross and James Jackson. The first stewardess board included, in addition to Louise Bratcher, Lucile Powell, Harriett Reid, Mary Steele, Isabel Brooks, Hortense Barnett, Cora Griffin, Georgia Chronic, Violet Brooks and Julia Espey. The church has met in several locations through the years, including Marshall Street, Atlanta Avenue and Hiburnia Avenue. In 1874 the church built a one-

After he returned from the war, William R. Wallace (seated at right), opened a saw mill and furniture shop on what is now Chamblee Dunwoody Road at Nancy Creek. Wallace and his wife, Nancy Ann, had seven children. The youngest, Carl, is pictured between his parents. In the back row are Alma Wallace (Mrs. W. A. Eidson), Ida Wallace (Mrs. C. M. Carroll), John L. Wallace, Dave Wallace, Mamie Wallace (Mrs. C. V. Hudgins) and Maude Wallace (Mrs. S. D. Johnson Sr.) (Chamblee First United Methodist Church; Vanishing Georgia Collection, Georgia Department of Archives and History)

room structure where the new county courthouse is now located. The Bethsaida Baptist Church in Stone Mountain's Shermantown black community was organized in 1868 under the direction of the Rev. R. M. Burson. [48]

As the local economy slowly began to recover, several new businesses opened in 1868. J. M. Phillips built a ginnery, near Rock Chapel; the establishment's last owner was Nathaniel Patch. The building was demolished about 1890.

William R. Wallace was one of three brothers, all Confederate veterans, who built mills in DeKalb shortly after the war. Wallace bought from Ezekiel Mason a site where now Chamblee Dunwoody Road (then called Roswell Road) crossed Nancy Creek for his home, as well as a sawmill and furniture shop. He built a house on a dramatic prominence overlooking the creek. Wallace sold his furniture in Atlanta, Canton, Alpharetta, Cumming and Gainesville. He furnished 1000 tables for the Cotton States Exposition in Atlanta. He stopped making furniture and closed his mill about 1906. Dr. L. C. Fisher purchased the property from the Wallace estate, after his death in 1909. The shop, mill buildings and equipment stayed on the property until 1925. Fischer created Flowerland on the slope running from the house to the creek. In the 1940s and '50s it was a floral showplace that caused a traffic jam on Chamblee Dunwoody Road, as spectators filed by to see the thousands of azaleas in bloom. The Fischer house currently is part of the Unity Church property.

William's brother, John, operated a furniture shop, sawmill and business village where Peavine Creek merged with the South Fork of Peachtree Creek. The village on the Seaboard Railroad, about a mile northwest of the spot where Emory University is today, once had a post office and a railroad flag station, both called "Wallace." The center of the village was where Williams Mill Road (now Briarcliff) intersected with Paces Ferry (now Clifton) Road. Ammi Williams owned 130 acres at this location in 1843, and the mill Wallace operated may have existed on the Williams property. After Wallace stopped operating the mill in 1900, the village continued to exist. There was a general store, post office, railroad flag stop, blacksmith shop (operated by Juhan L. Johnston), barbershop and a drug store (operated by Dr. W. W. Andrews, who later moved to Tucker). The entire village had disappeared by 1917 or '18.

The third brother, Thomas Wallace, had a mill and distillery on the DeKalb-Gwinnett County line, five miles southeast of Stone Mountain. The mill may have been in Gwinnett County, but Wallace's nearby home was in DeKalb. Wallace sawed lumber, built furniture, ground corn and manufactured corn whiskey under the name of "Stone Mountain Corn." Thomas Wallace died in 1928.

John Y. Flowers and Dr. J. N. Flowers operated the Flowers Corn and Wheat Mill on Nancy Creek, a short distance below William Wallace's sawmill and furniture factory. The Flowers mill was built in about 1868 by a Mr. Pannell. The mill closed about 1900. Anderson Glass, "a large colored man," opened a blacksmith shop in Doraville about 1868. It was last owned by Berry Jones. Kelly's Tannery began manufacturing "a superior article of oak sole harness and upper leather, and calfskin" in DeKalb in 1869. The location of the tannery is not known. [49]

The first efforts at quarrying Stone Mountain granite, between 1845 and '50, had failed. The Stone Mountain Granite and Railway Company, chartered by John T. Glenn, S. M. Inman and J. A. Alexander in 1869 was the first successful quarry company. [50]

Meanwhile, in Atlanta, the Workingsmen's Union started in 1869. Only 325 men in Atlanta had annual incomes over $1,000 in 1868, although the highest paid was a banker who took home $35,127. [51]

The Decatur Methodist Church approved a resolution expressing condolences to the family of Robert Melville Clarke on August 30, 1868. Clarke, the son of the Rev. William Henry Clarke and his second wife, Alice Moore Kirby, was killed in 1868 when he tried to stop a Negro youth from attacking a white child. [52]

On December 2, 1868, a DeKalb County native, William H. Hulsey, age 29, became the youngest Atlanta mayor since Moses Formwalt, 28, was elected 20 years earlier. Hulsey was the son of Eli J. and Charlotte Collier Hulsey, and the grandson of two DeKalb County pioneers, Jennings Hulsey and Merrell Collier. Hulsey had studied law in the office of Ezzard and Collier, then joined the Confederate Army where he quickly rose to the rank of colonel. After the war he became William Ezzard's law partner. [53]

The 1869 Georgia legislature refused to ratify the 15th Amendment allowing Negroes to vote. Gov. Bullock apparently thought the state's political climate volatile enough to request federal troops be returned to Georgia. Gen. Alfred H. Terry was sent to watch over the state, and Bullock ordered the legislature back into session in January, 1870. [54]

While the DeKalb Grand Jury of March, 1869, may have agreed with the politics of the Georgia legislature, it condemned its "reckless" spending:

"... We find the Roads in the Northern portion of the County in bad condition and recommend the property authorities to have the road leading from Decatur to Old Cross Keys put in good order, and bridge built over the North prong of Peachtree Creek on said road...

"We feel proud to report that but few misdemeanors under the penal and criminal codes have come before our body, and hope the morals of our County may still improve...

"We very much regret to see the disposition manifested so plainly in the last Legislature of the State, of such reckless expenditure of the public funds of the State that have to be raised by the Industry of the County. Men who will sit and deliberately vote themselves nine dollars per diem and other officers enormous salaries for services rendered. Believing that such a course, if persisted in, will impoverish and dishearten the people to such an extent, that there is danger of seriously injuring the credit of our noble Old State. We therefore hope the people will be careful in the future to select such men as will be in favor of economy and retrenchment before their constituents, and in legislative acts will not squander the hard earnings of the people by voting themselves so much money for such little services rendered..."

John W. Scruggs (Mayor of Stone Mountain), Foreman

Richard M. Morris	Andrew Fergason	John D. Wells
Shelton H. Campbell	John T. C. Wilson	John R. Mehaffey
James E. Elam	Joseph Owens	Vincent R. Tommey
Francis M. Wellborn	Milton C. Lively	John T. Willingham
John B. Swanton	George W. Morris	Newton M. Reid
James R. McAllister	Robert McWilliams	Edwin H. Guess. [55]
Leandrew Biffle	Robert L. Barry	
Samuel T. Corley		

Six months later, in September, 1869, the grand jury decided its members should have a little money spent on their comfort: "... We have also examined the public buildings and find them in much need of repairs. And we are gratified to learn that our worthy Ordinary is taking steps to have them made. But we would say to him, `be not weary in well doing,' but after having made those repairs, go on and have the jurors' seats in the Court Room cushioned; twenty-four good substantial split bottomed chairs for the Grand Jurors' room, one armed chair for the Solicitor; also one armed chair cushioned for the Judge..."

Edmond J. Bailey, Foreman [56]

The name of DeKalb County's Superior Court judicial circuit was changed in 1869, from Coweta, a name it had held since 1833, to Atlanta. The circuit covered Fulton, DeKalb and Clayton counties. John Collier was the last judge in the Coweta circuit; John D. Pope was the first under the new name.[57]

Possibly the saddest consequence of the Civil War was the number of orphaned children it produced. Since the end of the war, the Rev. Dr. Jesse Boring (1807-1890) had worked toward establishing an orphans's home. A charter was granted by the Superior Court of Fulton county in 1869 to The Orphan's Home of the North Georgia Conference of the Methodist Church. The first trustees were Judge John L. Hopkins, president; Judge T. M. Meriwether, vice-president; Charles H. Johnson; Dr.

Boring; W. R. Branham; W. H. Potter; L. J. Davies; Clement A. Evans; W. F. Cook; George N. Lester; Y. L. G. Harris and H. P. Bell.

William W. McAfee, John C. Hendrix and J. G. W. Mills, all members of Payne's Chapel in Atlanta, supported the project by pledging $300 in gold. Other contributors were John J. Thrasher, Givens W. Arnold, George Jarvis, Dr. Thomas Boring and members of DeKalb's Lively and McElroy families. With the blessing of the Methodist Conference, Boring purchased property in Norcross in early 1870. The home opened on April 26, 1871, with 19 orphans.

Two brothers, Wylie Edward and James Winfield Marchman may have been among those first orphan's home residents. Their father Coleman W. Marchman, a member of the Fulton Dragoons Cavalry, died of yellow fever at Camp Winder, Va. Their mother, Martha, tried to keep the family together, but in 1871 gave them to the orphanage. "The two boys soon became thoroughly unhappy and ran away. After some misadventure, they returned to their grandmother's home, a farm near Oak Grove Church," wrote a Marchman descendant in The Story of Dunwoody. The boys and their older sister, Fannie Gertrude Marchman, were raised by their grandmother. As adults, Ed Marchman settled in Dunwoody, and Jim in Atlanta. Martha Marchman married a man named Morris and lived on a farm on Elmwood (now Chrysler Drive).

Fannie Marchman remained in the Oak Grove community and married James Thomas Cheek. They raised seven children: Woodrow Wilson, Raymond Roosevelt, Ima, Mattie Lee, Rosa, James (died of whooping cough at the age of one year) and Ruth May. Descendants of Ed and Jim Marchman and Fannie Marchman Cheek still live in the DeKalb County area. [58]

The orphanage in Norcross burned in 1873. The trustees then bought from heirs of the recently-deceased William H. Clarke 247 1/2 acres near Decatur on then Flat Shoals Road (now Columbia Drive). The name was changed in 1934 from Decatur Orphan's Home to Methodist Children's Home at Decatur. The institution is still located on Columbia Drive today. It is said that the trustees chose Decatur for the new home because of the influence of Dr. Boring and Mrs. V. R. Tommey. [59]

News from the region was not all gloomy during the post-war years. The city purchased from DeKalb pioneer Chapman Powell and E. R. Sasseen property on Marietta Street that would serve as a new location for the state agricultural fair, which had outgrown its original site. Called Oglethorpe Park, the property would host one of the era's several successful expositions. Later exposition buildings would become the Exposition Cotton Mills and mill town. [60]

North DeKalb citizens were treated to an amazing sight in the waning days of 1869. Dr. Albert Hape and Professor Samuel A. King launched their gas-powered balloon, Hyperion, on December 10. The Atlanta Constitution reported the following day:

"Marietta and streets adjacent to it, near its junction with Walton, as well as the track of the State Road, and windows and house-tops were filled yesterday with people gazing at the balloon getting ready for its upward flight. At least 5,000 or 6,000 people were on the scene. Prior to its ascension, several balloons bearing the shapes of fishes, elephants, seals, hogs and men were sent up amid the cheers of the crowd. The balloon was filled from a main of the Gas Works. At half past two, Professor

King and Dr. Albert Hape, got into the basket, the cords were loosed, and the balloon went right up -- at first in a Northwest direction, then going rapidly in a Northeast direction.

"The balloon probably reached a height of one mile, and for half an hour could be plainly seen speeding on in its flight through the air.

"When Dr. Hape was going up, an old negro remarked to his friend, `If dat man owes you anyting, you'd better scratch um off.' Another wondered, `if dem folks had religion, as dey wou'd need it before dey got back.' Another said, `they'd be nearer heaven this time than they ever would get again.'

"Various were the conjectures as to the mode of their coming down. One sage individual suggested that when they wished to let the gas out, they'd rip a hole in the side.

"The weather was propitious, and the ascension a success. We trust the descension will be, also."

From the gondola, Professor King played his bugle which was said to be heard 12 miles away. Some onlookers thought the professor was Gabriel blowing his trumpet, signaling the end of the world. The flight came to an end in a cotton field in Alpharetta.

Saying the balloon was unsafe, King declined a second ride on New Year's Day, 1870, so Hape went alone. At about one mile high, the balloon exploded, and onlookers speculated where Hape's corpse might return to earth. An hour later, Hape rode into town on a horse. He had parachuted safely to the banks of the Chattahoochee River where he profoundly startled a Negro woman who was washing clothes. [61]

Four prominent DeKalb County men died in 1869: Bennett Lee, age 75, of the Stone Mountain District, Benjamin Crowley, 57, of the Panthersville District, Greenville Henderson, 77, of the Browning's District, and the Rev. Elijah Byrd, 83, a pioneer Methodist minister.

These deaths were offset on a single October day when a woman, forever nameless, gave birth to quadruplets. The Atlanta Constitution reported on October 19: "Old DeKalb Still Ahead -- We learn that a Lady near Lithonia, in DeKalb County, gave birth to four bouncing boys. Old DeKalb is preparing for the next war." [62]

With so many fathers killed in the Civil War, there was a crying need for a home for orphans. With the support of the Methodist Church, the Rev. Dr. Jesse Boring opened an orphanage in Norcross in Gwinnett County on April 26, 1871. The home burned in 1873. The trustees chose Decatur for its next location for the orphanage, purchasing 247 1/2 acres of land on what is now Columbia Drive from the estate of Methodist minister William Henry Clarke. The home still operates in the same location. (North Georgia Conference, Methodist Children's Home)

THE HISTORY OF DEKALB COUNTY, GA. 1822-1900 • CHAPTER 27

Older boys at the orphanage worked on construction jobs and grew crops for sale to help support themselves.

For ease of maintenance, little girls all got the same short haircuts. When they went out on the grounds of the children's home, youngsters were kept together by holding onto a long string.

Older girls at the children's home were responsible for doing the laundry. (North Georgia Conference, Methodist Children's Home)

ORPHAN'S MESSAGE.

"Inasmuch as ye have done it to one of the least of these, my brethren."

VOL. 7.   DECATUR, GA., SEPTEMBER, 1900.   NO. 8.

Works We Do.

This glimpse is of the actual work done in the Home by our orphans. Here is gardening, poultry raising, washing, cooking, ironing, milking, churning, sewing, carpentering, painting, wood cutting, shoe repairing, blacksmithing, nursing the babies, house keeping, etc., etc. Work helps to develop and elevate character.

Sunday School Day, Sunday Sept. 30, 1900.

You teach your scholars to live like Jesus who took the little ones in his arms and blessed them. Now have a review lesson on September 30, by seeing if the lessons are in their hearts and lives. See if they will feed and bless the orphans for Jesus' sake.

We have mailed each superintendent whose name we could get programs to be used on that Sunday. If not received, please write me.

Advertize our work-day thoroughly, also your Sunday-school service. If your pastor is absent, have the program at 11 or 7 o'clock and have a good stirring talk on the Home.

Scatter these messages on Sunday, September 16, so people can get ready for the work-day. Work up an interest—a big interest—in the orphans.

The orphans plead with God and with you.

The Methodist Children's Home published the Orphan's Message around the turn of the century. The newspaper encouraged citizens to donate money, materials and time to support the home. (Donald S. Clarke)

Chapter 27 Notes

1. Garrett, Franklin M., 1954, 1969, <u>Atlanta and Environs -- A Chronicle of Its People and Events</u>, Vol. 1, page 676.

2. Gay, Mary A. H., 1879, 1979, <u>Life In Dixie During The War</u>.

3. Garrett, Franklin M., 1954, 1969, <u>Atlanta and Environs -- A Chronicle of Its People and Events</u>, Vol. 1, page 673.

4. Garrett, Franklin M., 1954, 1969, <u>Atlanta and Environs -- A Chronicle of Its People and Events</u>, Vol. 1, pages 669-670.

5. Garrett, Franklin M., 1954, 1969, <u>Atlanta and Environs -- A Chronicle of Its People and Events</u>, Vol. 1, pages 674-675.

6. Garrett, Franklin M., 1954, 1969, <u>Atlanta and Environs -- A Chronicle of Its People and Events</u>, Vol. 1, page 675.

7. Garrett, Franklin M., 1954, 1969, <u>Atlanta and Environs -- A Chronicle of Its People and Events</u>, Vol. 1, pages 688-689.

8. Garrett, Franklin M., 1954, 1969, <u>Atlanta and Environs -- A Chronicle of Its People and Events</u>, Vol. 1, page 689.

9. Garrett, Franklin M., 1954, 1969, <u>Atlanta and Environs -- A Chronicle of Its People and Events</u>, Vol. 1, pages 681-682.

10. Hudgins, Carl T., 1952, "Mills and Other Early DeKalb County Industries (And Their Owners)," <u>The Collections of the DeKalb Historical Society</u>, Vol. 1.

11. Hudgins, Carl T., 1952, "Mills and Other Early DeKalb County Industries (And Their Owners)," <u>The Collections of the DeKalb Historical Society</u>, Vol. 1. Smith, R. Frank, August 1, 1922, "A Brief Historical Sketch of Indian Creek Missionary Baptist Church."

12. Garrett, Franklin M., 1954, 1969, <u>Atlanta and Environs -- A Chronicle of Its People and Events</u>, Vol. 1, page 689.

13. Garrett, Franklin M., 1954, 1969, <u>Atlanta and Environs -- A Chronicle of Its People and Events</u>, Vol. 1, page 676.

14. Garrett, Franklin M., 1954, 1969, <u>Atlanta and Environs -- A Chronicle of Its People and Events</u>, Vol. 1, page 678.

15. Clarke, Caroline McKinney, 1973, 1996, <u>The Story of Decatur</u>.

16. Gay, Mary A. H., 1879, 1979, <u>Life In Dixie During The War</u>, page 308.

17. Garrett, Franklin M., 1954, 1969, <u>Atlanta and Environs -- A Chronicle of Its People and Events</u>, Vol. 1, page 693.

18. Garrett, Franklin M., 1954, 1969, <u>Atlanta and Environs -- A Chronicle of Its People and Events</u>, Vol. 1, page 695.

19. Ford, Elizabeth Austin, 1950, "Mt. Pleasant Baptist Church For Negroes." Deed recorded in DeKalb County November 10, 1873.

20. Gay, Mary A. H., 1897, 1979, <u>Life In Dixie During The War</u>, page 291.

21. Garrett, Franklin M., 1954, 1969, <u>Atlanta and Environs -- A Chronicle of Its People and Events</u>, Vol. 1, page 701.

22. Garrett, Franklin M., 1954, 1969, <u>Atlanta and Environs -- A Chronicle of Its People and Events</u>, Vol. 1, page 705.

23. Tilly IV, Harwell Parks, 1993, <u>Stephen and Rebecca (King) Tilly and Their Descendants 1782-1992</u>.

24. Garrett, Franklin M., 1954, 1969, <u>Atlanta and Environs -- A Chronicle of Its People and Events</u>, Vol. 1, pages 706-707.

25. Garrett, Franklin M., 1954, 1969, <u>Atlanta and Environs -- A Chronicle of Its People and Events</u>, Vol. 1, page 709.

26. Garrett, Franklin M., 1954, 1969, <u>Atlanta and Environs -- A Chronicle of Its People and Events</u>, Vol. 1, pages 710-711.

27. Barre', Laura and Ken, 1995, <u>The History of Doraville, Georgia</u>. Tilly IV, Harwell Parks, 1993, <u>Stephen and Rebecca (King) Tilly and Their Descendants 1782-1992</u>.

28. Garrett, Franklin M., 1954, 1969, <u>Atlanta and Environs -- A Chronicle of Its People and Events</u>, Vol. 1, page 717.

29. Garrett, Franklin M., 1954, 1969, <u>Atlanta and Environs -- A Chronicle of Its People and Events</u>, Vol. 1, page 718.

30. Garrett, Franklin M., 1954, 1969, <u>Atlanta and Environs -- A Chronicle of Its People and Events</u>, Vol. 1, page 721.

31. Garrett, Franklin M., 1954, 1969, <u>Atlanta and Environs -- A Chronicle of Its People and Events</u>, Vol. 1, pages 721-722.

32. Candler, Charles Murphey, November 9, 1922, "Historical Address." Gay, Mary A. H., 1897, 1979, <u>Life In Dixie During The War</u>.

33. Green, J. Howell, August 1, 1920, "A Brief History of the Decatur Methodist Episcopal Church, South."

34. Garrett, Franklin M., 1954, 1969, <u>Atlanta and Environs -- A Chronicle of Its People and Events</u>, Vol. 1, page 733.

35. Garrett, Franklin M., 1954, 1969, <u>Atlanta and Environs -- A Chronicle of Its People and Events</u>, Vol. 1, page 734.

36. Garrett, Franklin M., 1954, 1969, <u>Atlanta and Environs -- A Chronicle of Its People and Events</u>, Vol. 1, pages 738-739, 771-772, 775.

37. Garrett, Franklin M., 1954, 1969, <u>Atlanta and Environs -- A Chronicle of Its People and Events</u>, Vol. 1, page 739.

38. Garrett, Franklin M., 1954, 1969, <u>Atlanta and Environs -- A Chronicle of Its People and Events</u>, Vol. 1, pages 747-748.

39. Garrett, Franklin M., 1954, 1969, <u>Atlanta and Environs -- A Chronicle of Its People and Events</u>, Vol. 1, pages 748-766.

40. Garrett, Franklin M., 1954, 1969, <u>Atlanta and Environs -- A Chronicle of Its People and Events</u>, Vol. 1, page 767.

41. Garrett, Franklin M., 1954, 1969, <u>Atlanta and Environs -- A Chronicle of Its People and Events</u>, Vol. 1, page 773.

42. Garrett, Franklin M., 1954, 1969, <u>Atlanta and Environs -- A Chronicle of Its People and Events</u>, Vol. 1, pages 776 777.

43. Garrett, Franklin M., 1954, 1969, <u>Atlanta and Environs -- A Chronicle of Its People and Events</u>, Vol. 1, pages 779-781.

44. Garrett, Franklin M., 1954, 1969, <u>Atlanta and Environs -- A Chronicle of Its People and Events</u>, Vol. 1, pages 781-782.

45. Garrett, Franklin M., 1954, 1969, <u>Atlanta and Environs -- A Chronicle of Its People and Events</u>, Vol. 1, page 786.

46. Garrett, Franklin M., 1954, 1969, <u>Atlanta and Environs -- A Chronicle of Its People and Events</u>, Vol. 1, page 702.

47. Garrett, Franklin M., 1954, 1969, <u>Atlanta and Environs -- A Chronicle of Its People and Events</u>, Vol. 1, page 794.

48. Antioch AME Church files, DeKalb Historical Society, Georgia Department of Archives and History. Joseph, J. W., and Kehoe, Lisa M, November 14, 1994, <u>Historic Sites Survey, City of Stone Mountain, DeKalb County, Georgia</u>.

49. Hudgins, Carl T., 1952, "Mills and Other Early DeKalb County Industries (And Their Owners)," The Collections of the DeKalb Historical Society, Vol. 1.

50. Workers of the Writer's Project of the Work Projects Administration in the State of Georgia, 1942, Atlanta -- A City of the Modern South, page 221.

51. Garrett, Franklin M., 1954, 1969, Atlanta and Environs -- A Chronicle of Its People and Events, Vol. 1, pages 817-820.

52. Gay, Mary A. H., 1897, 1979, Life In Dixie During The War, page 310.

53. Garrett, Franklin M., 1954, 1969, Atlanta and Environs -- A Chronicle of Its People and Events, Vol. 1, page 801.

54. Garrett, Franklin M., 1954, 1969, Atlanta and Environs -- A Chronicle of Its People and Events, Vol. 1, page 805.

55. Garrett, Franklin M., 1954, 1969, Atlanta and Environs -- A Chronicle of Its People and Events, Vol. 1, page 806.

56. Garrett, Franklin M., 1954, 1969, Atlanta and Environs -- A Chronicle of Its People and Events, Vol. 1, page 806.

57. Garrett, Franklin M., 1954, 1969, Atlanta and Environs -- A Chronicle of Its People and Events, Vol. 1, page 807.

58. Price, Vivian, July 24, 1991, "Marchman Family Put Down Roots In Oak Grove And They're Still There," DeKalb News/Sun, page 4B North. Davis, Elizabeth L., and Spruill, Ethel W., 1975, The Story of Dunwoody. Cross, Patricia Dian, personal collection.

59. Candler, Charles Murphey, November 9, 1922, "Historical Address." Garrett, Franklin M., 1954, 1969, Atlanta and Environs -- A Chronicle of Its People and Events, Vol. 1, pages 813-814.

60. Garrett, Franklin M., 1954, 1969, Atlanta and Environs -- A Chronicle of Its People and Events, Vol. 1, page 802.

61. Garrett, Franklin M., 1954, 1969, Atlanta and Environs -- A Chronicle of Its People and Events, Vol. 1, page 815.

62. Garrett, Franklin M., 1954, 1969, Atlanta and Environs -- A Chronicle of Its People and Events, Vol. 1, page 824.

Chapter 28

According to the U. S. census, DeKalb County had 10,014 citizens in 1870, half the number of people living in the city of Atlanta. Of that number, 2682 were Negroes, only 26 percent of the total population. The population of the town of Decatur was 401. [1]

Mills -- both grist and lumber -- were by far the most prevalent industry. Thirty six were listed in the 1870 census. Typical of these businesses was White's Mill on Doolittle Creek and Thompson's Mill on Snapfinger Creek. Paul Thompson, who operated Thompson's Mill in the late 1940s, recalled that the mill was said to be built between 1837 and 1840, and had been built by J. B. Badger. Subsequent owners included a man named Crockett and David C. Thompson and Thompson's father. David Thompson was treasurer of DeKalb County until 1915 when the office was abolished. He was never defeated in an election. Thompson's Mill, located in Land Lot 96 of the 15th District, was equipped to grind corn and saw lumber, as well as gin cotton. Thomas H. Fincher opened his cotton ginnery on his homeplace, on the south side of the Georgia Railroad, one mile west of the center of the Clarkston community. The ginnery operated for only 10 years.

The Manufacturing Schedule of the 1870 census listed the following industries in DeKalb County:

Evans' District

Name	Type of Business	Power Source	Capital Invested
G. Mehaffy	Sawmill	Steam	$ 1500
Daniel Morgan	Sawmill	Water	1500
J. N. Swift	Custom Gristmill	Water	3000
J. W. Fowler	Sawmill	Water	800
Swanton & Angier	Tannery	Steam	2500
Thomas Kelly	Tannery	Hand and horse	2000
E. Mason	Custom Gristmill	Water	5000
E. Mason	Sawmill	Water	1000
Samuel Durand	Grist and sawmill	Water	2000

Panthersville District

Name	Type of Business	Power Source	Capital Invested
Mary J. Terry	Sawmill	Water	$ 1000
McCurdy and Adams	Sawmill	Steam	2500
J. M. Thompson	Wagonmaking, repairing and blacksmithing	Hand	300
J. W. Kirkpatrick	Furniture	Steam	10,000
E. P. Sanders	Sawmill	Steam	2000
Mrs. Akers and sons	Gristmill	Water	1500
J. W. Beaty	Gristmill	Water	1000
Pitts and White	Gristmill	Water	1000
Pitts and White	Sawmill	Water	1000
Wright and Scully	Sawmill	Water	1000
R. B. Wilson	Gristmill	Water	800
McNaught, Ormond and Co.	Two paper mills	Water	65,000
John P. Ray	Gristmill	Water	4000
John P. Ray	Sawmill	Water	1000
Crockett and Wilkins	Sawmill	Water	1000
Robert Clarke	Gristmill	Water	10,000
Swift and Thompson	Gristmill	Water	2000
E. J. Hulsey	Grist and sawmill	Water	7200

Diamond's District

Name	Type of Business	Power Source	Capital Invested
Mary J. Barnes	Gristmill	Water	800
Mary J. Barnes	Sawmill	Water	500
Nathaniel Patch	Sash and blind factory	Water	500
James L. Kilgore	Gristmill	Water	1500
Zadok Baker	Gristmill	Water	1500
Zadok Baker	Sawmill	Water	1500
Jacob Chupp	Grist and sawmill	Water	2500
Elijah Steward	Grist and sawmill	Water	1800

Stone Mountain District

Name	Type of Business	Power Source	Capital Invested
Stone Mountain Granite Company	Quarrying and dressing granite	Hand and horse	$75,000
B. F. Veal	Gristmill	Water	3000
F. Maddox	Sawmill	Water	1000
Rufus Henderson	Gristmill	Water	1500
J. Wall and Co.	Sawmill	Steam	2000
Lively and McElroy	Sawmill	Steam	2500

C. P. Lively	Grist and sawmill	Water	1800
Flowers and Son	Gristmill	Water	3600
W. B. Wallis	Sawmill and cabinet shop	Water	1500

Cross Keys District

Name	Type of Business	Power Source	Capital Invested
J. B. Davidson	Pottery	Hand and horse	250 [2]

Citizens in Atlanta elected Decatur pioneer William Ezzard again in 1870; he became the only mayor to serve the city before the Civil War and after. Atlanta again was thriving and living up to its potential as a distribution center. In the outlying areas, large land holdings were being broken into smaller farms and town properties, since, without slaves, plantations were no longer manageable. [3]

Georgia Gov. R. B. Bullock spent much of the year in Washington, D. C., herding the Congressional Act of 1869, called "the Georgia Bill," through the U. S. House and Senate. The measure directed the governor to convene the legislature for the purpose of ratifying the 15th Amendment to the U. S. constitution. The legislators called for the 1870 session were the same ones from 1868, including the Negroes who were thrown out two years previously. All the legislators were required to swear that they had not participated in the late "rebellion." Even notaries public, town marshals and state librarians were prohibited. Exclusion based on race was prohibited. Gov. Bullock was authorized to call in the military to back his position. [4]

The "Georgia Bill" ensured Bullock a Republican legislature, which convened January 10, 1870 and immediately ratified the 15th Amendment and overturned the 1868 election of U. S. Sens. H. V. M. Miller and Joshua Hill in favor of a Republican senator and representative. On July 15, 1870, military rule was withdrawn, and Georgia once again was eligible for representation in Congress. The following year, 1871, Miller and Hill took their seats in the U. S. Senate, the first Georgians to do so since 1861. Gov. Bullock resigned and left Georgia under "suspicions that he is guilty of high crimes and misdemeanors" [5]

Oglethorpe College, which had been operating for 26 years before the Civil War near Milledgeville, tried to follow the state capital to its new location in Atlanta in 1871. The Atlanta City Council enticed the school with $40,000 in subscriptions raised through private donations. Classes were held in Atlanta City Hall during the 1871-72 school year, after which time the Oglethorpe trustees bought a residence on the southwest corner of Washington and Mitchell streets. Financial trouble forced the school to close in 1872. The city of Atlanta ultimately acquired the school property, where it later located the city's Girls and Boys high schools and city hall.

Oglethorpe would return 40 years later, and build a campus on Peachtree Road in north DeKalb County. One benefit to DeKalb from the failed school venture was the acquisition of a new citizen would prove to have a significant impact on education in Decatur. Donald Fraser (1826-1887) was graduated from Oglethorpe University in 1848 and came to Atlanta to teach ancient languages at the school. While in Atlanta, he and his family boarded at the Calico House, the home of one of his students, Piromis H. Bell. When the school closed, Fraser moved to Decatur and served as the pastor of Decatur Presbyterian Church from 1872 until 1887. [6]

The Donald Fraser School opened in Decatur in May of 1892, funded by townspeople and a gift from the Presbyterian Synod of Georgia. Here the school and Decatur Presbyterian Church are pictured in the winter of 1910. (DeKalb Historical Society)

Decatur Presbyterian Church incorporated a boys's high school in May of 1892 and named it for Fraser. Townspeople purchased shares in the school for $50 apiece, raising a total of $5,600 to launch the new school. The Presbyterian Synod of Georgia also gave $3,200 from the remaining funds of Oglethorpe College. Trustees of the school purchased the old Decatur Presbyterian Church building and its two-acre lot at Webster and Williams streets for $4,000. G. Holman Gardner was the first principal of the Donald Fraser School for Boys. Charles D. McKinney Sr. was the assistant principal. Trustees were J. C. Kirkpatrick, Frank J. Ansley, George Bucher Scott, Washington J. Houston, Milton A. Candler and the Rev. Frank H. Gaines. [7]

Decatur Presbyterian Church elders also helped the Rev. Myron D. Wood organize Rock Spring Presbyterian Church in Atlanta on November 12, 1870. [8]

DeKalb residents brought their best crops, livestock and hand goods to the state fair of 1870, and left with the lion's share of premiums. The fair was the largest to date. Opening on October 18, 1870, there was a record turn-out of 20,000 attendees on October 21.

Representing Lithonia were:
• John C. Ragsdale, a premium for his essay.

- Dan Johnson, best stock corn, best cotton yield per acre, best yield of sweet potatoes and best peas.
- Dr. W. P. Bond, best bread corn.
- Easom Bond, best sorghum syrup and finest sweet potatoes.

Winners from Decatur were:
- J. N Pate, best jack.
- J. G. Laird, best mare and mule colt.
- James Kirkpatrick, best mare and colt.
- Lizzie Swanton, best handiwork.
- Thomas (Uncle Tommie) F. Lowe, best old-time fiddling. Lowe defeated the previous champion, Atlanta marshal G. Whit Anderson in playing "Arkansas Traveler."

The community of Kirkwood was represented by a Miss Tarver, who won a prize for the most artistic painting, and George Kidd, who grew the best vegetables shown at the fair. [9]

The fair had two new events, only one of which proved to be successful. Dr. E. A. Billups proved to be the best trap-pigeon-shooter, with a Col. Dearing second best. Dr. Hape and Col. Morrison of Stone Mountain tied for third place. Only two birds of 27 released escaped. A medieval style tournament, featuring armored knights with lances on horseback resulted in the death of Michael E. Kenny who was thrown from a horse and killed. [10]

Rock Chapel Methodist Church, which survived Sherman's March to the Sea, burned in 1870 and was immediately rebuilt. The new building was sold to a black congregation in 1886, when a new Rock Chapel building was constructed. Edmund Lee gave yellow pine timber for the new church. Members David B. Chupp, Tandy Y. Nash, Easom J. Bond, Simeon Duncan and J. L. Chupp moved a sawmill to the site and prepared the wood. [11]

Mt. Zion African Methodist Episcopal Church was established in 1870 under the leadership of the Rev. Grannison Daniel. The church was first located near Lawrenceville Highway and called Rocky Knoll AME. An old railroad box car served as the first sanctuary and was located on land given by Judson Stokes. The church moved to its current location at 2977 LaVista Road in the 1890s. [12]

The Air-Line Railroad was quickly making its way from Atlanta through DeKalb on the way to its destination in Charlotte, N. C. Several towns sprang up along the way. The first to incorporate was Norcross in Gwinnett County on October 26, 1870. Stephen Tilly McElroy, who had recently moved from Chamblee, was one of the original commissioners. [13]

DeKalb lost several of its older residents in 1870. Thomas Barnes of Lithonia died in May at the age of 70. The McWilliams District was first Barnes's District for him. Decatur citizens who died were Allen Woodall, 63, on July 7; Jonathan B. Wilson, 68; and John Fannin, 76, on November 10. Barnes, Woodall, Wilson and Fannin all are buried in Decatur Cemetery. Zachariah R. Jones of the Panthersville District died at the age of 66, and is buried in Macedonia Baptist Church Cemetery. In addition, DeKalb's pioneer physician, Chapman Powell, died on May 30, 1870 at his home in Atlanta. He is buried in the Hardman Cemetery off Clairmont Road.

After enduring terrible tragedy, a young man who was to be influential in Decatur and DeKalb County was starting over in the early 1870s, with a new family and a new career. Born in Virginia in 1841, George Alexander Ramspeck was the son of German-born George P. Ramspeck and Charlotte R. Lewis. Before the Civil War, the family moved to Charleston, S. C., where the elder Ramspeck died and George was apprenticed to a printer at age of 11. The apprenticeship was to be the end of his formal education.

George A. Ramspeck married 16-year-old Eliza Florida Anderson, daughter of Robert and Eliza J. Anderson of Charleston, on August 25, 1863. The couple moved to Atlanta and later Decatur after the war, along with George's mother and several siblings. Florida Anderson Ramspeck died in Decatur in 1865, leaving George to raise a small daughter. The Atlanta Constitution ran an obituary:

Decatur Baptist Church's first sanctuary was this building, called "the little brick church." (DeKalb Historical Society)

"Departed this life in Decatur, Ga., on the 28th of December, 1865, Mrs. Eliza Florida Ramspeck, aged 19 years, 2 months, and 11 days. The subject of this brief notice was born in Charleston, S. C., the daughter of Capt. Robert and Eliza J. Anderson: and at the age of sixteen, was united in marriage with Mrs. George A. Ramspeck of the same city. Soon after the birth of her only child, a sweet little daughter, now only eighteen months old, she discovered symptoms of bronchitis. Having to fly with her family from Atlanta on approach of Sherman, and exposed to all the privations and hardships incident to frequent removal from place to place developed her disease, and terminated her brief career."

Little Florrie Ramspeck would live to be only seven years old. Her obituary read, in part: "Death's icy hand has called the sweetest flower from among that household circle to transplant to a brighter world..."

On December 31, 1868, George married Margaret Morgan, daughter of Joseph and Jane Morgan of Decatur. The couple had five children: George, Mary, Joseph Lewis, Helen and Jean. George left the printing business and opened a store in Decatur, which he operated until 1890, when he began to manufacture fertilizer. George Ramspeck had a reputation for a natural business sagacity. At the close of the Civil War, he held $50,000 in Confederate money. He hurried to Griffin (ahead of the news) and swapped his money for goods and a wagon to bring them back to Atlanta, where he sold them from a store on Whitehall Street.

The square in Decatur became home to the extended Ramspeck clan, including the families of George's brother, Charles W. Ramspeck, and sister, Mary Margretta (Mrs. Hal Jones). The Jones and Ramspeck families became prominent citizens of Decatur. George Ramspeck served two terms as mayor of Decatur and was a DeKalb County commissioner. George's brother Charles was chief of Decatur's volunteer fire department. Hal Jones was the first judge of the Decatur City Court.

George's niece, Annie Belle Jones, compiled a family and town history book. In her book was a newspaper article dated April, 1872, which gives a view of Decatur:

"The town of Decatur is evincing a spirit of improvement that is highly commended. The streets are being put in fine order and necessary improvements have been made to the public buildings.

"A town pump has been put up and the public square is to be enclosed and beautified. They have a mayor and town council. But we think the mayor of a town ought to be married now. The dignity of the office demands it." [14]

The Decatur Baptist Church completed its first sanctuary in April of 1871, with a dedication on May 27, 1871. The one-room chapel, 40x50 feet, built of red brick, was located on the lot that had been purchased from Milton Candler for $600. W. H. Strickland was pastor at the time of construction. During the church's early years its young members attended the Decatur Union Sunday school.

The church building had been made possible "largely through the untiring efforts of Miss Mary Gay, who for months traveled all over the country soliciting contributions, raising more than $2,000 in small sums."

With the exception of the addition of a vestibule and belfry, the building was not enlarged for 55 years. The "little red brick church" was demolished in 1922 to make way for a new building.

Decatur had a Baptist congregation for some years prior to the Civil War, but the congregation moved and was renamed Indian Creek Baptist. A new Baptist church had been organized on November 21, 1862, and had met in homes, in the county courthouse and the Decatur Presbyterian Church. A. T. Holmes was the first pastor. [15]

In 1871, the town limits of Decatur were extended to one-half mile in all directions from the courthouse.

The town of Doraville was the same size at its incorporation as the enlarged Decatur. Doraville, one stop south of Norcross on the Air-Line Railroad, was incorporated December 15, 1871, with corporate limits set at one-half mile in every direction from the railroad depot, which was located where the MARTA rapid rail station is today. The original council was made up of G. N. Flowers, L. T. Jackson, Samuel Harman, Samuel H. Braswell and William N. Leitch.

Doraville is said to have been named for Dora Jack, the daughter of an official of the Atlanta and Charlotte Air Line Railroad. In fact, there are several women by that name who could qualify as the inspiration for the town name. Prominent Doraville citizen John Y. Flowers is said to have suggested the name to honor his granddaughter, Dora Braswell Tapp. Dora was the daughter of Flowers's daughter Georgia Ann, who married B. H. Braswell. Their daughter, Grace Tapp, married Reavis Elbert Lively and became the mother of current Doraville Mayor Gene Lively. Another candidate, Dora Howell, was the daughter of Singleton Howell, suggested by several young railroad engineers who built the line through town.

Although born on August 7, 1882, 11 years after Doraville was incorporated, Dora Akin Jones lived her entire life in the town. She was the daughter of James Francis Akin and Nancy Martha McElroy, and the granddaughter of DeKalb pioneers Thomas J. Akins and Samuel McElroy Jr. Dora Akin

Jud and Dora (Darling) Tapp are pictured in the buggy about 1900. The town of Doraville may have been named for Dora. The original of this photo hangs in the office of Doraville Mayor Gene Lively, grandson of the Tapps. (City of Doraville)

married another Doraville resident, Carlos Dolos Jones, who was mayor of the town. Together they made significant contributions to Doraville and Prospect Methodist Church, of which they were lifelong members.

The settlement that would become Doraville began to grow when the railroad came through, but the town incorporated, it is said, because church leaders wanted control over two saloons in the area. The nearest churches were Prosperity Presbyterian and Prospect Methodist. Prosperity moved to the corner of Central Avenue and Church Street, its current location, in 1872 and changed its name to Doraville Presbyterian Church in 1890.

Until 1922 Doraville had only three postmasters: John Yancey Flowers (1815-1887), his son, George Newton Flowers (1837-1917), and his grandson, Dr. John Ebenezer (Ebb) Flowers ((1866-1955). Dr. Ebb Flowers was known in Doraville as something of a character. He kept postal records on the backs of letters, halves of used envelopes, any scrap of paper. His doctor's office, post office and country store were located in the same building next to the railroad depot on what is now New Peachtree Road. The doctor donated the land on which Flowers Park was developed. In addition to the doctor's office, turn-of-the-century Doraville contained two stores, a corn mill, the Presbyterian church, a barbershop and a small area of houses with swept yards.

Families who have had a significant impact on the history of Doraville include Akin, Atwood Autrey, Bankston, Barrett, Beaty, Blair, Bolton, Booker, Borders, Braswell, Brooks, Brown, BurrellChesnut, Christian, Cowan, Creel, Dabney, Dodgen, Dougherty, Epps, Evans, Flowers, Ford, Galloway, Gholston, Gregory, Graham, Grant, Hansard, Harmon, Henderson, Holbrooks, Hood, Jackson, James, Jett, Jones, Kinnard, Lamar, Langford, Lawson, Leitch, Leslie, Lively, Maloney, McCurdy, McDill, McElroy, Metcalf, Miller, Mize, Morris, Munday, Norman, Parsons, Patterson, Peeples, Pelfrey, Pittman, Pounds, Pressley, Rainey, Reeves, Ross, Smith, Spires, Stapp, Stevenson, Stewart, Strickland, Swicord, Tapp, Tilly, Warbington, Weldon, Wilson, Wood and Wylie.

The Greater Mt. Carmel African Methodist Episcopal Church was started in the late 1870s by the Rev. George Washington Gholston. Meetings were first held at the Gholston home on Chamblee Tucker Road in what is now the Embry Hills community. The congregation later rented the Odd Fellows Lodge Hall on New Peachtree Road in Doraville, then Barrett's store on New Peachtree. A school for black children also met at Barrett's store. Mary J. Gholston was the first teacher.

Land for a cemetery was obtained in 1888 a short distance north of town on New Peachtree at Winters Chapel. Family names in the Mt. Carmel cemetery include Allen, Brown, Colquitt, Etchison, Garrison, Graham, Hamilton, Hood, Howell, Jett, Judge, Lyons, Mayfield, McCrary, Myhan, Morehead, Morrison, Parson, Peeples, Rainey, Scott, Smith and Williams. [16] In 1912, the church built its first sanctuary adjacent to the cemetery from timber cut on the Gholston property. The church next moved to property now occupied by the General Motors plant. Construction of the plant forced the church to move to its current location on Carver Circle in about 1961. [17]

Redan First Baptist Church, first known as Woodville Baptist, was organized in 1871 with 14 charter members. The area now known as Redan in southeast DeKalb was first called McCarter's Station for K. F. McCarter who donated the right of way for the Georgia Railroad. The railroad was completed through the area in 1845. McCarter operated a fuel stop for the railroad, which may account for the settlement's other early name, Woodville. Reed Alford operated one of the first stores in the community. His wife's name was Annie. The town name is a combination of the first names of Mr. and Mrs. Alford. Other early setters were the Floyd, Holt, Johnson, Jones, Kilgo, Phillips, Reed, Street, Suber, Ozmer and Wellborn families. Although Redan has never been incorporated, it has a town cemetery, which has been in use since 1880. [18]

Decatur physician Dr. Peter F. Hoyle died on January 6, 1871 in Jacksonville, Fla. where he had recently moved. He was 58 years old. Other 1871 deaths included Dr. John W. Jones, April 27; William Nash, age 68, June 22; Daniel N. Pittman, 78, August 8. Nash and Pittman are buried in Stone Mountain Cemetery. Various sources give different death dates for DeKalb pioneer Thomas Akins. Akins died on either June 23, 1871 or March 10, 1873. There is no doubt, however, that the octogenarian is buried in Decatur Cemetery. [19]

The <u>Atlanta Constitution</u> reported on January 12, 1872 that post-war Reconstruction was finally over:
"The Downfall of the Radical Dynasty
"What a world of meaning in the expression, misrule ended! An oppressed people redeemed! The restoration of honesty to public office!" The occasion was marked by the inauguration of Gov. James M. Smith. Shortly thereafter, former Gov. Charles J. Jenkins returned to Georgia with the state seal. [20]

The first public schools opened in Atlanta on January 30, 1872, more than a year before DeKalb County would begin its first public system, with schools for students in grades one-eight. Three DeKalb schools -- Bouldercrest, Scottdale and Southwest DeKalb -- operated in the same locations through the mid-20th century. DeKalb's first public schools offered classes for for students in grades one-eight. [21]

DeKalb County held its first county fair October 15, 1872. The fair was remembered in the DeKalb New Era newspaper on June 2, 1921:

"The DeKalb County Fair at Lithonia yesterday was a most excellent success. There was a large attendance from all parts of the county and great interest manifested. The exhibition of articles was very gratifying. The ladies of course beat the men badly; their departments showing great numbers of articles.

"There was a good display of stock. DeKalb is coming back to pre-war times. There were displays of field crops and vegetables to cheer the lover of agricultural successes. The ladies, as we have stated, poured out in numbers and filled a large building with quilts, tidies and all sorts of needle work; with bread and preserves and jellies and all other fabrications of feminine industry and fancy. A jolly baby show enlivened the proceedings.

"Altogether the affair was a gratifying success, and everybody seemed pleased and left in the best of humor." [22]

The Rev. William Henry Clarke, the "large and powerful" Methodist preacher, died on May 1, 1872 at the age of 67. He is buried in Decatur Cemetery. John Wesley White, 47, of the Panthersville District, met a grisly end after his hand became caught in a gin he was feeding. He died on October 13, 1872 from his injuries, and is buried in the Clifton Methodist Church cemetery. Jacob Born, the Lithonia pioneer, died on April 11, 1872. [23]

Baseball fever hit DeKalb in 1873 as the Decatur Olympics sluggers took the field against the sandlot nine. A local newspaper covered the action:

"Atlanta vs. Decatur -- Decatur Victorious
by A Score of Thirty-eight to Twenty-four
A Splendid One
"On yesterday the Atlanta boys went to Decatur to play the first game of a series with the Olympics of that place. On their arrival at Decatur they repaired immediately to the ground and the game was soon under way. On the choice the Atlanta boys took the field and the Olympics the inning with Cassin at the bat. Before the game commenced the Atlanta's were the favorites, but the Decatur stock soon came up and they won the game after a hard struggle. During the game good fly catches were made by Messrs. Massey, Savage, and Houston, and batting by Woods, Clements, Adams and Austin.

"Captain Durham of the Decatur nine is an excellent player and `based' his men to perfection.

"The game went hard with the Atlantas, who expected an easy victory, but attribute their defeat to being out of practice. Next Saturday the second game comes off and we shall see if their excuse was a good one, for they shall have plenty of time for practice during the week. Mr. Billups is a splendid first baseman, and the Decatur boys may well be proud of him. The gentleman from `New York' needs spikes in his shoes for it appeared as if his head wanted to get underneath his feet. Mr. A's moustache is an impediment to his good playing. Cassin is rather loose, in fact too much so for a successful pitcher." [24]

The oldest recorded minutes of the Decatur City Commission date back to 1873. On February 3, L. J. Winn was requested to serve as chairman, T. R. Ramspeck as secretary and Hiram J. Williams (Decatur's Civil War postmaster) as treasurer. J. B. Swanton and W. L. Goldsmith were the other commissioners. Among the first orders of business for the commission was arranging to have trees trimmed in the town's square and business area. The job was done for 20 cents per tree.

Turner L. Evans was chosen town marshal at a salary of $240 per year, with an extra fee of $1 for each convicted criminal. Law-breakers could be fined a maximum of $25 or work on town streets for not more than 25 days. Decatur laws in 1873 prohibited:

• Public indecency, quarrelling, obscene, vulgar or profane language and acting in a disorderly manner to the disturbance of any citizen.

• Putting trash boxes, wood or other obstructions on the public square or any street or sidewalk.

• Willfully destroying or injuring any shade tree, or fastening a horse or other animal to a shade tree or fence so as to injure the same.

• Firing a gun, pistol or any other firearm.

• Fighting chicken cocks either with or without gaffs, and encouraging dog fights, and betting on the same.

• Allowing hogs, cattle, horses or mules (calves excepted) to run at large.

• Refusing to abate a nuisance.

Selling "spirituous or fermented liquors without a license" was considered a more serious offense in Decatur, punishable with a hefty $250 fine or working the town streets for 90 days. [25]

Rainbow Park Baptist Church was constituted as Beech Springs Baptist in 1873, and originally located near the Kirkwood community. The church's new building was dedicated on August 31, 1886, "the night of the Charleston earthquake.

"The effects of the quake were widespread and definitely felt in DeKalb. The tremulous motion lasted about three minutes." Church member Carl Foster remembered his mother, who was present at the service, as saying the quake caused great excitement and nearly broke up the meeting.

The church name was changed to Kirkwood Baptist on August 19, 1894, and the building moved in

September 1894. The structure was mounted on rollers and drawn by horses a distance of more than mile to the corner of North Howard and Hardee (now Delano). The church later moved to Rainbow Park Drive in Decatur and changed its name once again. [26]

A pioneer citizen of Atlanta, whose descendants would have a powerful impact on the city and DeKalb County, died on September 5, 1873. William Richard Venable had come to Atlanta in 1848 from his native Jackson County, Ga. His first job in the town as a bookkeeper for cotton merchant A. B. Forsyth. Venable was first elected clerk of the Fulton Superior Court in 1856, and had served in that capacity continuously since 1862. In 1850, Venable married Sarah Cornelia Hoyt, sister of Judge S. B. Hoyt. Their nine children included William Hoyt Venable, Samuel Hoyt Venable and Elizabeth Venable (Mrs. Frank Tucker Mason), all who were involved in the family's large granite quarries in Stone Mountain and Lithonia. At one point, William and Samuel Venable owned Stone Mountain, Arabia Mountain and Pine Mountain in DeKalb.

William H. Venable succeeded his father as clerk of Superior Court and was later president of the Georgia Senate. He marrried Sarah Ann Miller of LaGrange, and had four daughters: Coribel, Maude Gay, Robert Ridley and Lucille, who died as an infant. Samuel remained a bachelor, but built his mansion on Ponce de Leon Avenue, called Stonehenge, big enough for his extended family. Elizabeth Venable Mason was considered the mistress of Stonehenge and was called The Angel of Key West because of her work with wounded soldiers in a Florida hospital during the Spanish American War. [27]

Presbyterian minister Dr. John S. Wilson, who lived in Decatur from 1844 to 1859, died in Atlanta on March 27, 1873 at the age of 77. He is buried in Oakland Cemetery. James Oliver Powell, former DeKalb sheriff and son of DeKalb's pioneer physician Chapman Powell, died on April 3, 1873 at the relatively-young age of 46. He is buried in Decatur Cemetery. Other notable DeKalb County deaths in 1873 included Dr. James Corbin Avary, 55, who died on March 18; and Presbyterian elder Joseph Pitts, age 78, who died on August 23. Avary is buried in Decatur Cemetery, and Pitts in the Clifton Methodist Church cemetery. [28]

Confederate Gen. John B. Gordon of the Kirkwood community was elected to the U. S. Senate in 1873, and served until 1880. In the absence of Vice President Henry Wilson, Gordon presided over the Senate on March 25, 1873, the first time an ex-Confederate had been so honored. [29]

DeKalb County citizens met in Decatur in July of 1873 to discuss building the county's first public school. W. L. Goldsmith was president of the new citizens's group, with T. N. Wilson as secretary. Attendees purchased $1200 in subscriptions and proposed to raise $3000 more. [30]

Milton Candler's younger brother, Asa Griggs Candler, arrived in Atlanta on July 7, 1873 at the age of 21, having just completed an apprenticeship as a druggist in Cartersville. By 9 p.m. on his first day in town, he had landed a job in the drug store of George J. Howard on Peachtree Street. He worked until the store closed at midnight that night. He later married the boss's daughter, Lucy Howard. Having arrived in Atlanta with $1.75 in his pocket, Asa Candler became the richest man in town, and Atlanta's primary philanthropist. His impact on Atlanta and DeKalb during the next 56 years is incalculable. [31]

U. S. Sen. John B. Gordon was the featured speaker on Memorial Day, April 26, 1874 at a ceremony unveiling a monument to Confederate dead at Atlanta's Oakland Cemetery. Some 15,000 persons turned out for the occasion. The Atlanta Ladies Memorial Association had raised $8,000 to pay for the monument. The stone was donated by the Stone Mountain Granite Company. [32]

The career of Clarkston's best known writer, Mary Edward Bryan, was restarted on November 4, 1874, with the first edition of the Sunny South, a weekly literary newspaper. Bryan was associate editor of the paper; J. H. and W. B. Seals were editors and proprietors. In 1893, the Sunny South became a supplement to the Atlanta Constitution, and in 1907 it was incorporated into the Uncle Remus Magazine. The operation suspended publication altogether in 1913.

Bryan, described as a "beloved daughter of Clarkston and one of Georgia's most famous women," also was a "novelist and poet of high rank." The author of 15 books, she was among the highest paid women of her time. There is a granite memorial to Bryan on the grounds of the Clarkston Woman's Club.

Bryan "was a romantic writer and, although there was nothing immoral in her work, she did not hesitate to `call a spade a spade.'" [33]

Decatur's well-known tinware manufacturer, Walter Wadsworth, a native of Hartford, Conn., died on November 5, 1874 at the age of 73. He is buried in Decatur Cemetery. Andrew Rogers, 70, of the Panthersville District, died on April 18, 1874. He also is buried in Decatur Cemetery. Stone Mountain physician Dr. George K. Hamilton, 70, died on June 7, 1874, and is buried in Stone Mountain Cemetery. Wesley Braswell, 73, of Lithonia, committed suicide on March 6, 1874, and is buried in Lithonia Cemetery. [34]

Midway Union Sunday School was organized on May 17, 1874, with pioneer citizen John Cooper Austin as the first superintendent. The Sunday school closed after the Midway Presbyterian Church was organized on July 29, 1876. George W. Lyon (1822-1895), grandson of Revolutionary soldier Joseph Emanuel Lyon, is credited with founding the church, which was formed with members from churches in Augusta, Decatur and Indian Creek. The church's first structure, on Midway Road just off Covington Road, was made of a mixture of concrete, sand and rocks, similar to tabby. The Rev. Donald Fraser was the first pastor. Midway is the mother church of Ingleside Presbyterian, formed in 1900.[35]

Two north DeKalb Baptist churches -- Corinth and Olive Leaf -- consolidated in January of 1875, and kept the former's name. The original Corinth Baptist Church had participated in the formation of the DeKalb Sunday School Union in 1866.

The church began as a women's prayer group, which first met in W. S. (Bert) Johnson's blacksmith shop. The group was organized by Julia Carroll, wife of William Spencer Carroll. The first recorded minutes in 1889 showed 18 male members and 36 female members:

Male Members
R. F. Watkins	G. W. Lord	R. R. Purcell
L. W. Phillips	D. P. Donahoo	W. W. Penell
F. Gay	Terry Southern	W. J. Warbington
R. D. Yancey	T. F. Adams	Harvy McGinnis
	H. B. Baswell	Walter L. Blackwell

J. W. Jeffries
J. W. Spinks
W. S. Carroll
L. C. Brisco

Female Members
Laura E. Moncrief
M. E. Watkins
Minnie D. Watkins
Nancy Holbrooks
S. M. Gay
C. B. Flowers
M. F. Martin
Dice Lord
M. Purcell

T. R. Brown
T. S. Penell
Lilly K. Downs
Julia Carroll
Lavinia Robinson
Tobitha Phillips
Susan Yancy
Ida Yancy
S. A. Ellison
E. A. Donahoo
Annie Bently
Lavadah Holbrook
Elizabeth Brown
Lula Spinks

M. Carrie Evins
Margaret Adams
Emma Baswell
Martha Purcell
Carry Southern
Amanda L. Henson
Sarah E. Howard
E. E. Howard
Delaney Brown
Martha Brown
A. J. Penell
M. A. Brisco
M. C. Evins

Justinian Evins, the grandson of DeKalb pioneers, John L. Evins and Meredith Collier, was a deacon at Corinth, and church clerk for many years beginning in 1880. Evins, who died on June 9, 1930, is buried in the church cemetery in Chamblee. Among others buried there is James Henry Polk, Evins's brother-in-law and son of DeKalb state Sen. James K. Polk, who died on February 5, 1898.

The church's first building was constructed in 1881 on what is now Peachtree Road between the intersections of Hospital Avenue and New Peachtree Road. Early baptisms were conducted in nearby Folsom's Pond.

Corinth changed its name to Chamblee Baptist in January of 1920. The church moved in the mid-1990s to Forsyth County, and the name changed to Johns Creek Baptist Church. The church cemetery remains on the east side of Peachtree Road, Land Lot 299, in Chamblee. Families buried there include Adams, Bertling, Bloodworth, Brooks, Brown, Cain, Carroll, Clower, Collins, Cox, Donahoo, Donaldson, Evins, Ford, Fay, Gay, Holcombe, Honea, House, Hudgins, Hyde, Jameson, Johnson, Lively, Long, Martin, Polk, Ramsey, Robinson, Spinks, Turk, Wallace, Warren, Wilson, Wright and Yancy. [36]

The Calhoun brothers -- Ezekiel N. and James M. -- both died in 1875, E. N. on March 13 and J. M. on October 1. Both are buried in Atlanta's Oakland Cemetery. Ezekiel practiced medicine in Decatur from 1826 to 1854, when he moved to Atlanta. James followed his older brother to Decatur in 1829 and chose the law as his profession. He moved to Atlanta in 1849 and was Atlanta's mayor during the Civil War. Edward A. Center of Lithonia, a bachelor, died on July 25, 1875 at the age of 62. He is buried near his parents, John and Julia Center, in Rock Springs Cemetery near Lithonia. Jacob Chupp of Diamond's District died on July 17, 1875 at the age of 69, and is buried in his family cemetery. [37]

Three new industries opened in DeKalb in 1875, a sure sign that the local economy was sound. Crockett Distillery was located in Decatur, between Atlanta Avenue and Herring Street, 100 yards down Atlanta Avenue from McDonough Street. The distillery operated until 1900. J. C. Chupp constructed the Lithonia Mill, which ground corn and wheat and sawed lumber for a cabinet shop that was attached to the business. A. J. Almand later owned the mill, which closed in 1935. A. J. Almand was the father of Bond Almand, associate justice of the Supreme Court of Georgia in 1951. The Willis Wells Ginnery operated between Chamblee and Tucker from 1875 to 1890. [38]

The post-war trend for many DeKalb families was to sell the farm, pack up their belongings and move to the city in search of work. Just the reverse was true for the Medlock family. While Ponce de Leon Avenue beyond what is now Boulevard was considered the suburbs in 1875, the Medlock family decided they would like to live even farther from Atlanta.

John Parks (Buck) Medlock, born on June 6, 1837 in Gwinnett County, was the son of John Williams Medlock (1807-1882) and Sarah Jemison Ware (1807-1883). The family moved from Gwinnett to now Ponce de Leon Avenue when John Parks was 10 years old and the area was still DeKalb County. Buck Medlock married Virginia Vilenah Antoinette Mason on August 27, 1861; they set up housekeeping on land in the now Virginia-Highland area. Their daughter, William Vilenah, called Billie or Miss Willie, was named for both her parents. She was the only child born to the couple before Buck went off to war. Disabled, with wounded hands, Buck mustered out on June 24, 1863. Eight more children were born to the couple: Ida Ann, Charles Oscar, Jessie Istalena, Hugh Mason, Sarah Maude Ella, Madge Antoinette and James Wade.

In 1875, the family moved to a large tract of land at what is now Medlock Road and Scott Boulevard, lending their name to many landmarks still found near Decatur today. William Vilenah Medlock , who married Daniel W. Johnson, is probably the only woman in DeKalb County history to have two roads named for her: Willivee Drive, which runs between North Decatur and North Druid Hills roads, and Vilenah Lane off Oakdale Road in Druid Hills.

Also moving to DeKalb about this time was John William Warren. Warren and his wife, Emily Frances Stanton, came from Rockdale County and settled on Chamblee Tucker Road, where they raised eight children. One of their daughters, Abbie Warren, taught in DeKalb County public schools for 42 years. Warren Elementary School on Chamblee Tucker Road was named for J. W. Warren. [39]

A new post office opened in the community of Clarkston on October 9, 1876, with James J. Norman as postmaster. The area had been named New's Siding for Jacob New, a section foreman of the Georgia Railroad. The tract of land where town would be located had been owned by the Georgia Railroad before it was subdivided and sold. The post office, and subsequently the town, were named for W. W. Clark, a Covington lawyer and director of the Georgia Railroad and Banking Company. The town would not be incorporated for another six years, on December 12, 1882. Clarkston's principal early business was the general store operated by Hays Jolly, father of Clem and Tom Jolly. In the 1880s, store employee Henry Dawson would walk through town collecting orders and return to the store to fill them.

Mary E. Bryan once wrote that Clarkston had "magnificent trees, pure air, excellent water, an unequaled train service, good schools and churches, well equipped stores, a handsome Masonic lodge, many beautiful and some elegant homes and a grand university (Lamar University) in process of erection.

"The town is notable for its morality, its utter freedom from all objectionable characters -- white or black... There is no calaboose in Clarkston; none is needed. The marshall's office is a sinecure. there are no offenders against the law. The white citizens are intelligent, quiet, sociable -- the best of neighbors. The colored population are honest, industrious and respectful. No one ever hears of a row in their special part of town, where they have neat homes, churches, school houses and an imposing lodge building for the Knights of Pythias." [40]

The residents of the law-abiding town of Clarkston might have been amused to know that Atlanta's biggest crime problem in 1875 was "vagrant cows found out after respectable hours." When police officers impounded the outlaw cows, owners could get them back within 48 hours for a $2 fee. [41]

In the early years, Clarkston area youngsters attended a private school that was located between the town and Stone Mountain. Judge J. C. Estes, who was born in 1870, attended the school from 1876 until 1886. The tuition was five cents per day for lower grades and six cents per day for older students. J. C. recalled that the state paid three cents of the tuition, and parents like his father, Squire Z. Estes, paid the rest. Students went to school for six-eight weeks in winter, then larger children had to stop and help with farm work. They returned to school for 60 days in summer, then dropped out again to help with crops.

"Some of the larger ones attended two terms of four or five months each, and as they were eager to learn and applied themselves, were able to do it in that length of time," Estes said.

The school building was built of wooden planks, with gaps between the boards unsealed. There was a fireplace at one end. "There was a bench without a back on each side of the fireplace, and one across in front of it," Estes recalled. "Eight children sat on each of these. Then two benches back of the one facing the first place took care of the larger children. We would stick our feet under the bench in front of us as far as we could to try and get warmer...

"There was a wide plank hinged to the wall at the other end of the room from the fireplace. When no one was writing on it, it was let down out of the way." Ink was made out of "ink balls" from oak trees, as well as from mulberries. Estes said his first school book was a blue back speller, which cost his father 15 cents.

The school day lasted from 8 a.m. until 4 p.m., with one recess and a 10-minute break before lunch when students would to go to the spring to wash their hands and faces. Lunches were brought from home.

When little boys were not in school or working on the family farm, they played marbles. Larger boys played baseball. [42]

Greater Travelers Rest Baptist Church was organized in 1876 by the Rev. William Tillman, pastor of Atlanta's Wheat Street Baptist Church. Sam Stinson and others who lived on the McDonough Road about three miles outside the Decatur town limits had been conducting Sunday school work in the area for several months. Stinson also conducted weekly prayer meetings. The church chose its name because it first met in a building that had been used as a resting place by Union soldiers on their way through Atlanta in 1864. The church has moved several times over the years, and currently is located on Tilson Road near Decatur. [43]

Newspapers made the news in DeKalb and Atlanta in 1876. The DeKalb News was established in Stone Mountain in December by two young men named Carter. In Atlanta, three new writers -- Henry

W. Grady, Sam W. Small and Joel Chandler Harris -- started work at the Atlanta Constitution. [44]

John W. Fowler and his son, John W. Fowler Jr., both died in 1876. The elder Fowler was a veteran of the Creek Indian War of 1836 and a pioneer of the Indian Creek neighborhood. He died on November 19 at the age of 71. His son, a conductor on the Macon and Brunswick Railroad, died in Brunswick of yellow fever on October 14 at the age of only 37. Both are buried in Indian Creek Cemetery.

Michael Winningham, age 64, died on April 12, 1876; he is said to have dug the first grave in Stone Mountain Cemetery. Thomas Jefferson Dean of the Stone Mountain District, brother of Lemuel Dean of Atlanta, died on August 14, 1876 at the age of 74, and is buried in the Dean family cemetery. [45]

Washington J. Houston quit the railroad business in Atlanta in 1876 at the age of 45, and began a new career as a farmer and mill operator. Houston Mill opened on the south fork of Peachtree Creek, on Houston mill Road, between LaVista and Clifton, that same year. The mill produced well-known waterground cornmeal until 1940. With the exception of one term in the state legislature in 1894, Houston spent the next 35 years in quiet pursuits on the property he had bought some years previously from his father-in-law, Dr. Chapman Powell. While he considered himself retired, Houston nonetheless would be on the cutting edge of a technology that revolutionized life in DeKalb County.

Built in the 1880s, this plain clapboard building was probably Clarkston's first city hall. Classes were held at city hall when Clarkston Elementary School burned in the late 1930s. Ed Sutton, pictured here, was mayor in the late 1920s or early 1930s. (Vivian Price, personal collection)

Houston built DeKalb's first hydroelectric plant about 1900, which supplied Decatur with electric current for lighting. Houston, with his son, Washington Jackson Houston Jr., operated the Decatur Light, Power and Water Company. DeKalb's first electric light burned in the Houston home on Clairmont near North Decatur. The wonder of electricity would reach the town of Decatur three years later.

The mill also was a source of recreation for area residents. Houston's daughter, Sarah Amanda, recalled that "every first day of May, Pa would have the upstairs of the mill cleaned out, and wax cut up and strewn on the floor. Everybody from Decatur and miles around would come and bring a picnic dinner. The mill was a beautiful spot... Everybody danced the square dance and the Virginia reel and when the caller would say, `Sashay your partner, ladies,' we would have to get in the middle of the ring and cut capers to our partners. That is when we would blush and hang back, but the boys would pull us in and make us go through the motions." The mill pond also was the neighborhood swimming hole on hot summer days.

At Christmastime, Sarah Amanda and her sisters would walk from Clairmont and North Decatur Road

The family of Washington Jackson Houston Sr. lived in this house on Clairmont Road. The house contained the original cabin built by Dr. Chapman Powell, which was concealed by several renovations. Houston had purchased the property from Powell, who was his father-in-law. (DeKalb Historical Society)

to the brick courthouse on the Square in Decatur to see the lighting of the holiday tree. They left their horses at home to spare them from being frightened by the annual fireworks. [46]

The first telephones were installed in Atlanta in 1877, one year after Alexander Graham Bell had unveiled his amazing invention. It was 1884 before the contraption would come to Decatur. Back then a call from Decatur to Atlanta was considered long distance, and a call cost 15 cents for a five-minute conversation. Those who called Atlanta frequently could purchase books of 20 and 40 tickets. The original operators were boys, whose telephone manners were so rude they were replaced by women in 1888. [47]

Milton A. Candler was first elected to the U. S. House in 1877. The men of Decatur celebrated the victory with a torchlight parade from the town square to the Candler farm on Kirk Road. The Candler home would have been an exciting place to be in the waning quarter of the 19th century. John B. Gordon was a frequent Sunday visitor, riding over from Kirkwood to sit on the porch and talk farming and politics. [48]

Augustus J. Hulsey, the 30-year-old son of Eli J. Hulsey, died on February 17, 1877. He is buried in Atlanta's Oakland Cemetery. Diamond's District pioneer John C. Ragsdale died on March 21, 1877 at the age of 64. He is buried in the old Thomas Maguire family cemetery in Gwinnett County. [49] George Washington Scott, who had spent a night in Decatur in 1850, returned to the town in 1877. The intervening years had been a roller coaster ride.

Scott's mother Agnes Irvine was born on June 13, 1799 in Ballykeel, County Down, Ireland, and came to the United States in 1816 with her mother. At the age of 22, she married John Scott, a widower with five children, in Alexandria, Penn. John and Agnes had seven children: Susan, John, James Irvine, George Washington, William, Mary Irvine and Alfred. Agnes died in Alexandria on October 23, 1877.

Agnes's third son, George, was born on February 22, 1829 in Alexandria, but left there for Florida in 1850, because of poor health. To pay his expenses, he sold jewelry along the way. He settled in Tallahassee, Fla., where he made a fortune in business. He organized Scott's Cavalry in 1863 and "served with distinction." Scott married his boyhood sweetheart, Rebecca Bucher, in Pennsylvania, but returned to Florida. Scott was elected governor of Florida in 1868, but was disqualified by federal military authorities. The couple moved to Savannah in 1870, where Scott lost his entire fortune. He moved to Decatur to start over and to escape the coastal yellow fever epidemic.

In Decatur, he was once again highly successful in the commercial fertilizer business and later with Scottdale Textile Mills. Scott housed his family, including children George Bucher, Mary Hough and Nell, in a home on Sycamore Street where the Decatur Recreation Center is today. The house was originally built between 1835 and 1840 by Littlebury Harris for his brother-in-law, Charles Murphey. George W. Scott became a prominent elder in the Decatur Presbyterian Church, a relationship that would become more important to the town of Decatur as the years progressed. [50]

Two new post offices opened in DeKalb County in 1878. John M. Stodder was named postmaster at Edgewood on May 1, and Robert M. Clarke got the job at the new Panola Post Office on the South River on June 12. The town of Edgewood, so named because of its proximity to Atlanta, would be incorporated on December 9, 1898 by the Georgia legislature, but would merge with Atlanta on January 1, 1909, after a vote of its citizens. [51]

John Y. Flowers opened a steam-powered sawmill in the center of the town of Doraville in 1878. The mill, which was later owned by the Munday brothers and still later by a corporation, burned in 1921.[52]

Three DeKalb pioneers died in 1878: James H. Born of Lithonia, 98-year-old Joel Starnes and Thomas J. Perkerson, son of Dempsey Perkerson. Both Starnes and Perkerson died in Fulton County. Thomas Alexander, who passed through DeKalb on his way to fame and fortune, also died in 1878. He had come from Manchester, England to Brooklyn, New York at the age of 17, so poor he had to borrow two cents to pay his ferryage. He moved to Savannah in 1847 and Stone Mountain in 1852, pausing long enough to build a mill for Charles Latimer. One year later, he moved to Atlanta. When he died, he left the largest estate in Fulton County, more than half a million dollars. [53]

Dr. Thomas S. Powell founded the Southern Medical College in Atlanta in 1879. The college, its hospital and dental school merged with the existing Atlanta Medical College in 1898 and was renamed the Atlanta College of Physicians and Surgeons. The combined schools later would be incorporated

Singers learn to "shape" notes before they learn lyrics in sacred harp singing. James L. White, center, is pictured with his singing school students in this photo, taken about 1900. James White was the son of B. F. White, co-author of the Sacred Harp song book. (DeKalb Historical Society; Vanishing Georgia Collection, Georgia Department of Archives and History)

into DeKalb's Emory University Medical School and hospital. [54]

William Johnson proprietor of Johnson's Ferry on Chattahoochee, for whom today's Johnson Ferry Road in north DeKalb is named, died in 1879, but he was not destined to rest in peace. Johnson's body was snatched from its grave in a Cobb County cemetery. George Vaughn, a Negro janitor at the Atlanta Medical College, was charged with the crime. The body was never found, and Johnson's grave remains empty today. [55]

In the same year William Johnson died, Martin DeFoor and his wife, Susan were murdered. They were killed on July 26, while sleeping in their beds at their home near the Bolton community. DeFoor had come to DeKalb's Panthersville District in the mid-1840s, and had later moved to the Standing Peachtree community, taking over the operation of James McC. Montgomery's ferry. No motive for the killings was ever discovered, and the crime was never solved. Martin and Susan DeFoor are buried in the Montgomery family cemetery. [56]

Ezekiel Mason of Decatur also died in 1879. His home on the Square in Decatur had been headquarters during the Civil War for women who made uniforms for Confederate soldiers. [57]

Moments before his death on December 5, 1879, Benjamin Franklin White sang "Sounding Joy," one of the many songs he co-authored for The Sacred Harp. At the time of his death, White lived near Covington Highway in south DeKalb. White died from injuries he received in a fall near the home of his daughter in Atlanta. He is buried in Oakland Cemetery near his wife, Thurza Melvina Golightly,

420   THE HISTORY OF DEKALB COUNTY, GA. 1822-1900 • CHAPTER 28

who died in 1878. Their daughter, Martha America White, married the Rev. Elijah Henry Clarke.[58]

I. N. (Newt) Nash, a Confederate veteran who lost an arm at Gettysburg, returned home and opened a mill on Mill Street in Stone Mountain in 1879. During the last quarter of the 19th century, he also was the county's tax receiver "at first making his rounds over the county on foot, and later by horseback."[59]

Attempts to abolish the state's convict lease system began in 1876. One of the program's most outspoken opponents was DeKalb County state Rep. Robert Augustus Alston. "Robert A. Alston was the first man in Georgia to expose the enormities of the convict lease system whose existence was a blot upon the civilization of the nineteenth century... He dared to expose it, despite the lightning which he unloosed upon his own head and regardless of its powerful entrenchments."

B. F. White, co-author of *The Sacred Harp*, and his wife, Thurza Melvina Golightly White.

Alston was born on December 31, 1832 in Macon. As a young man he lived in Charleston, S. C., where he married Mary Charlotte McGill. During the Civil War, Alston enlisted first with the Charleston Light Dragoons and later Gen. John H. Morgan's cavalry. He was involved in 100 battles and never wounded. "He was in the fiercest combats and the wildest escapades which have made the memory of Morgan's men immortal... At the fight at Cynthiana, Ky., he had a biscuit shot from between his teeth."

While a prisoner of the Union Army, Alston demanded his release "on the ground that his detention was illegal, under the rules of war, and about forty letters to that General (Burnside) either convinced him of the correctness of the demand, or so thoroughly wore out his patience that the General ordered him out of prison, saying he preferred to die `by some other weapon than Bob Alston's pen.'" Upon their return from the war, Atlanta Mayor James M. Calhoun gave Morgan and Alston a hero's welcome and a huge party at the Trout House.

Alston bought land in what is now the East Lake community in 1856 and begun construction on his home, called Meadownook. The home contained expensive furnishings, including a number of rare paintings. The paintings were saved during the war by Alston's brother who hid them in some nearby woods. The house was saved from burning by Sherman's soldiers because Alston was a Mason. The structure still bears scars from the Battle of Atlanta in 1864, the heart of which took place just to the southeast. The Alston's entertained many noted guests at Meadownook, including Jefferson Davis, Alexander H. Stephens and John B. Gordon. The house said to be haunted with the ghosts of Civil War soldiers.

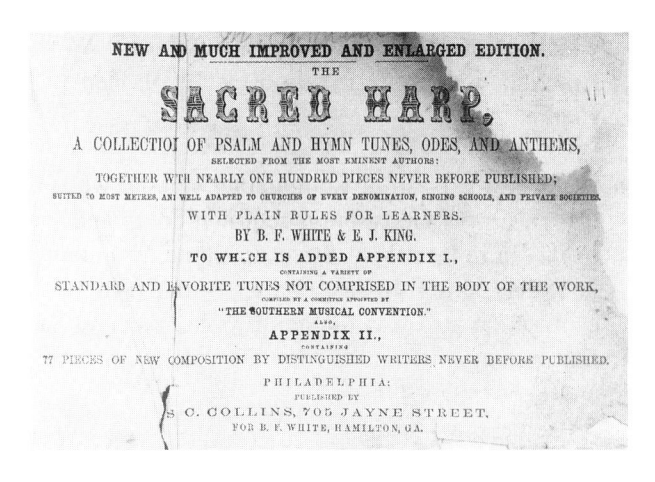

Pictured are the cover of B. F. White's Sacred Harp songbook and a page of the music and lyrics of "Sounding Joy." (Donald S. Clarke)

After the war Alston settled in DeKalb and engaged in farming, journalism and law. He was editor of ill-fated Atlanta Herald with Alex St. Clair Abrams, and was responsible for bringing the renowned Henry W. Grady to Atlanta.

Although he was a slave owner and worked after the war for restoration of the Democratic party, he "demonstrated his progressive positions on education, taxation, and other matters of concern to Georgians. "As chairman of the (Georgia House) Penitentiary Committee Alston demonstrated a leadership ability that gained national recognition. Following his report on the convict lease system... State and National Press releases reflected an exploding bombshell of public opinion. Alston was threatened and his wife was needled about his position but he remained firm in his convictions."

Alston compared work camps to Civil War prison camps. "The fearful mortality which prevails in many of the camps... is a reproach to our humanity." With poor medical care, an average of 10 percent of the prisoners died every year. With too few guards, 20 to 45 percent of the convicts escaped.

"We find in some of the camps," Alston wrote, "men and women chained together and occupying the same sleeping bunks. The result is that there are now in the Penitentiary twenty-five bastard children, ranging from three months to five years of age, and many of the women are now far advanced in pregnancy. This we regard as a flagrant wrong...

"To turn the prisoners over to private parties, who have no interest in them except that which is prompted by avarice, is to subject them to treatment which is as various as the characters of those who have them in charge and in many cases amount to nothing less than capital punishment with slow torture added."

Alston's stand on the convict lease system earned him threats from some who stood to lose money should the system be abolished.

In 1879, Alston had been asked by his friend, John B. Gordon, to sell Gordon's interest in a lease of 60 convicts at work on a farm in Taylor County. Edward Cox, a sublessee under Gordon, was incensed with Alston over the sale. On March 11, Alston and Cox argued over the transaction, and Cox promised to kill Alston before sundown. The two, both armed, met in the office of State Treasurer John W. Renfroe in the state capital at 3:30 p.m., where they engaged in another heated argument. Cox and Alston both drew their weapons. Alston managed to inflict a slight wound, but was hit in the right temple. He died at 6:40 p.m. at the residence of Dr. F. F. Taber at 82 Decatur Street in Atlanta.

He was survived by his wife, two sons and two daughters, as well as a younger brother, Thomas H. Alston. Thomas Alston's grandson, Wallace McPherson Alston, was president of Agnes Scott College. Alston was buried in Decatur Cemetery on March 13, 1879.

Cox was found guilty of murder on May 7, 1879 in Fulton Superior Court and sentenced to life at hard labor. He was later pardoned and operated a dairy farm in the Atlanta area until his death on March 1, 1901 at the age of 57. Cox also is buried in Decatur Cemetery, a only few feet away from Alston.

There was considerable reporting of Alston's death in newspapers all over the country.

The DeKalb Times printed this obituary:

"Under The Sod -- Funeral of the Late Colonel Alston
A Heartfelt Tribute to His Memory
The Concourse at the Grave
The Condition of his Family
The Evidence of Captain Nelms Before the Coroner's Jury

Robert A. Alston (1832-1879) was killed in a duel over Georgia's convict labor system. (DeKalb Historical Society, Georgia Department of Archives and History)

"The early trains yesterday morning brought in a number of people from the other cities of Georgia, who came to the city to pay their last respects to Colonel Alston. It was very soon evident that an immense crowd would go down to the funeral.

"It was universally remarked that no death that ever marked Atlanta's record with blood caused such widespread sadness as this. Strong men spoke with bated breath and moistened eyes, and parted with a silent pressure of the hand. `I never knew how tenderly I loved Bob Alston till I realized that he was dead,' said Captain Evan Howell, and this was an almost universal expression.

"`No death of the past ten years,' said Colonel Gus Bacon, with an honorable moisture in his eyes, `affected me so deeply. The first shock that benumbed me when I heard of it was this: There is no one that can fill his place. He was unique, lovable, the only Bob Alston that ever lived!'

"Said Mayor Huff, who had always been his devoted friend: `I do not believe there was a man in Georgia whose death would have caused so much personal grief as Bob Alston's death has done. There were tears shed for him in every city in Georgia yesterday, and I doubt not in every state in the union.'

Robert A. Alston built this home, which he called "Meadownook," shortly before the Civil War. The house was ransacked during the Union occupation in 1864, although some furnishings which had been hidden in the woods were saved. Located across from the East Lake Golf Club, the house is on the National Register of Historic Places. (DeKalb Historical Society)

"It was a sad and mournful crowd that boarded the train for Decatur. Nothing but praises of the dead man and sobs over his untimely taking off could be heard. At the church the vast crowd could not gain admittance, and as the cortege approached and the coffin was borne across the sward there were hundreds who bent their heads and gave way to their grief. The most touching thing, however, of the whole occasion was the simple and hearty grief of the country folks who had for years been the neighbors of Colonel Alston. The open-faced sorrow of these honest people told most eloquently of the love they bore him.

"He was the best friend we ever had," they said. It seemed to give them all relief to be able to testify to some stranger to the admirable virtues of their friend. `No woman that presses her firstborn baby to her heart had a gentler heart than he had,' said one of them in the rude beauty of plain speech to a clump of Atlantians. The feeling against Cox is intense and without qualification.

"The funeral of Colonel R. A. Alston yesterday was the concluding chapter of the tragedy of Tuesday last. We have seldom seen such an impressive occasion as was this funeral. At 1 o'clock a special train on the Georgia road carried out three hundred citizens of Atlanta, among whom were the Atlanta lodge of Free Masons and a detachment of the Atlanta Cadets, of which company Mr. Robert Alston Jr. is a member. The squad was commanded by Lieutenant Walter Venable.

"At the Decatur depot the Atlanta friends met a large number of residents of all parts of DeKalb county. Two o'clock was the hour appointed for the funeral, but long before that hour the Methodist church was full. At 2 o'clock the remains arrived from the family residence in Kirkwood. As they were taken out of the hearse the Atlanta and Decatur Masons opened their lines, and the coffin was borne through the crossed wands of Masonic mourning. The cadets stood in the rear with reversed arms. The metallic case was beautifully ornamented with white flowers and evergreens in designs of crosses and wreaths.

"The following gentlemen acted as pallbearers: Major J. B. Morgan, Major J. W. Warren, Judge Bryce, Mr. Z. D. Harrison, Mr. Frank Gordon, Colonel J. W. Nelms, Mr. Howard Van Epps. Mr. William James, Dr. A. W. Calhoun, Colonel Sam Williams.

The remains were carried into the densely-packed church and the choir sang a sad but sweet hymn with impressive effort. The pulpit was draped in mourning, but from the black cloth under the Bible descended an anchor of white flowers, a beautiful emblem of hope. The remains were followed by the stricken family. Mr. Gus Alston, of Eufaula, Alabama, arrived yesterday morning, and on his arm leaned the widow whom God's strange providence had bereft. The children of Colonel Alston and other relations followed. The solemn service of the dead was read by the Rev. Allen Thomas, pastor of the church, after which Rev. Dr. W. F. Cook offered a prayer of touching beauty.

"A remarkable incident is related in connection with Colonel Alston's membership with Decatur Methodist Church. About two years ago, when he felt it his duty to join the church, he preferred the Edgewood chapel and was about to join there, when he learned that Mr. Cox had an idea of joining the church also. He approached Mr. Cox and earnestly begged him to join the Edgewood church. Mr. Cox would not consent. At last Colonel Alston said: `Well, Ed, I'll join at Decatur if you will.' To this proposition an affirmative response was returned and these two men attended the solemn bonds together. Now, one is slain and the other is his slayer.

"The crowd at the church yesterday represented the officials of the state, the leading citizens of Atlanta and DeKalb county. Macon sent up Hon. A. O. Bacon, speaker of the house, Mayor Huff and the genial Charlie Herbst, who loved Alston like a brother.

"Outside stood hundreds about the doors and windows unable to gain entrance. There were scores of negroes present and some of them wept like children. Said a gentleman, `I believe every man, woman and child in DeKalb county loved Bob Alston.'

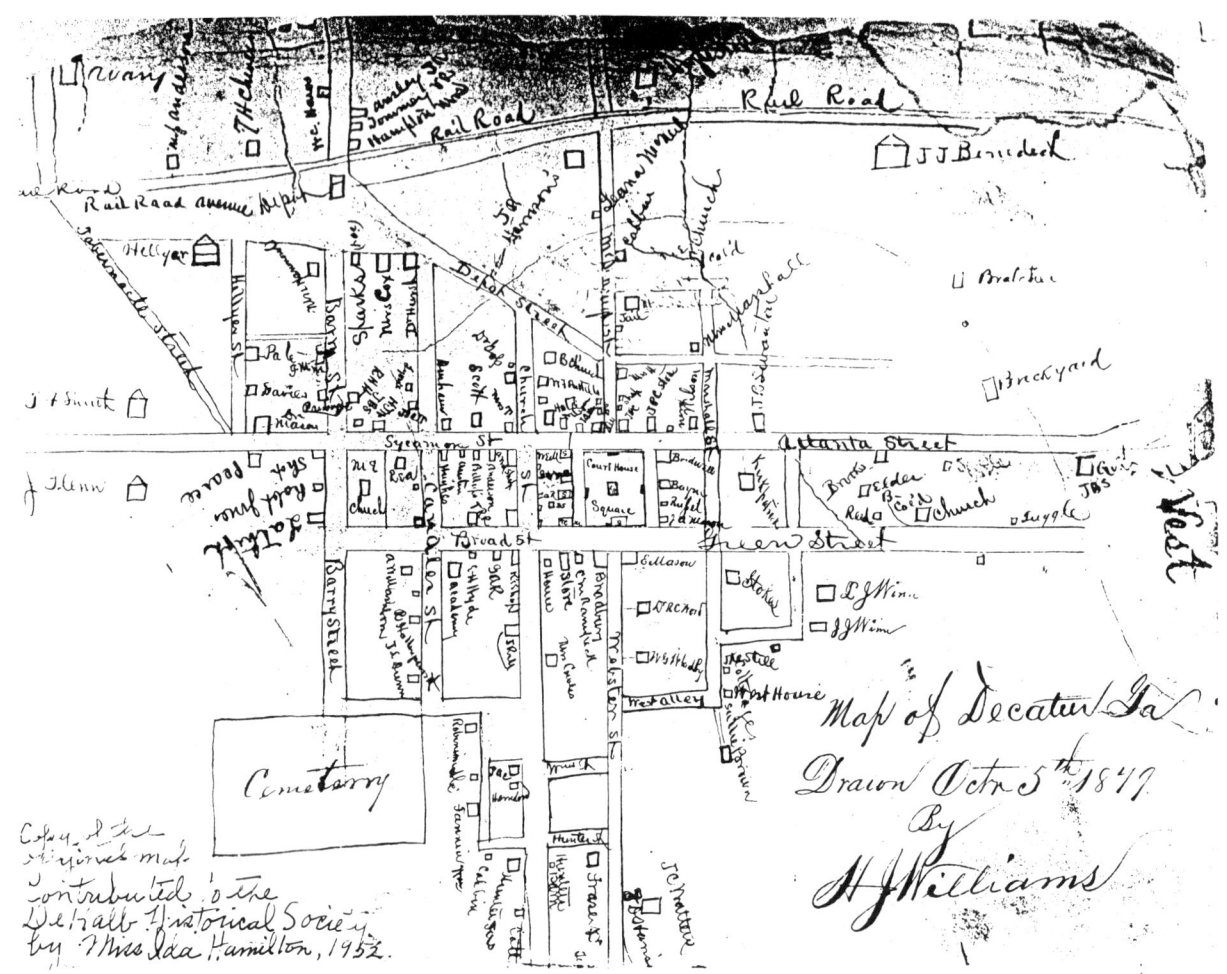

This map of Decatur shows the location of businesses, houses and other structures homes and businesses in the town in 1879. (DeKalb Historical Society)

"After the service at the church the crowd moved to the graveyard, where the remains were tenderly laid away in their last resting place. The Masons took charge of the corpse at the grave and never was the beautiful Masonic burial service more nobly performed.

"The ceremonies were conducted by Past Master Parkins, of the Atlanta lodge, who delivered a touching lecture on the occasion. All the funeral rites of this great order were performed over the dead brother, and the emblems placed in the graves with loving hands. After all this was the crowd slowly dispersed from the solemn scene and the clods fell on the coffin -- dust to dust, ashes to ashes. The grave was slowly filled and many a warm tear fell on its unfeeling clay. Silence and twilight came like twin angels to bless the scene with their sweet peace, and he who was so dearly loved here was left under the quiet stars in his last sleep -- awaiting the resurrection."

In its coverage of Alston's death, the New York Times condemned the South: "The killing of Colonel Alston is not only a fresh illustration of the slight value which the violent men of the south place upon human life, but also a striking example of the terrible risks which are run by those who attempt to correct abuses in that section of the country."

"Of the causes which really led to it no mention is made, but it is nevertheless, well known to those who have watched the course of recent political events in Georgia, that the killing of Colonel Alston was directly the result of his laudable effort to reform the penitentiary system of that state, a system which has long been a disgrace, not only to the commonwealth, but to humanity. The dead man was a democrat and had been a brave Confederate soldier.

"At the same time, however, he was always open to any argument which convinced him that his party was guilty of wrong-doing. At the last election he was chosen to the legislature, and acting as chairman of the penitentiary committee, he soon discovered that the unfortunate convicts, most of them negroes, were so maltreated by the men to whom they were leased by the state, that they were dying by the score, dying like dogs, in the swamps and remote places to which they had been taken by the contractors; dying from exposure, overwork and lack of food; dying because they were, in many cases, left without clothing, shelter or medical attendance."

In his description and account of his friend's death in the Atlanta Constitution, Henry Grady referred to `Bob' Alston's intensely religious character. `Alston was child-like in his faith he had absolute trust in prayer. I doubt if he ever closed his eyes at night without going on his knees. He prayed all the time and in all places. I have seen him go down on his knees in our old editorial room and pray aloud for help and guidance. And the first impulse that followed this prayer he would follow blindly and to the end. At heart he was profoundly religious, and his beliefs were old fashioned on all religious subjects...

"I might write forever about him. About his homelife, so soft, loving and gentle -- about the kindliness with which he placed his arm about me when I came to this city a friendless youngster..."

Alston was eulogized as "one of the most remarkable men in this country," certainly one of the most intriguing ever to live in DeKalb.

"The degree to which R. A. Alston appealed to a diverse coalition of social classes, and his liberal and deeply appreciated spirit towards the black man can be recognized in the beautiful testimony to his memory as expressed in the rare and previously unpublished broadside titled `Annual Decoration of the Grave of Robert A. Alston.' Alston Memorial Day was an annual event at the Decatur Cemetery for several years after Robert Alston's death.

"Annual Decoration
of the grave of
Col. Robert A. Alston.
To the Colored People of DeKalb County:

"Again you are called to the performance of a mournful duty. The affecting honors paid to the memory of Col. Robert A. Alston two years ago, fixed in the minds of his colored friends of DeKalb county a determination to annually render public homage to his virtues, character and achievements, and the undersigned committee were appointed to announce through this medium to the public, that on Saturday, the 25th of June, 1881, the Third Annual Decoration of the grave of Colonel Robert A. Alston will take place...

"It is desired by the Committee that every colored man and woman in the county, (and all others who may feel interested) shall be present and thus publicly testify exalted admiration of the life and services of him who was first and foremost to expose, condemn and denounce the workings of the abominable, blasphemous and vile penitentiary lease system, under which so many of our race are doomed to horror, agony and pollution, and whose highest object in life seemed to be the amelioration of the deplorable condition of the helpless and unfortunate..."

    L. G. Bivens, ch'm.
    Jethro S. Brooks
    L. M. Moss
    W. M. Rowe
    Elias Burdett

The convict lease system was abolished in 1909, 30 years after Robert Alston's death. [60]

Chapter 28 Notes

1. Garrett, Franklin M., 1954, 1969, Atlanta and Environs -- A Chronicle of Its People and Events, Vol. 1, page 852.

2. Garrett, Franklin M., 1954, 1969, Atlanta and Environs -- A Chronicle of Its People and Events, Vol. 1, pages 853-855. Hudgins, Carl T., 1952, "Mills and Other Early DeKalb County Industries (And Their Owners)," The Collections of the DeKalb Historical Society, Vol. 1.

3. Garrett, Franklin M., 1954, 1969, Atlanta and Environs -- A Chronicle of Its People and Events, Vol. 1, pages 825 and 828-829.

4. Garrett, Franklin M., 1954, 1969, Atlanta and Environs -- A Chronicle of Its People and Events, Vol. 1, page 830.

5. Garrett, Franklin M., 1954, 1969, Atlanta and Environs -- A Chronicle of Its People and Events, Vol. 1, pages 832, 870-871 and 879.

6. Author unknown, September, 1937, "Oglethorpe University, 1869-1875," The Atlanta Historical Bulletin, No. 11. Garrett, Franklin M., 1954, 1969, Atlanta and Environs -- A Chronicle of Its People and Events, Vol. 1, pages 846-47. Oglethorpe University files, DeKalb Historical Society.

7. Clarke, Caroline McKinney, 1973, 1996, The Story of Decatur 1823-1899.

8. Nix, Dorothy, personal collection, DeKalb Historical Society.

9. Garrett, Franklin M., 1954, 1969, Atlanta and Environs -- A Chronicle of Its People and Events, Vol. 1, pages 842-843.

10. Garrett, Franklin M., 1954, 1969, Atlanta and Environs -- A Chronicle of Its People and Events, Vol. 1, page 843.

11. Author unknown, 1984, "A Brief History of Rock Chapel Methodist Church."

12. Mt. Zion AME Church files, DeKalb Historical Society. Bak, Katherine, August 14, 1997, "Mount Zion African Methodist Episcopal Church," Community Review, page L14.

13. Garrett, Franklin M., 1954, 1969, Atlanta and Environs -- A Chronicle of Its People and Events, Vol. 1, page 848.

14. Harris, Joel Chandler, 1895, Memoirs of Georgia, Vol. 1. Ordner, Helen, July 24, 1991, "Gone With The Square," DeKalb News/Sun, page 3B.

15. Moncrief, Adiel J., n. d. "Historical Sketch of the First Baptist Church of Decatur." Ford, Elizabeth Austin, 1952, "A Precis of DeKalb's Early Church History," The Collections of the DeKalb Historical Society, Vol. 1. "Brief Synoptic History, First Baptist Church of Decatur, Georgia, Decatur Baptist Church file, DeKalb Historical Society.

16. Price, Vivian, tombstone inscriptions transcribed, January 13, 1997.

17. Author unknown, 1976, First United Methodist Church, Chamblee, Georgia, 1826-1976. Barre, Laura and Ken, 1995, The History of Doraville, Georgia. Candler, Charles Murphey, November 9, 1922, "Historical Address." Chesnut, Mr. and Mrs. J. David, personal collection. Flowers and McElroy genealogy files, DeKalb Historical Society. Jett, Fannie Mae, personal collection. Tilly, Harwell Parks IV, 1993, Stephen and Rebecca (King) Tilly and Their Descendants 1782-1992.

18. Nix, Dorothy, personal collection, DeKalb Historical Society. McVey, Virginia, April 20, 1966, "Redan Named After Store," Atlanta Journal.

19. Garrett, Franklin M., 1954, 1969, Atlanta and Environs -- A Chronicle of Its People and Events, Vol. 1, page 870. Clarke, Caroline McKinney, 1973, 1996, The Story of Decatur 1823-1899. Akin, Minnie Lee, and Lee, Kathleen Akin, 1982, The Akin Book.

20. Garrett, Franklin M., 1954, 1969, Atlanta and Environs -- A Chronicle of Its People and Events, Vol. 1, pages 873-874.

21. Garrett, Franklin M., 1954, 1969, Atlanta and Environs -- A Chronicle of Its People and Events, Vol. 1, pages 877-878. Nix, Dorothy, personal collection, DeKalb Historical Society.

22. Garrett, Franklin M., 1954, 1969, Atlanta and Environs -- A Chronicle of Its People and Events, Vol. 1, page 884.

23. Garrett, Franklin M., 1954, 1969, Atlanta and Environs -- A Chronicle of Its People and Events, Vol. 1, page 889. Clarke, Donald S., n. d., "The Reverends William Henry Clarke and Elijah Henry Clarke of Wesley Chapel Methodist Church."

24. Clarke, Caroline McKinney, 1973, 1996, The Story of Decatur 1823-1899.

25. Clarke, Caroline McKinney, 1973, 1996, The Story of Decatur 1823-1899.

26. Author unknown, n. D. "A Century for Christ, 1873-1973 -- A Baptist Church History -- Beech Springs, Kirkwood, Rainbow Park."

27. Garrett, Franklin M., 1954, 1969, Atlanta and Environs -- A Chronicle of Its People and Events, Vol. 1, page 892. Venable genealogy file, DeKalb Historical Society. Eldridge, Leila Venable Mason, 1952, "Stone Mountain," The Collections of the DeKalb Historical Society, Vol. 1.

28. Garrett, Franklin M., 1954, 1969, Atlanta and Environs -- A Chronicle of Its People and Events, Vol. 1, pages 899-900.

29. Garrett, Franklin M., 1954, 1969, Atlanta and Environs -- A Chronicle of Its People and Events, Vol. 1, pages 892-893.

30. Garrett, Franklin M., 1954, 1969, Atlanta and Environs -- A Chronicle of Its People and Events, Vol. 1, page 899.

31. Garrett, Franklin M., 1954, 1969, Atlanta and Environs -- A Chronicle of Its People and Events, Vol. 1, page 900.

32. Garrett, Franklin M., 1954, 1969, Atlanta and Environs -- A Chronicle of Its People and Events, Vol. 1, page 905.

33. Price, Vivian, September, 1982, Clarkston Centennial Edition, DeKalb News/Sun. Knight, Lucian Lamar, 1914, Georgia's Landmarks, Memorials and Legends. Garrett, Franklin M., 1954, 1969, Atlanta and Environs -- A Chronicle of Its People and Events, Vol. 1, page 905.

34. Garrett, Franklin M., 1954, 1969, Atlanta and Environs -- A Chronicle of Its People and Events, Vol. 1, page 908.

35. Nix, Dorothy, personal collection, DeKalb Historical Society. Ford, Elizabeth Austin, 1952, "A Precis of DeKalb's Early Church History," The Collections of the DeKalb Historical Society, Vol. 1.

36. Author unknown, 1975, A Century in North DeKalb -- the Story of the First Baptist Church of Chamblee, 1875-1975.

37. Garrett, Franklin M., 1954, 1969, Atlanta and Environs -- A Chronicle of Its People and Events, Vol. 1, page 923.

38. Hudgins, Carl T., 1952, "Mills and Other Early DeKalb County Industries (And Their Owners)," The Collections of the DeKalb Historical Society, Vol. 1.

39. Woodward, Johnnie, July 22, 1981, "Medlock Area Named For Farmer, Confederate Veteran," DeKalb News/Sun, page 5E. Author unknown, 1952, The Collections of the DeKalb Historical Society, Vol. 1. Chesnut, Mr. and Mrs. J. David, personal collection.

40. Garrett, Franklin M., 1954, 1969, <u>Atlanta and Environs -- A Chronicle of Its People and Events</u>, Vol. 1, page 926. Price, Vivian, 1982, Clarkston Centennial Celebration section, DeKalb News/Sun. Bryan, Mrs. Mary E., November 14, 1912, Illustrated Trade Edition, DeKalb New Era. Nix, Dorothy, personal collection, DeKalb Historical Society.

41. Garrett, Franklin M., 1954, 1969, <u>Atlanta and Environs -- A Chronicle of Its People and Events</u>, Vol. 1, page 911.

42. Author unknown, June 27, 1979, "Judge Estes Recalls Schoolhouse in Clarkston," DeKalb News/Sun, page 12E.

43. Nix, Dorothy, personal collection, DeKalb Historical Society.

44. Garrett, Franklin M., 1954, 1969, <u>Atlanta and Environs -- A Chronicle of Its People and Events</u>, Vol. 1, page 927.

45. Garrett, Franklin M., 1954, 1969, <u>Atlanta and Environs -- A Chronicle of Its People and Events</u>, Vol. 1, page 933.

46. Burbanck, Madeline, August 15, 1974, "The Druid Hills Letter," DeKalb New Era. Hudgins, Carl T., 1952, "Mills and Other Early DeKalb County Industries (And Their Owners)," <u>The Collections of the DeKalb Historical Society</u>, Vol. 1. Clarke, Caroline McKinney, 1973, 1996, <u>The Story of Decatur 1823-1899</u>.

47. Garrett, Franklin M., 1954, 1969, <u>Atlanta and Environs -- A Chronicle of Its People and Events</u>, Vol. 1, page 940.

48. Clarke, Caroline McKinney, 1973, 1996, <u>The Story of Decatur 1823-1899</u>.

49. Garrett, Franklin M., 1954, 1969, <u>Atlanta and Environs -- A Chronicle of Its People and Events</u>, Vol. 1, pages 940-941.

50. Alston, Wallace M., n. d., "The Significance of the Life of George Washington Scott." Scott genealogical files, DeKalb Historical Society. Clarke, Caroline McKinney, 1973, 1996, <u>The Story of Decatur 1823-1899</u>. Nix, Dorothy, personal collection, DeKalb Historical Society. Garrett, Franklin M., 1954, 1969, <u>Atlanta and Environs -- A Chronicle of Its People and Events</u>, Vol. 2, page 194.

51. Garrett, Franklin M., 1954, 1969, <u>Atlanta and Environs -- A Chronicle of Its People and Events</u>, Vol. 1, page 946.

52. Hudgins, Carl T., 1952, "Mills and Other Early DeKalb County Industries (And Their Owners)," <u>The Collections of the DeKalb Historical Society</u>, Vol. 1.

53. Garrett, Franklin M., 1954, 1969, <u>Atlanta and Environs -- A Chronicle of Its People and Events</u>, Vol. 1, page 950.

54. Garrett, Franklin M., 1954, 1969, <u>Atlanta and Environs -- A Chronicle of Its People and Events</u>, Vol. 1, pages 955-956.

55. Garrett, Franklin M., 1954, 1969, <u>Atlanta and Environs -- A Chronicle of Its People and Events</u>, Vol. 1, page 961-962.

56. Garrett, Franklin M., 1954, 1969, <u>Atlanta and Environs -- A Chronicle of Its People and Events</u>, Vol. 1, page 959-960.

57. Garrett, Franklin M., 1954, 1969, <u>Atlanta and Environs -- A Chronicle of Its People and Events</u>, Vol. 1, page 961.

58. Clarke, Donald S., n. d., "A Chronological History of the Life of Benjamin Franklin White."

59. Hudgins, Carl T., 1952, "Mills and Other Early DeKalb County Industries (And Their Owners)," <u>The Collections of the DeKalb Historical Society</u>, Vol. 1.

60. Garrett, Franklin M., 1954, 1969, <u>Atlanta and Environs -- A Chronicle of Its People and Events</u>, Vol. 1, pages 958-959, Vol. 2, pages 4-5. Author unknown, December, 1976, DeKalb Historical Society Bulletin, Vol. 1, No. 1.

Chapter 29

*I*n 1880, DeKalb's population grew to 14,497, a 45 percent increase over the previous census. Fulton County had three times the number of citizens as DeKalb, 49,137 at the time of the 1880 census. Atlanta had 37,409 residents, compared to fewer than 1,000 for Decatur. [1]

Decatur's town Square had changed little since before the Civil War. Families living around the courthouse included the Bradberrys, Bridwells, Browns, Crocketts, Coxes, Craigs, Jewetts, Joneses, Masons, Ramspecks and Russells. The office of the DeKalb Chronicle and two "bar rooms" also were located on the Square.

Annie Belle Jones, daughter of Hal Jones and Mary Margretta Ramspeck, was born at No. 3 East Court Square in 1873, and died there 78 years later. The home, with its wide verandas and large columns, was next door to the store owned by Annie's uncle, George Alexander Ramspeck. The site would later be occupied by the First National Bank. George Ramspeck, his wife and five children lived in a two-story Victorian house described by a newspaper of the day as "a very handsome residence, said to be the finest in the county."

Annie and her two sisters went to the Decatur Female Academy, taught by a Mrs. Stark and her daughter, Nora Bell. Her brother, George, attended the Donald Fraser School for Boys. Life in Decatur in the 1800s was simple and idyllic for families. Annie's only duties were to keep up with her school work and care for her canary.

The chief amusements for Annie and her family were Sunday buggy rides and visiting with Grandma (Charlotte) Ramspeck, whom her granddaughter recalled as always having her sewing scissors fastened at her waist, which she used for making silk "crazy quilts." There were fireworks on the Square at Christmas, and on Halloween young men tossed rag balls soaked in kerosene "for a fiery display." Annie's father, Hal Jones, wrote a humorous poem describing their lives:

> "And now to end these simple lines
> Let's dine as usual without wines,
> But don't forget we all are sinners
> And thank the lord for 'possum dinners." [2]

Young girls attended the Decatur Female Academy around the turn of the century, while boys attended the Donald Fraser School. (DeKalb Historical Society)

Shole's Georgia State Gazetteer and Business Directory for 1879 and 1880 described Decatur and other towns in DeKalb:

DEKALB COUNTY

Clarkston, Ga. R. R.
Five miles northeast of Decatur, the county seat, 11 from Atlanta and 160 from Augusta. Cotton the chief export. Methodist church and one school. Population 75. About 100 bales of cotton shipped annually. Mail daily each way. J. J. Norman, P. M. [1]

Cross Keys, A. & C. A.-L. Ry.
One and one-quarter miles distant is the depot and station for this place. Doraville, 3 miles distant, is the nearest express office. It is 9 miles north of Decatur, the seat of justice, and 12 1/4 from Atlanta. Nancy's Creek furnishes power for operating a mill. The place has two churches -- Methodist and

---

[1] Post Master.

George A. Ramspeck is pictured at his store, above (second from left), and at home with his family (far right). The little girl with the cat in the photo above is Ramspeck's niece, Bessie Jones. Both the store and the home were located on the Square in Decatur. The store burned about 1890. (DeKalb Historical Society)

Baptist -- on common school, and steam cotton gins. Cotton and wood form the chief exports. About 140 bales of cotton shipped per annum, most of which is carried to Atlanta by wagon. Population within a radius of 2 miles, near 400. Mail daily. G. L. Humphries, P. M.

Decatur, Ga. R. R.
A suburb of Atlanta, about 6 miles from the city, containing an estimated population of 700, and is

noted for its pleasant situation, pure air and water, and its religious and educational privileges, having three churches, Baptist, Methodist and Presbyterian-- and two excellent schools. County seat. H. J. Williams, P. M.

Doraville, A. & C. A.-L. Ry.
Ten miles due north of Decatur court house and 15 from Atlanta. It has a population of about 150, Presbyterian church, school and Southern Express office. Roswell, 10 miles north, uses this point for the shipment of cotton and factory goods. Mail daily by rail, and by hack from Roswell and Alpharetta. George N. Flowers, P. M.

Edgewood.
A suburb of Atlanta, about 3 miles from Decatur, -- its depot on Ga. R. R. -- extending from the corporate limits of Atlanta to Kirkwood, near Decatur. Its population of 250 or 300 persons is composed of business and professional men of Atlanta and their families. Although a comparatively new settlement, it is rapidly improving in population and wealth; contains a neat and well furnished church -- Methodist -- colored church, small public school, select school and many elegant residences and beautiful cottages. This location is most desirable, the climate very healthy and the society of the best. The accommodation train stops at any point for passengers to the city every morning and returns at evening. Kirkwood, a similar community, lies on the south side of the railroad but is without separate postal privileges. Mail daily each way by rail. Mrs. V. E. McFail, P. M.

Lithonia, Ga. R. R.
Early shipments of cotton from this place amount to about 2,200 bales. It is 13 miles southeast of Decatur, the seat of justice, 146 from Augusta, 25 from Atlanta, and a has a population of about 300; one steam saw mill, office of Southern Express Co., one common school and three churches -- Presbyterian, Methodist and Baptist. Mail daily each way. J. C. Johnson, P. M.; B. F. George, assistant.

Panola.
Decatur, the county seat, is 12 miles northwest; Lithonia, the nearest shipping point, 7 miles distant, via which the distance to Atlanta is 26 miles. From South River, power is derived to operate one saw and grist mill and cotton factory. Has about 200 inhabitants, one church -- Methodist -- and one common school. Weekly stages communicate with Lithonia. Warps and ropes are principal articles shipped. Mail daily by wagon. R. M. Clarke, P. M.

Panthersville.
A small settlement of 25 inhabitants, 7 miles south of Decatur, its nearest shipping, express and telegraph station, and 13 from Atlanta. Mails tri-weekly. No information received.

Smithton.
Is a small place, with perhaps 20 inhabitants, 3 miles southwest of Decatur, the county seat, and 4 from Atlanta. Two paper mills nearby (run by McNaught and Scrutchin and James Ormond, all of Atlanta), are operated by power from the Ocmulgee (South) River. Mail daily. Thomas J. Terry, P. M.

Stone Mountain, Ga. R. R.
A thriving little town of perhaps 750 inhabitants, 10 miles east of Decatur, the county seat, 16 miles from Atlanta, and 155 from Augusta. It has two academies, one common school, three churches -- Baptist, Methodist and Presbyterian -- and one saw mill and cotton gin operated by steam power.

The town of Chamblee was incorporated in August of 1908, one month before this photo of the depot was taken on September 11. Note the water tower on the left, and mule and house on the right. (Mr. and Mrs. J. David Chesnut; Vanishing Georgia Collection, Georgia Department of Archives and History)

Cotton and granite are the principal shipments; about 4,000 bales of cotton shipped annually. The mountain bearing the same name is about one and a half miles distant, and is one of the most interesting features of this section of the State. It is almost a solid mass of granite rising from a basin much lower than the surrounding lands, to an elevation 1,686 feet above the level of the sea and its value of quarrying can scarcely be estimated. Mail daily. S. Peck, P. M. [3]

Politics was a major source of conversation and debate in the county in the 1880s. Three politicians, including two from DeKalb, were at the height of their careers and powers during the decade. "The Bourbon Triumvirate," as the group was called, was made up of John B. Gordon, Joseph E. Brown and Alfred H. Colquitt. Colquitt was governor in 1880 and appointed Brown to fill the U. S. Senate seat vacated by Gordon, who resigned to become the attorney for the Louisville and Nashville Railroad. Some Georgians found the arrangement a bit too cozy. [4]

DeKalb residents Colquitt and Gordon were two of the best known figures in Georgia in the 1880s. Mrs. Gordon was a celebrity in her own right, having left her two children with Gordon's mother and gone with her husband to the battlefields during the Civil War. [5]

Members of the Chamblee family are pictured in front of Robert Chamblee's shoe shop in Gainesville. Robert Asbury Chamblee is pictured in photo at left. The town of Chamblee could have been named for Robert A. Chamblee or his father, Ransom Chamblee. (Alvin D. Chamblee)

T. Y. Nash, E. J. Bond and D. B. Chupp opened a cotton ginnery near Stone Mountain in 1880. T. Y. Nash was the father of L. T. Y. Nash, who served as DeKalb's commissioner of roads and revenues. The ginnery closed in 1910. [6]

Several well-known DeKalb County citizens died in 1880: Lemuel Dean, David Chupp of Lithonia, Judge John M. Born, Robert (Uncle Bob) Hollingsworth of Decatur, Leander Biffle (son of Revolutionary veteran John Biffle) and Decatur teacher Watson Kittredge, who moved to DeKalb from Spencer, Mass. [7]

DeKalb County got five new post offices in 1881:
- Redan, April 12, John T. Alford, postmaster.
- Snapfinger, June 15, Lorenzo M. Duren, postmaster.
- Saterfield, August 29, James F. Henderson, postmaster.
- Chamblee, October 20, James Monroe Bentley, postmaster.
- Dunwoody, November 18, Josephus Compton, postmaster.

Of these only Chamblee ever became an incorporated town. The Georgia legislature approved incorporation of Chamblee on August 17, 1908. [8]

The origin of the name of the post office and town of Chamblee, which had a population of 72 in

1890,[9] has been, and continues to be, the subject of considerable debate and research. There are two Chamblee families -- one white and one black -- whose family traditions state that the town was named for them.

The late Gordon Wallace, until his death in 1997 the oldest Chamblee resident, wrote in the history of the Chamblee (Prospect) Methodist Church:

"My father, William Dave Wallace, who was postmaster at Chamblee for a number of years... told me this story of how Chamblee received its name. It seems that about 1885, a few years after the Roswell branch railroad was built, the people comprising the small community known as Roswell Junction petitioned the U. S. Post Office Department to adopt this name and place a post office here. The petitioners were advised that `Roswell Junction' was not acceptable as a name (being similar to the name of Roswell, Ga. nearby) and requested a list of names from which to choose. A list was submitted, being names of prominent people in the community. However, in due time the Department advised that none of these names were acceptable either and suggested that another list be submitted.

"In the new list submitted, the name of a respected railroad laborer, a `section hand' in those times -- a black man held in honor then, as now -- by the surname of Chamblee, was included. From this new list the name of Chamblee was selected by the Post Office Department and accepted by the community..."[10]

Someone apparently intended for the town name to have been Edna. The name appears on the original application to the U. S. Post Office Department, dated September 14, 1881 and signed by George N. Flowers, postmaster of the Doraville post office, the branch nearest to the proposed site. "Edna" was crossed out and replaced by "Chamblee."

An exhaustive search of census, tax and other DeKalb County records indicates that no person named Chamblee lived in or near the town until considerably after incorporation.

The story of the naming of the town of Chamblee has been passed down verbally through six generations of the family of Alvin D. Chamblee, who lives in Roseville, Minn. Chamblee's great grandfather, Ransom Chamblee, was a slave in Hall County, Ga. After emancipation, Ransom Chamblee worked as a railroad laborer, and later in his son's shoe shop. Ransom Chamblee and his wife, Phyllis, had 10 children: Robert Asbury, Henry, Elizabeth, William, Austin, Hannah, Mary Jane, Evelina, Lula and June.

Their eldest son, Robert Asbury Chamblee (1862-1922), was a shoemaker, with a shop in Gainesville. Robert's wife, Georgia Ann James, daughter of Wesley James of Atlanta, was a school teacher. Robert and Georgia had five children: Leonard (who died as a child), Robert Wesley, Loran Delano, Harold and Edna Mae. Robert Wesley Chamblee, who lived to be 100 years old, was educated at Morehouse College in Atlanta and Columbia University in New York. He was vice president and general manager of the Atlanta Life Insurance Company. He died in 1984 in Chicago, Ill.

Although the town had not acquired the name of Chamblee until 1881, family records show that Marietta Chamblee Southard was born in Chamblee on May 26, 1859. She was the daughter of William L. (or John William) Chamlee (sic) and Minerva Westbrook of Cherokee County. In addition

Seated are William Turner Southard and his wife, Marietta Chamblee Southard. Their children, standing, left to right, are Lillian Southard Jones, Howard Southard, Ethel Southard Porter, Olin Southard, Bessie Southard House and Ernest Southard. This photo may have been taken at the family's home on Maxwell Street in Decatur. Marietta's family is one of the Chamblee families for whom the town could have been named. (Katherine Southard Stiltner)

to Marietta, William and Minerva had eight children: Columbus, John W., James A., William, Reuben T., Sherman F. Tilman F. and Jennie. Two of their children, John W. and Reuben T., are buried in the Winters Chapel United Methodist Church cemetery near Doraville. Reuben died in 1886 at the age of 19. Marietta's grandparents were Martin Chamlee and Polly Guthrie of Hall County. Her great grandparents were William Chamlee and Dorcas Seago, also of Hall County.

Marietta and other members of her family lived in Atlanta and worked at the Exposition Cotton Mills from the opening of the mill until she married William Turner Southard, son of Green W. Southard of the Panthersville District of DeKalb, on December 10, 1885. William Southard and Marietta Chamblee had five children: Lillian (married a Jones), Bessie (Mrs. Russell C. House), Olin, Howard and Ethel (Mrs. John L. Porter). Marietta Chamblee Southard died on March 7, 1943, and is buried in the Ousley Chapel Cemetery. Her obituary, published in the <u>Atlanta Constitution</u> and the <u>Atlanta Journal</u>, describe her as a member of a "pioneer family of the Chamblee section... the family for whom Chamblee was named." [11]

The Roswell Railroad, completed in 1881, was built to give the Roswell Manufacturing Company textile mills access to the main railroad line. The original line had three stops: Roswell (actually on the south side of the Chattahoochee River, Dunwoody and Roswell Junction (Chamblee). (Mr. and Mrs. J. David Chesnut; Vanishing Georgia Collection, Georgia Department of Archives and History)

The town of Chamblee was located at the junction of the Atlanta and Charlotte Air-Line Railroad (now Norfolk Southern Railway) and the Roswell Railroad, which operated from 1881 to 1921. The railroad had been the idea in 1853 of Barrington King, president of the Roswell Manufacturing Company, as a way to get the company's cotton and wool textile products to the main line railroad for distribution. Construction and financing problems and the Civil War interrupted the project. The Roswell Railroad, popularly called the Buckline, opened on September 1, 1881 with 9.8 miles of track, one locomotive, one passenger/baggage car, two box cars and four flat cars.

The railroad ran from Roswell Station, near the south bank of the Chattahoochee River and connected to Atlanta and Charlotte Air-Line Railway at a spot called Roswell Junction (later Chamblee). Twice-a-day runs also stopped at Dunwoody Station. Three houses were constructed on now Chamblee Dunwoody Road for railroad employees; one is still standing, across Chamblee Dunwoody from the Dunwoody Village shopping center, occupied by a business. Two stops along the line were added later: Wilson's Mill, in the area of Peeler and North Shallowford roads, and Morgan Falls in now Fulton County. The railroad had only one set of tracks; the train ran forward from Chamblee to Roswell and backward on the return trip.

Barrington King had intended that the railroad continue into the heart of Roswell. That part of his dream never came true, because bridging the river proved to be too expensive. King died before his vision became reality; work was completed under the supervision of King's son, James Roswell King,

Joberry Cheek's cotton gin and mill was located on the southeast corner of Mt. Vernon and Chamblee Dunwoody Road, the main intersection in the Dunwoody business district. (Vivian Price, personal collection; Vanishing Georgia Collection, Georgia Department of Archives and History)

and the firm of Grant and Alexander. Labor was provided by convicts leased from the state of Georgia.

Isaac Martin (Ike) Roberts was the only engineer in the railroad's 40-year history. He built a home near the Roswell Station in 1894; that home still stands today. Roberts died in 1930.

The Fulton Herald, on November 23, 1961, printed E. M. Jordan's memories of the Roswell Railroad in about 1900:

"The train consisted of an engine and a combination coach. The coach had a compartment for white people, one for colored people, a baggage compartment, a rest room, a heater, and a water cooler. There was a glass case containing a saw, an axe, and a crowbar. These were the emergency tools to be used in case the car turned over. (It never did.) The train also carried freight and hauled as many as five or six cars. The crew consisted of an engineer, fireman, conductor, and combination baggageman and brakeman... the engineer, Ike Roberts, conductor Pierce Sudderth, baggageman Hub Berry and several fireman were very fine people and were well known to the people living along the train route. The train made two rounds trips to Chamblee daily except Sunday, and remained in Roswell at night."[12]

The Dunwoody community was named for Charles Archibald Alexander Dunwoody who came to live in the community after the Civil War, building a home near the current intersection of Chamblee Dunwoody Road and Spalding Drive.

Early "downtown" Dunwoody included only a few businesses: P. L. Moss's store on Nandina Lane (where a well provided water for travelers and their animals); Cephus's blacksmith shop; Will Cheek and W. R. Nash's feed and grocery store; Dr. Puckett's livery stable and fertilizer store; and Joberry Cheek's cotton gin and corn mill on the southeast corner of Mt. Vernon and Chamblee Dunwoody. The train depot, post office, Dunwoody School and a few homes made up the balance of buildings clustered near what is now the primary intersection in Dunwoody. Dunwoody families included Austin, Carpenter, Cheek, Copeland, Donaldson, Eidson, Jordan, Lord, Manning, Marchman, Southern, Warnock and Womack.[13]

The Smith, Shippey, McElroy and Pounds Ginnery operated in Doraville from 1881-1883. It was later moved to the J. C. McElroy farm, where it was known as the McElroy and Pounds Ginnery. The ginnery was blown down by the notorious storm of 1884, which also destroyed many homes in the area. The McElroy-Pounds facility was rebuilt "and operated until the gin at Doraville was equipped for unloading unginned cotton by air suction," after which time the McElroy-Pounds Ginnery could no longer compete.[14]

The church that would later be known as Kirkwood Presbyterian was organized in 1881 at the corner of Boulevard and Warren Street. The name of the church was changed to Kirkwood in 1892. Kirkwood's most famous resident, John B. Gordon, was an elder. The church merged with Wee Kirk Presbyterian on Flat Shoals Road in 1963. Wee Kirk has a stained glass window dedicated to Gordon.[15]

DeKalb County residents undoubtedly visited the International Cotton Exposition in Atlanta's Oglethorpe Park, which ran from October 5-December 31, 1881. The fair featured exhibits from all the states and seven foreign countries. While textile machinery was the principal feature, there also were displays of sewing machines, musical instruments, carriages, wine, fruit, tea, coffee, minerals, photographs and women's handiwork. An opening day parade wound through the landscaped grounds. The highlight of the exposition was on October 27, when cotton picked in the early morning was woven into cloth and made into a suit worn by Gov. Colquitt at a reception that same evening.

The idea for the exposition originated with Edward Atkinson of Boston, and was supported by Atlanta journalist Henry W. Grady as part of his "New South" concept, as well as H. I. Kimball, president of

Pictured in about 1900 are Thankful Baptist Church leaders: James Bussey, Deacon Jake Sims, Deacon Arthur Kirkland and Deacon Claude Clopton.

Thankful Baptist Church, organized in 1882, is Decatur's oldest black church. (Vanishing Georgia Collection, Georgia Department of Archives and History, both photos)

the Atlanta Cotton Factory. William T. Sherman, the instrument of Atlanta's destruction 17 years previous, was a substantial subscriber to the fair.

The exposition facilities at Oglethorpe Park, in Atlanta's Marietta and Jefferson Street area, later became the Exposition Cotton Mill and mill town. [16]

The city of Decatur got a new charter in January of 1882, calling for a mayor and six-man council. Ernest M. Word was Decatur's first mayor under the new charter with a salary of $125 year. The mayor had his hands full three months later when a smallpox epidemic threatened and he had to devise a citywide plan for quarantine and providing health care to Decatur citizens. In July of 1882, the town council allocated $250 to help pay for a town clock and tower on the DeKalb courthouse. [17]

Decatur, being the county seat, had its share of lawyers, but few compared to Atlanta where, in 1882, there were 143 lawyers practicing, one for every 270 citizens, including women, children and Negroes.[18]

Lewis Stowers of near Lithonia, son of Revolutionary War veteran Lewis Stowers Sr., died in 1882, as

did John B. (Baptist) Twilley of the Panthersville District, and John Williams Medlock. [19]

Thankful Baptist, the oldest black church in the city of Decatur, was founded in 1882 by a group of new citizens who had recently moved from Augusta. They named their new church for the one they had left behind. They met in an abandoned log cabin until the owner "hitched up a pair of mules and pulled the shabby structure off its foundation." Members then built a new church near Peavine Creek.

The church later was located on Atlanta Avenue, and then on West College Avenue in Decatur. The Rev. Leon Tucker was its first full-time minister.

Other organizers of the church were Robert Tanksley, the Rev. Frank Paschal, Kittie House, Reese Howlworth (sic) and the Rev. Lewis Thornton. Nancy Wilson was the first person baptized at Thankful. Early members included the families of Lewis Parker, Alonzo Harvey, Smith Moore, George Temple, Phelix McWorter, Henry Randolph, Henry Ebster, Rufus Savage, Miles Clarke, Ed Smith, Peter Gibbs, Ellis Gibbs, Dick Gray, Henry Harris, T. I. Burdette, Sam Thurman, O. W. Lee and Wyatt Colquitt, as well as Harriet Jackson, Everline Walker, Milbra Bailey, Penny Benjamin, Cheney Fayette, Unice Burdette, Dorcas Reese, Lizzie Henderson and Mattie Jackson.

Although the church had an organ, the congregation preferred to sing shaped notes and the old favorite hymns like "Amazing Grace." Members frequently "shouted for joy" during the services.

In his history of Thankful Baptist Church written in 1926, church clerk D. G. Ebster recalled some memories of life in Decatur. D. G. Ebster, who was born in 1874, was one of three sons of J. H. and Nicey Ebster. D. G. had a twin bother, Joe, and an older brother named Luke. In 1881, D. G. recalled, his parents bought the boys their first school books, blue-back spellers, and slates and pencils. "We had no desk tablet, ink or anything like that; our slate took care of all of those things.

They went to school in the same dilapidated building used for Thankful church services. "We knocked down Jack Frost many a morning going to school." The children collected sticks and brush to burn in the one-room school fireplace. "We could see out of the top, sides or floor (of school building) without leaving our benches or boxes that we sat on. We had plenty of ventilation."

The Rev. Lewis Thornton was the first teacher. "He whipped children in those days.

"A good speller was somebody. I can remember some of our lessons -- ba-be-bi-bo-bu-by, etc., and when we got to baker, shady, lady and banquet we were considered good spellers. The highest aim of a student in those days was to spell `comprestibility,' and if you could spell that you were a professional speller."

Students had to "say a speech every Friday," like this one:
    "I can handle a musket,
    I can smoke a pipe,
    I can kiss a pretty girl
    At 12 o'clock at night."

Thankful Baptist was a member of the Hopewell Association (also called Hopewell Convention), which was organized in 1885 by the Rev. W. L. Jones and others at Hopewell Baptist Church in Norcross. [20]

A new black church also came to the Lithonia area in 1885. Fairfield Baptist Church, named for the beauty of its location, was organized on Redan Road, under the leadership of the Rev. A. D. Freeman.[21]

T. R. Floyd and Johnnie Longshore opened the Redan Cotton Ginnery in 1882. Longshore later sold his interest in the business to N. M. Read (sic). Others who owned the ginnery at one time included

W. P. Johnson, B. M. Johnson, L. O. Johnson, Marshall Floyd and S. D. Bryant. B. M. Johnson and his son, L. O. Johnson, also operated a ginnery and sawmill from 1890-1904 at their homeplace two and one-half miles south of Redan. The Redan Cotton Ginnery operated until 1936. [22]

The Atlanta Constitution reported on January 25, 1883 on the year's first meeting of the Decatur mayor and council:

"Decatur, Jan. 23, -- The last meeting of the mayor and council of Decatur was held last night for the purpose of making their annual reports, and to turn over to their successors the reins of the town government for 1883.

"H. R. Jewett, treasurer, submitted his report showing receipts and disbursements. Receipts from former treasurer J. A. Mason, $119.40; balance on liquor licenses, 1881, $50; liquor licenses to Crockett & Hunter, June, 1882 -- June, 1883, $100; street tax, 1882, $275.20; property tax, 1882, $378.73; fines, $112.40; cemetery lots, $27.70; other sources, $5, making total $6,698.43. Of this amount, the mayor, clerk, treasurer, marshal and sexton received for salaries $545. Paid expenses were -- quarantine, $61.90; vaccination, $67.50; appropriation on town clock, $400; schools, $25; street lamps and posts, $50; work on streets and in cemetery, and for bridge, lumber, nails, working implements, record books, trees, hitching posts, printing, etc., $431.87 leaving a balance in the treasury of $87.11.

"The report of Captain T. B. Watkins (town marshal) shows 134 persons in town subject to street tax, which amounts to $335, of which $275.29 was paid in money, $49.25 in work, and $10.55 uncollected. There were 729 days work done on the streets, 24 of convict labor, 98 in payment of street tax, and 607 of hired laborers. The marshal made 29 arrests, 32 cases by summons; fines paid were $127, all collected except $4.

The number of interments during the year was 38; 15 whites, 23 colored; 17 were males; 21 were females; 14 in early infancy (under 1 year); 5 between 5 and 10 years old; 4 between 10 and 25 years; 10 between 25 and 50 years old; 2 over 50 years of age; 3 age unknown. Four died from consumption; 5 from pneumonia, 10 from teething and troubles incident to infancy, 3 still births, 2 disease of heart, 2 from croup, 1 each from congestion, inflammation, crysipelas, scrofula and dropsy; 1 from violence, 6 from causes unknown.

"Mayor Word, was reelected, has conducted a prosperous and successful administration of one year."

H. H. Burgess came to Decatur in early 1883 to take the oath of office as DeKalb's tax receiver. It was the first appearance in public office of a member of a family that continues to be prominent in DeKalb County today. [23]

DeKalb County lost four of its older citizens to death in 1883: Frederick A. Williams, furniture craftsman and son of Ammi Williams; W. Ledbedder Williams and Harris Crowley, both of the Panthersville District; and Judge Walter R. Webster, former DeKalb ordinary. [24]

The DeKalb News published a report from its Rock Chapel community correspondent on October 18, 1883:

Some of the county's public officials are pictured in this photo, taken about 1890. At left is an unidentified man. Others, left to right are J. B. Stewart, county ordinary; Henry Burgess, clerk of Superior Court; Ben F. Burgess, who succeeded Henry Burgess as clerk; and George A. Ramspeck, county commissioner. (DeKalb Historical Society)

"Within two miles of this place there are two sorghum mills, two corn mills, one of which has ground 436 gallons, two merchant mills, five cotton gins, with a capacity of from one to three hundred bales, three saw mills with a capacity of from four to five thousand feet per day, two door, sash and blind factories, two school houses, four churches, two white and two colored, the latter of which are used by that class as school rooms. Who can beat this for community?" [25]

Two events occurred in Atlanta in 1884 that had a direct impact on DeKalb County residents. The Southern Baseball League was organized, and baseball fever soon would spread from the city to the suburbs. Construction started on a state capitol building in 1884. Limestone was imported from Indiana for use on the exterior, because Stone Mountain granite was deemed too expensive. [26]

DeKalb residents turned out in downtown Atlanta in 1884 to celebrate the election of Grover Cleveland, the first Democratic president in 24 years. The Atlanta Constitution reported: "The pent up enthusiasm of twenty years; the fruition of long deferred and oft defeated hopes; the wiping out of sectional lines; the breaking down of sectional prejudice; the burying of the bloody shirt. [2] All combine to bring the people on the streets and turn them wild with joy." [27]

I. N. Nash and his son-in-law John F. McCurdy took over operation of a cotton gin in Stone Mountain

---

[2] Term used to mean soothing sectional animosity.

Baseball was so popular with these Decatur third graders that they included their bat and glove in their 1904 class picture. (DeKalb Historical Society)

in 1884. They later moved the ginnery to an 800-acre farm they owned at the junction of Old Stone Mountain road and Tucker Road. Seven tenant farmers lived on the Nash-McCurdy farm. The ginnery closed in 1915. McCurdy was a deputy sheriff in DeKalb, a member of the board of education and president of the first bank in Stone Mountain. John Metcalf operated a sawmill, cotton ginnery, grist mill on what is now Peachtree Industrial Boulevard at McGaw Drive from 1884-1904. Metcalf headed one of several north DeKalb families that moved to Turner County in the early 20th century. [28]

Robert Jones, one of Decatur's oldest citizens and a former county sheriff and treasurer, died in 1884. Charles Latimer, father of Rebecca Latimer Felton, died at his home in Atlanta, and Decatur historian Levi Willard died in Springfield, Ohio. Among the other deaths in DeKalb in 1884 were George B. Hudson of the Browning's District, and Dr. William W. Durham, a well-known Atlanta and Decatur physician. [29]

Fourteen members of Prosperity Presbyterian Church in Doraville organized the New Hope Presbyterian Church in Dunwoody on October 18, 1884.

The Rev. C. E. Todd was New Hope's first minister and served until 1887. The Rev R. E. Patterson succeeded the Rev. Todd and served New Hope and Prosperity from 1887 until 1897 when he organized a Sabbath School called Miller's Mission. The school would become Antioch Presbyterian

Church and later Tucker Associate Reformed Presbyterian. The original 23 members of Miller's Mission also came from Prosperity Presbyterian. The Rev. Patterson died in 1899 typhoid, and is buried in Prosperity Cemetery.

Charter members of New Hope included the Weldon family (John, Charlie, David and William), Eliza Wing, Sarah Conway, Nancy Cowan, Mollie Copeland, Frances Copeland and Ludie McElroy. New Hope Church disbanded in 1917, selling its land to Nance's Creek Primitive Baptist Church in 1923. A new church was formed, called New Hope Primitive Baptist. The Primitive Baptist Church dissolved in 1931.

Georgia Duke sold land for the New Hope Cemetery on December 6, 1884 to W. A. Weldon, J. A. Weldon, G. W. Wing, E. J. Copeland and J. K. Cowan for $20. Families buried at New Hope include Adams, Anderson, Akins, Autry, Baldwin, Ball, Beam, Beavers, Bishop, Blackburn, Brannon, Braswell, Bratton, Brooks, Brookshire, Brown, Buchanan, Burnham, Camp, Carpenter, Charles, Cheek, Clanton, Cochran, Coker, Conaway, Copeland, Cox, Craven, Crook, Dickerson, Dodd, Donaldson, Dryman, Cuke, Fitts, Foster, Fuller, George, Graham, Grant, Harris, Haney, Hayden, Haynes, Hester, Hollifield, Hudson, Jackson, Jameson, Jones, Jordan, Kirby, Lewis, Lord, Loyd, Mann, Manning, Martin, McCoy, McElreath, McGinnis, Morris, Nash, Newhard, Orr, O'Shields, Pelfrey, Pettigrew, Pirkle, Rudisill, Rumsey, Samples, Sanders, Scruggs, Smith, Spruill, Sullivan, Thurman, Turner, Wade, Warbington, Warnock, Warren, Weldon, Whitlock, Wilson, Wenn and Yett. The oldest burial in the cemetery was that of William A. Weldon, who died on October 20, 1887 at the age of 65.

While New Hope church is gone, the cemetery is still active, cared for by a group of trustees. [30]

A debate that had been simmering in DeKalb since the mid 1850s heated up in 1885. A campaign to move the county seat from Decatur to Stone Mountain had been launched when Fulton was cut off from DeKalb, leaving Decatur on the western edge of the county.

In a letter to the DeKalb Chronicle in December, 1885, "William Why" explained why he felt the county seat should be moved.

"While at Decatur a few weeks since, the idea struck me forcibly that something should be done towards bringing before the people once again the much talked-of removal of the county site. To do the people of the lower part of the county justice, and to place all sections on an equal footing, the policy of its removal to my mind admits no argument.

"While we all admit that the present site is a very pleasant suburban retreat for Atlanta's tired populace, and while we are personally proud of her many attractions as such, we must not allow sentiment to displace judgment and the best interests of the people of the whole county. Now why is Decatur not the proper place for the county site? Surely every fair-minded person will admit that, situated as she is, almost on the edge of Fulton County, it works a very great hardship on the people of part of the county to be under the necessity of traversing the entire county in order to transact any business with its officials during sessions of court or otherwise.

"Now if my proposition -- that of the removal of the county site -- is wise, what more fitting time could arise for such removal than the present? Is not our jail and courthouse in a condition needing immediate attention? Needing such attention, and so very much, would it not be altogether economical to rebuild both outright than to expend double the sum in a few years in repairs on the present substitutes?

"Would it not be simply an act of humanity to give even the guiltiest wretch a pleasanter abode than our present jail, and but a simple act of justice to the innocent people around, who are liable at any moment to be placed with a pack of abandoned prisoners, freed by its insecurity? This being all true -- and surely none will gainsay it -- the plea of economy in expenditure of the people's money uselessly cannot be advanced, and the only question arising is, to what point shall it be removed?

"Taking all things into consideration, I can think of no better place than Stone Mountain, situated almost in the center of the county, a thriving, pushing business place full of vim and energy, and a trading place, for a portion of the county whose people Decatur never sees -- save when from compulsion they are obliged to call in county affairs -- it looms up prominently and forcibly as the place to which this removal should be made.

"Granting that new county buildings should be erected, is not Stone Mountain the proper place to procure building material at her very door, and at no cost of transportation, with which to erect a Courthouse which shall bespeak old DeKalb as the Banner County in her public buildings as well as in her democracy. I think so. Now, Mr. Editor, I commit what I have written to the calm and dispassionate consideration of the people of the whole county, and in doing so, desire to add that I am not advocating the claims of any section but what to me, appears to be for the interest of the county at large." [31]

The debate would continue for another 10 years before it was resolved.

Another controversy, this one over liquor sales, was settled in 1885, at least for a while. The campaign before the November referendum was heated, with "wets" sporting red badges and those favoring prohibition wearing blue ones. Prohibition became the law of the land in Atlanta and DeKalb. While Atlantans were given seven months to "go dry," the so-called "blue law" took effect immediately in DeKalb. The DeKalb Chronicle reported on November 19, 1885: "Stone Mountain's barroom closed last Saturday. There is now no whiskey sold in DeKalb County." The change did not last long in Fulton, however; the county repealed its prohibition laws at the election of 1887. [32]

J. W. Kirkpatrick became mayor of Decatur in 1885, the same year an ordinance was passed against "street walking." [33]

The Stone Mountain Judicial Circuit, covering DeKalb and Clayton counties was created September 8, 1885, and made permanent on October 4, 1887. DeKalb returned to the Atlanta circuit for a short time between those two dates. Richard H. Clark was named judge of the new circuit, with Henry Clay Jones of Decatur the solicitor general. When circuit was made permanent, Clark continued as judge, and John S. Candler became solicitor general. [34]

Residents of Kirkwood and Edgewood communities came out to observe a curious site in October of 1885. A team of 12 German artists arrived to examine Atlanta's Civil War battlefield in preparation for

The boll weevil had yet to make its appearance, and cotton was still king in DeKalb in October of 1894, when this photo was taken. When pickers came in from the fields, they dumped their cotton on the porch, where it stayed before being taken to the gin. Pictured, left to right, are Nancy Alice and Charles H. Cobb and their children: Nellie, Lovick, Clifford, Jennie Mae, Grady and Eugene. Their home was on McLendon Place in the Wesley Chapel community. (Vanishing Georgia Collection, Georgia Department of Archives and History)

painting a cyclorama, a circular panoramic picture, of the battle. The artists collected data daily at the site, constructing a 40-foot observation tower near Moreland Avenue and the Georgia Railroad from which to view the terrain. The painting was completed at the American Cyclorama Company in Milwaukee, Wisconsin in early 1887 at a cost of $40,000. The finished work weighed 18,000 pounds, and measured 50 feet high and 400 feet in circumference. The traveling exhibit featuring the painting was a failure, and the painting put up for auction. It was exhibited in Atlanta in the 1890s before being stored in a leaky Edgewood Avenue building, where it sustained weather damage. The painting finally found a safe home in Atlanta's Grant Park in 1898. [35]

Atlanta and Decatur innkeeper Dr. Joseph Thompson died in 1885, as did Henry B. Latimer, an Oglethorpe County native and early DeKalb settler who had moved to Gainesville in 1872. [36]

C. P. (Pink) Lively opened his corn mill on the North Fork of Peachtree Creek at what is now Briarwood Road. Washington J. Houston Sr. and W. B. Smith opened the new Smith-Houston Mill on the North Fork of Peachtree Creek about 300 yards from DeKalb-Fulton line in DeKalb. The waterpowered mill processed corn and wheat until about 1910. S. E. Guess, who lived near there in 1951, said a man named Kreigshaber converted the mill into a residence. The horsepowered Donahoo Ginnery, located on the northeast side of the Chamblee and Dunwoody Road opposite the current location of Chamblee High School, closed in 1885. It had been operated for some time by Mrs. Mary Donahoo. [37] Many DeKalb County farmers were still making their fortunes from cotton in 1885. V. C. Sparks and his son sold 423 pounds of cotton to Wallace and Liddell, dealers in cotton and general merchandise, in Norcross for $14.77 on October 6. [38]

The DeKalb Chronicle was in its heyday in the late 1800s, reporting on varied aspects of life in the county. News stories, editorials and advertisements in the November 26 and December 3 edition give interesting glimpses into the year of 1885:

"Southern Girls Beware
"Northern swindlers are fully aware of the fact, that all over the South, there are hundreds of young ladies who were once in affluence, but now are reduced to the necessity of working..." The editorial warned of advertisements "preying on need and innocence of young women."

"Jossey House
This popular hotel is now in full blast and is ready to furnish accommodations to the public. It has been renovated and all the modern improvements attached. Every attention given to boarders. Polite and attentive servants always in attendance. Address: W. W. Jossey, Decatur, Ga."

"Missouri Stokes is one of three Georgia delegates to the 12th annual Women's Christian Temperance Union meeting in Philadelphia." Some 294 delegates from 40 states and territories attended the meeting. Stokes was the state corresponding secretary for the WCTU.

"Winter is here. Today is Thanksgiving. Court next Monday. Xmas is right here. Indications are good for a snow. Quite a number of our people were at the election yesterday. Everybody will attend court come next week. The first "toot" of the Christmas horn was heard last Monday.

Wheat 6 1/2 per lb. Meal 67 1/2 per bushel at Wm. H. Howard's. Fresh fish and oysters Weds & Saturdays. Keg pickles 60 cents.

"Lamps, oils, baskets, home furnishing goods, notions, toys, boys' wagons, vases, ladies' work stands, balls, tops, dolls.

"William Kuhns, the well known artist, will fit up his tent on the vacant lot between the Chronicle office and Ramspeck's store, for the purpose of photographing any and all who desire pictures of themselves or their loved ones. Now is the time to have your pictures taken. Mr. Kuhns comes by the request of a number of our citizens. Don't fail to call on him at once. His time is limited." [39]

Dagmar Sams grew up in Decatur in the 1880s. She was the only daughter of Dade Sams and Julia Avary, the granddaughter of Dr. James C. Avary and the Rev. Marion Washington Sams. The Sams family lived in a house called Violet Cottage, near the railroad tracks,

Dagmar recalled her family's Christmas shopping expeditions:

"Bates Grocery Store was on Sycamore Street about midway of the block between East Court Square and church Street. About two weeks before Christmas every year Mr. Bates would send notes to his regular customers to say the store would be open certain nights ` next week' for customers to see his Christmas stock and place their orders for Christmas.

"Papa would commission my brother, Hansford, to have the lantern cleaned and filled for the night. I would be all bundled up and ready to go right after early supper. This was a big occasion. The stores didn't have all these good things every day of the years, as they do now.

"Mr. Bates usually had something new and unusual. He would say `Try one of these dates,' the first one I had ever seen." [40]

The Georgia legislature approved an act on December 8, 1886, creating the DeKalb County Board of Commissioners of Roads and Revenues. The provision became law in March of 1887. The DeKalb Chronicle reported the details on December 9, 1886:

"The bill of Mr. (Charles Murphey) Candler, to create a Board of Commissioners of Roads and Revenues, for the county, has passed both houses of the Legislature, and will become a law, upon the approval of the Governor, in time for the Board to be organized in March. The bill provides for a Commission, to consist of five persons, to be elected by the Grand Jury, at the spring term of the Superior court. They will receive $2 per day, actual service, and are exempt from jury and Militia duty. The board is to elect a clerk who may be one of its members, and whose salary, not exceeding $250 per annum shall be fixed by the board, prior to his election. The board will have exclusive jurisdiction over roads, bridges and all county property, and county matters and finances, and will meet at the Court House once a month.

"This bill was introduced by Mr. Candler, and great credit is due him and Senator (E. M.) Word, for the expeditious manner, in which it became a law. With good men elected by the grand jury, we believe it will work to the interests of the county. The whole success of the plan depends upon who will constitute the board of commissioners."

The first commissioners were named in the Chronicle three months later: "The five persons composing the commission of roads and revenues, of DeKalb County, as chosen by the grand jury are: T. U. Hightower, for three years; Thomas J. Flake, three years; E. J Bond, two years; L. N. Nash, two years; and William C. Holbrook, one year. These five gentlemen will make an able commission." [41]

As the board's name implied, its first job was supervision of the county's roads, a task the DeKalb Chronicle reported was long overdue:

"Panola, Feb. 4, 1886 -- Roads! Such roads! never were seen before in any county. If Job had to have traveled over them things would have been different with him...

"August 26, 1886 -- Dr. Bond, of Lithonia, while attempting to cross Snapfinger Creek, at the bridge, on the Covington Road, last Monday, dropped into a hole, just before reaching the bridge, the depth of which was sufficient to upset his buggy, and drowned his horse... The hole was about fifteen feet deep. The road commissioners are responsible for such accidents and should be held accountable. It is a disgrace to any civilized people that their roads should be in so dangerous a condition. We have traveled several of our public roads, and some of them are almost impossible, the Covington Road being one. It is a shame to our county, and a grave reflection on the road commissioners...

"Panola, September 16, 1886 -- The bridge, near John Leftwich, grows like a cow eating the grindstone, slowly."

The Decatur Post Office was made a money-order post office in 1886. The Chronicle published on August 26: "While this is a great convenience to the public, there is very little extra compensation for a considerable amount of extra work. Patrons of the office should bear in mind that the Postmaster depends for his salary, on the stamps cancelled by him, and people should mail as few letters as possible on the trains." Less than one month later, a citizen of the Pea Ridge community wrote to the Chronicle criticizing the service provided by Decatur Postmaster Henry R. Jewett: "Mr. Editor I wish you would tell us what's the matter with the Post Office at Decatur. We can't get our mail half the time. Surely it don't' take a month for a weekly Journal to come from Atlanta to Decatur. I heard a man say he received a Journal last Saturday, 11th, that was printed August 12th." [42]

The earthquake that disrupted the dedication of the Beech Springs Baptist Church broke windows and frightened citizens all over DeKalb. Residents described the quake, which occurred at 9 p.m. on August 31, 1886 as the same sensation as a heavily loaded train passing close by. Correspondents from across the county reported to the DeKalb Chronicle:

"Panthersville -- The earthquake was felt very sensibly in this section. A great many were badly frightened and left home and went to their neighbors to learn if it was felt anywhere except at their house. It was the heaviest shock we have ever felt and hope we may never feel another such one...

"Panola -- It has come and gone, may it stay gone. That earthquake shook up things generally. There were more scared citizens in old DeKalb, on last Tuesday night, than any night before or since...

"Doraville -- We were shaken up considerably on the night of the 31st of August. There were more scared people around here at that time than ever before. A great many thought it was burglars and took their guns and began to look around. I don't think I ever did laugh so much at one little foolish thing as I did when I heard about Mr. James L. Baxter. When his house first began to shake, he got his gun and crawled under the house saying,`I bet I will kill some man's dog.' I never did hear whether he killed him or not; very likely the latter." [43]

The unveiling of a monument to U. S. Sen. Ben Hill on May 1 drew an estimated 100,000 people to the intersection of Peachtree and West Peachtree streets in Atlanta. They came primarily to see the frail and aged president of the Confederacy, Jefferson Davis. Huge crowds greeted Davis at every train station between his home in Mississippi and his destination in Atlanta.

"Everybody in DeKalb, who can will go to Atlanta next Saturday to see Jeff Davis one more time before the Grand Old Man passes from earth to heaven," the Chronicle reported. "We hope on that day to hear the real, old fashion rebel yell, having never heard it. We reckon it will offend no one, but if so, let it offend."

Ten thousand Confederate veterans attended the event. Spectators climbed to rooftops and perched in trees to get a good view. The dedication also served as a kick-off to John B. Gordon's successful bid for governor. Gordon and Alfred H. Colquitt were the only two Georgia governors to call DeKalb County home.

The statue has since been moved to the grounds of the Georgia state capitol. Ben Hill is an ancestor of Georgia lieutenant governor, Pierre Howard. [44]

Events of the year, 1886, reflected the lifestyles of the past and the future in DeKalb County. The DeKalb Chronicle reported on February 18 that neighbors still gathered for old-fashioned cornshuckings. Fifty or sixty neighbors and their farm hands surrounded immense piles of corn, and shucked as much as 15,000 bushels of the grain. They worked until about midnight, and were rewarded with a memorable meal. "There was old ham, the sort that makes red gravy, and fresh pork and turnips, and cabbage and potatoes and chickens and chicken pie, and oysters and sardines and cheese, and pies and pound cake and pickles and preserves, world without end." [45]

What began as a headache remedy in 1886 would become one of the world's most popular soft drink in the 20th century. John Styth Pemberton had experimented with a variety of patent medicines at his Marietta Street home and laboratory. His syrup called Coca-Cola was just one of them. That same year, an ailing customer bought a bottle of syrup from soda fountain operator Willis E. Venable and asked for water, so he could mix and consume it on the spot. Venable suggested carbonated water, and a new taste treat drink was born. Asa Candler, himself a headache sufferer, began buying interests in Coca-Cola in 1888, and owned the formula outright by 1891. The Coca-Cola Company was chartered in 1892.

Before the 20th century, Coca-Cola was touted for its restorative qualities, as well as its refreshment value, as shown in this 1889 advertisement in the Atlanta Journal:
ASA G. CANDLER & CO.
sole proprietors of
COCA-COLA
Delicious, Refreshing, Exhilarating, Invigorating
The new and popular soda fountain drink containing the tonic properties of the wonderful coca plant and the famous cola nuts, on draught at the popular soda fountains at 5 cents per glass. [46]

The DeKalb Chronicle did not neglect the ladies in its coverage of the news in 1886. On January 14, the paper reported: "The latest Paris fancy for adorning evening dresses is to have a garland of natural flowers about the waist. It is stated that violets, lilacs and roses are the correct flower for this purpose." In September, the Chronicle turned its attention to "Chimney Pot Hats. Last year feminine headgear was all breadth. This year it is all height. Milliners have reverted to 1860 models." [47]

Four notable DeKalb citizens died in 1886: John K. McCarter of Lithonia, E. B. Walker of Kirkwood, the Rev. John McElroy of Doraville and Elijah Steward, son of DeKalb pioneer Absalom Steward. [48]

The editor of the DeKalb Chronicle sounded like the beleaguered neighbor of a zucchini farmer on March 4, 1886 when he wrote: "The time of the year is approaching when the editor will be called upon to accept cabbages, onions, turnips and other indigestible articles of food, on payment for subscriptions due him. Heaven pity the digestive organs of the country editor." [49]

The Chronicle reported on February 25, 1886 that DeKalb County ranked fifth in the state in manufacturing, at a time when steam was replacing water and mules as the power source for the county's industries. John T. Chewning opened his steam powered cotton ginnery in 1886 in front of his house on the Tucker Road (now LaVista), a few yards east of its junction with Oak Grove Road. The ginnery closed in 1892 or '93. [50]

It would be 52 more years before the DeKalb Chamber of Commerce would be formed, but there was no lack of good press, thanks to the Chronicle, which published this glowing report of the county on February 18, 1886:

"DeKalb County is the most populous county in Georgia, with the exception of the counties containing cities. She is also the most fertile county in this Empire State, with no exception, besides ranking with the foremost counties in wealth... In fact, DeKalb is the garden spot of Georgia, where all honest people can find homes and make a good living, if they are willing to work. There is no more productive soil to be found than the fertile lands of old DeKalb, and foreign emigrants need go no further for a healthy climate, productive soil, and hospitable people. Already several Northerners have cast their lot with us, and all, without a single exception, are happy and prosperous, and say they would not leave DeKalb for any country.

DeKalb has many and varied industries, all of which are prosperous and lucrative. Our manufacturers are all becoming wealthy; the laboring classes have good houses, and are contented; our merchants, all over the country, are doing a safe and profitable business; every profession, except doctors and lawyers, is remunerative; our farmers, the back-bone, are a happy and prosperous people, and have no desire to seek homes elsewhere; the fruit growers of DeKalb are making money, and thank their God for this goodly land.

"... At Stone Mountain and Lithonia the extensive rock quarries furnish labor for hundreds of workmen. Scott's Guano Factory, the cotton seed oil mills, Ramspeck's Guano Factory, and various industries over the county, furnish homes and bread for thousands of families. Besides all these, DeKalb County looks well to her educational advantages, and every community is blessed with one or more good schools, where none but able and competent teachers are employed. Also, our county is literally dotted with churches of every faith and order, all of which are well supported, and this speaks volumes for a town or a county...

"All in all, DeKalb is an ideal county, and fifteen thousand souls now living within her borders, will welcome as many more to her genial clime, fertile soil, and other happy advantages. DeKalb is, indeed and in truth, the Banner County of this Empire Southern State." [51]

The description of "ideal," however, apparently did not apply to the county's roads. Despite a new Commission of Roads and Revenues, the DeKalb Chronicle still reported on poor road conditions on March 10, 1887:

"It is very evident that DeKalb County needs a better road law than her present one, and our

The Stone Mountain Presbyterian Church near Second Street presents a picture pretty enough for a postcard against the backdrop of the giant granite rock. The photo actually was made into an engraved postcard. The church was torn down in the early 1930s. (Lee Collection, DeKalb Historical Society; Vanishing Georgia Collection, Georgia Department of Archives and History)

Representatives have not done their duty until they have made an honest effort to secure for us, a road law. We sincerely hope our coming grand jury will consider the inefficiency of our present road laws and recommend a remedy. It is too big a task to undertake the macadamizing of our roads, recommend a road tax either to be paid in cash or work, and let the working of all public roads to the lowest bidder, and pay the contractor directly out of the treasury to keep the roads in good condition. Put the contractor under a heavy bond, and force him to give us better roads. Or, if this will not do, recommend a law allowing each district to pass its own road laws. Anything rather than the present mode of going over our roads at break neck speed, digging up a little dirt here and there, often leaving the road impassable.

"We witnessed a squad of hands working the roads, and actually it was as much as we could do to keep up with them, and we were riding a horse. They were working toward town, and desired to spend the day in town. It took them just one half hour to work two miles of bad roads. This is about the average road working, and it will always be thus, so long as our present road laws are in force." [52]

DeKalb County got its second newspaper in 1887, which the Chronicle gracefully announced on December 8:

"The Lithonia New Era made its first appearance last Friday. It is a seven column folio, published by Steadman and Guinn, at Lithonia, 'The Birmingham of DeKalb.' The New Era is neatly printed and ably edited, and bids fair to become a permanency. We welcome brothers Steadman and Guinn to DeKalb County. With two fine newspapers, old DeKalb will soon be the foremost county in the State. She is a hummer anyhow." [53]

A comparatively inconsequential notice in the Chronicle on June, 1887 may have gone unnoticed by some citizens:

"Mr. and Mrs. C. M. Candler, Rejoiceth.
"It is a bouncing baby boy, and will do honor to the name of George Scott Candler." Scott Candler would grow up to receive a great deal of notice during an unmatched career in the 1930s and '40s as DeKalb's Commissioner of Roads and Revenues. His service in the post earned him the title of "Mr. DeKalb." Candler came from two distinguished lines of DeKalb County residents. He was the grandson of Milton A. Candler Sr. and Eliza Caroline Murphey, and of George W. Scott and Rebecca Bucher. He was the grandnephew of Asa G. Candler Sr., Judge John S. Candler and Methodist Bishop Warren A. Candler.

William Ezzard, the venerable pioneer attorney and judge of Decatur and Atlanta, died on March 25, 1887 at the age of 88. He had practiced law for 28 years in Decatur before moving to Atlanta in 1850. He is buried in an unmarked grave in Oakland Cemetery.

Other notable deaths in 1887 included Willis Wells of Stone Mountain, John Y. Flowers of Doraville and Judge Berry Ragsdale of the Panola area, who survived the five sons he lost in the Civil War. Samuel H. Venable, one of the owners of Stone Mountain, and A. B. F. (Bud) Veal were involved in an argument that resulted in a death in 1887. Charles D. Horn, a builder working on the state capitol, tried to stop an argument between Venable and Veal on August 7. Veal shot at Venable, but missed and hit Horn, who died at the age of 38. [54]

According to Dagmar Sams, there were three big events for children in DeKalb in the 1880s: his or her birthday, Christmas and the annual county Sunday School Celebration. The Tabernacle, an open-sided shelter, had been built about 1874 at the southeast corner of now College Avenue and Columbia Drive (then Flat Shoals Road). Families affiliated with churches of all denominations all over the county came to the annual celebration at the Tabernacle.

Children practiced for weeks on special songs they would perform, and got new clothes to wear especially for the occasion. Women worked for days preparing special picnic dinners. By 5 a.m. on the morning of the big day, wagons and buggies would begin arriving in Decatur. All roads into town would be clogged with dust, and the town would be filled with the sounds of mules braying and old friends meeting in joyful reunion. A crowd of 3,000 people could be expected at the annual event.

The children from Decatur Sunday schools met at one of the churches and marched together to the Tabernacle, led by Washington J. Houston and Milton Candler. Signs were placed in the Tabernacle designating seating areas for the different church groups. A big platform was constructed at one end of the Tabernacle. One by one groups from the various churches marched up, and sang the hymn they had been practicing.

The farm of of Ollie and Hannah Weaver was a picturesque scene in the Rock Chapel community in 1888. Hannah Weaver, who was a member of the Rock Chapel Methodist Church, was buried in an old slave cemetery on the property. (Vanishing Georgia Collection, Georgia Department of Archives and History)

"What they might have lacked in real musical training, they made up in volume," Dagmar said, adding that she recalled one particularly memorable version of "Bringing in the Sheaves." The best singers got a banner to keep until next year's celebration.

Noontime was devoted to eating and socializing. Friends went from family to family, responding to invitations to sample such homemade treats as pound cake, apple pie and watermelon pickle. Cakes of ice were floated in a nearby spring to keep drinks and watermelon cold. Refreshment stands offered red lemonade, chicken, candy and cake for sale.

The "Anniversary Exercises of the DeKalb County Sunday School Association at the Twenty-Second Annual Celebration in the Children's Tabernacle" were held on August 3, 1887. Milton A. Candler was president. Other Sunday school leaders were W. J. Houston, G. A. Ramspeck, W. P. Pattillo, J. R. Smith, I. N. Nash, Dr. (J. B.) Bond and B. F. George.

Participating Sunday schools that year were Beach (sic) Spring, Belmont, Bolton, Cedar Grove, Clarkston Methodist, Clarkston Union, Centre, County Line, Constitution, Cross Roads, Clifton, Decatur Presbyterian, Decatur Methodist, Decatur Baptist, Edgewood, Indian Creek, Kirkwood, Lithonia Union, Liberty, Lithonia Baptist, Mt. Cavalry, Woodville, Midway, Marvin, Mt. Pisgah, New Hope, Oak Grove, Ousley Chapel, Panola, Peoples, Peachtree, Pea Vine, Phillip's, Philadelphia, Poplar Spring, Rehoboth, Rock Chapel, Stone Mountain Baptist, Stone Mountain Presbyterian, Stone Mountain Methodist, Shady Grove, Sylvester, Salem, Union Hill, Walnut Grove and Wesley Chapel. [55]

Decatur's Negro community also used the Tabernacle for its annual Sunday school celebration, which was held in 1887 on August 27. The event began cheerfully, but ended in violence, due to some uninvited guests with whiskey and guns. A Decatur city court bailiff named Rodgers and several others had gone to the Tabernacle to hear the children sing. An attempt by the bailiff to arrest a drunken man brandishing a pistol developed into a shoot-out among three Negroes and four white men. Marshal J. F. (Tobe) Hurst was killed, former Marshal Tom Chivers was seriously wounded. DeKalb Sheriff H. C. Austin and W. F. Pattillo also were involved. Several Negroes were arrested. When a rumor began circulating that a mob was being organized in Stone Mountain, the prisoners were moved to the Fulton County jail.

At a subsequent meeting of the Decatur town council, W. W. Jossey was appointed temporary marshal and two extra law enforcement officers were added. [56]

J. W. Kirkpatrick was mayor of Decatur in 1887. Councilmen were George A. Ramspeck, F. M. Bridwell, John S. Candler, E. L. Grant, D. A. Laird and E. L. Hanes. Thomas H. Chivers (son of the poet by the same name) was marshal for part of the year, and also served as sexton of the cemetery. At a meeting early in the year, the council directed the street committee to put the town streets and street lamps in good condition, and voted $10 for cemetery maintenance. Councilman Hanes (editor of the Chronicle) introduced an ordinance requiring the town marshal to visit every home once a month to remind residents to keep their property clean. A council committee was appointed to investigate buying a fire engine. [57]

Decatur people "generally stood by each other in the time of trouble and in serious illness or death in those days," recalled Dagmar Sams. "Even though it might be someone you did not especially like, there was general sympathy and offers of help. When there was a death, a kind of hush would fall over the town.

"This was before the days of the telephone, of course, or when there were very few. When anyone died, it was the custom for the family to send a messenger around from house to house, maybe a Negro boy, or someone else, with a note written on a white card on a tray, a silver tray if the family had one. A little sprig of green or a little flower would be fastened on the card with a notice of the death, and perhaps a statement that the funeral plans would be announced later.

"The Church bell tolled just before the service and as the procession passed out of the Church."

T The Accommodation train was a popular means of travel between Decatur and Atlanta. Dagmar Sams remembered that children waited at the depot for their fathers to come from jobs in Atlanta on the Accommodation train. Capt. Virgil Boyd of Covington was conductor, and Bob Huson the engineer. Dagmar recalled that Boyd knew every passenger, his business, his family and his customary schedule. Henry Ansley, who lived on South Candler was a regular, and suffered from a hip wound received during the Civil War.

"If Captain Boyd did not see him waiting, he would swing off the train and peer down South Candler Street -- calling to the engineer, `Hold it, Bob, hold it! The Major hasn't gotten here yet. We've got two or three minutes to spare... He'll be here in a minute.. He's acoming, Bob, here he comes!"

Another Decatur resident who frequently rode the Accommodation train to Atlanta was George Washington Scott, who was described as one of the most generous and public-spirited citizens ever to reside in Decatur.

George Washington Scott, founder of Agnes Scott College. (Agnes Scott College)

Agnes Irvine Scott, for whom Agnes Scott College was named. (Agnes Scott College)

He and the Rev. Dr. Frank Henry Gaines proved to be a powerful combination toward the good of education. The Rev. Gaines arrived in Decatur in December of 1888 to become pastor of Decatur Presbyterian Church. In the summer of 1889, Gaines proposed to open a Presbyterian school for girls. "If you educate a man, you may produce a good citizen, but if you educate a woman, you may train a whole family," Gaines said. At a meeting of a few Decatur citizens, Scott introduced a resolution: "Resolved, That we determine to establish at once a school of high character." The group originally proposed to offer instruction for girls in the seventh grade and younger.

Stock in the school was offered to area citizens in an effort to raise $5000. Of the 108 shares purchased, Scott bought 40. The Decatur Female Seminary opened on September 24, 1889 in a rented residence on what is now College Avenue. There were with 63 students, including a few little boys. Three were boarders; the remainder were day students.

Gaines was the first chairman of the board of trustees and the first president of the school. Nannette Hopkins came from Virginia to be the first principal, intending to stay only one year. She was dean and "first lady" of the institution for 50 years. The school had only three teachers that first year:

This panoramic photo of the Agnes Scott College campus was made into an unusual folding postcard. At left is White House, the school's first building. In the center is Main Hall; Rebekah Scott Hall is at left. (Lee Collection, DeKalb Historical Society)

Mattie Cook, general assistant; Fannie B. Pratt, piano; and Valeria Fraser, art and physical education.

The second session opened on September, 1890 with 138 students, including 20 boarders. The school rented a big stucco house [3] for a dormitory.

The rented Allen residence, known as the White House, was the school's only classroom building for the first few years. In the spring of 1890 Scott proposed to give $40,000 for a permanent home for the school. Scott told Dr. Gaines: "The Lord has greatly prospered me in my business, and I don't want it to harden my heart. I have decided to give $40,000 to provide a home for our school." Scott traveled to colleges in the north to investigate school buildings. His trips and funding resulted in the red brick building now known as Main Hall. It was the first building in Decatur to have electricity and indoor plumbing. The building cost Scott $112,500, the largest gift to a college in Georgia at that time.

The building was dedicated during a Presbyterian Synod of Georgia meeting in Decatur on November 12, 1891. The seminary was renamed the Agnes Scott Institute for Scott's mother, Agnes Irvine Scott, "to whose character, intelligence and religious faith he attributed all his success."

George's older brother John, a U. S. Senator from Pennsylvania, was the dedication speaker. Of their mother, John said:

"It is not for the spirit of mortals to be proud; but if men, yea, men whose hairs are whitened with the light of years, may justly, at any time, feel any pride, I am sure it is when they mingle with that pride the gratitude, reverence and affection which are due to an intelligent, conscientious, good Christian mother. The pride and gratitude, reverence and affection, and of your commemoration. She met the duties of her sphere with the sublimest faith and trust in the goodness of God, and in His overruling providence. `There is a God who rules and reigns in the armies of heaven and who doeth His will among the inhabitants of the earth,' was one of her daily utterances to her children. She was a

---

[3] Now called Marble House, the structure is still standing across McDonough Street from Decatur High School.

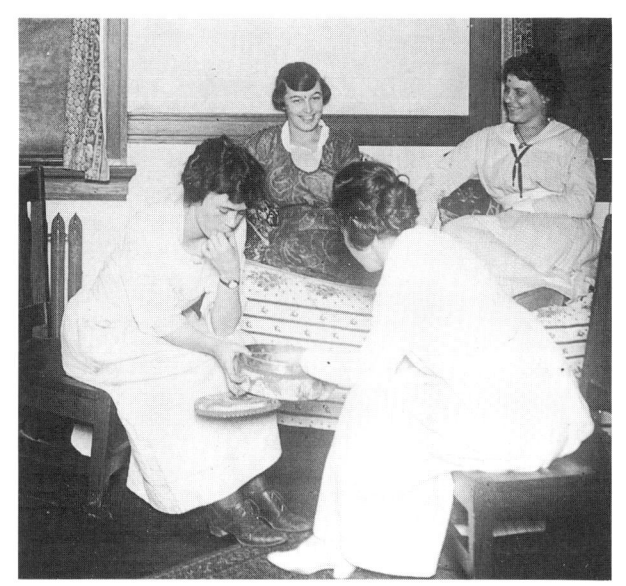

Agnes Scott College coeds share what appears to be a snack in one of the dormitory rooms. "Eating imprudently at night" was against the school's Rules for Domestic Government. (Agnes Scott College)

Before the turn of the century, Agnes Scott students wore hats even for strenuous outdoor activities. Note the student with the walking stick and another with a water pail and dipper. (Agnes Scott College)

Presbyterian, and loved her church. She believed in the sovereignty of that God as devoutly as in His goodness and mercy; and did not waste her time in metaphysical disquisitions, attempting to reconcile them, but diligently went about her duties and saw to it that no child of hers should go out into the world ignorant of the Shorter Catechism. Her early education had awakened in her the love of the true and the beautiful; hence, the first of all books to her was the Bible; and after this and her devotional books she appreciated Shakespeare and Burns. I have two treasures from her hand, both presented on the 14th of April, 1840 -- a copy of Shakespeare and a Bible. In the latter, written with her own hand, is an admonition which was the reflection of her own life: Proverbs c. 3; v. 5, 6. `Trust in the Lord with all thine heart, and lean not unto thine own understanding.' `In all the ways acknowledge Him and He shall direct thy paths'...

"And thus it was that in her home alike in pleasure, in sorrow, in the midst of the ever-recurring duties of wife, mother, friend, and counselor, she seasoned all her lessons with the truths of inspiration. A beautiful reflection of the character and spiritual life of Agnes Irvine Scott is found in a prayer written in her own handwriting in her Bible: `Heavenly Father, I leave all that belongs to me to Thee. Undertake Thou for them (her children). Bless them and make them blessings. Hide them under the shadow of Thy wings and direct their steps. May the grace of the Lord Jesus Christ be with you all.'"

Agnes Scott Institute became a four-year degree-granting college in 1906, with a curriculum expanded to include English, history, mathematics, Bible and pedagogy. Discipline remained strict, as reflected in the school bulletin of 1892:

"Rules for Domestic Government
"The following violations of the laws of health are prohibited:

"Eating imprudently at night; wearing thin shoes in cold weather; sitting on the ground or going outdoors with uncovered heads; too early removal of flannels, or the neglect to put them on at the approach of cold weather.

"No pupil is allowed to appear in a wrapper outside of her own chamber.

"Pupils will not be allowed to go to Atlanta oftener than once a quarter for shopping purposes.

"No one will be excused from breakfast except in case of illness.

"Visitors will not be received during school or study hours, nor the visits of young men at any time. Pupils are permitted to correspond only with such gentlemen as are especially named in writing by parents.

"All rooms will be inspected daily.

One young woman was expelled from the school because she was seen riding in a carriage "in an undesirable part of town." Another girl's fiance was told never to return to campus, because the engaged pair had been seen kissing good night.

George Washington Scott's birthday, February 22, is still celebrated as Founder's Day at the school. [58]

Agnes Scott students were allowed to form a bicycle club. The new sport of cycling caught on in DeKalb after the Bicycle Club of Atlanta was founded in 1888. Stone Mountain was a popular destination for racers and pleasure cyclists. Ladies wore long skirts and short Eaton jackets with leg-o'-mutton sleeves in cool weather and tailored shirtwaist dresses in summer. Men were decked out in tweed business suits and floppy caps. Proper bicycle etiquette was as important as the fashionable costume. Gentlemen cyclists were instructed: "Be ever ready to assist a female rider in distress on the road, without the formality of an introduction." Debate flourished from the pulpit on whether women should ride at all. [59]

Christmas in the 1880s in DeKalb, as remembered by Claude Candler McKinney (1877-1972), was a time of simple pleasures.

"We each hung up our stocking, and Santa filled it with fruit and nuts and raisins and candy. There would be one or two small gifts in the toe. We usually wanted a little `pen' knife to sharpen our pencils. We might get a tea set and maybe a new doll.
"The Negro servants would slip into the house soon after light to catch the family `Christmas Gif!' There were always bags of fruit, candy, and nuts for them, and a new piece of clothing for each.

"Mama (Eliza Murphey Candler) always had pretty bowls of fruit around on the tables and sideboard.

"But the really big excitement of Christmas Day was watching for the `Fantastics' to come riding up

Brown's Mill was located at the corner of what are now Flat Shoals and Snapfinger roads. (DeKalb Historical Society)

John Llewlyn Brown (1858-1934) was the owner of Brown's Mill. (DeKalb Historical Society)

the `avenue.' The boys and young men of Decatur on their horses would be dressed up in costumes,

and their horses decorated, too. They would ride through the streets in Decatur on Christmas morning, and then out to some of the homes not too far out from town.

"We children would run back to the house shouting, `The Fantastics are coming! The Fantastics are coming! Mama would be ready with fruit and cake or some other refreshments to serve them when they rode through the `big gates' and up to the house."

The Fantastics were still entertaining Decatur on Christmas when Scott Candler, Claude's nephew, was a boy.

"... Decatur was a `country town,' and it had preserved many of the quaint customs of the early settlers. One of these was the custom of `Riding Fantastic.'

"On Christmas morning, about nine o'clock, there would move a procession of gaily decorated horses, their riders in bright costumes and masks. The parade advanced with a great flurry of horns, a banging of firecrackers and a crack of blank cartridges.

"The procession always moved, without any apparent leader or order, up Candler Street to Sycamore, along Sycamore to the Court House, and north on Shallowford Road (now Clairmont). This Route practically covered the town of that time. None of the streets was paved; in dry weather they were deep in dust, and in wet spells they were a sea of mud.

"When the noise was heard heralding the approach of the Fantastics, children would drop their new Christmas toys and dash to the front yards' edges, where they were joined by the older people. It was a grand sight, the horses prancing, young men whooping and shouting, horns squawking, and explosions going off every few moments.

"All of the town dogs got into the act also, adding their yips and howls to the din... The word `fantasia' was applied long ago in Arabic countries and in North Africa to a showing off of horsemanship. In some way the custom of `Riding Fantastic' may have originated in some far, dim land. Who brought it to Decatur will never be known." [60]

Several churches in DeKalb made improvements during the final years of the 1880s. The trustees of Oak Grove Methodist Church bought two and one-half acres of land from James Francis Akins for $1. The trustees were J. M. Loyd, Jonathan Pennell, W. M. Henderson, J. M. Akins and W. B. Justice. Male church members were responsible for keeping a fire lit in the new sanctuary. Women kept the dust at bay, quite a job since no streets in the area were paved. Peachtree Baptist Church moved into a new sanctuary on Briarcliff Road. The old one had sustained considerable damage from Union soldiers during the Civil War. Rehoboth Baptist Church also constructed a new building, a frame structure seating 150 people and costing $3,000. A large part of the expenditure was for a big wood stove.

The church that had been known as Briarwood Methodist since 1858 changed its named to Ousley Chapel in the late 1880s, to honor its founder, the Rev. Newdaygate B. Ousley. Surnames in the Ousley Chapel Cemetery reflect the community: Adcox, Allen, Alexander, Barfield, Buttrill, Carpenter, Clay, Crowley, Doby, Fincher, Gladden, Hulsey, Jackson, Jarrett, Johnson, Lane, Leach, Lee, McCurdy, Parker, Porter, Puckett, Ramsey, Scott, Southard, Tucker, Tuggle, Walker, Wallace and Webb. [61]

Brown's Mill, located on Snapfinger Creek a mile downstream from Thompson's Mill, opened in 1888, and Carroll's Mill closed. It is not known when the corn and wheat mill opened, but it operated until its owner died, and then burned about 1890. The mill was located on the North Fork of Peachtree Creek, where Chamblee-Tucker Road crossed the creek at home. The three-story millhouse was operated by the first turbine in the area. "Mr. Carroll had a colored helper who played a fiddle for the amusement of his customers... The mill had the reputation for grinding slowly, and some of the customers claimed that a hungry hound dog could eat the meal as fast as it came from the mill." In 1887, Washington J. Houston added a new dimension to his business interests with the manufacture of white and red oak buckets. The <u>DeKalb Chronicle</u> reported on March 3 that Houston's new factory could turn out 100 buckets per day. By 1887, Houston's enterprises at his mill were substantial enough that the area was known as Houstonville. [4] [62]

In the late 1800s, the granite industry began to flourish, turning Lithonia and Stone Mountain into boom towns on the order of San Francisco during the 1849 gold rush.

Because granite was too heavy for a long haul by wagon, it had "no commercial value whatever" until the railroad come through in 1845. John T. Glenn, S. M. Inman and J. A. Alexander established the first commercial granite quarry in 1869, but it was not until 1880 that tools were invented which made commercial quarrying possible.

The first successful quarry opened in Lithonia in 1879. In 1880, DeKalb County produced granite for paving roads that was worth $13,000. The industry employed only 13 people. George Johnson and

---

[4] The Houston Mill property, northeast of now Emory University.

Cotton may have been king in other parts of the South, but granite was king in Lithonia in the 1890s. The final years of the 19th century were a decade of prosperity in southeast DeKalb County. This photo was taken about 1901 at Pine Mountain Quarry No. 3 in Lithonia. (Vanishing Georgia Collection, Georgia Department of Archives and History)

others built a spur railroad, called the Dinky, in 1889, capable of hauling 40 carloads of stone per day. Samuel and William Venable bought Stone Mountain in 1887 at a cost of $48,000, and opened the Venable Brothers quarries. By 1896, the mountain had yielded rock worth $750,000, and 1,000 people were employed in the granite industry in DeKalb. It is said that all the railroad cars of granite shipped around the world by the Venable brothers would stretch from New York to California. Stone Mountain granite was used in structures from the U. S. Naval Academy to the Panama Canal.

"To split the rocks, quarriers drilled holes and drove in iron wedges with sledge hammers. Sometimes workers hammered in wooden wedges. When soaked, the wooden wedges expanded, causing the stone to split. In the 19th century quarriers filled holes with gunpowder, which was detonated with a burning fuse. More recently, holes were plugged with dynamite, which was detonated electrically. The shock of explosives caused hairline fissures in building stone, however. This then allows water to infiltrate, where it can erode, freeze and crack the stone. To improve the quality of the stone at the end of the 19th century, quarriers introduced mechanized techniques using pneumatic shears, saws and hammers...

Stonecutters from Scotland, Wales, Italy, Sweden and Norway came to Lithonia to work in the granite industry. Lithonia was so rowdy in the "Gay '90s," it was said that the town made Dodge City "look like a Sunday School picnic." (DeKalb Historical Society)

"After quarrying, large blocks of quarry stone were broken or cut to about the final size at the quarry to ease handling and reduce shipping costs. Originally done with wedges. this is now done with sawing."

Workmen and stonecutters with special skills unknown in America came to Lithonia and Stone Mountain from Scotland, Wales and Italy, Sweden and Norway. Many married local girls and settled in DeKalb.

One of those stonecutters was John Keay Davidson Sr., who came from Aberdeen, Scotland to Lithonia in 1888. He and his sons, John Keay Jr., Norton A., Charles Lemuel Sr. and Wheeler, would found the Davidson Granite Company, which grew to be one of the best known in the world. [63]

The "Gay Nineties" were indeed gay in the prosperous town of Lithonia. Young ladies wore New York fashions and attended all the best schools. But, the prosperity had a down side. Street brawls and drunkenness were common, despite prohibition laws. "Compared to this town on a Saturday afternoon,

Dodge City out West was a Sunday School picnic. Local people like to think all the real bad characters were hanged publicly and thus excluded from their ancestry."

A list of Stone Mountain businesses and other interests from the 1880s reflects a bustling, good-sizes town: grist mills, D. Beauchamp and Robert Ray; general stores, S. H. Campbell and Son, Z. M. Matthews, J. T. Meador, E. L. Phillips, J. W. Scruggs, James R. Smith, John Swift, T. B. Thompson, A. J. Veal and Son, W. R. Wells and Son; physicians, J. Dillworth, John L. Hamilton, L. H. Jones and C. L. Summey; saloon, Gilham and Brown; general store and guano agents, Goldsmith and Daugherty; Baptist churches, the Rev. A. J. Goss, the Rev. P. B. McCurdy and the Rev. Elijah Wood; harness maker, Hiram Holley; Primitive Baptist church, the Rev. James T. Jordan; Presbyterian church, the Rev. J. F. McClelland; "guano, notary and justice," John W. McCurdy; shoemaker, John Miller; railroad agent, M. B. Ragsdale; attorney, W. M. Ragsdale; agent for the Stone Mountain Granite and Railroad Company, John Thomson; teacher, Mrs. Dora Turner; hardware store, T. P. Wells; dentist, L. D. Whitson; and watchmaker, Thomas Wholey. [64]

Even with the prosperity of southeast DeKalb, the income generated was nothing to compare with Atlanta, which boasted five millionaires in 1889. [65] Electricity changed the face of Atlanta's streets. Gas lights were replaced, and mule and steam were no longer used to power the street railroad cars. [66]

Several prominent DeKalb County residents died in 1889 including James W. Goldsmith of Stone Mountain, William Wright of the Panthersville District, Judge Charles W. McGinnis, Dr. J. L. Hamilton, Joseph Walker of Indian Creek Baptist Church, Lochlin Johnson Winn and James Veal, age 98, a War of 1812 veteran from the Stone Mountain District.

Chapter 29 Notes

1. Garrett, Franklin M., 1954, 1969, <u>Atlanta and Environs -- A Chronicle of Its People and Events</u>, Vol. 2, page 1. Hutcheson, Eleanor S., 1890, <u>U. S. Atlas 1890 and Complete Post Office Directory List of Post Offices</u>.

2. Ordner, Helen July 24, 1991, "Gone With The Square," DeKalb News/Sun, page 3B.

3. Garrett, Franklin M., 1954, 1969, <u>Atlanta and Environs -- A Chronicle of Its People and Events</u>, Vol. 2, pages 11-12.

4. Garrett, Franklin M., 1954, 1969, <u>Atlanta and Environs -- A Chronicle of Its People and Events</u>, Vol. 2, page 2.

5. Freeman, Douglas Southall, 1944, <u>Lee's Lieutenants</u>, Vols. 1, 2 and 3. Plant, Percy, 1957, "Historic DeKalb."

6. Hudgins, Carl T., 1952, "Mills and Other Early DeKalb County Industries (And Their Owners)," <u>The Collections of the DeKalb Historical Society</u>, Vol. 1.

7. Garrett, Franklin M., 1954, 1969, <u>Atlanta and Environs -- A Chronicle of Its People and Events</u>, Vol. 2, pages 10-11.

8. Garrett, Franklin M., 1954, 1969, <u>Atlanta and Environs -- A Chronicle of Its People and Events</u>, Vol. 2, page 19.

9. Hutcheson, Eleanor S., 1890, <u>U. S. Atlas 1890 and Complete Post Office Directory List of Post Offices</u>.

10. Author unknown, 1976, <u>First United Methodist Church, Chamblee, Georgia 1826-1976</u>.

11. 1850-1920, Cherokee, DeKalb, Gwinnett and Hall County census records. 1850-1920 DeKalb County tax records. 1870-1889, Atlanta City Directory. Chamblee, Alvin D., personal collection. Garrett, Franklin M., Necrology, Cemetery Records. Stiltner, Katherine Stiltner, personal collection. Turner, A. S., Funeral Home records. U. S. Postal Service records.

12. Hitt, Michael D., 1994, <u>History of the Roswell Railroad 1853-1921</u>.

13. Davis, Elizabeth L. and Spruill, Ethel W., 1975, <u>The Story of Dunwoody</u>. Dunwoody Elementary School students, 1982, "A Journey of 100 Years -- A Child's History of Dunwoody."

14. Hudgins, Carl T., 1952, "Mills and Other Early DeKalb County Industries (And Their Owners)," <u>The Collections of the DeKalb Historical Society</u>, Vol. 1.

15. Kirkwood Presbyterian Church file, Georgia Department of Archives and History.

16. Garrett, Franklin M., 1954, 1969, <u>Atlanta and Environs -- A Chronicle of Its People and Events</u>, Vol. 2, pages 31-32.

17. Clarke, Caroline McKinney, 1973, 1997, <u>The Story of Decatur</u>.

18. Garrett, Franklin M., 1954, 1969, <u>Atlanta and Environs -- A Chronicle of Its People and Events</u>, Vol. 2, page 47.

19. Garrett, Franklin M., 1954, 1969, <u>Atlanta and Environs -- A Chronicle of Its People and Events</u>, Vol. 2, pages 50-51.

20. Ebster, D. G., 1926, "History of Thankful Baptist Church." Nix, Dorothy, personal collection, DeKalb Historical Society.

21. Nix, Dorothy, personal collection, DeKalb Historical Society.

22. Hudgins, Carl T., 1952, "Mills and Other Early DeKalb County Industries (And Their Owners)," <u>the Collections of the DeKalb Historical Society</u>, Vol. 1.

23. Garrett, Franklin M., 1954, 1969, <u>Atlanta and Environs -- A Chronicle of Its People and Events</u>, Vol. 2, page 54.

24. Garrett, Franklin M., 1954, 1969, <u>Atlanta and Environs -- A Chronicle of Its People and Events</u>, Vol. 2, page 66.

25. Nix, Dorothy, personal collection, DeKalb Historical Society.

26. Garrett, Franklin M., 1954, 1969, <u>Atlanta and Environs -- A Chronicle of Its People and Events</u>, Vol. 2, page 79.

27. Garrett, Franklin M., 1954, 1969, <u>Atlanta and Environs -- A Chronicle of Its People and Events</u>, Vol. 2, pages 80-81.

28. Hudgins, Carl T., 1952, "Mills and Other Early DeKalb County Industries (And Their Owners)," <u>the Collections of the DeKalb Historical Society</u>, Vol. 1.

29. Garrett, Franklin M., 1954, 1969, <u>Atlanta and Environs -- A Chronicle of Its People and Events</u>, Vol. 2, pages 84-85.

30. New Hope Cemetery file, DeKalb Historical Society. Davis, Elizabeth L., and Spruill, Ethel W., 1975, <u>The Story of Dunwoody</u>. Miller, Mrs. Flora McElroy, n. d., <u>History of Doraville Associate Reformed Presbyterian Church</u>.

31. Garrett, Franklin M., 1954, 1969, <u>Atlanta and Environs -- A Chronicle of Its People and Events</u>, Vol. 2, pages 90-91.

32. Garrett, Franklin M., 1954, 1969, <u>Atlanta and Environs -- A Chronicle of Its People and Events</u>, Vol. 2, pages 95-98 and 159.

33. Clarke, Caroline McKinney, 1973, 1997, <u>The Story of Decatur</u>.

34. Garrett, Franklin M., 1954, 1969, <u>Atlanta and Environs -- A Chronicle of Its People and Events</u>, Vol. 2, page 90.

35. Garrett, Franklin M., 1954, 1969, <u>Atlanta and Environs -- A Chronicle of Its People and Events</u>, Vol. 2, pages 99-102.

36. Garrett, Franklin M., 1954, 1969, <u>Atlanta and Environs -- A Chronicle of Its People and Events</u>, Vol. 2, page 103.

37. Hudgins, Carl T., 1952, "Mills and Other Early DeKalb County Industries (And Their Owners)," <u>The Collections of the DeKalb Historical Society</u>, Vol. 1.

38. Chesnut, Mr. and Mrs. J. David, personal collection.

39. Nix, Dorothy, personal collection, DeKalb Historical Society.

40. Clarke, Caroline McKinney, 1973, 1997, <u>The Story of Decatur</u>.

41. Garrett, Franklin M., 1954, 1969, <u>Atlanta and Environs -- A Chronicle of Its People and Events</u>, Vol. 2, page 1072.

42. Garrett, Franklin M., 1954, 1969, <u>Atlanta and Environs -- A Chronicle of Its People and Events</u>, Vol. 2, page 110.

43. Garrett, Franklin M., 1954, 1969, <u>Atlanta and Environs -- A Chronicle of Its People and Events</u>, Vol. 2, page 115.

44. Garrett, Franklin M., 1954, 1969, <u>Atlanta and Environs -- A Chronicle of Its People and Events</u>, Vol. 2, pages 116-118. Plant, Percy, 1957, "Historic DeKalb." Candler, Charles Murphey, November 9, 1922, "Historical Address."

45. Nix, Dorothy, personal collection, DeKalb Historical Society.

46. Garrett, Franklin M., 1954, 1969, <u>Atlanta and Environs -- A Chronicle of Its People and Events</u>, Vol. 2, page 119-124.

47. Nix, Dorothy, personal collection, DeKalb Historical Society.

48. Garrett, Franklin M., 1954, 1969, <u>Atlanta and Environs -- A Chronicle of Its People and Events</u>, Vol. 2, pages 127-128.

49. Nix, Dorothy, personal collection, DeKalb Historical Society.

50. Nix, Dorothy, personal collection, DeKalb Historical Society. Hudgins, Carl T., 1952, "Mills and Other Early DeKalb County Industries (And Their Owners)," The Collections of the DeKalb Historical Society, Vol. 1.

51. Garrett, Franklin M., 1954, 1969, Atlanta and Environs -- A Chronicle of Its People and Events, Vol. 2, pages 108-109.

52. Garrett, Franklin M., 1954, 1969, Atlanta and Environs -- A Chronicle of Its People and Events, Vol. 2, page 132-133.

53. Garrett, Franklin M., 1954, 1969, Atlanta and Environs -- A Chronicle of Its People and Events, Vol. 2, page 131.

54. Garrett, Franklin M., 1954, 1969, Atlanta and Environs -- A Chronicle of Its People and Events, Vol. 2, page 161.

55. Clarke, Caroline McKinney, 1973, 1997, The Story of Decatur. Nix, Dorothy, personal collection, DeKalb Historical Society.

56. Garrett, Franklin M., 1954, 1969, Atlanta and Environs -- A Chronicle of Its People and Events, Vol. 2, page 133.

57. Garrett, Franklin M., 1954, 1969, Atlanta and Environs -- A Chronicle of Its People and Events, Vol. 2, page 133.

58. Alston, Wallace M., n. d., "The Significance of the Life of George Washington Scott." Clarke, Caroline McKinney, 1973, 1996, The Story of Decatur. Garrett, Franklin M., 1954, 1969, Atlanta and Environs -- A Chronicle of Its People and Events, Vol. 2, pages 194-197. Hutchens, Eleanor N., 1952, "Brief History of Agnes Scott College," The Collections of the DeKalb Historical Society, Vol. 1. McNair, Walter Edward, 1983, Lest We Forget -- An Account of Agnes Scott College. Scott genealogy file, DeKalb Historical Society.

59. Garrett, Franklin M., 1954, 1969, Atlanta and Environs -- A Chronicle of Its People and Events, Vol. 2, page 174-175.

60. Clarke, Caroline McKinney, 1973, 1997, The Story of Decatur.

61. Author unknown, 1954, "Rehoboth Baptist -- 1854-1954." Georgia Daughters of the American Revolution, 1950-51, Church Histories (Ousley), Vol. 405, pages 252-254. Nix, Dorothy, personal collection, DeKalb Historical Society.

62. Garrett, Franklin M., 1954, 1969, Atlanta and Environs -- A Chronicle of Its People and Events, Vol. 2, page 131. Hudgins, Carl T., 1952, "Mills and Other Early DeKalb County Industries (And Their Owners)," The Collections of the DeKalb Historical Society, Vol. 1.

63. Brewster, Gaines, February 28, 1974, "Rocks To Riches or How Granite Has Benefitted DeKalb." Brewster, Gaines, and Fossett, Fran, 1972, Charlie's World.

64. Brewster, Gaines, February 28, 1974, "Rocks To Riches or How Granite Has Benefitted DeKalb." Joseph, J. W., and Kehoe, Lisa M, November 14, 1994, Historic Sites Survey, City of Stone Mountain, DeKalb County, Georgia. Nix, Dorothy, personal collection. Stevens, O. B., commissioner, 1901, "Georgia Historical and Industrial," Georgia Department of Agriculture. Wesley, Cecil Cobb, August-September, 1961, "Lithonia -- Place of Stone -- A Brief History," Georgia Magazine, page 47.

65. Garrett, Franklin M., 1954, 1969, Atlanta and Environs -- A Chronicle of Its People and Events, Vol. 2, page 179.

66. Garrett, Franklin M., 1954, 1969, Atlanta and Environs -- A Chronicle of Its People and Events, Vol. 2, pages 182 and 188-191.

Chapter 30

*A*side from the bare totals, no census data exists for DeKalb County from the federal survey of 1890. However, the Georgia Statistical Register shows that DeKalb County had 17,189 inhabitants (and six post offices). The most populous town, of course, was Decatur, with 1013 residents, followed by Stone Mountain with 929, Chamblee with 72, Doraville with 63, and Edgewood with 53. The population of Kirkwood, which also had a post office, was not recorded. [1]

The 1890s were generally prosperous in DeKalb County, although farmers suffered from low cotton prices, unstable labor and a lack of credit. These conditions led to the establishment of the National Farmers' Alliance and Industrial Union, a political organization, which "grew like a mushroom overnight" in DeKalb, according to Rock Chapel resident J. B. Bond. The alliance gubernatorial candidate, William J. Northen, was elected governor of Georgia in 1890. [2]

While crime was negligible in Decatur and Atlanta in 1890, offenders knew neither city had jurisdiction in the no-man's land between the boundaries of the cities. Gambling dens and other havens for criminals thrived in the Edgewood area. The crime problem may have led to the incorporation of two small cities. Edgewood, named because of its proximity to Atlanta, was incorporated in 1898. It was absorbed into the city of Atlanta on January 1, 1909. Kirkwood was incorporated on December 20, 1899, and named for James H. Kirkpatrick, an early settler who owned all the land within the town limits. A post office had been granted to the community on March 31, 1891, with Raleigh C. Cassels as the first postmaster. The town became a part of Atlanta on January 1, 1922. DeKalb's two most famous citizens, John B. Gordon and Alfred H. Colquitt, were Kirkwood residents. Mrs. Alfred H. Colquitt was the honorary first president of the Women's Christian Temperance Union, and meetings were held at her house in Kirkwood. [3]

A former Kirkwood resident was fast becoming a well-known figure in Atlanta. David T. Howard had been a slave of Thomas Coke Howard, and was listed as one of the wealthiest black men in Atlanta in 1890. A railroad porter immediately after the Civil War, Howard made his fortune as an undertaker. [4]

The Atlanta suburbs were growing rapidly in 1890, causing the same kinds of disruptions familiar to area residents today. The body of John Williams Medlock had laid quietly in its grave for almost 10 years when a developer bought land, including the Medlock family cemetery, for a new residential

After the cotton, woolen and grist mills at Panola burned, the Panola Light and Power Company was built on the site shortly after the turn of the century. The company furnished electric power for Lithonia and Conyers. (Vanishing Georgia Collection, Georgia Department of Archives and History)

subdivision. Medlock's body was moved from its resting place near Ponce de Leon and Boulevard avenues to a new home in the Decatur Cemetery. [5]

As soon as new homes were built in the suburbs, they were snapped up by Atlantans looking to get out of the city to places where they could "enjoy the luxury of fresh air, pure water and plenty of room." And little wonder. Ditches served as sewers in the city of almost 40,000 people, and those ditches emptied into area creeks. It was during the 1890s that Atlanta developed a modern sewer system. Fewer than one in three Atlanta households had indoor plumbing in 1890. [6]

DeKalb County lost five of its prominent citizens to death in 1890: John N. Swift of Lithonia, Eli J. Hulsey of Panthersville, Decatur physician Dr. Robert Campbell Word, Decatur railroad agent John N. Pate and Edmund Lee of Rock Chapel Methodist Church.

Epworth Methodist Church was organized in the fall of 1890, with a few members of the old Edgewood Church. The new church name was suggested by Mrs. C. W. Smith. Early services were held at Mayson Academy. In 1892, Mrs. A. A. Bessent donated a lot on the corner of South Mayson Avenue and LaFrance Street. The sanctuary was struck by lightning in 1897, and totally destroyed by fire. The congregation rebuilt on the same site. The new church was struck twice more by lightning, and caught fire several times, but was never again destroyed. The church moved to the 1500 block of McLendon Avenue in 1925. [7]

Fire also destroyed Veal's Mill. The mill, located on Mountain Creek near what is now the Smokerise subdivision, was purchased by the father of C. W. Caldwell of Tucker about 1890. Caldwell hired the son of Henry See to operate the mill. See was killed in the fire in 1900. "Wheat threshing season was in July and then you left the grain to season and dry out. Consequently the wheat piled up and in August the mill ran night and day. It was believed the young operator of the mill went to sleep, the hopper ran out of grain and the mill stones ground out sparks setting the mill afire. It was not rebuilt."

The steampowered Chupp-Duncan-Braswell Ginnery operated between 1890 and 1925 near Lithonia. Owners at various times were J. L. Chupp, R. S. Duncan and E. R. Braswell. E. A. Warwick also operated a ginnery near the railroad depot in Clarkston about 1890. [8]

Agnes Scott Institute students attended church services at Decatur Presbyterian Church. Enrollment grew to such an extent in 1891, that the church was compelled to build a new sanctuary. William Bensel of Atlanta was the builder of the new brick and stone structure on Sycamore Street. Members of the church building committee were George W. Scott, Milton A. Candler, H. F. Emery, J. A. Mason and N. P. Pratt. An $18,000 building fund was raised by the congregation for the sanctuary which served the church for the next 60 years. [9]

Deaths in 1891 included former DeKalb County treasurer James R. McAllister, Dr. Hilliard J. Fowler, veteran of the Indian wars in 1830s, and Robert M. Clarke, well-known horse breeder and proprietor of Panola Cotton Mills on the South River. Clarke's mill, on the oldest industrial site in the Atlanta area, burned two years after his death, on September 1, 1893. Clarke had built the mill on land he purchased from Charles Latimer. The mill was never rebuilt. Across the river from the Panola mill was Oglethorpe Manufacturing Company, another textile mill that operated until about 1895. The flourishing town called Panola that surrounded the two mills disappeared when the businesses ceased to exist. The Panola Power Company later was built on the site of old Panola. [10]

Alf Chewning, pictured here with his wife, Delilah Rachel, was the first postmaster of Tucker. (From Cotton Fields to High Techology in Tucker, Georgia)

Another mill owner, Thomas F Scully, proprietor of the Sugar Creek Paper Mills, died in 1892. Other DeKalb County citizens who died in 1892 were William W. Veal of Stone Mountain, James J. Winn, Thomas N. Paden, Harris Goodwin and J. W. F. (Uncle Fletcher) Tilly. [11]

DeKalb's first Episcopal church, Holy Trinity in Decatur was established in 1892, with its first building on the northeast corner of Church Street and Trinity Place, which was named for the church. Holy Trinity moved to the corner of East Ponce de Leon Avenue and Sycamore Street in 1928. The church has sponsored three missions: St. Michael and All Angels, St. Bartholomew's and Holy Cross.[12]

The newly completed Seaboard Air-Line Railroad ran its first train from Monroe, N. C. to Atlanta on April 24, 1892. Stations between Athens and Atlanta included Tucker and North Decatur. New towns soon would appear at stops all along the line. [13]

Members of the John Montgomery family are shown at the Montgomery home in Decatur in this photo, taken about 1893. On the porch is Mary Powell Montgomery, daughter of James Oliver Powell, holding her first-born child, Allen. At left is Mary's mother, Sara Carroll Powell. At right is Jennie Powell Avery, Mary's sister. At the gate is Sadie Avery, daughter of Jennie. (DeKalb Historical Society)

Tucker was granted a post office on June 25, 1892, with Alpheus C. (Alf) Chewning as the first postmaster. The North Decatur Post Office opened on August 10, 1892, with Henry R. Schurter, postmaster. [14]

The town of Tucker, which has never been incorporated, was laid out by railroad officials, and said to have been named in honor of a railroad official. As is the case with several other DeKalb County towns, there are numerous other stories told about the naming of Tucker. The town may have been named for a Tucker family that lived in the area or a leading Baptist church official. In the late 1800s, Tucker consisted of Alf Chewning's dry goods store and a blacksmith shop operated by Edwin P. Dunagan. [15]

The Montreal Post Office, with William W. Wilcox as postmaster, opened on July 29, 1892, a few months before the Montreal Manufacturing Company was incorporated. The company, which made furniture, toys, tools, machinery and other articles of wood, metal and other materials, was granted by the legislature the unusual power to build railroads, bridges and other structures. Incorporators were James T. Carter, W. T. Evans, H. L. Talton and James W. Robinson. The company bought a "town block" in the town of Montreal, bounded by the Georgia, Northern and Carolina (Seaboard) Railroad and by Melrose Avenue and Atlanta Avenue. Construction started in 1893, but was quickly halted by a lien on the property. The DeKalb County sheriff sold the town block and partially constructed factory on January 1, 1895, for $250. The entire project was abandoned.

Before electric lights came to Decatur, Joe Osborne had the task of filling and lighting the oil lamps on the town's street corners. This photo was taken between 1890 and 1895. (DeKalb Historical Society)

Dr. Washington Jackson Houston Jr. and his wife, Emily Miriam Wing, raised their family in this house in Decatur. The house also served as Houston's doctor's office. Originally it faced the Square, but it was turned to face Church Street. (DeKalb Historical Society)

Montreal citizen and postmaster John J. Richardson later tried to convert the unused boiler to shred corn, with disastrous results. The boiler exploded. Richardson's hired man was killed. The boiler head later was found a mile away. The building of the railroad through Montreal inspired an attempted revival of the plant and subdivision of the land into lots, but this project also failed. "There is nothing left now to indicate the site of the factory building. In fact, there is nothing now to show on the ground that a village existed under the ambitious name of "Montreal." [16]

DeKalb got three additional post offices between 1891 and 1893. John W. McWilliams became postmaster at East Atlanta on April 13, 1891. The Ingleside Post Office opened on February 20, 1892, with Hiram C. Randall as postmaster. Multimillionaire George F. Willis turned Ingleside into the picturesque town of Avondale Estates, which was incorporated on March 16, 1925. John W. Wallace, one of three DeKalb County Wallace brothers, was named postmaster of his town, called Wallace, on September 28, 1893. [17]

For DeKalb's large Powell and Houston families, the years of 1892 and 1893 were filled with happy occasions, which were also Decatur's social events of the seasons.

Mary Parisade Powell and John Montgomery were the first couple married in Decatur's Presbyterian Church. Mary was the daughter of the late James O. Powell and Sarah Carroll. John was the son of William Montgomery and Caroline Franklin. John Montgomery would be elected mayor of Decatur in 1906.

Mary Powell's cousin, Sarah Amanda (Susie) Houston married Dr. Edward Conner Ripley on March 1, 1893. Houston and Ripley were the second couple married in Decatur's Presbyterian church. Susie Houston was the daughter of Washington Jackson Houston Sr. and Amanda Katherine Powell. Susie Houston's cousin, Annie Billups, and Dr. Will Goldsmith were the attendants. A local newspaper

The Weekes Brothers Grocery Store was a fixture on the Square in Decatur for 42 years. (DeKalb Historical Society)

covered the event: "There was a large and fashionable audience. Miss Billups wore a gown of creme cashmere trimmed with lace and ribbons. The bride, always handsome, looked handsomer than ever, daintily and becomingly attired in a gown of pale blue silk and white lace. She was indeed a picture of womanly beauty. Her bouquet was composed of white hyacinth and maidenhair fern." [18]

Susie Houston's older brother, Washington Jackson Houston Jr., married Emily Miriam Wing on October 10, 1893 at Decatur Methodist Church. Emily, the daughter of Hiram and Emily Berry Wing of Atlanta, had been voted the prettiest girl at Agnes Scott Institute. Houston would graduate from the Eclectic College of Medicine in 1898 and begin practicing in Decatur.

Houston's mother had decided that the family home on Clairmont Road, the same site where Chapman Powell had practiced medicine a half century earlier, was too far away from town. She purchased a lot on the Square in Decatur, where Houston built a home, which also served as his office. The home

Rock Chapel historian J. B. Bond is pictured with an unidentified lady friend headed for a Fourth of July outing. (Vanishing Georgia Collection, Georgia Department of Archives and History)

originally faced the Square, but later was turned to face Church Street. The structure still stands today at 410 Church Street, and houses a floral shop.

Houston was the first officially designated city and county physician, the forerunner of today's public health department. As such it was his duty to certify all DeKalb County inductees as fit for duty during World War I.

Houston and Emily Wing had five daughters: Mildred (Mrs. Swanson L. Craig), Mary (Mrs. John Meckerling), Katie Hazel (Mrs. Sidney Dean McDonald), Alice (Mrs. Paul Harold Milton) and Doris (Mrs. William Smith VanLandingham). The girls grew up on the Square in Decatur, playing Pop The Whip on Sycamore Street, and sledding on Atlanta Avenue. Every Saturday night, a choir and string band from Thankful Baptist Church would play on the sidewalk, while young people danced on the porch. [19]

The financial panic of 1893 certainly wasn't evident by reading the Atlanta Constitution's story about Decatur, published on May 25, 1893:

"The new electric line to Decatur (North Decatur line) that is so rapidly nearing completion is very naturally exciting a great deal of interest, not only in the line itself, but also in the town of Decatur, and it has brought the charming little suburb into prominence again in a very advantageous and conspicuous way.

This photo of downtown Decatur was taken shortly after the turn of the century. Identifiable businesses include the Decatur Furniture Company, Decatur Beauty Parlor, a shop selling electrical fixtures and the A. S. Adams Cates Company. Pictured, second from right, is Dean Livsey of Clarkston. (DeKalb Historical Society)

"It is not generally known what wonderful strides in the way of progress and improvements our little neighbor has made in the last few years, but such a gratifying fact, and the truth of the assertion can easily and plainly be proven to any one who takes a very little while, and it will amply repay any one, for there is no more pleasant or interesting trip that can be taken around the city.

"To a great many people, especially those who have not been there for a long time, and more especially to those who have never seen Decatur before, it is a revelation, and just at this season of the year it will captivate anybody.

"As a suburban place of residence for Atlanta it just simply has no equal, and with its three different lines of transportation that link it so closely to the city, it is now just as convenient for Atlanta people to live at as Inman Park, West End or nay of the immediate suburbs adjoining the city limits.

"Being only six miles east of Atlanta on the old reliable Georgia railroad and also having both a dummy line (South Decatur line, then operated by steam locomotives and an electric line running to it, its transportation facilities are perfect, and even if it keeps its present rate of growth and improvement it will only be a short time before it doubles in size and population.

"It has been steadily growing for a good number of years past but not until completion of the dummy line about three years ago did it seem to awaken to its many advantages and fully realize its importance and possibilities. Since that time, however, it has surprised itself, and the number of pretty new residences that have been built and other marked improvements will do credit to any place of twice its size.

Asa Griggs Candler Sr. built this home on Ponce de Leon Avenue in the Druid Hills subdivision. The house is now St. John's Melkite Catholic Church. (Lee Collection, DeKalb Historical Society; Vanishing Georgia Collection, Georgia Department of Archives and History)

"The population is now between 1500 and 2000 and a happier and more contented set of people would be hard to find.

"The conveniences of living in Decatur are just about the same as in Atlanta. There are plenty of nice first-class grocery stores, a good drug store, meat market, etc., with free deliveries and city prices.

"When it comes to school and church advantages Decatur is unsurpassed. Everybody knows what the Agnes Scott Female Institute is without any comment, for it has the reputation of being one of the very finest institutions in the South, and is the pride of Decatur. There is also a very fine boys' school[5] that bids fair to become a worthy companion to the Agnes Scott.

"As to churches there are already three flourishing ones, viz: Methodist, Baptist and Presbyterian, and a nice new Episcopal church is now in the course of construction.

"The society of Decatur cannot be excelled anywhere -- and all newcomers are warmly welcomed and made to feel at home.

---

[5] Donald Fraser School.

A public well on the courthouse square in Decatur, shown at far left, provided water for people and animals. Note the livestock wandering in the road and on the courthouse grounds. (Lee Collection, DeKalb Historical Society)

"The new electric line expects to be running cars to Decatur by next Saturday afternoon or Sunday, and it will be an invaluable addition to the already fine transportation facilities.

"Its route is on the north of the Georgia railroad all the way to Decatur and the dummy line is on the south side. Both lines run through a beautiful section of country and are doing wonders in the way of developments and improvements on their respective lines.

"The fare to Decatur on either one of these lines or on the Georgia railroad is only a nickel, and is no more than it costs to ride a few blocks in the city.

"All the country in the direction of Decatur is built up splendidly with beautiful homes, and it is by odds the prettiest direction and range of country out of Atlanta.

"The value of such a suburb as Decatur to a city like Atlanta is almost inestimable, but up to this time it has not been as fully appreciated by the Atlanta businessmen as it should be. When they realize, however, this summer that they can so easily and cheaply get out of the heat, noise and dust of the city in the evenings after a hard day's work, away from mosquitoes, and in such a few minutes to a nice cool country home, they will begin to see what a valuable suburb it is.

"To have such a place within such easy reach means a great deal to a city the size of Atlanta, for it not only obviates the necessity and expense of a man having to send his family off for the summer, away off up the country or to some out of the way place, but by sending them to such a place as Decatur he can have them nearby, can be with them every night, and will only have to lose a very few minutes from his business to do so. And too, besides that advantage very few places can be found that have a more delightful climate, finer water and better health...

"To sum up all of the advantages of Decatur, in a few words, she is the county site of DeKalb County, has magnificent transportation facilities, the very finest educational advantages, nice churches, good stores, a livery stable, telegraph, telephone and express offices, a first-class newspaper, unexcelled society, elegant climate and water and is as healthy a place as there is on the globe. There is also a good hotel and several first-class boarding houses that charge very reasonable rates. A movement is already on foot to furnish the town with electric lights, and the prospects for having them soon are first-class.

"The surrounding country is very pretty, affording beautiful drives and the pike road to Atlanta is also in splendid condition.

"Property is cheap and can be bought on very easy terms. There is an abundance of beautiful residence property with plenty of fine shade, and also a good many nice and pretty new residences for sale that have been recently built and gotten ready for newcomers. Then, too, there is plenty of good farming land nearby that can be bought very reasonable, and there is no better section of the state for truck and dairy farming.

"Not only as a place of residence is Decatur a good place to buy, but as a field for investment it has no equal near Atlanta, and anything in the way of property bought there or near there is sure to bring handsome returns and enhance rapidly in value.

"The thing to do, however, is just to get on one of the transportation lines, take a trip out there and see for yourself." [20]

The financial crisis of 1893 did halt plans for a subdivision that eventually would become a world-class residential area. Atlanta developer Joel Hurt began assembling farm land between Atlanta and Decatur in 1890. Famed Central Park designer Fredrick Law Olmsted completed the first draft of a plan for the Druid Hills community and the Ponce de Leon linear parks on August 8, 1893. Olmsted's plan was to replace the typical city grid pattern with gently curving streets lined with open meadows and small wooded areas. Homes would be placed on lots of one to 10 acres. The project was delayed until 1908 when the property was sold to a syndicate headed by Asa G. Candler. [21]

Tucker First Baptist Church was organized in 1893, and constructed its first sanctuary two years later.[22]

Two prominent DeKalb citizens died in 1893: Thomas C. Howard of Kirkwood and Easom J. Bond of Rock Chapel. Former DeKalb Sheriff and state legislator Daniel (Uncle Dan) Johnson died in 1894. Johnson Road is named for him. Death also claimed Robert M. Brown of Decatur and John Bryce, former judge of the DeKalb Inferior Court, in 1894. John B. Swanton of Decatur, son of Benjamin Franklin Swanton, died in 1895. DeKalb pioneer John Glen, later mayor of Atlanta, died in 1896. [23]

The first grand jury to serve in the new courthouse is pictured on the granite steps in early 1900. The identities of only a few are known. In the front row, left to right, are DeKalb Ordinary William M. Ragsdale, Henry George, DeKalb Superior Court Judge John S. Candler, William Parks Medlock and Thomas P. George. In the second row are Ben Burgess, unknown, Hamilton Weekes and F. L. Hudgins. The identity of the boy sitting on the railing is unknown. (DeKalb Historical Society)

Snow was 18 inches deep in February of 1895 when fire destroyed George Ramspeck's store on the Square in Decatur. That same year the Atlanta city limits were extended to the DeKalb County line at Moreland Avenue in 1895. [24]

Women made the news in 1895. DeKalb women got a glimpse of Susan B. Anthony at the annual meeting of the National American Woman's Suffrage Association in January. The Atlanta Chapter of the United Daughters of the Confederacy was organized on July 18 at the home of Mrs. Edward C.

The cornerstone was laid on DeKalb's new courthouse on November 24, 1898. This building burned in 1916, but the granite walls survived the blaze and formed the exterior of what is now known as DeKalb's Old Courthouse on the Square. The building is home to the DeKalb Historical Society. (DeKalb Historical Society; Vanishing Georgia Collection, Georgia Department of Archives and History)

Peters. Mrs. C. Helen Plane was elected president. In 1909, Mrs. Plane would propose carving a monument to the Confederacy on the north face of Stone Mountain. [25]

The financial impact of the Cotton States Exposition lifted the Atlanta area out of a depression in 1895. Some 800,000 visitors attended the event at Piedmont Park from September 18 through December 31., with 25,000 viewing the opening parade. Rebecca Latimer Felton was a member of the Board of Women Managers, chairing the Awards Committee. However, the fair itself, which cost almost $3 million to stage, had to be rescued by a group of civic-minded Atlantans. [26]

DeKalb citizens Piromis H. Bell and T. J. Flake helped organize Atlanta's popular Burns Club on the anniversary of the Scottish poet's birth, January 25, 1896. [27]

Methodist Bishop and Emory College president Atticus G. Haygood, who lived for a while in Decatur, died in 1896, as did Stone Mountain Circuit Judge Richard H. Clark. John Bolton Johns, the 90-year-old pioneer of the Rehoboth community, also died in 1896 from injuries he sustained when knocked down by a calf. [28]

The 43-year-old debate over the location of DeKalb's county seat would be settled in 1897. In a countywide referendum on December 2, 1896, voters chose Stone Mountain by a vote of 814 to 160. Opponents of the outcome challenged the validity of the election, but the Supreme Court of Georgia reaffirmed the vote in March of 1897. Citizens who wanted to keep Decatur as the county seat then appealed to the Georgia legislature in November of 1897. The lawmakers voted 85 to 60 for removal, two votes short of the required two-thirds majority. A vote the following day to reconsider was defeated 52 to 36. State legislator William M. Morris of Decatur was a leader in the effort to keep the county seat in Decatur. [29]

With the issue decided, bids were reopened on January 26, 1898 for the sorely-needed new courthouse. Plans for the building, described in the DeKalb New Era, "called for a building (on the same site) 101 x 110 feet; height from basement floor to the crown on the brow of Justice, 126 feet. In the basement will be heating apparatus, fuel room closets, a room for holding elections and a county court room.

"The first floor will be occupied by the county officers, including the county school commissioners and justice of the peace for the Decatur District. An arrangement made by Ordinary (William R.) Ragsdale provides for a special room for ladies equipped with toilets, etc.

"The second floor will be taken up with the superior court room, grand jury room, two witness rooms, jury rooms and prisoners' room. The court room, when completed, will be one of the nicest in the State. The dome is to be framed of heart pine and covered with heavy galvanized iron, the roof being red tile. The inside finish is to be native hard pine oil finish. The whole building when finished will be a modern, up-to-date structure, with best arrangement of offices possibly, amply large for the convenient transaction of business and safety of the papers and records." [30]

Granite for the new courthouse came from the Lithonia quarry of Carl T. Wells, son-in-law of John Wilson McCurdy. Walls made of two layers of brick, made in Decatur, were overlaid in the interior with marble from Alabama. The new courthouse was completed at a cost of $60,000. [31]

John Brown Gordon built this home, called Sutherland, on the site of his Kirkwood home that burned in 1899, the same year Kirkwood was incorporated. Gordon was governor of Georgia from 1886-1890. He died in 1904. (Brooke Collection, DeKalb Historical Society)

On April 7, 1898, the Atlanta Constitution reported on the demolition of DeKalb's old brick courthouse:

"... The work of tearing away the old courthouse of DeKalb County, to make place for the new one which is to be erected there was begun yesterday morning. The cupola of the old building has been dismantled. The old clock that for so many years has told the time to the citizens of the county and rung the hours, was taken down, and the large bell, that could be heard for miles, was brought from its high place to the ground.

"The work will progress with haste and in a few weeks the walls of the historic old building will be scattered to the ground, a mass of broken bricks. These walls are nearly two feet in thickness and after nearly a century (sic) of seasoning, have become as one stone.

"A temporary house is being erected on the public square where the county offices will be placed until the handsome new building is completed, which, it is expected, will be a year."

The cornerstone of the new courthouse was laid on November 24, 1898 with impressive Masonic ceremonies. A highlight of the ceremony was a short address on the history of the county by Milton A. Candler. County officials moved into the new building in 1899. Fire gutted the entire interior of the granite courthouse in September of 1916. Thanks to fireproof vaults, few records were lost to the flames. [32]

F. M. Wellborn of Redan, Allen Veal of Stone Mountain and Samuel McWilliams of Panthersville died in 1897. Decatur saloon keeper James Pickens Crockett, 58, committed suicide. It was said that Crockett had a large bank account, considerable real estate and $40,000 in gold hidden in his house at the time of his death. [33]

Mason's Mill, located on Burnt Fork Creek off Peachtree Creek, burned in 1898. It was owned by J. A. Mason, onetime treasurer of DeKalb County. The miller was "Ketch" Wilson. [34]

Of Georgia's 3,531 soldiers in the Spanish American War, only five were from DeKalb: James Alexander Campbell of Decatur, John S. Candler (later Georgia Supreme Court justice), William Schley Howard, Wiley West (later Decatur postmaster) and Joseph Edward Smith. [35]

Back home, the Atlanta Relief Association, made up of young women, was organized on May 30, 1898. Ella M. Powell, granddaughter of DeKalb pioneer Chapman Powell, was chosen president. Elizabeth R. Venable was chairman of the Executive Committee. The association worked in hospitals and raised money for the support of soldiers through events like the barbecue at the Venable place near Stone Mountain on June 11. Elizabeth Venable had been visiting Key West, Fla. in February, 1898 when the battleship Maine was destroyed. Her brothers, granite magnates William and Samuel Venable, were there building fortifications. Elizabeth formed her own one-woman relief organization, tending to the needs of wounded soldiers from the battleship. [36]

In 1906, Nettie Southern and Glen G. Austin were the first couple to be married in the Dunwoody Baptist Church. (The Story of Dunwoody)

The largest crowd ever assembled in Atlanta saw the Confederate Veterans's Reunion on July 20, 1898. John B. Gordon was commanding general of the event. Visitors streamed into the city from DeKalb in wagons and via the trains and trolleys. [37]

That same summer, the Atlanta Athletic Club was organized on August 15, 1898. The club built a seven-hole golf course in 1906 at DeKalb's popular resort, East Lake. A 13-year-old local boy named Bobby Jones captured the imagination of the sporting world when he played in his first tournament at East Lake in 1915. [38]

A new post office opened in Klondike on the Rockdale County line on January 4, 1898. The community had been named to commemorate the recent gold rush to Klondike in the Yukon Territory. The post office had only two postmasters -- James J. Robertson and Edward C. Powell -- before it was discontinued in April of 1902.

A new store that opened on the Square in Decatur in 1898 had considerably more staying power than the Klondike Post Office. The Weekes Brothers Grocery and General Merchandise Store was a fixture on East Court Square until 1940. Hamilton Weekes was the first of three Weekes brothers to move to Decatur. [39]

The coldest winter temperature ever recorded in DeKalb County, eight degrees below zero, hit in mid-February of 1899, accompanied by four and one-half inches of snow. [40]

An interdenominational Sunday school was organized later in the year in Dunwoody. The Sunday school group would later evolve into the Dunwoody United Methodist Church. The earliest officers of record are those from October 20, 1901: Henry Spruill, superintendent; D. N. Thurmond, assistant superintendent; J. B. Cates, treasurer; Nettie Southern, secretary and chorister; and Columbia Cheek, assistant secretary. Teachers were Columbia Cheek, Joberry Cheek, Laura Puckett and Henry Spruill. The church's first building, costing $500, was built on a lot donated by John Cates. The church remains in the same location today. The first marriage ceremony performed in the church was that of Nettie Southern and Glenn G. Austin in 1906. Mrs. Austin was a popular teacher and principal of Dunwoody Elementary School for many years. [41]

The year, 1898, saw the deaths of Dr. J. J. Cowan, Dr. W. P. Bond and Judge Isaac Newton Wilson. The Rev. Samuel C. Masters, pioneer Methodist minister and legislator, died in 1899 at the age of 90., as did Atlanta and Decatur lawyer William H. Dabney. DeKalb farmer Robert F. Davis was shot and killed by a Negro farm hand in 1899. [42]

At the close of the 19th century, DeKalb County was still a primarily rural county, despite its proximity to the city of Atlanta. The county's fewer than 20,000 residents were spread out over an area of 271 square miles, an average of a spacious 74 square miles per person. Major population centers were the county seat, Decatur, with 1418 residents, Lithonia with 1208 and Stone Mountain with 835.

Three lines of electric railway and the Georgia Railroad linked Decatur and Atlanta.

At the close of the century the county's public school fund contained $11,256.25. There were 2750 students in 55 white public schools, and 1500 students in the county's 17 black public schools.

The total value of real estate and personal property owned by DeKalb citizens was $5,086,306, with 98 percent of that property owned by white residents.

DeKalb farms produced 3,184,985 pounds cotton, 1,167,319 gallons of milk, 331,022 pounds of butter, 167,848 dozen eggs and 21,294 pounds of honey in the closing year of the 1890s. Its farms were home to 300 cows (mostly Jersey), 290 sheep, 5,916 cattle (including 170 working oxen), 1043 horses, 1465 mules, two donkeys, 5746 swine and 74,482 domestic fowls of all kinds. [43]

Chapter 30 Notes

1. Hutcheson, Eleanor S., 1890, U. S. Atlas 1890 and Complete Post Office Directory List of Post Offices.

2. Garrett, Franklin M., 1954, 1969, Atlanta and Environs -- A Chronicle of Its People and Events, Vol. 2, pages 204-206. Nix, Dorothy, personal collection, DeKalb Historical Society.

3. Candler, Charles Murphey, November 9, 1922, "Historical Address." Clarke, Caroline McKinney, 1973, 1997, The Story of Decatur 1823-1899. Garrett, Franklin M., 1954, 1969, Atlanta and Environs -- A Chronicle of Its People and Events, Vol. 2, pages 208-209 and 275.

4. Garrett, Franklin M., 1954, 1969, Atlanta and Environs -- A Chronicle of Its People and Events, Vol. 2, page 214.

5. Garrett, Franklin M., 1954, 1969, Atlanta and Environs -- A Chronicle of Its People and Events, Vol. 2, page 220.

6. Garrett, Franklin M., 1954, 1969, Atlanta and Environs -- A Chronicle of Its People and Events, Vol. 2, pages 209-210 and 221.

7. Author unknown, 1983, "History of Epworth United Methodist Church."

8. Hudgins, Carl T., 1952, "Mills and Other Early DeKalb County Industries (And Their Owners)," the Collections of the DeKalb Historical Society, Vol. 1. Nix, Dorothy, personal collection, DeKalb Historical Society.

9. Garrett, Franklin M., 1954, 1969, Atlanta and Environs -- A Chronicle of Its People and Events, Vol. 2, pages 228-229.

10. Chapman, Ashton, May 21, 1933, "Felton Home To Be Restored," The Atlanta Journal. Garrett, Franklin M., 1954, 1969, Atlanta and Environs -- A Chronicle of Its People and Events, Vol. 2, pages 246, 275.

11. Garrett, Franklin M., 1954, 1969, Atlanta and Environs -- A Chronicle of Its People and Events, Vol. 2, page 272.

12. Nix, Dorothy, personal collection, DeKalb Historical Society.

13. Garrett, Franklin M., 1954, 1969, Atlanta and Environs -- A Chronicle of Its People and Events, Vol. 2, page 252.

14. Garrett, Franklin M., 1954, 1969, Atlanta and Environs -- A Chronicle of Its People and Events, Vol. 2, page 275.

15. Turner, Dewey L., 1986, From Cotton Fields to High Technology in Tucker, Georgia.

16. Garrett, Franklin M., 1954, 1969, Atlanta and Environs -- A Chronicle of Its People and Events, Vol. 2, page 275. Hudgins, Carl T., 1952, "Mills and Other Early DeKalb County Industries (And Their Owners)," the Collections of the DeKalb Historical Society, Vol. 1.

17. Coe, Martha, June 27, 1879, "Avondale Has Grown Up Just Like Willis Wanted," DeKalb News/Sun, page 6G. Garrett, Franklin M., 1954, 1969, Atlanta and Environs -- A Chronicle of Its People and Events, Vol. 2, page 275.

18. Clarke, Caroline McKinney, 1973, 1997, The Story of Decatur 1823-1899.

19. Ordner, Helen, 1989, "Prime Business Site Remembered As Home To Pioneer Houston Family," DeKalb News/Sun. Weaver, J. Calvin, 1951, "100 Years of Medicine in DeKalb County -- 1822-1922."

20. Garrett, Franklin M., 1954, 1969, Atlanta and Environs -- A Chronicle of Its People and Events, Vol. 2, pages 287-288.

21. Ragsdale, Spencer, 1991, "Green Was Olmsted's Color, Ponce de Leon Was His Canvas," DeKalb News/Sun.

22. Nix, Dorothy, personal collection, DeKalb Historical Society.

23. Garrett, Franklin M., 1954, 1969, Atlanta and Environs -- A Chronicle of Its People and Events, Vol. 2, pages 291-292, 304-305, 332 and 343.

24. Garrett, Franklin M., 1954, 1969, Atlanta and Environs -- A Chronicle of Its People and Events, Vol. 2, page 307. Ordner, Helen July 24, 1991, "Gone With The Square," DeKalb News/Sun, page 3B.

25. Garrett, Franklin M., 1954, 1969, Atlanta and Environs -- A Chronicle of Its People and Events, Vol. 2, page 310.

26. Garrett, Franklin M., 1954, 1969, Atlanta and Environs -- A Chronicle of Its People and Events, Vol. 2, pages 312-316.

27. Garrett, Franklin M., 1954, 1969, Atlanta and Environs -- A Chronicle of Its People and Events, Vol. 2, pages 340-341.

28. Garrett, Franklin M., 1954, 1969, Atlanta and Environs -- A Chronicle of Its People and Events, Vol. 2, pages 342-343.

29. Clarke, Caroline McKinney, 1973, 1997, The Story of Decatur 1823-1899. Garrett, Franklin M., 1954, 1969, Atlanta and Environs -- A Chronicle of Its People and Events, Vol. 2, page 348.

30. Garrett, Franklin M., 1954, 1969, Atlanta and Environs -- A Chronicle of Its People and Events, Vol. 2, pages 348-349.

31. McCurdy, Julius Augustus, 1979, The Stone Mountain McCurdys -- The Ancestors and Descendants of John Wilson McCurdy and His Wife, the Former Sarah Jane Carter, and Phillip Burford McCurdy and His Wife, the Former Celia Ann Carter. Old Decatur Courthouse files, DeKalb Historical Society. Stevens, O. B., commissioner, 1901, Georgia Historical and Industrial, Georgia Department of Agriculture.

32. Garrett, Franklin M., 1954, 1969, Atlanta and Environs -- A Chronicle of Its People and Events, Vol. 2, page 349.

33. Clarke, Caroline McKinney, 1973, 1997, The Story of Decatur 1823-1899.
Garrett, Franklin M., 1954, 1969, Atlanta and Environs -- A Chronicle of Its People and Events, Vol. 2, pages 350-351.

34. Hudgins, Carl T., 1952, "Mills and Other Early DeKalb County Industries (And Their Owners)," the Collections of the DeKalb Historical Society, Vol. 1.

35. Garrett, Franklin M., 1954, 1969, Atlanta and Environs -- A Chronicle of Its People and Events, Vol. 2, pages 354-35. Trotti, Louise Haygood, 1952, The Collections of the DeKalb Historical Society, Vol. 1

36. Garrett, Franklin M., 1954, 1969, Atlanta and Environs -- A Chronicle of Its People and Events, Vol. 2, page 354.

37. Garrett, Franklin M., 1954, 1969, Atlanta and Environs -- A Chronicle of Its People and Events, Vol. 2, pages 359-363.

38. Garrett, Franklin M., 1954, 1969, Atlanta and Environs -- A Chronicle of Its People and Events, Vol. 2, pages 368-369.

39. Clarke, Caroline McKinney, 1973, 1997, The Story of Decatur 1823-1899.

40. Garrett, Franklin M., 1954, 1969, Atlanta and Environs -- A Chronicle of Its People and Events, Vol. 2, page 374.

41. Davis, Elizabeth L., and Spruill, Ethel W., 1975, The Story of Dunwoody.

42. Garrett, Franklin M., 1954, 1969, Atlanta and Environs -- A Chronicle of Its People and Events, Vol. 2, pages 371 and 385.

43. Nix, Dorothy, personal collection, DeKalb Historical Society. Stevens, O. B., commissioner, 1901, Georgia Historical and Industrial, Georgia Department of Agriculture, pages 631-632.

🌿 EPILOGUE 🌿

For the first 50 years of the 20th century, DeKalb County would remain a tranquil rural counterpoint to Atlanta's burgeoning metropolis. Nonetheless, the events of years after the turn of the century would be exciting.

That tiny invader, the boll weevil, forced DeKalb farmers to stop depending on cotton. What seemed like a disaster at the time turned out to be the catalyst for a prosperous new era in agriculture. DeKalb became the leading producer of dairy products in the Southeast. Agricultural methods developed by local farmers like R. J. Sams had farmers all across the nation looking to DeKalb for leadership in modern techniques. DeKalb County was described as the "Pearl of the Piedmont."

President Theodore Roosevelt visited Chamblee in 1905, and President-Elect William Howard Taft stopped in Decatur in 1909.

Asa G. Candler began development of his posh Druid Hills subdivision in 1908, with Fredrick Law Olmsted's sons carrying out their father's design for the parks along Ponce de Leon Avenue. Asa's brother, Judge John S. Candler, built the first home in Druid Hills. Asa gave a few acres to another brother, Methodist Bishop Warren A. Candler, for the campus of Emory University, which opened in 1915. Oglethorpe University made a successful comeback that same year, choosing the Brookhaven community for its new home. The school's dynamic president, Dr. Thornwell Jacobs, created a worldwide controversy over his search for the grave of Georgia's founder, James Edward Oglethorpe.

The 61-year saga of the Confederate memorial carving on Stone Mountain began in 1909. Man had to overcome the physical difficulties of creating a three-acre work of art hundreds of feet off the ground, a challenge that could, and did, end in death. Even more complex were the financial problems, mismanagement, politics and personal animosities that plagued the project from beginning to unveiling.

The statue of "Justice" on the cupola of DeKalb's courthouse came crashing down on a night in September, 1916, when the building burned. The granite walls held, and the courthouse was rebuilt. "Justice" was never replaced.

In 1917, the U. S. Army built a city almost overnight at Camp Gordon in north DeKalb. Thousands of soldiers, including the famed Sgt. Alvin York, trained there for the war in Europe.

Crowds gathered on the Square in Decatur on November 9, 1922 to hear Charles Murphey Candler deliver his historic address on the gala occasion of DeKalb's centennial celebration. All Decatur watched breathlessly two years later as Dr. Washington J. Houston accomplished a dramatic rescue of workmen from the city water tank.

The story of Louie and Dock, DeKalb's fearless crime fighters, was the stuff of ballads. Their big black Lincoln was the only car on the road that could catch the moonshiners that plagued the county in 1927. On an icy night in January, that Lincoln became their coffin.

The Ku Klux Klan raised its ugly head in the 1930s. Their burning crosses atop Stone Mountain could be seen for miles around. Tobie Kendall Grant, the daughter of a slave fortune-teller, was not intimidated. "If any of them Ku Kluxers come Klucking around here, I'll put a hex on 'em," she said.

Scott Candler was elected county commissioner in 1939. His progressive improvements and unique vision for the county earned him the title of "Mr. DeKalb."

Soldiers returned to DeKalb in 1941, transforming old Camp Gordon into the Naval Air Station, where pilots would train for World War II. The post-war years saw tremendous growth in DeKalb County, including the organization of the DeKalb Historical Society in 1947.

Most recent history has seen DeKalb County move from being a sleepy country place to Atlanta's "bedroom community" to an economically and socially diverse county looking forward to the 21st century.

Appendices

TABLE OF CONTENTS

APPENDICES	i
Appendix 1: Land Lottery Grantees	ii
Appendix 2: Government Officials	ix
Appendix 3: Justices of the Peace	xix
Appendix 4: Militia Officers	xxi
Appendix 5: 1830 Census Index	xxv
Appendix 6: 1850 Census Index	xxxix
Appendix 7: 1860 Slaveholders	lxiii
Appendix 8: Confederate Companies	lxvii
Appendix 9: Timeline	lxxix
Appendix 10: Historic Places	lxxxiii

Appendix 1

Original Land Lottery Grantees in the 14th District of Henry (later DeKalb and Fulton) County, Ga.

ADAMS, Miles
ADAMS, William
ALEXANDER, John
ANDREWS, David
ANTONIO, Charles
ARCHER, Thomas
ARNOLD, Charley
AXSON, Samuel I.

BACHLOTT Sr., John
BACON, Nicholas H.
BAILEY, Dawson
BAKER, Jean (wid.)
BARNES, Lewis B.
BARTLETT, Myron
BATES, Daniel
BEARD, John
BEASLEY, William M.
BECKMAN, Benjamin
BENTON, Jeremiah
BOATRIGHT, John
BOGAN, Elizabeth (wid.)
BRADDY, Lennear
BROCK, John
BROOKS, Brooks
BROWN, Henry
BROWN, Robert
BRYANT, James (orp.)
BUCKLEY, James K.
BUSTIAN, William

CALDER, John
CALHOUN, Jasper
CALLAHAN, Moses L.
CAMPBELL, Thomas
CANNON, Hugh
CAREY, Alex
CARSON, John E.
CARTER, John R. C.
CARTER, Winnefred
CASTLEBERRY, John

CASY, Ausbun I.
CHAMPEON, Murphy
CHANCE, Mason
CHRISTLER, Wesley
CLAREY, Jeremiah
CLARK, Johnson
CLEMENTS, Polly (wid.)
COLMAN, Hezekiah
COOK, Benjamin
CRAFT, Garrett
CRAIG, William
CREWS, Martin

DANIELS, David
DAVID, Jacob W.
DAVIDSON, Isham
DAVIS, James G.
DAVIS, Richard
DEADWYLER, Martin
DELISLE, John G.
DIBY, Joseph (orp.)
DICKEN, Elizabeth (wid.)
DICKEY, Robert
DISMUKES, William
DISMUKES, William
DIXON, William
DORE, Endicott F.
DOSS, Jane (wid.)
DOUGLAS, Eaton
DUFFIE, William
DUNN, Jesse
DURHAM, Nancy (wid.)
DYKES, Elias

ECHOLS, J. D.
EDGAR, Absolom
EDINFIELD, John
EDWARDS, Penelope (wid.)
ELLIS, Stephen
EMANUEL, L. B.

ETHERIDGE, Thankful (wid.)

FENNEL, Dempsey
FINCH, Charles
FIRK, Charles
FLOYD, Joseph
FORD, William
FUN, Paul
FURHARD, James

GARNER, Thomas W.
GARTRELL, John (orp.)
GENTRY, Elisha
GILBERT, Charity (wid.)
GLASCOCK, Thomas
GLOVER, John P.
GOARE, Robert
GOVENSTEIN, Mary (wid.)
GREEN Sr., James
GREENE, Pleasant
GRIFFIN, Dempsey
GRIFFIN, Lewis L.
GRUBBS, J.
GUISE, Thomas

HALE, Nancy (wid.)
HALE, Mary (wid.)
HAMILTON, Pierce
HARDEGREE, Pleasant
HARRIS, Amos
HARRIS, Jesse (orp.)
HARRIS, L. F.
HARVEY, Jonathan
HATHORN, Jane (wid.)
HAYLES, John
HAYMEN Sr., Stowten
HAYSLIP, Lot W.
HEARD, Bernard (wid.)
HEARN, Elisha
HENRY, Henderson

HERRIN, Ann (wid.)
HOLLANDS, Archibald
HOLLY, Alex. P.
HORTON, John
HOWARD, Nathan
HOYTON, Sarah L.
HULL, Ann (wid.)
HUNNINGTON, Alfred I.
HUSTON, John
IVEY, Elias
IVIE, Benjamin

JACKSON, William
JARRETT, Thomas
JARRETT, Thomas
JENKINS, Daniel
JENKINS, Susannah (wid.)
JOHNSTON, Isham
JONES, Gabriel
JONES, Henry
JONES, Weldon
JORDAN Sr., Benjamin
JORDAN, Zachariah
JUSTICE, John

KAPMAN, Joseph
KELLEY, Morris (orp.)
KELLY, Edward
KENNINGTON, John

LANE, Jesse
LANE, William
LARD, Robert
LEVERETT, John R.
LILES, Pleasant
LINSEY, Ephria (orp.)
LITTLE, William
LYNCH, Berry E.

MAGBY/MAGBEE, Laban
MALONE Sr., William
MANLEY, Isaac D.
MANLEY, John T.
MARSH, Robert
MASONS, John (orp.)
MAUYAN, James
MC CAY, Charlotte (wid.)
MC COY, Henry

MC CRARY, John
MC CUNE, Joseph
MC KEE, Thomas
MC NIEL, James
MILLER, Peter Samuel
MITCHELL, John
MOORE, James R.
MOTE, Silas
MURPHY, Robert

NEATHERLIN, William
NELSON, David D.
NOBLES, Thomas

ORR, Jonathan

PADGETT, Elisha (orp.)
PADGETT, William
PATRICK, William (orp.)
PATTEN, John
PEARMAN, Sterling
PENNY, Alford
PETTYJOHN, William
PIERCE, Jacob W.
PONDER, James
POPE, John
POSEY, Thomas
POURRIA, Peter
POWELL, Sion
PRITCHARD, John B.

RAGAN, Jeremiah
RANSOME, Chivears
RATTEREE, A.
REDMOND, Robert
RICHARDSON, George
ROBERTS, Betsy (wid.)
ROBERTS, Willis
ROGERS, Ellis
ROBINSON, Abel L.

SAFFOLD, Catherine (wid.)
SAMFORD, Thomas
SANDERS, Jordan
SCOGGINS, Sanders I.
SCOTT, Absolam
SCOTT, Richard (orp.)
SEGARS, Mary (wid.)

SHELTON, Savannah
SHEPARD, Joshua
SHERMAN, Clement
SHORT, David (orp.)
SLEDGE, Whitefield
SMITH, Andrew
SMITH, Isabel
SMITH Jr., John
SMITH, Rollins
SMITH, William
SNOW, Fountain
STAFFORD, Robert
STEELE, J. A. and S. E. D.
STEELY, Hukel
STILES, Benjamin E.
SWANSON, Lemuel
SWIFT, John N.
SWITZER, Williamson
TAYLOR, Taylor
TERONDET, James C.
TERRELL, Sarah A. (wid.)
TERRY, Richard
THOMAS, Bernard G.
THOMAS, Stephen
THORNTON, Reuben (orp.)
THWEATT, Thomas
TOLBERT, Frederick G.
TUDER, Thomas
TURNER, Green B.

VEITCH, Walter
WALLER, John T.
WARD, Enos W.
WARD, Leonard
WATSON, Claiborn
WAYNE, James M.
WELCH, George W.
WELLS, Thomas
WEST, John West (orp.)
WESTMORELAND, John
WICKER, John A.
WIGLEY, Nancy (wid.)
WILKINSON, Sidney
WILLIAMS, George
WILLIAMS, George
WILLIS, Jonathan W.
WILSON, James (orp.)
WIMBERLY, Zachariah

WINGATE, Richard B.
WISE, John
WOODALL, Martin

WOODRUFF, Littleberry

YARBROUGH, Randall

YOUNG, Marmaduke N.

ZACHRY, William [1]

Original Land Lottery Grantees in the 15th and 18th Districts of Henry (later DeKalb) County, Ga. [1] [2]

ADAMS, Samuel R.
AKIN, John
AKINS, Thomas J.
ALDERMAN, David
ALFORD, Erasmus
ALLBRIGHT, Joseph
ALLEN, Lucretia (wid.)
ALLEN, William
ALLIN, Elizabeth J. (wid.)
ANDREWS, Owen Jr.
ARNOLD, Salmond
ARNOLD, Sumner W.
ARNOLD, William
ASHLEY, Robert
ASKEW, James L.
ATCHISON, John
ATKINSON, James

BACON, Thomas D.
BAGLEY, Ranson T.
BAILEY, Caty (wid.)
BAILEY, William
BAINES, John
BAKER, William
BALDWIN, Anderson
BALDWIN, john
BALDWIN, John
BALLARD, Nancy
BANKS, Nathaniel
BARRETTE, John
BASINGER, Elizabeth (wid.)
BASKINS, William O.

BAZEMORE, Blunt (orp.)
BEAL, Richard K. (orp.)
BECK, Samuel
BELL, Bazdell
BELL, George
BELL, Olive T. (wid.)
BELM, William F. (orp.)
BISHOP, William (orp.)
BLAND, William
BLEDSOE, Margaret (wid.)
BOLTON, Langston
BOMAN, Thomas
BOND, Easom
BOND, Gabriel
BOWEN, Nathan (orp.)
BOX, Phillip M. (orp.)
BOX, Shadrock (orp.)
BOYD, James (orp.)
BRADDY, John
BRADY, Samuel Jr.
BRANTLEY, Ann
BRASSELTON, Reubin
BREWAR, James
BREWER, Barrett
BREWER, Randal
BRIDGES, Hardy
BRITT, Joel
BRITTON, Henry L.
BRITTON, Stephen
BROOK, Sarah (wid.)
BROWN, Dempsey
BROWN, Elijah
BROWN, Jesse Sr.

BROWN, John
BROWN, Philip
BROWN, Robert
BROWN, Uriah
BRUTON, Benjamin
BURDELL, Humphreys (orp.)
BURNETT, Robert (orp.)
BURNS, Robert
BURNS, William
BURTON, William
BUTLER, Macksill
BUTLER, Samuel
BUTT, Joseph J.
BYNE, George

CALHOUN, James
CALHOUN, John L.
CANE, James
CANNADY, Henry Jr.
CANNON, Edward
CANNON, Ricahrd
CARLETON, Eliza (orp. Jacob)
CARR, James
CARRELL, James
CARTER, Elizabeth (wid.)
CARTER, Jacob
CARTER, Wiley
CHADBOURN, Jacob
CHEVERS, Abner
CHILDS, Elisha
CHURCHWELL, James

---

[1] Free, white males older than the age of 18, widows and orphans each were allowed one draw in the lottery.

[2] Although many "fortunate drawers" did not take up their lots, the reader will doubtless recognize names of families who did settle in DeKalb.

CLAY, Eve (wid.)
CLEMENTS, John (orp.)
COBB, Jacob
COBB, Wiley
COCHRAN, William
COCKRAN, Hugh
COLEMAN, Harriett (wid.)
COLLINS, John
COLLINS, Joseph
COLLY, James Jr.
CONE, Joseph
CONE, William
COOK, Arthur (orp.)
COOK, Francis
COOK, Phillip
COOKE, John G.
COOPER, Arthur
COOPER, Henry
COOPER, Mary A.
COPE, John
CORNWALL, Daniel
COSBY, Nancy (wid.)
COUCH, Benjamin
COXE, Thomas I.
CRAPON, P. H.
CRAVEY, James (orp.)
CRAWFORD, Thomas
CRAWFORD, William H.
CREAMMER, Hugh S.
CRENSHAW, James
CROPPEE, Edward
CURTIS, Sampson

DANIEL, Elizabeth (wid.)
DANIEL, Matthew
DARDEN, James
DAVIS, Thomas (orp.)
DAVIS, William
DAY, Charles
DAY, Zachariah
DEAN, Also
DEAN, Silas
DEES, Thomas
DENMARK, Redding (orp.)
DENNARD, Isaac
DENNIS, Mathias
DENT, Mary M. (wid.)
DOMINY, James (orp.)

DORSEY, Seth
DOTTONS (orp.)
DOUGLASS, John
DOYLE, Francis
DREW, Asa
DRIGORS, William
DRISKELL, William
DUNAWAY, William
DUNLAVEY, Daniel
DUNN, James
DUPREE, Jessee
SURHAM, Samuel D.
DYER, Martin
DYKES, William

EAKEN, Jane (wid.)
EARNEST, Elisha C.
EASON, Whitmill
EASTERLING, Shadrack
ECHOLS, Mary (wid.)
EDMONDS, Anthony
EDMONDS, Henry
EDWARDS, Asa
EDWARDS, Henry L.
ELDER, Joseph M.
ELKINS, William
ELLIOTT, James (s/Geo.)
ELLIOTT, Thomas
ELTON, Anthony M.
EXLEY, Solomon

FAGG, Thomas M.
FAIN, John
FAIRCLOTH, Benjamin
FAIRCLOTH, Thomas
FALLIN, Charles Sr.
FANIN, Lauchlan Jr.
(Elbert)
FARMER, John
FAVOR, John
FERRELL, John
FINNEL, Ann (wid.)
FLEMING, William W.
FLEWELLEN, Ann (wid.)
FLINE, Augustus
FLOYD, Margaret (wid.)
FOREST, Martin
FORT, Owen C.

FOSTER, John D. L.
FOSTER, Richard
FOX, Josiah (orp.)
FRANKLIN, Easum D.
FREEMAN, Tyre
FRYER, Ryan
FULLER, Aphred
FURGASON, William H.

GAINES, Levingston P.
GAMBLE, John Sr. (orp.)
GARLINGTON, James
GARNER, John
GARRETT, Samuel T.
GAUDRI, John B.
GAULDING, Thomas (Rev.)
GEORGE, Tunstall B.
GILBERT, Jesse
GILBERT, John F.
GILLOM, Suky C. (wid.)
GILMORE, John H.
GILMORE, John H.
GLASS, Thomas Jr.
GLAZE, Samuel
GLAZA, Susannah (wid.)
GLORE, Asa
GNANN, Solomon (s/And.)
GODFERY, Thomas
GODIN, William
GOODSON, Jordan
GOOLSBY, John Sr.
GRAHAM, Archibald
GRAHAM, Joseph (orp.)
GRANAD, Martin
GREEN, Mary (wid.)
GRESHAM, Josiah
GRESHAM, Sterling
GRIFFIN, Thomas
GRISUP, James

HAIESLEY, William
HALL, John W.
HAMBLETON, Solomon
HAMBLETON, Stewart
HAMP, Benjamin
HANCOCK, John
HANCOCK, John
HANNAH, Thomas

HARKINS, William
HARRIS, Benjamin
HARRIS, John
HARRIS, William
HARRISON, David
HARRISON, Joseph
HARRISON, Samuel (Capt.)
HARRISS, Mary Ann (wid.)
HATTOX, John
HAUK, Andrew
HAWK, Thomas
HAY, John E. (orp.)
HEARD, John
HELDEBRAND, William
HERREDGE, John
HESTERLY, Francis
HICKS, Daniel
HILL, Mordica
HILL, Samuel B.
HILLIARD, Silas
HOLCOMB, Henry D.
HOLLAND, William R.
HOLLINS, James
HOLLOWAY, William
HOLMES, Adam T.
HOOPER, Joicy (wid.)
HOPPS, Richard (orp.)
HORN, Joel
HOUSE, James
HOWIT, Georgie W. (orp.)
HOYLE, William S.
HUDSON, Charles
HUNT, George
HURST, James
HUTCHENS, William
HUTSON, James
HUTSON, Sarah (wid.)
HUTTO, John

IRWIN, Prudence (wid.)
IRWIN, Robert

JACK, Harriot (wid.)
JACKSON, Burk
JACKSON, Luke
JACKSON, Peter Jr.
JACO, Philip
JAMES, Stephen

JARRETT, Peter
JEMISON, John
JOBSON, Francis W.
JOHNS, John
JOHNSON, Burrell
JOHNSON, Henry
JOHNSON, Locklin
JOHNSON, Nancy L. (orp.)
JOHNSON, Robert (orp.)
JOHNSON, Thomas
JOHNSON, Lodowick
JOHNSTON, William
JONES, Edward
JONES, Josiah W.
JONES, Lucy (wid.)
JOWELL, Mark M. R.
JOYCE, Henry
JOYCE, Sabrim (wid.)

KEINNER, Henry
KELLEY, Marvel
KELLY, William
KENNEDY, Francis (orp.)
KILBY, William
KING, Amos
KING, William
KINGERY, Daniel H.
KNIGHT, John

LAIN, Daniel T.
LAMB, John
LANDRUM, Jacob
LANE, Joseph
LATHAM, Henry
LAW, William
LAWSON, David
LE CROY, John
LEE, Eaton
LEE, Margaret (orp.)
LEE, Oliver (orp.)
LEE, Peter (orp.)
LEWIS, Nathaniel
LIGON, Henry
LILES, John
LINDSEY, Caleb
LINDSEY, Phebe (wid.)
LINEBAUGH, Cutlip
LINSEY, Nelson

LITTLE, Uriah
LIVELY, Luke W.
LLOYD, Virginia (orp.)
LOCKETT, Green H.
LOCKLIN, Samuel
LODGE, John
LONG, Philip
LOW, William
LUCAS, John M.
LUMPKIN, George W.
LUMPKIN, George
LYON, Thomas

MAGNOURK, Benjamin
MALONE, Daniel
MALONE, Robert
MALPER, John H.
MARABLE, George
MARK, Joseph (orp.)
MASON, Alex (orp.)
MATHEWS, Allen
MATHEWS, Joshua W.
MAYS, William
MC BRIDE, Andrew
MC CAND, Charles
MC CLENDON, Joel
MC CLENDON, John Sr.
MC CLOUD, James and John M. (orp.)
MC CLOUD, William and Simeon (orp.)
MC CORD, James
MC COY, Ann (wid.)
MC CROMICK, Matthias
MC DANIEL, John
MC DANIEL, John
MC DONALD, Braddock
MC DONALD, Charles (orp.)
MC FARLIN, Charles
MC KUNE, Jamison M. (orp.)
MC MICHAEL, William
MEACHAM, Henry Sr.
MILLICAN, Andrew
MILLICAN, Robert
MITCHELL, Green
MONROE, John

MORDEICA, Sampson
MORGAN, Stokely
MORIN, John
MORRIS, Isaac
MORRIS, John
MORRIS, Thomas
MULKEY, Jonathan
MULLIN, Eleanor (wid.)
MUNCURS, Benjamin
MURPHY, Sarah (wid.)
MURREY, Jehu
MURRY, John (orp.)
MYERS, Lewis
MYHAND, James

NICHOLS, Ambers
NIXON, Evey (wid.)
NORMAN, William
NORTHEART, Alexander
NUNNALLY, William B.
NUTT, John (orp.)

OTWELL, William M.

PACE, William (JP)
PARAMORE, William H.
PARKER, James
PARKER, John
PARKMAN, Samuel B.
PATE, Thomas D.
PAYNE, Edwin
PERMENTER, Susannah (wid.)
PERSON, Samuel (orp.)
PETERS, William M.
PETREE, John G.
PHILBRICK, Samuel
PHILLIPS, Martin (orp.)
PHILLIPS, Sally (wid.)
PIELLE, Reubin
POE, John
POPE, James
PRITCHARD, Sterling L.
PRUETT, Jacob Jr.
PURVISE, William

RAGLAND, Abner
RATCLIFF, Mark

RAY, Elizabeth (wid.)
REAVES, Thomas
REDD, Charles A.
REDFIELD, Elias
REEVES, John
REGDON, Stephen
RENTFROE, Ephraim
REYNOLDS, George
RICE, Leonard
RICHARDSON, Jacob
RIGGINS, Thomas
RIGGINS, Thomas
ROBERTS, Robert
ROBERTSON, Abner P.
RODDENBERRY, Richard
RODGERS, Isaac
RODGERS, Ledford
ROGERS, Hesekiah
ROGERS, James P.
ROWLAND, Nathan
RUFF, Stephen
RUFF, William
RUSHIN, Sarah
RUSSEL, Mary (wid.)

SALTER, Mary
SANDERS, Isaac
SANKEY, William D.
SAPP, Jason
SAPP, Wyley
SAWYER, Charles
SCHRODER, Shadrack (orp.)
SCOTT, William Jr.
SEALS, Arnold
SEARS, Frederick
SECKINGER, Benjamin
SELF, Rebecca (wid.)
SHADROCK, Mary Ann (wid.)
SHARYER, William
SHAW, Thomas B.
SHEERWOOD, Benjamin
SHEPPEARD, Jacob Jr.
SHIVER, Fleming
SHUFFIEL, Austin (orp.)
SHUFFIELD, Isham
SIMMONS, Thomas C.

SKINNER, Charles
SLAUGHTER, Augustin
SMITH, Andrew A.
SMITH, Dred
SMITH, Gilham M.
SMITH, James
SMITH, James
SMITH, John P.
SMITH, John Sr.
SMITH, Joseph
SMITH, Robert S. Jr.
SMITH, Sidney
SMITH, Wiley
SOLEY, William
SORROW, George P.
SPEARS, Messer
SPENCE, Aaron (orp.)
SPIVY, Mary (wid.)
SPRATLEN, Jesse
STARNES, Frederick Sr.
STEPHENS, John
STEWART, James B.
STEWART, Joseph
STIBBINS, Catharine (wid.)
STILES, Joseph C.
STILES, Richard Wayne
STIMPSON, James
STINSON, Michael
STONE, Henry
STONE, Walter
STOWERS, Thomas
STUART, John S.
SUGGS, John
SUMMERILEN, Henry
SUMNER, Sumner
SURRENCY, Elizabeth (wid.)
SURRENCY, James D. Jr.
SUTTON, Margery (wid.)
SWINNEY, Rossey (wid.)

TAFF, William
TAFF, William B.
TAFT, Oray
TANNER, William H.
TAYLOR, Abralom
TAYLOR, Angalina (wid.)
TAYLOR, Bartholomew

TAYLOR, James
TAYLOR, William S.
THOMAS, Benjamin (orp.)
THOMAS, William
THOMPSON, David
THOMPSON, Randal
THOMPSON, William
THORNTON, Isaac
TILLMAN, John
TISON, Calvin
TOMLINSON, William
TOWNS, Bartlett
TRAWICKS, Robert (orp.)
TRICE, William Jr.
TUCKER, Elizabeth (wid.)
TURNER, Bartholomew
TURNER, John M.

UMPHRES, Uriah

VEASEY, Abner
VEAZEY, Thomas

WADE, Joshua A.

WALKER, Henry
WALKER, Samuel Jr.
WALL, David
WARD, Francis (orp.)
WARREN, Allen (orp.)
WATKINS, Benjamin T.
WATKINS, John D.
WATKINS, Phillip
WATKINS, Thomas A.
WATKINS, William
WEEKS, Bartemus
WEST, Elizabeth (wid.)
WEST, William
WHEELER, Thomas
WHITE, Alexander
WHITE, John
WHITE, Zachariah
WHITEHEAD, Amos P.
WHITEHEAD, Benjamin
WHITEHEAD, Reason
WHITMAN, John L.
WILKERSON, Carter
WILKS, Nancy (orp.)
WILLIAMS, Jemima (wid.)

WILLS, John
WILLS, Jonathan
WILLS, William D. (orp.)
WILLS, Zechariah
WILLIS, Britton
WILLIS, Henry
WILSON, Bennet
WILSON, Eaton P.
WILSON, William L.
WINN, Allen B.
WOLF, David
WOOD, Demcy Jr.
WOODALL, Abner
WRIGHT, Charles
WRIGHT, Christiana
WRIGHT, James
WYATT, Joseph

YORK, Solomon
YOUNG, Daniel
YOUNG, Mary A. (orp.)
YOUNG, Nancy M. (orp.)
YOUNGBLOOD, Asa
YOUNGBLOOD, Bossell [2]

Appendix 2

First DeKalb County Government Officers
(commissioned from Fayette County on March 18, 1822)

John S. Welch, sheriff
Thomas A. Dobbs, clerk of Superior Court
Jonathan Dobbs, clerk of the Inferior Court
John Calhoun, coroner
James Adams, surveyor [3] [3]

DeKalb County Sheriffs

March 18, 1822-May 31, 1823	John S. Welch
May 31, 1823-January 15, 1824	Lochlin Johnson
January 15, 1824-January 15, 1826	George Harris
January 15, 1826-January 15, 1828	David R. Sullivan
January 15, 1828-January 15, 1830	John Brown
January 15, 1830-January 9, 1832	Isaac N. Johnson
January 9, 1832-February 15, 1833	John Brown
February 15, 1833-January 10, 1834	Dr. Chapman Powell
January 10, 1834-January 10, 1836	Isaac Johnson
January 10, 1836-January 10, 1840	Shadrick (Shadrach) Farmer
January 10, 1840-January 8, 1842	John Jones
January 8, 1842-January 8, 1844	John W. Fowler
January 8, 1844-January 8, 1846	Spencer P. Wright
January 8, 1846-January 22, 1848	Thomas Perkerson
January 22, 1848-January 12, 1850	John Jones
January 12, 1850-January 16, 1851	Allen E. Johnson
January 16, 1851-January 8, 1852	Edwin G. Collier
January 8, 1852-January 10, 1854	Thomas J. Perkerson
January 10, 1854-January 12, 1856	Spencer P. Wright
January 12, 1856-January, 1858	John W. Fowler
January, 1858-February, 1860	John Y. Flowers
February, 1860-January, 1862	William Wright
February, 1860-January, 1862	James Oliver Powell
January, 1864-January 22, 1866	Oliver Winningham
January 22, 1866-August 8, 1868	James Oliver Powell
August 8, 1868-February, 1871	James R. Smith
January, 1871-January 3, 1873	James Hunter
January 3, 1873-January, 1875	John Baxter
January, 1875-February 8, 1887	James Hunter
January 8, 1887-1898	Henry C. Austin
January, 1898-January, 1902	C. H. Talley
January, 1902-January, 1908	E. O. Reagin

---

[3] All served until January 15, 1824, except Welch who resigned May 31, 1823 and was succeeded by Lochlin Johnson.

January, 1908-January, 1912   B. A. Morris
January, 1912-January, 1924   J. A. McCurdy [4] [5]

DeKalb County Clerks Of Superior Court

1822 Thomas A. Dobbs	1860 T. R. Hoyle	1900 Henry H. Burgess
1824 Thomas A. Dobbs	1862 John M. Hawkins	1902 Henry H. Burgess, dec.
1826 Daniel Stone	1864 John M. Hawkins	1903 Benjamin F. Burgess
1828 Daniel Stone	1866 John M. Hawkins	1904 R. J. Freeman
1830 Daniel Stone	1868 H. J. Williams	1906 Benjamin F. Burgess
1832 Charles Murphey	1870/1 H. J. Williams	1908 Benjamin F. Burgess
1834 John Glen	1873 H. J. Williams	1910 Benjamin B. Burgess
1836 John Glen	1875 H. J. Williams	1912 Benjamin F. Burgess
1838 John Glen	1877 J. R. Russell	1914 Benjamin F. Burgess
1840 John Glen	1879 J. R. Russell	1916 Benjamin F. Burgess
1842 John Glen	1881 J. R. Russell	1918
1844 John Glen	1883 J. R. Russell	1920
1846 Daniel Stone	1885 J. R. Russell	1923 B. F. Burgess
1848 Robert M. Brown	1887 J. R. Russell	1925 B. F. Burgess
1850 Robert M. Brown	1889 Henry H. Burgess	1927 B. F. Burgess
1850 Robert M. Brown	1891 Henry H. Burgess	1929 B. F. Burgess
1852 Robert M. Brown	1893 Henry H. Burgess	1931 B. F. Burgess
1854 Robert M. Brown	1895 Henry H. Burgess	1933 B. F. Burgess
1856 Robert M. Brown	1896 Henry H. Burgess	1935 B. F. Burgess
1858	1898 Henry H. Burgess	1936-1969 Ben B. Burgess [4]

DeKalb County Clerks Of Inferior Court/Ordinary Court Clerks [6]

Inferior Court Clerk	1844 Elzy B. Reynolds	1860 K. A. Russell
1822 Jonathan Dobbs	1846 Henry B. Latimer	1862 James Oliver Powell
1824 Daniel Stone	1848 Alexander Johnson	1864 John M. Hawkins
1826 Charles Murphey	1850 Alexander Johnson	1866 John M. Hawkins
1828 Charles Murphey	**Ordinary Court Clerk**	**Ordinary Court Clerk**
1832 Elzy B. Reynolds	1852 Alexander Johnson	1867 Thomas Hoyle
1834 Elzy B. Reynolds	1854 Alexander Johnson	1868 James S. Wilson
1836 Elzy B. Reynolds	1856 Alexander Johnson	1871 Walter Webster
1838	1858 Alexander Johnson	1873 John B. Steward
1840 Elzy B. Reynolds	1860 J. B. Wilson	1875 John B. Steward
1842 Elzy B. Reynolds	**Inferior Court Clerk**	1877 H. V. Bayne

---

[4] DeKalb County Sheriff's Department records also show that James Mc. Montgomery served as sheriff from 1834 to 1836. <u>Memoirs of Georgia</u>, Vol. 1 (1895, The Southern Historical Association) shows that Charles Melton Jones was sheriff of DeKalb County before the Civil War.

[5] DeKalb Historical Society files and McCurdy family history records show that J. A. McCurdy died in office April 22, 1928.

[6] E. Katherine Anderson, in her sketch of James McConnell Montgomery, wrote that he was clerk of the DeKalb Court of Ordinary in 1823 and kept the records in books he bought himself until the Inferior Court appropriated $5. (Source: December, 1937, Atlanta Historical Bulletin, No. 12.)

1879 H. V. Bayne
1881 John B. Steward
1883 John B. Steward
1885 John B. Steward
1887 John B. Steward
1889 William R. Ragsdale
1891 William R. Ragsdale
1893 William R. Ragsdale
1895 William R. Ragsdale
1896 William R. Ragsdale
1898 William R. Ragsdale
1900 William R. Ragsdale
1902 William R. Ragsdale, dec.
1904 James R. George
1906 James R. George
1908 James R. George
1910 James R. George
1912 James R. George
1914 James R. George
1916 James R. George
1918
1920
1923 James R. George
1925-47 V. S. Morgan [5]

Original Justices of The DeKalb County Inferior Court
Charles Gates Sr. • Joseph D. Shumate • William Baker
(commissioned February 6, 1822 in Fayette, retained in DeKalb)
Andrew Camp • Absalom Steward
(commissioned March 4, 1822 in Henry, retained in DeKalb) [6]

Justices Of The DeKalb County Inferior Court
with date of commission

George Clifton, May 31, 1823
Joseph Morris, June 7, 1824
Joseph Morris, January 27, 1825
George Clifton, January 27, 1825
William Correy, January 27, 1825
William Towers, January 27, 1825
John Reid, February 14, 1826
James Paden, October 29, 1827
James Lemon, January 21, 1828
William Latimer, July 18, 1828
James Lemmon, January 16, 1829
James Paden, January 16, 1829
John Jennings, January 16, 1829
Thomas Ray, January 16, 1829
George Clifton, January 16, 1829
John Dobbs, January 10, 1833
Thomas Ray, January 10, 1833
Edward Jones, January 10, 1833
Moses Murphey, January 10, 1833
Lodowick Tuggle, January 10, 1833
John McCulloch, April 10, 1834
James Lemon, February 12, 1835
Isaac N. Johnson, February 6, 1836
Isaac N. Johnson, January 10, 1837
Lochlin Johnson, January 10, 1837
James Lemon, January 10, 1837
Lodowick Tuggle, January 10, 1837
John N. Ballinger, January 10, 1837
Robert Jones, January 25, 1838
William Johnston, January 14, 1841

David D. Anderson, January 14 1841
William Hairston, January 14, 1841
John N. Ballinger, January 15, 1845
William Hairston, January 15, 1845
Lawrence S. Morgan, January 15, 1845
Ezekiel A. Davis, January 15, 1845
Lochlin Johnson, January 15, 1845
John N. Bellinger, January 4, 1849
Ezekiel A. Davis, January 4, 1849
Lawrence S. Morgan, January 4, 1849
James A. Hayden, January 4, 1849
Peter F. Hoyle, January 4, 1849
Peter F. Hoyle, January 8, 1853
James Payden, January 8, 1853
J. A. Hayden, January 8, 1853
S. G. Howell, January 8, 1853
Stephen Terry, January 8, 1853
William A. Powell, January 5, 1854
John Bryce, March 16, 1854
Simeon Smith, March 16, 1854
Berry Ragsdale, January 12, 1857
Daniel Johnson, January 12, 1857
Thomas J. Dean, July 1, 1859
E. J. Bailey, July 1, 1859
P. F. Hoyle, January 10, 1861
E. J. Bailey, January 10, 1861
T. J. Dean, January 10, 1861
Z. R. Jones, January 10, 1861
C. W. McGinnis, January 10, 1861 [7]

DeKalb County Coroners

1822 John Calhoun	1860	1900 R. E. Jones
1824 Willeford Grogan	1862 William Wilson	1902 T. C. Robertson
1826 Larkin Carlton	1864 John B. Wommack	1904 R. E. Jones
1828 Larkin Carlton	1866 H. R. Jackson	1906 R. E. Jones
1830 William Carson/ William Gresham	1868 Henry Jackson	1908 R. E. Jones
1832 Joel Morton	1871 William Dickerson	1910 R. E. Jones
1834 Joel Morton	1873 William Dickerson	1912 R. E. Jones
1836 Joel Morton	1875 M. A. Veal	1914 R. E. Jones
1838	1877 T. L. Evans	1916 R. E. Jones
1840 William Betts	1879 T. L. Evans	1918
1842 Joel Morton	1881 T. L. Evans	1920
1844 Moses D. Harris	1883 Morgan Veal	1923 R. M. Thompson
1846 William Johnson	1885 Morgan Veal	1925 E. Thomas
1848 William Johnson	1887 W. R. Hurst	1927 Emsil Thomas
1850 William Johnson	1889 Henry Gentry	1929 Emsil Thomas
1852 William Johnson	1891 R. E. Jones	1931 Emsil Thomas
1854 William Johnson	1893 R. E. Jones	1933 E. Thomas
1856 John Hawkins	1895 R. E. Jones	1935 E. Thomas
1858 Robert M. Wilson	1896 R. E. Jones	1937 E. Thomas
	1898 R. E. Jones	1939-43 Paul O. Estes [8]

DeKalb County Surveyors

1822 James Adams	1862	1902 T. C. Jackson
1824 Bennet Conine	1864 Robert Jones	1904 C. S. Mercer
1826 James Anderson	1866 Robert Jones	1906 C. S. Mercer
1828 James Anderson	1868 Robert Jones	1908 C. S. Mercer
1830 James Anderson	1871 E. M. Kittridge	1910 Thomas C. Jackson
1832 James Anderson	1873 E. M. Kittridge	1912 Thomas C. Jackson
1834	1875 Frank L. Guess	1914 Thomas C. Jackson
1836 Samford Gorham	1877 Frank L. Guess	1916 M. F. Mable
1838	1879 E. M. Kittridge	1918
1840 Palmer R. Phillips	1881 E. M. Kittridge	1920
1842	1883 Frank L. Guess	1923 M. F. Marble
1844 John Morse	1885 Frank L. Guess	1925 M. F. Marble
1846 Stephen Terry	1887 Frank L. Guess	1927 M. F. Marble
1848 Stephen Terry	1889 Frank L. Guess	1929 M. F. Marble
1850 Robert Jones	1891 Frank L. Guess	1931 M. F. Marble
1852 Malcolm McLeod	1893 Frank L. Guess	1933 T. O. Jackson
1854 Robert Jones	1895 Frank L. Guess	1935 T. O. Jackson
1856 Robert Jones	1896 Frank L. Guess	1937 T. O. Jackson
1858	1898 T. C. Jackson	1939-43 T. O. Jackson [9]
1860	1900 T. C. Jackson	

DeKalb County Treasurers

1822	1828	1834
1824	1830	1836 James Lemon
1826	1832	1838

1840
1842
1844
1846
1848
1850
1852
1854
1856
1858
1860
1862
1864 Levi Willard

1866 John N. Pate
1868 John N. Pate
1871 John N. Pate
1873 Robert Nones
1875 J. R. McAllister
1877 J. R. McAllister
1879 J. R. McAllister
1881 J. R. McAllister
1883 J. R. McAllister
1885 J. R. McAllister
1887 J. G. Rankin
1889 James A. Mason
1891 James A. Mason

1893 James A. Mason
1895 J. L. Johnson
1896 J. L. Johnson
1898 J. L. Johnson
1900 J. L. Johnson
1902 J. L. Johnson
1904 D. C. Thompson
1906 D. C. Thompson
1908 D. C. Thompson
1910 D. C. Thompson
1912 D. C. Thompson
1914 D. C. Thompson
1916 post abolished [10]

DeKalb County Tax Receivers

1850 John Hawkins
1852 Hugh M. Boyd
1854 John C. Ragsdale
1856 John C. Ragsdale
1858 James M. Reeve
1860 L. B. Underwood
1862 W. W. Davis
1864 W. J. Williams
1866 I. N. Nash
1868 J. W. Nash
1871 I. N. Nash
1873 Crawford W. Johnson
1875 Crawford W. Johnson

1877 W. J. Williams
1879 J. L. Teat
1881 J. L. Teat
1883 H. H. Burgess
1887 H. H. Burgess
1889 William G. Akins
1891 I. L. Teat
1893 I. L. Teat
1895 I. L. Teat
1896 I. L. Teat
1898 I. L. Teat
1900 S. D. Warren
1902 S. D. Warren

1904 C. E. Gibbs
1906 C. E. Gibbs
1908 C. E. Gibbs
1910 C. E. Gibbs
1912 C. E. Gibbs
1914 C. E. Gibbs
1916 M. D. Grogan
1918
1920
1922
1923 W. H. Bond
1925 W. H. Bond
1927 W. H. Bond [11]

DeKalb County Tax Collectors

1850 Francis M. White
1852 John Smith
1854 Ezekiel A. Davis
1856 Ezekiel A. Davis
1858
1860 Simeon Smith
1862 W. W. Davis
1864 W. W. Davis
1866 Henry Gentry
1868 H. V. Bayne
1871 H. V. Bayne
1873 Philip B. McCurdy
1875 I. N. Nash
1877 James T. Veal
1879 James T. Veal

1881 Thomas R. Floyd
1883 Thomas R. Floyd
1885 Thomas R. Floyd
1887 J. F. Henderson
1889 Thomas H. Weaver
1891 J. N. Nash
1893 J. N. Nash
1895 J. N. Nash
1896 J. N. Nash
1898 J. N. Nash
1900 J. N. Nash
1902 J. N. Nash
1904 J. R. Floyd
1906 J. R. Floyd

1908 E. O. Reagin
1910 E. O. Reagin
1912 J. E. Forrester
1914 J. E. Forrester
1916 J. E. Forrester
1918
1920
1922
1923 C. H. Talley
1925 C. H. Talley
1927 C. H. Talley [12]

DeKalb County Tax Commissioners

1929 W. H. Bond   1931 W. H. Bond   1933-45 Homer H. Howard[13]

DeKalb County Road Commissioners/County Commissioners

Road Commissioners
1823
James McC. Montgomery
Henry Logan
Ebenezer Pitts
Samuel Prewett
T. A. Dobbs
James Hicks
January, 1826
John Beasley
Abraham Chandler
Charles Bonner
Benjamin Plaster
February, 1826
Gettin's District
Thornton Ward
Dempsey Perkerson
Lochlin Johnson
Scaif's District
Samuel L. Wilson
Adam Poole
Daniel Childs
Merritt's District
Meredith Collier
James Campbell
1836
Militia District 469
Moses Bibby
Richard C. Todd
Dempsey J. Donnally
Militia District 479
Nathaniel Mangum
Constantine Wood
John White
Militia District 487
Joseph D. McEver
John Jones
James A. Barr
Militia District 524
Josiah Power
Reuben Martin
John Isom
Militia District 530
Samuel L. Wilson

Charner Humphries
Edward White
Militia District 531
Robert Jones
William Jackson
James Paden
Militia District 536
John McGinnis
George L. Black
William Fowler
Militia District 563
James Diamond
John Hoyle
John P. Carr
Militia District 572
Willis Langston
John T. Dabney
Thomas J. Akins
Militia District 637
Ransom Seay
David D. Anderson
John W. Fowler
Militia District 686
James W. Reeve
John L. Evins
Hastings D. Palmer
Miitia District 722
Hardy Pace
John M. Harris
Isaac Reid
Militia District 683
Benjamin J. Camp
Charles Latimer
Josephus Harrison
1840
Militia District 469
Spencer B. Crow
James McCurdy
George Elliott
Militia District 479
James Donehoo
Jacob Redwin
James Blackstock

Militia District 487
Joseph D. McEver
Palmer R. Phillips
George Thomas
Militia District 524
Josiah Power
John Bellinger
John Austin
Militia District 530
Thomas J. Perkerson
Charner Humphries
William Willis
Militia District 531
Jonathan B. Wilson
Chapman Powell
John Bryce
Militia District 536
Zachariah R. Jones
John H. Jones
Hugh M. Boyd
Militia District 537
John Evans
Thomas Atwood
William Meadow
Militia District 563
James Diamond
James R. Henry
Elijah Steward
Militia District 572
James Milican
Thomas J. Akin
John Burns
Militia District 683
James W. Givins
John Swift
William Miller
Militia District 686
James W. Reeve
William Johnston
Hastings D. Palmer
Militia District 722
Britton Sentell
Thomas Farr
Henry Irby

1845
J. B. Wilson
E. Mason
John Collier
J. W. Kirkpatrick

1846
William Willis
Aaron B. Knight
Robert Orr
Noah Hornsby

1846
New Militia District 1026
Edwin G. Collier
Joseph H. Mead

Alexander F. Luckie
Willis Buell

1847
Daniel Johnson
P. F. Hoyle
Ezekiel A. Davis
Joseph Pitts

1877
John B. Steward

Board Of Commissioners
1886
George Ramspeck
---- Flake

Judge Ragsdale
John McCelland

1907-1918
Robert T. Freeman

1918-1929
L. T. Y. Nash
Judge Ragsdale

1930-1939
C. A. Matthews

1939-1954
Scott Candler [14]

DeKalb County Justices of the Peace
(with date of commission)

Frederic Hilsback, April 17, 1823
Daniel Gober, June 3, 1823
James Jett, June 3, 1823
John Henry, July 3, 1823
James Blackstock, July 17, 1823
Oliver Houston, July 17, 1823
Joseph Hubbard, August 9, 1823
Micajah Harris, December 11, 1823
James Hendley, June 7, 1824
Matthew R. Grace, July 26, 1824
Burwell Smith, January 11, 1825
James Henly, January 11, 1825
Micajah Harris, January 21, 1825
Leonard Randal, January 21, 1825
James Hicks, January 21, 1825
William Hudspeth, January 21, 1825
Willis Langston, January 27, 1825
Gresham Durham, January 27, 1825
Samuel L. Wilson, January 27, 1825
John Hewitt, January 27, 1825
Westley Camp, January 27, 1825
Lewis Brantly, January 27, 1825
Zarah Wilkerson, January 27, 1825
David R. Sillilvan, January 27, 1825
Daniel Gober, January 27, 1825
William Session, January 27, 1825
Nathaniel Greer, January 30, 1825
Meredith Colyer, May 27, 1825
Nathan Williford, June 30, 1825

Joseph Hubbard, September 24, 1825
James Blackstock, November 16, 1825
James Campbell, January 26, 1826
Thornton Ward, February 15, 1826
John Morris, February 15, 1826
Shadrack Farmer, February 15, 1826
James R. George, April 20, 1826
John G. W. Brown, August 11, 1826
Levi Dempsey, February 1, 1827
Ransom Thompson, February 23, 1827
William Stoker, February 23, 1827
Samuel Dodson, March 29, 1827
Israel Hendon, March 29, 1827
Moses Murphy, April 21, 1827
Elijah Bankston, April 21, 1827
James Malden, May 1, 1827
John Gaddis, May 1, 1827
Alexander Corry, June 28, 1827
William T. Cowan, February 4, 1829
Lemuel Dean, February 4, 1828
George Heard, February 4, 1828
John Williamson, March 31, 1828
Levi Dempsey, April 3, 1828
James S. Malden, April 10, 1828
John Johnson April 25, 1828
John Evans, May 31, 1828
Westley Camp, July 8, 1828
Jessee Norwood, July 24, 1828
James W. Reives, September 11, 1828 [15]

U. S. Representatives From DeKalb County

43rd Congress -- March 4, 1873-March 3, 1875
  5th District James Crawford Freeman
44th Congress -- March 4, 1875-March 3, 1877
  5th District Milton Anthony Candler
45th Congress -- March 4, 1877-March 3, 1879
  5th District Milton Anthony Candler
46th Congress -- March 4, 1879-March 3, 1881
  5th District Nathaniel Job Hammond
47th Congress -- March 4, 1881-March 3, 1883
  5th District Nathaniel Job Hammond
48th Congress -- March 4, 1883-March 3, 1885
  5th District Nathaniel Job Hammond
49th Congress -- March 4, 1885-March 3, 1887
  5th District Nathaniel Job Hammond [16]

State Senators From DeKalb County

James Mc. Montgomery, 1823
Lochlin Johnson, 1824-25
Tully Choice, 1826
William Ezzard, 1827-1830
Jesse F. Cleveland, 1831-34
Stephen Mays, 1835
Isaac N. Johnson, 1836
Jonathan B. Wilson, 1837-40
James Diamond, 1840-41
Charles Murphey, 1842
John Jones, 1843

39th District
Charles Murphey, 1845
James P. Simmons, 1847
Charles Murphey, 1849-50
James P. Simmons, 1851-52

DeKalb County
John Collier, 1853-54
Charles Murphey, 1855-56
Thomas Akins, 1857-58
Samuel F. Alexander, 1859-60

34th District
Samuel F. Alexander, 1861-63
James Polk, 1863-67
Milton A. Candler, 1868-72
Samuel J. Winn, 1873-74
---- Winn, 1875-76
George W. Bryan, 1877-79
William Parks Bond, 1880-81

Tyler M. Peeples, 1882-83
James E. Brown, 1884-85
E. M. Wood, 1886 (died)
J. L. Hamilton, 1887
George H. Jones, 1888-89
C. T. Zachry, 1890-91
Charles W. Smith, 1892-93
Charles H. Brand, 1894-95
Thomas D. Stewart, 1896-97
William M. Morrison, 1898-99
W. T. Smith, 1900-01
Paul Turner, 1902-04
Charles Murphey Candler, 1905-06
E. Winn Born, 1907-08
S. C. McWilliams, 1909-10
J. W. Mason, 1911-12
M. D. Irwin, 1913-14
E. M. Smith, 1915-17
Alonzo Field, 1917-18
Oscar Adelbert Nix, 1919-20
Robert W. Campbell, 1921-22
Arthur Whitaker, 1922-24
Carl N. Guess, 1925-26
Richard Paul Lester, 1927
Clarence Rowland Vaughn, 1929-31
John Wesley Weekes, 1932-33
Robert Walker Campbell, 1933
Clarence Rowland Vaughn, 1935
Paul Leonard Lindsay, 1937-40 [17]

State Representatives From DeKalb County

1823
James Hicks

1824-25
James Hicks

1825
James Hicks
George Clifton

1826
Thomas Akin
Jacob R. Brooks

1827
Jacob R. Brooks

Thomas Akin
1828
Stephen Mays
Thomas Akin
1829
Thomas Akin
Stephen Mays
1830
Thomas Akin
Stephen Mays
1831
Stephen Mays
George D. Anderson
1832
George D. Anderson
Stephens Mays
Thomas Akin
1833
George D. Anderson
Stephen Mays
John Dobbs
1834
Stephen Mays
Moses Murphy
John Dobbs
1835
James Diamond
Moses Murphy
John Dobbs
1836
James Diamond
Abner Murphy
Chapman Powell
1837
James Montgomery Calhoun
James Lemon
John L. Evans
1838
John L. Evans
James Lemon
Meredith Collier
1839
Charles Murphey
Meredith Collier
Hastings D. Palmer
1840
Charles Murphey
Hastings G. Palmer

Meredith Collier
1841
Charles Murphey
Hastings D. Palmer
John N. Ballenger
1842
John M. Born
John N. Ballenger
Thomas Farr
1843
John M. Born
Daniel Johnson
William Gilbert
1845
John M. Born
Daniel Johnson
1847
Thomas M. Darnell
Jonathan B. Wilson
1849-50
Thomas Akin
Jonathan B. Wilson
1851-52
J. N. Bellinger
John M. Born
1853-54
Greenville Henderson
G. K. Smith
1855-56
P. F. Hoyle
1857-58
James J. Diamond
1859-60
John G. Ragsdale
1861-62-63 Ex.
Milton A. Candler
1863-64 Ex.-64-65 Ex.
E. A. Davis
1865-66-66
Oliver Winningham
1868 Ex.-69-70 Ex.
W. H. Clarke
1871-72-72 Adj.
Washington L. Goldsmith
1873-74
S. C. Masters
1875-76
Oliver Winningham

1877
M. R. Ragsdale
1878-79 Adj.
Robert A. Alston
1880-81 Adj.
Henry Clay Jones
1882-83 Ex.-83 Ann. Adj.
Oliver Winningham
Henry Clay Jones
1884-85 Adj.
G. L. Humphries
William Parks Bond
1886-87 Adj.
C. Murphey Candler
George W. Johnson
1888-89 Adj.
C. Murphey Candler
George W. Johnson
1890-91 Adj.
W. C. Holbrook
T. Y. Nash
1892-93
John Nunnally
1892
J. B. Stewart
1893
Milton A. Candler
1894-95
W. J. Houston
John W. McCurdy
1896-97 Adj.-97
William Billups Henderson
William Morrison
1898-99
James R. George
John W. Mayson, M. D.
1900-01
James R. George
William Schley Howard
1902-03-04
John W. Mayson, M. D.
C. Murphey Candler
1905-06
Hooper Alexander
John W. Mayson, M. D.
1908-08-08 Ex.
C. Murphey Candler
Hooper Alexander

1909-10
Alonzo Field
Hooper Alexander
1911-12 Ex.-12
Alonzo Field
Hooper Alexander
1913-14
Alonzo Field
R. Frank Smith
1915-15 Ex.-16-17 Ex.
Leslie J. Steele
R. Frank Smith
1917-18
J. L. Chupp
Leslie J. Steele
1919-20
Paul L. Lindsay
Carl N. Guess
1921-22
Ralph McClelland
Carl N. Guess
Leslie J. Steele
1922-23 Ex.-24
Carl N. Guess
Leslie J. Steele
Albert J. Woodruff
1925-26 Ex.-26 2nd Ex.
James Curran Davis
Paul L. Lindsay
John Wesley Weekes
1927
James Curran Davis
Paul L. Lindsay
John Wesley Weekes
1929-31 Ex.
Hooper Alexander
Robert C. W. Ramspeck
John Wesley Weekes
1931
Henry Arthur Beaman
Roy Clark Leathers
Paul Leonard Lindsay
1933
Carl Thomas Hudgins
Paul Leonard Lindsay
Aubrey Mell Turner
1935
Paul Leonard Lindsay
David Henry Ansley
Carl Newton Guess
1937-38 Ex.
Charles Murphey Candler Jr.
Aubrey Mell Turner
Augustine Sams
1939 Ex.-39-40
Augustine Sams
Aubrey Mell Turner
Charles Murphey
Candler Jr. [18]

Appendix 3

First Justices of the Peace for Each Militia District of DeKalb County, Ga.
researched and compiled by Donald S. Clarke

469th Militia District (Cook's)
now in Fulton County (Cook's Center Hill, Peachtree and Collins areas)

Name	Commission Date
Richard Respess	March 20, 1822
Ebenezer Pitts	March 20, 1822

Note: When these men were commissioned, the district was still part of Fayette County.

479th Militia District (Stone's)
now in Fulton County (Adamsville, East Point, College Park areas)

Name	Commission Date
James H. Kidd	April 25, 1822
James Hicks	April 25, 1822

Note: When these men were commissioned, the district was still part of Fayette County.

487th Militia District (Philips's)
Lithonia and southeast DeKalb area

Name	Commission Date
Elijah Bankston	May 30, 1822
Merrill Collier	May 30, 1822

Note: When these men were commissioned, the district was still part of Henry County.

524th Militia District (Shallowford)
Doraville and Dunwoody areas

Name	Commission Date
Daniel Gober	June 3, 1823
James Jett	June 3, 1823

530th Militia District (Blackhall's)
now in Fulton County
(Blackhall, South Bend, Hapeville and College Park areas)

Name	Commission Date
James Blackstock	July 17, 1823
Oliver Houston	July 17, 1823

531st Militia District (Decatur)

Name	Commission Date
Joseph Hubbard	August 9, 1823
Micajah Harris	December 11, 1823

536th Militia District (Panthersville)
Panthersville and east Atlanta areas

Name	Commission Date
Zarah Wilkerson	January 27, 1825
David R. Sellivan	January 27, 1825

563rd Militia District (Diamond's)
part of Stone Mountain, Lithonia and Redan areas

Name	Commission Date
James Hendly	June 7, 1824
Burwell Smith	January 11, 1825

Note: Hendley recommissioned January 11, 1825.

572nd Militia District (Browning's)
part of Tucker, Clarkston and Stone Mountain areas

Name	Commission Date
Willis Langston	January 27, 1825
Grisham Durham	January 27, 1825

637th Militia District (Evans's)
Clarkston, Redan, Stone Mountain areas

Name	Commission Date
Moses Murphy	April 21, 1827
Elijah Bankston	April 21, 1827

683rd Militia District (Lythonia)
Lithonia and parts of Redan areas

Name	Commission Date
William J. Cowan	February 4, 1828
Lemuel Dean	February 4, 1828

686th Militia District (Cross Keys)
parts of north DeKalb and Buckhead and Oak Grove areas of Fulton County

Name	Commission Date
Levi Dempsey	April 3, 1828
James W. Reeves	September 11, 1828

722nd Militia District (Buckhead)
now in Fulton County
(Buckhead, Oak Grove and part of Collins areas)

Name	Commission Date
Jesse Fulcher	January 16, 1829
John Beasley	January 16, 1829

1026th Militia District (Atlanta)
now in Fulton County

Name	Commission Date
Willis Buell	March 30, 1847
Wiley Buel	January 22, 1849
Edwin P. Collier	January 22, 1849

Note: Wilis Buell was the only justice of the peace in the district from 1847-1848. Wiley Buel may be the same man as Willis Buell.

1045th Militia District (Stone Mountain)

Name	Commission Date
Elijah Stewart	February 9, 1850
Benjamin F. Veal	February 9, 1850

1327th Militia District (Clarkston)

Title	Name	Commission Date
N. P.	W. E. Moon	September 25, 1880
J. P.	W. C. Moore	January 17, 1885

Note: Beginning in 1868, each militia district had one justice of the peace and one notary public.

1349th Militia District (Mill)

Title	Name	Commission Date
N. P.	James R. Cobb	April 8, 1882
J. P.	Robert McWilliams	Jan. 17, 1885

1379 Militia District (Edgewood)

Title	Name	Commission Date
N. P.	James R. Mayson	Sept. 29, 1884
J. P.	E. W. Brooks	January 17, 1885

1398th Militia District (Redan)

Title	Name	Commission Date
N. P.	N. M. Reid	August 19, 1886
J. P.	J. L. Floyd	September 27, 1886

1416th Militia District (Doraville)

Title	Name	Commission Date
N. P.	J. C. McElroy	March 19, 1888
J. P.	Charles J. Carroll	Nov. 11, 1887

1448th Militia District (McWilliams)

Title	Name	Commission Date
N. P.	W. B. Watts	March 12, 1890
J. P.	M. O. Wiggins	April 8, 1889 [19]

Note: Justices of the Peace and Magistrates generally were addressed as "Squire." (Source: Garrett, Franklin M., 1954, 1969, Atlanta and Environs -- A Chronicle of Its People and Events, Vol. 1, page 73).

Appendix 4

First Company Grade Officers Listed In Each Militia District Of DeKalb County, Ga.
researched and compiled by Donald S. Clarke

469th Militia District (Cook's)
now in Fulton County

Rank	Name	Commission Date
Captain	Levi Merritt	April 17, 1823
1st Lt.	Curtis Calldwell	September 18, 1823
2nd Lt.	John Pow	September 18, 1823
Ensign	Cary Woff	September 18, 1823

479th Militia District (Stone's)
now in Fulton County

Rank	Name	Commission Date
Captain	Nalley Gilmore	August 2, 1822
1st Lt.	Edward Staggs	August 2, 1822
2nd Lt.	Seaborn Kidd	August 2, 1822
Ensign	Isaac Calhoun	August 2, 1822

487th Militia District (Philips's)

Rank	Name	Commission Date
Captain	Orasamus Camp	November 8, 1822
1st Lt.	William Biffle	November 8, 1822

No 2nd Lt. listed until January 25, 1827; no ensign listed until January 21, 1835

524th Militia District (Shallowford)

Rank	Name	Commission Date
Captain	William Conn	June 10, 1825

no 2nd Lt. or ensign listed unti August 9, 1827; no 1st Lt. listed until August 24, 1827

530th Militia District (Blackhall's)
now in Fulton County

Rank	Name	Commission Date
Captain	Henry Logan	November 18, 1823
1st Lt.	Joseph Hathorn	November 18, 1823
2nd Lt.	Elisha Ataway	November 18, 1823
Ensign	Nelson Brown	November 18, 1823

531st Militia District (Decatur)

Rank	Name	Commission Date
Captain	William Hughey	August 9, 1823
1st Lt.	John Granger	October 3, 1823
2nd Lt.	Jesse Townsend	October 3, 1823

No ensign listed until June 10, 1825

536th Militia District (Panthersville)

Rank	Name	Commission Date
Captain	William Jordan	August 29, 1823
1st Lt.	Thomas S. Robertson	August 29, 1823
2nd Lt.	Irwin Stricklin	August 29, 1823
Ensign	Aaron Starnes	August 29, 1823

563rd Militia District (Diamond's)

Rank	Name	Commission Date
1st Lt.	Matthew Henry	June 28, 1825
2nd Lt.	Simeon Smith	June 28, 1825
Ensign	Tyrey Pearce	June 28, 1825

No captain listed until October 21, 1830

572nd Militia District (Browning's)

Rank	Name	Commission Date
1st Lt.	William Bell	September 16, 1825
2nd Lt.	Wilson G. Griffin	June 8, 1826
Ensign	Hinson Harris	June 8, 1826

No captain listed until June 19, 1827

637th Militia District (Evans')

Rank	Name	Commission Date
Captain	John Brockman	May 17, 1827
1st Lt.	Lotspeech Lewis	May 17, 1827
2nd Lt.	Elbert Harris	May 17, 1827
Ensign	Elijah Stancil	May 17, 1827

683rd Militia District (Lythonia)

Rank	Name	Commission Date
Captain	Burgess Reeves	February 18, 1829

No 1st Lt. or 2nd Lt. listed until October 25, 1830; no ensign listed unitl July 23, 1838

686th Militia District (Cross Keys)

Rank	Name	Commission Date
Captain	Samuel N. Malony	March 7, 1828
Ensign	William Carroll	November 1, 1828

No 1st Lt. listed until December 31, 1831; no 2nd lt. listed unti September 19, 1836

722nd Militia District (Buckhead)
now in Fulton County

Rank	Name	Commission Date
Captain	William H. Fain	January 12, 1829
1st Lt.	Hardy Harris	January 12, 1829
2nd Lt.	James Baxter	January 12, 1829
Ensign	John Atwood	January 12, 1829

1026th Militia District (Atlanta)
now in Fulton County

Rank	Name	Commission Date
Captain	Thomas Dillon	April 13, 1847
1st Lt.	Willis Carlisle	April 13, 1847

No 2nd lt. listed for this district; no ensign listed until March 16, 1849 [7] [8]

---

[7] No company grade militia officers commissioned in DeKalb County after 1849. No commissions in militia districts created after 1849 (districts 1045, 1327, 1349, 1379, 1398, 1416 and 1448).

[8] This list does not include those officers in independent companies, such as cavalry, artillery, riflemen, guards, light infantry, etc., or field grade officers, the majors of the battalions and the lieutenant colonel and colonel of the regiment. When DeKalb County was first established, it only had three militia companies, enough for one battalion, which was attached to another county's regiment in order to have the minimum required two battalions per regiment. DeKalb's regiment was in the First Brigade of the 11th Division of the Second Grand Division of the Georgia Militia in 1837. Officers listed may not have been the first officers in a district. Some of DeKalb's early company grade officers may have been commissioned before a district number had been assigned to their company.

Appendix 5

1830 (First) DeKalb County Census Index

Heads of Households

Page 25
- Hiram Buckly
- J. McC. Montgomery
- Elijah Paty
- Martin Adams
- Westly Martin
- Abram Chandlor
- Joel Moreton
- William Bullard
- John C. Atwood
- William G. Martin
- John Pope
- Elijah Crawford
- John Roe
- David Pope
- C. D. Scoggin
- Furny Hutchins
- John Golden
- John Dobbs
- Whitfield Caldwell
- Edward Hagin
- Samuel Akridge
- Jonathan Luther
- Lindsy Elseberry
- David Cotton
- Meredith Colyer
- Samuel Walker
- Aaron Poor
- Daniel Bruce

Page 26
- Jesse Cleveland
- William Ezzard
- William Gresham
- William Malone
- William M. Hill
- James H. Kirkpatrick
- George Hammond
- Loughlin Johnson
- William Paty
- Robert Smith
- H. L. Norman
- John Mason
- Alexander Courie
- John Hughey
- Isaac Towers
- J. McLean
- J. C. Ostin
- William Sceaf
- Isam N. Johnson
- Mason Shumate
- James Liggin
- William Sansome
- William Abright
- Benjamin Wooton
- Robert F. Davis
- G. S. Fisher
- J. P. Fones
- C. Powel

Page 27
- S. M. Malony
- J. F. Adair
- Joel Akins
- B. M. Owens
- James Brewer
- William Jackson
- Joseph Shaw
- Allen Loveless
- Lemuel Hilburn
- Samuel Birdine
- Loderick Tuggle
- Oliver Clarke
- James A. Jett
- Ruben Cone
- George Heard
- Francis Smith
- John M. Daniel
- Gillum Goodman
- J. D. Holbrooks
- J. C. Johnson
- John Martin
- Nathan Wansly
- William Lattimer
- E. N. Calhoun
- J. B. Wilson
- John Simpson
- William Robuck
- John Holly

Page 28
- Elijah Twilly
- Aaron Starnes
- J. W. Fowler
- William Smith
- M. Hilburn
- J. V. George
- Daniel Stone
- Gairy Adams
- Naman Hardiman
- Ruben Harris
- Jesse Cox
- Allen Hardiman
- David Hubbard
- Lotte Morgan
- Robert Malone
- Wyley Browning
- John Evans

Archbald Walraven
William Pierce
Jesse H. Fulcher
Richard Boswell

Elias Campbell
Miles Paty
John Paty
Sanders Scoggin

William McGriff
Josiah Land
Jacob White

Page 29
Polly Cannon
John Beasly
William M. Beasly
Thomas Farr
William H. Farr
James Baxter
William Bruce
Howard Smith
Tirza Baxter

Ruben Baxter
Charles Isham
George Thomasson
Nelson Thomasson
James Fulcher
Polly Fulcher
Hardy Pace
Britain Centil
Loughlin Arnold
Edmond W. Runnels

Penelope Conn
Susannah Magby
James Tremble
John Tremble
Joel Babb
William Babb Jr.
William Babb Sr.
John Babb
John Goodwin

Page 30
Benjamin Maddox
James Morgan
Ryal Fowler
Micajah Goodwin
Thomas Akins
Jincy White
William Hutchenson
Jesse Mitchell
Turner Hutchenson

William Williamson
William Parmer
George W. Baily
Mary Ann Davis
Willis Robertson
John Dial
Benjamin Rhodes
Rhadford Gunn
Benjamin B. Hall
Mary Powers

John Woodall
A. H. Wilber
John King
David Isham
William Worthy
Samuel Worthy
John Worthy
William Baggwell
Kindred Baggwell

Page 31
James Donnalson
Wyley Robason
Michael Allbright
John Daniel
Elijah Copeland
Baily Jett
Donnalson Scission
James Hammond
George Carpenter

David McDowel
Stephen Martin
Newton Randal
John Hawkins
Thomas Atwood
Young T. Standiver
Hiram Perry
William Reeves
James Philips
Thomas M. Wood

Uriah Sprayberry
Nancy Wadkins
Benjamin Howard
Elijah Bird
Assa Glore
Charles Lattimer
J. V. George
James Morris
Edward S. Callehan

Page 32
Joel Swinny
William T. Cown
James B. George
Elijah Bankston
John Biffle

Philip Anderson
Andrew Camp
Moses Forrester
George Moon
John Rieves
Henry Ellison

John Center
James D. Puckett
John L. Bradly
Stephen Chandler
Nimrod Argo
James McGraw

Nelson Anderson
John Reed
Burges Rieves
John Waldrope

John Covington
Daniel Franklin
James T. White
Thomas Liggett

Samuel Dean
John M. Burnes
William Johnson

Page 33
Dempcy J. Connally
Hiram C. Harris
William Rutledge
John Tillah
James Sprayberry
Allen Bates
Allven T. Fones
James Jordan
Richard L. Eskey

William Millar
David Argo
Abram Glore
Joseph Jolly
P. H. Burford
Henry Hughey
Drury Fowler
Samuel Cone
James W. Pollard
G. S. Smith

James Guess
E. Heard
John Gillum
Sarah Shaw
Tunison Coryell
Matilda Cockram
Peter Wallace
James Jones
Jacob Parker

Page 34
Austin H. Green
Moses Hammelton
Jesse Fain
Lucy Carrol
James White
Zabad Hearn
John Glenn
Jonathan Waits
Cynthia Philips

George White
John M. Gilbert
Nancy Adams
Thomas Petty
Elizabeth Jennings
Gilbert D. Greer
Jack Morris
Jane Simms
Thomas Copeland
John Koil

Richard Bass
William Bass
William Padon
Thomas Hannah
John King
Polly Chesnutt
John Pendly
Jane Bosworth
William Olliver

Page 35
Federick Baldwin
James Tally
Walter Wadsworth
John Gordon
Matthias Garryson
Thomas Cotton
James Santford
James Lemmons
William Loveless

James Kirkpatrick
Simeon Williams
Tully Choice
John V. Kilgore
James Anderson
James Nesbitt
William Pollard
Robert Ware
Else Harris
Zilpha Rich

Sara Tomlinson
John Brown
Joseph Tompson
John Whoopper
John Breedlove
Thomas Bradford
Thomas Ray
L. H. Tomlinson
Daniel Durham

Page 36
Nathan Williford
William Dickson
John McGinnis
John Sloan
Ulysses McC. Montgomery

Susannah Pugh
Stephen C. Turner
William Davis
Olliver Hackett
Aaron Herrin
Hosea Mainer

Levi Merrett
Clarrissa Merrett
Joseph Garrett
James H. Holly
Henry Scoggin
Sally Bankston

Lucy Mitchell
Charles Coursey
Briant Miles
William Sanders

Micajah Martin
George Huston
Edward Sanders
Joseph Land

Bartlett Grogan
Jacob Land
Thomas Landers

Page 37
Ebenezer Pitts
Solomon Sweat
Alford Mainner
Thomas Hoopper
Peter Johnson
John Gassaway
John Patterson
Isham Dison
Nathan Jordan

Elbert White
Charlotte McLeod
Jesse Patterson
Stephen Petty
David White
Nancy Cheattam
William Fain Sr.
Greenbery Fain
William Debro
James Dunnahoo

William Fain Jr.
Abram Fain
Benjamin Wallace
Joel Fain
Thomas Cannady
Greenberry Baker
Moses Petty
Izbel Grant
James Turner

Page 38
Francis Derrett
Samuel Turner
Matthias Turner
Jerre Waits
David Waits
Elizabeth Dunlap
John Dunlap
Levi Peacock
John Sewel

Samuel Sewel
Moses Tremble
Jacob Redwine
John M. Smith
John Dorsey
John Holbooks
Daniel Ferguson
Thomas L. Thomas
Thomas Smith
Joseph Stone Sr.

James Harlin
Ashly Blackstock
William C. Baker
Nancy Adams
James Blackstock Jr.
James Russel
Andrew Derrett
Thomas Hornsby
Noah Hornsby

Page 39
Aaron Roberts
James Brewster
Moses Hornsby
James Blackstock Sr.
Kindred Blackstock
Micajah Little
John Deacon
David Connally

Robert Wood
Aaron Roberts Jr.
James Oliver
John Williamson
Henry C. Channel
John Waits
John McCammon
Sarah Smith

John A. D. Childers
Nancy Reed
James McGriff
Dennis Hopkins
Augustin Young
James Milligan
Joel Farmer
Britain Harris

Page 40
William C. Milligan
Willis Lankston
William Slay
Nathaniel Beauchamp
Samuel Henderson

Richard Grogan
J. T. Baker
Nathan Beauchamp
Thomas Rainey
Alexander Hewett
James Baker Jr.

Thomas J. Akens
William Beauchamp
John Cockram
William Cowey
Isaac Baker
Richard Wilson

Nicolas Rhodes
Charles McGrady
William Tally
Daniel R. Fones

Page 41
Martin Holcombe
Drury Graden
John Cudd
Lemuel Lunceford
Malakiah Reeves
John H. Walker
John Hayse
Shadrach Morris
John Rainey

Page 42
John Blake
Westly Bains
John Graden
James H. Holbrooks
David Wilson
Jordan Webb
Stephen Spruel
Henry Meadcalf
Richard Gober

Page 43
Johnston Williams
Joel Scales
Meredith Brown
Joseph Boswell
James Foot
Isaac Hughes
Amassa May
Isaiah Herrin
William W. White

Page 44
Thomas Stevens
William P. Foster
Charity Ellisson
Charles Varner
James Atwood

Gilbert Cone
William Wilson
James W. Rieves
John Meadcalf

Noah Slay
Greeville Henderson
James Wafford
Richard Litteral
John R. Greenlee
Larkin Knash
Peter Thiess
John Winters
Larkin Knash
Azzariah Pogue

Joseph Powers
William Conn
Elisha Cockram
Peter Bowman
Jesse Gilbert
Elizabeth Wright
Leonard Hornsby
James Adams
Isham Hendon
Andrew White

Peter Brown
Jethro Baker
David Hutchins
Henry Tandy Walker
Burrel Hutchins
Richard Shipp
Sylvanus Walker
Elijah Baker
Tandy Green
John Phillipps

Thomas Harris
Moses P. Harris
Charles Harris
Stephen Jett
Isaac Reed
Nathaniel Reed

Levi Johnston
William T. Whitfield
Nicholas Campbell

John Adams
Ambrose Tuning
Abner Coleman
John Dabbs
Samuel Dabbs
Wyley Gober
Thomas Gaddy
John McCoy
Britain Davis

Andrew Griffin
Harman Cumins
John Evans
Andrew Nelson
Andrew McCullins
Joseph Blackstock
Austin Crow
William Ford
David Miles

Abner Magaherty
Enoch Boyle
Dennison Crow
Thornton Simms
John McDonald
Joseph Burrows
John Robason
Samuel Arledge
James Hughey

Isaiah Kirksey
William Malony
William Spruel
Willis Cox
Thomas Cupp
Michael Cupp

Lucinda Casselberry
Walnor Cupp
John Wilson
Jonathan Hightower

Philip Woodall
Jubal C. Heard
Ann McGloughlin
Jacob Poss

Elizabeth Woodall
Joseph Knight
William Simms

Page 45
John Carter
Joshua Crow
Dukason Mizzuki
Samuel Wilson
Leonard Griffin
Bradly Smith
Joshua Townsend
Moses Heirs
Nelson Ginnings

Humphry Berditt
Samuel Conn Sr.
Eli Donnaldson
Samuel Abernatha
Willis Fortner
Betsey Donnaldson
William Taylor
William Heard
Joseph Powers
Nathan Danger

John Gober
James King Sr.
Daniel Gober
James King
Hasting Palmer
Asa White
Jackson H. Randal
David B. Ellington
Jesse Harris

Page 46
James M. Watson
Tubal C. Cawley
Alfred Edwards
Robert Walker
Thomas Hayse
Charles C. Hickman
Benjamin Chapman
Abner Farrow
Levi Dempey

James B. Hairston
Samuel Dodson
William Burns
John McCulloch
William Ward
William W. Lewis
Moses Murphy
James L. Mann
James Blanks
Lewis Wolf

Agnes Atwood
William Taylor
Peter Ball
Sarah Taylor
William Donnaldson
Ruthy Taylor
William Grant
John Allbright
Robert Martin

Page 47
Andrew Martin
Austin Martin
John Gaddis
William S. Heard
John Williford
Nancy Martin
Obadiah Scisson
John Murfy
William B. Scisson Sr.

William Scisson Jr.
William Southerlin
Jacob Donnalson
Robert Akels
James H. Davisson
John Johnson
William A. Rogers
John Hughey
Mason Doherty
Willy Downs

Jesse J. Jones
Thomas W. Slaughter
Thomas Austin
William Towers
Jacob R. Brooks
Stephen Mays
John Townsend
Leonard Simpson
William McKelpin

Page 48
James Campbell
Carter Mahaffy
Ozburn Willkinson
Ryal Clay Jr.
James Casselberry

Stephen Terry
Edward Mobly
James Ward
Greenberry Butler
Archibald Johnson
William Boyle

Thomas Oliver
Daniel Johnson
Andrew Nelson
Alfred B. Edwards
Benjamin Master
John Rowel

William Dobbins
Richard C. Todd
James Sweat
Bartlet C. John

William W. Malony
James Blackstock Jr.
Ambrose Hill
Benjamin Loky

Simeon Smith
Andrew Boyd
Dillan Johnson

Page 49
John Morris
Loughlin Adams
William B. Wooten
David Sanders
Hugh Horn
Daniel Hughes
Christopher Sewel
William Willis
Joel Herring

Richard Orr
Merrel Emmery
Hiram H. Emmery
Marzel Willis
Jacob Wolf
Richard B. Hornbuckle
Abner Connally
James Mangram
William Mangram
John Eaton

John Blailock
William Ottery
William Williams
James Watwood
John Wilson
Elias Maddin
William Eades
Abner Crow
William Reedy

Page 50
Richard Talliaferro
Dudly Jettur
James M. Wright
William Sceaf
Santford Moore
William A. Fullar
Adam Pool
Louny Sceaf
Thomas Ward

Burrel Morris
Willis B. Hicks
Matthew Knight
Kellis Brown
James Bruce
George Foot
Nancy Terrell
William S. Brown
Mary Brown
James Calee

William Terrell
Daniel Chiles
James Hanson
J. Westly Cox
Richard Hull
William B. Cox
Mary Cox
John Fuller
Ceely Brown

Page 51
Richard Taliaferro
Mozley Davis
John W. Walker
Thomas Eli
David Thurmond
Benjamin Little
Benjamin Thurmond
George Watts
Edward Watts

William Thurmond
Richard Thurmond
Daniel Melton
Michael Reeves
Ellenor Barnes
Polly Twilly
William Brooks
James Buchanon
Jesse Clay

James Smith
Aaron Knight
William Stinson
James Yancy
John L. Parker
Richard Head
William Morris
Lemuel Cobb
Harrison Williams

Page 52
James Hunt
Martha Vaden
George Clifton
Benjamin B. Auvery
Aaron Clifton

Levin Clifton
Fanning Brown
John Cowan
Moses Black
Elijah Turner
Thomas Fowler

Thomas Espey
Demcy Perguson
William Morris Sr.
Thomas Lemmons
James B. Broughton
George Wilson

Thomas Cook
Thomas B. Lanier
Samuel Cobb
William Clemons

Page 53
William Hornsby
James Twilly
Edward Wade Jr.
John Parker, from N. C.
Richard Burnett
William Dozer
Edward Wade Sr.
James Nichols
William Redd

Page 54
William Jameson
James Jones Jr.
William Terry
William Malony
Ann Gillaspey
Zachariah Jones
William Harris
Alexander Nelson
Wyley Davis

Page 55
James Scisson
John Blackstock
Philip Houseworth
Lewis Towers
Andrew Rogers
Ellenor Brown
Seamon Powel
George Rogers
Abram Houseworth

Page 56
Archibald Hollin
Nathaniel Guess
James Wambel
David Reed
William Herben

William Hyde
Stephen Williams
Green Aulman
Micajah Pope

William Cornelius
James Brown
William Wood
John Rapshaw
William Hellerbrand
J. G. W. Brown
Hugh Baity
Mary Broughton
Barnett Downs
John Gilbert

William Hudgens
Thomas White
Darkey Hughey
William T. Brawner
John M. C. Flowers
Asa C. A. Simmons
William Grimes
Joseph Hollinsworth
Aaron Hollinsworth
Edward Bunt

Zachariah Baily
Peter Gray
George Barber
Ellenor Stancel
Edward Howard
John Stephenson
James Miller
Samuel Barber
Joel Driggers
William Nichols

William Anderson
Robert Anderson
D. D. Anderson
William Center
John W. Betts
Henry Johnson

Briant Cash
Martha Butler
Joshua Gammon

William Broughton
Sterling Harris
James Jones
Benjamin Lewis
Sarah Jones
John H. Jones
Wright Martin
William Morris
Samuel Gill

William Moreton
Josiah Rounceville
Jinnings Hulsey
William Callihan
Whitfield Hull
Briant Hambrick
Joseph Hambrick
Joshua Callihan
John Bolland

Robert Rounceville
John Gunn
Gillum Goodman
William Anderson
Joseph Thomas
George Elam
Edward Jones
Mary McCarty
Jordan Creel

William West
Berry Shumate
William A. David
James Paden
Robert Biggers
John Perguson

M. L. Anderson
John F. Bowen
Titus Starnes
Newman Pounds

Page 57
Harman Kolb
Alexander Stephenson
Izrael Hendon
George Thomas
John Turner
Nathaniel Center
Thomas W. Garner
William Elam
Martin Butlar

Page 58
James McKleroy
Milton Victors
William C. Williams
Billings B. Bird
John B. Badgers
John Barnett
Young Browning
John Veal
John Patricks

Page 59
Thomas Wooton
Thomas Richardson
William Gates
Henry Gothard
William Hazlett
James Manning
Robert Ellisson
Elliot Wood
John M. Wood

Page 60
John Criswell
John Sanders
John Thompson
James Thompson
Elijah Pierce

M. M. Lead
John L. Black
George Heard
Henry Swinny

John Terry
Louis Brantly
James B. Robason
Samuel McCandles
Robert Givens
William Hairston
Jonathan Rieves
Joseph Wooton
Elisha L. Hendon
Zachariah Holloway

Solomon Tingle
Jarrett Ellisson
Wyley Scoggin
Samuel Reed
James McGriff
John P. Carr
Benjamin Carr
Joel Starnes
Aaron Haygood
Wyley Goss

John Insly
Jesse Corbett
Cornelius Foster
Mary Ellisson
William Elliott
Isaac Wadkins
James Pope
Randol Arnold
Hiram Spraberry
J. L. Davis

John Henry
William Henry Sr.
Mathew Cockram
Thomas Henry
William Clark
William Henry Jr.

Merrel Colyer
Jacob Moore
John Easter

James Loyd
Thomas Hendon
George Hall
Joseph Hall
Hiram Wilbanks
John Spraberry
Cynthia Mercer
Jesse Jordan
Benjamin Spraberry

Josiah Grimes
John Manning
Frances Carter
Thomas Jinks
Henry Swinny
Jacob New
Joel New
William Holly
Ruben Bishop

Jacky Montainvill Cawly
Hannah Snow
Stephen Whitly
James Henly
Richard Bond
James Insly
Hammelton Ware
Vardy Bonds
George Maddox

James Smith
Simeon Smith
Burrel Smith
John B. Ayres
Allen Cambron
Richard Bond

Baily Cambron
Absalom Steward
Thomas Johnson
Thomas Garrett

Page 61
Henry Curton
Hily Curton
John Tollison
Samuel B. Hill
Nancy Ellen
Elizabeth Doherty
Nancy Thompson
Davis Gresham
Jesse Wood

Page 62
Samuel J. Anderson
John Hambrick
James Jefferson Evans
Alexander Vaughn
John Evins
Ludlow Williams
Mary Jones
William Veal
James C. Scott

Page 63
Wyley Glover
Thomas Durham
William Turner
Kenneth Gillis
Bennell Tankesly
Wyley Browning
Isaac Mitchell
Jacob Smith
John Wooldredge

Page 64
Ellis Swinny
Robert Cassey
William Gilbert
Abner Simpson
John Simpson

William Patrick
William Briant
James Diamond
Solomon Sanders

William H. Jordan
Ryal Clayton
Santford Britain
Loughlin Fanning
Benjamin Fannin
John Fannin
Darcus Crawly
Jesse Lane
Susannah Vinson
L. P. Hairston

James Smith
Colly Hicks
Elihu Smith
Hetty Hicks
John Wilson
Eliza Wadkins
William Lewis
Amos Towers
Martha Roe
John H. Brockman

William Hardiman
William Mason
Ford Mason
Walter Manning
Peter Windham
James Carpenter
William Eskew
Tederick Lee
William Anderson
Uriah Cassey

William Shaw
Thomas Johnson
William Cash
Telman Pruitt
James Cash
William Wallace

Holloway Sanders
Thomas Norton
Charles Jordan

Josiah McLean
William Austin
Jesse Williams
Nathaniel Wade
John Pickens
William Gant
Dempcy Sanders
Thomas Mahaffy
John Terry

John Henry
Samuel Bird
Panel Padon
Joab Binion
Peter C. Balenger
James McCurdy
Polly Pierce
Isaac Steel
Rachel Smith

Joseph Devenport
Robert Lemmons
William Harris
Wisdom Gober
Thomas Gober
Charles Lively
Santford Gorham
Lazarus Gorham
Silas McGrawdy

John Martin
Jerre Jones
Howard Cash
William Cruce
Henry Cash
Peter Cash

William Coody
Garland Dabney
John Hardiman
John Little

Thomas Venable
William Copeland
William Tapp
Joseph McDonnald

Elizabeth Harris
John McDonnald
Charles Whitlock

Page 65
James Casselberry
F. L. Goze
Andrew Browning
Edward Level
Henry Gulledge
Henry Judson
William Towers
Wade Wallace
Robert Caruth

James Spencer
William Talton
John McWilliams
Olomon Dodgens Jr.
Olomon Dodgens Sr.
Jacob Caheely
William Dodgen
Larkin Dodgen
Joseph Crockett
Joseph Gragan

Samuel House
Ruben Wright
William Wright
Jesse Wallace
Daniel D. Baker
Alexander Johnson
James Bell
Charles Sawyers
James Shaw

Page 66
Thomas Wilson
John Jinnings
William Ferrel
Littleton Jackson
Samuel L. Paris
John Ivy
Milly Harden
Robason Hendon
William Morris

Alexander McCarty
Felix Harden
Jesse Farmer
Jesse Swinny
William Swinny
James Buys
Levi Betterton
Brooks Harper
James Akens
Benjamin Ellis

Benjamin Jamison
Nancy Rutledge
John F. Smith
James Willis
Jesse Warren
Josiah Melton
John C. Turner
William V. Griffith
Henry Holcombe

Page 67
Lewis D. Veal
Benjamin Simms
William R. Lester
Mason Wraggsdale
Marget Waddle
James Hayse
Edmond Strange
Elizabeth Carter
Richard Clayton

William Johnson
Nancy Hill
William Burnett
John Farris
William Knash
Thomas Milligan
Joseph Woodruff
Thomas Ward
John Barnett
Robert Wood

William Meddows
Robert Scott
Samuel Cawly
William Hodge
James Doherty
Edward L. Knash
Hitson Tollison
Dicy Simpson
Elijah Hughes

Page 68
Jesse Pierce
J. William Pierce
Booker Johns
Cynthia Williams
Samuel Ingram

Polly Beavers
Jesse Waldrope
Lewis Jarrel Dupree
John Powers
Isaiah Parker
Daniel Fones

Leonard Winters
Wyley Jones
Lewis Kennon
Robert McCord
John Jones
Roger Murfy

William Martin
Jesse Hearst
Albert Bates
John Beauchamp

Page 69
Stephen Hightower
Edmond Lewis
Thomas Lawrence
John Jett
James Jett
William Bell
Joseph Morris
Tassie Jarmin
John Dabbs

Page 70
James Lowry
David Holcolmbe
Henry Jones
Nancy Irby
Joseph Tremble
John W. Tremble
Constant Irby
Solomon Williams
Ruben Holcolmbe

Page 71
Samuel McKleroy
James Wilson
Stephen Mitchell
Thomas Adams
Salathiel A. Lester
John Ridling
Thomas D. Harris
Joseph Steward
John Blufort

Page 72
Jonathan Davis
Josiah Johnson
John Defurr
Ozburn Mullins
Robert Steward

James P. Barnes
Elisha Jordan
Bird Wammack
Thomas J. Wammack

Nathan Slay
Zadock Johnson
Enoch Morris
Lemuel Edwards
Ruben Mayfield
William Guess
Cairy Spillars
Sophia Guess
Mary Hammelton
William Rainy

Oliver Johnson
James Goodwin
Lewis E. Walker
Samuel Conn
James Hoopper
Drury Morris
Buly Lynch
William Tate
Joseph Gault
John Waits

John McKleroy
Lewis Thomas
Wootson Roberts
Rebecca Balenger
Jesse Roberds
Elijah Stancel
Neelly Goodwin
Samuel Loury
M. P. Belknap
David Reed

William Tatum... E. J.
John A. Craddick
Elizabeth Duncan
Eli Thomas
James Collins
Ryal Harvel

Coleston Copeland
Izrael Millar
Abram Hill

John Rainey
Daniel Smith
John Bruce
Lewis Clarke
Thomas Gober Jr.
Ella Moore
Thomas Yarborough
John Wheeler
Jonathan Holcolmbe

Jesse Wallace
Davis Reed
William Wilson
Nancy Vann
Gardner Cone
John Mincy
Greevill Pullin
Rebecca Burton
Stephen Tillah

Nathan Morgan
William Baker
Thomas Brown
Joseph Johnson Sr.
Thomas Smith
James Harris
William Harris
John Martin
Samuel Brown

John Kelly
Edward Harris
William Harris
Samuel Quinton
Else Harris
John Harris

John Mariner
James B. Waller
James Barnett
Dillan Fulcher

William Quinton
John Gay
Samuel Quinton
Henry Cupp Sr.

Henry Cupp Jr.
Haily Shaw
Nathaniel Krenshaw

Page 73
John Kembel
John Gay Jr.
James Lockaby
Betsey Williams
Hester Paris
Joseph Philips
Sabard Beauchamp
William Thompson
George Tomlinson

John McTeer
John Thompson
John Parsons
Harman Channel
John Mullins
James L. Pair
Richard Coleman
Thomas W. Blainy
Irvin Stancel
Thoms Higgins

James Murfy
John Floyd Jones
John L. Holcombe
Thomas Woodall
Abram Tumblin
Moses Bibby
John Waldraven
Miles Glasco
Polly Pakins

Totals

1344 total households,
  88 (6.5 per cent) headed by women
White males -- 4295
White males younger than 15 -- 2184
White males between 90 and 100 -- 2

White females -- 4081
White females younger than 15 -- 2129
White females between 90 and 100 -- 1

Total white population -- 8,376

Male slaves 782
Male slaves younger than 10 -- 315

Female slaves -- 671
Female slaves younger than 10 -- 313

Free black males -- 9
Free black females -- 9

Deaf and dumb citizens -- 1
Blind citizens -- 3

Largest categories:
White males ages 0-5 -- 970
White females 0-5 -- 922

Total population 10,047

Census-taker's Comments

The extent of my division which extends into the Cherokee Country agreebly to an act of the Legislature of Georgia commencing at the Buzzard Roost on the Chattahooche along an old indian trail which passes the Buffalow Fisher thence leaving Duk Scotts on the left hand thence by Jacksons (or Tarehonies) thence to the Missionaries on the Hightower waters by the indians call'd Etowa until the said trail (the direction of Sally Hughes's) intersects the road leading from Gates's Ferry to Duk Roes the distance forty miles from thence along the said Road to Gates ferry forty miles, thence with the meanders of the River down the same to the said Buzzard Roost on the Chattahooche River a distance from forty to fifty miles.

James McC. Montgomery
Asst. to the Marshal
25th October, 1830

I, James Mc. Montgomery, Assistant to the Marshal of the District of Georgia, do hereby certify that the number of persons within my Division, consisting of the County of DeKalb, is as appears in the foregoing schedule, subscribed by me this twenty fifth day of October, in the year one thousand eight hundred and thirty, amounting to four thousand, three hundred and one free white male persons, four thousand and eighty seven free white females, seven hundred and eighy six male slaves, eight hundred and eighty three female slaves, eight free male persons of color, and nine free female persons of color, among which are one male and one female which are blind, and one female which is both deaf and dumb. The aggregate amount is ten thousand and seventy four.

                    J. Mc Montgomery
                    Assistant to the Marshal
                    of the District of Georgia [9] [21]

---

[9] "Sally Hughes's place" was located across the Etowah River where now U. S. Hwy. 41 crosses the river, near Cartersville.

Appendix 6

1850 DeKalb County Census Index
(Heads of Households Only)
Anderson's District

Name	census page no.	Name	census page no.
ADKINS, Jeptha V.	2	HUEY, John	12
ADKINS, Joel	1	JOLLY, Jesse	75
ALMAN, Henry	9	JOLLY, Robert	74
ALMAN, Simeon	16	JONES, John	11
ANDERSON, David	55	LYNCH, John	23
ANDERSON, Robert	36	MAHAFFY, Thomas	32
ANDERSON, Samuel J.	65	MALONEY, Isaac N.	20
ANDERSON, Sarah	37	MALONEY, James R.	22
ASKEW, James	66	MC ALPIN, Floyd	47
ASKEW, Richard H.	61	MC ALPIN, James M.	46
AUSTIN, John C.	77	MC LAINE, James M.	3
AUSTIN, Nathaniel	5	MITCHELL, James W.	14
AYERS, William	4	MORGAN, Daniel	50
BOLTON, Thomas C	42	MORRIS, James S.	43
BRAZIER, Elezabeth	7	PARKER, Andrew	48
BROWN, William M.	70	PARKER, James	26
CALAHAN, Thomas	33	PICKENS, Reuben	35
CASE, James	15	PEYTON, Susan	76
COCHRAN, George	30	POTTS, William	41
COGGIN, Joshua	71	PRICHARD, Joseah	49
DAVIS, Moses W.	73	RAGSDALE, John	24
DICKERSON, Michael	38	RAY, William	69
ELAM, James E.	57	SCOTT, Joseph	56
EVANS, John	52	SEAY, Bernard	21
FERRILL, John	53	SHEPPERD, William	59
GANT, William	63	SMITH, James	31
GOSS, Elizabeth	44	SMITH, John M.	29
GOSS, James	39	THOMPSON, Nancy	64
HADDEN, J. M.	60	TOWERS, Francis M.	19
HAMBRICK, James	54	TOWERS, Isaac	18
HAMBRICK, James M.	62	TUGGLE, Lodowick	17
HAMBRICK, John	34	VAUGHAN, Alexander	40
HAMBY, Jesse	68	VEAL, Francis	27
HAMOND, Matthew	10	VEAL, William	28
HARELL, Jane	102	WEBB, Matilda	45
HOLCOMB, Sarah E.	67	WOOD, Charles H.	58
HOLT, Andrew J.	25	WOODSON, Benjamin	72
HOWARD, Moses	8	WOOLLY, Elias	13
HOWARD, Samuel S.	6		

Atlanta District

Name	census page no.	Name	census page no.
ADAIR, G. O.	111	BROWN, Edgefield	205
ALDRICH, H. T.	110	BROWN, Nancy	412
ALEXANDER, A.	70	BRUCE, Daniel	369
ALLISON, Amos	69	BRYANT, Harrison	198
ALMON, Asmon R.	203	BRYANT, James W.	132
ALMOND, Green B.	183	BRYANT, Littleberry	167
ARMSTED, William	398	BUCHANAN, Henry	200
ARMSTEAD, John	399	BURDETT, Mrs.	47
ASKEW, Simmeon	346	BURWELL, Jessee	259
BAKER, Jessee	43	BUSHTIN, William	274
BAKER, Joseph S.	262	CAIN, John	312
BAKER, R. S.	41	CAIN, John R.	240
BARNES, Micaja	32	CAMERON, Charlotte	18
BARNES, Thomas	415	CANANT, O. H. P.	147
BARNES, William	275	CANANT, O. H. P.	379
BATEMAN, Jeremiah	297	CARLYLE, Willis	314
BATES, Joshua	249	CARMICHAEL, Richard H.	362
BAXTER, John W.	9	CARTER, Margaret	250
BEACH, Alexander	148	CARTER, Thomas W.	76
BEACON, Emaline	2	CASH, Willis M.	105
BEALL, W. T.	272	CENTER, William	238
BECK, Martha A.	13	CHAMBERLAIN, Robert	216
BECK, Sarah	25	CHEEK, Pendleton	142
BEGALY, Alitha	191	CHRISTIAN, John	151
BELFORD, Katharine	136	CLARK, David	10
BELL, Charles	229	CLARK, Jessee	282
BERRY, John	176	CLARK, Robert	175
BIGGERS, Stephen	267	CLEMENTS, John	386
BISHOP, Graham	251	COATS, Henry	60
BLACKMON, James	396	COBB, John	273
BOMAR, B. F.	49	COLLINE, James	408
BOOTH, Jeptha	26	COLYER, John	33
BORING, John M.	74	COLYER, Martha	327
BOSWORTH, Josiah R.	134	COMBS, Laura	303
BOWEN, Hiram	114	COMES, Jane	279
BOWEN, Stephen	115	CONE, Rewbin	373
BRADLEY, William	286	CONLY, Patrick	331
BRADSHAW, Harriet	20	COOK, G. W.	101
BRADY, A. J.	71	COOK, William M.	108
BRADY, John W.	197	CORRY, Alexander	320
BRASE, Peter	162	COSBEY, Martha	112
BRAY, Bannister R.	354	COWAN, William	218
BRAZELL, William	22	CRABB, B. F.	99
BRIDWELL, J. W.	34	CRAVEN, Isaac N.	290
BRIGHT, W.	7	CRAWFORD, David	59

Name	census page no.	Name	census page no.
CRAWFORD, Elisha B.	188	GILLAND, James	57
CRAWFORD, James	187	GILLING, Thomas	97
CRAWFORD, Mozes	164	GILMER, William	228
CRAWFORD, William	338	GLAZIER, William	21
CRISWELL, Thomas	394	GLEN, John	287
CROCKET, David M.	252	GLOVER, Wiley	317
CROFT, William	253	GOLDSBERRY, William	414
CROSSLY, Lovebery	417	GOLDSMITT, George W. T.	413
CROW, Jackson T.	19	GORDAN, N. E.	63
DABBER, Stephen	375	GREEN, Jessee	113
D'ALVIGNEY, P. P. Noel	255	GRUBBS, James M.	361
DANIEL, Amarcah	300	GRUBBS, T. J.	359
DANIEL, David G.	352	GURLEY, Nancy	234
DANIEL, Margaret T.	230	GUTHRIE, Henry	109
DANIEL, Thomas V.	94	HAAS, H.	212
DARBY, James	268	HAAS, Jacob	211
DAVIS, Andrew J.	209	HACKET, Rutha	14
DAVIS, John W.	103	HANTULER, C. R.	280
DAVIS, William R.	130	HARDEN, James L.	30
DEVARK, Timothy	82	HARDMAN, William B.	171
DOONAN, T.	383	HARRIS, James	185
DULIN, Addison	72	HARRIS, William	307
DURHAM, Martha C.	67	HARVEL, William H.	258
ECKMEND, John G.	269	HATHAWAY, Mrs.	45
EDDLEMAN, Francis	102	HAVENS, William H.	149
EDGAR, Betsey	124	HAWREY, Edward S.	154
EDMUNDSON, Mary A.	265	HAYNES, Isaac	281
ELMORE, Alfred	223	HAYNES, Rewbin	38
EVANS, John W.	8	HAYNES, William	125
FARRIS, William E.	178	HEARN, Thomas	116
FAYETT, James	177	HEMBREE, Martha	395
FIELDS, Gabriel	78	HENRY, William	98
FLEMING, Robert N.	204	HERRING, William	96
FLOYD, Tabitha	79	HIGGINS, Green	173
FORMWALT, M. W.	357	HIGGINS, William P.	193
FORSYTH, Ambrose	304	HIGHTOWER, R. H.	129
FORSYTH, William	301	HILBURN, N. C.	391
FOSTER, John A.	155	HILL, Thomas C.	309
FOWLER, Asa	319	HOLCOMB, H. C.	305
FRANKFORD, S.	90	HOLLIDAY, William C.	128
FRAZER, George R.	378	HONEYCUT, E. T.	121
FRAZIER, Julia	172	HOUSE, Paschel	174
GARDNER, Rewbin	62	HOUSTON, Oswal	310
GARNER, Nancy	27	HUDSON, Charles A.	358
GIBSON, Andrew	405	HUMPHRIES, J. T.	224
GILL, A. B.	276	IMMEL, P. J.	88

Name	census page no.	Name	census page no.
IVEY, Sarah	318	LINN, Reese	66
IVEY, William	315	LITTLE, Harvey	289
JACKSON, Wesley T.	44	LONG, C. W.	83
JEPSON, Lemuel	135	LOYD, James	377
JOHNS, Phebe	402	LUCKY, Alexandre F.	411
JOHNS, W.	401	LUMPKIN, Jessee	120
JOHNSON, Allen	384	LYNCH, James	86
JOHNSON, Jacob N.	341	LYNCH, Michael	291
JOHNSON, Richard	208	LYNCH, Patrick	292
JONES, Edward	206	LYON, Vinson	340
JONES, John	247	MACRAW, Thomas	263
JONES, John	40	MALONE, Elizabeth	93
JONES, John T.	170	MANGUM, Nathaniel	131
JONES, Thomas M.	222	MANGUM, R. E.	55
JONES, William B.	351	MANN, John	326
KAY, William	89	MANN, William J.	91
KELLUM, A. R.	77	MANUEL, David E.	195
KELLY, Daniel	356	MARTIN, William G.	242
KELSEY, Joel	257	MASSEY, James E.	12
KELTON, Catharine	5	MC AFEE, William M.	335
KENADY, James	308	MC CAY, John	239
KENNAN, Patrick	157	MC CLENDON, Thomas	388
KERSHAW, John	201	MC CLOBOY, Hugh	278
KICKLIGHTER, F.	380	MC CONNELL, William	237
KIRKSEY, James	39	MC CRARY, Micagah	202
KIRKSEY, James E.	363	MC CULLOUGH, Michael	158
KIRKSEY, John	37	MC DANIEL, J. O.	139
KITE, Bankston	42	MC DANIEL, Philip E.	140
KNOTT, Benjamin	189	MC DANIEL, S. J.	141
KONTZE, Christian	336	MC GINNIS, J. L.	381
KROG, Freddrick	164	MC GINNIS, William	220
KYLE, John	233	MC GINTIS, Joel T.	330
KYLE, John	283	MC LAW, W.	393
KYLE, Thomas	325	MC MUFFIE, Dunan	406
KYLE, William	165	MC WATERS, Alexander	199
LAMB, B. T.	92	MEAD, Joseph H.	214
LANGFORD, John W	156	MEDLIN, John W.	410
LANIER, W. P.	85	MEYER, David	95
LATIMER, Henry B.	374	MIMS, John F.	392
LAWSHA, Lewis	56	MITCHELL, Josiah	226
LEDBETTER, John	29	MOODY, Anderson	382
LEE, Joel	347	MOONEY, Alfred	133
LEE, John	232	MORRIS, B. M.	231
LESTER, Harrison	344	MORRIS, L. G.	194
LESTER, James M.	121	MOSS, Rhoda	277
LESTER, German M.	80	MULLINBRINK, H.	87

Name	census page no.	Name	census page no.
NEESE, Andrew	266	ROSSER, James R.	64
NEESE, Jordon A.	345	ROUNDTREE, James	296
PACE, Drewry	179	ROURKE, W. W.	104
PARK, Samuel H.	180	RUCKER, Louisa V.	169
PARR, Charles D.	256	RUFF, Milley	313
PAYNE, Edwin	348	RUSK, Thomas	126
NICHOLS, William	65	RUTHERFORD, Telman	190
NORCROSS, J.	329	SANTO, Mrs.	186
OLIVER, John S.	371	SARTAIN, Sarah	294
ORME, W. P.	334	SCARBORO, John	36
OSLIN, R. E.	311	SCHOENBERRY, Jinenlan	370
PARKER, Anderson	84	SCOTT, Reubin	322
PARKER, William C.	117	SHACKELFORD, Stephen J.	235
PARKS, Henry	343	SHAW, George	54
PEACOCK, Ava	107	SHEAD, James	342
PEACOCK, J. T.	106	SHIVERS, Thomas	306
PEARCE, Martha	337	SHUBURN, George	192
PENDLY, Benjamin F.	196	SIKES, Wiley	16
PERRY, Francis	390	SIMMES, William D.	225
PERRY, Mordran	389	SIMMS, Cicero	418
PETERS, Richard	51	SIMPSON, Elijah	6
PILGRIM, G. A.	143	SIMPSON, Joana	15
PLUMMER, James R.	248	SIMPSON, L. C.	75
PLUMNER, Edward	17	SMALL, William J.	159
POWELL, Irbin	323	SMITH, George T.	81
POWELL, Lewis	23	SMITH, John D.	68
RABUN, William	227	SMITH, Jos. S.	332
REED, Mary	28	SMITH, L. Windsor	1
REID, Mary Agnus	270	SMITH, T. M.	127
RENNEAU, Jessee	58	SMITH, William	166
REYNOLDS, Elza B.	366	SPALDING, Albert	152
RHODES, Mrs. A.	160	SPANN, John M.	254
RHODES, A. S.	150	STOCKTON, Anderson	35
RHODES, John R.	229	SULIVAN, Jeremiah	122
RHODES, Nancy	365	SWEAT, Riley	407
RHODES, T. B.	364	SWINEGAN, Pauline	385
RICE, William H.	146	SYLVEY, Drewry H.	153
RICHARDSON, William	372	TAYLOR, Samuel	328
RICHARDSON, William B.	368	TERRY, Stephen	210
RILEY, S. T.	298	THOMAS, Thomas L.	215
RILEY, William H.	213	THOMASON, G. W.	353
ROBINSON, Elizabeth	302	THOMPSON, Joseph	376
ROBINSON, George	73	THOMPSON, Robert C.	260
ROBINSON, R. P.	61	THURMOND, Benjamin	349
ROBINSON, Rachel	288	THURMOND, David	243
ROGERS, Benjamin P.	138	THURMOND, William	350

Name	census page no.	Name	census page no.
THWEAT, Thomas	118	WHEAT, Basil	416
TILLER, John	46	WHITAKER, Vincent	293
TODD, Richard C.	400	WHITAKER, William	367
TOMLINSON, John	392	WHITE, Henry	244
TONEY, James	397	WHITE, James	11
TRAIL, Eliza C.	236	WHITE, James	245
TRAMMEL, John C.	48	WHITNEY, Zeno W.	219
TURNER, David G.	4	WILEY, John T. W.	145
VAUGHN, Henry A.	217	WILLIAMS, Drayton	50
VAULT, Mahala E.	31	WILLIAMS, John H.	3
VEAL, Mary	24	WILLIAMSON, John	285
WALKER, Edward	100	WILLIFORD, Benjamin N.	137
WALKER, James F.	403	WILMOTH, William	246
WALKER, M. T.	163	WILSON, Almida	52
WALKER, Martin T.	123	WILSON, Moses	161
WALKER, Sam	404	WILSON, Winney	153
WARD, Patrick J.	144	WING, Edward	168
WARE, A. C.	241	WINGFIELD, W. S.	339
WATSON, George W.	181	WOOD, Nimrod	207
WEAVER, John	387	WOOD, Winston	360
WELLS, Amanda	182	WOODING, Alford	355
WELLS, Jeremiah	184	WOODRUFF, John	409
WELLS, Mary	295	WORNER, Ferdinand	221
WESTMORELAND, Harrison	271	WRIGHT, U. L.	333
WHEAT, Augustus	261	YARBOROUGH, William	316
		YOUNG, Joice	321 [22]

Blackhall District

Name	census page no.	Name	census page no.
ALEXANDER, A. C.	63	BRYANT, Heth	29
ANDERSON, John	41	BUTLER, Patrick	33
ARMSTRONG, William	34	CALDWELL, Charlott	134
AUSLY, William	101	CALDWELL, Joseph	52
AVERY, William	50	CAMPBELL, Mary	68
BAKER, Elisha	109	CARTER, Rhoda	26
BAKER, Jethro	105	CARTER, Samuel	81
BELK, Warren A.	47	CASH, Polly	28
BETTS, William	140	CASON, William	74
BIRD, Nelson	57	CHAFFIN, Thomas	49
BOTHWELL, Samuel	42	CHESHIRE, Hezakiah	137
BROWN, Gideon	8	CLARADY, Abraham M.	67
BROWN, James M.	21	CONELLY, Abner	96
BROWN, Merideth	3	COOK, Frances	11

Name	census page no.	Name	census page no.
COOK, Jack L.	62	JONES, James V.	134
COOKRUN, S. R.	141	JORGUET, William J.	17
CRAWFORD, Robert	123	LIDDEL, Benjamin	118
CRAWFORD, Terry	108	LOFTEN, James B.	73
CROWELL, E. G. D.	103	MAGUIRE, Mary	20
DAVIS, James	127	MANGUM, James	51
DAVIS, Thomas W.	18	MANN, Ezekiel C.	44
DEARING, William	10	MARCHMAN, Wiley C.	78
DUFFY, William M.	135	MARRIS, Nancy	66
ELLIS, John E.	23	MC COOL, A. P.	99
ELLIS, William N.	112	MC COFFEY, James	77
EVANS, John L.	22	MC DANIEL, Henry T.	76
FERRELL, Joseph	107	MC DONALD, Alexandre	70
FORD, Bennet T.	59	MC DUFFIE, Neal A.	119
GAMMON, Berry	40	MC GERITY, Solomon	125
GAMMON, Joshua	39	MIDDLETON, James	38
GAMMON, Samuel	45	MITCHELL, Darel D.	54
GARRISON, Aaron	129	MITCHELL, Elden	58
GIDDINGS, George	79	MITCHELL, H. F.	53
GINNINGS, Flavius J.	138	MITCHELL, Mary	65
GREEN, William J.	85	MOBBS, George W.	114
GRIFFIN, Francis	27	MOORE, Gibson	106
GRIFFIN, Leroy	6	MORGAN, Winney	46
GRIFFITH, Thomas H.	128	MORRIS, Andrew	15
HARDY, Berry	102	MORRIS, Mathew	24
HARIS, Mary	130	MORRISON, Angus	120
HAWKINS, Andrew J.	4	ORR, Robert	87
HEAD, James	30	PADUE, James	139
HEAD, Mary	113	PATRICK, Jonathan	64
HEAD, Richard	31	PATRICK, John	61
HEAD, William	110	PEGG, Samuel S.	9
HEELY, Michael	116	PERKINS, William A.	32
HENDESON, Esham	35	PERKINSON, Thomas J.	48
HENDON, John	36	POOL, Allen J.	2
HERRING, James F.	82	POOL, Adam	1
HERRING, Joel	83	POOL, Thomas	25
HERRING, N. W.	84	POWELL, Silas J.	94
HILL, James R.	71	PRICE, Robert M.	13
HOLBROOK, Greenbery	55	RATAREE, Alexander	97
HORNBY, Thomas	60	PRUIT, Ervin J.	104
HUCHENS, Judge	86	RATAREE, John	95
HUCHINS, Levi	117	ROBINSON, W. G.	133
HUMPHRIES, Charmer	75	SHEUMATE, Frances F.	136
HUTCHINS, Meredith	111	SMITH, James M.	93
JETER, William W.	24	SPENCER, William	12
JOHNS, Granbury	80	STEPHENS, Isham	56

Name	census page no.	Name	census page no.
STEPHENS, Jonathan V.	14	WALKER, Mrs.	115
STEWARD, Thomas	98	WALLACE, Nicholas	116
TALIAFERRO, Susan	5	WALLAM, Benjamin	69
THORERMEND, Benjamin	43	WATTS, Edward	121
THOURMOND, John	126	WHITE, Daniel P.	89
THOURMOND, William	122	WHITE, Henry M.	92
TOMLINSON, Archibald	7	WHITE, J. J.	90
TOMLINSON, Leonard	16	WHITE, Jacob	91
WAITES, Daniel D.	19	WHITE, James V.	37
WALKER, John M.	132	WHITE, Mary	88
		WHITE, William W.	72

Browning's District

Name	census page number	Name	census page no.
AIKIN, James	74	GOSA, Aaron	55
AIKIN, Thomas J.	70	GOSA, Bird	56
BAGWELL, John	40	GOSA, John	23
BAXTER, George	64	GREEN, Larken	93
BAXTER, James	51	GULLIDGE, Henry	87
BAXTER, Robert	9	GUNTER, James P.	54
BLAKE, John	45	HARALSON, P. A.	28
BOOGS, Nancy	86	HARDMAN, John	16
BROWNING, A.	32	HARDMAN, Josiah	62
BUCKHANNAN, John W.	92	HARRIS, John C.	8
CAMPBELL, Malinda	80	HENDERSON, Greenville	35
CAMPMIRE, Delia	14	HENDERSON, J. B.	37
CARROLL, James	63	HENDERSON, Major E.	44
CARTER, T.	6	HENDERSON, Rufus	38
CASH, Howard	82	HENDERSON, Thomas	68
CASH, Nancy	81	HENDERSON, William G.	36
CASH, Stephen P.	42	INGE, Cherrye	65
CASH, Washington	84	JACKSON, William	24
CASH, William	41	JEFFERS, John E.	50
CASH, Winston H.	77	JOHNSON, W. H.	10
CHEWNING, Ambrose	85	JOHNSTON, R. Wiley	47
COCKRAN, John	53	JOHNSTON, Thomas T.	46
COCKRAN, Seaborn	22	JOHNSTON, William	27
CONN, William A.	39	JOHNSTON, William B.	12
DABBS, Jesse	59	JOLLY, Joseph	83
DABNEY, Garland	20	KELLEY, A. A.	5
DEAN, Hiram	26	LANG, John C.	30
FLOWERS, John Y.	48	LEACH, Arthur	3
FLOWERS, Stother	66	LEACH, J. I.	4

Name	census page no.	Name	census page no.
LEVEL, John W.	61	SHANNON, Moses M.	43
LIVELY, Mary	71	SHOEMATE, Benjamin F.	88
LIVELY, Milton C.	72	SMITH, George P.	58
LITTLE, Caroline	18	THOMAS, John T.	29
MC CORD, Robert	60	THOMPSON, Thomas	1
MC MICKEN, John H.	76	TOWERS, Isaac	89
MITCHELL, L. W.	33	TOWERS, Mary	19
NASH, John	7	TUCKER, T. O.	11
NASH, Larkin	15	WAITS, Maxmillian	94
NASH, Miles P.	17	WASHINGTON, Ellmunda	90
NASH, William	25	WEBB, Robert H.	78
OSBURN, John	79	WELLS, Willis L.	13
PARISH, Isaac	91	WHITLOCK, Charles	21
PEYTON, Valentine	75	WIGGINS, John	31
PRICHARD, Jordan	2	WILSON, William B.	49
REEVES, Ezekiel	34	WOOD, Robert	9
RICHARDSON, Esther	52	WRIGHT, Spencer P.	73
ROSS, James	69		
ROSS, Robert	57		

Buckhead District

Name	census page no.	Name	census page no.
ABERNATHY, James	39	FARR, Thomas	17
BEASLY, Cintha	56	GATES, John	54
BEASLY, Philip T.	18	GILMORE, Sanford	32
BELLINGER, John N.	69	GOLDING, Coleman	60
BRYANT, Asa	9	GOODWIN, Solomon	64
CAGLE, William	47	GOODWIN, Sterling	62
CAIN, Harrison	46	GROGAN, Bart	8
CAMPBELL, Elias	5	HARRIS, Reuben	16
CAMPBELL, Elizabeth	20	HATCHER, Johnathan	10
CAMPBELL, Thomas	6	HERD, William G.	38
CANNON, Mary	13	HILDEBRAND, William H.	33
CANNON, William	19	HILL, Elias	27
CAWHERN, Mary	41	HILL, Elias	58
CHANDLER, Harrison	42	HOPKINS, Solomon	35
COLLIER, Willey	4	IRBY, Henry	1
DAVIS, James	12	ISOM, Charles	29
DOUGLAS, Elbert	63	ISOM, John	30
DOWERS, Jackson	44	JETT, Ferdnan	50
DOWERS, John M.	49	JETT, Richard	51
ELLINGTON, David	3	JETT, Stephen	48
FARR, James	24	JOHNSTON, Willis	55
FARR, Milton	11	KIRKSEY, Isaiah	34

Name	census page no.	Name	census page no.
MC CRARY, Thomas	7	SENTELL, Elizabeth	31
MC LAUGHLEN, Nancy	37	SMITH, Augustus	66
MODLIN, Nathan	15	SMITH, William	53
MORGAN, Eldridge	61	SMITH, William B.	70
ONEAL, James	65	STOWERS, Orpha	25
PACE, Solomon K.	14	THOMASSON, Nelson	28
PATRICK, William A. K.	26	TOMLIN, Mary	59
PERKINS, Reuben	71	TOWNSEND, Joshua	40
PHILLIPS, Meredith	52	WALRAVEN, Berry	2
PLASTER, Sarah	22	WILLIAMS, Ichabod	36
POSS, Sally	43	WILLIAMS, James	45
RANDALL, P. H.	57		
RAY, Lydia	67		
RICHARD, Obadiah	68		
ROWELL, William	21		
ROWELL, William Jr.	23		

Casey's District

Name	census page no.	Name	census page no.
AKRIDGE, J. T.	55	COSEY, Charles P.	47
AKRIDGE, Simeon	54	COSEY, James A.	53
ALSOBROOK, Wilson	117	COSEY, Robert C.	52
ANDERSON, John S.	1	COSEY, William	48
ALLARD, Morris R.	72	DAVIS, Benjamin P.	82
BASKINS, John	91	DAVIS, Elizabeth	103
BAUGH, Absalom	44	DAVIS, George W.	62
BONDS, James	74	DEAN, Henry G.	9
BOSWELL, Allen	105	DONAHOO, Elijah M.	65
BOWEN, Charles	41	ECHOLS, Joseph	86
BOYD, John	40	ECHOLS, Robert	77
BOYD, Samuel	112	ECHOLS, Thomas	80
BROCKMAN, Elijah	20	ELLIOTT, Edmond	104
CAMPBELL, Delagall	50	ELLIOTT, George	101
CAPE, James R.	39	ELLIOTT, Henry	57
CAPE, Lewis	38	ELLIOTT, Marshall	102
CARTER, Moore A.	51	FLETCHER, William	4
CARTER, Wilson	93	FOSTER, Prudence	84
CASEY, Ausburn J.	10	GILHAM, Nancy	16
CASEY, Elisha L.	66	GOLDING, John	90
CASEY, Hiram	67	GOLDING, Osborn	89
CASEY, JohnA.	6	GOODWIN, Jesse	64
CHRISTIAN, William J.	17	HAWS, Rebecca	113
CONLEY, Cornelius M.	109	HIGGINS, Moses	25
COOK, Jesse M.	64	HIGGINS, Reuben	24

Name	census page no.	Name	census page no.
HOOPER, Enoch	17	NORTON, Silas M.	85
HOOPER, Hiram	13	PITTS, Philip	68
HUDSON, Calvin	111	POPE, John H.	60
HUDSON, David	95	RAMEY, Pitt M.	56
HUDSON, Jane	94	RAY, Joseph	46
HUDSON, Notley	30	REESE, Franklin	69
HUDSON, Wesley	92	REID, Benjamin	35
HUGER, Peter	96	ROMAN, Alexander	70
JARRALL, Thomas	115	SANDERS, John K.	106
JETT, James A.	58	SIMMS, William	34
JOHNS, John D.	79	SIMPSON, Griffith	11
JOHNS, Sarah	37	SMITH, Thomas M.	114
JOHNS, William	43	STARNES, Joel	75
JOINER, Daniel P.	49	STARNES, Mansel B.	76
JONES, Samuel J.	59	SWEAT, Solomon	29
JONES, William	2	THOMPSON, Annanias	7
LANGSTON, James	97	THOMPSON, Isaac	8
LEACHMAN, Matthew	98	TOWNLY, Zachariah	12
MARTIN, Ewel	110	TURNER, Matthew	5
MASON, James L.	18	TURNER, Stephen C.	45
MASON, William C.	21	VAUGHN, Jesse	3
MCCORMICK, James A.	23	WADKINS, Strauder	99
MCCORMICK, John P.	22	WALKER, William	61
MCDONALD, William	116	WATERS, William J.	88
MCGRIFF, Edward L. Jr.	15	WEBB, Alfred	42
MCMASTER, John	63	WELLS, Elizabeth	87
MITCHELL, Andrew B.	78	WOOD, Elias	28
MONTGOMERY, Elizabeth	14	WOOD, James	32
MORRIS, Enoch	31	WOOD, Jesse	81
MORRIS, Ira L.	27	WOOD, Moses	33
MORRIS, Joseph	71	WOOD, William	26
MORRIS, William H.	73	WOOD, Zilpa	36
NETTLES, Solomon	83	WOODALL, William M.	100
		WINGFIELD, William	108

Cross Keys District

Name	census page no.	Name	census page no.
ADAMS, Enos	88	ARENDALL, Loughlin	66
ADAMS, Jesse H.	47	AUSTIN, William	69
ADAMS, John Jr.	93	BEATENVAW, Adam	29
ADAMS, John Sr.	92	BELLINGER, John F.	27
ADAMS, Salathiel	91	BOGGS, Andrew J.	30
ALLEN, William	41	BRADDEN, Thomas M.	40

Name	census page no.	Name	census page no.
BRAZIL, Asa	77	LOWERY, James	85
BRAZIL, William H.	13	MANN, Jesse	39
BURDETT, Thomas S.	61	MARTIN, Henry H.	60
CAMPBELL, Chesley C.	9	MARTIN, Jesse G.	59
CARLYLE, William	79	MCCRAVY, Eli	46
CARPENTER, Willis	12	MCELROY, John	3
CASH, Jasper	32	MCELROY, Samuel Jr.	6
CHESNUT, Alex	4	MCELROY, Samuel Sr.	8
COOK, James	45	MCELROY, William	36
DALE, Samuel	63	MEDLOCK, Thomas L. D.	99
DALE, William	64	MILLER, Israel	2
DODGIN, Elizabeth	100	MILLICAN, Andrew	44
DONALDSON, A. B.	101	MITCHELL, John W.	70
DONALSON, M. S.	56	MORGAN, Henry M.	74
EADES, T. M.	31	MORRIS, Gideon	1
EADES, Thomas V.	51	NORTON, James	57
ELLIOTT, James	16	POSS, John	24
EVANS, George W.	80	POWER, Josiah	50
EVANS, John L.	65	PRESSLEY, Daniel	35
GADDY, G. W.	58	RAINEY, Bennet	15
GARNER, Kindred	14	RAINEY, Charles	22
GIBSON, Elizabeth	17	REEVES, James W.	37
GOBER, Thomas C.	95	REEVES, William D.	49
GOODWIN, Harris	78	REYNOLDS, David	18
GRIER, Henry M.	97	RIDLING, John M.	43
HARRIS, B. S.	52	SPRUILL, James	68
HEFLIN, L. F.	82	SPRUILL, Stephen	42
HELTON, Peter	83	SPRUILL, Stephen Jr.	67
HELTON, Temperance	84	SPRUILL, W. E.	71
HOOPER, James	10	STEWARD, Joseph	34
HOUSE, Jacob	21	TALBOT, Clinton T.	53
HOUSE, Philip	20	THOMPSON, John	23
HOUSE, Samuel	76	TILLY, Ebenezar	103
HUMPHRIES, George W.	33	TILLY, John W. P.	102
JEFFERS, Robert D.	7	TILLY, Stephen	28
JETT, John	5	TIMMONS, Thomas T.	11
JOHNSTON, John	94	TRIMBLE, James	75
JOHNSTON, John	38	WOMMOCK, George W.	26
JOHNSTON, Susan C.	90	WOMMOCK, John B.	25
JOHNSTON, Thomas J.	87	WILLIAMS, Robert	72
JOHNSTON, William	89	WILLIAMS, Solomon	73
JONES, Hartwell	96	WILSON, David	81
JONES, Nancy L.	19	WILSON, George W.	62
LANCEFORD, Lemuel	54	WILSON, William	86
LORD, Jabez	98	WILSON, William C.	55
		WRIGHT, Henry E.	48

Cross Roads District

Name	census page no.	Name	census page no.
ANDERSON, William H.	61	MAULDING, Drury	66
ARGO, Nimrod	21	MCCARTER, John R.	42
ARGO, Willis	19	MCELROY, Archibald	48
BIFFLE, Leander	65	MCELROY, George W.	46
BISHOP, Jackson	36	MEADOR, Vashti	25
BLACKMON, John	49	MILES, James	40
BORN, Jacob	4	MILLER, Barron	17
BORN, James H.	7	MILLER, Harvest	16
BORN, John M.	8	MILLER, John W.	26
BORN, William	5	MILLER, William	34
BOYD, Andrew	11	MITCHELL, John M.	62
BRADLY, John L.	68	MITCHELL, Rebecca	33
BURFORD, Philip H.	69	MORRIS, Renly	30
CENTER, John	9	NEW, Henry	14
CHANDLER, Ira	35	NEW, William N.	10
CHANDLER, Nicholas	50	PEARCE, George W.	47
CHAPMON, Phebe	55	PENDLY, William R.	1
CLARK, William H.	56	PHILLIPS, James	53
COWAN, James K.	51	PHILLIPS, Paschal C.	52
DUNCAN, Philip	12	POTTS, Samuel	27
ELAM, William	32	RAGSDALE, Elijah	45
ESTES, Celia	15	REID, Mary	23
ESTES, Reuben	37	REID, William J.	22
GEORGE, James R.	57	RICHARDSON, Elizabeth	13
HAIRSTON, Milas	64	RICHARDSON, James	20
HAIRSTON, William	63	SCOTT, James C.	28
HOLLINGSWORTH, Henry	59	STUDDARD, John	3
HOWELL, Elizabeth	54	STUDDARD, William	2
HULL, B. F.	18	TERRY, James	60
JACKSON, Melton	41	WAITS, John	67
JAMES, John	39	WEBB, Archibald	38
JORDAN, William	70	WELLS, Andrew	6
KILGORE, William	43	WHALEY, Thomas	44
KIRBY, Hampton	58	WIGGINS, Walton	31
LOWRY, George W.	29	WOOTEN, Joseph	24

Decatur District

Name	census page no.	Name	census page no.
ADAMS, Daniel	28	ANDERSON, Jesse	40
ADAMS, Gardner	31	AUSTIN, Thomas	21
ALEXANDER, A.	85	BIRD, Elijah S.	75

Name	census page no.	Name	census page no.
BLACKSTORK, James	46	KNIGHT, Thomas	83
BOWIE, Jane E.	36	LINSEY, Cullen	74
BROWN, Robert M.	27	MASON, Ezekiel	23
BROWNING, Willy	6	MCALLIST, James R.	58
BUCHANNAN, R. C.	8	MCCARRY, Nancy	34
BUCKANNEN, James B.	63	MCGUINES, James	38
BUTHE, Elizabeth A.	47	MCNEAL, James	44
CALHORNE, E. N.	53	MORGAN, DeWitt C.	66
CALHOUN, James M.	62	MORGAN, L. S.	67
CAMERON, Nancy	37	MURPHY, Charles	68
CHUNING, W. F.	59	NESBIT, Eliza	49
DAVID, William A.	5	PENDLEY, Jane	7
DAVIS, Robert	39	POWEL, William A.	25
DEARING, William	79	REIVES, Joseph A.	43
DELAY, Hiram R.	19	REYNOLDS, Thomas	50
DORSEY, Henry A.	77	ROBINSON, Jessee	86
DOUGLASS, Thena	72	ROBINSON, Sarena	41
DURHAM, John	13	ROPE, Thomas	81
EZZARD, William	30	ROSSER, Elijah	33
FARRAR, Jesse C.	11	ROSSER, Isaac	35
FERRELL, James	2	SCOTT, Lucinda	14
FLOYD, D. A.	52	SHUMATE, Benjamin D.	12
FLOYD, David	51	SIMPSON, Jno.	24
GEORGE, T. R.	73	STONE, Daniel	70
GRANT, Lemuel P.	71	SWIFT, John N.	32
HALL, H. T.	4	TILLEY, Wesley	64
HALL, Thomas F.	20	VEAL, William	22
HILL, Henry B.	80	WADSWORTH, Walter	55
HILL, William	1	WAITS, Jeremiah	82
HOLLY, Hiram J.	16	WALLACE, Thomas	84
HOLLY, J. M.	15	WILKERSON, Elizabeth	48
HOLLY, John B.	9	WILLIAM, Levi	54
HOLSONBACK, Eli	65	WILLIAMS, Amrose	60
HOYLE, Peter F.	69	WILLIAMS, Jesse L.	56
HUMPHRIES, Merrill	17	WILLIAMS, John J.	61
IVEY, Thomas P.	76	WILLINGHAM, Rely M.	45
JOHNSON, Nathaniel	78	WILLSON, J. I.	29
JOHNSTON, Alexandra	26	WILLSON, Samul H.	18
JONES, Robert	42	WILSON, John S.	57
KIRKPATRICK. J. W.	3	WOODALL, Allen	10

Diamond's District

Name	census page no.	Name	census page no.
ADAIR, William F.	3	JACKSON, Littleton	83
ALFORD, Nancy	25	JOHNSTON, Thomas	16
ANDERSON, David	76	KILGORE, Theophelus	64
ARGO, William	6	LEE, Edmond	40
BAILEY, E. J.	58	LEE, Z. J.	44
BARNETT, William	87	LUCKEY, J. I. B.	24
BISHOP, Reuben	11	LYNCH, Thomas	4
BOND, Joseph B.	31	MANNING, Richard	20
BRAWNER, John	53	MARBUT, William G.	1
BRAZIL, Wesley	17	MARBUT, Michael	2
BUNT, Abington	85	MARBUT, Young	46
CAMPBELL, Thomas	51	MCGAFFY, James	39
CHUPP, David	9	MINOR, Lazrus	47
CHUPP, Jacob	65	MISE, Henry	82
COCKRAN, Charles	49	NEW, Edwin	62
CORLEY, Mountville	13	NEW, James	61
CORLEY, Sarah	14	NEW, Joel	60
CORNWELL, John O.	78	NEW, William	86
DAVIS, Lewis	63	PARKER, William	71
DEAN, Jefferson	77	PEARCE, Elizabeth	80
DICKENS, William	83	PEARCE, Elizabeth	27
DRAKE, Brackston	12	POSS, Nicholas	69
DRAKE, James	42	PYRON, William H.	72
EMMERSON, James P.	77	RAGSDALE, Mark M.	34
EVANS, James M.	29	RICHARDSON, Thomas	57
FERRELL, Tarner	59	SMITH, Orlando	75
FLOYD, Richard	21	SMITH, William B.	73
FOGERTY, Cornelius	37	SPIVY, John	45
GARRETT, Thomas	66	STEWART, Absalom	53
GODDARD, Clement	26	STUDDARD, Anderson	23
GODDARD, James	22	TAYLOR, James D.	48
GODDARD, William	56	TURNER, John C.	55
GRAHAM, Joseph W.	7	VAUGHAN, Griffin	74
GRAHAM, Josiah	41	WADE, James	79
HASLETT, William	15	WADE, Thompson	70
HEARN, C. C.	19	WATTS, William	38
HENRY, Joseph T.	52	WEAVER, Drury A.	68
HOLT, James	50	WEAVER, Henry	67
HUDGINS, Alfred	32	WESLEY, Mavin	35
HUDGINS, John	32	WHITLEY, Needham	5
HUDGINS, Noel	36	WHITLEY, Zechariah	81
HUDMAN, Elizabeth	80	WHITLOW, J. I. J.	30
HUMPHRIES, Sterling	43	WHITLOW, W. D.	28
IVY, A. F.	84	WINGATE, William	8
IVY, Martin B.	54	WILSON, William	10

Hulsey's District

Name	census page no.	Name	census page no.
ARMSTRONG, John	49	KENADY, George R.	79
BOYD, Lawson	51	KEYS, John	4
BRANTLY, William	34	LYONS, George	42
BROCKMAN, Henry	77	LYONS, Johnston	48
BUSBY, William	1	LYONS, Thomas	44
BUTLER, Elizabeth	11	MCPEAK, John	30
CAPPS, Catharine	10	MCPEAK, William	29
CENTER, Nathan	63	MITCHELL, Alexander W.	45
CLELAND, John	7	MITCHELL, Isaac	37
COE, Hayden	39	MOORE, William	73
COLLIN, Edwin	82	MOORE, William	57
COLLINS, Meredith	81	MORRIS, John H.	46
DEAL, Marcellus	62	PHILIPS, John M.	53
DONALSON, Silas H.	80	PLASTER, Edwin	78
ELAM, George	55	POPE, Abel	16
EMORY, Hiram	84	POPE, Felix	17
GARNER, George	64	POPE, James	12
GOWENS, Alexander	14	POTTS, Moses J.	38
GOWENS, Solomon	13	POWELL, John A.	22
GRESHAM, Davis E.	61	REAGAN, Jones	8
HAMBRICK, Joseph	35	RICHARDSON, Isaac B.	36
HARRIS, William	74	RICHARDSON, John W.	2
HOLLINGSWORTH, John	23	ROBINSON, James B	60
HOOKS, McKinzie	41	ROBINSON, Thomas	56
HOOPAUGH, Mariah	9	RUSSELL, Jane	19
HOUSEWORTH, Michael	18	SCOTT, Wiley W.	52
HOUSEWORTH, Philip	32	SIMMS, Alfred	24
HOUSWORTH, Abraham	33	SPRAYBERRY, Freeman	5
HOWARD, Asa W.	69	STAPLES, William	27
HOWELL, Lewis	67	STEPHENSON, John	59
HUDSON, James M.	68	STEPHENSON, William M.	58
HUFF, James R.	76	STOWERS, Lewis	21
HULSEY, Juinius	40	STOWERS, Lewis	26
JENKINS, Jesse	6	STOWERS, Thomas	31
JOHNSON, Perry	83	STREET, William B.	3
JOHNSTON, Daniel	75	TANNER, Silas	47
KEMP, Nancy	43	TOWNSEND, Mansel	28
KELLY, John	65	TWEEDLE, Hiram	15
KELLY, Martha	66	WEBB, Elijah	72

Panthersville and Flat Shoals Districts

Name	census page no.	Name	census page no.
ABBOTT, David	105	CHAPMAN, Eli T.	3
ADCOCK, Thomas	156	CLARK, Mary	67
ANDERSON, Nelson	54	CLARK, Thomas	34
ARES, William	196	CLARK, William	35
ARGO, David	137	CLAY, Elizabeth	101
AVERY, George W.	94	CLAY, Jeddy	102
AWTRY, Araminta	120	CLAY, John A.	56
AWTRY, Eldridge	9	CLAY, Nathan	99
BADGER, J. B.	125	COLB, James L.	146
BADGER, Sabra	126	COLB, Nancy	142
BALL, Elizabeth	79	COLB, Robert M.	145
BARTLETT, James	58	COLB, William T.	203
BATY, James W.	91	COLLIER, Merrill	110
BETTERTON, Levil	36	CONNALLY, William F.	108
BIRD, Charity	83	COOK, Allin J.	190
BIRD, Elijah	127	COOK, William	171
BIRD, John	36	COWAN, James	57
BLACKMON, Daniel	219	CRAWFORD, Esther	131
BOHANNON, Isaih W. D.	157	CROWLEY, George W.	73
BONDS, John	22	CROWLEY, Mary J.	150
BOYD, Andrew	25	CROWLY, Harris	74
BOYD, Kizziah	52	CRUSE, David	103
BOYD, Peter	20	DARNALL, Thomas M.	159
BROUGHTON, Rutha	87	DAVIS, Ethan	207
BROWN, Benjamin C.	208	DAVIS, Margaret	153
BROWN, Emanuel	170	DEARING, Thomas	216
BROWN, Faming	163	DEFUR, Martin	213
BROWN, Jackson G.	114	DEFUR, Sydney	174
BROWN, James	198	DENSON, Obadiah	78
BROWN, James	168	FARLOW, James	62
BROWN, James	31	FARRIS, John	209
BROWN, James W.	37	FLOWERS, Reuben	44
BROWN, Joel	215	FORD, Colemond	193
BROWN, Killis	214	FORD, William	195
BROWN, Samuel	167	FOWLER, Alfred	141
BROWN, William	217	FOWLER, Joel	107
BROWN, William D.	14	FOWLER, K. J.	71
BROWN, William S.	218	FOWLER, Mary V.	140
BUNT, Edmond	7	FOWLER, Samuel	204
BURDETT, Richard T.	130	FOWLER, Thomas	143
BURNS, James	63	FOWLER, William	206
BUSBY, Elias	128	GARR, Michael A.	23
BUTLER, James	42	GARR, Russel W.	49
CAGLE, Robert	21	GUNNELS, William B.	18
CARTER, Maleshial	81	HARRIS, David H.	189

Name	census page no.	Name	census page no.
HARRIS, Jackson	20	MORE, John	53
HELTERBRAND, John E.	69	MORGAN, Abram	90
HEWEY, John	166	MORGAN, Seth	161
HILDEBRAND, J. Y.	202	MORRIS, Garret L.	59
HOLLINGSWORTH, Robert	149	MORRIS, J. L.	201
HUCHINS, Wiley	66	MORRIS, John	211
HUDGENS, William P.	81	MORRIS, Nancy	47
HUDGENS, William W	81	MULLICAN, Berry	2
HUDGINS, L. Z.	93	NICHOLS, James	184
HULSY, William	33	NICHOLS, Sam	183
JOHNSON, Laughlin	85	NIGHT, Matthew	48
JOHNSTON, Andrew	5	NOLAN, Isaac	133
JOHNSTON, Catharine	4	OSMORE, Robert	135
JOHNSTON, Galin	144	OWENS, Benjamin	28
JONES, Edward	152	OWENS, Richard	41
JONES, John	148	PACE, Charles	86
JONES, John H.	45	PARKER, David	165
JONES, Zachriah R.	80	PARKER, John	164
JORDAN, Jesse	138	PARKER, Mary	162
KERBY, John	109	PARRIS, Ezekiel	186
LANGFORD, Basil F.	113	PERKINSON, Dempsy	32
LATTIMER, Charles	17	PITTS, Augustus S.	205
MALDING, Benj.	43	RAGSDALE, Berry	10
MALDING, Richard	24	REEVES, Burgess	6
MCCLOUD, John	104	RHODES, Nicholas	172
MCCLOUD, Malcolm	132	ROBINSON, James A.	16
MCEVER, Joseph	11	ROGERS, Andrew	182
MCGUINES, C. W.	151	ROSSER, David	194
MCGUIRE, Jane	98	SCREWS, Enoch	77
MCKEE, Martine	26	SIMMS, Alfred	54
MCKEEVER, William	124	SIMMS, Leonard	61
MCLANE, James W.	139	SIMMS, Reddick	55
MCLANE, William S.	169	SIMMS, Thornton	1
MCWILLIAMS, Alexander	115	SIMPSON, Levi	27
MCWILLIAMS, Alexander	97	SKELTON, Charles S.	12
MCWILLIAMS, David M.	179	SPRAYBERRY, Bryce	39
MCWILLIAMS, John	71	SPRAYBERRY, Robert	134
MCWILLIAMS, John G.	95	STEWARD, John	119
MCWILLIAMS, Nathaniel	60	STINSON, Joseph	132
MCWILLIAMS, Robert	96	STUBBS, James	46
MCWILLIAMS, Robert	70	STURGESS, Laban	75
MCWILLIAMS, Samuel	175	SWINNEY, Hariet	15
MITCHELL, Everett	118	SWINNEY, Matilda	116
MITCHELL, William	40	THOMAS, John H.	123
MOORE, James	200	TERRELL, William	192
MOORE, Thomas	197	TERRY, Thomas	13

Name	census page no.	Name	census page no.
TERRY, William	111	VICKORY, Middleton	72
THOMAS, George	8	WADKINS, Tabitha	89
THOMAS, Joseph	68	WALDRIP, David	38
THURMAN, Richard	191	WATTS, George	187
THURMOND, James C.	160	WEBB, Bryce	122
THURMOND, Richard	188	WEBB, John	176
TOLER, Margaret	112	WESTBROOK, Milly	29
TUGGLE, Alexandra C.	155	WHITE, James	173
TURNER, Case	177	WHITE, John	159
TURNER, Elijah	64	WHITE, Thomas	19
TURNER, Elisha	180	WHITE, William	92
TURNER, John B.	65	WHITEFORD, Mary A.	178
TURNER, Nathan	106	WIGGINS, James M.	121
TURNER, Thomas C.	199	WIGGINS, William	117
TURNER, William	185	WILEY, William	51
TWILLY, Cyrus	88	WILKINS, Thomas W.	30
TWILLY, James	84	WINN, James W.	82
TWILLY, John B.	100	WRIGHT, William	212
VAUGHN, Elijah	154	YANCEY, Sanford B.	210

Shallowford District

Name	census page no.	Name	census page no.
ABERNATHY, John	45	DUDLEY, George A.	48
ABERNATHY, Thomas	46	ELLIS, Isaac	37
ADAMS, Walter	59	FEE, Samul	23
AIKIN, William G.	56	GARMAN, William	33
AUSTIN, Thomas F.	43	GROGAN, William	22
BALL, James	52	HACKET, William	8
BALL, Peter	50	HALL, Cyntha	32
BELL, John	49	HARDMAN, E. C.	1
BINION, Job	25	HEARD, William	110
BRIGHTWELL, William B.	40	HITSON, Boyce	4
BUCKHANNON, John D.	41	HITSON, Zechariah	5
BUTLER, James J.	13	HOWELL, Frederick	3
BUTLER, Joseph	11	HOWELL, Simpson	2
BUTLER, Milton	12	HUTCHURSON, William	36
CAHEELY, Elizabeth	62	ISOM, David	9
CALDWELL, Clayton C.	58	JONES, John	7
CARPENTER, John	14	LEWIS, William	53
CARPENTER, William	15	LONGSHORE, David	66
COPELAND, Elijah	10	MARBUT, Eucledus	63
CROSSLY, Gardner	6	MARBUT, John P.	65
DEAS, James	29	MARTIN, Stephen	60

Name	census page no.	Name	census page no.
MAYFIELD, Elisha	21	STEAN, William	19
MCEWEN, Edward	44	STEEN, George	24
METCALF, William F.	61	STEEN, John	26
MINOR, Mark	64	STEWARD, Thomas	68
NORRELL, John	31	SULLIVAN, William	30
POSS, Adam	54	WAITS, Absalom	47
POWERS, Samuel	57	WAITS, John W.	38
POWERS, William	35	WALLACE, John	16
ROBERTS, James H.	51	WALLACE, William	17
SENTILL, William W.	39	WALLACE, Zechariah	18
SINGLETON, Cyntha	28	WING, John L.	27
SMITH, John	20	WOODALL, James	55
SNEAD, John G.	67	WRIGHT, Lewis	42

Stone Mountain District

Name	census page no.	Name	census page no.
ALEXANDER, John	45	HICKS, John	69
ALEXANDER, Thomas	48	HICKS, Milly	13
BEAUCHAMP, John	11	HOLCOMB, John	58
BEAUCHAMP, William	37	HOLCOMB, John C.	59
BINION, Abram	81	HOWARD, S.	34
BLOODWORTH, William R.	33	JARRET, John	14
BRADY, William	10	JIMMERSON, Hannah	65
BURDETT, Joshua	70	JOHNSON, Andrew	44
CAMPBELL, Thomas M.	51	JONES, Francis A.	57
CORNWELL, Hiram	16	JORDAN, Solomon E.	62
DANEL, James M.	29	KEMP, Andrew	47
DEAN, Lemuel	27	KEMP, William	46
DIAMOND, James J.	40	LAMPSON, Henry	36
DICKENS, Ephraim	97	LANGFORD, Jesse	89
FARMER, William	60	LEE, Bennett	8
FOWLER, A. C.	66	LEE, Cynthea	43
FOWLER, John W.	71	LEE, James	7
GARRETT, James J.	53	LEE, William	90
GOLDSMITH, William	55	LEVERETT, John E.	2
GOODE, Joseph	23	LEVINGSTON, Charles	64
GUEST, Thomas K.	6	LOVELESS, William	78
HAMBRICK, Levi	54	LOWERY, Marshal W.	95
HAMILTON, George K.	28	MASON, John	88
HARRIS, Henson C.	20	MASON, William	85
HAYS, Elizabeth	93	MATHIS, Thomas	6
HICKS, CalyJane	17	MCCARDY, Clarissa	84
HICKS, Jeremiah	15	MCKEE, William M.	4

Name	census page no.	Name	census page no.
MEESE, Washington	31	STEWART, A. G.	18
MILLICAN, Henry	98	STEWARD, Elijah	19
MILLICAN, James	99	STONE, Micajah	96
MILLICAN, Thomas	82	THOMAS, Winford	72
MINOR, George W.	5	THOMPSON, A. J.	74
NORMAN, H. S.	68	TOWERS, Lewis	56
PARKER, Isaiah	79	TURNER, John B.	25
PAYNE, Alex.	61	TURNER, William B.	26
PEW, Elenor	63	VEAL, B. F.	49
PICKENS, Robert	9	VEAL, J. J.	52
POOL, Adah	21	VEAL, Morgan	22
RICE, Charles H.	3	WADE, David	12
ROSS, A. M.	100	WADSWORTH, Archibald	30
RUSSAW, William C.	41	WALDROP, Davidson C.	75
SANDERS, E. B.	92	WARREN, E. P.	76
SANDERS, James	91	WEBB, Milbry	35
SHIPERD, William M.	67	WELLS, M. W.	73
SIMMS, William	50	WIGGINS, Lewis	24
SMITH, George K.	39	WILLINGHAM, Michael	32
SMITH, Simeon	1	WOOD, I. J.	38
		WOODRUFF, Nancy	94

Stone's District

Name	census page no.	Name	census page no.
ARMSTRONG, John	62	CONNELLY, Thomas W.	65
AVERY, Henry W.	35	CONNELY, Charles W.	59
BAKER, Julius	87	COOK, John	115
BAKER, Larkin	86	DANIEL, Burgess	78
BAKER, Green W.	83	DANIEL, John M.	77
BAKER, Oliver	104	DIGGS, John	63
BAKER, William	6	DONAHOO, James	20
BANKSTON, Henry	24	DUKES, James L.	103
BOND, John	61	EDMOND, Pitt R.	18
BUES, John	15	ELLIS, Shadrick	127
CARROLL, William	43	ELLIS, Shadrick	38
CASH, John H.	100	EWING, Joseph	121
CASON, Edward	151	FAIN, Elizabeth	114
CHILDRESS, Jesse	52	FAIN, John J.	109
CHURCHHILL, William D.	73	FERGUSON, Elizabeth	120
COCKRUM, Elizabeth	11	GAINS, James	112
COCKRUM, Lewis M.	16	GILBERT, William	49
COLLINS, James	60	GILHAM, John	5
CONELLY, Christopher	66	GITTING, James	4

Name	census page no.	Name	census page no.
GRANT, David	45	MCDANIEL, Premascus	19
GRANT, Joseph	84	MCFALLS, Jacob	30
GRAY, James D.	80	MCGEE, Marat	22
GREEN, Cintha	7	MCVAY, Anna	42
GREEN, L. B.	75	MIMMS, Azariah	125
HALEY, A. M.	26	MORGAN, Charlott	97
HANIGAN, Christian	53	MYERS, James D.	146
HARVILL, Coleman P.	145	PAYNE, Joseph	57
HARVILL, Levi H.	144	PAYNE, Moses	56
HATHCOCK, William	123	PEACOCK, M. J.	99
HAWES, Claiborn	17	PEOPLES, H. T.	149
HEROD, Henry	122	PETTY, Anderson	47
HERRING, Edmond R.	27	PETTY, James	117
HIGGINS, Isaiah	10	POWELL, Thomas	47
HIGGINS, Joel	14	OTTO, Christian	31
HOLBROOK, John B.	70	REDWINE, Jacob	107
HOLBROOK, Martha A.	79	REDWINE, James C.	124
HOLBROOK, William	76	REDWINE, John	110
HOLDER, Greenberry	132	REDWINE, William P.	108
HOLDER, John	133	RICH, Levi	44
HOLSCLAW, W.	13	ROBBINS, James Y.	91
HORNSBY, Henry	142	ROBBINS, Sydna	92
HORNSBY, John	135	ROBERTS, Aaron	64
HORNSBY, N. K.	130	ROBERTS, James	74
HORNSBY, Noah	143	ROBERTS, Willis	54
HORNSBY, Thomas	134	ROBERTS, Willy	140
HUCHINS, Harris	55	RUSSELL, James	131
HUGHS, James	23	SEWEL, Isaac	113
HUGHS, Jonathan	138	SEWEL, John E.	119
HUGHS, Rebecca	33	SEWEL, Samuel	111
HUGHS, Zachariah	34	SHEARIN, John G.	88
JARRELL, Enoch	14	SHEARIN, Rebecca	89
JINKINS, Isaack	128	SHIPPY, James	51
KENNADY, James	46	SHIPPY, William	139
KENNADY, Thomas	46	SMITH, A. S.	21
KNIGHT, Nathaniel	2	SMITH, David D.	71
LEE, James	129	SMITH, James T.	67
LEE, John	126	SMITH, John M.	105
MADASON, Andrew	50	SMITH, John T.	37
MANOR, James	1	SMITH, Riley	41
MANOR, Joseph	3	STONE, Flora	118
MATHIS, Arthur	101	SUTTLES, Micajah	136
MCCLESKY, James	39	SUTTLES, Wiley	116
MCDANIEL, Green	85	THRASHER, John J.	72
MCDANIEL, James	69	TOMLINSON, Summer	145
MCDANIEL, John	8	TURNER, James	90

Name	census page no.	Name	census page no.
VINCENT, Amos	28	WILLIAMS, J. J.	106
WAITS, John	94	WILLIS, Joseph	32
WAITS, Osbern R.	81	WILLIS, Margaret	152
WAITS, William	82	WILLIS, William	58
WALLACE, Henry	23	WILSON, Custus A.	25
WALLACE, Joseph	141	WILSON, Elizabeth	40
WALLACE, William L.	93	WILSON, Gilford B.	98
WALLACE, Simeon H.	68	WILSON, Peter	96
WARREN, James B.	29	WINBURN, David	150
WEAVER, James B.	12	WOOTEN, Daniel B	137
WELLS, Mary	147	YANCY, Robert	9

Town District

Name	census page no.	Name	census page no.
AVRY, John	53	EVANS, James M.	15
BAKER, James A.	55	FANNING, John	21
BALLINGER, Joseph T.	31	GHOLSTON, Gilbert C.	34
BATEY, James	80	GHOLSTON, Zechiariah	37
BATY, David	81	GOBER, Emily	78
BRANDON, William R.	40	GOBER, John E.	7
BRYCE, John	32	GRIER, Robert D.	93
BURDETT, Benjamin	29	GUESS, James	95
BURDETT, Samuel	26	GUESS, William R.	96
BURDETT, William	24	HARDMAN, F. M.	76
CAMPBELL, William	10	HARDMAN, Martha P.	89
CANNON, John	87	HARDMAN, Rennew J.	13
CASH, Lewis L.	8	HARDEMAN, Allen	18
CASH, Robert	9	HARRIS, William	63
CHANDLER, Robert B.	97	HAWKINS, John	42
CLAY, Green	72	HAYS, John	12
CLAY, Jesse Sr.	58	HENDRICKS, William	23
CLAY, Joseph	73	HOUGHTON, D. D.	83
CLAY, Joseph W.	57	HUEY, Joseph	16
CLAY, Samuel	60	HUEY, Mourning	38
CLOWLY, Seaborn	43	HUEY, Thomas	45
COCHRAN, Alex	51	JACKSON, Andrew	47
COOPER, John	2	JACKSON, Daniel E.	1
CROCKET, Robert	25	JACKSON, William J.	46
DABBS, John	92	JETT, Richard	98
DABBS, William C.	77	JOHNS, John R.	4
DEAN, Elbert	70	JOHNSTON, John	91
DEAN, Elizabeth	71	JONES, Jesse J.	44
DIGGS, Thomas	3	JONES, Sarah	19

Name	census page no.	Name	census page no.
KIRKPATRICK, James H.	74	SHERMAN, Henry	5
KITRIDGE, Watson	6	SHOEMATE, Abner O. H. P.	41
LANGFORD, Gower	86	SHOEMATE, Mason P.	39
MARTIN, Melinda	62	SOUTHARD, Green	49
MASON, William	11	SMITH, Robert H.	88
MCALISTER, Elizabeth	79	SPENCE, David	85
MCCULLOUGH, John	33	STARNS, Shubal M.	69
MCDUFFY, Daniel	61	STEEL, Isaac	84
MELTON, Archibald	65	STEEL, Michael A.	20
MELTON, Daniel	64	STEPHENS, Thomas J.	99
NOILS, Charles	68	STEPHENS, William H.	94
NOILS, William	67	THURMOND, John	66
PATTERSON, James L.	82	TERRY, Thomas	54
OSBURN, Randall P.	48	TUNING, Levi	28
OWENS, Nicholas	56	TURNER, Elesha	50
PADEN, John	22	VOSS, John	35
PENION, Richard	27	WALKER, Joseph	36
PITTS, Joseph	59	WEAVER, Jackson	52
PLASTER, Benjamin	100	WHITLOCK, William	14
POWELL, Chapmon	75	WILLIAMS, Alvin	90
RAY, Patterson	17	WILLIAMS, James	30

Appendix 7

DeKalb County Slaveholders In 1860
Total Slaves: 1929 (934 males, 995 females)

Slaveholders With 20 Or More Slaves (16)

William H. Clark, 69
S. F. Alexander, 31
C. Murphey, 31
Ann Dougherty, 29
John McColouch, 28
James Paden, 28
L. W. Chewning, 27
P. L. Hoyle, 27
Samuel House, 25
Watson Kittridge, 25
Phillip Housworth, 23
James B. Roberson, 23
John Caloway, 21
Gardner Corley, 21
George K. Hambelton, 20
James Paden, 20

Slaveholders With 10-20 Slaves (49)

James C. Avery, 19
Benjamin Burdett, 19
Lewis Ethridge, 19
George P. Key, 19
William C. Daniel, 18
Richard Holt, 18
C. Latimore, 18
Phillip H. Bufford, 17
George Lyons, 17
E. A. Center, 16
Est. of Thos. H. Chivers, 16
James H. Norris, 16
Joel R. Chivers, 15
W. W. Durham, 15
John A. Fowler, 15
Thomas Barnes, 14
E. H. Clark, 14
A. S. Fowler, 14
H. I. Fowler, 14
Greenville Henderson, 14
Daniel Johnson, 14
E. Mason, 14
James F. Strubbs, 14
John H. Swift, 14
Autery A (sic), 13
James Crockett, 13
James R. George, 13
P. C. Phillips, 13
Thomas L. Roberson, 13
B. F. Veal, 13
Lochalin Johnson, 12
Thomas Johnson, 12
Naoma Johnston, 12
E. Watington, 12
John F. Balinger, 11
John W. Fowler, 11
William Mason, 11
Vashti Meadows, 11
R. H. Morris, 11
Robert H. Smith, 11
E. A. Turnner, 11
John Brice, 10
Jacob Chupp, 10
R. W. Cobb, 10
Thomas Johnson, 10
James Phillips, 10
Bery Ragsdale, 10
John C. Ragsdale, 10
Sarah Reeve, 10

Slaveholders With Nine Slaves (10)

Killis Brown
F. H. Gay
M. Harry
R. D. Isner
C. M. Jones
John Lamar
Lasrus Minor
John D. Sharp
William A. Shields
S. P. Wright

Slaveholders With Eight Slaves (18)

James C. Avery, Agent
William M. Barton
John Y. Flowers
H. P. Fowler
P. F. Hoyle, in trust
Z. R. Jones
M. C. Lively
C. Murphey, Guardian
Samuel Patty
Dempsey Perkison
Joseph Pitts
William Shepard
Henry Sherman
Mary W. Stokes
Steven Tilley
William Veall Sr.
Nancy Wiley
William L. Williams

Slaveholders With Seven Slaves (17)

William Barnett	Fielding Maddox	Lewis Starnes
R. M. Brown	William Marley	Nathan Turner
Pheba Chapman	D. A. Newsom	Ann Williams
James S. Elliott	Rebecca Rainey	James J. Winn
James M. Evins	Ezekiel Reeve	Benjamin Woodson
Elizabeth Gowing	Simion Smith	

Slaveholders With Six Slaves (16)

Nancy Akins	Thomas J. Deaver	A. J. H. Pool
E. J. Bailey	Rusell W. Garr	Augustus L. Potts
Thomas Buchanan	John Hardman	M. A. Steel
M. A. Candler	? K. Humphries	Sintha Stone
Seaborn Cochran	Charles Lattimer	Joseph Walker
Seabron Crowley		

Slaveholders With Five Slaves (15)

Thompson A. Browning	William C. Hightower	R. Nash, Guardian
James T. Cobb	Henry Hollingsworth	William J. Palmer
D. A. Cook	? L. Humphries	Samuel Potts
E. A. Davis	Hester A. Jones	Sarah Rainey
John R. George	I--- Morgan	L. Tuggle

Slaveholders With Four Slaves (28)

John C. Austin	H. C. Harris	Robert McWilliams
J. W. Buchanan	A. T. Holmes	John W. Miller
Tarlton Carter	Arrann Johnson	R. Nash, in Trust
B. F. Chapman	Susan C. Johnston	Drewry Pace
Warren J. Clark	Martha Jones	J. C. Turnner
William A. Cook	B. G. Kelley	James Veal
H. Crowley	J. L. Kilgore	Elija Watts
A. Fuller	J. T. Lock	S. P. Wright, interest for minor
W. D. Gholston	John P. Marbit	
Harris Goodwin	Luther Mason	

Slaveholders With Three Slaves (33)

? E. Brown	John H. Jones	Reubin B. Perkins
R. M. Brown	Thomas J. Lyons	George M. Phillips
J. W. Christain	S. C. Masters	John M. Phillips
B. Christon	George W. Matheney	Margaret Rozen
Feraby Clark	James A. Miller, interest	James Smith Sr.
J. E. George	James Millican	Brice M. Sprayberry
James Hambrick	Jane Morgan	Mathew Stephens
J. C. Harris	Garet Morris	Ebenezar Tilley
Henry F. Holmes	Nancy Morris	A. Weller
Samuel E. Jackson	Thos G. Paden	John J. Whitlaw
Naoma Johnston	John H. Pate	Charles Whitlock

Slaveholders With Two Slaves (46)

Thomas T. Armstrong	Mary E. Fox	Reuben Mitchell
L. H. Austin	Martin Goodwin	R. N. Morris
James Ball	William Hairston	Isarisah Parker
Lydia A. Bowen	Sintha Hardman	John M. Ridling
Asa Braswell	J. T. Henry	Jasper Smith
James M. Carroll	George W. House	Phon Stephenson
John Cochran	M. Houseworth	J. W. Stewart
William Cobb	W. M. Kiley	J. W. F. Tilley
J. J. Cowen	Jane Johnson	L. B. Underwood
Benjamin Crowly	Malinda Mann	Alexander Vaughn
Elizabeth Ealim	Aberham Martin	W. W. Veal
John F. Evans	Thomas D. Mathews	William Veal Jr.
John Fannin	John R. McCarter	T. P. Wells
Coleman Forn	Juda McClendon	W. L. Wells
A. C. Fowler	John McWilliams	William Wright
J. M. Fowler		

Slaveholders With One Slave (58)

John Bird	John Jones	John Ozmer
Elija Bishop	Robert Jones	Reubin B. Perkins
Joshua J. Bishop	F. W. Kendrick	J. L. Phillips, Agent
Jacob M. Born	Ann Kirkpatrick	James O. Powell
David Chesnut	B. Lankford	J. Prickett
James M. Coe	Edmon Lee	John G. Rainey
A. R. Craven	Dilthey Levert	Mary A. Reese
W. A. Evans	T. Levert	James Reeve
John Evins	Helen M. Luckey	James M. Reeve
J. B. George	E. Marbut	W. C. Reusson
?. Goldsmith	J. R. McAllister	Joseph Scott
J. W. Goldsmith	F. T. McCalpin	George K. Smith
S. H. Harris	Judea McClendon	William Sprayberry
D. Herrin	C. H. McCurdy	Laborn Sturgess
P. H. Hightower	John G. McWilliams	Thomas Thompson
Robert Hollingsworth	H. S. Miller	James W. Vincent
Dicy Hulsey	James Minter	J. B. Walker
Larking Nash	George W. Mitchell	W. W. Williams
J. B. Johns	J. N. More	T. F. Williamson
William Johnson	Seth P. Morgan	J. B. Willson [23]

Appendix 8

Confederate Army Companies From DeKalb County [10]

Co. E, 7th Regiment
Georgia Volunteer Infantry, Army of Northern Virginia, C. S. A.
"DeKalb Light Infantry"
May 29, 1861

Officers

Fowler, John W., captain
Powell, John J., 1st lieutenant
Hawkins John M., 2nd lieutenant
Wilson, James L., jr. 2nd lieutenant
Brown, Moses L., 1st sergeant
Morgan, Dewitt C., 2nd sergeant
Jackson, Daniel E., 3rd sergeant

Fowler, John W. Jr., 4th sergeant
Norman, Hugh Heard, 1st corporal
Norman, William L., 2nd corporal
Davis, Robert L., 3rd corporal
Powell, George W. L., 4th corporal
Galliger, Charles T., musician

Privates

Arwood, Thomas W.
Austin, Joseph V. *
Austin, William C.
Betts, James M. *
Biggers, William G.
Bohnefeld, Carl
Bohnefeld, Richard (Dick)
Bostick, James G.
Bradbury, Aaron G. (Crack)
Bradbury, William W. *
Brimm, William W.
Brown, James Freeman
Brown, Robert M.
Burnham, Julius W. *
Butler, Thomas C.
Caldwell, Curtis C.
Carroll, John
Carroll, Thomas H. *
Carroll, William *
Cash, Rush H.
Chamberlin, Elliott R.
Chamblee, William
 Nicholas *
Chandler, David P.
Chewning, John C.

Cochran, John B.
Cochran, William M.
Crocket, A. J.
Crockett, George W.
Crockett, Joel J.
Crockett, Wilkes W.
Davis, Ezekiel A.
Davis, James L. *
Deal (Deel), George S.
 (Joseph S.)
Degnan, James
Dilda, James *
Dilda, Joseph *
Dilda, William A. *
Durham, George *
Eads, John M. *
Eskew, Thomas J. *
Floyd, Thomas L. *
Ford, John
Ford, J. Landrum
Fowler, Joel M.
Garner, George W.
Gentry, Henry
Gholston, William D. *
Gordon, William

Graham, Frank M.
Hadden, Robert J.
Haynes, George W.
Haynes, William Pope
Henderson, Elijah
Henderson, Greenville A. *
Henderson, Thomas *
Henderson, William G.
Herron, William T.
Hightower, Paschal H.
Holmes, Samuel D.
Holt, Francis M. *
Holt, Samuel F. (Samuel L.)
Hopkins, George Wiley
Hudson, Thomas Pliney
Hunter, James
Johnson, Thomas P.
Jones, William B.
Kearney, John Joseph
Kimbrell, James M. *
Lawhorn (Lawhon), William
 Riley
Leavell, George W.
Lively, Henry H.
Martin, John A.

---

[10] * died while in service or as result of service.

Mashburn, Aaron W.
Matthews, John Francis *
Mayson, Asbury S.
Mayson, William Jefferson *
McAllister, George Clint
McAllister, William Oscar *
McCulloch, Charles E.
McCulloch (McCullough), James W. *
McCulloch (McCullough), John
McWilliams, James M.
Medlock, John T.
Mills, George W.
Mills, William Hugh (Wig)
Morgan, William W. *
Morton, Edward L.
Moseley, Enoch F.
Nash, Francis M. *
Nash, John F.
Nash, Thomas Washington
Nash, William Milton *
Norman, John M.
Ozmer, John W.
Packer, Redding D. *
Pate, Patrick H.
Peelen (Peeler), Thomas E. *
Pennell (Pinnell), James P.
Pickens, Reuben
Pitard, Robert Pinckney *
Potts, James G.
Potts, James J. *
Potts, Martin E.
Powell, Leonard C.
Richardson, James L.
Richardson, Robert
Robertson, William M. *
Rowe, Seaborn
Singleton, John Washington
Skelton, William J. D. S.
Stokes, David Plinty
Tarleton (Talton), William E. *
Teat, Irvine L.
Terry, Andrew Jackson
Thomas, Andrew J. *
Thomas, George A.
Thomas, William B.
Webb, James A.
Weed, James H. (James A.)
Weed, John D. B. *
Weed, William R.
White, Josiah H.
Wilson, Hugh J. Marion
Wilson, Virgil Alonzo
Wooddall, Hamilton Garmany
Wooddall, James Allen
Wooddall, John Smith

Co. A, 38th Regiment
Georgia Volunteer Infantry, Evans' Brigade, Gordon's Division, Wright's Legion Army of Northern Virginia, C. S. A.
"Murphey Guards"
September 26, 1861

Officers

Flowers, John Y., captain
Pool, A. J. H., 1st lieutenant
Rankin, John G., 2nd lieutenant
Miller, W. A. C., junior 2nd lieutenant *
Jett, James S., 1st sergeant *
Wells, George, 2nd sergeant
Pool, W. H., 3rd sergeant
Rainey, John G., 4th sergeant
Holcombe, A. M., 5th sergeant
Hawkins, John M., 5th sergeant
Harris, Sterling G., 1st corporal
Wilson, R. M., 2nd corporal
Cochran, S. W., 3rd corporal
Harris, Edmond (Edward), 4th corporal
Dodgen, William O., musician
Jenkins, William H., musician
McClendon, William, musician

Privates

Adams, John A. *
Akins (Aiken, Charles Thomas *
Anderson, George J.
Arnold, B. W. *
Austin, A. C. *
Austin, John Thomas
Austin, W F. *
Baker, W. M. *
Ball, John W.
Ball, Peter M.
Ball, William M.
Baxter, Francis M. *
Baxter, John
Binion, Joseph D.
Braswell, G. A. *
Braswell, Samuel H.
Campbell, Benjamin M. (Benjamin W.)
Campbell, George M. *
Carpenter, John J.

Carroll, J. M.
Carter, John D.
Carter, William J. *
Cash, L. J.
Chamblee, W. L.
Chesnut, D. A.
Chesnut, G. R. M. *
Coggin, J. F.
Conn, William A.
Copeland, Obediah B.
Corley, R. J. *
Davis, William Caleb *
Dees, David
Dickerson, W. F. A.
Dodgen, J. N.

Ealum (Elum), Joel R. *
Edwards, William A.
Eidson, A. J.
Eidson, John *
Eidson, Robert
Eidson, R. S.
Eidson William M. *
Eidson, Z.
Elliott, Joseph E.
Estes, Gainham T. *
Evans, John L. *
Evins, Nelson H.
Fields, William A.
Flowers, Asbury P.
Flowers, James A. *
Gaddy, G. W. *
Gardner, Andy J. *
Gardner, Charles *
Gardner, James R. *
Gardner, William *
Goss, John W.
Green, David A. *
Gresham, J. W. *

Hall, John W.
Hambrick, James F. *
Hambrick, J. T. *
Hambrick, Robert C. *
Hardman, E. C.
Hardman, J. S. W. *
Harmon, Francis M.
Harmon, James P.

Harmon, John T.
Harmon, J. B.
Harmon, R. A. *
Harris, J. C.
Hix, A. H.
Holly, H. J.
Holmes, James M.
House, David C. *
House, George W.
House, John T. *
House, Thomas J.
Ivey, Aaron H.
Ivey, Joseph J. *

Jenkins, J. D.
Jenkins, W. C.
Johnson, G. F. M. *
Johnson, J. T. M.
Johnston, W. J.
Jones, C. M.
Kite, Claiborn
Lafoy, John A.
Lang (Long), John W. *
Lang (Long), William B.
  (Wiley B.)
Langford, Josiah C.
Lanier, Pessley *
Lanier, William L. *
Lawhorn, Joel J.
Leavell, E. F.
Leavell, F. M.
Lord, Russell D.
Lord, S. M.
Lord, William J. *
Luckey, J. R.
Lynch, Thomas

Maddox, Thomas L. *
Marable, John J.
Marbut, John S. (John T.) *
Marlow, William T.
  (William L.) *
Martin, Benjamin S.
Martin, James *
Mason, Cornelius A.
McCandless, Jesse A.
McCurdy, John Wilson
McCurdy, Phillip Burford

McElroy, Samuel B. *
Medlock, Eli W.
Miller, Andrew J.
Miller, Charles *
Miller, David Y. *
Miller, H. B. *
Miller, N. R.
Miller, Robert W. *
Mitchell, William H.
Morris, D. C. *
Nash, John Miles *
Nash, J. N.
Nash, Miles H.
Newsom, Moses H.
Parrish, Isaac N. *
Poss, James *
Powers, Asbury H.
Powers, J. W. *
Powers, Patrick H. *
Powers, William H. *

Rainey, John M.
Ray, John P.
Ray, Robert A.
Reeves, James Andrew
 Jackson
Reeves, William P.
Ridling, M. V.
Ridling, Thomas C.
Robinson, Robert M.
Sellers, John A. *
Simpson, Robert M. *
Simpson, William M. *
Singleton, William Leonard
Smith, Tilnon P. *
Stewart, E. P.
Stewart, Thomas H.
Stewart, William D. *
Tankersley, J. M. *
Thomas, Thomas Jefferson
Thoams, Wyett L.
Thomas, Zephaniah
Thompson, G. F. M. *
Thompson, Joseph Maxine *
Thompson, Richard Govan *
Tucker, John T. *

Verdin, William J.

(William V.)
Waits, Newton *
Wallace, George W. *
Warnock, John C. *
Warnock, Patrick *

Warnock, William R.
Wells, Willis Virgil *
West, John P. *
Williams, William Jasper
William, William W. *

Wilson, John Hamilton
Wilson, Thomas
Wilson, Thomas M. *
Wilson, W. A. *

Co. K, 38th Regiment
Georgia Volunteer Infantry, Evans' Brigade, Gordon's Division, Wright's Legion, Army of Northern Virginia, C. S. A.
"DeKalb, Fulton and Bartow Avengers"
(also known as Co. G and New Co. B)
September 26, 1861

Officers

Wright, William, captain
Robinson George F., captain
Gober, Julius J., 1st lieutenant *
Goodwin, Gustin E., 2nd lieutenant *
Stubbs, George W., jr. 2nd lieutenant *
Johnston, 1st sergeant *
Henry, William Robert, 2nd sergeant
Maddox, Joseph A., 3rd sergeant *
Hudgins, Francis L., 4th sergeant

Morris, Enoch H. C., 5th sergeant *
Gazaway, Francis M., 1st corporal *
Ward, William O., 2nd corporal *
Gazaway, James H., 3rd corporal
Walker, James M., 4th corporal
Tony (Toney), Charles W., musician
Tony (Toney), James, fifer
Wade, George W., musician

Privates

Adams, Enos
Adams, John *
Akers, John H. *
Almand (Almond), A. W. *
Anderson, James Lewis
Armstrong, James J.
Autry, Isaac W.
Autry, William Allen
Bailey, Luke R.
Ball, James E. *
Bayne, Hendley V.
Bowman (Boman), William M. *
Boyd, John B.
Brisentine (Brisendin), William H.
Brooks, William A.
Brown, Allen
Brown, Illis
Brown, Lewis
Burdett, Humphrey M.
Burdett, John S.

Caudle, John H. W. H. (see Co. M)
Chandler, James E. *
Chandler, John W. *
Chandler, William B. *
Childress, Joseph H.
Childress, William A.
Collier, James S. *
Collier, John E. J.
Connor, B. G.
Cook, George G.
Cook, James R. *
Cordell, J. H.
Cowan, John Jordan
Cowan, John S. *
Cowan, Zach J.
Daniel, Jesse F.
Dorris, John M. *
Ellis, William H. *
Ennis John
Ennis, William
Farr, David N.

Fletcher, Richard H.
Gazaway, John
Gazaway, William
Gentry, Asbury M. *
Goodwin, Charles H. *
Goodwin, William M. *
Goos, William T.
Grogan, Gideon F. *
Grogan, Jerry H.
Grogan, Joseph D. *
Grogan, Josiah T.
Guess, Franklin L.
Hammond, Joshua T. (see Co. M.)
Head, Henry Tandy
Henry, Jesse L.
Hildebrand, William B. H.
Hornbuckle, H. H. *
Jones, Charles S. W. *
Jones, James H.
Jones, John W.
Jones, Jordan M.

Jones, J. H.
Jones, Robert F. *
Jones, R. D. F.
Kelly, John F.
Kelly, John H.
Kelly, J. T.
Lee, A. J.
Lee, George *
Little, William J.
Mangham, Wiley
Martin, Benjamin S. (see Co. A)
McClain, Berryman S. *
McGuire, William R.
Mitchell, Elisha J.
Mitchell, James R. *
Morgan, William A.
Nash, John W. *
Owens, William L.
Phillips, John W. *
Pruett, Jerry J.
Richardson, Daniel D. *
Richardson, Josephus S. *
Richardson, William M.
Seals, Benjamin A.
Smith, William A. *
Stowers, Asbury M.
Swiney, James M.
Swiney, S. J. J. *
Thomas, Thomas Jefferson (see Co. A)
Thompson, John B.
Tweedle, M. J.
Vaughn, J. S.
Vaughn, Robert L.
Vaughn, W. T.
Victory, Middleton
Wade, Enoch D.
Wade, F. M.
Wheeler, Amos *
Wiggins, Ellis W. *
Wiggins, George W.
Wiggins, Jackson C. *
Wiggins, James M.
Wiggins, M. O.
Wiggins, R. W. *
Wilkins, James B.
Wilson, Aaron, Jordan *
Wilson, Benjamin L. *
Wilson, J. H. *
Wood, William B. (William R.)
Wright, William A.

Co. D, 42nd Regiment
Georgia Volunteer Infantry, Army of Tennessee, C. S. A.
"DeKalb Rangers"
March 4, 1862

Officers

Clay, Nathan, captain
White, William C., 1st lieutenant
Young, James H., 2nd lieutenant *
Wright, Marshall J., jr. 2nd lieutenant *
Turner, Nathan, 1st sergeant *
Fowler, Josiah M., 2nd sergeant
Jackson, Thomas J., 3rd sergeant
McWilliams, Galen J., 4th sergeant
Hollingsworth, Robert, 5th sergeant
Kendrick, Franklin W., 1st corporal
McWilliams, David, 2nd corporal
Parker, Robert J., 3rd corporal
Jordan, James Henry, 4th corporal

Privates

Adams, Henry
Adcock, James A.
Adkins, William T. *
Argo, Charles W.
Armstrong, Benjamin F. *
Armstrong, Jamems I.
Armstrong, J. T.
Armstrong, Lawson M.
Ayers, Benton B.
Ayers, Daniel
Ayers, Russell T.
Bird, John W.
Bishop, Elijah
Bishop, John T. *
Blackstock, George
Blackstock, John B. *
Blackstock, Terry T. *
Brown, Denson
Brown, Jackson (Jack)
Brown, John F.
Brown, John W. *
Brown, William A.
Burgess, Albert C.
Burgess, Henry Harris
Cagle, James K. P.
Cagle, Robert Montgomery *
Campbell, Oliver P. *
Campbell, S. H.
Cardin, Benjamin F.
Chewning, David *
Clarke, Elijah H.
Clay, Cleveland
Clay, James W.
Clay, Jesse W. *
Clay, Joseph A.
Clotfelter, David F.
Cobb, James H.
Collier, Joseph M. *
Collier, William T.
Crockett, Joel J.
Crossley, Joseph M.

Crowley, James L.
Crowley, J. K. P.
Darby, James W. *
Dooley, Barney J.
Eades (Edes), Samuel T. *
Ellison, William *
Fargason (Farbarson),
 William C.
Farris, Ezekiel
Ford (Fort), Bennett F.
 (Bennett T.)
Green, James T. W.
Greer, John W.
Hamby, Andy C.
Harris, Elbert F.
Harris, George W.
Henry, Cyrus V.
Henry, Flavius J. *
Higginbotham, William W.
Holcomb, Henry C.
Huey, Jesse Marion *
Irwin, John
Jackson Daniel E.
Jackson, James W.
Jackson, John A. M.
Johns, Joseph G.
Jones, James Green Berry *
Kelly, James *
Kelley, James H.
Kelley, Robert Jackson
King, William B.
Lacy, Adiel S.

Lee, A. J.
Lyon, George W.
McCanless, Blount W. G.
McClane (McLane),
 William H.
McLeod, Angus
McWilliams, James L.
McWilliams, James M.
McWilliams, John W.
McWilliams, Samuel
Merriett, James B.
Miles, James F.
Miller, William A.
Mitchell, A. M.
Mitchell, Benjamin G.
Moore, Daniel
Moore, George W. *
Moore, James
Moore, John
Morgan, Alexander L. *
Morgan, DeWitt C.
Morris, Richard M.
New, Jarrett *
New, Joel
New, Samuel C. *
Ozmer, George Smith
Ozmer, John W.
Pace, William Henry
Perkins, Berry C.
Perkins, George W.
Richardson, William A.

Rutledge, James M. *
Scarborough, William H. *
Sheppard, David C.
Sheppard, John T.
Sheppard, William M. *
Simpson, Andrew J.
Simpson, Thomas E.
Smith, William T. *
Spain, William S. *
Stephens, J. J. (I. J.)
Talton, Martin P. (Martin T.)
Tanner, S. T.
Thomas. A. L. *
Thomas, B. T.
Thomas, George M.
Thomas, John H. *
Thomas, William B.
Thornton, Lewis N. *
Turner, Elijah F. *
Turner, L. H.
Turner, Thomas C.
Tweedell (Tweedle),
 Lewis H. *
Twilley, James W.
Vaughn, James J. *
Waldrop, Robert W.
Warren, Jesse J.
Warren, John H. *
Webb, Thomas C. *
Webb, William Henry
White, Nicholas W.

Co. D, 38th Regiment
Georgia Volunteer Infantry, Evans' Brigade, Gordon's Division, Wright's Division, Army of Northern Virginia, C. S. A.
"McCullough Rifles"
April 1, 1862

Most of the members of Co. D were originally in Capt. John Y. Flowers's Co. A (Murphey Guards), mustered into service at Camp Kirkpatrick in DeKalb County. The company was divided in 1862, and the new company took on the name of McCullough Rifles. Following is a roster of the officers of Co. D and only the those men added to the original Co. A:

Officers
Rainey, John G., captain
McCurdy, John Wilson, 1st lieutenant

Wells, George R., 2nd lieutenant
Baxter, John, junior 2nd lieutenant

Hambrick, Robert C., 1st sergeant
McCurdy, Phillip Burford, 2nd sergeant
Gresham, J. W., 3rd sergeant
Lafoy, John A., 4th sergeant
Carter, John D., 5th sergeant

Hall, John W., 1st corporal
Smith, Tilnon P., 2nd corporal
Ray, Robert A., 3rd corporal
Nash, John Miles, 4th corporal

Privates

Baxter, George
Coggin, William M.
Collier, John E. J. (see Co. K)
Estes, Hilliard
Goza, Robert D.
Grogan, Joseph T. (Josiah T.) (see Co. K)
Grogan, William D.
Huff, J. H. *
Huff. Thomas P.
Jackson, Henry B.
Jeffers (Jeffares), Bennett Rainey
Mason, William S. *

Mehaffey, Francis M.
McCurdy, Stephen C. *
Nash, William T.
Perlinski, Julius (see regimental musician)
Rosenthal, Adolphus *
Singleton, James Madison
Smith, Isaac H.
Smith, Thomas *
Verdin, L. N.
Wells, W. S.
Williams, T. J.
Woods, S. J. *

Co. F, 36th Regiment
Ga. Volunteer Infantry, Army of Tennessee, C. S. A.
April 10, 1862

Officers

Morton, Edward L, captain
Jones, Charles Melton, 1st lieutenant
Hudson, George Baylis, 2nd lieutenant
Wilson, William E. C., jr. 2nd lieutenant *
Beatty, Sanford H., 1st sergeant
Donaldson, William J., 2nd sergeant
Smith, James R., 3rd sergeant
Moseley, James A., 4th sergeant

Jeffares, John E., 5th sergeant *
Henderson, Rufus, 1st corporal
Thurman, James, 2nd corporal
Holcombe, John J., 3rd corporal
Jones, J. Thomas, 4th corporal
Robinson, James P., musician
Robinson, John W., musician

Privates

Adams, James F.
Adams, Salathiel L. *
Adams, Walton D.
Akins, Thomas B.
Akins, William G.
Allen, John J.
Allen, William *
Anderson, William B. *
Bagwell, John
Ballenger (Ballinger),
Barnes, James D.
Bostick, James F. *
Braswell, George W.

Bunt, Joseph S.
Cash, James E. *
Cash, Lifus W. (Lifus C.)
Cash, L. W. (L. M.)
Cash, Robert W.
Chapman, B. F.
Chewning, Richard A.
Clarke, William B. *
Cochran, Augustus T. *
Cochran, William M.
Conn, William A.
Davis, James L. *
Delong, James M.

Donahoo, B. M. *
Donahoo, W. J. *
Dooly, Barnett J.
Dougherty, Charles L. *
Dougherty, Moses Ezekiel
Evans, James M.
Finch, H. H.
Flowers, Strawner V. *
Floyd, D. Samuel
Fowler, John W. Jr.
Gittens, Robert F. M.
Goff, W. A.
Goza, Thaddeus

Hampton, W. M.
Hardman, George D.
Harris, William D.
Henderson, William G.
Henderson, W. N.
Hill, William B.
Hix (Hicks), John T.
 (John S.)
Ivins (Evans), James M.
Joice, James M.
Jolly (Jolley), John
Jolly (Jolley), Robert
Jolly (Jolley), William
 H. H. *
Jones, Benjamin
Jones, George W.
Jones, J. F.
Kearney, Benjamin W. *
Kittredge, A. A.
Kittredge, E. M.
Lunsford, Andrew J.
Maddox, H. T.
Maddox, John F. *
Maddox, John P.
Maddox, William C.
McAlister, Wallac E.
McCrary, Andrew
McElroy, John N.
McElrow, Stephen Tilly
McMichen, Andrew M.
McMichen, John Johnson
McNeely, Robert O.
Middleton, Stephen S.
Moore, William M.
Morgan, Henry B.
Morton, Warren F.
Munday, James B.
Nash, Edward Newton
Nash, John W. *
Nash, Willard P. *
Nash, William Riley
Pace, Edward J. *
Payton, William R. *
Pinnell, William M.
Potts, James J. *
Pritchard, J. Thomas
Pritchard, Marion D. *
Ray, James P.
Ray, William T.
Ridling, George M. *
Ridling, William J.
Roberts, James A. *
Robinson (Robertson),
 Jesse I.
Rutledge, Joseph S.
Seay, John A.
Sherman, George W.
Simpson, A. J. *
Sprayberry, Pinkney
Sprewell (Spruill),
 William M.
Stanford, David
Steward, John B.
Talton, Thomas E.
Thrasher, W. J.
Tucker, Alvin H.
Tucker, Chadick W. *
Turner, John W.
Walker, James T.
Wamack, Lyddmell B.
 (Bob)
Weaver, John P.
Wells, Marion M. *
Wells, Thomas P.
Wells, Wilber H.
 (William H.) *
Wells, W. R.
Williams, J. Frank *
Williams, W. F.
Woodson, John F.
Wright, Charles Tolbert
Wright, John S.

Co. B, 66th Regiment
Georgia Volunteer Infantry, Army of Tennessee, C. S. A.
July 16, 1863

Officers

Jordan, Columbus M., captain *
Wright, J. A., 1st lieutenant
Walker, A. H. C., 2nd lieutenant
Jolley, James W., jr. 2nd lieutenant
Worley, Martin V., 1st sergeant
Saulsbury, James L., 1st sergeant (see Co. D)
Arrington, M. G., 2nd sergeant *

Wright, Lewis C., 3rd sergeant
Dodd, Benson W. (Benjamin W.) , 4th sergeant
Bentley, James C., 5th sergeant *
Craig, J. S., 1st corporal
Bowdoin, J. D., 2nd corporal
Harris, Jasper F. M.
Sasnett, Fred G., 4th corporal

Privates

Aroner (Arriner), Isaac
Arrington, C.
Atcherson, James *
Bacon, John F.
Beaver, John H.
Bilbo, T. J. (James T.,
Joseph T.)
Boles, John H.
Bowdoin, Eletia F. *
Brace, R. H.
Bridges, Jordan
Brinson, John A.
Bucklew, J.
Carlisle, Mathew
Chance, John T.
Colbert, Mason
Crenshaw, Joseph
Darden, Madison

Dodd, Edward C.
Dodd, M. *
Dodson, Levi
Etchieson (Etcherson),
  Allen S. *
Evans, Isaac
Evans, John T. *
Forsyth, Thomas J.
Fricks, W. S.
Gentry, Benjamin P.
Gentry (Gurtry), Jeremiah P.
  (Jeremiah H.)
Guthiel, Adam
Haines, Adam (Allen)
Hanson, David W.
Harris, John H. *
Harrison, William
Haynes, David V.
Haynes (Haines), Thomas
Head, George W.
Henderson, James J.
Hicks, Berry
Hicks, S. A.
Hodge (Hodges), James R.
  (James B.) *
Hopper, John R.
Hulsey, William
Inglet (Inglett), Geldin R.
  (Gillroy R.)
Inglett (Inglet), G. T.
Inglett, J. J.
Inglett (Englitt, Inglet),
  Samuel J.
Inglett (Inglet), Thomas A. *
Inglett (Inglet), William J. L.
Jackson, William
Jordan (Jorden), John
King, James
Kinnoman (Kinnaman),
  Henry L. (Henry S.) *
Knox, James M.
Langford, William H.
Langston, Asa F.
Latimer (Lattimer), S. W.
Little, John A. J. *
Little, John J.
Little, M. A.
Love, Stephen *
Mauldin, C. W.
McKinney, William D.
Moore, R. G.
Marrow (Morrow), H. B.
Parr, W. E.
Pierce, John W. *
Powell, J. A.
Raimey (Rainey), Josiah *
Raimey (Rainey), L. Terrell
Sargeant, James S.
Smith, George
Stinson, Jesse J.
Stone, Thomas L.
Strickland, Drury *
Summery (Summers), Jacob
  R. (Jacob B.)
Teal (Teale), Luther
Turner, Abner James
  (James A.)
Turner, James W.
Victor, T.
Wilder, John F.
Williams, William C.
Wilson, Robert H.
Wright, J. S.
Young, Hiram L.
Zimmerman, Benjamin B.

Co. E, 66th Regiment
Ga. Volunteer Infantry, Army of Tennessee, C. S. A.
August 1, 1863

Officers

Brown, Moses L., captain (drill master at Camp of Instruction, Decatur, Ga., Sept. 17, 1863)
Stone, Osborn M., 1st lieutenant
Smith, John F. (John T.), 2nd lieutenant
Brown, James F., jr. 2nd lieutenant
Wooten (Wotten), John D., 1st sergeant
Kirkland (Kirklain), Williamson, 2nd sergeant
George, Jephthah E. (Jeptha), 3rd sergeant
McKoy (McKay), James B., 4th sergeant
Bryant, William, 5th sergeant
Mustin, David K. (Mastin, Lane K.), 1st corporal *
Mann, Stephen, 2nd corporal
Kelley (Kelly), Sanford, 3rd corporal
Tuggle, Bennett S., 4th corporal *

Privates

Abee, Simeon *
Baty (Beatty), Sandford H.
Bell, K S.
Berry, Richard
Bishop, D. G.
Bloodworth, Milus E.
Boyle, Wiliam R.
Brown, Zachariah Taylor
Bugg, Hampton C.
Burney, John H.
Burton (Barton, Benton), John H.
Campbell, William H.
Cannady (Kannady, Laurens), Lazarus *
Canady (Kannady), William
Clay, John M. S.
Cobb, Thomas S.
Cooper, John N.
Cramer, Samuel A.
Crosley, Minor G.
Darden, E. Burch
Deadwiley (Deadwaly), Charles P.

Drennan, John W.
Driscoll (Driswold),
  James B.
Dyer, Albert N.
Dyer, Lucius M.
Ellenburg, John
Ethridge, Manley (Manly)
Feagin (Fragans),
  Humphrey P.
Finley (Fealey, Fendley),
  Alfred *
Furr (Farr), W. J.
Gaulding, William D.
Gilliam, John
Gober, Dempsey M. C.
  (Denice)
Grow, J. A.
Hadley, P. S. *
Harris, John C.
Heinz, John C.
Hendley, Phillip L.
Hendon, George M.
Henry, John C.
Hines, Levi S.
Hudgins, Bartlet L.
Hudgins, William P.

Jackson, John M. *
Jackson, S. R.
Kelly, J. T. *
Kimbrough, John P.
King, William D.
  (William B.)
Kirk, Henry J.
Kiser, Pinckney L.
  (Pinckey L.)
Landon, Elijah S.
  (Elijah L.) *
Lee, George W.
Lee, James B.
Livsey, Joseph
Marshall, Dillard L.
McIntyre, Phillip
Miles (Myles), Milton L.
Miller, James
Minor, Andrew J.
Mitchel (Mitchell), James L.
Moon, Isaiah
Moore, B.
Moore, James B.
Northrup, George M.
  (George N.)
Pate, H. M. R. *

Payson, C.
Perry, A. B. (R. B.)
Phillips, John C. (John S.)
Price, John W.
Rector, Henry B.
Reeves, Hiram
Reees, Thomas
Renfrow (Renfroe), Marion
  J. (Martin)
Sims, William R.
Smith, Charles
Smith, Frederick H. *
Smith, Gideon (E. Gideon)
Smith, J. *
Snellings, Elisha A.
Sparks (Sharpe), Leonard *
Sprayberry, William H.
Thomas, John H.
Tomlinson (Thomelson),
  Wilford T. (Wilford F.)
Upchurch, Claiborn D.
Vaughn, Henry A.
Walker, Henry S.
Warren, Edmond P.
  (Edward P.) *
Wright, Thomas

Co. H, 66th Regiment
Georgia Volunteer Infantry, Army of Tenessee, C. S. A.
August 8, 1863

Officers

Belisle, Lorenzo D., captain
Rasberry, J. M., 1st lieutenant
Quillian, Wiley H., 2nd lieutenant
Woodbridge, O. G., 2nd lieutenant
Orear (O'Rear), Daniel, jr. 2nd lieutenant *
Holmes, E., 2nd sergeant
Hogan, Hamilton, 2nd sergeant

Harris, J. S., 3rd sergeant
Jackson, Joseph, 4th sergeant *
Williams, Joel, 5th sergeant
Trulove (Truelove), William, 1st corporal
Doss, W. J. (or W. G.), 2nd corporal
Barrow (Barron), John, 3rd corporal
Shaver (Shafer), Hiram, 4th corporal

Privates

Adams, Charles
Allen, James M.
Bacon, James
Bancroft (Barcroft), Henry
Beaty, (Battey) Joseph
Belisle (Belesles), John H.
Blake, James

Bollinger (Ballinger),
  Frederick R.
Bond, C. (see Co. I)
Boris, C. S.
Brannan, (Brannon) J. W.
Brock, M. L.
Brooks, Wilson W.

Brown, D. E.
Bryant, James R.
Cable (Coble), William R.
Caker (Coker), Robert Mills
Campbell, Miles H.
Clayton, Jesse C.
Coleman, Peter (see Co. A)

Cowart (Comer), William H. *
Cruse (Crews), James E.
Cullain (Cullan), Patrick
Davis, John
Day, James
Dial (Deal), D. W.
Echols, E. B.
Echols (Eckols), James M. (James W.) *
Evans, John M.
Finley, Alf (See Co. E)
Fitts, William P. *
Floyd, Mathew
Foster, James
Fricks (Frix) W. C.
Garrison, T. A. (F. A.)
Gay, J. M.
Gray (Grey), T. P.
Gregory, John *
Gunn, J. M.
Gunn, P. L.
Hailey (Haley), J. M.
Hampton, G. W. *
Harris, Parker C.
Harrison, B. A. *
Harwell, J. J.
Holcomb, A. H.
Howard, W. R. *
Hubbard, John *
Hurt, William A.
Jackson, Seaborn
Johnson, A. S.
Kanady (Kennedy, Canaday), S. H.
Kanada, William (see Co. E)
King, Daniel
Leverett (Loverett), T. B.
Martin, C. *
Masters, W. T.
Meade (Mead), J. H. *
Milan, Luke
Millwood, H.
Mise (Mize), A. W.
Moulder (Molder), A. C.
Murrah, George W.
Musick, G. W. *
Nix, B. F.
Oaks (Oakes), G. W.
Payne, Thomas S.
Peck, Jacob Y. *
Pendry (Pendrey), James E.
Pittman, John D. *
Pugh, S. O.
Quillian, George K.
Richards, R. W.
Ridley (Riley), Peter
Russell, Drayton P.
Sears, J. W.
Sewell, J. A.
Simmons, C. P. *
Smith, Alpha
Stidham (Stedham), Elihu *
Stephens (Stevens), Henry C. *
Summers, H. J.
Terry, William
Thaxton, W. C. *
Thornton, William *
Townes (Towns), Thompson P. (P. T.)
Vandever (Vandiver), H. P.
Voils (Voyles), Perry
Wacaser (Wacassey), David
Walker, C.
Ward, W. T.
Watson, George W.
Weathers, J.
Wiggins, A.
Williams, Alexander G.
Wood (Word), Willis

Co. A, 10th Regiment Cavalry Georgia State Guards
August 4, 1863

Officers

Candler, Milton A., captain
Masters, Samuel C., 1st lieutenant
Wright, William, 2nd lieutenant
Belisle, William, 3rd lieutenant
Morris, George W., 1st sergeant
Kirkpatrick, James W., 2nd sergeant
Walker, Joseph, 3rd sergeant
Winn, Samuel G., 4th sergeant
Turner, Edwin A., 5th sergeant
Pitts, A. L., 1st corporal
McWilliams, J. T., 2nd corporal
McGinnis, Charles W., 3rd corporal
Tilley, J. W. F., 4th corporal [24]

Appendix 9

Abbreviated Timeline Of DeKalb County History

6000-2000	B. C. Ice Age closes. Archaic Period begins. Small camp sites found in DeKalb. Soapstone bowl forms were carved by these Indians.
2000 B. C.-500 A. D.	Woodland Period begins. Indians build stone wall on top of Stone Mountain.
500 A. D.-1500 A. D.	Mississippian Period. More permanent Indian villages appear at creek bottoms of DeKalb.
1550 A. D.-1840 A. D.	Historic Period. Europeans infringe on native culture of Indians. DeKalb becomes hunting grounds of Creek and Cherokee Indians.

1700s

1732	England's King George II grants charter to Oglethorpe for founding of Colony of Georgia.
1790	Alexander McGillivray, half-breed chief of the Creek Indians, meets on Stone Mountain with subordinate chiefs who were to accompany him to New York to discuss a treaty with the U. S. government.
1790	Col. Marinus Willett, personal friend of George Washington, in *A Narrative of Military Action* writes "while encamped at Stoney Mountain (sic) where I ascended the summit."

1800s

1802	U. S. agrees to remove Creeks and Cherokees from North and Northwest Georgia for cession of Alabama and Mississippi lands plus $1,250,000.
1813	George Gilmer leads state militia to put down raids of Creek Indians at Standing Peachtree.
1820	James Mc. Montgomery establishes DeKalb County's first settlement, at Standing Peachtree on the Chattahoochee River.
1821	Creek Indians cede territory that will become DeKalb County. Henry County created.
1822	DeKalb with population of 2,500 created from Henry, Fayette and Gwinnett counties, December 9.
1823	Decatur named county seat, December 10.
1823	First academy established by legislature, located at Decatur.
1823	Macedonia Baptist Church constituted, oldest church in county.
1824	Nance's (Nancy) Creek Primitive Baptist Church organized.
1824	Utoy Baptist Church organized in what is now Fulton County.
1825	Decatur Presbyterian Church organized as Westminister Presbyterian Church.
1825	Rock Chapel Methodist Church organized.
1825	Hardman Primitive Baptist constituted, mother of Indian Creek and Decatur churches.
1825	J. Mc. Montgomery named postmaster at the Standing Peachtree, DeKalb's first post office.
1829	"Neat brick courthouse" replaces small log courthouse on Decatur Square.

1829	Sherwood's Gazetteer reports Decatur contained a courthouse, jail, academy and about 50 houses and stores.
1830	First DeKalb census in the county records 8,388 whites, 1,669 slaves and 17 free Negroes. Territory surveyed includes Cherokee Indian lands across the Chattahoochee River.
1832	Legislature provides for creation of Decatur Burial Ground.
1833	Meteor shower prompts local preacher to warn "the end of the world is at hand," November 13.
1839	Town of New Gibralter (sic) incorporated. Name changed to Stone Mountain in 1847.
1840	County's second census shows 10,466 inhabitants -- 8,456 whites, 2,004 slaves and 2 free persons of color.
1842	DeKalb's "neat brick" courthouse burns, replaced by similar structure.
1842	First train from Atlanta, then Terminus, runs on December 24, 20 miles to Marietta.
1843	Marthasville, later named Atlanta, incorporated.
1846	Southern Central Agricultural Association holds first Georgia Fair at Stone Mountain.
1847	Marthasville becomes Atlanta.
1847	Third courthouse is completed, identical to the second, except for addition of a portico, two granite columns and exterior steps to the second floor, all on the east side.
1850	Census records 14,398 residents, including 2,994 slaves and 32 free persons of color.
1853	Fulton County carved from DeKalb.
1856	Lithonia incorporated, formerly little settlement of Crossroads.
1857	Hannah Moore Female Academy incorporated in Decatur, county's institution of higher learning.
1860	The first census after Fulton is cut off from DeKalb records a total population of 6318, including 464 slaves, less than half of the 1850 population.
1861	DeKalb sends two pro-Union delegates to Secession Convention. Delegate Charles Murphey dies on opening day of session.
1861	"War, the unthinkable, war!" -- Diary of Benjamin T. Hunter, principal of Lithonia Academy.
1861	First four DeKalb Confederate army companies leave for battle.
1864	Union soldiers invade DeKalb.
1865	James Johnson appointed provisional governor for territory of Georgia.
1870	State of Georgia readmitted to Union, July 15.
1870	Census reports 10,014 inhabitants in DeKalb, including 2682 Negroes, half the number living in Atlanta.
1871	December 15 Doraville incorporated, December 15.
1871	Methodist Children's Home founded.
1873	First public schools, now known as Scottdale, Bouldercrest and Southwest DeKalb opened for children in grades one-eight.
1880	DeKalb emerges from Reconstruction into prosperous era.
1880	Census records 14,497 residents, a 45 percent increase over 1870.
1882	Clarkston, incorporated, December 12.
1886	DeKalb is fifth in Georgia in manufacturing.
1890	No census data exists for DeKalb. The Georgia Statistical Register and U. S. Postal Service records show 17,189 persons living in the county.
1890	Decatur Female Seminary is renamed in honor of Agnes Scott, mother of Georgia W. Scott.
1896	Campaign fails to move county seat from Decatur to Stone Mountain.

1898   Cornerstone laid for new granite courthouse.
1898   Edgewood incorporated, becomes part of Atlanta in 1909.
1899   Kirkwood incorporated, becomes part of Atlanta, 1922. [11] [25]

---

[11] Original expanded Timeline by Dorothy Nix dedicated to James A. Mackay, DeKalb Historical Society president, 1985-1987.

The Benning House, at left, is located at the corner of Oakdale Road and Benning Place in the Kirkwood community. It was built by Judge Charles Whitefoord Smith. The Seminary in Lithonia was built for the Malone family between 1895 and 1906, and later housed a school. (DeKalb Historical Society)

Appendix 10

National Register of Historic Places Listings in DeKalb County And Other Historic Sites

STRUCTURES AND PLACES

1. Briarcliff, 1260 Briarcliff Road, Atlanta, former home of Asa G. Candler Jr. (son of Asa G. Candler Sr.), [12] built in 1922, property once contained a zoo, now DeKalb Addiction Clinic.

2. Callanwolde, 980 Briarcliff Road, Atlanta, former home of Charles Howard Candler (son of Asa G. Candler Sr.) and Flora Glenn Candler, begun in 1917, finished in 1920 because of construction delays caused by World War I, now DeKalb fine arts center.

3. DeKalb Avenue-Clifton Road Archaeological Site (Arizona Street railroad/MARTA underpass).

4. Neville and Helen Farmer "Lustron" House, 513 Drexel Ave., Decatur, 1949, made from porcelain enameled steel panels.

5. Mary Gay House, built about 1850, originally faced the Square on West Ponce de Leon, later at 524 Marshall Street, off West Ponce de Leon, now in the Adair Park Historic Complex, Trinity Place,

---

[12] Asa Griggs Candler and his five children built some of Atlanta's most opulent dwellings. Today none is owned by the Candler family, only two are private residences.

Decatur, home of Mary Ann Harris Gay, author of Life In Dixie During The War, now headquarters of the DeKalb Junior League.

6. William T. Gentry House, 132 E. Lake Drive, S. E., built about 1913-1914.

7. Cora Beck Hampton School and House, 213 Hillyer Place, Decatur, one-story cottage and one-room school, the house built about 1880 and the school in 1892.

8. Agnes Lee Chapter House of the United Daughters of the Confederacy, 120 Avery Street, Decatur, built in 1916.

9. Old DeKalb County Courthouse, Decatur, exterior dates to 1898, interior rebuilt after 1916 fire, built from Stone Mountain granite quarried in Lithonia.

10. Russell and Nelle Pines "Lustron" House, 2081 Sylvania Drive, Decatur, similar to the Farmer house, built in 1949.

11. Pythagoras Masonic Lodge No. 41, 136 E. Ponce de Leon Ave., Decatur, built 1924-25.

12. Scottish Rite Hospital for Crippled Children (South DeKalb Community Health Center/Oakhurst Community Health Center), 321 W. Hill Street, Decatur, builb about 1918-1920.

13. The Seminary (formerly the Malone House), 6886 Main Street, Lithonia, built between 1895 and 1906.

14. Smith-Benning House, 520 Oakdale Road, N. E., Atlanta, built in 1886.

15. Soapstone Ridge.

16. Steele-Cobb House, "Briarpatch," 2632 Fox Hills Drive, Decatur, built about 1855.

17. Swanton House, originally located uphill from current location, Adair Park Historic Complex, Trinity Avenue, Decatur, house is now located where Swanton's tannery once stood, original two-room cabin built between 1823 and 1830, Benjamin Franklin Swanton purchased from Ammi Williams.

18. Zuber-Jarrell House, 810 Flat Shoals Ave., S E., built between 1904 and 1906 by John William Zuber, Atlanta lumber dealer.

DISTRICTS

1. Avondale Estates Historic District, developed in 1924 by George F. Willis as a model residential suburb

2. Brookhaven Historic District, east of Peachtree-Dunwoody Road and north and east of Peachtree Road, dates from early 20th century.

3. Cameron Court District, east of Briarcliff Road between Ponce de Leon Avenue and North Decatur Road.

The Avary-Fulton House is located at 205 South Columbia Drive in Decatur. (DeKalb Historical Society)

The Cora Beck Hampton Holleyman House and Schoolhouse at 213 Hillyer Place in Decatur were built between 1880 and 1892. (DeKalb Historical Society)

4. Candler Park Historic District, roughly bounded by Moreland, DeKalb, McLendon and Harold avenues, Matthews Street and Clifton Terrace.

5. Druid Hills Historic District, Ponce de Leon Avenue east of Briarcliff Road, adjacent to Emory University District, conceived by Joel Hurt and developed by a syndicate led by Asa G. Candler Sr., first home built in 1909 for Judge John S. Candler (brother of Asa Sr.). Includes:
• **Alpha Delta Pi Sorority's national headquarters**, 1386 Ponce de Leon Ave., Atlanta, built in 1911 as home for Clyde L. King family.
• **St. John Lutheran Church**, "Stonehenge," 1410 Ponce de Leon Ave., N. E., Atlanta, former home of Samuel H. Venable, built in 1912 of Stone Mountain granite from the Venable quarry.
• **888 Oakdale Road**, N. E., designed in 1913 by prominent architect Neel Reid, who designed several houses in the area.
• **Druid Hills Parks and Parkways**, designed by Fredrick Law Olmsted in 1893, wide Ponce de Leon Avenue planned for through commercial traffic, smaller road for Sunday carriage rides and walking, "linear" parks separate the two roads, with alternating open meadows and wooded areas.

6. Emory University District, several buildings on campus built beginning in 1915. Includes:
Lullwater House, 1463 Clifton Road, home of Emory University president, built for the Walter T. Candler (son of Asa G. Candler Sr.) family in 1926 of stone quarried on the property (formerly owned by DeKalb pioneer Dr. Chapman Powell).

7. Oglethorpe University Historic District, Peachtree Road in the Brookhaven community, oldest building, Lupton Hall, built 1916, architectural style inspired by school attended by James Edward Oglethorpe, Corpus Christi College in Oxford, England.

8. South Candler Street/Agnes Scott College Historic District, Decatur. Includes :
• **Agnes Scott Hall**, 1890
• **Rebekah Scott Hall**, 1903
• **Charles Murphey Candler House**, 158 S. Candler Street, birthplace of longtime DeKalb Commissioner Scott Candler Sr., originally four rooms, second story added later, purchased by Candler

shortly his after marriage to Mary Hough Scott in 1882. Charles Murphey Candler was a nephew of Asa G. Candler Sr.
- **Candler-Clarke House**, 146 S. Candler Street, built by Milton A. Candler, father of Charles Murphey Candler, in 1889. Caroline McKinney Clarke, granddaughter of Milton A. Candler and author of The Story of Decatur, lived her entire life there.
- **Scott-Sams House**, 312 S. Candler Street, built between 1875 and 1885 by Bucher Scott, son of George W. Scott, founder of Agnes Scott College, later owned by Bucher Scott's daughter, Mrs. Hansford Sams.

HISTORIC, BUT NOT ON THE REGISTER

Biffle Cabin and **Thomas-Barber Cabin**,, Adair Park Historic Complex, Trinity Place, Decatur, maintained by the DeKalb Historical Society.

Solomon Goodwin House, 3967 Peachtree Road, Brookhaven, said to have been built by Solomon Goodwin about 1831, may have been built by John Harris Goodwin, Solomon's son, or John Dobbs, designated the oldest extant house in DeKalb County by a state of Georgia Historical Marker, originally located closer to intersection of Peachtree and North Druid Hills roads.

East Lake Country Club, 2575 Alston Drive, S. E., Atlanta, built in 1904, championship golfer Bobby Jones learned to play here.

Meadownook, 2420 Alston Drive, S. E., built 1856-1861, home of Robert Alston, state representative who was killed in 1879 by a political opponent.

Stephen B. Spruill House (Spruill Art Center), 4681 Ashford Dunwoody Road, Dunwoody.

Cary Spruill House, corner of Ashford Dunwoody and Mt. Vernon, Dunwoody.

Samuel House House (Peachtree Golf Club), 4600 Peachtree Road. N. E., Brookhaven, built about 1858 by Samuel House from bricks handmade from native clay, served as Sherman's headquarters on July 18, 1864.

Macedonia Baptist Church, 3420 Panola Road, DeKalb's oldest church, established 1823.

Donaldson House, 4831 Chamblee Dunwoody Road, Dunwoody, built shortly after the Civil War by James Donaldson, now home of Mr. and Mrs. J. David Chesnut.

Williams-Evans ("High") House, 309 Sycamore Street, Decatur, built in the 1830s.

Walters ("Marble") House, 119 North McDonough, Decatur, built in 1885, once used to board Agnes Scott College students.

Chapman Powell Cabin, Stone Mountain Park Antebellum Complex, "Mammy's Cabin," built about 1826 by one of DeKalb County's first physicians, Martha Bulloch Roosevelt (mother of President Theodore Roosevelt) visited there. Stone Mountain Park had cabin cut down from its original size when it was installed in the Antebellum Complex.

Stillwell House, 992 Ridge Avenue, Stone Mountain, built about 1850, dance floor on the third floor, purchased in 1868 by the Rev. Jacob M. Stillwell, pastor of the Stone Mountain Baptist Church. Tradition holds that Stillwell, for whom dancing was a sin, said he "had about as much need of a dance hall as a possum has for a petticoat." While the Rev. and Mrs. Stillwell were out of town, their nine children invited their friends to a dance, complete with a band from Atlanta. The Stillwell family owned the house until 1942. There is no record of the fate of the children.

Ashe House, 5329 Mimosa, Stone Mountain, built about 1836, said to have been used by Andrew Johnson as hotel, tavern or storehouse, a hospital between 1852 and 1884 hospital, later a hotel, then a residence, walls are constructed of two layers of brick with airspace in between.

Lyon House and Smokehouse, Lyon Road overlooking the South River, original portion of house (now the kitchen area), said to have been built when the area was Henry County (before 1822), basement (partially underground) served as slave quarters.

John B. Johns House, Johns Road, Tucker, said to have been built in 1829.

Towers-Fowler-Thompson House, property first owned by William Towers in 1822, then by Alexander C. Fowler (son of John W. Fowler) in 1854, moved from original site Northern and Rockbridge roads about 1984.

Avary-Fulton House, 205 South Columbia Drive, built by Dr. James C. Avary about 1868, later home to the Rev. Atticus Greene Haygood, bishop of the Methodist Episcopal Church South.

Pearce-Glenn House, 428 Sycamore, built by John Pearce in 1876, Pearce also built a windmill and water tank on the property, said to have had the first running water in Decatur.

Decatur First United Methodist Church Chapel, Sycamore Street and Columbia Drive, Decatur, built in 1897 of native granite.

Stone Mountain Park covered bridge. [13] [14] [26]

---

[13] Many National Register sites in DeKalb are private properties and/or residences. Most require prior approval before visiting.

[14] Space prohibits listing all the historical structures in DeKalb County. More on these and other properties may be obtained from the DeKalb Historical Society.

Appendix Notes

1. Atlanta Historical Society Bulletin.

2. Lucas Jr., Rev. Silas Emmett, 1986, The Fourth or 1821 Land Lottery of Georgia, Southern Historical Press.

3. Bryan, Mrs. Mary Givens, 1952,"DeKalb County Officers", The Collections of the DeKalb Historical Society, Vol. 1, pages 28-30. Garrett, Franklin M., 1954, 1969, Atlanta and Environs -- A Chronicle of Its People and Events, Vol. 1, page 27.

4. Collins, L. Clyde, November 14, 1989, Findings Relating to the History of the DeKalb County Sheriff's Department; and Collins, Clyde, Flake, Andrew and Taulbee, James Larry, n. d., A History of the DeKalb County Sheriff's Department: 1822-1992, unpublished manuscripts. Bryan, Mrs. Mary Givens, 1952, "DeKalb County Officers," The Collections of the DeKalb Historical Society, Vol. 1, pages 28-30. Nix, Dorothy, personal collection, DeKalb Historical Society.

5. Nix, Dorothy, personal collection, DeKalb Historical Society. Bryan, Mrs. Mary Givens, 1952, "DeKalb County Officers," The Collections of the DeKalb Historical Society, Vol. 1, pages 28-30.

6. Garrett, Franklin M., 1954, 1969, Atlanta and Environs -- A Chronicle of Its People and Events, Vol. 1, page 27.

7. Bryan, Mrs. Mary Givens, 1952, "DeKalb County Officers," The Collections of the DeKalb Historical Society, Vol. 1, pages 28-30. Hays, Louise Frederick, 1936, Georgia Service Records -- State and Federal Officers, 1777-1936 -- County Officers, 1777-1800, with Sheriffs and Justices of the Peace Through 1815; Military Officers, 1777-1860, Vols. 1 and 2, Georgia Department of Archives and History.

8. DeKalb Historical Society records.

9. Bryan, Mrs. Mary Givens, 1952, "DeKalb County Officers," The Collections of the DeKalb Historical Society, Vol. 1, pages 28-30. Nix, Dorothy, personal collection, DeKalb Historical Society.

10. Nix, Dorothy, personal collection, DeKalb Historical Society.

11. Nix, Dorothy, personal collection, DeKalb Historical Society.

12. Nix, Dorothy, personal collection, DeKalb Historical Society.

13. Nix, Dorothy, personal collection, DeKalb Historical Society.

14. Nix, Dorothy, personal collection, DeKalb Historical Society. Garrett, Franklin M., 1954, 1969, Atlanta and Environs -- A Chronicle of Its People and Events, Vol. 1.

15. Bryan, Mrs. Mary Givens, 1952, "DeKalb County Officers," The Collections of the DeKalb Historical Society, Vol. 1, pages 28-30.

16. Nix, Dorothy, personal collection, DeKalb Historical Society.

17. Nix, Dorothy, personal collection, DeKalb Historical Society.

18. Nix, Dorothy, personal collection, DeKalb Historical Society.

19. State of Georgia Justice of the Peace Commission Books, Georgia Department of Archives and History. Executive Register for Notaries Public, Georgia Department of Archives and History.

20. State Militia Officer Commission Books, Georgia Department of Archives and History.

21. 1850 Georgia census records. McCurdy Census Abstract, DeKalb Historical Society. Hollingsworth, Leon S., typescript, Georgia Department of Archives and History. Garrett, Franklin M., 1954, 1969, Atlanta and Environs -- A Chronicle of Its People and Events, Vol. 1, pages 83-97.

22. One head of household in the 1850 DeKalb County census (Atlanta District) appears with no surname; the first name is Antoine.

23. 1860 DeKalb County, Ga. Slave Schedule.

24. Henderson, Lillian, Roster of the Confederate Soldiers of Georgia 1861-1865, compiled for the State of Georgia. Candler, Charles Murphey, Historical Address, November 9, 1922, pages 25-27. Confederate muster rolls and service records, Georgia Department of Archives and History.

25. Nix, Dorothy, DeKalb Historical Society executive director, 1980-1987, with assistance from Cindy Platto, Wynne Christensen, Fran Broadnax Franz, Deborah Gaudier, Delia Gilliland, Alice Park and John Worth.

26. Historic Preservation Division, Georgia Department of Natural Resources, August, 1997. DeKalb Historical Society files. Coe, Martha, June 27, 1979, "Avondale Has Grown Up Just Like Willis Wanted," DeKalb News/Sun, page 6G. Ford, Elizabeth Austin, 1852, "Some Old Houses of DeKalb County," The Collections of the DeKalb Historical Society, Vol. 1. Martin Jr., Albert, August 27, 1996, personal interview. Nix, Dorothy, personal collection, DeKalb Historical Society. Powell Jr., George Travis, 1985, Thomas Powell and John Hardman, Vol. 1. Price, Vivian, Sept. 11, 1991, "If Houses Could Talk," DeKalb News/Sun, pages 8-10B. Sawyer, Elizabeth M., and Matthews, Jane Foster, 1976, The Old In New Atlanta.

INDEX

INDEX

A

Abernathy, Samuel	112
Adair Park	76, 90, 188, 295
Adair, George W.	239, 316, 209
John Fisher	316
Thomas Owen	316
William F.	243
Adams, Daniel	293
Gardner	293
Gary E.	131
James	67, 187, 190
John E.	210
Martin	129
Norman	327
Salathael	240
Adams	112
Adkins, Jeptha R.	337
Agnes Lee Chapter, UDC	295
Agnes Scott College	160, 351
Agnes Scott Institute	329
Aiken, W. G.	311
Akers, John H.	335
William	85, 257
Akin, Thomas	85, 275, 278
Akin, Thomas J.	231
Akins, Daniel W.	118
J. M.	214
James F.	118
James Francis	117, 118, 214
Matilda Caroline	117
Thomas	113, 210, 225
Thomas J.	117, 118, 200, 245, 296, 317
Akridge, Simeon	274
Alexander, A.	294
Aaron	286
Alford, Annie	182
J. T.	326
John T.	318
Allen, E. G.	318
Nathaniel	252
W.	210
William, Dr.	157
Allman, A. W.	366
Alman, Azmon R.	225
Almand, A. R.	261
John Parks	324
Almond, Green V.	263
Alston, Robert	338
Robert Mrs.	336
Anderson, Charles	71
D. D.	225
David	131
David D.	200, 305
George	126, 267
George D.	131, 221
James	188
Jesse	293
Joseph J.	209
Mary	78
Nelson	211, 326
O. D.	210
Phillip	211
R. C.	208
Robert C.	208
S. J.	208
Samuel	131
William	71
William B.	221
William U.	131
Andrew, James C.	261
Andrews, Garnett	252
Angier, N. L.	307
Needom L.	260
Archaic Period	2
Arendall, L.	304
Telephus	111
Argow, W.	208
Armistead, David	313
George	313
Robert	241
Arms, Frederick	239
Frederick C.	236
Arnold, C. W.	307
Askew, James	211
Assafoetida	173
Atalanta	246
Atkins, Joel	210
Atkinson, Robert	80
Atlanta	245, 256, 262, 310, 347, 354, 358-359, 364
Atlanta Amateurs	336
Atlanta and Dahlonega Plank Road Company	298
Atlanta Bank	307
Cemetery	298
Daily Intelligencer	280
Fire Company No. 1	157
Gas Light Co.	305
Grays	326, 328
Historical Society	75
Hotel	298, 310
Medical College	313
Paper Mill	328
Pioneer Historic Society	245
Pioneer Citizens Society	75
Rolling Mill	334
Atlatl	2
Atwood, T.	210
Thomas	231
Austen, John B.	211
Austin, J. C.	318, 326
John	231
John C.	314
Larken	211
Thomas	85, 200, 293
Toliver L.	211
William C.	297, 298
Avary, James C.	314
James C., Dr.	85
Avery, Benjamin	209, 222
George	222
George W.	263
John	239
William	97, 232, 279, 309
Awtry's Mill	199, 233
Ayers, R. T.	312
W. R.	226
William R.	314
Ayres, William R.	307

B

Badger, Joshua B.	317
Ralph	268
Roderick D.	317
Bagwell, Elizabeth	311
Emeline	311
John	311
Bailey, John	236
S. T.	85, 124
Samuel T.	128
Baker, Green W.	198
Green	87
Jesse	231

Joseph	256, 299	Belisle, L. D.	328	James Sr.	79
Joseph S.	259	Bell, Henry B.	276	K.	210
William	67, 71, 85, 190	Henry Bibb	335	Blair, R.	208
Bale, James A.	186	James	283	Ruth	56
Balenger, John N.	216	James Sr.	276	Blake, William	71
Ball, Dicey	112	Marcus Aurelius	276, 324	Blalock, J.	210
James	318	Piromis Hulsey	276	Bogle, Harriet N.	104
James E.	338	Bellenger, John N.	225	Boling, Barnet	213
Peter	112, 298	Bellinger, J. N.	279	Bolton, Henry H.	302
Ballenger, David	113	John	231, 240	John Q.	211
John, Dr.	113	John F.	309	Julia	283
Martha	114	John N.	230, 241	Thomas C.	229, 257
Banigan and Kelly's Caravan		John N. Mrs.	93	Bomar, Benjamin F.	273, 279
of Animals	252	John Nelson	308	Bond	95, 96
Bankston	96	Joseph T.	279	E. J.	85
Elijah	79, 80, 92	Belmont	165, 201, 241	Easom J.	97
John	153	Benedict, Maggie	336, 365	J. B.	85
Barbashela Creek	90, 92	Benino, Abram	335	Joseph	313
Barker Greys	328	Benson, S. E.	208	Joseph B.	95, 237
Barnes, Thomas	275, 313	Berditt, Humphrey	79	Joseph Ballenger	96
W. H.	336	Betterton, Levi	211, 240	Joseph T.	317
William H.	336	Betts, William	230	W. P., Dr.	85
Barnett, John	209	Bibby, Moses	200	Bonner, Charles	185
Miles	209	Biffle, John	75, 80, 95	Bookout, John	257, 258
William	240, 309	Leander	76, 93	Boren	96
Baron DeKalb Chapter,		Leandrew	211, 263	Boring	96
DAR	152	Sarah	257, 258	Boring, John M.	240
Barr, James A.	200	Biggers, Robert	230	Borman, Henry G.	211
Bartlett, Frederick W.	259	Bigham, Benjamin H.	199	Born, J. M.	269
Bartow Avengers	327	Bilious fever	187	James H.	326
Bartram, William	32	Billups, Alice F.	152	John M.	313, 318
Bates, B.	210	Alice Pharr Houston	158	John W.	85, 315
Battle of Atlanta	359	John	257, 298	William L.	85, 315
Battle of Chickamauga	338	Lanier	56	Bowie, Jane E.	293
Battle of Cold Harbor	335	Lanier Richardson	158	John	329
"Battle of Decata, Near		Binion, J. S.	211	Boyce, Ker	252
Atlanta, July 20, 1864"	358	S. E.	208	Boyd, Hugh M.	221, 231
Battle of Decatur	354	Samuel	85	Bradberry, J. W.	210
Battle of Peachtree Creek	356	Bird, Elijah	132, 200, 230	T. C.	211
Baugh, Nancy	109		302-303, 314	Thomas C.	198
Baxter, Robert	309, 316	Elijah L.	294	Bradbury, William	329
Beach, Solomon S.	331	Elijah, Rev.	96	William W.	186
Beal, William T.	245	John	233, 301, 303	Bradford, John	208
Beall, Sarah	159	John Mrs.	301	John R.	208
Beasley, John	70, 185	Bishop	96	Bradley, John	239
William	79, 80	Black, Garland D.	309	John L.	221, 237, 245
William M.	297	George L.	221	Brandon, W. R.	211
Beaty, James M.	337	I. R.	281	William R.	245, 316
Beauchamp, John W.	20	Blackhall	64	Brantly, Joseph	211
John William	182	Blackstock, James	67, 72, 85,	Braselton, Reuben	71
William	85, 119, 182, 230,		124, 189, 230-231, 293	Braswell	96
	275	James M.	313	Asa	114

Hamp	315	Bryan, Mary E.	317	Green B.	239, 244
S. H.	113	Bryant's	64	Green Berry	267
Breedlove, J. A.	211	Bryant's Minstrels	326	Butt, William M.	307, 308
Sucky	257, 258	Bryant, Samuel	311	Buzzard's Roost	33, 35, 194
Brewster, Hugh	79, 80	Bryce, Elizabeth	131	Byrd, Elijah	113
James	190, 198	John	85, 131, 210, 231,		
Briarwood Methodist			245, 252, 278, 313, 337	**C**	
Church	115	Robert	211	Cagle, Robert	326
Brimm, W. W.	125	William	130	Cain, Jacob T.	196
Britain, Mourning	186	Buchanan, H. F.	312	Calburt, L.	208
Britt, Joe	311	James B.	293	Caldwell, James	196, 225
Brockhan, Carston	297	R. C.	292	Joseph	97
Brockman, Henry	279	Buckhead	64, 70, 222	Calhoun, E. N.	198, 212, 239,
Brookhaven	37, 111, 202	Buckley, Hiram	190		252, 267, 293
Brooks, George	229	Buell, William	305	E. N., Dr.	85
Jacob R.	72, 85, 87, 109,	Willis	262	Ezekiel	208
	124	Wyllys	300	Ezekiel N.	207
Brooks, Joshua	187	Buffer zone	31	Isaac	187
Broughton, Mary	105	Buice, Lester	312	J. M.	252, 255
Brown	96	Bull, Orvill A.	199	James	155, 267
Alfred B.	105, 231, 232	Bullard, Robert W.	273	James M.	85, 209, 223, 241,
Cole	284	Bulloch County	118		244, 252, 256, 293, 298,
Cynthia	367	Bulloch, Agnes	276		302, 308, 313, 337, 347,
Edgefield	231	Martha	152		359
Fanning	85, 87, 126, 230,	Bullock, J. T.	208	John	67
	240	Burch, Allen	67	Lowndes	267
H. W.	331	Burdett, B. A.	211	Ned	267
J.	211	Benjamin	309, 324	Pickens	267
James Mrs.	331	Elizabeth	112	Pickens Noble	335
John	85, 127	Mary	226	Calico House	324
Joseph E.	317, 331, 338	R.	211	Callahan, William A.	211
Killis	240, 263, 309, 324	Samuel	257	Callaway, W. A.	226
Meredith	80, 185, 305	T.	211	Callehan, Joshua L.	211
Meredith G.	79	Burdette, Benjamin	242	Camden, S. C.	60, 75
Mollie G.	327	Mary Jane	242	Cameron, Allen	80
Moses L.	328	S.	311	Julia	105
Peter	71, 231	Burford, Clarissa	276	Nancy	293
R. M.	239	Philip H.	200, 276	Camp Creek	71
Robert M.	245, 293	Philip Terrel	75, 78	Camp Fire Girls	56
Robert M. Sr.	85	Burgess	96	Camp Gordon	159
S. E.	326	Burke, Thomas	245	Camp of instruction	328
T. E.	217	Burnet, William	209	Camp Randolph	328
Thomas	187	Burnett, L.	208	Camp, Andrew	67, 71
Browning's	64	Burnham, Elisha B.	97	Benjamin J.	200
Browning's District	119	Burns, James	245, 263, 314	Campbell County	34, 76
Browning, A.	233	John	231	Campbell, Catherine	120
Andrew	119, 181	Burrus, A. B. Mrs.	56	G. Chesley	214
Thompson A.	181	Burt, Edmund	211	J. W.	361
Tom	119	James	211	James	185, 190
Willis	292	Burton, C.	211	Jesse H.	299
Bruce's Bridge	298	Butler, Elizabeth A.	293	John	71
Bruce, William	79, 80	G. B.	85	John W.	120

Candler, Asa Griggs 159, 324
  Charles Murphey 63, 85, 96,
    159-160, 325, 351, 361
  Eliza Murphey 327, 361
  George Scott 160
  John S. 159, 303
  Milton A. 157, 196, 197,
    327-328, 361, 366
  Milton Anthony 159
  Milton Anthony Jr. 160
  Samuel Charles 159, 160
  Scott 229
  Warren A. 159
Cannon, Allen 79
Carath, Robert 119
Carlisle, Willis 236
Carlton, James 274
  Larkin 85, 132, 189
Carpenter, F. O. 112
  John 263, 318
Carr 95
  Benjamin 85
  John P. 96
  William 80, 190
Carral, L. 210
Carroll, J. M. 85
  Sarah 156
  Sarah Frances 118
  Thomas 70
  William 195
Carson, Ephraim 80
  William 85, 130
Carter, Celia Ann 276
  Elizabeth May 201, 203
  John 70, 185
  Sarah Jane 276
  William 70
Carver, P. 210
Casey, H. 310
  Hiram 279
Cash, Amanda Jane 120
  Esther 258
  George Washington 334
  George 335
  J. L. 210
  James 119, 120
  James Ellis 334
  Lewis L. 120
  Lucinda 120
  Mary (Polly) 120
  Oliver P. 334, 335
  Oliver Perry 120

  Peter 75-77, 119, 120
  Peter Jr. 120
  S. P. 311
  Stephen 119
  W. 210
  Washington 120
  Wesley 120
  William 79, 119
  Willis 213
  Winston H. 337
Cass, Lewis 275
Cawly, Samuel 79
Cedar Grove Cemetery 75, 79
Cedar Grove Methodist
  Church 97
Center, E. A. 210, 326
  Edwin A. 313
  Nathan 317, 318
Centers for Disease Control
  and Prevention 158
Central of Ga. Railroad 258
Cession, Indian 47
Chambers, Elizabeth 79
Chamblee 7, 79, 111, 112, 117
Chamblee First United
  Methodist Church 114
Chamblee, Alvin D. 439
  John William 335
  Ransom 439
  Robert Asbury 439
  Robert Wesley 439
  William Nicholas 335
Chamlee, Martin 440
  Nelle Sherwood 280
  William 440
Chandler 96, 113
Chandler's Bridge 233
Chandler's, A. 200
Chandler, Abraham 70, 72, 87,
  185, 200
  Frances 151
  James E. 335
  James W. 211
  Joel 75, 76
  John Sr. 80
  John W. 335
  Lewis 211
  W. B. 338
Chapman, Benjamin 233
  Eli T. 337
  William 274
Charles Town 26

Charlton, Robert M. 284
Chatooga County 104
Chattahoochee River 6, 25,
  33, 46, 52, 63, 71, 109
Chattanooga, Tenn. 347
Cheek, Bunyan 311
  Myra 311
Cherokees 31
Cheshire, Hezekiah 203, 237,
  240
Chesnut, David 214, 337
Chestnut, Alexander 314
Chewning, Ambrose 334, 335
  Jesse 328
  T. E. 312
  Virginia 255
  W. F. 293
  William F. 240
Childers, John 79
Childress, John A. D. 197
  Naomi 203
Childs, Daniel 185
  Ralph 209
Chivers, Harriett 260
  T. H. Mrs. 367
  Thomas Holley Jr. 260
  Thomas Holley 259, 260
Choice, C. 210
  Cyrus 210
  J. 208
  Josiah 213
  T. 210
  Tully 85, 135
Chupp's Mill 231
Chupp, D. B. 231
  David 317, 324
  David B. 97
  J. L. 97
  Jacob 85, 231, 326
Chupp 96
Church of the Immaculate
  Conception 260
Churchhill, S. B. 311
Clapp, Joseph B. 259
Clark, Henry 113, 269
  Oliver 85, 125
  William H., Rev. 85
Clarke, Caroline McKinney 160
  Elijah Henry 241, 242
  Eugenie A. 242
  Jennie 239
  John 63

Oliver	188	
Robert M.	197, 307, 338	
William H.	197	
William Henry	159, 239, 241, 338, 365-6	
William Jr.	241	
Clarkston	117, 348	
Clay, Green B.	318	
Nathan	328	
Samuel C.	316	
Clear Creek Post Office	196	
Cleland	96	
Cleveland, Barnett F.	186, 198	
Grover	212	
J. F.	124	
Jesse F.	85, 135, 186, 197	
R. M.	252	
Clifton Methodist Meeting House	196	
Clifton's Bridge	200	
Clifton, Aaron	196	
Cloth making	168	
Cloud's Tower	181	
Cloud, Aaron	181, 182, 261	
Ezekiel	80	
Cobb	96	
Cobb County	104	
Cobb's Legion	327	
Cobb, George S.	221	
Howell	338	
James T.	85	
Josiah F.	200	
Lemuel	85, 190	
Lovick	243	
Coc-lan-poo-chee (Yellow) River	89	
Cochran, Charles J.	240	
John	263	
S.	311	
Seaborn	313, 318	
William	181	
Cock-fighting	273	
Cockran, Alexander	211	
Coker	109	
Colburn, John	359	
Coleman, Richard	79	
Colley, Martin	262	
Samuel	80	
Collier homeplace	93	
Collier Place	93	
Collier's Mill	275	
Collier, Aaron	196	
Edwin G.	230, 262, 273, 275
Emiline (Emily)	110
George	280
George Washington	34, 259
Henry G., Dr.	93
James	335
John	85, 199, 237, 239, 241, 244, 266, 274, 308, 310, 313
Meredith	71, 85, 87, 110, 185, 196, 221, 233, 262, 273
Merrell	212, 232, 233, 276
Merrill	85, 93, 324
Collins Memorial Methodist Church	242
Collins, James A.	103, 239, 262, 273, 282-3, 287, 307
James D.	242
James W.	284
Mildred	239
Sallie	283
Colquitt, W. T.	187
Walter T.	129, 135
Conally, D. J.	210
Conant, Oliver Hazard Perry	298
Cone, Francis H.	276
Lucinda	131
R.	126
Reuben	63, 66, 72, 85, 124, 135, 186, 188, 217, 239, 259, 264, 282, 287, 305
Samuel	79
Confederate money	366
Conine, Bennet	124
Conley Creek	2
Conn, Samuel Sr.	79
William	190
Connally, C. M.	262
Christopher	232, 257
Cornelius (Neal) McCarty	104, 217, 240, 275
D. J.	217
David	198
Dempsey	103
Dempsey J.	101
Thomas W.	279
William F.	279
Conner, John	239
Consolidated Quarries	231
Convict lease system	166
Cook's	64
Cook, Allan J.	97
John	80
John R.	209
Tallulah House	368
Cooley, Emily A.	126
Martin	262
Coop and black	126
Cooper, Amanda	311
John	311
Mark A.	251, 252, 298
R. J.	367
Thomas L.	308
Copeland, William	80, 229
Copenhill	356
Coplin, William	80
Corby, Bernard	239
Corinth (Chamblee) Baptist Church	110
Corinth Sunday school	196
Corlee, James	185
Corley	96
S. T.	226
Corn	32
Corn-shuckings	171
Cornwell, Betty	182
Edward	297
Nancy	95
Corr, John P.	200
Corry, Alex	85
Alexander	124, 130, 135, 188-9
Sarah Jane	299
Cotterill, R. S.	33
Country Life in Georgia in the Days of My Youth	167
County Line Church	52
Covington, James	213
Covington	71
Cowan, James J.	263
James K.	211
John F.	211
Cowen, J. S.	208
Cowles, Clifford A.	160
Cox, Jeps	153
Cozart, G. P.	252
Hubbard W.	313
Craig, W.	210
Crane, James	303
M. A.	303
Crawford, George W.	252

THE HISTORY OF DEKALB COUNTY, GA. 1822-1900 • INDEX   499

J. T. S.		210	Daniel, Dovey	215, 216		120, 123-126, 130-131, 181,
M.		210	Mary		299	186, 188-190, 197-198,
Moses B.		211	W. C.		325	208, 217-218, 220-222, 225,
Creek Confederation		31	William C.		252	230, 232, 236, 238-240,
Crockett		96	Darby, Mary		201	243-245, 259, 267, 269,
Davy		96	Darnall, T. M.		275	274, 288, 292, 298, 301,
J. W.		96	Thomas M.		274	305, 310-311, 314, 316,
James		85	Darnell, Thomas M.		239	326, 336, 345, 349, 350,
James W.	306, 307, 316		Daughters of the American			352, 354, 356, 358, 361,
Joe		191	Revolution	63, 75		364, 366
Robert	212, 221, 297		David, W. A.		210	Baptist Church 226
Cross Keys	64, 70, 109, 115,		William A.	210, 297, 257,		Building and Loan
		349		292, 307		Association 278
Cross Keys Post Office		197	Davidson Granite Company		315	Cemetery 75, 77, 78, 158,
Cross Roads	94, 165, 189, 315		Davidson, Charles L.		315	193, 230, 242, 260,
Crow, F.		209	James A.		189	296, 338
S. B.		233	John Keay Jr.		315	Circuit 113, 115
Spencer B.		231	John Keay Sr.		315	Electric Light, Power
Crowder, Elizabeth		193	Norton A.		315	and Water Company 158
James		193	Wheeler		315	Female Academy 166
Crowell, William	305, 313,		Davis, A. E.		255	Female Seminary 160
		314, 316	Anna		327-8	Gold Mining Company 188
Crowley, Allen		222	C. R.		210	Methodist Episcopal
Benjamin		306, 316	E. A.	85, 124, 131, 208		Church 131
George W.		313	Ezekiel A.		263, 279	Presbyterian Church 78, 130,
Harris	307, 314, 318		James L.		335	159, 196, 226, 261,
James		210	Jefferson		337, 347	264, 316, 329, 336
Martha		255	John W.		128	Union Sunday School 196
S.		210	M. W.		208	Watchman, The 193
Sarah		226	Moses W.	85, 208, 257, 297,		Woman's Club 174
Seaborn		324			314	Decatur, Stephen 67
Crystal Mountain		25	Robert		293	DeFoor, Martin 105
Cullen, John		131	Robert F.	85, 208, 279		DeKalb (Cotton) Mfg. Co. 197
Cumming, W.		252	Samuel		189	Academy 109, 130, 132, 193
Cunningham, John		252	William M.		196	Cavalry 209
Cureton, H. J.		210	Davison, James H.		252	County Academy 124
Currey, Benjamin F.		195	Davney, John T.		208	County Bible Society 132
Curry, Alexander		131	de Chozas, Pedro		25	County Sunday School 196
			De Foor, Martin		275	Gazette, The 193
D			de Luna, Tristan		25	Historical Society 76, 78,
D'Alvigny, D. N. B.		257	de Soto, Hernando		25	90, 188
Noel		298	Dean, Henry G.	105, 232, 297		Independent Guards 210
D'Antignac, William M.		252	Lemuel	211, 226, 233, 252,		Light Infantry 207, 212,
Dabbs, John	80, 212, 221,				263, 278	327, 329
		239, 245	Mary Jane		182	Sunday School Assoc. 157
Dabney, A. B.		208	Nancy E.		106	DeKalb, Johann, Baron 59
John T.		200, 222	S. H.		182	Delay, Hiram R. 293
William		328	Samuel H.		181	Dempsey, Alvin 214
William H.	217, 241, 244		Thomas J.		313, 314	Levi 87, 189
Daily Examiner		279	Dearing, William		252, 294	Densmore, Harriet 311
Dalrymple		112	Death		171	Destroying the railroad 349
Dalton		345	Decatur	63-65, 76, 88, 94,		Devil's Cross Roads 18, 177

500 THE HISTORY OF DEKALB COUNTY, GA. 1822-1900 • INDEX

Diamond	96	
Diamond family cemetery	95	
Diamond's District	96	
Diamond's	64	
Diamond, E. M.	208	
F. C.	208	
Franklin	323	
G. B.	210	
Green B.	211	
James J.	323	
James	67, 85, 87, 94, 186, 200, 212, 230-231, 233, 239, 252, 279, 323	
Nancy Cornwell	323	
Rebecca	323	
William Winfield	323	
Dickson, David	131	
M.	126	
William	131	
Diggers, Joel	211	
Dillon, Thomas	80	
Dimond, E. M.	208	
F. C.	208	
"Dixie"	326	
Dixon, Jordan	208	
Doane, J. T.	280	
Dobbs, J. H.	210	
John	80	
Jonathan	67	
Mary Jane (Jennie)	117	
T. A.	70, 85	
Thomas A.	66, 67, 124	
Doby, William	226	
Dodgen, Emily	201, 203	
Dodson, James W.	211	
Samuel	85	
Donald Fraser School for Boys	160, 261	
Donaldson, Silas H. Mrs.	93	
W. J.	86	
William	80	
Donehoo, Elijah	304	
James	186, 231	
Dooley, Nancy	112	
Doolittle Creek	52	
Doonan, Terrence	280	
Doraville Associate Reformed Presbyterian Church	214	
Doraville	110-112, 116	
Dorsey, Henry A.	294	
Dougherty, C.	252	
Douglass, Aunt Seney	267	
Thena	294	
Dowis, J. M.	335	
Doyle, John M.	239	
Duffee, Patrick	245	
Dulin, Addison	282, 283	
Al	264	
Dulley, Henry	182	
Dunahoo, Patrick	239	
Duncan, Simeon	97	
Dunegan, Thomas	239	
Dunning, Vol	268	
Dunwoody	443-444	
Dunwoody, Charles Archibald Alexander	443	
Dunwoody Baptist Church	311	
Duren	96	
Durham, Daniel	221, 230	
Isaac	80	
John	292	
S. D.	153	
W. W.	366	
Duty, Thomas	80	
duVinage, Lucia Augusta	280	
Dyre, W.		
E	208	
Eagle's Nest	180	
Earthquake	325	
Eaton, John	97	
Ebenezer Methodist Church	241	
Ebenezer Methodist Episcopal Church	201	
Echota Trail	52, 53	
Edes, Samuel	208	
Edison, Bois	237	
Edmonson, Lud	274	
Edna	439	
Edwards, H.	210	
Lemuel B.	230	
Thomas	208	
Eidson, Boice	240	
Elam, George	212	
John	257	
Eldridge, Leila Venable Mason	17	
Electric lights	158	
Eliotte, James	209	
Elliott, George	231, 239	
James S.	323	
Joseph	114	
Ellis, Shadrick	80	
Ellsberry, Lindsey	87	
Elom, James	208	
Elsberry, Lindsey	190	
Emancipation Proclamation	338	
Embry, Abel O.	199	
H. H.	153	
Hiram H.	237, 245	
Emmett, Daniel Decatur	326	
Emory Presbyterian Church	157	
Emory University Hospital	158, 324	
Medical School	314	
Ensibia Academy	226	
Entrenchment Creek	7	
Entrenchments	351	
Erminger, John	297	
Ervin, Robert M.	348	
Eskew, Richard E.	297	
Richard H.	226	
Estes, Eli O.	337	
Zephenia	311	
Etowah Trail	123	
Evans's District	92	
Evans, J. M.	324	
James R.	86	
Jefferson	209	
John	87, 97, 225, 230, 231, 239, 252, 255-256, 289, 299	
Mary	255	
Evans	64, 96	
Evins, Georgia Ann	110, 368	
Jack	111	
James J.	209	
James R.	278	
John L.	111, 200, 233, 278, 368	
John Leroy	109	
Justinian	110	
Mitchell Mrs.	93	
Nancy Baugh	111	
Susan	110	
Thomas M.	240	
Thomas Mitchell (Mitch)	110	
William Crawford	110	
Evins	109	
Ewings, John	257, 258	
Ezzard, William	86, 124, 129, 135, 188, 199, 210, 238-239, 241, 244, 255-257, 259, 267-268, 293, 296, 298-299, 302, 307, 328	

F

Fain, Jesse	188, 199
William	187
William Sr.	80, 199
Fair, David N.	335
Fall, Abram B.	241
Fannin, Loftin	70
Farley, Kate Elizabeth (Mrs. Broddie)	117
Farlow, Nancy	79, 101
Farm products	169
Farmer, Joel	212
S.	210
Shadrack	225
Shadrick	190, 245
Farr, Thomas	198, 231, 297
Farrar, Bob	268
J. C.	210
Jesse	292
Jessee C.	210
Larkin	268
Farrel, James	232
Farrell, James	210
William	131
Farrer, Laura C.	255
Farris, James	232
R.	210
Fayette County	34, 63, 67
Fee, Samuel	305
Fellowship Cemetery	75
Fellowship Primitive Baptist Church	119, 332
Cemetery	76, 119
Felton, Rebecca Latimer	165, 166, 174, 181, 218, 253, 316
William	174
William H.	166
Fenner, J. A. Mrs.	367
Ferrel, James	211
Ferrell, James	292
Ferries	71
Fillmore, Millard	275, 314
First Baptist Church of Atlanta	299
of Decatur	157, 312
First Battle of Manassas	328
First census	194
First hanging	193
First known murder victim	128
First newspaper	193

First Presbyterian Church of Atlanta	264
First school	124
Fitzpatrick, John	245
Flake's Mill	231
Flake, T. J.	93, 231
Flake	96
Fleming, E. H.	208
Fletcher, R. H.	335
Flint Judicial Circuit	64
Florida	236
Flournoy, Thomas	252
Flowers family slaves, Sam and Tilda	111
Flowers, George Newton	114
John Y.	86, 111, 197, 214, 279, 313-314
John Yancey	114
John Yancey, Dr.	110
Flowers	109
Floyd, D. S.	293
David	293
John	42
Fonerden, William Henry	264
Fones, Daniel	75, 76, 119
Foote, G.	210
George W.	239
Foraging parties	362
Ford, C.	210
Coleman	209
Elizabeth Austin	17
Harold A. Mrs.	78
Foreacre, G. T.	331
Green J.	328
Formwalt, Moses	282, 284, 307
Moses W.	273
Forster, W. P.	190
Forsyth, A. B.	283, 287
Fort Delaware	340
Fort Field	185
Fort Mitchell	42
Fortification Field	89
Foster, Frances S.	126
Ira R.	298
Thomas	252
V. Mrs.	299
William P.	198
Fowler	96, 113
Fowler Guards	328
Fowler's Mill	275, 307
Fowler, A. T.	326
Alexander C.	181

Drury	86, 132
H. J.	314
Hilliard J.	307
J. W.	209, 255
John	209
John W.	86, 200, 208, 226, 241, 252, 255, 257, 307, 327, 333
John Y.	327
Lou	327
Minty	86, 96, 197, 200
Franklin County	123
Franklin, David	80
James Samuel	102, 105
John	101
Frazier, J. A.	312
Free and Rowdy Party	300
Frost, Edward D.	126
J.	208
Fuller, John	75
William Allen	75
Fulton County	34, 51, 64, 123, 310
Furgerson, Angus	230
Daniel	190
Furlow, Elizabeth	165

G

Gaar, Russel W.	317
Gaddis, T.	210
Gaddy, George	114
T. A.	208
Thomas	210
Galier, James	71
Gambling	274, 300
Gannon, L. V.	236
Gant, Elizabeth	257, 258
Gardner, Thomas	211
Garnett, Charles F. M.	252
Garr's Mill	231
Garr, Russell W.	231
Garrard, William	20
Garrett, Franklin M.	63, 77, 96, 111
John	260
Thomas	80
Garrison's Mill	200
Garrison's Mills	221
Garrison, Matthias	200
W.	210
Gassaway, F. M.	335
Gatehouse, Abraham	71

Gates's Ferry	194	Givens, James W.	96, 201, 225, 232, 237, 231	Goodwin	109, 111
Gates, Charles	86			Gordon, E. Mrs.	299
Charles Sr.	67	Joseph W.	86	John B.	160
Horatio	60	Robert	80, 86, 201	Thomas	75
Gaudier, Deborah	79	Glascock, Thomas II	233	Goulding, Francis R.	177
Gay, Franklin H.	337	Glen, John	67, 86, 186, 208, 241, 252	Goza, Aaron and John	119
Joshua	80			Grace, Matthew R.	70
Mary	329, 334, 335, 340, 347, 352-3, 357-9, 361, 367	Glendale Paper Mill	328	Graham, W. H.	239, 262
		Glenn, John	197, 210, 255	William H.	310
		L. J.	327	Grand jury	212, 213, 220, 222, 225, 230, 232-233, 235, 237, 239-240, 244-245, 257, 263, 274, 275, 278-279, 296, 303-305, 307-308, 313-314, 316-318, 323, 326, 332, 337
Mary Ann Harris	294, 296	Globe Hotel	267		
William	294	Globe, The	197		
Gazaway	96	Glore, Asa	211		
Gaziway, J.	210	Gober, Daniel	67		
Gentry, A. M.	335	Elizabeth	215, 216		
George Stitt's landing	185	James	189		
George, Banks	86	Julius J.	335	Grandpap House, The	115
Henry	315	Thomas C.	239, 240, 263	Granite industry	315
J. E.	318	William	245	Granite	16
J. V.	132	Godard, Thomas	187	Grant, John	282
J. W.	86	Goddard, John	187	L. P.	287, 307
James L.	326	Godwin, J.	210	Lemuel	259
James R.	95, 212, 269, 279	Goff, John	185	Lemuel P.	217, 294
James R., Rev.	86	Gold strike	188	Ulysses S.	348
James S. (Jimmie)	328	Golden, John	217	Graves, John W.	251
Jeptha V.	132	Golding, Wineford	257, 258	Gray, Elizabeth	93
T. B.	294	Goldsberry, William	292, 305, 309	Greathouse, Jacob	80
Tunstal B.	317, 245, 275, 309			Green's Ferry	304
		Goldsmith, A. J.	86	Green's Mill	199
Tunstall B.	86	James W.	86	Green, A. H.	199
Walter F.	166	Leomi B.	278	Alston H.	86, 258, 263
Georgia Gazetteer	177, 187	William	86, 233, 307	Alston Hunter	266
Militia, 54th Regiment	210	Goodman, S.	210	Clem	268
Railroad	179, 217-8, 220, 243, 315, 351, 354, 356	Goodwin family cemetery	111, 203	J. Howell Mrs.	56
				Will	267
		Goodwin Home Club	203	Greenwood, A. B.	210
Railroad and Banking Company	217-8, 276	Goodwin House	202	Alfred B.	213
		Goodwin's Station	203	G.	210
Gettysburg, Pa.	338	Goodwin, Augustine E.	335	Gresham, John	80
Gholston, Zachariah	230, 237	Charles H.	335	Josiah	109, 119
Gibbs, Laura L.	152	Emily Dodgen	335	Margaret Kate	119
Thomas Fortson	307	Franklin	203	Mary Howard	119
Gilbert, Jeremiah S.	97	Harris	201, 203, 304, 318	William Collins	119
Joshua	331	John	80	William	66, 86, 124
William	80, 239	Nealy	190	Gresham-Weed Cemetery	119
Gill, R. G.	210	Sarah Elizabeth Catherine	203	Griffin, Charles W.	208
Gillem, John	208			Ely, Dr.	97
Gillis, Kenneth	188	Solomon	37, 111, 201, 318	J. M.	94, 96
Gilmer, George R.	187, 222	Solomon Jr.	201, 203	R.	210
George Rockingham	42	Starling	201, 203, 304, 314, 316	R. A.	208
George	223			Griffin	96
Gittens, Richard	318	W. F.	338	Griffis, Thomas H.	275

THE HISTORY OF DEKALB COUNTY, GA. 1822-1900 • INDEX   503

Griffith, C. W.	208	John	199	Joel Chandler	295
W. G.	231	John H.	211	John	198
Grining, Jamima	119	Hamby, Micajah	316	John C.	237, 306, 307
Grisham, Billy	127, 135	Hamilton, A. P.	126	John L.	313
Josiah, Rev.	86	Doc	244	John M.	200, 222
Grogan, Gideon	335	George K.	86, 305, 313	Micajah	70
Henry	221	J. L.	182	Susan	280
J. D.	335	Thomas, Dr.	252	Thomas	130, 209
Wileford	124	Hammond, Joshua	335	Thomas D.	222
Williford	190	Hancock County	101	Thomas J.	208
Grogen, W. S.	210	Hand-to-hand fighting	356	Harrison, Hezekiah	211
Grogin, Henry	70	Hanleiter, C. R.	259, 279	James	211
Richard	70	Cornelius R.	264	Joseph	201
Groves, Elizabeth	276	Hannah Moore Female Colle-		Josephus	200
Guen, C. R.	210	-giate Institute	173, 316	Hart, C. C.	324
Guess, Francis L.	221	Hannah Moore Institute		Haven, W. H.	257
H.	210	for Girls	130	Hawes, Claiborn	263
James	198, 212, 222	Haralson, Cammilus A.	307	Hawkins, John	274
Thomas K.	261	Kinchin L.	239, 241	John M.	309, 367
Guiton, N.	210	Harbour and King	190	Lizzie	367
Gumbles, W. L.	210	Hardee, William J.	356	W.	209
Gunby, William T.	307	Hardman Cemetery	156, 158	William	208
Gunn, Bedford	153	Hardman Primitive Baptist		Hayden, J. A.	279, 307
Bedford, Rev.	86	Church	158-159, 226	Julius A.	282, 298, 301,
John	71, 189	Hardman's Meeting House	153		305, 308
Radford	112	Hardman, Allen	222	Hayes, John	75, 78, 120
Gunnell, William	80	D. C.	211	Haygood, F. M.	172
William R.	75, 76	Elizabeth (Betsy)	151	Green B.	313
Guthrie, Polly	440	J. B.	210	Haynes, James	211
Gwinnett County	35, 46, 52,	John	225, 263	R. O.	336
	67, 71, 87, 90, 109	Joicy	153	Reuben	283
		Naman	71, 86, 151, 153,	W. A.	336
H			189-190, 198, 200, 221	Hays, John	80
Hadden, Jonathan	131, 313	Namon	153	W.	208
Hairston	96	Samuel J.	156	Hazelet, William	279
Hairston, Albert M.	317	Uriah	151	Hazelett, William	257
Albert Miles	90, 91	Varner	189	Heard, Alexander A.	210
Lucinda A.	118	William	70, 151, 189, 243	George	86
Peter and Martha Baker	90	Hardwick, R. S.	252	J. A.	208
William	86, 87	Thomas W.	166	William G. (Buck)	297
Hale, James	119, 153	Harmony meeting house	189	William	70, 80, 189, 222
Sarah Fowle	188	Harper, James	252	Henderson's Mill	316
Hall, Davis	288	Harralson, Emeline	256	Henderson, A.	119
George	96	Harrel, W.	210	Green Ville	119
H. T.	292	Harrington, J. C.	252	Greenville	119, 296, 310
James	211, 221	Harris, Benjamin	80	Nancy	119
Joseph	211	Charles	71, 86	Rufus A.	316
Thomas F.	293	Edward C.	190	Samuel	197
Young	92	George	124, 128, 135	W. M.	214
Hallaway, Zachariah	86	Hand	255	Hendley, James	70
Hambrick, J.	211	Handy	237, 257, 263	Hendon, Israel	95
J. M.	326	Hardy	131	Hendrick, Thomas	70

Henry County 59, 71, 76, 119	Hodges House 191	Washington and Anthony 111
Henry, J. L. 335	Hodges, James N. 213	Paschal 301
James R. 208, 231, 239	Hog Mountain 42, 56, 70	Philip H. 368
John 67	Holbrook 109	Phillip 110
Joseph T. 337	William 113	S. 257, 258
M. B. 208	Holbrooks, John B. 190	Samuel 110, 111, 113, 114,
Mathew 71	Holcomb, Henry 112	118, 202, 258, 297,
Milton B. 208	John 279, 313	317, 348, 368
Henson, William 275	Holcombe, A. M. 226	Suky 258
Herd, J. 208	H. C. 259, 264	Thomas 80
Herring, Joel 210, 222, 257	Henry and Priscilla 112	House 96, 111
William 313	John 314	Houston, Amanda
Herron, Frank 327	Holland, Archibald 197	Katherine 156, 363
Hesterly, Green Mrs. 93	E. W. 307	Anna Shaw 264
John 190	Edmund W. 308, 309	Oliver 67
Hiburn, Matthias 213	Hollaway, Zachariah 124	Oswald 157, 273, 301, 332
Hicks, Charles C. 86	Holley, James M. 297	W. J. (Wash), Dr. 152
James 64, 70, 86, 87	Holliday, Anne 120	W. J. 264
Riall B. 222	Cooper 280	Washington 157
Higgin's Shop 263	Hollingsworth, Henry 245	Washington J. 256, 264,
Higgins, Thomas 189	Robert 86, 245, 275	273, 299
High Tower Path 46	Holloway, Zachariah 72, 92-3	Washington Jackson 156-157,
Hightower Trail 25, 37, 51,	Holly, Hiram J. 293	332, 350
53, 63, 94, 109	J. M. 292	Washington Jackson Sr. 363
Hightower, Aaron 210	James M. 222, 305	Housworth, Abraham 199, 257
J. C. 211	John B. 292	Howard, Asa W. 86, 211,
P. H. 326	Holsomback, Eli 294	314, 316
William O. 337	Holt, A. J. 260	Benjamin 212
Hightower 96	Hines 86, 125, 129	Edward 211, 212
Hilburn, Charles 211	Richard 87	Elizabeth 337
Nathaniel G. 222, 301	Honor Farm 231	James J. 211
R. F. 210	Hood, John Bell 347	Nathan 233
Hill, Billy 267	Hook, Daniel 313	Nathaniel 211
E. Y. 275	Hooker, Joseph 358	Pierre duVinage Jr. 280
Edward Young 173, 199, 302	Hooper, Charles J. 131, 210	Pierre duVinage Sr. 280
Henry B. 294	James 75, 189	Thomas Coke 280
Joseph 70, 71	John W. 86	William Schley Jr. 280
Lucinda Ivy 232	W. 210	William Schley Sr. 280
Thomas C. 232	Hopewell Presbyterian	Howell's Ferry 189
W. M. 239	Church 214	Howell, Clark 189, 298, 307
William 70, 86, 292	Hopkins, Dennis 198	Isaac 187, 189
William M.	Hornady, Henry C. 299	Hoyl, Levi 208
(Uncle Billy) 126, 232	Hornbuckle, H. H. 335	Hoyle's mill pond 268
Hillburn, M. 198	Hornsby's Post Office 230	Hoyle, Eli W. 335
Hillsman, T. J. Mrs. 346	Hornsby, Joseph 230	Fredonia 336
Hillyer, Junius 252	Leonard 190	G. 336
Hilsback, Frederick 67	Noah 212	Georgia 328, 336
Hinsen, Joel C. 296	W. 210	John 200
Hinton, James W. 268	Hotze, Henry 326	P. F., Dr. 86
John W. 283	House, George Washington 114	P. F. 196, 263, 366
Hodge, Pat 285	Jacob G. 118	Peter F. 294, 297, 325
Patterson M. 275	Slaves: Kitty, Rolly,	Hoyt, Cornelia 102

Samuel B.	102	
Hubbard, Joseph	70, 71	
Hudgins, Carl	53	
W. P.	226	
Hudson, G. B.	318	
Jason Lester	358	
W.	233	
Wesley	217	
Hudspeth, William	70	
Huey, Henry	80	
John	230, 240, 313	
Huff, Sarah	368	
Hugh, Jennie	329	
Hughes, P. A.	312	
Sally	194	
Hughs, Isaac	212	
Huie, Joe	113	
Hull, Asbury	252	
Hulsey, Eli	252, 281	
Eli J.	86, 93, 211, 231, 245, 263, 276, 309	
J. M. C.	327, 335	
Jennings Sr.	94	
Jennings	75, 78, 87, 94, 324	
Mary Jane	276, 324	
William M.	279	
Humber, Elizabeth	104	
Humphries, Charner	200, 201, 231, 239, 266, 282, 287, 310	
George W.	309	
Giles F.	317	
J. T.	307	
John R.	310	
John T.	301	
Merrill	293	
Hunnicutt, Calvin	280	
Calvin Mrs.	283	
E. T.	308	
Hunt, James	197	
John J.	260	
Hunter	96	
B. T.	196	
James Mrs.	325	
Hurt, Augustus F.	356	
George M. Troup	359	
Hutchins, N. L.	252	

I

Independent Volunteer Rifle Company	210
Indian Creek Baptist Church	226
Sunday school	197
Infairs	170
Inge, Charles	230
Ingram, Sally	75
Intrenchment Creek	185
Inzer, Elizabeth	119
Robert D.	119
Irby, Henry	222, 231
Irbyville	222
Irwin, David	302
Isom, John	200, 298
Ivey, H. P.	209
Ivy, Hardy	86, 222, 232
Thomas P.	294

J

J. B. Johns School	312
Jack and ginnet	252
Jackson County	43, 90, 92, 101, 102
Jackson, Andrew	41, 46, 103, 188, 194, 208, 212, 213, 233
Daniel E.	317
James	92
Littleton	225
Thomas J. (Stonewall)	338
William	63, 86, 87, 200, 221, 230, 233
Jackson	96
James, Georgia Ann	439
John H.	158, 280
Wesley	439
Jarrell, George R.	111
Jarrell	109
Jeffers, Robert P.	214
Jefferson, Thomas	35
Jenkins, Evan	71
Jennings, John	86, 222, 225
Jeter, J. J.	210
Jett, Adam	112
James	67, 87
James A.	263, 274
John	316
Stephen	189
Theofilus	70
Jettar, Dudley	80
Johns, J. B.	311
John B.	311, 335
John Bolen	311
John C.	211
Johnson, A.	210
Aleck	267
Alexander	230, 233, 239, 293
Allen E.	301, 309
Andrew	181, 182, 211, 297, 307
Angus	200
Arch	210
Archibald	86
B. M.	315
Billy	335
Black	274
D.	210
Daniel	86, 210, 263, 314
Edwin	221
Elizabeth	311
Gabe	86, 96
H. H.	211
Herschel V.	310
Isaac N.	153
J. W. P.	208
John	125, 153, 186, 198
John G.	211
John Gerdine	186
Lochlin	67, 86, 89, 131, 135, 185, 190, 200, 221-222, 245, 332
Locklin	221
Nathaniel	294
Patsey	153
Samuel	311
Thomas D.	305
W. M.	311
William W.	86, 96
William	221, 252, 261
Johnson	96
Johnston	109
Johnston's Mill	198, 304
Johnston, Albert Sidney	340
Dorothy Ann	110
Jackson	110
John S.	335
Joseph E.	347
Levi	80
Martha Maria	111, 117
Nancy	311
Nancy Elliott	110
W. C.	311
William	109, 110, 198, 200, 225, 231, 304

William W.	201	
Jolly, J.	211	
Jones, Aaron	239	
Adam	301	
Benjamin O.	307	
Charles Melton	118	
Elijah E.	252	
Hon T.	209	
J. J.	197	
James	153, 197, 200	
Jesse J.	305	
Jesse L.	257	
Jesse P.	132	
Jesse Potter	135	
John	87, 200, 208, 241, 257, 301	
John H.	231	
L. E.	197	
M. H.	208	
Oliver H.	339	
R. F.	335	
Robert	190, 200, 225, 279, 293, 306, 307	
Robert F.	335	
Robert Sr.	87, 358	
Samuel G.	260	
Seaborn	87, 226	
T.	210	
T. M.	307	
William	252	
Wilson P.	260	
Wylie	117, 118	
Z. R.	196	
Zachariah R.	231, 257, 274, 275, 316, 326	
Jordan	112	
Dickson	232	
Nathan	70	
Solomon E.	316	
Vincent	211	
William	71, 209	
Zachariah	71	
Judson, D. N.	111	
Justice, W. B.	214	
Justices		
of the Inferior Court	64	
of the peace	64	

K

Kell, John	185	
Keller, H.	210	
J. M.	210	
Kemp, Thomas M.	211	
Kennedy, J.	210	
James	275	
John Pendleton	314	
Thomas	193, 198, 239, 279	
Thomas A.	215	
W. A.	331	
Kennon, Owen H.	104	
Kentucky	243	
Key, George	314, 326	
Susan Bell	276	
T. T.	197	
Kiddoo, David	87, 124, 135	
Kile, John	230	
John Jr.	275	
John Sr.	236	
Thomas	273	
Kilgore, J. L.	324	
J. V.	190	
Killian, Daniel	261	
King, Barrington	298, 307	
Sarah S.	118	
Kirby, Alice Moore	241, 242	
Francis	241	
Melinda	241	
Timothy	297	
Kirkpatrick, Alex	87	
Alexander	124, 130	
George	267	
J. H.	256	
J. W.	244, 292, 366	
James H.	87, 131, 135, 212, 239	
James H. Mrs.	316	
James W.	87, 306	
Jane	338	
John	366	
John C.	328	
John L.	131	
Kate W.	230	
Washington	267	
Kirksey, Isaiah	198	
Kirkwood	356	
Kittredge, E. M.	318	
Watson	87, 124, 131, 135	
Klondike	79	
Knight, Aaron	80, 97	
Lucian Lamar	217	
Nathaniel	266	
Thomas	294	
Knoll, James H.	71	
Kontz, Christian	297	
Kurtz, Wilbur G. Sr.	56	
Kurz, Harvey Mrs.	367	
Kyle, Maria Gertrude	236	

L

Lagget, Alsey	258	
LaGrange Female College	105	
Lakewood Fairgrounds	257	
Land Lot 246	65, 94	
Landers, John	80	
John K.	297, 305	
Landrum, Elish	209	
Langford, B.	196	
Langston, Willis	200	
Lankford, N. M.	117	
Lasseter, Henry Z.	211	
Thomas A.	211	
Lassiter, Jacob	201	
Late Archaic period	6	
Latham, Thomas A.	302	
Latimer's Station	169	
Store Post Office	197	
Store	165	
Latimer, Charles	87, 169, 197, 200, 211, 241, 257, 274, 276, 279, 286, 323	
Eleanor	166	
H. B.	87, 258, 262	
Henry	303	
Henry B.	210, 212, 215, 300	
William	131, 165	
William M.	197	
LaVelle, Jean	119	
Lawless, John	71	
Lawly, John	56	
Lewis	56	
Lawson, Mary Barry	241	
William	190	
Leavel, Raihe	119	
Leavell, Edward	119	
Francis Marion	119	
John W.	119	
Nancy E.	119	
Rachel M.	119	
William Jasper	119	
Ledbetter, Lewis L.	239	
Lee's Mill	231	
Lee, Drewry	181	
Drury	87, 182	
Franklin	279	
W. H. Mrs.	231	

THE HISTORY OF DEKALB COUNTY, GA. 1822-1900 • INDEX 507

Wright	211
Zachary	231
Lee	96
Leggett's Hill	359
Lemon, James	78, 87, 130, 190-191, 196, 213, 220
Robert	78, 87, 130, 233
Lester, German	284
James M.	308
W.	208
Levell, Edward	75, 76
W. W.	210
Lewis, David W.	252, 298
Liddell, Haney Mrs.	93
Ligon, James	87, 212
Lucy	241
Linsey, Cullin	294
Lithonia	64, 67, 79, 94, 96, 165, 231, 244, 315, 356, 363
Lithonia Baptist Church	269
Lithonia Methodist Church	324
Little, Benjamin	222
Live Oak Quarry	6
Lively Cemetery	339
Lively, Elizabeth Ann	117
Gene	111
Judith Matilda C.	117
Laura Ann N.	117
Milton Charles	111, 118
Milton Charles II	117
Nancy Lena	117, 118
William Washington (Billy)	111
Log Cabin Post Office	233
Logan, Henry	70
Long, James	252
Josiah	217
Stephen Harriman	216, 231
Longshore, Dave	315
Loomis, Laura	345
Lord, Jabez	324
Lovejoy, Samuel	201, 233
Lovelace, Hazel	237
Loveless and Jones	198
Loveless, William	260
Loveliss, A.	211
Lowe, Thomas F.	336
Lowry, Ella Mrs.	117
Loyd, J. M.	214
Jabey M.	113
Jabez	118
Jabez M.	117, 324, 339
Jake	114
James	239, 259, 262, 287, 307
Luckie, Alexander F.	262, 279
Lumpkin, Joseph Henry	284
W.	252
Wilson	235
Lunceford, Lemuel	304
Nancy	153
Lyle, D.	252
Lynch, James	280
Patrick	297
Lyon, George	237, 313, 337
Johnson	211
Joseph Emanuel	75, 76, 89, 337
William L.	209

M

Macedonia Baptist Church	95, 75, 169
Macedonia Primitive Baptist Church	153, 159, 337
Macedonia Sunday school	196
Mackin, Michael	211
MacLeod, Malcolm	87, 126, 225, 237, 258
Macomeson, John	80
Macomson, John	229
Mad Dog of the Eutassies	35
Maddox, J. A.	366
John C.	87, 314, 315
Madison Female College	166
Maffett, John	75, 78
Maguire, John E.	87
Thomas	356, 363, 364
Main Hall	351
Maner, Hosea	217, 222
Mangum apple	340
Mangum, James	340
James, Rev.	87, 97
Nathaniel	200, 217, 237, 239, 241
R. E.	239
Robert E.	305, 307
William	97
Mann, Samuel	328
William J.	297
Marbut	96
Euclidus (Clide)	323
Johnnie (John P.)	315
Young	323
Margerum, G. V.	262
Markham, William	308, 338
Marshall, John	188
Rebecca	165
Marshbank, Mary Ann	76
Marthasville	235-236, 239, 243-245
Marthasville Post Office	236
Martin's Ferry	190
Martin, Alfred	203
Catherine	112
Charles	197
J.	210
J. J.	211
James	80
Larkin	112
Loving	233
Matt	252
Milly	112
Nancy	112
Reuben	112, 190, 200
Stephen	225
Wesley	190
Will	311
William	211, 222, 298
Mason's dry goods store	267
Mason, Charley	237
E.	244
Ezekiel	87, 131, 293, 297, 307, 327, 345, 366
Ezekiel Mrs.	327
John	230, 245
William	209
William P.	87, 263
Massey, R. J.	179
Masters's Cemetery	303, 76
Masters, Samuel C.	87
Mauze, Mary (Polly)	120
Maxey, John J.	313
Maynard, Poole	15
Mayne, Permelia	186
Mays, Dennis	187
Stephen	197
Mayson, James L.	279, 299
McAdoo, William	294
McAfee, William W.	296
McAlister, J. R.	87
McAllister, James R.	279, 293, 314
McAlpin, Floyd F.	316

James M.	317	
McAlpine, James M.	211	
McCammon, John	80	
McCarter, John K.	324	
William	70	
McClain, James W.	226, 314, 317	
William L.	337	
McClean, Ephraim	186	
McClure, Samuel B.	71	
McColl, A. P.	309	
McConnell, Elizabeth	101	
William	288, 301, 302	
McCool, Andrew P.	97	
McCoy, John	267	
William	267	
McCrary, Lizzie	367	
Nancy	293	
Thomas B.	131	
McCulloch, Ben	340	
James Mrs.	327	
James W.	335	
John	327	
McCullough Rifles	327	
McCullough, John	87, 131, 239, 307, 322	
Michael	239	
McCurdy, James	230, 231, 233	
James Robert	276	
John	276	
John W.	87	
John Wilson	276	
Julius Augustus Jr.	278	
Julius Augustus Sr.	278	
P. B.	87	
Philip Burford	276, 278	
Robert	276	
Stephen Cicero	276	
Walter Sr.	278	
William Tarlton (Dr. Bill)	277	
McDanel, A.	210	
McDaniel, I. O.	307	
Ira O.	279, 281, 307, 308, 310	
John	70, 225, 232	
John B.	209	
McDill, Margaret (Peggy)	116	
McDonald, C. J.	126, 252	
Charles J.	4, 129, 135	
John	257	
William	153	

McDowell, Ephraim	209	
Robert	80	
McElroy, Archebal	211	
Archibald	337	
Elizabeth	214	
Frances Rebecca	117	
John	116, 214, 318	
John Calvin	116	
John Ebenezer	117	
John T. Pressley	117, 118	
John, Rev.	87	
Mary Elizabeth	117	
Nancy Martha	117	
Samuel	116, 212, 336	
Samuel Bryson	117, 335, 336	
Samuel Jr.	115, 117, 214	
Samuel Sr.	87, 115, 117, 214	
Stephen Tilly	339	
Steven Tilly	115	
William	87, 115, 117, 214, 296, 324	
William Samuel	117	
McElroy	111	
McEver, Joseph D.	200, 231	
William	257, 258	
McGee, John W.	225	
McGillivray, Alexander	36	
McGinnis	96	
McGinnis, C. W.	87, 131, 208	
Charles W.	233, 297, 316	
J. L.	211	
J. S.	209	
James	293	
John	197, 200	
John S.	208	
Joseph L.	208	
McGrady, Silas	71, 125, 189	
McGriff, Thomas	212	
McGuffey	95, 96	
McIntosh, Chilly	47	
William	47, 88	
McKee, Mc.	211	
McKeever, J. D.	211	
McKenzie, D.	252	
McKinley, Charlie	267	
McKinney, Samuel Branch	160	
McKoy, John	340	
John J.	327	
McLain, Andrew	211	
J. W.	87	
McLean, J. W.	211	
McLeod, J.	211	

John Jr.	210	
N.	210, 211	
William	258	
McLeond, J.	210	
McNaught, William	328	
McNeal, James	292, 293	
McNeil's saddlery	267	
McNeil, Daniel	307	
James	75, 77, 338	
Martha Jane	338	
Sarah	77	
McNeill, Daniel	87, 316	
McOlister, Sister	153	
McPherson, James	281	
McShaffery, Michael	297	
McSheffrey, Daniel	301	
McWilliams, Alexander	245	
J. G.	211	
James	275	
John	131	
John G.	222, 314, 316	
R.	196	
Robert	87, 297, 324	
Mead, Joseph H.	262	
Meador, John T.	337	
Meadow, John	87	
William	181, 231	
Means, Alexander	261	
Medlin, J. A.	308	
Medlock, John W.	339	
Susannah Elizabeth (Susan)	114	
Megee, Marat	240, 263	
Mehaffey, Thomas	91, 92	
Meigs, R. J.	103	
Menifee, Willis P.	307	
Merret, John	210	
Metcalf, Francis	114	
Meteor shower	170	
Methodist Episcopal Church-South	159	
Methodist meeting house	190	
Mexican War	258, 287	
Milican, James	231	
Miller, A. J.	252	
James	211	
John W.	296, 337	
William	92, 231, 240	
William A.	309	
Millican, James	190, 222, 314	
Thomas	80	
Mills, E. R.	252	

THE HISTORY OF DEKALB COUNTY, GA. 1822-1900 • INDEX 509

J. S.	315	Ulysses	196	Mt. Charlotte Sunday	
Mills	221	William	101	school	197
Milson, J. B.	336	William Allen	157	Mt. Vernon Sunday school	197
Milton County	316	William F.	101	Mt. Zion Methodist Church	97
Mims, John F.	264, 276, 307-8	William R.	104	Murphey Guards	327
Miner, Samuel Wright	193	Moore's Mill Road bridge	186	Murphey, Charles	87, 127,
Minor, E. A.	56	Moore, Ernest	157		159, 198, 241, 244, 267,
Mark H.	226	Holladay	211		294, 302, 308, 324-325, 327
W. H.	87	James	239, 240, 305, 313,	Eliza Caroline	159
Mississippian period	7		314, 324	Eliza Word	159
Mitchell, Alexander		John	97, 245	Moses	87, 222, 230
Weldon	301	Judy	257, 258	Robert	87
John	185	William A.	196	Roger	80, 158
Margaret	156, 295	Moral Party	300	Murphy, John	80
Peter	240, 275	Moreland Avenue	356	Moses	211
Samuel	235, 236, 286	Morgan County	117-119	Murrel's Row	273, 281, 287,
Solly	96	Morgan, Billy	328		300, 301
Stephens	56	DeWitt	328	Murrel, John A.	273
Mize, James	211	J.	256, 294, 299	Muskogee	31
Monroe County	46, 111	Jane	327, 366	Muster day	201
Monroe Railroad	235	Joseph	87, 198, 220, 328,	Myley, George S.	252
Montgomery family			338		
cemetery	106	L. S.	87, 131, 240, 261,	**N**	
Montgomery Ferry	275		263, 279, 294	Nancy Creek Primitive Baptist	
Montgomery's Ferry	233	Lawrence S.	225	Church	79, 117, 119,
Montgomery, Adecia F.	101	Lawrence Sterne	337		203, 308
G. C.	52	Morgen, L. S.	208	Cemetery	111, 203
Hugh	194	Morris Church	97	Nancy's Creek	109
Montgomery, Hugh Brown		Morris, E. H. C.	335	Nash, J. E.	208
Troup (Troup)	101	Francis M.	211	John	317
Hugh Lawson	101	Garret L.	97	John W.	335
J. McC.	87, 190, 232	J. L.	324	Larkin	119, 307
James	101, 103, 105, 130,	James	189, 197	Tandy Y.	97
	186, 190, 222, 229	Joe	87	Neighbors, A.	211
James F.	239, 257	Joel	335	Nelson's Ferry	128, 222
James Floyd	103, 104	John	70-72, 200, 221, 230	Nelson, John B.	72, 87, 124,
James Mc.	125, 135, 194, 217	John B.	97		128
James McConnell	75, 42, 78	Joseph	71, 72, 124	John H.	252
James Sr.	101	William	66, 75, 124, 221,	L. B.	258
John Allen	157		274	Nesbit, Jeremiah	80
John Mrs.	152	William B. Sr.	75, 79	William	56
Lucinda	101	Morrow, P. G.	252	New Gibraltar	182
Mary Powell	157	Mortin, Lizzie	367	New Hope Cemetery	311
Nancy	102	Morton, E. L.	327	New Hope Church	346, 347
Nancy Farlow	104, 105	Ed	367	New York Giants	221
Nunan Tarpley	101	Edward L.	325	New, Jacob	80
Rebecca	101	Joel	233	William	87, 279
Rhadamanthus J.	125	Lizzie	367	Newhard, Lizzie Cheek	311
Rhoda Narcissa	105, 232, 101	Moseley, William	326	Nichols, James	131
Sarah	101	Mosely, William	87, 314, 316	William	80
Sophronia	101	Mountain Creek	94	Nisbet, Eliza	293
Telemachus F.	125			Eugenius A.	302

William	255	Paden, James	87, 129, 190, 198, 200, 212, 221, 235, 309	Peck, J. C.	331
Nissen, James	298			Peel, Alfred	114
Nixon, M.	211			Pegg, Samuel G.	97, 309
W.	211	Virginia	156	Pendley, Jane	292
Norcross	117	Pakanahuili	34	William	87, 315
Norcross and Prospect Charge	113	PaleoIndian Period	1	William R.	324
		Palmer, Hastings D.	200, 222, 231, 240	Pennell, Jonathan	214
Norcross Methodist Church	117			Peoples, J. J. Mrs.	299
Norcross, J.	265, 274	William	80, 368	Perkerson, Angus M.	97, 367
Jonathan	104, 125, 243, 245, 258, 266, 273, 279, 282-284, 288, 298, 300, 307-309	Panola	94	Dempsey	36, 87, 94, 185, 200, 222, 367
		Panthersville District	93, 96		
		Panthersville	64, 221, 229-231	Elizabeth (Lizzie)	367
		Paramore, B.	208	John	232
Norman, Harris S.	314	Pardo, Juan	25	T. J.	87, 262
Norton, James	211	Parker, Dicey	119	Thomas	367
Nowland, Michael	245	I., Rev.	95	Thomas J.	230-1, 241, 266
		Isaiah	87, 119, 153, 182, 252, 332	Thomas Jefferson	97
				Perkins, Reuben B.	317
O		Isaih	119	Peters, Dick	243
O'Brien, Michael	239	John G.	221, 225	Ellen	286
O'Neill, William	239	Lucrecy	153	Richard	245, 255-257, 260, 287, 298-299, 307
Oak Grove Methodist Church	314	Sarah	119		
Oakland Cemetery	285, 307, 345	William	199	Pettet, Thomas	187
Ocmulgee Association of the Baptist Church	95	William C.	305	Petty, J.	210
		Parkhurst, J. C.	361	T.	210
Oglesby, H. J.	252	Parks, Harwell H., Rev.	115	Philadelphia Church	52
Oglethorpe Infantry	328	W. J.	97	Phillips	64
Oglethorpe Mfg. Company	197	William, Rev.	87	James	95, 212, 257
Oliver, A.	208	Parks	95	John M.	314
Henry	358	Parr, Charles D.	209, 221, 237	John W.	335
William	80	Pate, J. N.	366	Palmer R.	230, 231
Original county boundary	63	John N.	186, 323, 329	Paschal C.	314
Ormond, James	328	Rebecca	78	Phinizy, Jacob	252
Orr, Matthew J.	209	Patey, Miles Mrs.	93	John	252
R.	210	Patrick, John	240	Pickens, Reuben	208
Robert	209, 233, 240, 275	Patrick	95	Pickins, R.	208
Ousley Methodist Church	115, 466	Patterson, John	199	Pillam, David R.	124
		Robert	80	Pittman, Daniel N.	260
Ousley, Newdaygate B., Rev.	466	Paupers	257	Pitts, A. L.	87, 296
Ousley, Newdigate B., Rev.	115	Payne, Edwin	283, 297	Augustus L.	309, 324
Overby, B. H.	308	Payton, Randolph	334	Ebenezer	70, 87
Owens, Richard	309	Pea Ridge	311	Joseph	87, 131, 263, 309
Ozmer, John H.	303	Peachtree Baptist Church	266	Plant, Percy	18
Robert	87, 263	Peachtree Creek	7, 33, 42, 52, 53	Plaster, Benjamin	87, 185, 197, 215-6
		Peachtree Golf Club	114	Benjamin Sr.	215
P		Peachtree Road	56	Edwin	215, 216, 225, 237, 257, 262, 297, 305
P. T. Barnum's circus	253	Peachtree Trail	56		
Pace's Ferry Post Office	226	Peacock, Lewis	190, 297	Piety	216
Pace, Hardy	197, 200, 212, 226	Peak, S. D. Mrs.	256	Sally	215, 216
		Peale, Emeline	256	Pleasant Hill Baptist Church	119
Paden's grist mill	267	Peavine Creek	52	Poe, Edgar Allen	259

Pony Boys	123	Price, Martha	303	Rebel yell	358
Pool, Ephraim M.	213	Peland	303	Redan	7, 90
Silas	182	Primitive Baptist Church of		Redwin, Jacob	231
William N.	182	Christ at Hardman's	153	Reeve, Dicey	111
Poole, A. J. H.	326	Pritchard	96	Ezekiel	257, 326
Adam	185, 189, 230	Pritchett, Joel	71, 87	James M.	337
Alfred J. H.	113, 117, 306-307, 338	Proffitt, Sally	120	James W.	79, 197, 200, 231, 232, 239, 307
Ephraim M.	196	Prohibition	306	John W.	113
Judith Matilda C. Lively	339	Promised Land plantation	356	William	75, 79, 229
Silas	275	Prospect Cemetery	114	Reeves, A.	211
Thomas M.	97, 196, 237	Prospect Methodist Church	111-112, 214, 308	Ezekiel	239, 311, 314
Poolesville Post Office	196	Cemetery	117	George W.	239
Poor school	124	Prosperity Presbyterian Cemetery	117	Joseph A.	293
Pope, Hunter	160	Prosperity Presbyterian Church	214, 314	Mary	311
Porter, Jane	160	Providence Baptist Church	311	Rehoboth Baptist Church	311-312
Post, Lindsey M.	189	Public education	304, 305	Rehoboth School	312
Potts, Samuel	275	Public school system	317	Reid	95
Samul	211	Pullin, Greenville	71	Reid's Shantee	222
Powell, Amanda Katherine	156, 157, 264	Putnam County	77	Reid, Isaac	200
Betsy Hardman	155	Pyron, William H.	275	James R.	132
Chapman	37, 87, 151, 153, 155, 158, 231, 264, 304, 327, 332, 363	Pyson, William H.	211	John	186, 232, 275
		Pythagoras Lodge	155, 239, 241, 326	Respess, Richard	185
Chapman, Dr.	87			Reynolds, E. B.	200, 208, 257
Claiborn	284	**Q**		Elzey B.	67, 239
Fielding Travis	156	Quiltings	171	Thomas	293
George T. Jr.	152	Quinn, Patrick	236, 239	Rice, Charles H.	260
George Washington Lindsey	156			Z. A.	259, 264
Irbin	274	**R**		Zachariah A.	279
James Oliver	156, 157, 332, 349	Ragan, James J.	316	Richard, J. S.	252
		Ragsdale	96	Richards, William C.	181
John Jefferson	156	Berry	275, 313, 314	Richardson, D. D.	335
Leonard Chapman	156	John C.	87	J. S.	335
Mary Jane Elizabeth (Mollie)	156	Rainey, James	208	James	211
Moses	208	John	197, 230	Riddling, J. M.	87
Moses Jr.	151	Rainy, John	221	Ridge, John	201
Nancy Pope	151	Ramsey, R.	210	Ridling, John M.	113, 313, 316
Sarah Carroll	156, 157, 350	Randal, Newton	190	Riley, John T.	193
Seamore	80	Randall, Hardy	326	Ripley, E. E. Mrs.	152
William A.	186, 293, 305, 327	Leonard	87, 124	Roark, William W.	301, 307
		Randon, W. R.	318	Roberson, W. T.	209
William Alfred	156	Rankin, John G.	327	Roberts, Isaac Martin	442
Power, James	197	Rape, Thomas	294	Jesse	112
John	210	Rapshir, Aaron	213	Thomas	229
John G.	211	Ratteree, Alexander	230	William H.	311
Josiah	200, 231, 239, 263	Ray, John	222	Willis	190
Prewett, Samuel	70, 87	P. M.	226	Robertson, James B.	263, 326
Prewitt, Samuel	124	Thomas	87, 153, 190, 191	Thomas L.	313, 314, 318
		Rebeckah Scott Hall	351	William	190
				Robinson	95
				Bolling H.	207

Hut	274	
James	297, 305	
Jesse	294	
Lavena	293	
Luke	96, 226	
Luke, Rev.	95	
Robuck, Willis	153	
Rock Chapel Camp Ground	313	
Rock Chapel Methodist Church	96	
Rock Chapel	94, 231	
Rock Mountain Association	226	
Rock Mountain Post Office	181	
Rock Mountain	177	
Rockbridge Baptist Church	97	
Roe, H. C.	208	
John C.	314	
Rogers	96	
Andrew	131	
William	87	
Rollings, Davis	70	
Roosevelt, Theodore	152	
Ross, Elizabeth	117, 118	
Rosser, Elijah	186, 293	
Isaac	293, 332	
Roswell	71, 347	
Roswell Junction	439	
Roswell Railroad	441-443	
Roswell, William R.	263	
Roussom, William	182	
Rowdy Party	301	
Rowe, Isac T.	211	
Royal, W. H.	259	
Rozan, J. H.	315	
Rucker, Jett	280	
Jett W.	279	
Jett Willis	156	
Ruggles, W. B.	280	
Rutledge, Samuel	190	

S

Sacred Harp	286
Saffold, A. F.	252
Sally Hughes's place	52
Samuel, Sam	226
Sanders, Holloway	211
John	80
Sandtown	8, 33, 52, 70, 123, 124, 190, 193
Sandy Springs	111
Sandy Springs Cemetery	79
Sanford, E. V.	20

Jesse	189
Savage, Charles	297
John T.	221
Saxton, Elizabeth (Bessie)	203
Scaife, William	87
Schley, Marie	255
William	209, 216
Scott Manufacturing Co.	329
Scott, Carhart and Co.	264
Scott, George Bucher Mrs.	230
George Washington	160, 298
H.	210
Lucinda	292
Mary	160
Milton Mrs.	77
Winfield	223
Scottdale Mills	160
Scruggs, John W., Sec.	316
Scrutchins, Thomas	328
Scully, Thomas F.	328
Seabrooks, Theressa	226
Seago, Dorcas	440
Seals, John H.	317
Seay, R.	211
Ransom	222
Ranson	200
Secession Convention	159, 324-325
Second Battle of Manassas	335
Sentell, Britton	231
William W.	222, 297, 298
Sequoyah	41, 195
Sewell, Christopher	221
James L.	211
Sexton, Walter Alonzo	354
Shackleford, John	260
Shallow Ford Trail	37, 53
Shallowford	64
Sharpsburg, Md.	335
Shaw, Anna S.	157
Sheibly, P. M.	126
Shelverton, William R.	296
Shepard, William	313
Shepherd, David M.	314
William	314
Sheppard, William	337
Sherman's Sentinels	362
Sherman, Henry	314
William Tecumseh	347
Sherwood Forest	93
Sherwood, Adiel	177, 186
Shewmate, B. F.	209

Shields, W. A.	324
Shifflett, Joyce	79
Shoal Creek	7
Shorter, Eli S.	64
Shumate, B. D.	190, 261
Benjamin F.	305, 337
Berryman D.	87, 245, 292, 297, 305
Joseph	104
Joseph D.	67, 71, 72, 101, 124, 130, 186
Lucinda	305
Mason D.	87, 131, 135, 261
Siege of Atlanta	359
Silliman, David R.	87
Silliven, David R.	127
Silvey, John	280
Simmons, Asa	87
E. C.	209
Eleanor Terry	331
Elvaline	156
Mary	156
Thomas	221, 331
Simpson, Christopher	284
D. M.	211
David M.	87
Griffith	208
J. M.	210
John	198, 245, 293
L. C.	313
Leonard	87, 130
Leonard C.	239, 241, 244, 252, 273, 300, 307-308
Sims, Leonard	324
Skins, Thomas	210
Slabtown	273, 281, 301
Slater, J. T.	239
Slaughter, Thomas W.	96, 214
Slave weddings	171
Slay, Thomas	80
William	222
Sloan, John	80
Smallpox	32, 174, 203, 285, 308, 338, 279
Smith, A.	211
Bartley M.	307, 328
Brantley	211
Britain	70, 71
Burrill	71
Charles Whitfoord	303
D. C.	334
G. K.	87

George Gilman	275, 280	Southern Miscellany,		Stephenson, John	87, 95, 212, 245
George K.	181, 193, 310, 324	The	264, 279		
George Kerr	241	Special Field Order No. 39	350	M. F.	18
Hoke	157	Spier, John, Rev.	96	M. R.	87
J. J.	211	Spivey, John B.	312	William	87
James	263, 309	Sprayberry, B. F.	303	Stevens, Mary	294
James M.	317	Benjamin	87, 96	Thomas	87, 294
James Sr.	314	Brice M.	211	Thomas J.	245
John M.	125, 190, 257	Harris	87, 201	Stevenson, John	214
John M., Rev.	87	Harvey J.	211	William	214
Joicy	151	Jincey	258	Steward's Store	231
Jonas S.	273, 280	Uriah C.	201	Steward, Absalom	67, 71, 182
L. A. Mrs.	255	Uriah C., Rev.	87	Austin G.	208
N. N., Dr.	104	Uriah, Rev.	96	Belle	329
Noah	113	William H.	303	Elijah	87, 231, 297
Painter	284	Sprewell, William	211	John Barnett	182
Riley	211	Spruill, Geraldine (Gerry)	110	Stewart, A. C.	209
Robert	198	Hugh	110	John W.	337
Robert H.	87, 198, 304, 317, 337	Stephen T.	110	Joseph	87, 214, 305, 314
		William	80	William	182
Sidney	190	Spruill	109	Stidham, John	262
Simeon	87, 257, 263, 297, 313, 326, 328	St. Philip's Episcopal Church	260	Stidman, John	262
				Stinsom, William	129
Thomas	190	Stagecoach line	165	Stocks, Thomas	252
Tullie	198	Stancil, Levi	96	Stoker, William	71
William	209, 221	Stancil	95	Stokes, Joseph	294
William R. (Long Billy)	126	Standing Peach-tree	106	Mary	294, 340, 366
William R.	87	Standing Peachtree	8, 33, 35, 41, 52-53, 56, 70-71, 79, 93, 101, 103, 105, 222, 231-232	Missouri	327, 336, 340, 346
Snake Nation	273, 281, 285, 300-301			Missouri Horton	294
				Thomas	345, 346
Snapfinger Creek	90, 91			Thomas J.	294
Snead, John G.	317	Stanton, Emily Frances	415	Thomas J. (Thomie)	340
Snellville	75	Starnes, Aaron	190, 209	William B.	241
Soap Factory	96	Joel	87	William H.	346
Soapstone Ridge	2, 53	Shubel	211	Stone Mountain	15, 25, 36, 52-53, 78, 177, 212, 244, 251, 256, 279, 289, 314, 362, 364
Soapstone	2	Starnes	96		
Social Circle	365, 366	Starns, Mansfield	211		
Solomon Goodwin House Foundation	204	State Guards	328		
		Stavens, Titus	209	Stone Mountain Academy	182
South River Association	312	Steele, Isaac	87, 200	Stone Mountain Assoc.	312
South River Post Office	222	Leslie J.	303, 326	Stone Mountain Authority	160
South River	2, 36, 52, 53, 63, 71, 78, 89, 94	M. A.	87	Stone Mountain Baptist Church	260, 278
		Michael A.	296, 324		
Southard, Green W.	440	Stegall, Washington	274	Stone Mountain Creek	7
H. H.	211	Stell, John D.	307	Stone Mountain Inn	251, 252
Marietta Chamblee	439	Stephens Rifles	327, 340	Stone Mountain Methodist Church	311
William Turner	440	Stephens, Alexander H.	276		
Southeastern Fair	257	Alexander Hamilton	224	Stone Mountain-Sandtown Trail	52-53
Southern Central Agricultural Association	298	John	87		
		Reuben	80	-Standing Peachtree Trail	52, 53
Southern Central Agricultural Society	251	Thomas	197		
				Stone, Cynthia	366

D.	153	Talbot, Lucy	165	Thrasherville	233
Daniel	87, 124, 127, 131, 186, 215, 294	Taliaferry, Edward M.	97	Thurman, Benjamin	222, 232, 237
Frank	328	Talliaferro, Edward	257	Mary J.	221
Joseph	189, 211	Tankersly, Bennett	80	Thuston, William	282
Rosella	366	Tanner, Jefferson	211	Tidwell, M. M.	302
Story of Decatur, The	160	Thomas	80	Tiller, Elisha	310
Stowers, Benjamin	232	William H.	232, 263	Tilley, Ebenezer	87, 305, 307, 324
Henry	213	Taylor, Zachary	275	J. W. F.	324
Lewis	75, 199	Telford, David	71	Stephen	87
Lewis Sr.	79, 229	Mary Brown	78	Wesley	294
Strange, Susannah	101	Telitha	347, 358, 362, 366	Tillman, D. R.	71
Strong, Cicero H.	309	Temperance rallies	268	Tilly, Ebenezer	114, 314
Noah	298	Terminal Station	225	Fletcher	115
Stubbs, George W.	335, 366	Terminus	235	Harwell Parks	115
James F.	275, 313, 316	Terrell, William	75, 79, 80, 229, 275	John William Fletcher	114
Joel H.	182	Terrell-Ford Family Cemetery	79	Mandy	114
Sturgess, Laban	324	Terry's Mill	221	Margaret Malinda	112
Sugar Creek Paper Mills	328	Terry, Bill	221	Mattie	157
Sugar Creek valley	356	Eleanor	221	Newdigate Owenby	115
Sullivan, Patrick	239	Ellen M.	221	Newton	117
Thomas A.	186	Green B. H.	222	Sarah Ann	114
Summers, J. J. Mrs. (Margaret)	324	Sarah	79	Stephen	112, 113, 212
Summey, S. J.	338	Stephen	225, 239, 284, 307	Tilly	96, 111
Sunday School Union	196	Thomas	221, 331, 332	Toby	347, 352, 353, 358
Susan Creek	7	William	225, 275	Todd, R. C.	153
Suttles, William	75, 79, 80	William M.	221	Tomlinson, Archibald	245
Swanton house	354	Thomas Moore's Mills	263	George	191
Swanton, B. F.	255	Thomas Terry's mill pond	356	Leonard H.	196, 222
Benjamin	366	Thomas, Emmsy	76	Tooke, George	198
Benjamin Franklin	188, 354	George	231, 237, 245	Towers, Elizabeth Akins	90-91
John	188	George and Martha	90	Isaac	80, 87, 90, 311
John B.	328	Joseph	239	Isaac Jr.	70
Sarah Elizabeth	188	Thomas L.	190	John L.	208
Sweat, Nathaniel	217	Thomas-Barber Cabin	90	Laura	226
Solomon	217	Thompson, Asa	87	Lavinia	90
Sweeny, Thomas W.	354	C.	210	Lewis	87, 126, 226, 240, 252
Swift, Eleanor	165	Chesley	211	R.	208
John	231	James	268	Royal	208
John N.	87, 293, 305, 307	James D.	187, 208, 209	Sarah	153
Thomas	165	John W.	187	Temperance	311
Swiney, Jesse	210	Joseph	259, 307	William	87, 90, 91, 153, 186
W.	210	Joseph C.	187	Towns, George W.	266
Swinney's Mill	189	Joseph, Dr.	87	Townsen, John	213
Swinney, Ellis	190	Martin	119	Townsend, John	71, 190
James	71	Randsom	187	Trammell, L. A. Mrs.	255
Joel	71, 186	Thomas	314	Trimble, John	75, 79, 80, 222
Sylvester Church	332	Young	268	Troup, George M.	47, 103, 187
		Thomson, J. Edgar	245, 260	George M., Gov.	128
T		Thrasher, John	196		
Taft, William Howard	157	John J.	224, 230, 235		

THE HISTORY OF DEKALB COUNTY, GA. 1822-1900 • INDEX 515

Tucker	76, 119	
Tucker Baptist Church		278
Tuggle, Bennett H.		318
Elizabeth		312
Lodawick		190
Lodowick	197, 222, 232	
Ludowick		306
Mary Pinckney		277
Turner		95, 96
E. A.		326
Ed		364
Edward A.		309
J. B.		182, 208
Sebie Loutelia		156
Silus		211
Thomas		214
William		209
William B.		182
William P.		211
Twain, Mark		294
Tygers		32

U

"Uncle Joe" Starnes	95
"Uncle Mack"	347
Underwood, L. B.	326
Union Station	235
University Apartments	158
University of Georgia	104
Utoy Creek	33, 190
Utoy Post Office	215
Utoy Primitive Baptist Church	
	96
Church Cemetery	79

V

Vaughan, Alexander	226, 337	
Vaughn, A.		208
Alexander		307
Veal		95
Veal, Benjamin F.		314
James		313
James J.		211
Wesley		313
William		293
William W.		211
Venable Quarries		278
Venable, Cynthia		103
Nathaniel		102
William Richard		102
Veteran's Administration Hospital		158

Vicksburg		328
Villa Allegra		260
Vines, Benjamin		190

W

Waddail, Clark R.		305
Waddle, Alfred S.		211
Wadkins, Benjamin		80
Wadsworth's Mill		296
Wadsworth's tin ware shop		267
Wadsworth, John		239
Walter	87, 212, 293, 296	
Wagnon, Thomas P.		80
Waits, Jeremiah		294
Walcott, Walter	225, 239	
Waldraven, Peter J.		211
Waldrop, David		36, 94
Waldrup, Davidson G.		275
Walker, J. B.		318
J. E.		210
Jane		226
Joseph	87, 126, 197, 209, 225-226, 230, 317, 337	
Joseph E.		311
Mary		311
S.		210
Samuel	216, 263, 283	
W. H. T.		356
Wallace		391
Wallace, Gordon		439
John		391
Thomas	294, 391	
William Dave		430
William R.		390
Wallis, Jessie		119
Walraven, A. J.		210
Walter Candler estate		158
Walton Spring		275
Walton, A. W.		287
Anderson W.		273
L. W.		282
Wamble, Roanah		257
Wansley, Nathan W.		128
War, Francis		225
Ward, Elizabeth		93
Nancy		94
Robert		132
Thomas		97
Thornton	71, 185	
Ware, Hambliton		211
Robert		132
Warner, Hiram		199

Obediah		199
Warnock, Jane and Andrew		112
Warren, Abbie		415
B. H.		252
Guy L.		260
Jesse		208
John William		415
Washburn, Hiram		126
Washington Hall	259, 264	
Washington, George	36, 60, 306	
Washingtonian Society		268
Wates, Rachel	257, 258	
Watkins, Henry		92
John D.		252
Watson, James M.		221
Robert		208
Thomas E.		166
Watts, Edward		240
George		80
Jacobus		130
William		70
Watts		95, 96
Wayside Home		339
We-La-Nee (South) River		89
Wear, D. G. Mrs.		256
Weaver, J. Calvin, Dr.		152
James H.		311
Webb, Jordan	190, 222	
M.		208
Preston		323
Weddings		170
Weed, John D. B.		335
Weekes, Wesley Hamilton		295
Weelaunee		36
Weems, D. R.		210
Welch, John		71
John S.		67
Weldon, James		215
Wellborn		96
Wells, Andy		315
Carl T.		277
J. S.		208
W. W.		318
Willis L.	239, 314	
Wells		109
Wesley		96
Wesley Chapel Camp Ground		96
Wesley Chapel Cemetery	90, 91, 93, 96, 303	

Wesley Chapel Methodist
    Church 96, 241-242
    Sunday school 196
West View Cemetery 93, 282
Westbrook, Minerva 439
Western and Atlantic Railroad
    217, 224, 232, 245
Western Reserve Historical
    Association 367
Westminster Presbyterian
    Church 130
Wheat, A. W. 279
Wheeler, Amos 366
  Charles L. 259
  Joseph 352
Whidby, William G. 157, 317
Whitaker, Jared I. 308, 313
White Hall 233, 282, 304
White Hall Tavern 201
White's Mill 296
White, Benjamin F. 242
  Edward 200
  Isaiah 209
  J. P. 296
  James 66, 87, 124, 188, 226
  James M. 296
  John 198, 200
  John W. 296
  Joseph R. 208
  Martha America 242
  Nettie 79
  Rolly 274
  Susan A. 296
  William N. 265
  William R. 123
  William W. 232
Whitesides, J. A. 252
Whitley, Graner 75-77, 119
Whitlock, Charles 119, 230
Whitlow, J. I. 324
Wiggins, E. W. 335
  J. C. 366
  J. M. 210
  Sarah 257, 258
Wild Boys 126
Wiley, William 70
Wilkerson, Elizabeth 293
Wilkes, T. U. 226
Willard, Josiah 268, 328
  Levi 87, 125, 131, 170,
    178, 191, 196, 293,
    328, 361

  Levi Mrs. 327
Willett, Marinus 36
Williams, A. 211
  Ammi 87, 128, 135, 188,
    217, 259, 287, 293,
    340, 345
  Ammi Mrs. 361
  Anson 70
  Elijah 190
  Frederic 131
  Frederic A. 128
  H. H. 211
  Hiram 56
  Hiram J. 329
  Ichabod 326
  Isham 56
  Jacob 153
  James E. 287
  James S. 231
  Jesse 190
  Jesse L. 233, 293
  Jimmie 113
  John J. 293
  Laura 131, 336, 340
  Mary 153
  Mary T. 153
  Sarah 153
  Simeon 232
  Stephens 71
  Thurza 153
  William L. 317
Williamson, John 215, 216
  Sally 216
Williford, Ben 284
  Benjamin N. 301
  Nathan 80
Willingham, J. T. 326
  Riley M. 293
Willis, James 209
  John 209
  Joseph 239, 263
  William 231
Wilson 96
Wilson's wool hat plant 267
Wilson, B. L. 338
  Beattie 326
  J. B. 208, 244, 293, 314
  J. H. 338
  James 331, 332
  James L. 317
  John 331, 332

  John S. 166, 173, 264, 293,
    316
  John S., Dr. 125, 130
  Jonathan 156, 366
  Jonathan B. 87, 135, 231,
    275, 302
  Jonathan B. Mrs. 327
  Jordan 335
  Louisa Ann 156
  Nancy 158
  Robert K. 296
  S. B. 211
  S. L. 190
  Samuel H. 293, 297
  Samuel L. 165, 185, 200
  Scott 268
  T. D. 211
  Thomas 259
  Walton (Watt) 331
  William 186
Winn, Catherine 196
  James 366
  James J. 87, 125, 317, 318,
    307, 328
  James J. Mrs. 230
  L. J. 326
  Paul 230
  Paul P. 328
Winningham, Michael 182
Winship, Joseph 307, 308
Winston, Thomas 118
Winters 115
Winters Chapel United
Methodist Church cemetery 440
Wolfe, Henry 197
Woman of Achievement
    in Georgia 296
Women's Christian Temperance
    Union 295
Wood, C. 210
  Carey 252
  Charles H. 275
  Constantine 200, 210
  Edward D. 307
  Elliott 80
  Isham J. 241, 244
  Jesse 263, 309
  Mary C. (Polly) 119
  William L. 317
Woodall's tan yard 267
Woodall, A. 211
  Allen 292

John	80, 190	Wright, Catharine	222	Yellow River	7
Joseph	71, 190	David	190	Yellow River	
Woodbury, Josephine Frances		Nancy	120	Association	95, 153, 225
	88	S. P.	311	Yellow River Baptist	
Wooding, Alfred W.	298	Spencer P.	241, 305, 314	Association	110, 119
Woodland period	7	U. L.	264, 280	Young, Augustine	70
Woodson, Benjamin	226, 314	Wade H.	185	Bob	56
Green	311	Weldon E.	252	Celia Strickland	56
Wooten, Thomas	80	William	87, 211, 296, 327	Elizabeth Ann	104
Wooton, Thomas	80	William D.	316	Gustin	56
Wootton, Joseph	95	Wyatt, Adecia Montgomery	104	J. H.	326
Worbington, J.	208			James H.	335
Word, Eliza	159	**Y**		John	56
Joyce J.	131	Yancy, E.	210	Robert	56
Robert C.	131	Yarbrough, C. H.	259		
Sarah Joyce	159	George W.	242, 266		
Worthy, William	80, 197	John W.	268, 283		

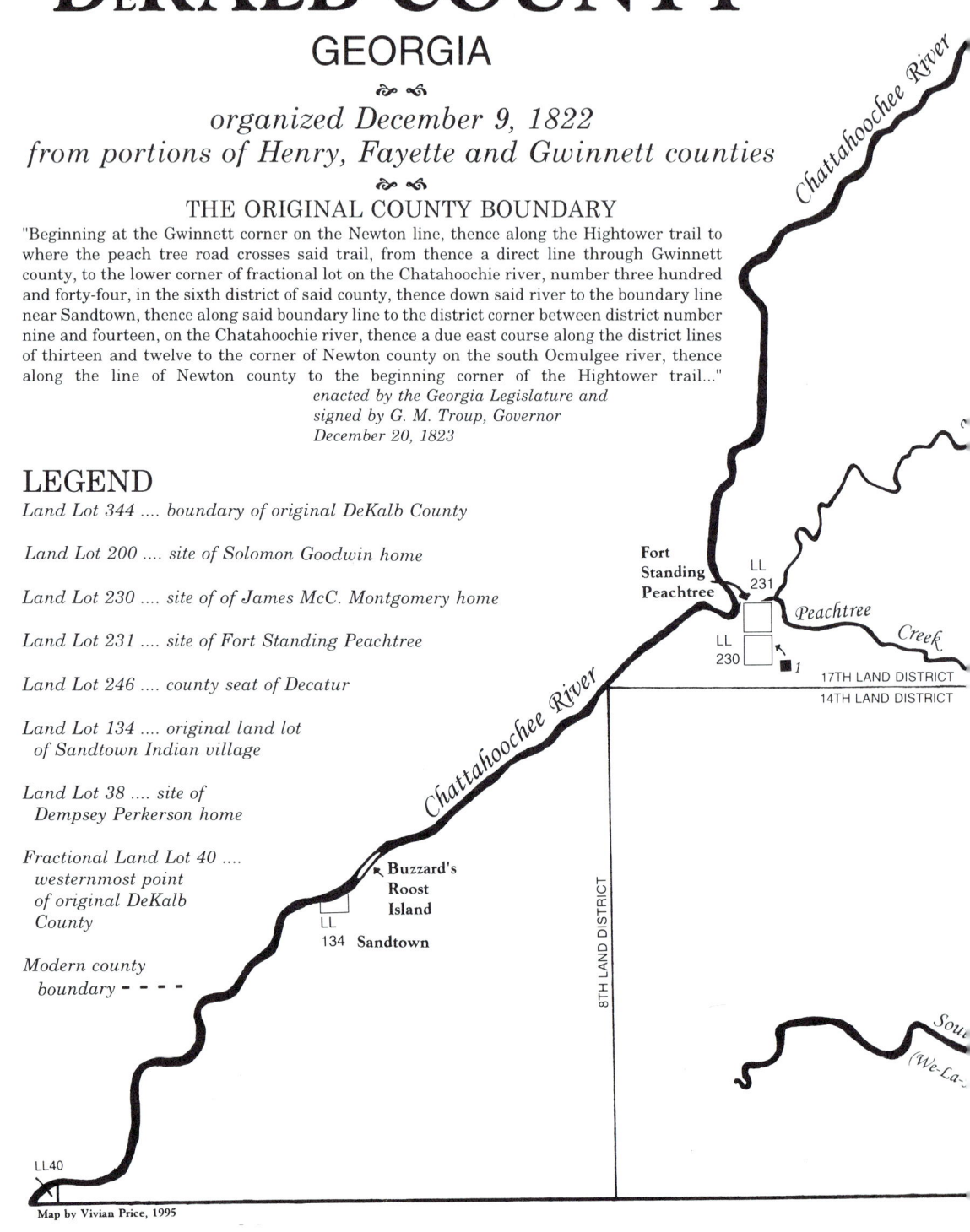

DeKALB COUNTY
GEORGIA

organized December 9, 1822
from portions of Henry, Fayette and Gwinnett counties

THE ORIGINAL COUNTY BOUNDARY

"Beginning at the Gwinnett corner on the Newton line, thence along the Hightower trail to where the peach tree road crosses said trail, from thence a direct line through Gwinnett county, to the lower corner of fractional lot on the Chatahoochie river, number three hundred and forty-four, in the sixth district of said county, thence down said river to the boundary line near Sandtown, thence along said boundary line to the district corner between district number nine and fourteen, on the Chatahoochie river, thence a due east course along the district lines of thirteen and twelve to the corner of Newton county on the south Ocmulgee river, thence along the line of Newton county to the beginning corner of the Hightower trail..."

enacted by the Georgia Legislature and
signed by G. M. Troup, Governor
December 20, 1823

LEGEND

Land Lot 344 .... boundary of original DeKalb County

Land Lot 200 .... site of Solomon Goodwin home

Land Lot 230 .... site of of James McC. Montgomery home

Land Lot 231 .... site of Fort Standing Peachtree

Land Lot 246 .... county seat of Decatur

Land Lot 134 .... original land lot of Sandtown Indian village

Land Lot 38 .... site of Dempsey Perkerson home

Fractional Land Lot 40 .... westernmost point of original DeKalb County

Modern county boundary - - - -

Map by Vivian Price, 1995